# The Safe Hiring Manual

The Complete Guide to Keeping
Criminals, Imposters and Terrorists
Out of Your Workplace

By Lester S. Rosen

©2007 by Facts on Demand Press
PO Box 27869
Tempe, AZ 85285
(800) 929-3811

www.brbpub.com

# The Safe Hiring Manual

*The Complete Guide to Keeping Criminals, Imposters and Terrorists Out of Your Workplace*

*First Edition - Fourth Printing, Revised and Updated in 2007*

©2007 By Facts on Demand Press
PO Box 27869
Tempe, AZ 85285
(800) 929-3811

ISBN: 1-889150-44-4
Written by Lester S. Rosen
Edited by Esther Lynn Dorbin, Michael L. Sankey, Robert Peterson, and Peter J. Weber
Cover Design by Robin Fox & Associates

**Cataloging-in-Publication Data**

    Rosen, Lester S.
      The safe hiring manual : the complete guide to
    keeping criminals, imposters and terrorists out of the
    workplace / Lester S. Rosen, author ; Michael L .Sankey,
    editor.
      p. cm.
      ISBN: 1-889150-44-4

      1. Employee screening.  2. Employee selection.
    I. Sankey, Michael L., 1949-  II. Title

    HF5549.5E429R67 2004        658.3'112
                    QB104-200237

The material in this book is presented for educational and informational purposes only and is not offered or intended as legal advice in any manner whatsoever.  The materials should not be treated as a substitute for independent advice of counsel. All policies and actions with legal consequences should be reviewed by your legal counsel. Specific factual situations should also be discussed with your legal counsel. Where sample language is offered, it is only intended to illustrate a potential issue. A sample policy cannot address all specific concerns of a particular company and should not be relied on as legal advice.

# Acknowledgements

First and foremost, this book is dedicated to my wife Donna for her unending support and everything that she does, as well as my daughter Alexandra.

My gratitude as well extends to a number of people who assisted in different but vital ways. I would like to thank and acknowledge the professional talents of Carl Ernst, Derek Hinton, Wendy Bliss, Larry Henry of the Boone, Smith, Davis, Hurt and Dickman law firm in Tulsa, Oklahoma, Dr. John Schinnerer, Dr. Marty Nemko, Dennis DeMey, Bruce Berg, Rod Fliegel of the San Francisco office of the Littler law firm and attorney Barbara de Oddone. A special thanks to Craig Caddell of ReferencePro.com.

This book also a large debt of gratitude to Michael Sankey, CEO of BRB Publications, Inc., who personally undertook the laborious task of formatting and editing this book for publication.

I would also like to thank Greg Pryor for valuable research and the editing performed by Esther Lynn Dobrin and Peter J. Weber.

To everyone at Employment Screening Resources (ESR) and to our key advisor Stanley Abrams, I thank you for your dedication and professionalism.

In a large sense I'd like to thank all of the employers, human resources professionals, security and risk management professionals, and members of the screening industry I have worked with over the years and spent time with who have contributed to my knowledge of this subject.

You have all made this book possible.

Les Rosen

September, 2007

# Table of Contents

# Section 1: Setting a Legal Foundation for a Safe Hiring Program

Is This Any Way to Run a Railroad?    The Economic Fallout From a Bad Hire; What Can Employers Do?

Definition of a Safe Hiring Program;    Anatomy of a Safe Hiring Program; The S.A.F.E. System;    Reasons Why Safe Hiring Is Such a Challenge;    4 Biggest Benefits From a SHP;    What a SHP Does NOT Do;    Risk Managemnt Calculation for Safe Hiring; The ROI of a Screening Program;   Answers to 10 Frequently Expressed Concerns by Employers

How Negligent Hiring Lawsuits Start;    A Safe Hiring Program Shows Due Diligence; Avoiding a Negligent Hiring Lawsuit;    Proving Negligent Hiring;    Defenses Against Negligent Hiring Lawsuits;    Due Diligence After Hiring;    Take the Safe Hiring Audit

The Elements of a S.A.F.E. System;    Key Terms: Policies, Practices and Procedures; Example of a Safe Hiring Program Using the S.A.F.E. System;    Sample Language in Employee Manual for Background Screening;    Sample Policy on Employment Background Screening; The Safe Hiring Checklist

# Section 2: An Essential Starting Point — The AIR Process (Application-Interview-Reference)

# Section 3: Employer & Vendor Guidelines to Background Screening Tools

# Section 4: A Crucial Safe Hiring Program Reference Library

# Section 5: Appendices

# ➢ Introduction
# To The
# Safe Hiring Manual

The process of matching the right person to the right job is a subject that affects nearly everyone — employers, employees or job applicants, or a professional in human resources, security, staffing, or recruiting — or when a serviceman comes into your home, how safe should you feel?

The purpose of this book is to bring together in one place the information an employer needs to keep a workplace safe and profitable. There are any numbers of books aimed at helping employers find the ideal candidate for a position. The critical topic, where information is harder to come by, is how to determine who NOT to hire, and why.

This book is geared to help employers identify candidates who pose a risk to the employer, co-workers, or the public — how to protect your workplace from hiring a person with an unsuitable criminal record, false credentials, or a person whose aim is to harm this country.

The tools, skills, knowledge, and resources aimed at keeping an unqualified person from the workplace falls under the general term "safe hiring." Putting everything together in a comprehensive program to exercise "due diligence" in hiring is referred to as a "Safe Hiring Program," or SHP.

The first eighteen chapters of the book cover the all the features of a Safe Hiring Program. Chapters 19 through 30 are intended as a Reference Library on Safe Hiring, presented to readers as an added set of guides, helping you become knowledgeable about a variety of safe hiring practices.

A number of themes recur throughout this book. From the employer's point of view, one consistent theme is the old adage "an ounce of prevention is worth a pound of cure." When an employer fails to exercise due diligence in hiring and just one bad hire slips through, the results can be disastrous. Since 9/11, safe hiring and employment screening have become a greater factor of American life. Just as everyone who goes into an airport is screened to ensure everyone's safety, safe hiring and pre-employment screening protects employers and employees alike.

Another critical theme is that due diligence and safe hiring is not a sign that Big Brother has arrived, or that privacy and civil liberties are being sacrificed for the sake of security for a few. An essential theme in this book is, as Americans, we do need to balance our needs for security in the workplace with fundamental American notions of privacy and fairness. Balance! To quote Benjamin Franklin, "They that can give up essential liberty to obtain a little temporary safety deserve neither liberty nor safety."

We will look at privacy considerations as well as the proper use of information in a legal and non-discriminatory fashion. A Safe Hiring Program is conducted with the consent of job applicants. You will also learn about criminal records — that a criminal record may not be used automatically to deny employment without a job-related justification to do so. As a society, we want ex-offenders to have jobs in order to become law abiding and tax paying citizens, however not every ex-offender is a good fit for every job. Chapter 29 contains advice for ex-offenders on how to deal with a past criminal record during the job-hunting process.

Employers have long recognized that employee problems are caused by problem employees. The goal of this book is to help an employer not to hire a problem employee in the first place. By using this book, you will gain new tools, skills, knowledge, and resources that can be used to implement the very best Safe Hiring Program.

For updates and supplemental material that the author may add,
please refer to www.esrcheck.com/safehiringupdates.php

# Section 1

# Setting a Legal Foundation for a Safe Hiring Program

This section examines two important elements of a Safe Hiring Program.

Overall, the establishment of an organizational commitment and infrastructure is essential to a proper Safe Hiring Program.

The **S.A.F.E System** outlines how a company sets in place the necessary and critical **Policies, Practices and Procedures**.

Going hand-in-hand with a S.A.F.E. System is the implementation of Legal Compliance Practices.

# Chapter 1

# The Parade of Horribles

## Is This Any Way to Run a Railroad?

This is a true story—

> A carpet-cleaning firm in California hired its new employees on the "warm body theory." If the employer needed to hire someone quick and the person applying claimed he had relevant experience — and the applicant looked good to the hiring manager — then no background checking was done, no criminal history, and no reference check.

> A newly hired employee was immediately sent into people's homes to clean carpets. Within a month, a horrible event occurred — the new employee committed a brutal murder. The victim was a woman whose carpets were being cleaned. As the facts came out it became apparent this employee's past-employment claims were false. He had been convicted of a violent crime and had been in prison for the past ten years.

> If the employer had just taken two minutes to pick up the phone and call the *supposed* past employment references, then the employer would have immediately discovered the applicant's fraudulent past-employment claims. Had the employer done a simple background check, it would have raised red flags. A two-minute phone call or a simple record check would have saved a life.

### Employers Must Know Whom They Are Hiring

Ask any labor lawyer, human resource manager or security professional whether an employer should engage in pre-employment screening. Their response: it is an absolute necessity. The exercise of due diligence is a must in today's environment, and proper due diligence includes verifications, background checks — a complete pre-employment screening.

How ridiculous is the following?

1. On a busy downtown street, you look for a person walking by that appears to be "reasonable" — based upon whatever criteria you wish to use for "reasonable."

2. You have a five-minute conversation with this person who proceeds to tell you all about himself.

3. Since this person still appears to be "reasonable," you say to him, "Here are the keys to my house. Come over and walk inside anytime, day or night — my house is your house."

Now, compare that to the current system in place in America for hiring a great many workers—

1. A worker sends in a resume, which is merely a marketing device whereby an applicant tells an employer what the applicant chooses to reveal.

2. The applicant comes in for an interview and talks about himself or herself.

3. The interviewer makes a judgment about the person based upon whatever criteria the interviewer is using. If the judgment is positive, within a short period of time a hiring decision is made.

Once a worker is hired, this person literally has the keys to your economic house. This person now has access to your assets, your clients, your co-workers, your money, your reputation and even your very existence. If you make a bad-hiring decision, the results can be devastating. At the root of the problem is the fact that one of the most utilized hiring tools in America is simply the use of gut instinct.

# The Economic Fallout From a Bad Hire

For almost every any firm in the U.S., the direct cost associated with labor is either the first or second largest line item in a budget; this includes revenues spent for pay, benefits, recruiting and training. If firms add in the cost of managing and dealing with employees, the figure is even greater. In a study published in 2003, CFO Research Services[1] found that companies spend about 36 percent of their revenues on "human capital." That figure was even higher in some industries, such as financial services or the pharmaceutical industry.

Yet many employers spend more time and effort choosing a copier or deciding between competing brands of laptops than they do in selecting employees.

Consider the following nightmare that could easily happen to any employer—

The telephone rings late Friday afternoon just as you are tying up the loose ends after the course of yet another tough week. A panic-stricken voice informs you that Pat in accounting has assaulted a co-worker and has threatened to harm a supervisor. As the mess is being sorted out more facts come to light. Pat did not really have the work experience he claimed. A co-worker says that Pat was stealing money.

Now everyone in the company – from the CEO down to your co-workers – asks the same question: how did Pat get hired in the first place? The CEO also wants to know how much this mess will cost the company.

The following statistics are circulated by ADP (a payroll processing firm), compiled by their employment screening division—

- 30% of all business failures are due to employee theft and related forms of dishonesty

---

[1] in collaboration with Mercer Human Resource Consulting

- The direct and indirect average cost of employee turnover is equal to 150% of the annual salary

- 51% of all resumes, applications, and references provided by applicants contain inaccurate information

- 7% of applicants have had a criminal record within the last seven years

At the end of this chapter is an excellent article about ADP's Annual Hiring Index Study.

## Replacement Costs and Damage Control

The direct economic cost of replacing a single bad hiring decision can be very expensive. Staffing industry sources estimate the cost of a single bad hire can range from twice the yearly salary to a much higher multiplier, depending upon the position. The time, money, and energy spent recruiting, hiring, and training is wasted. Add to the equation the amount of time lost between the date a bad hire is identified to when a suitable replacement is trained and in place.

An employer must also consider costs that are hard to quantify such as loss of productivity, knowledge, know how, and disruption to the workflow. With a 10% turnover rate, a firm will spend a substantial amount of its revenue on employee replacements.

Even more difficult to measure are other intangible costs that should also be taken into consideration when calculating the long-term fallout from a bad hiring decision—

- Lost customers or business causing damage to a firm's credibility

- Damage to employee morale

- Brand destruction

- Litigation

Firms spend millions of dollars to brand their products or services. One bad hire can create irrevocable brand destruction. A fast food worker can contaminate food or a hotel worker can assault a guest. With just one highly publicized incident millions of dollars spent building brand identification is lost.

Termination lawsuits, harassment claims, negligent hiring lawsuits and customer dissatisfaction all undermine a company's finances and reputation. The financial costs to defend these suits can be staggering, and the damage these suits can cause to relationships with customers and employees may cause the business to fail.

## Litigation and Attorneys' Fees for Bad Hires

If the matter turns into litigation, then the legal fees stemming from a single incident can easily soar into six-figures, and jury awards can be astounding. Employers have a duty of due diligence in hiring, and if their hiring practices cause harm to co-workers or members of the public, an employer can be sued for negligent hiring. Employees can be sued for negligent retention when they fail to terminate, discipline, or properly supervise another employee after learning this person is dangerous or unfit.[2] Even the bad employee may sue, claiming wrongful termination.

According to the Insurance Information Network of California, lawsuits for negligent hiring, retention and out-of-court settlements in California due to workplace violence averaged over $500,000; jury verdicts in these cases averaged about $3 million.[3] In another study quoted in *The Reish & Luftman Practical Guide to Employment Law*, October, 2002, employers in California in 1999 lost sixty percent of negligent hiring cases. There is no reason to believe the figures are significantly different in other states.

According to a very detailed legal article on negligent hiring lawsuits—

> "One of the fastest growing areas of tort litigation involves the imposition of liability upon third parties for intentional or criminal acts committed by one person against another." *29 Am Jur Trials, Sec. 1*

This in-depth article was written for the purpose of assisting lawyers who are either suing employers or defending employers in negligent hiring lawsuits. The fact that how-to books are written expressly for lawyers about negligent hiring cases should be a wake-up call to employers. *Safe Hiring* is a priority if employers want to stay out of court.

An example of just how dramatic jury verdicts can be was demonstrated by the 1998 Massachusetts case of *Ward, et al. v. Trusted Health Resources, Inc.* A health care facility failed to check the background of ex-felon Jesse Rogers. The facility had hired Rogers to care for a 32-year-old quadriplegic with cerebral palsy and his 77-year-old grandmother. Weeks after he was removed from the assignment due to failure to consistently show up for work, Rogers murdered both the patient and the grandmother formerly in his care. A jury awarded a 26.5 million dollar verdict.

Believe it or not, the *Ward* case is not the highest amount awarded in a negligent hiring case. In 2001, a New Jersey jury awarded $40 million in damages to the estate of a home health care patient stabbed to death in her own home by an employee of a home health care provider. This health care provider had not performed a background check even though the attacker told his employer he had a criminal record. If a background check had been performed, then the employer would have also uncovered the soon-to-be murderer's history of mental problems.

Negligent hiring cases are not limited to just health care. Firms from all industries have been subject to lawsuits and claims of negligent hiring stemming from not only acts of violence, but also workplace theft and embezzlement. A firm can be sued for hiring employees who steal confidential information for the purpose of fraud or identity theft, or sued for hiring a person who harasses his or her co-workers.

These jury verdicts and settlements underscore the legal duty of employers to exercise due diligence in hiring.

Once litigation starts, HR and security managers will find that in addition to their normal duties they now have a second, nearly full-time job — dealing with the discovery process, the learning curve accompanying the litigation process, and managing the ensuing organizational fallout.

---

[2] see the discussion on Negligent Hiring in the Chapter 3

[3] this does not even include attorney fees, which can easily reach into the six-figures

**Author Tip** ➡ A cartoon on the author's wall shows a terminated employee being escorted out of the building with his box of personal items. As he is leaving, the escort says "Don't worry. If it is any conciliation, we are also going to fire the *idiot* who hired you." Unfortunately, a bad hiring decision can also have negative career repercussions for the hiring manager. The HR or security manager can come under fire even if not involved in the hiring decision.

One of the goals of this book is to supply the tools so you will not be that "idiot."

## Workers with Criminal Records and the Cost of Workplace Violence

Statistics maintained by firms that perform pre-employment screening and background checks unanimously agree — unless a firm engages in due diligence in hiring, **it is a statistical certainty that the firm will eventually hire someone with a criminal record**. These industry statistics show that as much as ten percent of the applicants who are screened have criminal records. Of course, not all ten percent would necessarily be dangerous or disqualified from being hired. Some of the criminal matters can be for minor acts, or the record may have already been disclosed to the employer.[4]

The impact of violence on the American workplace is staggering. As estimated in Chapter 24, cost in lost wages alone is 55 billion dollars per year. That figure does not take into account the human suffering associated with workplace violence, or the economic and legal fallout.

Experts who study workplace violence have concluded it is difficult to predict ahead of time who will be violent. However, experts have also found there is an important common denominator when it comes to workplace violence — a history of past violence. Given the reluctance that many employers have in giving a reference that may reveal past violence, a criminal background check is often the most recommended method to help avoid workplace violence in the first place.

## Effects of Resume Fraud

Industry statistics, such as the ADP Study, clearly demonstrate that resume fraud is as high as 40%. In other words, in 2 of every 5 resumes an employer receives, there are material misstatements or omissions that go beyond the acceptable bounds of puffing up a resume. These resumes venture into the world of fantasy, make-believe and deception. Every applicant has the right to put a best foot forward in a resume, but when the applicant is untruthful, there is a problem.

Examples of resume fraud can be as simple as claiming to have worked at a job for a longer period than is accurate. There can be outright distortions such as an overstatement of title or inaccurate claims of promotion, e.g. claiming to be a supervisor when the position is really a file clerk. In more extreme instances, some applicants go so far as to make up jobs, degrees, credentials entirely.

*Business Week* underscored the issues involved in false credentials at the executive level with an article called **ResumeGate** appearing in its February, 2003, issue. The magazine asked the question, "Is it

---

[4] the rules concerning the proper use of criminal records in hiring are discussed in Chapter 11

really so hard to write an accurate resume?" The article pointed out certain executives who have not managed to do so. On this list are—

- Ram Kumar, Research Director of Institutional Shareholder Services, falsely claimed a law degree

- Kenneth Lonchar, former CFO of Veritas, falsely claimed an MBA from Stanford

- Ron Zarrella, CEO of Bausch & Lomb, falsely claimed an MBA from New York University

- Bryan Mitchell, Chairman of MCG Capital, falsely claimed a BA in economics from Syracuse University

The resume fraud issue has also surfaced in the sports world. George O'Leary lost his job as football coach at a major university because he claimed he had an advanced degree that he did not earn.

## Potential Shareholders' Suits, Corporate Fraud and Honesty Issues, and Sarbanes-Oxley

It is only a matter of time before publicly-traded firms are the subjects of shareholder lawsuits for loss of value as a result of negligent hiring. A California-based software firm failed to perform a simple background check on its CFO. When it was revealed that the CFO did not in fact have an MBA as he claimed, the stock's value plummeted fifteen percent, and a major analyst lowered his rating on the firm's stock from "out-perform" to "neutral." How can a publicly-traded company not justify spending five minutes and a few dollars in order to make sure there was a qualified, truthful person running their finances?

In the current business climate, corporate honesty and integrity are also emerging as critical issues. Spectacular corporate and financial fraud cases such as those involving Tyco, Enron, and WorldCom have placed a new emphasis on honesty as a critical element of corporate life. Under the Sarbanes-Oxley Act[5], publicly-held corporations are now held to a standard of exercising proper control over their financials, which means knowing whom they are hiring. Without a Safe Hiring Program, a firm is at increased risk of finding itself the main subject of the next negative headline.

## Employee Theft and Fraud

Another reason why employers need to be very concerned about who they hire is employee theft. Consider these startling facts and figures reported on *Business Week Online*, May 20, 2003—

- Employee dishonesty costs U.S. businesses over $50 billion annually

- Over 46% of inventory shrinkage is due to employee theft

Another reason for concern is embezzlement. As discussed in detail in Chapter 23, embezzlers are typically difficult to spot once hired. They often come disguised as the perfect employee. In order to obtain a position of trust, this employee often makes himself or herself indispensable and highly

---

[5] The Sarbanes-Oxley Act is discussed in detail in Chapter 23

regarded. In order to prevent the embezzlement from being discovered, the embezzler must typically go through extraordinary steps to prevent anyone from finding out what he or she is doing. If an embezzler were to take a vacation or miss a day of work, an employer may discover something amiss.

According to research cited in an article called *Getting Wise to Lies* found in the May 1, 2006 issue of *Time Magazine*, there is "a lot of evidence that those who cheat on job applications also cheat in school and in life." That was the opinion of Dr. Richard Griffith, director of the industrial and organizational psychology program at the Florida Institute of Technology. Dr. Griffith is the editor of a book on job applicant faking, titled *A Closer Examination of Applicant Faking Behavior* (2007). He is concerned that if an applicant fakes a degree, how can the employee be trusted to tell the truth when it comes to financial statements.

These observations confirm what many employers, security and human resources professionals already know – that if an applicant lies in order to get into a job, there is no way of knowing what lies or acts of dishonesty will occur when they are working for you. What is the best strategy to keep embezzlers and cheats out of your workplace? Due diligence in safe hiring!

## The Cost of Firing and the Importance of Documentation

If a firm determines it must terminate an individual, the firm may risk litigation for wrongful termination regardless of the reason for the termination. There will be attorney fees. This explains why some employers have a fear of firing.

Consider the following scenario experienced by many firms—

First, an employer takes steps to avoid the necessity firing the person. The employer may move the person into a different position, trying to find a position where the employee will do the least harm. Perhaps the employer will place the employee on a 90-day improvement plan.

When the employer finally realizes that it is not going to work out, the employee is let go. Afterwards, the HR or legal department discovers the firm did not sufficiently document the reasons for termination. The next week the former employee files a lawsuit for wrongful termination.

Once a firm recognizes an employee will be terminated, it must begin the process of documenting the reasons. Merely saying, "It just didn't work out," is usually not a sound basis for termination. If the employee happens to be a member of a protected classification under discrimination laws, then it is even more critical to be able to document a bona fide business reason for the termination.

*The lesson—* take steps to avoid hiring a problem employee in the first place.

# ADP's Sixth Annual Hiring Index

ADP issues a yearly hiring index showing the degree of fraud, discrepancies, or criminal records found in background screening. In the 2003 Hiring Index, ten percent, or approximately 300,000 records, contained an area of concern or data inconsistency.

Below is an excerpt from that study.

> "ADP's Hiring Index is comprised of calculations based on the number of background verifications performed by the company during the previous calendar year. Since its inception, the Hiring Index has shown the different areas in which candidate screening can help employers by highlighting where data inconsistencies on a candidate's resume can exist. Specifically, the Hiring Index measures the number of data incidents found in criminal records, employment history, education and credential records, as well as driving, credit and workers' compensation claim records."

The 2003 Hiring Index showed these facts among records checked—

- 5% had a criminal record in the last seven years
- 44% had a driving record with one or more violations or convictions
- 24% had credit records showing a judgment, lien or bankruptcy, or had been turned over to a collection agency
- 9% had a previous workers' compensation claim
- 51% of employment, education or credential reference checks revealed a difference of information between what the applicant provided and what the source reported
- 8% of the information differences were received with negative remarks from the source in regard to the applicant[6]

Another survey, conducted in 2004, supports the conclusion that employers face serious issues when hiring. According to an online survey by the Society for Human Resource Management (SHRM) in May, 2004, a random sample of email responses showed that 88% of employers found some degree of inconsistencies in resumes. Only 2% never found inconsistencies and just 9% said they do not investigate the backgrounds of applicants.

For employers, human resource professionals, and security managers, these figures are certainly something to think about.

# What Can Employers Do?

Given the enormous price tag of a bad hiring decision it is no surprise that employers of all sizes are looking to various tools in hopes of boosting the effectiveness of the hiring process. However, the good news is that employers do not need to live through this "Parade of Horribles." There is something employers can do — institute a **Safe Hiring Program**.

---

[6] to review the entire study, go to www.investquest.com/iq/a/aud/ne/news/adp51903study.htm

# Chapter 2

# The Solution: A Safe Hiring Program (SHP)

A fact of business life is: *employee problems are caused by problem employees*.

Each new hire represents an enormous investment and potential risk to an employer. Ironically, many employers spend more time, energy and money shopping for a new piece of office equipment than they do on a new hire.

Despite inherent challenges in weeding out problem applicants, there are steps employers can and should take. The best way for employers to make one of the most critical decisions in their business is to institute a Safe Hiring Program (SHP).

## Definition of a Safe Hiring Program

A Safe Hiring Program (SHP) is a series of policies, practices and procedures designed to minimize the probability of hiring dangerous, questionable, or unqualified candidates, while at the same time helping to identify those candidates who are capable, trustworthy, and best suited to the job requirements.

An SHP is part of the fabric of how a firm operates its businesses. The program—

- dictates the types of precautions to be taken and sets limits for eligibility for employment
- incorporates screening and selection procedures, clearly stating qualifiers and disqualifiers
- utilizes a series of overlapping tools, recognizing that no one tool is perfect, and
- recognizes that due diligence requires multiple approaches

Moreover, a Safe Hiring Program—

- maps out the events in the hiring process
- dictates policy in order to ensure all candidates are treated equally and fairly, and
- establishes legally defensible practices for dealing with undesirable or potentially problematic applicants

These practices are to be supported by documented procedures.

Yes, safe hiring is not something that occurs without some effort. Without a safe hiring program, it is a statistical certainty that an employer will eventually hire someone with an unsuitable criminal record or false credentials, creating a very real possibility of a legal and financial nightmare.

# Anatomy of a Safe Hiring Program

Given the enormous price tag of a bad hiring decision, it is no surprise that employers of all sizes are looking to various tools in hopes of boosting the effectiveness of the hiring process. The tools used include honesty and skills testing, behavior-based testing, group interview techniques, criminal record checks and verification of previous employment. Not one of these tools alone has proven 100% effective in weeding out bad candidates; each tool should be used in conjunction with all the tools documented in your overall Safe Hiring Program.

A Safe Hiring Program consists of five core areas—

| Core Competencies | Key Components |
|---|---|
| 1. Organizational Infrastructure | Have organizational commitment and structure to a Safe Hiring Program. The **S.A.F.E System**[1] sets in place the critical *Policies, Practices and Procedures* necessary for a Safe Hiring Program. |
| 2. Initial Screening Practices | The **AIR Process** (for *Application, Interview and References)*[2] begins from the first job announcement or advertisement. It may also include an initial identification check. |
| 3. In-Depth Screening Practices | These practices include a criminal record check and other tools described throughout the book. |
| 4. Post-Hire Practices | Practices include a continuing commitment to a safe workplace even after an applicant has been hired. |
| 5. Legal Compliance Practices | Practices include an awareness of the legal and regulatory environment surrounding safe hiring and compliance. |

The above sounds good, but how does one start? …By deciding to incorporate the elements of the S.A.F.E. System into an overall Safe Hiring Program that is implemented on a company-wide basis! In this way, large organizations can ensure that hiring managers within different divisions and even different physical locations follow the same procedures.

# The S.A.F.E. System

S.A.F.E. stands for—

**S** — Set-up a program that consists of documented policies, practices and procedures to be used throughout the organization in order to achieve safe hiring.

**A** — Acclimate/Train all persons with safe hiring responsibilities, especially hiring managers.

**F** — Facilitate/Implement the program.

**E** — Evaluate and audit the program.

---

[1] more about the S.A.F.E. System is presented in Chapter 4
[2] AIR Process tools are analyzed in Chapters 7, 8, and 9

Item "E" includes making sure that everyone involved understands their own compensation and advancement is judged in part by the attention they pay to the hiring process. Organizations typically accomplish those things that are measured, audited, and rewarded — so do that in your hiring program.[3]

**A key concept presented in this book is "pre-employment screening" or as it is sometimes called, "employment screening." This process is also referred to as "background checks."**

**A Safe Hiring Program is NOT the same thing as pre-employment screening.**

Pre-employment screening is only one part of the total approach to a Safe Hiring Program. Pre-employment screening is certainly a critical part, but there is much more to an SHP.

The background screen occurs when an employer or an outside professional firm assembles information such as criminal records, credit reports, or credentials verifications on an applicant.

Many firms make the mistake of believing that safe hiring is an event that is typically outsourced to a screening firm or investigator. The misconception is that, in order to show due diligence, employers merely need to spend money to perform background checks and criminal record searches. These firms somewhat incorrectly view pre-employment screening as a process that begins after a hiring manager selects an applicant, then submits the name to the firm's security or human resources department, or chooses to outsource by calling in an employment screening firm for a background report or to conduct the screening tasks.

The key point to remember is— an effective Safe Hiring Program is much more than just pre-employment screening or background checks. In fact, in an effective SHP, the primary tools are processes that occur in–house as part of a routine, documented hiring program. For example, one of the most effective tools for safe hiring is the application, interview and reference checking process, also known as the *AIR Process*. This multi-step process, examined in detail in this book, is not only one of the best lines of defense against a bad hire, but the cost is right — virtually nothing. The only cost is a commitment to safe hiring.

# Reasons Why Safe Hiring is Such a Challenge

Even though everyone agrees that safe hiring and due diligence are missions critical for any business, there are still numerous employers who find safe hiring to be a challenge. Sadly, there are many employers that either do nothing when it comes to due diligence, or do way too little.

Here are some of the issues that face employers—

## Compliance With Hiring Laws

The laws associated with employment screening have sought to achieve a balance between privacy and due diligence. Although a number of laws limit, prohibit, or regulate obtaining and using background information, there is a great deal of information an employer is entitled to obtain and use in making the best hiring decisions. Certainly, all citizens have a reasonable expectation to privacy and a right to be

---

[3] refer to Chapter 4 for a detailed explanation of the S.A.F.E. System and how it is used to create a Company Safe Hiring Program

treated fairly, yet, at the same time, an employer has the right to make diligent and reasonable job-related inquiries into a person's background so that the company, its employees, and the public are not placed at risk.

Therefore it is vital to keep the scope of reference checking and screening within specified legal boundaries. There are certain matters that are not valid predictors of job performance, and delving into them can be considered discriminatory. This can include information about religion or race, national origin, marital status, age, medical condition, and so forth. An employer cannot ask reference questions or obtain background information on those subject areas that cannot legally be raised in an interview situation with an applicant face-to-face.

## There is No Instant Database That Gives All the Answers

In a perfect world, an employer needs only to go on the internet, put in an applicant's name and identity, then up pops an instant thumps-up or thumbs-down result. Wow, with the click of a mouse, the employer would know if the person has a criminal record and if his or her credentials are accurate.

Unfortunately, there is no magic database in existence. There is no national credentials database where an employer can instantly confirm an applicant's past employment or education. There is no public record database where an employer can instantly find out if the applicant has a criminal record, a problematic driving record, or a job-related civil lawsuit.

Some employers have been given the legal authority to obtain government criminal records when filling positions involving security or access to groups at risk. In many states, for positions involving access to vulnerable patients or children, screeners for hospitals and school districts can submit applicant's fingerprints to be checked by the FBI or state authorities.

However, for most private employers, the challenge is more pressing because of the fact a criminal record check is not nearly as effective a tool as most employers might believe. Although certainly a criminal check is an essential part of any hiring program, it does not necessarily provide complete protection — there are over 10,000 courthouses in 3,500+ jurisdictions in the U.S.A. Since employers cannot search every jurisdiction, there is always the possibility of missing a criminal record from a court not searched. The possibility of errors are compounded by the fact the searches are conducted by human beings who enter names in computers, scan listings of names, or engage in some other activity that ultimately depends upon human intervention. There is always the possibility of error. Even official government "rap sheets" are subject to error.[4]

There are privately-assembled multi-jurisdictional databases but these too can lead to false negatives — that is, a person with a criminal record comes up clean

Confirming education credentials and past employment is equally labor intensive. Although some colleges and universities allow online record verifications and electronic transcripts, employers must still identify and individually go to each relevant school database. Past employers must be contacted, which is a process that presents its own difficulties.

---

[4] reasons for errors on government records are discussed in Chapter 12

# There Are No Magical Tools That Find an "Honest" Person

In the wake of Enron, WorldCom and what appears to be a general collapse of corporate ethics and morality, more emphasis is now placed on the age-old question asked by Greek philosopher *Diogenes*, *"How do you find an honest person?"*

Part of the challenge in safe hiring is that by definition, employers are seeking an elusive quality. Ultimately, the ability to find an honest person depends on the correct use of a number of overlapping tools. These include 1) a number of objective fact-finding tools (pre-employment screening and reference checks); 2) tools used to convince applicants to be self-revealing (applications and interviews), and 3) to a subjective extent, instinct and intuition. However, reliance only on instinct and intuition can be dangerous. Consider this fact— for every dishonest person ever hired there was someone who sized up the person hired and concluded that this person would be good for the job.

There is no surefire test or method that will tell an employer if a particular person is an honest person.[5]

# It is Almost Impossible to Spot Liars at Interviews

Even if Diogenes had found an honest person, there is a body of modern evidence that suggests it is difficult for anyone, from ancient philosophers to modern day employer, to use an interview to determine who is really who. Employers have a distinct challenge when it comes to spotting liars; industry statistics suggest that as many as 30% of all job applicants falsify information about their credentials, but trying to spot liars at interviews is, well, difficult if not impossible.

There are lists of so-called "tell-tale signs" that a person is lying. For example, employers might observe if a person is avoiding eye contact, fidgeting, or hesitating before answering. Unfortunately, it can be a costly mistake for an interviewer to think lying can always be detected by such visual clues, "tells" or by relying upon one's own instinct or intuition since some of the so-called "visual clues" can simply be a sign of nervousness about the interview, or stress, and not an intent to lie. In fact, accomplished liars are more dangerous because they can disguise themselves as truthful and sincere. An experienced liar will often show no visible signs.

The problem is further complicated because many people feel they can detect who is lying and who is not. Studies have demonstrated that most people are poor judges of when they are being told the truth and when they are being deceived. Paul Ekman, a psychology professor in the Department of Psychiatry at the University of California Medical School in San Francisco, is the author of thirteen books, including *Telling Lies*.[6] Ekman has tested about 6,000 people professionals trained to spot liars, including police officers, lawyers, judges, psychiatrists, and agents of the FBI, the CIA and the Drug Enforcement Administration, to determine if they can tell if someone is lying. According to his research, most people are not very accurate in judging if a person is lying. The average accuracy in studies is rarely above 60%, while chance is 50%. Even among professional lie catchers, the ability to detect liars is not much better than 50%. In one study, custom agents who interviewed people at custom stations did not do any better than college students.

---

[5] Chapter 23 addresses ways to incorporate some effective honesty and integrity testing

[6] published by W.W. Norton, 2001

Another researcher at the same school, Dr. Maureen O'Sullivan, tested 13,000 people for the ability to detect deception. Using three different tests, only 31 subjects — nicknamed "wizards" — could *usually* tell whether a person was lying about an opinion, how someone is feeling, or about a crime.[7]

Some interviewees tell lies they have ingrained in their life story. They have created identities and legends of their own and, when they tell their stories, they are not fabricating on the spot. They put "it" on their resumes and talk about it and tell their friends about it. It becomes part of their personalities and personal histories because they have told it so often. It becomes second nature as they retell it again and again.

That does not mean that some liars cannot be detected at interview. John E. Reid and Associates offers a one-day course specifically designed around interviewing of applicants. [8]

Employers, HR and Security professionals should remember that as valuable as instinct may be, it does not substitute for factual verification of an applicant's credentials through background checks and other safe hiring techniques.

## The Effects of Corporate Culture and Other Impediments

At some firms, efforts at safe hiring may be impeded by the simple fact that it has historically not been done. Pre-employment screening, reference checks, and criminal background checks are relatively new on the corporate scene. Although a recent study by the Society of Human Resources Management[9] suggests the use of screening tools is on the rise, there are some employers who are still reluctant to engage in background screening out of a concern that an applicant may find it insulting. There is even more reluctance to perform screening for higher-level positions, especially positions that have a C in the title such as CEO or CFO. The higher a person is in the organization, the more harm that person can do.

# The Four Biggest Benefits From The SHP

Employers do not have to sit back and wait to be victimized. By addressing workplace problems at their main source – ***problem employees*** – employers can substantially lessen risks to their businesses.

To prevent the hire of potentially problematic individuals, businesses are responsible for taking appropriate steps toward the development of policies and countermeasures before the hiring process begins. All relevant departments and personnel must be familiar with – and committed to – their company Safe Hiring Program. Properly implemented, an SHP helps employers in four key ways—

---

[7] more information about these studies is available at www.paulekman.com

[8] information on John E. Reid and Associates one-day course specifically on interviewing applicants is at www.reid.com/training-interview-dates.html

[9] issues common to this Study by the Society of Human Resources Management are discussed in Chapter 10

## 1. Deterrence

Making it clear that screening is part of the hiring process can deter potentially problematic applicants and discourage applicants with something to hide. An applicant with serious criminal convictions or falsified information on his or her resume is less likely to apply at a firm that announces pre-employment background checks are part of the hiring process. Do not become the employer of choice for people with problems when simply having a screening program can deter those problem applicants.

## 2. Encourage Honesty

The goal of a safe hiring program is not to find only "perfect candidates." Many candidates who may have some blemish on their record may be still well-suited for employment. However, employers need to be fully informed when making a hiring decision. Having a Safe Hiring Program encourages applicants to be especially forthcoming in their interviews. Making it clear that background checks are part of the hiring process is strong motivation for applicants to reveal information about themselves they feel may be uncovered by a background check.

## 3. Fact-Finding

Although instincts play a large role in hiring, basing a decision on hard information is even better, and safer. Effective screening obtains factual information about a candidate in order to supplement the impressions obtained from an interview. It is also a valuable tool for judging the accuracy of a candidate's resume. Facts limit uncertainty in the hiring process.

## 4. Due Diligence

Implementing a Safe Hiring Program helps an employer practice due diligence in their hiring. Having an SHP is a powerful defense in the event of a lawsuit.[10]

# What The SHP Does NOT Do

Although it is important to understand the benefits of a Safe Hiring Program, it is also important to be clear on what the SHP does not do. While a properly implemented program can considerably minimize the risk of hiring a problem employee, it is not a guarantee that every person with an undisclosed criminal record or false credential will be identified.

The world's experts on background screening and pre-employment investigations are probably the FBI and the CIA. They spend millions on pre-hiring investigations. Yet, from time to time, there are newspaper stories about how the FBI hires spies and the CIA hires crooks. If the world's experts do not have a 100% success rate with millions of dollars to spend and full access to governmental databases, what chance do private employers have?

---

[10] more information about exercising due diligence is contained in Chapter 3

As the term suggests, background screening is a large-scale process that operates on a cost/benefit basis. A firm is looking at confirming known information (such as past employment or education) or doing quick and cost-effective checks of readily available public documents such as criminal records.

Background screening is not meant to be a full investigation, where the investigator develops leads and intensely focuses on the individual. During an investigation the investigator is focused on one person (as opposed to a group) and is doing an in-depth examination (as opposed to using diagnostic tools) where the information is either hidden or not readily apparent. Thus, investigations are typically much more expensive than a background screening.

As a result, when performing a background screening, it is possible something will fall through the cracks. Given that screening is relatively inexpensive, employers cannot expect a foolproof process for the prices being charged. However, screening is extremely effective at keeping the workplace safe, productive, and reasonably trouble-free. Screening also demonstrates due diligence, which is important if a problem employee is hired and the employer needs to defend their hiring practices in a lawsuit.[11]

# Risk Management Calculation for Safe Hiring

Another way of analyzing the value of a Safe Hiring Program is to utilize risk-management analysis. Risk can be defined as *the possibility of suffering loss*. Risk management means *the systematic identification of the risks involved, and determining the best course of action to avoid or minimize the risks*. It can also be thought of as a cost-benefit analysis.

The Federal Aviation Administration (FAA) has prepared an excellent introduction to risk management. According to the FAA—

> "Risk management…. is pre-emptive, rather than reactive. The approach is based on the philosophy that it is irresponsible and wasteful to wait for an accident to happen, then figuring out how to prevent it from happening again. We manage risk whenever we modify the way we do something to make our chances of success as great as possible, while making our chances of failure, injury or loss as small as possible. It is a commonsense approach to balancing the risks against the benefits to be gained in a situation and then choosing the most effective course of action."

One key principle of risk management is to *Accept No Unnecessary Risk*. According to the FAA—

> "Unnecessary risk is that which carries no commensurate return in terms of benefits or opportunities. Everything involves risk. The most logical choices for accomplishing an operation are those that meet all requirements with the minimum acceptable risk. The corollary to this axiom is "accept necessary risk" required to successfully complete the operation or task."[12]

As a part of a risk management process, it is critical to fully identify all of the risks that can be encountered, and to demonstrate the cost of avoiding the risks.

In the case of safe hiring, the risks are well known. As seen throughout this book, the cost of controlling the risks of a bad hire is marginal in comparison to the benefits gained. The most effective

---

[11] screening and due diligence is discussed in Chapter 3

[12] for more information about the FAA material, see www.asy.faa.gov/Risk/SSHandbook/Chap15_1200.PDF

screening tools cost an employer very little. The portion of the Safe Hiring Program that involves utilizing outside professional services has a cost that is minimal compared to just one bad hire. Any risk-management analysis will come to one conclusion — a firm is taking an unnecessary risk when they do not engage in a safe hiring program.

# The ROI of a Screening Program

Employers justify the costs associated with employment screening because of the clear Return on Investment — the ROI — these programs bring to the workplace.

There are two costs associated with a screening program. First is the cost of the in-house time and effort needed to pursue a safe hiring program; second, the cost of any outsourced services. These costs will be covered in greater detail in a later section. In the meantime, let us assume, as a general rule, the cost of a background screening is less than the cost of an employee's salary on his or her first day on the job. Of course, applicants may be screened at different levels so the cost is not the same for all candidates. A screening for a janitorial position may be less costly than a more in-depth screening used for an executive position. However, since the executive also gets paid more, the cost of a screening as a percentage of salary still works out as less than that new executive's first day's salary.

## Two Approaches to Calculating ROI

Because the purpose of background screening is to prevent harm, it is often difficult to quantify the ROI of events that did *not* happen. As seen in Chapter 1, a firm hit with even a single incident of workplace violence or related legal action immediately recognizes the advantages of a Safe Hiring Program.

**Method One: Making a Judgment as to the Value of Avoiding the "Parade of Horribles."**

Assume an average background check performed by a third party firm is $65, and during a twelve month period a firm submits 100 names to a screening firm. Keep in mind that most employers only screen finalists, not all who apply. The third-party costs of this service would be $6,500.

Given the fact that industry sources indicate that up to ten percent of all screened workers have criminal records, a firm would have to decide if it was worth $6,500 to avoid hiring ten workers with some sort of criminal record. A judgment has to be made as to whether it is worth that cost in order to avoid hiring problem employees. Given the impact that even one "bad hire" can bring, it would appear to be a very small price to pay.

**Method Two: Calculation of Benefit from Lack of Turnover**

One way benefits of a Safe Hiring Program can be measured is by estimating the average costs associated with a single employee turnover. An easy way to consider these costs is by building a "turnover calculator" that breaks down all the costs associated with having and filling a vacancy on an item-by-item basis.[13] When the expenses involved are broken down to basics, it is easy to see how such costs can add up to a sizeable figure.

---

[13] an example of a *Turnover Cost Calculator Form* appears in Appendix 3

# Answers to 10 Frequently Expressed Concerns of Employers

Even with all of the advantages of a Safe Hiring Program, many employers have questions and concerns about implementing safe hiring and background checks. These are the ten most common concerns that employers express regarding safe hiring or a screening program.

## 1. Is an SHP legal?

Employers have an absolute right to select the most-qualified candidate for a job. The only limitations on employers are the ones that employers already understand and abide by in all of their workplace policies. For example, employers must ensure that all selection procedures are non–discriminatory, based upon factors that are valid predictors of job performance and do not invade privacy rights or other laws.[14] A safe hiring program easily falls within these limitations.

If a firm utilizes a pre-employment screening agency, then a federal law called the Fair Credit Reporting Act (FCRA) balances the right of an employer to know whom they hire with the applicant's rights of disclosure and privacy. Under this law, the employer first obtains the applicant's written consent to be screened. In the event negative information is found, the applicant must be given the opportunity to correct the record. Employers should set up a **consistent** policy so similarly situated applicants are treated the same. A qualified screening company will assist an employer with legal compliance issues.

## 2. Does safe hiring invade privacy?

No. Employers can find out about only those things that an applicant has done in his or her "public" life. For example, checking court records for criminal convictions or calling past employers or schools does not invade a zone of personal privacy. Employers are looking only at information that is a valid and non-discriminatory predictor of future job performance. As a general rule, an employer will not ask for any information that an employer could not ask an applicant in a face-to-face interview. Employers should also take steps to maintain confidentiality within their organization, such as keeping reports in a separate file from the personnel files. To maintain privacy, most background firms offer internet systems with secured websites.

## 3. Is safe hiring cost-effective?

In a Safe Hiring Program, the cost to select one new employee will typically cost less than the cost of that new employee on his or her first day on the job. That is pocket change compared to the damage one bad hire can cause. In addition, if an employer utilizes an outside agency, the service is typically used only to screen an applicant if a decision has been made to extend a job offer. Not all applicants are screened. It is ironic that some firms will spend hours shopping for a computer

---

[14] privacy rights and other laws are discussed in depth in Chapter 5

bargain yet at the same time try to save money by not adequately checking out a job applicant, which represents an enormous investment. Problem employees usually cause employee problems, and money is well spent to avoid problems in the first place.

## 4. Does safe hiring discourage good applicants?

Employers who engage in a safe hiring program do not find that good applicants are deterred. Job applicants have a desire to work with qualified and safe co-workers in a profitable environment. A good candidate understands background screening is a sound business practice. It is not an invasion of privacy or an intrusion.

## 5. Does background screening delay hiring?

No. Background screening is normally done in 48 to 72 hours. Most of the necessary information is obtained by going to courthouses or calling past employers or schools. Occasionally there can be delays beyond anyone's control such as previous employers who will not return calls, schools that are closed for vacation, or a court clerk who needs to retrieve a record from archive storage.

Furthermore, an organization that is careful in its hiring practices should find a lower rate of negative "hits" during background checks. As discussed in later chapters, there are a number of steps a firm should take to ensure safe hiring well before a name is submitted to a background screening company. These techniques include making it clear your firm does background checks in order to weed out bad applicants, knowing the "red flags" to look for in an application, and asking questions in interviews that will help filter out problem candidates.

## 6. Does safe hiring have to be outsourced to be effective?

Not at all. In fact, the most effective safe hiring tools are completed in house and cost nothing. Firms that take time to thoroughly develop an application process, an interview process, and a reference checking process receive a great deal of protection. Many firms do outsource part of the task, such as criminal record checks, because of the specialized skills, knowledge, and resources that are involved in a correct check. Typically these tasks, although vital, are not part of a firm's core expertise and can be performed by a third party more quickly and efficiently.

## 7. If we outsource, is it difficult to implement?

Even for an overburdened HR, security, or risk management department already handling numerous tasks, outsourcing background screening can be done very quickly and effectively. A qualified pre-employment screening firm can set up the entire program and provide all the necessary forms in a short time. Many firms have internet-based systems that speed up the flow of information and allow an employer to track the progress of each applicant in real time.

## 8. How do we select a service provider if we outsource all or part of it?

An employer should apply the same criteria they would use in selecting any other providers of critical professional services. An employer should look for a professional partner and not just an information vendor selling data at the lowest price. For example, if an employer were choosing a law firm for legal representation, it would not merely select the cheapest — the employer would clearly want to know it is selecting a firm that is competent, experienced, knowledgeable, as well as reputable and reasonably priced.[15] The same criteria should also apply to critical HR services. A screening firm should have an understanding of the legal implications of background checks, particularly the Federal Fair Credit Reporting Act. A list of screening firms that have voluntarily agreed to an industry code of ethics by joining the National Association of Professional Background Screeners (NAPBS) is available at www.napbs.com.

## 9. Do we risk being sued by an applicant?

Unfortunately, anyone can go to the courthouse and sue anyone else. On a risk/management basis however, the advantage of performing pre-employment screening clearly outweighs the possibility that an applicant may sue. Statistics overwhelmingly show that employers do not need to be concerned, as a practical matter, about applicant lawsuits. On the other hand, it is an absolute certainty, without screening, an employer becomes the employer of choice for everyone with a problem, and will hire unsuitable criminals and applicants with false credentials. An employer can be protected by following certain basic guidelines in a fair and legal screening program.

## 10. Is it worth the time and energy to even think about safe hiring, given everything else an employer has to do?

Since the fundamental rule in running a business of any size is that employee problems stem from *problem employees* — it is time and money well spent to avoid hiring a problem in the first place. As outlined in the next chapter, if there is an incident of workplace violence or litigation due to a bad hire, then a firm would want to pay almost anything to avoid the bad hire in the first place. Use of a legally sound screening program can protect against the vast majority of employee issues.

Both employers and applicants have learned that pre-employment screening is an absolute necessity in today's business world. More importantly, we have learned due diligence in hiring is a way to keep firms safe and profitable in difficult times.

---

[15] how to select a screening firm is discussed in detail in Chapter 10

# Chapter 3

# Due Diligence and Negligent Hiring

Every employer carries around a large invisible burden when they hire. That burden is the obligation — the duty — to exercise reasonable care for the safety of others. The legal description of the duty of care is called "**due diligence**." The employer's duty to exercise due diligence means the employer must consider if a potential new employee represents a risk to others in view of the nature of the job.

> **Question:** What is a term that can be used to describe an employer who fails to exercise due diligence in the hiring process?

> **Answer:** The term "defendant," as in a party who is sued for damages in a civil lawsuit for failure to perform a legal duty.

When an employer fails to exercise due diligence and a person is harmed by an employee, that employer can be sued. The name of the legal action is called, "**negligent hiring**," sometimes referred to as "**the negligent hiring doctrine**."

Negligent hiring is the flip side of "due diligence." If an employer hires someone who they either *knew* or in the exercise of reasonable care *should have known* was dangerous, unfit, or not qualified for the position, and it was foreseeable that some sort of injury could happen to someone as a result, then the employer can be sued for negligent hiring. This is called the "knew or reasonably should have known" standard.

Obviously, most employers will not hire someone they know is dangerous or unfit for a job. It is the "**should have known**" part that gets employers into difficulties.

The threat of being sued for negligent hiring is far from theoretical. As discussed in Chapter 1, lawsuits for negligent hiring are one of the fastest growing areas of tort litigation. Employers are being hit with multi-million dollar jury verdicts and settlements as well as enormous attorneys' fees.

## How Negligent Hiring Lawsuits Started

Assume you have an employee who is driving to an assignment and gets into an accident, or, while on the job, an employee accidentally injures someone while trying to perform his or her duties. In these cases, most employers would agree an employer would expect to be liable. In fact, there is a legal theory called **Respondent Superior**, which means literally that the *Master* must respond when their employee commits a wrongdoing while engaged in the scope and course of his duties. The law refers to this as *vicarious liability*.

What happens if an employee decides to beat up someone on the job? What happens if an employee meets someone on the premises, goes to that person's home and commits a sexual assault or a theft?

In these scenarios, an employer may say, "Wait a minute, I have looked through the job descriptions and the job says nothing about assaults, thefts, or sexual offenses on or off the job. He was not doing those things in the performance of his duty. These were independent and intentional acts he committed."

The employer would be right to a point. Under the **traditional** legal theory of **Respondent Superior**, the employer likely could not be sued successfully. However, such a limitation would result in innocent victims being denied their day in court and negligent employers not being held responsible. As a result, the ability to bring a lawsuit for **negligent hiring** was developed in order to afford relief to victims injured by the negligent actions of an employer, where the negligence had foreseeable consequences and caused the injury.

The right to bring a lawsuit for negligent hiring as well as negligent supervision, training or promotion, is established primarily through case law and is legally recognized in the majority of states. As of June, 2004, a fifty state survey revealed that forty-six states have judicially recognized the concept of negligent hiring or retention. The four states that have not formally recognized the concept have not declared an injured party cannot sue for negligent hiring. To date, this is yet to be the subject of a case reported from a state appellate court.

> **Author Tip** ➡ To determine if your state has a Negligent Hiring Doctrine, visit your local law library where you can search the Westlaw or Lexis systems using a topic heading of "Agency and Employment" or "Master and Servant."

# A Safe Hiring Program Shows Due Diligence

Understanding how due diligence is associated with the liability for negligent hiring is critical for any employer. If a bad hire does something to force an employer to defend in court, then an employer must show how it took appropriate measures of due diligence.

Firms that do not perform due diligence are sitting ducks for litigation, including attorneys' fees and big damage awards. Employers that implement and follow a Safe Hiring Program (SHP) show due diligence measures that are a powerful legal protection. Fortunately for these employers, the cost of exercising due diligence through a SHP is very modest. Even if there is a cost involved, employers need to measure the risk of hiring blind with the considerable and near certain risk of litigation and attorney fees stemming from a single bad hiring decision. As the old saying goes, it is a matter of paying now or paying later.

Conversely, a SHP protects the employer in case a bad hire slips through. Despite an employer's best efforts at safe hiring, there is always the possibility someone will be hired who causes harm. If an employer can convince a jury that the employer exercised due diligence and acted in a reasonable fashion, then the employer has a powerful defense against a lawsuit.

**Author Tip** ➡ When an employer obtains criminal records, the employer needs to carefully evaluate if the information obtained truly shows due diligence. For example, one "national" database service advertises they provide criminal conviction, sexual offender registry data, and incarceration record information from across the United States. This particular service is advertised for a fee of only a few dollars per name searched. For an employer seeking a cost-effective due diligence solution, this search may seem like a good deal at first blush. Unfortunately, because of the nature of this sort of database search, there is a strong possibility that a criminal record can be missed. As explained in Chapter 12, database searches can be valuable *secondary tools* to supplement the more accurate on-site court search of public records. Databases are also problematic due to issues of timelines, completeness, accuracy, and coverage. A database search can create a false sense of security. The fact that a name is not in a criminal database search, despite the use of the term "national," does not mean a person does not have a record or is not a criminal. Conversely, just because a name is in a database does not mean the person is a criminal.

If an employer relies primarily upon a $2.00 search and a criminal record is missed, then the employer would have a challenging time convincing a jury that a $2.00 search demonstrates due diligence.

# Avoiding a Negligent Hiring Lawsuit

What must an employer do to AVOID negligence in hiring? This is the million-dollar question. The answer is — it depends. What does it depend upon? We will discuss that in the next six pages.

## Non-Regulated Private Employers — A Moving Target

Some employers have obligations or standards created by law. However, for the vast majority of private employers, liability depends upon the jury's view of the facts in each particular case. Generally, due diligence is a moving target. Unless an employer is governed by federal or state statutes, there is no one thing an employer can do to makes itself 100% immune from being sued. In other words, with some limited exceptions discussed below, there is not a national standard of care that, if followed, insures an employer is not negligent as a matter of law.

Generally speaking, the employer's duty of care is commensurate with the reasonably anticipated risk to third parties. That is where a Safe Hiring Program comes in. The SHP consists of a number of overlapping tools and procedures that, when combined, create an ample defense against a negligent hiring lawsuit.

## Public Employers Also Must be Concerned

Public entities, ranging from local school districts, counties, states and the federal government, also hire employees. Although governmental entities enjoy immunity from being sued, there are tort claim acts that allow lawsuits in certain situations. For example, the Federal Tort Claims Act (FTCA) allows a person to bring a lawsuit against the U.S. government for personal injury, wrongful death, or property damage under the following four conditions—

- The injury must have been caused by a U.S. government employee acting negligently or wrongfully (but not intentionally).

- The employee must have been acting within the scope of his office or employment.

- The injured party must comply with the claims procedures, which include submitting a claim to the appropriate federal agency within two years from the date of injury.

- A lawsuit can only be filed if the agency either denies the claim or six months pass with no action, whichever comes first.

The federal law also excludes a number of possible causes of action such as injuries caused by a government contractor, or caused by government employees acting in accordance with the law or carrying out discretionary duties.

Although some protections and some procedural barriers exist when it comes to a public employer getting sued for negligent hiring, public employers need to exercise due diligence in their hiring as well.

## Mandated Background Checks

Some private employers have obligations created by state or federal law to perform background checks or not hire individuals with certain criminal matters in their past. When determining what is proper due diligence, an employer must be aware of any rules or regulations affecting its particular industry. For example, every state has a myriad of laws requiring a criminal record background check before someone can be hired within a certain industry (heath care, child care, etc.), or be licensed by a state licensing board (nurse, private investigator, etc.).

Employers and boards regulated by a federal or state law will likely already be aware of that obligation by virtue of being in that industry. Many public positions also require background checks. It is beyond the scope of this book to attempt to summarize the vast number of specific state laws that require background checks. However, it is clear that any private or public employers who violate the rules on mandatory checks can be sued if their failure results in harm to a co-worker or third party.

## Abiding by State Laws and Industry Standards

There can also be standards which force employers to practice due diligence. The legislatures in several states have created standards that provide strong incentives to use background checks as a means to avoid negligent hiring. Below are two examples.

- In accordance with **Fla Stat Ann** § 768.096, a Florida employer who conducts a background investigation of an employee, including utilization of the Florida Crime Information Center system, is presumed not to have been negligent in the hiring of an employee. The election by an employer not to conduct an investigation under § 768.096 does not raise a presumption that an employer failed to use reasonable care in hiring an employee.

- A similar law went into effect in **Texas** in 2003. This law created an incentive for "in-home service" or "residential delivery" companies to perform background checks on their employees. If an employer runs a background check using the Texas online database and the report comes back clear, then the employer has the protection of a rebuttal presumption that the company did not act negligently. Texas Department of Public Safety (DPS) has established an internet site for criminal records, registered sex offenders, and deferred adjudications.[1]

---

**Legal Presumption and Rebuttable Presumption Defined—**

A legal presumption is a fact the law assumes to be true. However, once a fact is assumed true, the other party can then offer evidence to "rebut" or disprove the presumption. The advantage to an employer when there is a "rebuttable presumption" of acting with due diligence is the employer starts off not having to prove anything. The suing party has the obligation of presenting evidence to disprove the employer's due diligence.

---

In addition, employers should consider general industry standards and guidelines, even if they are not mandatory. For example, in Chapter 22 on Terrorism, there is a discussion of certain rules the federal government has strongly suggested, but not mandated, for the food industry.

Finally, an employer may consider if a member of its industry has been sued for negligence in connection with hiring, and the outcome. Not only can an employer learn from what has happened to other firms, but a verdict can create an industry standard that other employers may be held to as well.

---

**Author Tip** ➡ The American Society for Industrial Security at www.asisonline.org is currently working with the National Association of Professional Background Screeners, at www.napbs.com, to develop guidelines for employment screening, including the level of screening recommended or required for certain occupations and certain industries.

---

# Proving Negligent Hiring

To prove negligent hiring, an injured party (or the surviving family members suing for a wrongful death claim in the event the victim died) must prove the following—

1. Injury
2. Existence of a duty of care owed toward the plaintiff
3. The employer breaches the duty of care
4. Causation between the negligent hiring and the injury

Following are detailed breakdowns about each of these four points proving negligent hiring.

---

[1] refer to http://records.txdps.state.tx.us

# 1. Injury

For a lawsuit to be brought, the plaintiff must allege there is an injury. The injury can include injuries that are physical (assault, murder, sexual offenses), emotional or psychological (infliction of emotional distress), property loss or damage (theft, destruction), or even identity theft.

Examples of injuries in negligent hiring cases include—

(1) The plaintiff, Welsh Manufacturing, brought suit against the security guard company it hired, Pinkerton's, Inc. As a result of three major thefts resulting in losses in excess of $200,000, a security guard was found to have been a co-conspirator in connection with those thefts.

(2) The plaintiff, an industrial contractor, brought suit against the company it hired to perform janitorial services. A janitor stole cash from a desk on subsequent nights and burned down the building in order to cover up the theft.

(3) The plaintiff, a hitchhiker, brought suit against an employer of a truck driver. A rape was committed by the truck driver after he offered the plaintiff a ride in his truck.

(4) The plaintiffs, the parents of a disabled minor daughter, brought suit against a home health care agency. A substitute home health aide provided by the agency injected the daughter with a large unauthorized insulin dose, causing a seizure.

(5) The plaintiffs, parents of a murder victim, brought suit against their daughter's employer. A co-worker at her office murdered her at her own apartment after gaining access to her address at work.

(6) The plaintiff, a female employee, brought suit against her employer. A co-employee harassed her using cruel practical jokes, obscene comments, behavior of a sexual nature, unwanted touching of employee's person, and veiled threats to her personal safety.[2]

# 2. Existence of a Duty of Care Owed Toward the Plaintiff

The injured party must show there is some connection or relationship between itself and the employer, so the employer owes a **duty of care**. This can occur in numerous situations, such as a co-worker on the job, a member of the public in a location where customers are expected to have contact with employees, tenants in an apartment building injured by a maintenance worker, and other situations where the victim and the dangerous employee are expected to come into contact. In other words, an employer breaches a duty of care if it creates a situation where a third party is expected to be brought into contact with the employee who causes the injury, under conditions for which there is an opportunity for an injury to occur. It does not matter that the particular injury was foreseeable, just that any injury was foreseeable.

Certain employers have a **higher duty of care** because of the unique situations of the job. **An employer's duty of care will increase with the degree of risk involved with the position** For example, consider the nature of the authority and position of trust a security guard holds. Many courts

---

[2] (1) *Welsh Mfg., Div. of Textron, Inc. v. Pinkerton's, Inc.,* 474 A.2d 436 (R.I. 1984); (2) *Lou-Con, Inc. v. Gulf Building Services, Inc.,* 287 So.2d 192 (La.App. 4th Cir. 1973); (3) *Malorey v. B & L Motor Freight,* 146 Ill. App. 3d 265 (1986); (4) *Interim Healthcare of Fort Wayne, Inc. v Moyer ex rel. Moyer,* 746 N.E.2d 429 (Ind.Ct.App. 2001); (5) *Gaines v. Monsanto Co.,* 655 S.W.2d 568 (Mo.App. E.D. 1983); (6) *Watson v. Dixon,* 502 S.E.2d 15 (N.C.App., 1998).

impose an even higher standard of care on a security guard business than other types of employers since there is a greater likelihood of harm to third parties. *Welsh Mfg., Div. of Textron, Inc. v. Pinkerton's, Inc.*, 474 A.2d 436 (R.I. 1984). In other words, when the job enables a person to act under some color of authority, a greater risk is involved because a person can potentially abuse that authority.

Similarly, courts have held employers who send workers into people's homes to a higher standard. This is on the theory that when an employer hires an employee who is given a unique opportunity to commit a crime, the employer has a higher duty of care. Examples are firms that clean carpets, deliver or fix appliances, or perform pest control services in a home. An example is a homeowner who brought suit against the exterminating service she hired when one of its employees raped her in her home. *Smith v. Orkin Exterminating Co., Inc.*, 540 So.2d 363 (La.App. 1st Cir. 1989).

Other examples of higher duties of care can be medical professionals, home health care agencies or childcare workers that serve a vulnerable population particularly at risk. Another example is a worker hired in a call center who has access to sensitive financial information such as credit card numbers, or personal information such as SSNs.

## 3. The Employer Breaches the Duty of Care

The employer breaches or violates the duty of care when an employer has either actual knowledge of the employee's unfitness or, in the exercise of reasonable care, would have knowledge the employee was dangerous, unfit, or not qualified. In other words, if the employer does not perform a reasonable background check, a jury could find the duty of care has been breached.

- In a case against the Episcopal Diocese of Pittsburgh, a court found the jury could find that defendants breached their duty to properly hire, train, and supervise a priest because they failed to discover he was not sufficiently trained and experienced in counseling, he had problems with alcohol and his personal life, and he had a propensity to engage in dual relationships with female communicants. *Podolinski v. Episcopal Diocese of Pittsburgh*, 23 Pa. D. & C.4th 385, (Pa.Com.Pl. 1995)

- In a Wisconsin case, a court held it is foreseeable that failing to properly train or supervise a loss prevention associate would subject shoppers to unreasonable risk, injury, or damage. If the defendant fails to properly hire, train, or supervise its employees, then it breaches its duty to shoppers at its store. The jury determined the defendant negligently hired, trained, or supervised its employees and therefore breached its duty to its patrons. *Miller v. Wal-Mart Stores, Inc.*, 580 N.W.2d 233, 261 (Wis., 1998).

- In a case involving a nightclub bouncer punching a patron, a court held that by the very nature of the job, a bouncer has significant interaction with the public and is routinely placed in confrontational situations with patrons. Therefore, hiring a bouncer who is known to have violent propensities would likely be a breach of the duty. *Hall v. SSF, Inc.*, 930 P.2d 94, 99 (Nev., 1996).

The level of the duty of care an employer must use is determined by the mythical "reasonable person standard." No one has yet located that person, although many lawyers have spent considerable time looking for the "reasonable person." The following is how one leading legal textbook describes the degree of care an employer must exercise.

---

### Employer's Duty of Care Explained in Legalese

"As a general rule it may be stated that the degree of care required to be exercised by an employer in selecting or retaining an employee is the degree of care that a person of ordinary prudence would use in view of the nature of the employment and the consequences of the employment of an incompetent person. Such degree of care should be commensurate with the nature and danger of the business and the grade of service for which the employee is intended, as well as to the hazard to which other employees would be exposed from the employment of a careless or incompetent person."

*9 2Am Jur Trials, Sec. 10. Negligent Hiring and Retention of Employees.*

---

## 4. Causation Between the Negligent Hiring and the Injury

The plaintiff must show the negligence was the cause of the injury. That means the injuries were a logical consequence of the employer's misconduct or incompetence. If an employee attacks a victim and causes injuries, there is no question the attack was the actual or physical cause of the injury. However, see discussion below for a defense based upon a lack of causation.

# Defenses Against Negligent Hiring Lawsuits

There are defenses an employer can raise in a lawsuit for negligent hiring. In the real world, an employer cannot count on a defense being successful. It is much better not to get sued in the first place. When an injury occurs and a lawsuit is initiated, most employers would have paid anything to avoid it. Some of the defenses listed below are intertwined and could be used in more than one category.

### Investigation would not have revealed anything negative

Even with more investigation, the employer would not have discovered anything that was relevant to the injury. A New York court held that a grade school principal's failure to perform a background check on a person recommended as a volunteer art teacher before permitting him to work with students, including a student he later molested, could not serve as a basis for a cause of action for negligent hiring, in absence of any evidence the volunteer had a criminal history and where a routine background check would not have revealed his propensity to molest minors. *Koran I v. Board of Education*, 683 N.Y.S.2d 228 (1998).

### Lack of foreseeability

The most successful defense has been the injury that occurred was not foreseeable. A successful foreseeability defense proves the knowledge gained through a proper background check in light of the hazards of the job would not indicate a given injury would occur. For example, information that a school bus driver had been terminated from his former position for tardiness did not demonstrate the subsequent employer should have known the driver posed a risk of engaging in sexual misconduct with children. *Giraldi by Giraldi v. Community Consol. School Dist.*, 279 Ill. App. 3d 679 (1996).

In a California case, the owner of a beauty school hired an employee to manage and supervise student training. The employee met a minor who was the son of a student at the school. As a result of meeting the minor through the school, the employee met the minor outside of the school and engaged in an illegal sexual encounter. The employee had previously been convicted of sexual offenses against children. The court held that the beauty school was not liable because even if they did a background check, nothing would have been revealed related to managing a beauty school. The past offenses did not involve students or customers of a hairdressing establishment and there was no indication the employee posed a threat to minors he may encounter in the course of his work. The court further held that an employer is not responsible for guaranteeing the safety of everyone an employee may incidentally meet while on the job. *Federico v. Superior Court*, 59 Cal. App. 4th 1207 (1997)

## Lack of causation

An employer can argue there was no causal or factual connection between the failure to investigate and the injury. For a victim to sue, she must show "but for" the employer's act or omission, she would not have been injured. For example, in one case the plaintiff was injured when he was struck by a car driven by an intoxicated employee of a car repossession firm hired to repossess the car. The plaintiff alleged the firm was negligent in hiring the employee without a repossessor license. The court determined that not being licensed to repossess was insufficient to establish the employee's unfitness as a repossessor. Additionally, there was no evidence that being unlicensed to repossess cars caused the accident. *Jones v. Beker,* 260 Ill. App. 3d 481 (1994).

In another case involving the issue of causation, a court held that a construction company was not liable to a plaintiff employee on theories of negligent hiring and supervision, where another employee of the construction company shot the plaintiff off the job site as a result of an altercation the previous night. Even though there was evidence the employee who did the shooting was aggressive and used drugs, the plaintiff failed to show the construction firm did anything more than hire the two employees to work at the same time so hence they knew each other. The plaintiff failed to show the defendant's alleged negligent hiring and supervision actually caused the shooting. *Escobar v. Madsen Constr. Co.*, 226 Ill App 3d 92 (1992, 1st Dist).

## Superseding or intervening cause

Related to the causation and foreseeability issue is the issue of proximate cause. An employer can argue that its negligence in hiring was not the legal or "proximate" cause of the injury because there was a superseding or intervening cause that was unexpected or was not reasonably foreseeable. An employer may have started a chain of events that led to an injury by making a bad hire, but some courts have held that the result was so unexpected that the employer cannot be held liable.

For example, in a case in New Mexico the employee delivered a television to the victim's apartment. Three nights later the employee returned, entered the apartment without permission and raped the victim. Even though the employee would not have meet the victim "but for" being hired to deliver a television, the court ruled that at the time of the crime the employee was on his own time, was not acting within the scope of his employment, was not in the employer's business vehicle, and had no authority from the employer to enter the apartment. In addition, he did not enter the victim's apartment to repair an appliance and the offense did not occur in or near the business. The employer knew the employee had a prior criminal record and that a purse belonging to a rape victim had been found near its place of business. However, on those facts, the court held that the act of the employee was independent of the employer and too attenuated to be attributed to the employers. *F&T Co. v. Woods*, 92 N.M. 697 (1979).

However, employers should not assume that they avoid liability just because their employee acted on his or her own or committed an intentional act. The "superseding cause" defense is determined on a case-by-case basis and other courts have found employers liable for acts committed by employees where the employer should have known about the employee's dangerous propensities. In another New Mexico case, a hotel was found liable for the sexual assault of a minor guest by an employee on the hotel premises while the employee was working. The employee had consumed alcoholic beverages during working hours. According to the court—

> "There was evidence from which a jury might find that defendant was aware or should have been aware that (the employee) had a drinking problem and a propensity for violence. Two incidents had occurred on hotel property shortly before the assault that gave rise to this lawsuit. (The employee) was terminated from his job as dishwasher for drinking prior to the incident that gave rise to this lawsuit. Shortly after that termination, (the employee) went to defendant's place of business to inquire about re-instatement. He was drunk, interfered with the kitchen's operation, and became violent when he was asked to leave the premises. He was forcibly subdued by defendant's security personnel and he left under threat of criminal prosecution. Further, defendant later rehired (the employee) as a steward. (the employee's) position as a steward required him to help in the preparation of banquets. He had some contact with customers and other invitees in this connection. He was not closely supervised and had access to alcoholic beverages, which he consumed with some regularity while on duty. Other employees were aware of (the employee's) behavior in this regard."

The court held the employer was on notice of the dangerous propensities and the behavior was foreseeable. *Pittard v. Four Seasons Motor Inn*, 101 N.M. 723 (1984).

In a Georgia case, two 14 year-old girls sued a landlord for hiring a manager who abused them. The landlord argued that anything the manager did was on the manager's own time. However, the court held the girls would not have met the manager in the first place if the landlord had not initially hired the manager. It was alleged that the landlord was on notice that the manager had dangerous tendencies, and that the landlord could be sued for creating an opportunity for abuse. *Harvey Freeman & Sons, Inc. v. Stanley*, 259 Ga. 233, 378 S.E. 2d 857 (1989).

In another case, a nine-year old girl was raped at a city playground by a city employee with a background of violent criminal behavior. He had been assigned to the children's playground generally alone and unsupervised. The City tried to defend on the basis the employee was not acting in the scope of employment, but the rape was an intervening and superseding cause breaking the chain of causation. The appellate court ruled the sole issue was in fact whether the city was negligent by allowing the employee access to the playground, and there was sufficient evidence for a jury to find that a violent assault was foreseeable when a violent employee was knowingly assigned to a children's park. *Haddock v. City of New York*, 140 A.D.2d 91, 532 N.Y.S.2d 379 (1988).

In reviewing these cases, the courts consider a number of factors such as the vulnerability of the victims, the existence of a special relationship or duty of care between the employer and the victim, what the employer either knew or reasonably should have known about the employee, the connection of the injury to the employer's businesses, and the foreseeability the employee may harm someone in a way that has some connection to the employer.

### Industry standard

Employers have asserted that when their background check follows industry practice or state procedure they cannot be liable for negligent hiring. However, neither compliance with an industry standard nor with state law alone insulates an employer from potential liability for negligent hiring. For example, in an Illinois case, the defendant was an investigative agency that responded to claims of insufficient background checks by asserting that it followed the industry standard. The court stated that compliance with what other firms do was no indication it had met its pre-employment screening obligations. It was inadequate to claim the defendant followed the industry standard because it is possible a whole industry could be reckless in performing background checks. *Easley v. Appollo Detective Agency,* 69 Ill. App. 3d 920 (1979).

### Cost

Although cost can be a consideration in a claim of negligence, it is unlikely to prevail as a defense to negligent hiring given the relatively low cost of a background check. In one case, an applicant for a truck driver position gave negative answers on his application to questions about criminal convictions and vehicular offenses. Later, a seventeen-year-old hitchhiker was raped and beaten by the truck driver. The employer had only verified the response to the questions about vehicular crimes. A criminal records check would have revealed convictions for violent sex crimes and an arrest for attacking two teenaged hitchhikers. The employer asserted a defense that imposing the requirement of doing criminal background checks was too costly a burden to place on employers. The court dismissed this defense because it considered the cost minor when compared to the possible harm not performing the check could cause. *Malorey v. B & L Motor Freight,* 146 Ill. App. 3d 265 (1986).

Even small employers cannot claim that cost prevented them from exercising due diligence. As outlined in Chapter 20, small business are well able to implement due diligence at very little cost.

### The worker was an independent contractor

An employer may try to contest liability by claiming the worker was an independent contractor. That would be an uphill battle. First, a court may well look at the real nature of the relationship, not what an employer chooses to label it. If an employer classifies a worker as an independent contractor and issues a 1099 form at the end of the year instead of a W-2 is probably irrelevant. The IRS has published guidelines on how to differentiate between independent contractors and employees. The real issue of whether the worker was, in fact, an independent contractor or an employee is the degree of control the business can exercise over the worker.[3]

Even if the individual was, in fact, an independent contractor, courts have found an employer may be liable for the negligent hiring of an independent contractor when the employer knew or should have known the independent contractor was not competent. A firm risks being sued for negligence for its own independent failure to adequately investigate the firm it hired, or to require that its contractor hire safely. If the task involved some peculiar risk of harm, the lawsuit may allege a failure to adequately supervise or train the contractor.

Courts have even found that a business can be held liable for negligent hiring when it hires an independent contractor that in turn negligently hires someone who causes an injury. In an Iowa case, a victim brought an action against both a cable television company and its independent contractor who employed a cable installer who raped her. The cable company argued it was not liable since the rapist worked for the contractor and was not employed by the cable company. The court held that both the cable company and its independent contractor could be held liable for the negligent hiring of the rapist. The independent contractor who employed the rapist could be liable under a general allegation of negligent hiring. The cable company had an independent duty towards its customers, and could not abandon that duty simply by hiring a contractor. D.R.R. v. English Enterprises, 356 N.W.2d 580 (Iowa App. 1984). For additional information about the responsibility of employers and independent contractors, see Chapter 16.

# Due Diligence After Hiring

Liability does not end with the hiring process. In fact, employers can be sued for failure to exercise due diligence in retention, supervision, or promotion as well.

## Negligent Retention

An employer may be liable for negligent retention when during the course of employment, the employer becomes aware or should have become aware of problems with an employee who indicated his unfitness, and the employer fails to take further action to prevent such conduct such as investigation, discharge, or reassignment. In a Minnesota case, the court ruled a church could be sued for negligent retention if the church knew or should have known about the propensity of a church pastor to engage in sexual misconduct with persons who sought spiritual or religious advice from him. *Olson v. First Church of Nazarene*, 661 N.W.2d 254 (Minn App, 2003). In an action a co-employee brought after being assaulted, evidence that an employee had been fired previously after lunging with clenched fists at a supervisor was enough for a jury's conclusion the employer should have known of the employee's propensity to react violently when angry. Therefore, when the employee was rehired after he threatened

---

[3] see www.irs.gov/businesses/small/article/0,,id=99921,00.html. See also add'l discussion in Chapter 16

to bring a racial discrimination claim, the defendant was liable for negligent rehiring and retention. *Tecumseh Products Co., Inc. v. Rigdon*, 552 S.E.2d 910 (Ga. App. 2001).

## Negligent Supervision

Under this theory, employers are subject to direct liability for the negligent supervision of employees when third parties are injured as a result of the tortuous acts of employees. The employer's liability rests upon proof the employer knew or, through the exercise of ordinary care, should have known the employee's conduct would subject third parties to an unreasonable risk of harm. Before the employer is held liable, there must be facts or occurrences that put the employer on notice that the supervised person poses a danger to third parties. In an Arkansas case helpful to employers, a retailer was sued for invasion of privacy and outrageous conduct when a store security officer conducted an investigation of theft from the store. The court found there was no evidence that put the employer on notice that the employee would be overzealous or aggressive in an investigation and the allegation was dismissed. *Addington v. Wal-Mart Stores, Inc.*, 105 S.W.3d 369, 458 (Ark.App.,2003).

## Negligent Promotion

For someone to successfully recover damages, it must be proven the employer knew or should have known the employee was incompetent or unfit to perform the job to which he was promoted. As a matter of law it was not negligence for a garage owner to promote an employee to the position of night garage manager without making a detailed investigation at that time of his possible criminal past, because at the commencement of his employment more than three years earlier the employee was successfully bonded, his previous job checked out satisfactorily, and during the interim period of employment he performed exemplary service for the employer. *Abraham v. S. E. Onorato Garages,* 50 Haw. 628 (1968).

## Negligent Failure to Warn

The duty of care can even extend to a duty to warn consumers that a former dangerous employee was terminated and no longer works for the employer. An electronics services company terminated an employee who the employer either knew or should have reasonably known had a propensity towards violence. The employee had entered the victim's home on various occasions for business reasons. After the employee was terminated, he gained entry into the victim's home by pretending he was there for business purposes and raped the victim. The court held that because the employee had been to the victim's home in the past on the employer's behalf, a special relationship had developed between the victim and the employer, and the employer had a duty to warn the victim the employee was no longer employed. *Coath v. Charles W. Jones Company*, 277 Pa. Super. 479 (1980).

## Employer Unaware of Past Conduct or Employee Hides It

Claiming that an employer had no duty to conduct a background check because the employer was not aware of a criminal record, or that the applicant hid it or lied about it, was rejected in a case decided by the Fourth Circuit Court of Appeals in 2004. The Court held that a janitorial service that did not check backgrounds could be sued for negligent hiring when an employee attacked a college student, and a background check may have shown prior physical assault on a woman. The court rejected the defense that there was no duty to check since the applicant denied a criminal conviction on a previous application and there was nothing to put the employer on actual notice of a prior criminal history.

The janitorial firm was hired by a college on the condition that background checks be performed. The janitorial service failed to conduct a background check despite having employed the attacker on several different occasions before the attack. A lower court agreed with the janitorial service that the case should be dismissed because the employee had previously indicated no criminal record on an application and the janitorial service had no reason to suspect a criminal record.

The Appellate court reversed, and determined there was sufficient basis for the case to proceed to a jury trial. The Appellate Court, citing an earlier court decision, determined an employer can be liable for the acts of an employee on a theory of negligence when:

> "an employer in placing a person with known propensities, or propensities which should
> have been discovered by reasonable investigation, in an employment position in which,
> because of the circumstances of the employment, it should have been foreseeable that the
> hired individual posed a threat of injury to others." [4]

According to the Court, it was a jury issue if a background check may have revealed a criminal complaint filed in a neighboring county by a woman that the employee had previously attacked.

## In Conclusion—

When an employer fails to conduct due diligence on an employee, and someone is harmed in a situation where damage was foreseeable, the employer cannot escape liability because it did not know about the hire's past criminal conduct. The fact that an applicant denies a criminal record or the employer does not know about it is not an excuse. To avoid liability, employers should be proactive in conducting background checks.

# Take the Safe Hiring Audit

The goal for any employer is to stay out of court, if possible, in the first place. Since anyone in the U.S. has the right to file a lawsuit against anyone else for just the cost of a filing fee, employers may have no choice in the matter. The next best thing an employer can do is to take steps to minimize the possibility of being sued for negligent employment related practices and, if sued, to maximize its ability to defend itself. An effective tool to control the risks associated with litigation is a Safe Hiring Program.

A *25-point Safe Hiring Audit* is presented in Chapter 19. This test allows an employer to judge the effectiveness of its Safe Hiring Program and how well the program would stand-up in court if the employer is required to explain to a jury what precautions were taken.

---

[4] see *Blair v. Defender Services*, 386 F.3d 623 (4th Cir., 2004)

# Chapter 4

# How to Implement the S.A.F.E. System

As we have learned, an effective Safe Hiring Program is much more than just pre-employment screening and background checks. Now let us set up and document your own Safe Hiring Program

## The Elements of the S.A.F.E. System

The S.A.F.E. System is the creative driving force behind a Safe Hiring Program. This is what S.A.F.E. stands for—

**S** — Set-up a Safe Hiring Program that consists of documented policies, practices and procedures to be used throughout the organization to achieve safe hiring.

**A** — Acclimate/train all persons with safe hiring responsibilities, especially hiring managers.

**F** — Facilitate/Implement the program.

**E** — Evaluate and audit the program by making sure that everyone responsible understands their compensation and advancement is judged in part by the attention they pay to the hiring process. Organizations typically accomplish those things that are measured, audited, and rewarded.

Let us take a look at each of these elements—

 ## Set-up a Program of Policies and Procedures to be Used Throughout the Organization

This is done in four steps.

1. **Who is in charge**— For any program to succeed, someone in the organization must have both the responsibility and the authority to carry out the program. Unless someone is firmly accountable and holding others accountable, it is hard to succeed.

2. **Policies**— Have internal policies and procedures in place. A sample policy memorandum is contained at the end of this chapter.

3. **Set-up the elements for safe hiring**— The critical elements are the Application, Interview, and Reference Checking Process, also called the **AIR Process**. These are done within an organization, and are a matter of training and commitment. Typically it is not a line item in the budget.

4. **Criminal check**— Once an applicant has gone through the AIR process, then a criminal check program can be conducted.

# A Acclimate/Train All Persons with Safe Hiring Responsibilities, Especially Hiring Managers

It is recommended that each hiring manager go through training on the **AIR Process**. The program would include the importance of safe hiring and pre-employment screening, how to implement the **AIR Process**, and why it is personally a matter of importance to hiring mangers that due diligence be demonstrated in the hiring process. It is critical that all training be documented so that there is no question in the event of a lawsuit that there was adequate training.

# F Facilitate/Implement the Program

In order to facilitate the program, it is recommended that each hiring manager be provided with a Safe Hiring checklist that goes into every applicant file. A sample checklist is attached at the end of this chapter. The elements on the checklist may vary for each firm. The checklist makes it easier for hiring mangers to follow the program since it creates a routine and provides a clear audit trail.

# E Evaluate and Audit the Program

As a general rule, members of an organization accomplish those things that are measured, audited, and rewarded. As a result, a Safe Hiring Program will be most effective if hiring managers clearly understand they will be audited periodically on how well they implement and follow the system. Otherwise, the hiring manager may just assume the Safe Hiring Program is just a flavor of the day from the central office and no one will follow-up. If regional and division managers routinely ask to see a number of files in order to ensure the Safe Hiring checklists are in the file, then the hiring managers will quickly understand this is something they must do. Compliance with the system must be part of a hiring manager's evaluation for purposes of salary and promotion. In turn, the regional managers must be held accountable by their supervisors who make sure they are checking. The audit trail must go to the top. Only in that way will every member of the firm understand that safe hiring is, in fact, a priority.

# Key Terms: Policies, Practices, Procedures

Public records and screening expert Carl R. Ernst describes Policies, Practice and Procedures—

**Policy:** A policy is a general statement of a principle according to which a company performs business functions. A company does not need to maintain policies in order to operate. However, practices and procedures that exist without the underpinnings of a consistent policy are continually in jeopardy of being changed for the wrong reasons, with unintended legal consequences.

**Practice:** A practice is a general statement of the way the company implements a policy. Good practices support policy. To implement the policy statement example above, your company could establish a practice of validating the existence and currency of the registered entity on the public record.

**Procedure:** A procedure documents an established practice. Use of forms is one of the useful ways procedures are documented. For a firm that has a practice of checking past court records for criminal records, the procedures would be the documentation on how it is done, as well as the documents showing it was done.

**Policies, practices and procedures that are not in writing are worthless.** To the extent that policies, practices and procedures are documented in writing, it is possible to independently verify from the procedure whether employees are conforming to the practice, and therefore to the policy. This kind of documentation makes it easy to perform reliable audits. However, if policies and practices are not documented in writing, the only documentation available is the results of actions of employees documented in paper output, such as copies of filings, search requests and search reports, and vendor invoices. In addition, it is also worthless having policies, practices and procedures unless an employer can also demonstrate with documentation that there was training, implementation, and auditing to ensure that programs were followed.

# Example of a Safe Hiring Program Using the S.A.F.E. System

The remainder of this chapter consists of a sample internal polices and procedures memo from ABC Company that covers the basics of their Safe Hiring Program. It is an excellent example of how an S.A.F.E. System is implemented.

This memo assumes the ABC Company is outsourcing the employment screening aspect of the Safe Hiring Program to a third party firm. However, if a company intends to perform those functions in-house, then the memo must be adjusted accordingly. At the end of this chapter is a separate policy statement that an employer can utilize in their employee manual. In succeeding chapters, details of each element of the Safe Hiring Program are discussed. A safe hiring audit is provided in Chapter 19.

# ABC Company Memo

### Safe Hiring Statement

To ensure that individuals who join this firm are well qualified and have a strong potential to be productive and successful, and to further ensure that this firm maintains a safe and productive work environment that is free from any form of violence, harassment or misconduct, it is the policy of this company to exercise appropriate practices to screen out applicants whose employment would be inconsistent with this policy.

These practices include certain procedures that occur prior to an offer being made, including adherence to the Application, Interview, and Reference checking (The AIR Process) outlined below. In addition, this firm will perform pre-employment screening and credentials verification on applicants who are offered and accept an offer of employment. A pre-employment background check is a sound business practice that benefits everyone. The fact that a candidate is subject to a pre-employment screening is not a reflection on any particular applicant and is not a sign of mistrust or suspicion. All finalists are subject to this procedure. The success of our firm depends upon our people and although we operate in an environment of trust, our firm still must verify that all employees are both qualified and safe. All finalists for any position at this firm are subject to the same policy.

Therefore, offers of employment are conditioned upon the firm's receipt of a pre-employment background screening investigation that is acceptable to the firm at the firm's sole discretion.

All procedures will be reviewed by legal counsel to ensure they are in strict conformity with the Federal Fair Credit Reporting Act, the Americans with Disabilities Act, state and federal anti-discrimination, privacy laws and all other applicable federal and state laws. All pre-employment background screenings are conducted by a third party to ensure privacy. All reports are kept strictly confidential, and are only viewed by individuals in this firm who have direct responsibility in the hiring process. All screening reports are kept and maintained separately from employee personnel files. Under the **Fair Credit Reporting Act (FCRA)**, all background screenings are done only after a person has signed a release and received a disclosure[1]

## Overall Procedures—

Following after the company's Safe Hiring Statement, next the firm's policies need to be documented. The following sections contain the considerations.

1.  The Safe Hiring Program will be coordinated by either the Human Resources Department or Security Department, hereinafter referred to as the Program Administrator.

2.  The Program Administrator is responsible for implementation of procedures to ensure that all steps in the Safe Hiring Program are documented.

3.  The Program Administrator is also in charge of implementing, training, and auditing adherence to this program, including periodic assessments to measure and evaluate the effectiveness of

---

[1] Additionally, the disclosure should includes language about the impact of state laws if the employer operates in more then one state. Also, the impact of any union contract should also be considered.

the program, review potential improvements, and to ensure continuing legal compliance. The Program Administrator is also responsible for full documentation of the program, and maintaining ongoing documentation of the program's operation. as well as all training. The Program Administrator will oversee training, keeping record of who participated, dates of attendance, and the training material as well as an monitoring of training's effectiveness.

4.  The Program Administrator is also responsible for maintaining and updating his or her knowledge of the legal and practical aspects of safe hiring and background checks.

## Application, Interview and Reference Checking Processes - AIR Process

Following is a statement of best practices the firm will utilize in the application, interview, and reference checking stage of the hiring process. The Program Administrator is responsible for developing procedures for the implementation of these practices. These duties include—

1.  Developing forms that must be completed and placed in each applicant's file before the employment decision is made final.

2.  Training all persons with hiring responsibility in these procedures, and document the training.

3.  Institute and document procedures to ensure these practices are being followed.

### APPLICATION STAGE – Use and carefully review application forms

1.  **Use an application form, not just resumes**.

    [**Note:** Use of an employment application form is considered a *best practice*. Resumes are not always complete or clear. Applications ensure uniformity, include all needed information that is obtained, prevent employers from having impermissible information, and provide employers with a place for applicants to sign certain necessary statements.]

2.  **Make sure the application form contains all necessary language**.

    Use the broadest language possible for felony and misdemeanor convictions and pending cases. One of the biggest mistakes employers make is to ask only about felonies on an application form. Misdemeanors can be very serious also. Employers should inquire about misdemeanors to the extent allowed by law in their state.

    a.  Include a statement that criminal records do not automatically disqualify an applicant. This is important for EEOC compliance. Employers need to understand that background screening is conducted to determine whether a person is fit for a particular job. Society has a vested interest in giving ex-offenders a chance. However, an employer is under a due diligence obligation to make efforts to determine if a person is reasonably fit for a particular position. For example, a person just released from of custody for a violent crime would not be a good candidate for a job required to go into people's home, but may perform very well on a supervised work crew. If a criminal record is found, then an employer must determine if there is a business reason not to hire the person, based upon 1) the nature and gravity of the offense, 2) the nature of the job, and 3) when the crime occurred. There are also limitations to the use of arrests not resulting in a conviction, and a number of states also have rules about criminal records.

b.  Statements that lack truthfulness or contain material omissions are grounds to terminate the hiring process or employment no matter when they are discovered. This is particularly important if a criminal record is found. Although a criminal record may not be used automatically to disqualify an applicant, the fact that an applicant has lied about a criminal matter can be the basis for an adverse decision.

c.  Include other standard statements in the employment application that are approved by the Human Resource department and legal counsel. These can include statements that employment is "at will," and "we are an equal opportunity employer and our firm has an arbitration policy when it comes to disputes concerning employment, such as employment is at-will."

d.  Require a release for a background check in the application process.

e.  Have each job applicant sign a consent form for a background check, including a check for criminal records, past employment and education. Announcing that your firm checks backgrounds may discourage applicants with something to hide, and encourage applicants to be truthful and honest about mistakes they have made in the past. If a firm outsources to a third party vendor, then under the Federal Fair Credit Reporting Act there must be a disclosure on a separate stand-alone document.

3.  **Review the application carefully**.

In most instances, when there is an employee problem or lawsuit, a careful review of the application would have alerted the employer in advance they were hiring a lawsuit waiting to happen. Look for the following red flags—

1.  Applicant does not sign application.

2.  Applicant does not sign consent to background screening.

3.  Applicant leaves criminal questions blank[2]

4.  Applicant self-reports a criminal violation[3]

5.  Applicant fails to explain why he or she left past jobs.

6.  Applicant fails to explain gaps in employment history.

7.  Applicant gives an explanation for an employment gap or for the reason leaving a previous job that does not make sense.

8.  Applicant uses excessive cross-outs and changes, as though making it up as they go along.

9.  Applicant fails to give complete information, i.e. insufficient information to identify a past employer, leaves out salary, etc.

10. Applicant fails to indicate or cannot recall the name of a former supervisor.

---

[2] the honest criminal syndrome - the applicant does not want to lie about a criminal past

[3] taking into account that applicants can self-report matters incorrectly

## INTERVIEW PROCESS STAGE — The Five Questions

**Always ask these five questions during the housekeeping stage of the interview**. Since they have signed a consent form and believe we are doing checks, applicants have a powerful incentive to be truthful.[4]

1. We do background checks on everyone to whom we make an offer. Do you have any concerns you would like to discuss? Good applicants will shrug off this question.

2. We also check for criminal convictions for all finalists. Any concerns about that?[5]

3. We contact all past employers. What do you think they will say?

4. Will a past employer tell us that you were tardy, did not perform well, etc.?

Also, use the interview to ask questions about any **unexplained employment gap.**

## REFERENCE CHECKING STAGE —
## Check References and Look for Unexplained Employment Gaps

All past employers for a period of 7-10 years must be contacted. All efforts to contact past employers as well as the results of any conversations must be noted and documented. Even if a past employer will not provide qualitative information about the applicant's potential performance, it is critical to verify, at a minimum, his or her start date, end date, and job titles.

The Program Administrator will create forms that are to be used to assist in the process. These will include a call history to document who was called and when, as well as the results of the call. The Program Administrator will also ensure there is proper training on legal and illegal reference questions. The Hiring Manager will make the decision necessary to determine if a candidate should be offered a position. However, Human Resources or a third-party screening firm will call past employers to confirm dates of employment and job titles in order to ensure that all finalists have been subject to the same process and that no one is hired unless the firm has made reasonable efforts to confirm past employment. The firm will not contact the current employer without an authorization, but reserves the right to call the current employer after the applicant has begun employment, or to ask the applicant for a copy of their paycheck stub to confirm current employment. [6]

Verifying past employment is one of the single most important tools an employer has. It is as important as doing criminal checks. Why? Past job performance can be an important predictor of future success. Some employers make a costly mistake by not checking past employment because they believe past employers may not give detailed information. However, even verifying dates of employment and job titles are critical because an employer must be concerned about unexplained gaps in the employment history. Although there can be many reasons for a gap in employment, if an applicant cannot account for the past seven to ten years, that can be a red flag.

In addition, documenting the fact that an effort was made will demonstrate due diligence.

---

[4] these questions are the equivalent of a New Age lie detector test. Good applicants will shrug it off and applicants with something to hide may reveal vital information

[5] make sure the wording of the question reflects what an employer may legally ask in that state

[6] see Chapter 9 for additional information on past employment checks

It is also critical to know where a person has been because of the way criminal records are maintained in the United States. There are over 10,000 courthouses in America. If an employer knows where an applicant has been as a result of past employment checks, it increases the accuracy of a criminal search, and decreases the possibility an applicant has served time for a serious offense.

## The Pre-employment Screening Process

1. All pre-employment screening will be conducted through a third party Consumer Reporting Agency (CRA).

2. The Program Administrator will—

    a. Administer and coordinate the pre-employment screening program.

    b. Approve all forms utilized in the process and ensure that all forms are utilized consistently.

    c. Submit names and background requests to the CRA.

    d. Receive reports from the CRA.

    e. Contact the CRA as necessary to review the report or receive additional information.

    f. Review all reports, and in the case of negative or derogatory information, take appropriate action by contacting the hiring manger.

    g. Ensure that in the event an adverse decision is intended, the firm will take appropriate measures under the **Fair Credit Reporting Act.** That includes providing an applicant with a copy of the Consumer Report and statement of rights prior to the adverse action. If the adverse action is final, then the Program Administrator shall also cause a second notice, required by the **FCRA,** to be sent. The Program Administrator may delegate these duties to the CRA.

    h. When an exception is made to hire an applicant despite negative or derogatory information, the administrator will ensure the file properly documents the reasons for the decision.

    i. Maintain the background reports in complete privacy and confidence, and ensure only individuals with hiring authority are made aware of report contents, and further ensure that all reports are only ordered and utilized for screening purposes.

    j. Supervise the storage of all release forms and screening reports in a secure area, separate from employee personnel files.

    k. Select a CRA to perform pre-employment screening services through a Request for Proposal (RFP) process,[7] and approve all billing submitted by the CRA.

    l. Ensure the program is administered uniformly and consistently, and in compliance with all applicable laws including the Fair Credit Reporting Act, state and federal discrimination laws, and laws regulating the gathering and use of information in the employment process.

---

[7] see Appendix 3 for a Request for Proposal (RFP) form

m.  No information shall be requested, obtained, or utilized that would be in violation of any state or federal law, rule, or regulation.

n.  Perform such other tasks and duties in order to carry out the aims and purposes of the pre-employment screening policy.

## Mechanics of Screening Program

1.  All applications for employment will contain approved forms for pre-employment screening that all applicants must sign and date when applications are returned **OR** prior to a candidate being selected as a finalist or being offered employed, the candidate shall sign approved forms necessary for pre-employment background screening.

2.  All forms, including the original application and resume, shall be transmitted to the CRA by the Program Administrator.

3.  All offers of employment are conditional upon receipt of a background report that is satisfactory to the firm. In a situation where an offer is made prior to the receipt of the background report, the offer letter shall state, in writing—

    a.  "This offer of employment is conditional upon the employer's receipt of a Pre-employment background screening investigation that is acceptable to the employer at the employer's sole discretion."

4.  No employment will commence prior to the completion of the background report unless the Program Administrator and department head/Vice-President determines there is an exceptional circumstance. In that case, the employment will be conditional on a satisfactory report, as indicated above.

## Standards for Screening

The Program Administrator shall determine for each position, in consultation as necessary with the hiring manager, what level of pre-employment screening is required, taking into account the nature of the position, including duties and responsibilities—

1.  Does the position have access to money or assets?

2.  Does the position carry significant authority or fiduciary responsibility?

3.  Does the position have access to members of the public or co-workers so that any propensity to violence or dishonesty could foreseeably cause harm?

4.  Would the position be difficult to replace in terms of recruitment, hiring and training?

5.  Would a new hire's falsification of skills, experience, or background put the firm at risk, or lower the firm's productivity?

6.  Would a bad hire expose the firm to litigation or financial claims from the applicant, co-workers, customers, or the public, or other risks?

7.  Is there a statutory or legal requirement for certain positions to be screened?

The Program Administrator will designate which position shall be screened at which level. Additional screening may be requested as necessary for a particular position by a hiring manager or the Program Administrator. All screenings will be done consistently and uniformly. Once it has been determined that a particular position requires a particular level of pre-employment screening, all finalists for that particular position will be screened at the same level.

The four levels listed below are examples of screening that can be utilized—

1. **Individual**— For casual or temporary labor. Recommended search: County criminal search in local county or county of residence and other individual reports such as a Social Security trace and driving record.

2. **Basic**— For entry level employees, retail or manufacturing or positions where the employer has internally checked references and education. Recommended search: A full seven year on-site criminal records check for felonies and misdemeanors, Credit Report or Social Security and identity check, and driver's license check.

3. **Standard**— For more responsible positions and permanent hire. Recommended search: The Basic search above plus verification of the last three employers (and references if available) and highest post high school education.

4. **Extended**— For positions involving increasing responsibility or supervision of others. Recommended search: The Basic and Standard search above, plus checking Superior Court civil cases in the last two relevant counties for litigation matters that may be job related.

The Program Administrator can review other available tools such as a sexual offender search or a criminal database search as long as it is used as a supplement source of information and not a primary source.

## Analysis of Information

1. In the event derogatory or potentially negative information is found as a result of a pre-employment screening report, the Program Administrator will immediately notify the hiring manager or other management or hiring authority.

2. The following are general guidelines as to what information is considered potentially negative or derogatory. This list is not intended to be exhaustive or exclusive. There may be other factors which are appropriate for the position or the applicant under consideration. The decision to hire or not hire is not based upon any rigid matrix or pre-determined formula, but is based upon a consideration of the totality of the circumstances. General guidelines include—

   - The applicant or employee seeking hiring or promotion is found to have engaged in dishonest, misleading, or untruthful conduct, including but not limited to misrepresentations or omission of material facts during the selection process. This can include but is not limited to discrepancies or falsehoods in past employment, education and credentials, or in identification of the applicant.

   - The applicant or employee seeking hiring or promotion is found to have engaged in violence, wrongdoing, or other conduct inappropriate in the workplace.

- The applicant is found to not have the necessary skills, experience, abilities, aptitude or qualifications to successfully fulfill the job requirements.

- The applicant or employee has been convicted of any felony or misdemeanor that may be legally considered in the hiring process. That finding may preclude an applicant from effectively performing his or her job duties, or may create a security or safety issue in the workplace. It is this firm's policy that a criminal conviction does not automatically preclude a person from being hired. In the event this firm confirms the applicant has a criminal record, the hiring decision will be based upon a careful consideration of the nature of the position in question, the nature and gravity of the offense, the amount of time that has passed since the conviction, and whether there is a business justification for not hiring the applicant. The firm has a strong commitment to maintaining a safe working environment for the benefit of everyone. Criminal convictions for a felony or misdemeanor offense involving acts of violence, theft or dishonesty, weapons, or moral turpitude are likely to adversely affect the workplace. In addition, being on active probation or parole is also likely to affect job performance and the workplace. For these reasons, the firm will closely scrutinize the application of any candidate with such a criminal conviction, or who is currently on probation or parole, consistent with the firm's policy of not automatically excluding any applicant with a criminal record.

- The criminal record makes the applicant unable or ineligible to perform the essential job functions or creates a potential legal liability for the firm. For example, the applicant must drive a vehicle as part of the job responsibility and does not have a valid license or a clear driving record.

3. When a background report is returned with derogatory or potentially negative information that would reasonably impact a hiring decision, the Program Administrator will contact the hiring manager or other appropriate person to review the information. The Program Administrator will normally provide a verbal summary rather than the actual written report in order to limit confidential material from circulating within the company.

4. If the hiring manager, the Program Administrator or management believes that the information will form the basis of an adverse action or termination based upon the application of the guideless reviewed above, then the Program Administrator will document the basis of the decision, including specifically the job-related basis for the adverse action or termination.

5. In the event of an intended adverse action or termination, the Program Administrator will also initiate the adverse action notification procedures required by the Fair Credit Reporting Act.

6. If the hiring manager believes the negative information should not preclude employment or promotion, the hiring manager will seek approval from the respective department head or Vice-President who will decide the issue in consultation with the Program Administrator and legal counsel, if appropriate. If the decision is to offer the position despite negative information, then the reasons for the decision shall be appropriately documented in writing and provided to the Program Administrator. The purpose is to protect the firm by showing the negative information

was considered in light of all available information about the candidate and the position, and the firm exercised discretion only after a due diligence inquiry. The documentation is needed in the event the decision is challenged in the future. For example, an applicant with negative information may object to not being hired because a previous candidate with similar negative information did get hired. The previous candidate who was hired may have had excellent references or past work history that justified hiring despite negative information. In addition, if a person with adverse information is hired and that person commits an act resulting in harm to the firm or causes litigation, the fact the person was hired only after a screening process in which all facts were carefully considered would tend to establish due diligence.

# Sample Language in Employee Manual for Background Screening

Many employers do not refer to pre-employment screening in their Employee Manuals. Even when employers screen current employees for purposes of promotion, reassignment or retention, there are no legal requirements that compel employers to refer to "screening" in their handbooks. However, there is also no reason not to include mention in the employee handbook.

An Employee Manual is one of the most effective ways to communicate general policies and procedures to employees. A well-written manual helps avoid misunderstandings about policies or benefits, helps avoid lawsuits and thereby enhances morale. Manuals also promote consistency of treatment and reduce the risk of charges of discrimination being made.

The following sample policy on employment screening is suggested language for an Employee Manual. The text can be modified as appropriate for firms that choose to include their employment screening policy in the employee handbook. Because no one handbook applies to all businesses or all situations, this language is a general suggestion.

# Sample Policy on Employment Background Screening

To ensure that individuals who join this firm are well qualified and have a strong potential to be productive and successful —and to further ensure that this firm maintains a safe and productive work environment free of any form of violence, harassment or misconduct — it is the policy of this company to perform pre-employment screening and credentials verification on applicants who are offered and accept an offer of employment. A pre-employment background check is a sound business practice that benefits everyone. It is not a reflection on a particular job applicant.

Offers of employment are conditional upon the firm's receipt of a pre-employment background screening investigation that is acceptable to the firm at the firm's sole discretion. Any applicant who refuses to sign a background screening release form will not be eligible for employment.

To ensure privacy, all pre-employment background screenings are conducted by a third party. All screenings are conducted in strict conformity with the Federal Fair Credit Reporting Act (FCRA), the Americans with Disabilities Act (ADA), and state and federal anti-discrimination and privacy laws. All reports are kept strictly confidential, and are only viewed by individuals in this firm who have direct responsibility in the hiring process. All screening reports are kept and maintained separately from your personnel file. Under the Fair Credit Reporting Act, all background screenings are done only after a person has received a disclosure and has signed a release. In addition, you have certain legal rights to discover and to dispute or explain any information prepared by the third party background-screening agency. If the employer intends to deny employment wholly or partly because of information obtained in an pre-employment check conducted by the company's consumer reporting agency, then the applicant will first be provided with a copy of the background report, a statement of rights, and the name, address and phone number of the consumer reporting agency to contact about the results of the check or to dispute its accuracy.

The firm also reserves the right to conduct a background screening anytime after the employee has been hired to determine eligibility for promotion, re-assignment, or retention in the same manner as described above.

Applicants also are expected to provide references from their former employers as well as educational reference information that can be used to verify academic accomplishments and records. Background checks may include verification of information provided on the completed application for employment, the applicant's resume, or on other forms used in the hiring process. Information to be verified includes, but is not limited to, Social Security Number and previous addresses. Employer may also conduct a reference check and verify the applicant's education and employment background as stated on the employment application or other documents listed above.

The background check may also include a criminal record check. If a conviction is discovered, then the employer will closely scrutinize the conviction in view of our policy of ensuring a safe and profitable workplace. A criminal conviction does not necessarily automatically bar an applicant from employment. Before an employment decision is made, a determination will be made whether the conviction is related to the position for which the individual is applying, or would present safety or security risks, taking into account the nature and gravity of the act, the nature of the position, and the age of the conviction.[8]

Additional checks such as a driving record or a credit report may be made on applicants for particular job categories if appropriate and job-related. Employment screening assessments to determine an applicant's job fit may also be required of all applicants for employment. Skills tests related to the demands of the job may also be required.

This firm relies upon the accuracy of information contained in the employment application as well as the accuracy of other data presented throughout the hiring process and employment, including any oral interviews. Any misrepresentations, falsifications, or material omissions in any of the information or data, no matter when discovered, may result in the firm's exclusion of the individual from further consideration for employment or, if the person has been hired, termination of employment.

## The Stages of Hiring

Safe Hiring procedures may also depend upon the stage of the hiring process. Essentially, hiring is done in three stages: 1. Pre-offer; 2. Post-offer; and 3. Post-hire. Certain task can only be performed post-offer such as a workers compensation records inquiry. (See chapter 15). Other tasks can only be performed post-hire (i.e. after the applicant has come onboard), such as the I-9 procedure. (See chapter 17).

## Conclusion— Implementing Your Safe Hiring Program

In conclusion, each firm that implements a Safe Hiring Program will undoubtedly customize the details to accommodate its particular needs. However, employers, at a minimum, should address the issues raised in the example above.

The remaining pages in this chapter present the **Safe Hiring Checklist.**

Section 2 of this book examines the **AIR Process**, **Legal Compliance**, and the **Background Screening Elements**.

---

[8] there is further language which deals with the obligation of a current employee to report an arrest or conviction in Chapter 11, Important 'After the Hire' Issues

# The Safe Hiring Checklist

To be completed for every new applicant before being hired

Applicant: _____

Position: _____

Hiring Manager _____

| Task | Yes/No/ NA | Date/ Initials | Notes/Follow-up |
|---|---|---|---|
| **Application Process—** | | | |
| Did applicant sign the consent form? | | | |
| Is application complete? | | | |
| Did applicant sign and date application? | | | |
| Did applicant leave criminal questions blank? | | | |
| Did applicant indicate a criminal record? | | | |
| Did applicant explain why left past jobs? | | | |
| Did applicant explain gaps in job history? | | | |
| Any excessive cross-outs or changes seen? | | | |
| **Interview Process—** | | | |
| Did applicant explain any excessive cross-outs/changes? | | | |
| **Leaving past jobs**: Did applicant explain? | | | |
| **Leaving past jobs**: Was verbal reason consistent with reason on written app? | | | |
| **Employment Gaps**: Did applicant explain? | | | |
| **Employment Gaps:** Are verbal explanations consistent with written app? | | | |
| *Security Question. 1* – "Our firm has a standard policy of background checks and drug tests on all applicants. Do you have any concerns you would like to share with me about our procedures?" | | | Answer: |

| | | | |
|---|---|---|---|
| *Security question 2* – "If I were to contact the courthouse or police department, would we locate any criminal convictions or pending cases?" | | | Answer: |
| *Security question 3* – "If I were to contact past employers pursuant to the release you have signed, what do you think they would tells us about you?" | | | Answer: |
| *Security question 4* – "If I were to contact past employers pursuant to the release you have signed, would any of them tell us you were terminated or were disciplined?" | | | Answer: |
| *Security question 5* – "Please explain any gaps in employment." | | | Answer: |

**Reference Checks[9]—**

| | | | |
|---|---|---|---|
| Have references been checked for at least last 5-10 years, regardless of whether past employers will give details? | | | |
| Have efforts been documented? | | | |
| Discrepancies between information located and what applicant reported in application:<br> a. dates/title salary/job title<br> b. reason for leaving | | | |

**Background Check—**

| | | | |
|---|---|---|---|
| Submitted for background check? | | | |
| Check completed? | | | |
| Background check reviewed for discrepancies/issues? | | | |
| If not CLEAR or SATISFACTORY, what action is taken per policy and procedures? | | | Describe: |

*Notes: Use back if necessary. Sign and date all entries.*

---

[9] reference checks can either be performed by employer or by a third party

# Chapter 5

# Complying With Discrimination and Privacy Laws

## Discrimination Laws

The regulatory environment has a wide application to many facets of the employment relationship. As presented earlier, one of the core components of a Safe Hiring Program is "an awareness of the legal and regulatory environment surrounding safe hiring and compliance." The main emphasis deals with these elements of a SHP—

1. The application stage
2. The interview stage
3. Reference questions
4. The use of records and information, particularly criminal convictions

Each of these stages is discussed in the appropriate chapter. This Chapter 5 examines overall issues related to discrimination within these stages.

Federal and state anti-discrimination laws make it clear that decisions based on prohibited criteria are illegal. These criteria include race, color, national origin, religion, ancestry, medical condition, age, marital status, sex, or exercise of family care or medical leaves. These are prohibited criteria because they are not valid predictors of job performance or bona fide occupational qualifications (BFOQ). In the past, prohibited criteria have been found to cause unfair treatment and discrimination. This type of discrimination is called **"disparate treatment."** A person is being pre-judged based upon membership in a group or status instead of who he or she can accomplish as an individual. The word "prejudice" simply means to "pre-judge" a person based upon the color of the person's skin, country of origin, sex or some other criteria that has nothing to do with job performance.

The situation becomes complicated because information that appears neutral on its face can be utilized in a discriminatory way. This is called **"disparate impact"** and occurs when employer selection processes that appear fair on the surface actually result in a screening out of identifiable groups from employment. For example, credit reports and criminal records are perfectly legal for employers to obtain provided the methods used comply with various state and federal rules. However, the use of credit reports or criminal records can have a discriminatory impact if they are used in such a way that results in a disparate impact upon certain groups. The generally accepted limitations to the use of these records are discussed in later chapters and in Appendices 1 and 2.

Employers do need to have a basic understanding of the statutes, cases, and regulations on both the federal and state levels that affect how any employer can legally collect and utilize personal information about job applicants in order to make hiring decisions.

# Federal Discrimination Laws

There are a number of federal laws that prohibit discrimination in employment. The Equal Employment Opportunity Commission (EEOC) enforces these laws at the federal level. The EEOC also provides oversight and coordination of all federal equal employment opportunity regulations, practices, and policies. According to the EEOC website at www.eeoc.gov, these are the primary federal laws that prohibit job discrimination—

- **Title VII of the Civil Rights Act of 1964 (Title VII),** which prohibits employment discrimination based on race, color, religion, sex, or national origin; see www.eeoc.gov/policy/vii.html

- **Equal Pay Act of 1963 (EPA),** which protects men and women who perform substantially equal work in the same establishment from sex-based wage discrimination; see www.eeoc.gov/policy/epa.html

- **Age Discrimination in Employment Act of 1967 (ADEA),** which protects individuals who are 40 years of age or older; see www.eeoc.gov/policy/adea.html

- **Title I and Title V of the Americans with Disabilities Act of 1990 (ADA),** which prohibit employment discrimination against qualified individuals with disabilities in the private sector, and in state and local governments; see www.eeoc.gov/policy/ada.html

- **Sections 501 and 505 of the Rehabilitation Act of 1973**, which prohibit discrimination against qualified individuals with disabilities who work in the federal government; see www.eeoc.gov/policy/rehab.html

- **Civil Rights Act of 1991**, which (among other things) provides monetary damages in cases of intentional employment discrimination; see www.eeoc.gov/policy/cra91.html

The federal laws only affect employers above a certain size. For example, the Civil Rights and the Americans with Disabilities Act cover employers with fifteen or more employees based upon the number of employees during each working day of twenty or more calendar weeks of the current or preceding calendar year. However, the Age Discrimination Act utilizes twenty employees as the threshold. As a practical matter, even small employers who believe they fall below the federal limits are well advised to take these federal laws into consideration. First, it can be complicated to determine how many employees a small firm has for purposes of determining if the law applies. All employees including part time and temporary workers are counted. An employer may not count "independent contractors," but the possibility exists that the contractors may be counted if in fact they are really engaged in an employment type relationship, regardless how the employer chooses to compensate them. If an employer has two or more separate businesses, there are circumstances where the businesses will be counted as one for purpose of determining the employee count.

The rules about counting employees to determine if a firm is large enough to meet the threshold for application of federal civil rights laws can also be very complex. In addition, there are states where state laws can be in effect even if a federal law technically does not apply, discussed below. More importantly, if a small employer engages in any conduct that would have been a violation of federal law if they were larger, an aggrieved applicant or employee may still be able to go to court stating an alternative cause of action such as intentional infliction of emotional distress.

The Civil Rights Act and the Americans with Disabilities Act (ADA) are probably the two most well-known laws that apply to discriminatory hiring practices. These laws prohibit any non-job-related inquiry, either verbal or through the use of an application form, which directly or indirectly limits a person's employment opportunities because of race, color, religion, national origin, ancestry, medical condition, disability (including AIDS), marital status, sex (including pregnancy), age (40+), exercise of family care leave or leave for an employee's own serious health condition.

These laws generally prohibit any type of questions of applicants which—

- Identifies a person on a basis covered by the Act; or,

- Results in the disproportionate screening out of members of a protected group; or,

- Is not a valid predictor (not a job-related inquiry) of potential successful job performance.

## More About the Americans with Disabilities Act (ADA)

This federal law regulates hiring of Americans with disabilities and has broad implications. In terms of background screenings, an employer may not use or obtain any information that violates the rights afforded under this law. The most obvious impact of the law relates to medical records, disabilities, and worker's compensation records. Screening firms may provide worker compensation records, but only under the strict procedures mandated by the Americans with Disabilities Act (ADA).

One occasion where the ADA (and similar state laws) may raise a concern is for criminal convictions involving drugs or alcohol. Under the ADA, an employer cannot discriminate on the basis that an applicant is an alcoholic or a former drug user. However, the ADA and similar state laws do not protect a person who is currently using drugs or abusing alcohol. Where a person is otherwise qualified for a position, and the background screening reveals a drug or alcohol conviction, an employer should carefully review the totality of the circumstances involved before denying employment on that basis. Certainly, the current use of illegal drugs is not protected. The decision may also depend upon the position in question. For driving positions, for example, an employer may certainly evaluate driving-related convictions more seriously.

# State and Local Discrimination Laws

To add to the complexity for employers, a number of states and local jurisdictions have their own rules governing discrimination. The Federal Equal Employment Opportunity Commission website indicates over 100 state and local fair employment practice agencies, or FEPA's. Most states have their own Civil Rights Acts as well as an agency within state government that enforces these state laws. State laws can vary from the federal rules in terms of the size of the employer covered and what constitutes a violation.

Even local jurisdictions and cities can regulate employers. For example, the City and County of San Francisco have the San Francisco Human Rights Commission that can investigate and mediate complaints of discrimination for employees of any San Francisco employer, regardless of size.

Here is where it gets even more complicated for employers—they are generally subject to the most stringent discrimination laws in their jurisdictions. For example, even though the Federal Civil Rights Act limits jurisdiction to employers with fifteen or more employees, a California employer is subject to the California Fair Employment and Housing Act (FEHA) that has jurisdiction starting at five employees. Other states apply the discrimination laws to all employers. Most states have websites for the agency that enforces civil rights and fair employment practices law. For example, see the site for the state of Michigan at www.michigan.gov/mdcr/. To access data concerning civil rights and discrimination laws for each state, see the CCH Business Owners Toolkit at www.toolkit.cch.com/text/P05_0160.asp.

# Specific Issue for Employers – How to Avoid Previous Names and Marital Status Discrimination

One of the areas where the discrimination laws have an effect on safe hiring is the use of previous names in a criminal search. The issue arises because past names are a necessary identifying piece of information. For example, when searching for criminal records, researchers base the search on the last name. However, if an applicant at one time was known by a different name, a complete criminal search must be conducted under BOTH names. The most typical situation where an applicant has a previous name is in the case of a woman who marries and changes her name.

The problem is that by referring to a name as a maiden name, an applicant potentially is being identified on the basis of their marital status or sex, which can be a violation of federal and state discrimination laws. In California for example, asking for an applicant's maiden name has been specifically labeled as an unacceptable question by the California Department of Fair Employment and Housing, the California agency charged with enforcing the California civil rights laws. Consequently, a previous name search should **not** be referred to as a "maiden name" search, since that clearly indicates that an employer is obtaining information on martial status, which is a prohibited basis upon which to make an employment decision. That is why any application or consent for background screening should always include the phrase "previous name" instead of "maiden name."

Is this an example of a distinction without a difference, or political correctness going to far? No. Marital status has been a traditional basis for a woman to be the subject of discrimination. The fact is that whether a man or woman is married is simply not a valid basis to predict job performance. However, the reality has been that a woman applicant who is married may be the subject of discrimination based on a belief that she may leave the job to have a family. By phrasing it as a "previous name," the same information is obtained for purposes of a background check, but the application information is facially neutral. In addition, a female applicant is not discouraged from applying based upon an apprehension that by asking for a "maiden name," there is a likelihood of discrimination.

# How to Avoid Age Discrimination

## Using the Date of Birth Information on the Job Application

Most authorities agree that any information tending to reveal age should not be requested on an application form or during an oral interview. Asking for date of birth during the selection process could violate the federal **Age Discrimination in Employment Act** as well as various state civil rights laws. Asking for date of birth tends to deter older applicants from applying. If the application material contains date of birth information, the inference is that a firm may be methodically denying consideration of older workers. Many states have rules that prohibit an employer, either directly or through an agent, from seeking or receiving information that reveals date of birth and age before an offer is made. For example, the *California Pre-employment Inquiry Guidelines* by the California Department of Fair Employment and Housing (DFEH) lists specific age questions that cannot be asked.

Special problems are faced when an applicant's date of birth is not available. When researching court records, the date of birth is probably the most important factor needed to identify an individual since many court records do not contain Social Security Numbers. In fact, in some jurisdictions, a criminal search cannot be conducted without a date of birth. It is also needed in many states in order to obtain a driving record, thus the date of birth is key piece of identifying data on DMV records.

Under the **Federal Age Discrimination Act of 1967**, there is **not an absolute** prohibition against asking for date of birth or age. **That is a common misconception among employers.** In fact, the **EEOC** has specifically ruled that asking for date of birth or age is not automatically a violation of the act. However, the **EEOC** ruling indicated that any such request would be **closely scrutinized** to ensure that the request has a permissible purpose. The EEOC also indicated that the reason for asking for date of birth should be clearly disclosed so that older applicants are not deterred from applying.[1]

According to the EEOC website at www.eeoc.gov/types/age.html —

> **"Pre-Employment Inquiries**
>
> The ADEA (Age Discrimination in Employment Act) does not specifically prohibit an employer from asking an applicant's age or date of birth. However, because such inquiries may deter older workers from applying for employment or may otherwise indicate possible intent to discriminate based on age, requests for age information will be closely scrutinized to make sure that the inquiry was made for a lawful purpose, rather than for a purpose prohibited by the ADEA."

If a firm does screening in-house, then the firm may consider performing all screening and obtaining information **post-offer**. This provides maximum protection since there can be no inference that age played a role in the decision to hire or not hire.

What if an employer outsources background screening to a private firm? The screening firm will normally need date of birth to perform the service.

---

[1] see 29 Code of Federal Regulations Part 1625

There are several options. First, consider outsourcing to a screening firm only post-offer. If a conditional offer of employment is made that depends upon a background screening report, then asking for the date of birth post-offer is probably safe. The downside however, is that it is an administrative burden for most employers to coordinate giving offers, then collecting the date of birth and then transmitting it to a screening firm. Most employers have a practice of requiring all applicants to fill out a consent form for the background screening firm at the same time the original application is filled out, and the screening firm's forms will typically need date of birth information.

Another possible route is to only request the date of birth information on the **screening firm's form**, and not on any employer form. Furthermore, the applicant release forms should **not** be made available to the person or persons with hiring authority so as to avoid any suggestion that age information was used in any step of the hiring process. Most employment screening companies recommend that employers keep the screening forms and reports separate from the employee's personnel file or application papers.

In addition, to further protect the employer, the form used for the screening company can have such additional language as—

- The information requested on the screening firm's form is for screening and verification of information only and has no role in the selection process.

- All federal and state rights are respected in the employer's screening process.

- The year of birth is optional on the form.

- The information is used for identification only and that without such information the screening process may be delayed.

Another option is an employer can require a screening firm to takes steps to remove all references to age and date of birth in its reports so that employers will not receive age information.

Another option some employers have used is to setup a system that communicates the date of birth directly to the screening firm so that the data is never in the employer's possession. This can be done by establishing a special "800" phone number the applicants call to leave their date of birth, or with a tear-off form that the applicant mails in. One downside to these types of workarounds is they will likely delay screening reports because of the extra steps involved.

Another option is to have someone in the office such as a receptionist physically separate the screening firm's form from the application so there is no question that a decision maker has not viewed the date of birth before the applications are reviewed. Also new are online options where an applicant can supply the date of birth as part of the application process, but only the screening firm will be able to see it.

Most employers choose the option of asking applicants to place date of birth on the screening company forms. For questions about a form's legality, an employer should consult their legal counsel or seek advice from their attorney or contact the appropriate local or state authority or federal EEOC office.

# Privacy Laws

The second major area of legal concern for employers is privacy. Employers have a legal duty to respect the privacy of applicants and employees in a variety of areas, such as privacy limitation when it comes to what information an employer can obtain, how to protect the data, who else can see the data, and the rights of applicants and employees to discover what data has been obtained. With news media revelations in 2005 of large-scale theft of data from firms that store large amounts of personal and identifiable data, maintaining privacy has become a very critical concern.

The subject matter of workplace privacy is very broad, and spans a whole range of issues from electronic monitoring of email, searches of personal belongings and physical surveillance to regulating workplace behavior and dress codes, off the job conduct, and the protection and dissemination of confidential information. For purposes of this book, the concern is focused on gathering, utilizing and protecting information necessary for hiring and retention decisions. Privacy is also addressed in the following chapters—

- Privacy issues related to defamation are covered in
  Chapter 9 on Legal and Effective Past Employment Checks.
- International privacy and data protection are addressed in
  Chapter 21 on International Screening.
- The employer's duty to protect confidential information is covered in
  Chapter 17 on Identity Theft.
- The duty of a pre-employment screening firm to protect the confidentiality of data is
  addressed in Chapter 6 on the Fair Credit Reporting Act, and in
  Chapter 10 on Working with Screening Firms.
- Privacy and drug testing are addressed in Chapter 25 on Drug Testing

*The right to privacy* is guaranteed to every American citizen by the United States' Constitution. Although the federal constitutional protections do not extend to private employers dealing with job applicants and employees, most states have passed privacy legislation that recognizes a right to privacy to employees of private employers. Many states have passed privacy laws that cover specific situations, such as states that do not allow consideration or regulation by an employer of various forms of "off-duty" conduct.

There is a "common law" right to privacy in employment matters as well. A common law right means a legal right created by precedents set by court cases, instead of laws created by a legislative body. Common law rights include—

- The right to avoid public disclosure of private information
- The right to be protected from false or misleading statements being made in public
- Unreasonable intrusion into private affairs, either physically (such as a polygraph test)
  or otherwise invading an area of personal privacy
- Infliction of emotional distress by outrageous conduct

## Safe Hiring Programs and Privacy

There is no reason why a well-designed Safe Hiring Program should violate any statutory or common right to privacy. The processes outlined in this book are NOT intended to pry into an applicant's private life, turn employers into "big brothers," or turn hiring managers or HR professionals into the "hiring police." In fact, the type of information an employer obtains is job-related information about how a person has conducted themselves in their "public" lives — an area of their life that is visible to the public. For example, where a person has worked or attended school are generally not confidential matters. Anyone who was interested could see where the applicant was working or studying. Those activities are done in the open. In addition, if a person has a criminal record, that too is a matter of pubic record. A Safe Hiring Program does not invade a zone of privacy that a reasonable person would feel unduly invades those areas that society generally keeps private and confidential. The one tool that comes closest to butting up against a reasonable expectation of privacy would be credit reports, which are discussed in Chapter 13.

In addition, all of the Safe Hiring techniques recommended in this book are done with an applicant's expressed consent. As outlined in Chapter 7 on Applications, a conscientious employer will require each applicant to consent to and *authorize in writing* a background screening. If pre-employment background screening is outsourced to a background screening firm pursuant to the FCRA, then by federal law there must be written authorization and disclosure.[2]

Of course, just because information may not be private does not mean it is not confidential. If an employer locates a criminal record, efforts must be made to limit that information to just those in the company with a need-to-know for purposes of making a hiring decision. Personal identifiable information such as a Social Security Number is confidential and must be safeguarded. The right to privacy extends to how information obtained in a Safe Hiring Program is stored in order to protect against unauthorized viewing or theft. Another consideration is computer security when applicant data is transmitted or stored over a network. Maintaining confidentiality and security is a critical employment screening task.

As mentioned throughout this book, employers who engage in a Safe Hiring Program do not find that good applicants feel their privacy rights are being violated provided there are safeguards and assurances in place that the information will be kept confidential and used for legal purposes. Honest candidates understand that background screening is a sound business practice that helps all concerned. Job applicants want to work with qualified and safe co-workers in a profitable, professional environment.

## Employer's Choice: to Screen In-house or to Outsource?
## — and Privacy Considerations

In conducting pre-employment investigations, an employer essentially has two choices. The employer can either conduct the investigation in-house or outsource to a third party.

One advantage of outsourcing background screening is that screening companies must abide by the **Fair Credit Reporting Act (FCRA)**, which is the "gold standard" of privacy. Under the FCRA, all

---

[2] an exception is for truck drivers, and even then there still must be authorization

background screening is done with the applicant's written authorization as well as a disclosure of rights. There are limits to what may be obtained and for what reasons and who can access the information. There are also rules about maximum accuracy and re-investigation. By following the FCRA, employers have less concern that an applicant can allege a violation of privacy since everything is done pursuant to federal law at the onset. How the FCRA protects privacy is discussed in Chapter 6.

However, if an employer performs in-house applicant screening, then the employer no longer has the protection of the FCRA. In this situation, the employer's actions are governed by privacy law considerations. As a result, the employer needs to have an in-depth understanding of the privacy law framework within their jurisdiction or at the location where the job is being performed.

> **Author Tip** ➡  Essentially, an employer who does in-house screening or investigations must be aware of the general balancing test that attempts to reconcile the employer's need to have certain information with the privacy rights of job applicants and current employees. While it is not unlawful for an employer to conduct its own background checks, and considering the promulgation of more laws intended to preserve individual rights to privacy, employers can be at risk when performing screening in-house. To minimize risk, firms that do their own screening should act as though the FCRA applied.

For an applicant or current employee to allege a violation of a privacy right, generally the person must show that his or her reasonable expectation of privacy was seriously invaded by the employer.

In analyzing an invasion of privacy claim in an employment context, courts will first look to see if the employer invaded an employee's or applicant's protected privacy rights. If the employer's action did intrude upon privacy rights, then the court will examine—

1. Did the employer's action further a legitimate and socially beneficial aim?
2. If so, did the purposes to be achieved outweigh any resulting invasion of privacy?
3. Was there a less intrusive alternative that could have accomplished the same aim without invading privacy?

California has led the nation in issues involving employee privacy. A leading case is *Hill v. National Collegiate Athletic Association,* 7 Ca. 4th 1 (1994). In the Hill case, the issue was whether a college athletic association could require student athletes to sign consent forms for drug testing. The California Supreme Court ruled that the drug testing requirement was an invasion of privacy in that drug testing required an intrusion into bodily integrity. The court further held that the NCAA failed to show that the particular program it proposed furthered the intended goal, that the benefits did not outweigh the intrusion of rights, and there were less intrusive means to accomplish the goal.

There are other privacy matters that are not a matter of balance but have been made illegal directly by statute. For example, in 1988, the U.S. Congress enacted the Employee Polygraph Protection Act.[3] This act severely limits the ability of most private employers from using a polygraph or lie detector test for

---

[3] Employee Polygraph Protection Act, 29 U.S.C. Sections 2001-2009

job applicants or current employees who are being investigated. Although there are some narrow exceptions, as a practical matter this law ended the use of lie detectors.

## The Disturbing Trends of Data Sent Overseas and Use of Home Operators

A developing trend among some U.S. firms is to send Personal and Identifiable Information (PII) data abroad to call centers and data centers in order to take advantage of low-cost foreign labor. Privacy advocates are concerned when these U.S. firms send sensitive information such as medical records, Social Security Numbers beyond the privacy protections of the U.S.

In California for example, bills have been introduced in the past to firms to disclose to consumers if their personal data is sent overseas, or to ban the practice all together." In Washington D.C. efforts have been made to make regulatory agencies take action to protect privacy rights from being harmed by this overseas outsourcing of data. Even for international verification of employment or education, employers should carefully monitor if and how PII is sent outside of the U.S. If a background firm performs international verifications, employer should determine how PII is protected. A suggested practice is to only share personal information with the foreign employer or school directly, and not send personal information to an unregulated agent outside the U.S.

An employer should also carefully consider utilizing a background firm that uses home-based operators to make employment and education verification calls. Not only would that raise quality issues, but does an employer really want their applicant's personal data such as date of birth or social security number spread out on kitchen tables and dorms rooms across America. See Chapter 10 for more information. For additional information on issues associated with sending out of the United States or the use of home operators, see www.ESRcheck.com/safehiringupdates.php.

# Discrimination and Privacy — Conclusion

Legal limits and privacy/confidentiality are two important concepts presented in this chapter that will be revisited throughout this book and are intertwined with a Safe Hiring Program.

**Legal limits on what an employer can and cannot find out about applicants**. The primary law that affects this issue is equal employment opportunity laws on the federal, state and sometimes even the local level. The basic rule is that an employer can ask an applicant either directly on an application or interview — or find out indirectly through a past employment reference check — anything that is—

1. A valid predictor of job performance.
2. Not barred specifically by an equal employment law, such as questions concerning race ethnicity, religion, age, or sex.
3. Not prohibited due to a disparate impact even though neutral on its face,
   such as the use of arrest records.
4. Not prohibited by a specific statute, such as the prohibition on lie-detector machines.
5. Not prohibited due to illegal procedures, such as failure to follow the FCRA.

The role of **privacy rights and confidentiality** is the second key point in a Safe Hiring Program. An employer who follows the FCRA should not run afoul of privacy rights.

# Chapter 6

# Keeping It Legal – The Fair Credit Reporting Act

## A Basic Understanding of the FCRA is Important

When an employer uses a third party to help conduct a background check, there is a critical federal law the employer must be familiar with and follow. The law is called the **Fair Credit Reporting Act (FCRA).** Even though the name of the law uses the term "Credit," the FCRA goes far beyond credit reports. The FCRA establishes specific requirements and rules for a pre-employment background report, called a **Consumer Report,** which is usually much broader in scope than just a credit report.

A Consumer Report can include a wide variety of obtained information concerning job applicants, such as criminal and civil records, driving records, civil lawsuits, reference checks, and any other information obtained by a **Consumer Reporting Agency.** Therefore, the FCRA fundamentally controls the information on applicants that is assembled, evaluated, or disseminated by certain third parties and used for employment purposes.

When first passed in 1970, the FCRA was primarily meant to promote confidentiality, privacy, accuracy, and relevancy regarding information gathered about consumers. The law was extensively amended in 1996 with changes effective September 30, 1997. That amendment substantially overhauled the use of consumer reports for employment purposes by providing greater protection to consumers. Other important amendments were made in 1998 and additional amendments were passed in 2003.

### FCRA Definitions — Important Terms Found in the FCRA

**What is a Consumer Report?  (FCRA Section 603(d))**

A consumer report is a report prepared by a consumer reporting agency that consists of any written or oral or other communication of any information pertaining to the applicant's or employee's credit worthiness, credit standing, credit capacity, character, general reputation, personal characteristics, or mode of living, if this information is used or expected to be used or collected for employment purposes.

**What is an Investigative Consumer Report?  (FCRA Section 603(e))**

An Investigate Consumer Report is a special type of consumer report when the information is gathered through personal interviews (by phone calls or in person) of neighbors, friends, or associates of the employee or applicant reported on, *or* from other personal acquaintances or persons who may have knowledge about information bearing on the applicant's or employee's credit worthiness, credit standing, credit capacity, character, general reputation, personal characteristics, or mode of living, if this information is used or expected to be used or collected for employment purposes. The Investigative Consumer Report includes reference checks with former employers about job performance. However, a report would NOT be an Investigative Consumer Report if it were simply a verification of former employment limited to only factual matters such as the date started, date ended, salary, or job title. Once a reference checker asks about eligibility for rehire and job performance, then the report then becomes an Investigative Consumer Report.[1]

## What is a Consumer Reporting Agency (CRA)? (FCRA Section 603(f))

A Consumer Reporting Agency, or CRA, is any person or entity which, for monetary fees, dues, or on a cooperative nonprofit basis, regularly engages in whole or in part in the practice of assembling or evaluating consumer credit information or other information on consumers for the purposes of furnishing reports to third parties. It includes private investigators that "regularly" engage in pre-employment inquires.

## What is Meant by Employment Purposes? (FCRA Section 603(h))

A report is prepared for employment purposes when the report is used for the purpose of evaluating an applicant or employee for employment, re-assignment, or retention. Under the FCRA, a Consumer Report for employment purposes is considered a **"Permissible Purpose."**

## What is Meant by Adverse Action? (FCRA Section 603(k))

Adverse action in relationship to employment means a denial of employment or any other decision for employment purposes that adversely affects any current or prospective employee.

---

### An Important Area NOT Covered by the FCRA—

What if a business needs to investigate another business before entering into an economic relationship, such as investing, joint venturing, licensing agreements, merger or acquisition, or to just check out trade credit? A business may simply want to check out a competitor. The research may involve criminal or civil records, judgments, liens or bankruptcies or even a business credit report such as a Dun and Bradstreet report.[2] None of these investigations are covered by the FCRA, even if done by a third party. This is because the investigation is not focused on an individual and the **FCRA only protects individuals.**

What if a business wanted information about the people behind the other business? Any business relationship ultimately depends upon the integrity of the people involved. All the agreements and lawyers in the world cannot protect you or your business if the people you are dealing with lack integrity. Even in that scenario, a firm or a third party working on their behalf may check public records and even call schools and employers as long as the purpose is NOT employment. Here are three important considerations—

---

[1] Per FCRA Section 606(d)(4), if the information is adverse to the consumer's interest, the CRA must either obtain confirmation of the information from an additional source with independent knowledge or ensure the person interviews is the best possible source of information.

[2] Learn more about Dun and Bradstreet reports at www.dnb.com/us/

1. Even if the investigation is for business due diligence, under no circumstances can the business or their agent pull a personal credit report on any individual involved without consent. A personal credit report is ALWAYS covered by the FCRA, and can only be pulled for FCRA approved purposes.

2. If the economic transaction really amounts to starting an employment relationship, such as the acquisition of a small corporation where the principal is going to work for the acquiring company, this could trigger the need for full FCRA compliance.

3. There may be other laws that apply as well. In some states, the investigation can only be conducted by a state licensed private investigator.

## The Four Groups Affected

The FCRA addresses the rights and obligations of four groups. The descriptions below are focused on the groups as they relate to employment.

1. **Consumer Reporting Agencies (CRA's).** Again, these are third parties such as background screening firms or private investigators that provide Consumer Reports. [3]

2. **Users of consumer information.** These are primarily employers who hire CRA's to prepare Consumer Reports.

3. **Furnishers of consumer information.** Furnishers can include credit card companies that report payment histories to the three national credit collecting agencies, also past employers and schools — anyone who answers telephone calls from Consumer Reporting Agencies.

4. **Consumers.** The FCRA provides the consumers (applicants) with a host of rights in the process. These rights are discussed throughout this chapter and in Chapter 29.

There is bad news and good news about the FCRA. The bad news is that the FCRA is a very complex and convoluted law that makes little sense if an employer sits down and tries to read it. Anyone wanting to read the law can go to the website for the Federal Trade Commission (FTC), the federal agency charged with administering the law. Web links to review the law are available at the end of this chapter.

The good news is that there are only four basic steps an employer needs to know about the FCRA in order to begin a background screening program through an employment screening firm. These steps are explained in detail in the next section of this chapter.

Here is an important fact to keep in mind— The basic purpose of the law is to regulate what third parties do. The FCRA kicks in when a pre-employment background pre-screening is conducted by the Consumer Reporting Agency. Therefore, if an employer works with a professional pre-employment background firm, which is a CRA, the employer should select the firm based in part upon the background firm's knowledge of the FCRA. A competent background firm should know how to fully

---

[3] Some private investigators have incorrectly assumed that the FCRA does not apply to them because they have a state license. Nothing can be further from the truth. Any P.I. who "regularly" does pre-employment screening is also a CRA, and absolutely subject to the rules and regulations of the FCRA. There is no exact definition of the term "regularly" but any investigator who does more than one background screen for employment purposes must assume the FCRA applies.

comply with legal requirements of the FCRA, including the preparation of all documents and forms needed for a fully compliant screening program.

> **Author Tip** ➡ Employers risk legal liability if the procedures utilized to check on applicants infringe on legally protected areas of privacy. By following the FCRA, an applicant's privacy rights are protected. For this reason, many legal experts advise employers to engage the services of an outside screening firm. See Chapter 10 for a discussion on the pros and cons of outsourcing.

When engaging the services of a CRA, both the employer and the CRA must understand how critical it is to follow the FCRA. Failure to do so can result in substantial legal exposures, including fines, damages, punitive damages, and attorneys fees. Below is a brief summary of the substantial penalties involved for **NOT** following the FCRA.

| FCRA Sec. | Type of Non-Compliance | Maximum Possible Penalties |
|-----------|------------------------|----------------------------|
| 616 | Willful failure to comply with FCRA — applies to both employer and CRA | Attorney's fees / Punitive damages / $1,000 nominal damages even if no actual damages |
| 617 | Negligent non-compliance — applies to both employer & CRA | Actual damages/attorney's fees (no punitive damages or nominal damages) |
| 619 | Obtaining a report under false pretense — applies to both employer and CRA | Fine and two years prison |
| 620 | Unauthorized disclosure of consumer information by CRA officer or employee | Fine and two years prison |
| 621 | Administrative enforcement against CRA's engaged in a pattern of violations | Civil penalties |

## New Legal Development

In a 2007 case, the U.S. Supreme Court case broadened the definition of "willful" under the FCRA to include reckless conduct. This can have serious impact for employers and consumer reporting agencies. For more details, see: www.esrcheck.com/safehiringupdates.php.

# The FCRA in Four Easy Steps

To utilize the services of a Consumer Reporting Agency, you do not need to know all of the ins and outs of the FCRA. What **is necessary** for any employer is to understand the basic FCRA requirements in order to make sure that any supplier of hiring-related services is in compliance. Here are the four primary steps an employer needs to understand in order to make sure their program is in compliance—

# Step 1— Employer Certification[4]

The FCRA created a unique self-policing system. Prior to receiving a Consumer Report (remember, that is shorthand for a background report), an employer must first certify to the Consumer Reporting Agency in writing the employer will follow all the steps set forth in the FCRA. The employer certifies it will do the following—

- Use the information for employment purposes only.

- Not use the information in violation of any federal or state equal opportunity law.

- Obtain all the necessary disclosures and consents as required by the FCRA (steps 2 and 3 below).

- Give the appropriate notices in the event an adverse action is taken against an applicant based in whole or in part on the contents of the Consumer Report (see step 3 below).

- Give the additional information required by law if an Investigative Consumer Report is needed.

These requirements are explained further in a document prepared by the Federal Trade Commission titled *Notice to Users of Consumer Reports*. The FCRA requires a Consumer Reporting Agency to provide a copy of this document to every employer who requests a report. A copy of this notice is reprinted in Appendix 1.

# Step 2— Written Release and Disclosure

Before obtaining a consumer report from a Consumer Reporting Agency, the employer must obtain the applicant's written consent and also provide that applicant with a clear and conspicuous written disclosure that a background report may be requested. The disclosure must be provided in a separate, stand-alone document in order to prevent it from being buried in an employment application. The 1998 amendment to the FCRA clarified that the disclosure *and* the consent may be in the same document. However, the Federal Trade Commission, which enforces the FCRA, cautions that this form should not contain excessive information that may distract a consumer.

As a general practice, the Consumer Reporting Agency will provide employers with all the forms needed for the Disclosure and Release. A special procedure is necessary when the employer requests a Consumer Reporting Agency to obtain employment references. When the Consumer Reporting Agency is merely verifying factual matters such as the dates of employment or salary, no special procedure is necessary. However, as mentioned previously, when the Consumer Reporting Agency asks for information on topics such as job performance, that falls into a special category of consumer report called an "Investigative Consumer Report." When an Investigative Consumer Report is used, there are some special procedures to follow—

- There must be a disclosure to the applicant that "an investigative consumer report" is being requested, along with certain specified language. Unless it is contained in the initial disclosure, the consumer must receive this additional disclosure within three days after the request is made.

- The Disclosure must tell the applicant they have a right to request additional information about the nature of the investigation.

---

[4] see FCRA Sections 604 and 606. This also applies to Step 2 - Written Release and Disclosure, below.

- If the applicant makes a written request, then the employer has five days to respond with additional information and must provide a copy of a document prepared by the Federal Trade Commission called "A Summary of Your Rights Under the Fair Credit Reporting Act," provided by the CRA.

As a practical matter, a Consumer Reporting Agency should handle all of these requirements for an employer as part of their services. Still, an employer should be aware there are legal issues involved in preparing a proper form. Not only is there required information that must be conveyed to applicants, but also wrong language or excessive language can put an employer at risk. There is also the issue on asking for date of birth, as covered in the previous chapter.

Another concern is if a release or disclosure form contains a release of liability meant to protect the employer, the furnisher of information sources, or the screening firm. A release can potentially be contrary to public policy by requiring an applicant to give up rights. A release can also violate the rule against excessive verbiage on a form, which could detract from a consumer's clear understanding of the documents signed. In response to this issue, some firms use separate release forms and disclosure forms, while only placing the release of liability language on the release form. A good idea for firms that utilize release of liability language on a form is to consider adding the phrase, "to the extent permitted by law" after the release language.

In 1998, Congress passed one exception to the FCRA rules concerning these various notices. The trucking industry has an exception allowing for telephonic or electronic communications from commercial drivers. The reason is that commercial drivers may be hired over the phone from truck stops, and there is not an opportunity to obtain a written release or give certain notices.

### Where does an employer obtain these forms?

In order to utilize the services of a third party firm, the employer will need a certification form for the applicant to sign, along with an authorization and disclosure form. Yet, there are no industry-accepted or standardized forms in use. However, forms are available from a variety of sources. Many law firms will provide forms to their business clients. Nearly every background screening firm will provide forms. Part of selecting a screening firm is determining their ability to provide legally compliant forms. The pre-employment screening industry now has a national trade association, the National Association of Professional Background Screeners, which may suggest formats for the required forms in the future.[5]

## Step 3— Pre-Adverse Notice

When an employer receives a Consumer Report and intends not to hire the applicant based on the report, the applicant then has certain rights. If the "adverse action" is <u>intended</u> as a result of a Consumer Report, then the applicant is entitled to certain documents, see FCRA Section 604. <u>Before</u> taking the adverse action, the employer must provide the following information to the applicant—

- A copy of the consumer report
- The FTC document "A Summary of Your Rights Under the Fair Credit Reporting Act." This document is usually provided by the screening service.

---

[5] see the National Association of Professional Background Screeners at <u>www.napbs.com</u> and in Chapter 27

The purpose is to give an applicant the opportunity to see the report with the information being used against them. If the report is inaccurate or incomplete, the applicant then has the opportunity to contact the Consumer Reporting Agency to dispute or explain what is in the report. Otherwise, applicants could be denied employment without knowing they were the victims of inaccurate or incomplete data.

---

**Pre-Adverse Notice Sample Letter**

Dear Applicant,

A decision is currently pending concerning your application for employment at (the above employer)(this company). Enclosed for your information is a copy of the consumer report that you authorized in regard to your application for employment, together with a "Summary of Your Rights Under the Fair Credit Reporting Act."

If there is any information that is inaccurate or incomplete, you should contact this office as soon as possible so an employment decision may be completed.

Sincerely Yours,

*List the Consumer Reporting Agency's name, address and phone number below, including toll free numbers*

---

As a practical matter, by the time an applicant is the subject of a Consumer Report, an employer has spent time, money, and effort in recruiting and hiring. Therefore, it is in the employer's best interest to give an applicant an opportunity to explain any adverse information before denying a job offer. If there was an error in the public records, giving the applicant the opportunity to explain or correct it could be to the employer's advantage.

If there are other reasons for not hiring an applicant in addition to matters contained in a consumer report, the adverse action notification procedures still apply. Whether the intended decision was based in whole or in part on the Consumer Report, the applicant has a right to receive the report. In fact, these rights apply even if the information in the consumer report is not negative on its face. For example, an applicant may have a perfect payment record on his or her credit report, but an employer may be concerned the debt level is too high compared to the salary. The applicant still is entitled to a notice of pre-adverse action because it is possible the report is wrong about the applicant's outstanding debts. In a situation where the employer would have made an adverse decision regardless of the background report, following the adverse action procedures is still the best practice for legal protection.

A question that arises is how long an employer must wait before denying employment based upon information contained in a Consumer Report. The Fair Credit Reporting Act is silent on this point. However, many legal authorities advise an employer should wait a "reasonable" period of time before making the final decision. This period should be the time needed for an applicant to meaningfully review the report and make known to the employer or the Consumer Reporting Agency any inaccurate or incomplete information in the Consumer Report. A Consumer Reporting Agency should be able to assist employers in complying with these requirements. This does not mean an employer is required to hold the job open for a long period of time. After the first notice is given, and the applicant has had an appropriate opportunity to respond, an employer may either 1) wait until there has been a re-investigation, or 2) fill the position with another applicant.

As a practical matter, most employers find this provision of law does NOT impose any hardship or burden. While in rare situations an employer may question on how to proceed, the clear advantages of pre-employment screening far outweigh any complications that can theoretically arise from compliance.

# Step 4— Notice must be given to an applicant after an adverse action[6]

If, after sending out the documents required in Step 3, the employer intends to make a final decision not to hire, the employer must take one more step. The employer must send the applicant a Notice of Adverse Action informing the job applicant that the employer has made a final decision, and must provide a copy of the FTC form "Summary of Your Rights under the Fair Credit Reporting Act."

Many employers find it difficult to believe that Congress intended an applicant be notified twice, both before an adverse action and after. The law clearly requires two notices. This is also the interpretation of the Federal Trade Commission staff. The purpose is to give job applicants the maximum opportunity to correct any incomplete or inaccurate reports that could affect their chances of employment.

A special problem arises when an employer brings a worker on premises before the background check is complete, only to later find the background report uncovers negative information that may have disqualified the person. An employer may be tempted to simply call the person in, hand them the report, a final paycheck, and both letters at the same time. However, this does not give the applicant a reasonable time to review, reflect, and respond to the report. If the background report was incomplete or incorrect, there is not a meaningful opportunity for the applicant to exercise their rights under the FCRA. The best procedure is to follow the FCRA by providing the worker with their report, a statement of rights, the first letter and an opportunity to offer any response. The second letter should be delayed until a reasonable time has passed for an applicant to respond. Although it is administratively more difficult than giving two letters at once, two letters at once may violate an applicant's rights.

---

**Notice of Adverse Action Sample Letter**

Dear Applicant,

In reference to your application for employment, we regret to inform you that we are unable to further consider you for employment at this time. Our decision, in part, is the result of information obtained through the Consumer Reporting Agency identified below.

The Consumer Reporting Agency did not make the adverse decision, and is unable to explain why the decision was made.

You have the right to obtain within 60 days a free copy of your consumer report from the Consumer Reporting Agency as identified below and from any other consumer reporting agency which compiles and maintains files on consumers on a nationwide basis.

You have the right to contact the Consumer Reporting Agency listed below to dispute any information contained in the report that you believe may be inaccurate or incomplete. A copy of your rights under the "Fair Credit Reporting Act" is enclosed, entitled "Summary of Your Rights under the Fair Credit Reporting Act."

Sincerely Yours,

*List the Consumer Reporting Agency's name, address and phone number below, including toll free numbers.*

---

[6] see FCRA sec. 615

Attached in Appendix 1 is a copy of the summary of rights that should be given to a job applicant any time an employer sends either a pre-adverse action or a post-adverse action letter.

# Other Important FCRA Provisions

In addition to the four steps above, a CRA has other obligations. Observance of these obligations may also become important when an employer selects a CRA to assist with background investigations.

1.  **A CRA must follow reasonable procedures concerning identity and proper use of information per FCRA 607(a).** Per the requirements of the FCRA, every consumer reporting agency shall maintain reasonable procedures designed to avoid violations of section 605 (relating to what may be reported) and to limit the furnishing of consumer reports to the purposes listed under section 604. These procedures require that prospective users of the information identify themselves, certify the purposes for which the information is sought, and certify that the information will be used for no other purpose. Every consumer reporting agency is required to make a reasonable effort to verify the identity of a new prospective user and for the uses certified by a prospective user prior to furnishing the user a consumer report. No consumer reporting agency may furnish a consumer report to any entity if it has reasonable grounds for believing that the consumer report will not be used for a purpose listed in section 604. Lesson— A CRA must know the client and the limitations on what can be reported. These rules are of particular importance in view of well-publicized incidents in 2005 of the theft of data from firms where criminals posed as legitimate users and were able to set-up accounts in order to steal personal information, using it to commit crimes.

2.  **CRA must take measures to ensure accuracy of report (FCRA 607(b)).** Whenever a consumer reporting agency prepares a consumer report, it shall follow reasonable procedures to assure maximum possible accuracy of the information concerning the individual about whom the report relates. Lesson— The CRA should have written procedures that are followed and enforced to ensure maximum accuracy.

3.  **CRA must provide the Employer with the FTC prepared summary, "Notice to Users of Consumer Reports: Obligations of Users under the FCRA."** See FCRA Sec. 607(d).[7]

4.  **CRA must provide Employer with FTC summary, "Summary of Your Rights,"** **with every report.** See FCRA 604(b)(1)(B).[8]

5.  **A CRA may only include certain items of information in a consumer report.** FCRA Section 605 specifically limits certain information—
    a.  Bankruptcy cases older than 10 years, from the date of entry of the order for relief or the date of adjudication, as the case may be.[9]

---

[7] a copy of Notice is in Appendix 1
[8] a copy of Summary is in Appendix 1
[9] see Chapter 15 for limitations on bankruptcy as related to employment

b. Civil suits, civil judgments, and records of arrest older than seven years from date of entry. Due to the 1998 FCRA amendment, this section now only refers to a seven-year limitation on arrests, but *not* criminal convictions. There are no limits under the federal FCRA for reporting criminal convictions although there are some state limits.

c. Paid tax liens older than seven years from date of payment.

d. Accounts placed for collection or charged to profit and loss which are older than seven years.

e. Any other adverse item of information, other than records of convictions of crimes, which are older than seven years. Note that criminal convictions are excluded from the limitations, which leaves a seven-year limitation on using arrests without dispositions.

The FCRA, however, provides that these exceptions do not apply to an individual whose annual salary is reasonably expected to equal $75,000 a year or more.

6. **Rules concerning accuracy in reporting adverse public records.** If a CRA reports items of information as matters of public record but are likely to have an adverse effect upon a consumer's ability to obtain employment, the CRA must maintain strict procedures designed to insure that whenever public record information that is likely to have an adverse effect on a consumer's ability to obtain employment is reported, it is complete and up to date. For purposes of this duty, items of public record relating to arrests, indictments, convictions, suits, tax liens, and outstanding judgments shall be considered up to date if the current public record status of the item at the time it is reported. See FCRA Section 613(a)(2). The duty to accurately report a criminal matter under FCRA section 613 is typically satisfied by a CRA sending a researcher directly to the courthouse and pulling any public record to insure it is accurate and up to date, and to also look for identifiers. See FCRA section 613(a)(2). However, the FCRA does provide an alternative procedure under FCRA section 613(a)(1). Instead of going to the courthouse, a CRA can notify the consumer of the fact that public record information is being reported by the consumer reporting agency, together with the name and address of the person to whom such information is being reported.[10] However, in some states there is arguably the question: *is this alternative procedure advisable?* These states generally require that whenever a criminal matter is reported, reasonable procedures be followed such as double-checking any database "hit" against the actual records at the courthouse. In California for example, a background firm can only report a criminal conviction or other matters of public record for employment purposes if "it is complete and up to date," which is defined as checking the status at the time the matter is reported.[11] Double-checking a database "hit" at the courthouse certainly affords employees, applicants, and background firms the most protection and the highest degree of accuracy. The duty to deal with adverse information in a public record can have an important impact when using criminal record databases.[12]

---

[10] see FCRA Section 613(a)(1)

[11] see California Civil Code section 1786.28(b)

[12] this is discussed in-depth in Chapter 12. For a list of states that currently have their own requirements for accuracy as well as the text of the state statues, see www.ERcheck.com/safehiringupdats/php

7. **Re-investigation rule.** When a CRA prepares an investigative consumer report, no adverse information in the consumer report (other than information which is a matter of public record) may be included in a subsequent consumer report unless such adverse information has been verified during the process of making such subsequent consumer report, or the adverse information was received within the three-month period preceding the date the subsequent report is furnished. See FCRA Section 614.[13]

8. **Disclosure rules.** Upon request, a CRA must disclose to a consumer what is in the consumer's file upon request, identify sources, identity everyone who procured a report for employment for the past two years, and comply with various rules, e.g. provide trained personnel who can explain to a consumer any information in the report. See FCRA Sections 609 and 610.

9. **Duty to investigate.** If an applicant contests what is in the report, the CRA has an obligation to investigate and determine accuracy within 30 days, and to take appropriate actions. The CRA must give notice to the report furnisher within five days. Various other duties are dependent upon results of re-investigation. See FCRA Sections 611 and 612. CRA must carefully follow a series of rules in terms of various notices and responses and have a FCRA compliance procedure in place.

# Federal Lawsuit Demonstrates What Employers Should NOT Do

An opinion issued by the U.S. District Court in Northern District of Illinois in 2003 provides a case study on what an employer and screening firm should NOT do when it comes to safe hiring.

According to the allegations filed in the case, the plaintiff was contacted by a major hotel and offered a position. On his first day, he completed several forms, including an employment application where he truthfully stated he had no criminal record.

The application contained an authorization for a background check that the plaintiff did not initial. There was no indication in the court's opinion that any separate disclosure was signed as required by the FCRA.

After employment began, the major hotel hired a screening firm to do a background check. The screening firm mistakenly reported that the plaintiff had been convicted of a misdemeanor and served six months in jail. According to the court opinion, the plaintiff in fact did **NOT** have a criminal conviction. Neither the major hotel nor the background firm investigated the denial, and the plaintiff was terminated. To make matters worse, the plaintiff alleged that after he was fired the major hotel told third parties that he was fired because he lied on his application and spent time in jail. The plaintiff eventually found a new job, but at a substantially lower compensation.

---

[13] This only applies to matters that are adverse on its face. Employment or education verification is not adverse on its face, even if it becomes adverse in the context of the application, such as the information shows an applicant lied about job history.

Assuming all these facts were true, how many mistakes did the major hotel and the background firm make? Here are some of them—

- Failed to provide a separate Disclosure for the background check under the FCRA.

- Failed to comply with the adverse action rules under the FCRA. If the consumer applicant had the chance to explain, it could all have been cleared up.

- Failed to re-investigate when told information was wrong.

- Although the reasons for the mistaken criminal records are not clear, the question arises if reasonable procedures were used in obtaining the background data.

# The Fair and Accurate Credit Transactions Act — FACT — An FCRA Amendment

On December 4, 2003 President Bush signed into law H.R. 2622, known as the *Fair and Accurate Credit Transactions Act, (FACT)*. This amended the Fair Credit Reporting Act.

This wide ranging law dealt with a number of topics such as identity theft, increased consumer access to their credit report, pre-emption of certain state financial laws by the federal law, and increasing the accuracy of credit reports. Once fully implemented the new law allows consumers to receive a free credit report once a year from nationwide consumer reporting agencies and to have access to their credit scores. The law also allows for fraud alerts to be placed in credit reports and to block credit reports

For purposes of employment, these are some of the critical developments of FACT—

1. **Truncation of Social Security Number.** FCRA Section 609 was amended to allow consumers to request that the first five digits of his or her Social Security Number to be deleted from any disclosure to the consumer. The purpose is to help combat identity theft, since identity theft often occurs at the consumer's mailbox.

2. **Statute of limitations.** FCRA Section 618 sets the period of time that someone may sue for a violation of the FCRA. The statute of limitations has been extended from two years from the date of violation, to two years from the date of the discovery of the violation by the consumer, and up to five years from the date of the actual violation. Consumer reporting agencies should plan on keeping records for at least six years to allow time for the statutory period plus the normal delay time experienced in receiving notice of a lawsuit.

3. **Investigation of current employees.** Employers now have the ability to conduct third party investigations of current employees without disclosure or having to first get written authorization.

## Fixing a Flaw — Investigation of Current Employees

For employers, this was probably the most critical issue the FACT amendment addressed. A little history. When the 1997 amendments to the FCRA were first enacted, many security professionals, as well as labor attorneys and human resource professionals, had widely interpreted the notice and disclosure requirements as applying only to pre-employment hiring and not post-hire workplace investigations. However, in 1999, attorney Judy Vail sent a letter to the Federal Trade Commission (FTC), the federal agency that enforces the FCRA, asking whether the FCRA applied to investigations of sexual harassment claims against current employees.[14] In what was commonly referred to as the Vail letter, the FTC flatly stated that investigation of current employees by third parties who regularly conduct such investigations are covered by the same FCRA rules used for pre-employment screening.

There are many situations when a firm may wish to use a third party to *investigate* a current employee. If there are allegations of sexual harassment, employers have a duty to conduct a thorough, prompt and fair investigation, and that is often done by hiring an outside professional. If there is suspicion of misconduct, such as theft, drug dealing, or other criminal conduct, then the expertise of an outside investigator may also be required.

However, when investigative secrecy is required, it is difficult to conduct an effective third-party investigation under FCRA ground rules as interpreted by the Vail letter. As soon as the target is tipped off, it is very easy to destroy evidence, influence witnesses, or attempt to derail the investigation.

Another problem was securing witness cooperation. The FCRA provides a mechanism for the object of the inquiry to obtain a copy of the report, thereby revealing information sources. The result is that witnesses cannot be promised anonymity, discouraging witnesses from assisting an investigation.

Before the FACT amendment, to comply with the FCRA a third-party investigator had to obtain written authorization from the subject of the report. The employee must also receive a stand-alone disclosure that a consumer report is being prepared.

A number of court cases whittled away at the Vail letter. Finally the issue was put to rest by the FACT legislation. The FCRA was amended so that an employer would not need to obtain a written release and authorization in order to conduct investigation of current employees, where the investigation involved one of the following—

- Suspected misconduct relating to employment;

- Compliance with federal, state, or local laws and regulations;

- The rules of a self-regulating organization;

- Any pre-existing written policies of the employer.

---

**Author Tip ➡ Future Consents**

In order to protect the right to conduct future investigations when necessary, employers may consider adding the following language to their authorization forms— "This authorization and release will remain valid for future preparation of a consumer report or investigative consumer report for purposes of retention, promotion, or re-assignment unless revoked in writing."

---

[14] the FTC staff had a practice from 1997 to 2001 of issuing staff opinion letters in response to inquiries

## Even With FACT Act, Limitations Still Exist

First, the investigation cannot be made for the purpose of investigating a consumer's credit worthiness, credit standing, or credit capacity. A credit report is always covered by the FCRA. Secondly, the matter cannot be reported to an outside person or entity except for certain governmental agents and agencies.

Finally, there is still a procedure in place that must be followed if there are any adverse actions as a result of the investigation, such as termination or discipline. After taking any adverse that was based in any part on the report, the employer must provide the consumer with a summary of the nature and substance of the investigation. However, there are limits on providing the source of the information.

# State Laws Controlling CRA Activities

A number of states have their own rules and laws for regulating the background reports performed by Consumer Reporting Agencies. It is important for employers outsourcing their screening to use a vendor that is fully familiar with the applicable state laws.

There may be situations where a CRA can legally report a criminal matter, but a specific state rule limits the employer's use of that same information. For example, under the FCRA and under many state laws, a CRA may report an arrest not resulting in a conviction. However, the employer may be under some separate state limitation on how the arrest is utilized. The lesson is when it comes to state rules, an employer needs to be aware that there are potentially separate rules that control what a CRA can transit to an employer, and separate rules that control how the employer can use the information.

## Subtle FCRA and State Law Differences

Differences between the FCRA and state laws can be very subtle. Here are examples—

- In New Jersey, a CRA must not only notify a consumer within five days that a dispute is considered frivolous (which is similar to FCRA 611), but must also state reasons why.

- In New York, if an item of information is corrected or can no longer be verified, an agency must mail a corrected copy of the consumer's report to the consumer at no charge. A mailing is not required under FCRA § 611.

- In Massachusetts, the final adverse action letter must be in minimum 10 point type, sent within 10 days, with specified language.

- In Texas, a CRA must mail a corrected copy to everyone who requested a consumer report in the past six months.

- California, Minnesota, and Oklahoma have a "check the box" requirement where an applicant can check a box and is entitled to a copy of the report. In addition, California has two other possible boxes to check — one for credit reports and one for employers who do their own background reports. See the article "Only in California" in Appendix 5.

**Same states are stricter**— At least twenty states <u>arguably</u> have stricter state FCRA rules. The twenty states are Arizona, California, Colorado, Georgia, Kansas, Kentucky, Louisiana, Maine, Maryland,

Massachusetts, Minnesota, Montana, New Jersey, New Hampshire, New Mexico, New York, Oklahoma, Rhode Island, Texas, Washington. Also, state law effecting screening can change anytime.

## Examples of Different State Rules

The following list of states and state rules are *not* intended to be a comprehensive or definitive statement of current state laws. These examples are only illustrations of some of the differences found in some states. Of course, this list is subject to change without notice due to legislative action in a state.

- Special rules concerning the notice and initial disclosure— CA, MA, MN, NY, OK
- Rules for notice of Investigative Consumer Report (ICR) to consumers— CA, ME, MA, MN, NJ, NY
- Rules for Nature and Scope letter that is given to a consumer if they request more information about an ICR— ME, NY
- Special rules for pre-adverse action and post-adverse action letters— GA, KS, LA, ME, MD, MA, MN, MT, NH, RI, WA
- Right of applicant to know if report requested— ME, NY
- Disclosures to consumer by agency— AZ, CA, CO, GA, ME, MD, NJ, RI
- Disputed accuracy rules— AZ, CO, MA, ME, MD, NJ, NY, RI, TX
- Rules on timing of notice for ICR— CA, ME, MA, MN, NJ, NY
- States that have separate rule just for credit reports where there is some complication about how and if the rules also apply to pre-employment reports— CA, NM, NV, RI
- States that prohibit the CRA from utilizing arrests not resulting in convictions. This is a separate set of rules where the CRA itself is under a state mandate (as opposed to employers being under the mandate). Examples include Kentucky, New Mexico, New York.
- States that have a seven-year limitation on reporting criminal convictions and impose that state law directly on a Consumer Reporting Agency. Even though the federal FCRA was amended in 1998 to do away with the seven-year limitation on reporting criminal convictions, some states still have a version of a seven-year limitation law.

## More About the Seven-Year Rule

According to Derek Hinton, author of *The Criminal Record Handbook*,[15] the U.S. states that still restrict reporting of criminal information by a background firm to seven years are California, Colorado, Kansas, Maryland, Massachusetts, Montana, New Hampshire, New Mexico, New York, Texas, Washington. However, Kansas, Maryland, Massachusetts, New Hampshire, and Washington waive the time limit if the applicant is reasonably expected to earn $20,000 or more annually. In New York the exception is

---

[15] *The Criminal Records Handbook* published 2004 by BRB Publications, Tempe, AZ  www.brbpub.com

$25,000. In Colorado and Texas the amount is $75,000. With exceptions, California's rule is a prohibition on any conviction older then seven years.[16]

This leads to two immediate problems—

First, it is harder to create a workable national rule when some states have their own state-imposed limitation. So that there is no issue in determining applicable state law, as a matter of practical convenience some screening firms simply adopt the seven-year rule nationwide. This has some logic since cases older than seven years could potentially be stale under EEOC standards. However, it can also lead to serious cases not being reported in states with no seven-year rule, and it can lead to situations where a CRA is aware that an applicant has a criminal conviction, but by law must keep it under wraps and sit on potentially important information.

The second problem is the question "when does the seven years begins to run?" The general rule is that the seven years begins to run from the date the consumer is free of physical custody, regardless of whether the person was on parole or probation. However, if the consumer violates probation or parole and went back into custody even for one day, the clock would arguably start to run all over again. See 'When Does the Seven Year Limit Begin' on the following page.

The following are some further complexities associated with the seven-year rule imposed by states.

1.  It is arguable that some of these seven-year restrictions are not enforceable because they are "pre-empted" by the FCRA, meaning that the federal rules override the state limitations. However, that depends upon a complicated analysis of both federal and state law, as described later in this chapter. State laws cannot be ignored.

2.  The lack of a national rule when it comes to the seven-year rule also creates a potential confusion when more then one state is involved. This confusion can occur if the applicant, the employer, the screening firm, or the job location are physically located in different states and one of them has a seven-year rule.

3.  The state of Nevada also has a seven-year restriction but that appears to only apply to a report issued for credit purposes and not employment.

4.  The seven-year rule applies to what a background firm can report. This rule does not apply to employers who do their own criminal checks in-house.

5.  However, even an employer who does their own search in-house must still be aware that if they utilize records older then seven years, they need to consider the EEOC implications. See Chapter 11 for a discussion of how the EEOC affects the use of older criminal records.

6.  If an employer does their own search to avoid the seven-year rule, the employer must be careful to use the same time period for all similarly situated applicants so no applicant can claim disparate treatment.

7.  An employer who does their own search in-house must be cautious about utilizing any outside researchers, since that can trigger the application of the FCRA or state law versions of the FCRA.

---

[16] except in the event some other government regulation requires a criminal search to go back further

See the section 'Conducting Internal Investigations' on how an internal investigation can inadvertently trigger the FCRA.

# When Does the Seven Year Limit Begin?

An ongoing question for employers, screening firms, and criminal record search firms is "When does the seven years begin?" The Federal Trade Commission published commentaries to the FCRA, contained in the Code of Federal Regulations.[17] The FTC commentaries are intended to be interpretations of the law and clarify how the FTC will construe the FCRA in light of congressional intent as reflected in the statute and legislative history. According to page 514 of the commentary, the reporting time period is calculated as follows—

> The seven-year reporting period runs from the date of disposition, release or parole, as applicable. For example, if charges are dismissed at or before trial, or the consumer is acquitted, the date of such dismissal or acquittal is the date of disposition. If the consumer is convicted of a crime and sentenced to confinement, the date of release or placement on parole controls.[18] The sentencing date controls for a convicted consumer whose sentence does not include confinement. The fact that information concerning the arrest, indictment, or conviction of crime is obtained by the reporting agency at a later date from a more recent source such as a newspaper or interview does not serve to extend this reporting period.

However, nothing is as easy as it may seem. The difficulty is that a court record will only indicate the date the sentence was imposed by the court and the length of the sentence. It is not always possible to tell from the docket or court record when the confinement actually ended, since the release date from custody is often NOT contained in the court file. The date is actually contained in files maintained by the county jail or probation office for a county sentence, or by the state Department of Corrections for a state prison sentence. Information from these offices is not easily accessible without a subpoena.

Assume a screening firm did a background check in California in 2004. California has a seven-year rule. Suppose the court docket shows the consumer applicant was convicted of a serious crime in 1995, which is beyond the seven years, but received a 3-year prison sentence. There is no indication the applicant re-offended. Under the FCRA, the criminal conviction is reportable because there is no limit on reporting convictions.[19] *Is it reportable in a state such as California that has a seven-year reporting limit?* Based upon the sentence imposed, the consumer's sentence would have gone into the seven-year period and is reportable. *What happens if the*

---

[17] Code of Federal Regulations, 16 C.F.R. Ch. 1 (1-1-97 edition) Pt. 600 App.

[18] confinement, whether continuing or resulting from revocation of parole, may be reported until seven years after the confinement is terminated

[19] although the EEOC rules may apply

*person was released early, or was given credit for time served?* The background firm is in a catch-22. If a background agency did not report that, and the applicant was hired and re-offended on the job or harmed the public, the background agency would have exposure to fault. If the background firm reports it, there is a possibility that, in fact, the person was out of custody early and did not go within the seven years. However, since custody information is generally not public record, it is an unknowable fact to an employer or CRA. Most CRA's, if they are concerned about the issues involved with legal compliance, will take the position that a determination must be made on the publicly available information, and that assumptions cannot be made either way about early releases.

The logical conclusion is the FCRA intends to not count as part of the seven-years rule any time not spent in confinement. The seven years starts when a person is out of custody, even though he or she may still be on parole or probation.

This point also demonstrates that even in states with a seven year limit, a CRA must go back further then seven years, since a case is still reportable that is older than seven years if a person was incarcerated during the past seven years due to the case. Sometimes, a case older than seven years is brought back into the seven years rule if a person is jailed for having violated probation or parole within the seven year period. The seven years starts over again.

The lesson— a screening firm or court researcher should not limit their research to the past seven years since reportable older cases can be missed.

# Doing Background Screening in All Fifty States? Which State Law Applies?

A recurring issue for large firms with facilities in multiple states is 50-state legal compliance. As seen above, the rules for pre-employment background screening have become Balkanized, meaning many states have their own rules and regulations. This is similar to the early days of the railroads—one state had one type of rail, and the next state had a different rail, so at state borders things usually came to a halt. Compliance does become challenging for large employers trying to exercise due diligence across state lines, but challenging is not the same as impossible. Compliance just requires a little more work.

## FACT Act, Pre-emption, and National Standards

As mentioned previously, in late 2003 President Bush signed the Fair and Accurate Credit Transaction Act (FACT). The primary thrust of FACT was to extend the FCRA federal pre-emption of conflicting state laws in the area of consumer credit. Congress and the financial industry were concerned that the FCRA allowed states to begin passing their own laws in 2004, undermining a uniform national credit reporting system. The FACT Act prevented that. The FACT ACT also increased identity theft protection, provided for free yearly credit reports, and changed the rules concerning investigation of current employees.

Although the FACT Act establishes that the FCRA takes priority over state laws when it comes to areas involving credit reporting, the inter-relationship between federal and state law is still complicated when it comes to employment issues.

FCRA section 625 (as amended in the 2003 FACT Act) provides that, in certain areas, state laws that exist prior to September 30, 1996 could prevail over the FCRA. Any state limit in effect on reporting criminal convictions prior to that date would be valid, although under federal FCRA rules there is no limit on how far back a background firm can go on reporting a criminal conviction.

For example, California had a seven year limit in place prior to September 30, 1996, that did not allow criminal record to be reported beyond seven years unless the applicant made over $30,000 a year. That was changed in 1998 to $75,000 a year and in 2002, California changed that limit to place a prohibition on reporting any convictions older then seven years regardless of salary.[20] The California law contains an exception if the investigative consumer report is to be used by an employer who is explicitly required by a governmental regulatory agency to check for criminal convictions older than seven years when the employer is reviewing a consumer's qualification for employment.[21] An argument can be made that by changing the law, any California limitation is now null and void, and is pre-empted since the current law was not passed prior to September 30, 1996, and California now falls under the federal rules, which have no limit on reporting convictions. To date, no one has stepped forward as a guinea pig to test this theory. Similarly, Texas has a statute with a $75,000 limit that was effective September 1, 1997, that arguably has no force and effect under the FCRA.[22]

## The Forms Issue

A major issue for multi-state employers is which form to use. A fifty-state form would be a challenge due to the number of states with their own rules. If a form is written to accommodate all of the various state rules, one could argue such a form would be improper as it violating the FCRA mandate "…a clear and conspicuous disclosure has been made in writing to the consumer at any time before the report is procured or caused to be procured, in a document that consists solely of the disclosure."[23] Multi-state employers should work with CRA's that understand each of the separate state rules discussed above. This understanding should not only include forms, but also the different rights afforded to applicants at different stages of the process, as outlined in the previous sections.

## Which State's Laws to Follow

In order to give applicants all of their rights under state law, the next issue is which state's laws apply. Assume that a California resident is applying for a job in Ohio with a firm that is owned by a company in New York, and that a California screening firm does the background check. Both California and New York have a seven-year restriction on criminal records, but Ohio does not. Even though the applicant

---

[20] see California Civil Code Section 1786.18

[21] see Civil Code 1786(b)(2)

[22] see B & C Code Title 2, § 20.05. Further analysis of the seven-year limitations and if subject to pre-emption is found at www.esrcheck.com/safehireupdates.php

[23] see FCRA section (b)(2)

would likely move to Ohio if he gets the job, at the time of the search is he still a California resident. If the candidate has a criminal record in California older then seven years, can it be reported for a job in Ohio by a California screening firm? Can the candidate sue in California or New York for reporting a conviction that was too old under California and New York law, even though it would be permissible under the laws of Ohio?

*Here is a rule of thumb—*

The employer should first consider the **law of the state where the employment is to occur. However,** an employer or screening firm needs to understand where a consumer can possibly sue them, and consider the laws of that state. If the laws are contradictory, then a choice must be made as to the state that would most likely have jurisdiction over a lawsuit.

There are several issues to consider when deciding which state's laws to follow.

1.  The first issue is **what claims can be brought in what court**. This is sometimes referred to as "subject matter jurisdiction." This can be a complex issue since there are two court systems in the U.S. — federal courts and state courts. A legal action for violations of the FCRA may be brought in federal court since FCRA Section 618 provides for federal jurisdiction. However, a consumer cannot bring claims in a federal FCRA lawsuit in the nature of defamation, invasion of privacy, or negligence since those are pre-empted by FCRA section FCRA 610(e) except as to information furnished with malice or willful intent to injure. However, there are state claims that can be litigated in federal court, such as violation of a state's civil rights statutes. To get around federal limitations on certain claims, a plaintiff may attempt to bring an action solely under state law in state court. An employer or screening firm sued in state court under state law may argue that the claim is still pre-empted under federal law and ask for removal to federal court. [24]

2.  The second issue is **venue**. Venue means a place where an act or injury occurred. It is the proper place (or to use a legal word, forum) for the lawsuit.

3.  The third issue is **jurisdiction**. Jurisdiction means ability of court to exercise power over a business or a person.[25] Just because the applicant may have been injured in Ohio does not automatically mean an Ohio court has any power over the New York employer or the California based CRA. For the applicant to go into an Ohio court and to file a lawsuit, the Ohio court must have personal jurisdiction over the parties.

---

[24] However, one federal district court in the Eastern District of Kentucky has ruled in 2006 that FCRA Section 610(e) does NOT prevent a consumer from suing for a state court claim for defamation because FCRA Section 610(e) only provide immunity for disclosures required under law, but does not give immunity where a consumer report is inaccurate. This can have important implications for background firms. For a more detailed discussion, see: www.ESRcheck.com/safehiringupdates.php

[25] This is different from choice of law or Conflict of Law. In general terms, Conflict of Law means which law a court should apply in a lawsuit where the case has a relationship to more than one state. Factors include the place where injury occurred, place where conduct occurred that caused injury, the domicile of the parties, and where the relationship between the parties is centered. Jurisdiction refers to the power of the court to even exercise control over the parties to the lawsuit in the first place.

## Long Arm Statute

The topic of jurisdiction fills numerous law books. One of the key concepts is called a Long Arm Statute, which allows a state to have a long reach when it comes to exercising personal jurisdiction over people and businesses. States can assume broad jurisdiction, based on such concepts as minimum contacts or systemic and continuous activity in a state. Another basis for a state court to obtain jurisdiction is when a business intends to conduct business in that state.

For employers, the issue is generally very simple—the firm can generally be sued in any state where it does business, which is very broadly defined. Similar rules apply to screening firms. A screening firm can be sued in any state where it does business. Legal cases suggest if a screening firm has an interactive website where the screening firm conducts background checks, then that firm is doing business in all fifty states. Additionally, the screening firm can likely be sued in any state where it solicits business or has clients.

Understanding where a lawsuit can be brought is the key to choosing which state laws to apply. In the example above, the issue is whether a California court would likely exercise jurisdiction in a lawsuit against a California screening firm and a New York employer, when the criminal record was appropriate to report under Ohio law but not under California law.

What does all this mean? As a general rule, firms that hire in more then one state should first consider the law of the state where the employment occurs. However, the employer should also consider if other states may be likely to allow a consumer to sue for a violation of their state law. This can include the state where the consumer resides, the state where the employer is located, or the state where the consumer reporting agency has its place of business.

The result, of course, is that employers and screening firms are occasionally left to take their best "guess" about what law to apply, since there is not a clear national rule. In addition, employers can find themselves in the position of having to apply different rules to different applicants. Until Congress pre-empts the area with a clear national rule, this will be a confusing area for employers.

# Does the FCRA Apply to Employers Who Perform Background Checks In-House?

Employers with an in-house security department may decide to avoid the requirements of the FCRA by conducting their own investigations. On its face, the FCRA only applies to third parties and not in-house resources. With that in mind, many employers believe that if internal security or Human Resources perform the background checks, the FCRA mandates are not applicable. Unfortunately, these employers may still find that their actions inadvertently trigger the FCRA compliance rules.

For example, suppose an in-house security department hires a court retrieval service or an investigator merely to go to a courthouse to pull criminal records. According to an opinion letter by the FTC legal staff,[26] some court researching firms and private investigators can, in fact, be Consumer Reporting Agencies. If an employer happens to select a court researcher to obtain records who happens to qualify

---

[26] see the Slyter letter dated June 12, 1998, available at www.ftc.gov/os/statutes/fcra/slyter.htm

as a Consumer Reporting Agency, then what the employer thought was an in-house report suddenly turns into a Consumer Report. At this point, even though the investigation started out as an internal security procedure, hiring a consumer reporting agency can mean that all FCRA rules apply. This includes the need for written consent and disclosure and adverse action letters. Starting an in-house investigation without FCRA consents turns into an FCRA covered investigation.

Similarly, an employer who directly accesses an online database to obtain information about an applicant may also invoke the FCRA. In general, there are two types of databases an employer may access. If an employer accesses a public records database maintained by courts or other public entities, then the employer is not going through a third party and the FCRA is probably not invoked.[27] However, if an employer utilizes a *commercial database* that compiles public records, the FCRA is arguably invoked. An example is an online criminal record service that compiles millions of criminal records from public sources. The FCRA may come into play in this situation because an employer is accessing information assembled by third parties that bears upon an individual's character, general reputation personal characteristics, or mode of living as defined in the FCRA. In addition, some online commercial databases do not permit their data to be used for any FCRA-covered purpose, such as employment. These databases require a user to agree that the information can only be used as a source of "lead-generation" to conduct further investigation, such as going to the courthouse to confirm a criminal conviction. More information about the use of these databases is contained in Chapter 12.

The best advice for private employers who do in-house screening? Act as though the FCRA applies!

## Conducting Internal Investigations

A policy least likely to trigger the FCRA is for an internal security department to only obtain records that any member of the general public can obtain, and only to use their own internal employees to obtain the records. An example of the latter is a company sending its own employees to a courthouse to obtain criminal records.

Additionally, if the employer operates per the FCRA, the applicant would have the right to first review the report before any decision is finalized and to clarify any mistakes. If corporate security does not follow the FCRA, and the applicant is erroneously denied employment without a pre-adverse action letter and the opportunity to be heard, then the employer could be held liable for illegal employment practices if the rejected applicant pursues legal recourse.

When considering whether to conduct internal investigations, companies must also consider pertinent state laws. There are two sets of laws any employer must consider. The first set is the myriad of labor laws that apply to all information obtained by employers, regardless of who obtains it. Examples are the discrimination rules discussed in Chapter 5.

The second set of laws to consider is state FCRA-type laws. If an employer accidentally triggers the federal FCRA, the employer may be sued under state law as well.

In addition, there is a new trend aimed at applying FCRA-type protections to applicants who are screened in-house. Many privacy advocates consider the fact that internal investigations are not

---

[27] additionally there may be state laws that apply

regulated as a loophole in the FCRA. Here is the issue— Suppose an employer utilizes a screening firm and operates under the FCRA. If negative information is found, the applicant has a right to receive an adverse action letter and has the opportunity to review and respond before the action is made final. However, if an employer conducts the investigation, the employer does have to follow the FCRA procedures, including the adverse action sections, since the FCRA only applies to outside agencies. An employer can simply deny employment and never tell the applicant. The problem is that there have been documented cases of employers getting the information wrong and the applicant never knew why they were not getting a job, or there were errors in the public records.

# The Story of Mr. Lewis

In a lawsuit filed by Scott Lewis in Ohio, Mr. Lewis alleged that he suddenly lost his current job and had severe difficulty getting a new job. He could not figure out why suddenly no one wanted to talk to him. He reported that on one occasion he called the employer back after believing he had a good interview and was told he was an unsavory character and if he contacted the employer again the employer would contact the police.

According to the case allegations—

"Plaintiff states that, after months of searching for employment with no success, he engaged a private investigator to determine the reason for his repeated rejections. The investigator conducted a criminal background check on Plaintiff, which, according to Lewis, produced a record consisting of various felony convictions, including a 1996 murder conviction, all of which properly belong to Timothy Lockhart. Plaintiff contends that whomever entered Mr. Lockhart's arrest data entered the last four digits of his telephone number as the last four digits of his Social Security Number. This error resulted in Mr. Lockhart's information being entered under Plaintiff's Social Security Number. Thus, any third party who did a search using Plaintiff's Social Security Number would retrieve Mr. Lockhart's criminal history."

— *Lewis v. OPEN*, 190 F.Supp. 2d 1049 (S.D. Ohio, 2002).

The problem, according to Mr. Lewis, was that private employers accessed a private database in Ohio and obtained information about applicants. If the information was erroneous, as it was in this situation, the applicant would never know because private employers had no FCRA duty to give the applicant a copy of the report or a chance to explain.

Essentially, a person could be "blackballed" and never know it.

Partly in response to the facts in the Lewis matter, California passed the nation's first law that attempted to regulate in-house employer investigations. Effective in 2002, the law required that information about public records obtained by an employer, even without the use of an outside agency, must be provided to an applicant, unless that applicant waived the right. California employers are required to follow a series of steps when they do an in-house investigation that gives FCRA type protection, including adverse action notices if public record is obtained and used adversely.[28]

---

**Author Tip ➡    Beware of online websites that will get you the dirt on anyone!**

Most internet search engines will reveal a number of websites offering to sell all sorts of data about anyone, and "do-it-yourself background checks" is a popular subject for spam email. Some of these sites advertise they have billions of records on Americans — all it takes is a credit card and supposedly anyone can find out anything about anyone. Putting aside the significant privacy issues, there is one important piece of advice for employers: ***Do not use these sites for employment unless you really know what you are doing***. Since the use of these sites is likely to fall under the FCRA if used for employment, an employer needs to proceed with caution. A clue is these sites either do not even mention the FCRA or mention it only briefly in passing. In a Safe Hiring Program, an employer needs to work one-to-one with a professional with an understanding of the FCRA. These do-it-yourself internet sites typically have no one to talk with who can give employers the professional assistance they need. An additional problem with these sites is that employers may not know the source, accuracy, or integrity of the data. If an employer does an online criminal search, an employer may be getting a questionable "database search," which is subject to the limitations and issues discussed in Chapter 12.

Conclusion— online websites may be helpful for limited purposes, but employers need to proceed with extreme caution when using them.

---

# Sources of Information About the FCRA

1. The FTC's home page for the FCRA is at www.ftc.gov/os/statutes/fcrajump.htm. The text of the FCRA is available online at www.ftc.gov/os/statutes/031224fcra.pdf

2. Following the 1997 amendments, the FTC staff wrote letters in response to questions that were published online. The staff letters are online. These letters do not carry the force of law, but they are persuasive. They may eventually form the basis of any commentary published by the FTC; *see* Cast letter-October 27, 1997; *see* www.ftc.gov/os/statutes/fcra/index.htm

3. Commentary for FCRA prior to amendments effective 1997 can be found in 16 CFR Ch. 1(1-1-97 edition). Future FTC commentaries on the FCRA are likely.

4. FCRA required documents are also found on the FTC website and in Appendix 1. These are—

   a. General Summary of Consumer Rights

   b. Notice of Furnisher Responsibilities

   c. Notice of User Responsibilities

---

[28] see CA Civil Code section 1786.53

# Section 2

# The AIR Process — An Essential Starting Point

Section 2 examines the first true stages
of a Safe Hiring Program.

**The A.I.R. Process**
   stands for *Application, Interview* and *References*.

**The A.I.R. Process** involves the initial
   screening practices usually performed by the employer.

The Safe Hiring Checklist, found at the back of Chapter 4,
is an excellent resource to help employers
implement their Safe Hiring Programs.

# Chapter 7

# Why Applications Are Vital

## The Application Process Starts BEFORE The Application Is Filled Out

When does the application process start? From the point of view of a Safe Hiring Program, it starts before applications are printed or given out. It really starts when the job is first created.

First, an employer needs to create a job description. This is important for a number of reasons. Having a job description that clearly defines the essential function of the job and core competence not only helps identify and select the right candidate during recruitment, but also provides legal protection when it comes to claims of discrimination or compliance with the Americans with Disabilities Act (ADA). It is essential to have a job description in the event a criminal record is disclosed or discovered. This helps insure the employer is consistent with the requirements of the Federal Equal Employment Opportunities Commission (EEOC), as explained in Chapter 5.

A job description should clearly indicate the levels of education and experience required of candidates. Those who do not have the required education or experience may be discouraged from applying. If a candidate misleads an employer about knowledge, skills, or experience, then the fact that the requirements were clearly set forth in the job description will assist the employer in the event there is a rejection or termination. An employer can always take the position that dishonesty on an application is grounds for termination. However, the employer's position is buttressed when it is clear from a well-written job description there were certain requirements for the position, that the job description was provided to the applicant, and the applicant misled the employer about his or her qualifications.

Numerous resources and websites, as well as commercially available software, can assist an employer in preparing job descriptions. One useful site, found at www.acinet.org/acinet/jobwrite_search.asp, contains a job description writer feature. Employers may also use the job descriptions formulated by the National Academy of Science, Committee on Occupational Classification and Analysis. This organization created the *Dictionary of Occupational Titles* or DOT.[1] See their web page at www.wave.net/upg/immigration/dot_index.html for an online dictionary of jobs.

---

[1] this DOT is not to be confused with the Department of Transportation and DOT drug testing

Managers' job descriptions are also a critical consideration. Does part of the written job description indicate a manager's duty to "record, report, and address issues of workplace misconduct such as acts of workplace violence, or harassment, or drug abuse"? Placing these duties in the written job description of supervisors serves to re-enforce their role in workplace safety.

## Inform the Applicant About the Background Check

As part of any recruitment effort, the employer is well-advised to place applicants on notice that the firm practices safe hiring with background checks. The goal is to get maximum advantage from safe hiring by discouraging applicants to hide something when applying. Employers can place a phrase in the job announcement, bulletin, classified advertisement, or internet site that indicates the firm requires background checks.

The most likely effect is that applicants with something to hide will go down the block. Let a competitor be the employer of choice for people with problems. Announcing a company background check policy does not keep good applicants from employers no more then security checkpoints at airports stop people from flying.

# Using the Application Form as a Hiring Tool

One of the most critical safe hiring tools is the application process. Done correctly, the application process protects the employer. Although it seems obvious, the most important aspect of the application process is to use a proper job application form. Consider it a best practice. A professionally reviewed, pre-printed job application should allow the employer to legally obtain the necessary information to begin the hiring process. Applications ensure uniformity and that all needed information is obtained. Also, applications protect employers from having impermissible information a resume may contain. The application provides employers with a place for applicants to sign necessary statements that are part of the hiring process.

As a rule of thumb, resumes are not always complete or clear. If an employer insists upon using resumes, then the employer is well-advised to always use a standardized application form as well. Learn more about using resumes later in this chapter.

## Revealing Negative Information

Negative information honestly disclosed and explained on an application or in an interview may very well have no effect, especially if the applicant otherwise has an excellent and verified work history. However, when an applicant has failed to honestly disclose negative information such as the existence of a criminal conviction, then the employer's concern turns to the lack of honesty involved. If the applicant is dishonest and negative information is first revealed by a background check, then the failure to hire may be justified. That is why it is important to have broad enough language in the application to cover all relevant offenses.

**Author Tip** ➡ All applications should have this language: "The information provided by the applicant is true and correct, and that any misstatements or omission of material facts in the application or the hiring process may result in discontinuing of the hiring process or termination of employment, **no matter when discovered.**"

# The Reasons Employers Should Not Rely on Resumes

Some employers still hire based primarily upon a resume. This is a major mistake. For an applicant, a resume is a marketing tool. Many resumes start by describing the type of job that an applicant is looking for, or a statement of skills and experience. In a resume, an applicant picks and chooses whatever information he or she wants to share. Many job hunters use a resume writing service, and while there is nothing wrong with using a service to prepare a professional looking resume, the service typically will attempt to enhance the applicant's experience. The service's goal is to get the applicant to the interview stage.

Employers, however, need facts in order to make hiring decisions.

## Resumes May Have Information an Employer Should Not Have

For some reason, job applicants often feel compelled to reveal things about themselves that an employer does not need or legally should not know. Resumes often reveal volunteer affiliations, hobbies, interests or memberships in groups that reveal such prohibited information as race, religion, ethnicity, sexual orientation, or age. For example, a resume may reveal a person does volunteer time with a church, or belongs to a group that is clearly associated with a particular race or nationality. The problem is the Federal EEOC and equivalent sets of individual state's rules prohibit an employer from obtaining or using such information. An applicant cannot volunteer irrelevant information an employer should not possess. Having this information in the form of a resume in the employer's file is not a good practice in the event the employer is ever the subject of civil litigation or a government investigation into their hiring practices.

## Resumes May Not Have Information an Employer Needs

As mentioned previously, resumes may amplify facts and experience. At the same time, resumes may not give an employer all the information needed to make an informed hiring decision. With a proper application, an applicant cannot skip over jobs he or she rather not mention. An application can allow an employer to spot unexplained employment gaps. Also, job applicants typically do not self-reveal their criminal records in a resume.

> **Author Tip** ➡ Because employment applications provide legal and practical advantages, some firms astutely reject resumes and may return them to applicants. Jobseekers are told they must fill out the company-approved application only.

# Ten Critical Items Every Application Needs

It is much easier for an employer to prescreen candidates using a standardized application. An employer trying to screen a large number of resumes can more easily compare applicants.

Ten critical things need to be addressed in every application as part of a Safe Hiring Program—

1.  The application needs to clearly state that "there will be a background check" or "a background check will be performed." A well-worded application form discourages applicants with something to hide, and encourages applicants to be open and honest.

2.  There should be the broadest possible language asking about convictions and pending criminal cases. This is covered in detail later in this chapter.

3.  An application should state that "untruthfulness or material omissions are grounds to terminate the hiring process or employment, no matter when discovered." This is critical when an applicant is not truthful about a criminal conviction.

4.  The form should clarify that "a criminal conviction is not automatic grounds for rejection." As discussed later in Chapter 11, it could be a form of discrimination to automatically reject an applicant because of a criminal record. The keyword is "automatically." Without the statement that there is no automatic rejection, an applicant may be deterred from applying in the first place out of fear of being automatically rejected upon honestly answering the question. The chilling effect on an applicant could be a form of discrimination in itself, which is why this additional language is necessary. Conversely, if a person has lied about a criminal violation, then dishonesty may become the basis for disqualification.

5.  The application form should indicate the applicant consents to "pre-employment background screening, including verifying educational and professional credentials, past employment and court records." Such a release may discourage an applicant with something to hide, or encourage an applicant to be forthcoming in an interview. If an employer uses an outside service to perform a pre-employment screening, the federal Fair Credit Reporting Act requires there must be a consent and disclosure form separate from the application.

6.  The consent portion on any release form used for a background check must indicate the release is "valid for future screening for retention, promotion or reassignment (unless revoked in writing)." This is helpful, for example, when an employer needs to conduct a post-employment investigation into allegations of sexual harassment or other workplace problems.

7.  The application form must ask for ALL employment for the past 5-10 years. This is critical. A standardized application form makes it easier to spot unexplained gaps in employment. That is an important step in the hiring process and a critical part of exercising due diligence. Even if an employer hires a background company to perform a pre-employment criminal check,

records can be missed because there is no national criminal record resource available for use by private employers. Criminal checks must be done in each county where the applicant has lived, worked or attended school. If a person has an uninterrupted job history, an employer may have more confidence that the applicant has not been in serious trouble over the years.

8. The form should ask about addresses for the last seven to ten years. This helps in determining the scope of any criminal record search.

9. The form should allow the applicant to indicate whether the current employer may be contacted for a reference.

10. Finally, an employer can cover other standard matters. Examples include: the organization's "at will" policy; the employer is "a non-discriminatory employer;" uses mandatory arbitration in disputes; and requires that applicants provide original documents to verify their identity and right to work in the United States.

---

**An Example of an Application Language Law**

A good example of #4 above is an Illinois law that was passed in 2004. The Illinois law requires employers to modify their employment applications to "contain specific language which states that the applicant is not obligated to disclose sealed or expunged records of conviction or arrest." This law also bars employers from asking "if an applicant has had records expunged or sealed." 20 ILCS 2630/12 (2004).

---

# The Critical Areas and Questions Applications Must Avoid

Federal and state laws prohibit any non-job related inquiry, either verbal or through the use of an application form, which directly or indirectly limits a person's employment opportunities because of race, color, religion, national origin, ancestry, medical condition, disability (including AIDS), marital status, sex (including pregnancy), age (40+), exercise of family care leave or leave for an employee's own serious health condition. There are other areas that an employer may go into, but with limits, such as criminal records.

Employers want to avoid application questions and interview questions that directly identify a person as a member of a protected group. However, even questions that appear neutral on their face can be illegal if the question results in a disproportionate screening of members of a protected group or is not a valid predictor of job performance. Examples include application questions about arrests.[2]

As a rule of thumb, an employer cannot ask anything in an application that an employer cannot ask in a face-to-face personal interview. In Chapter 8 on interviews, there is an in-depth chart listing questions that are prohibited. These same rules apply to applications.

---

[2] arrests is discussed in detail in later chapters on criminal investigations and criminal records

# 10 Sure Signs of a Lawsuit Waiting to Happen

After going through the process of preparing an effective application and utilizing it instead of a resume, many employers make the fatal mistake of not reading the application carefully. This is a major mistake. Employee lawsuits often catch employers by surprise. Another way employers are bitten by their applications happens when, upon closer examination, the employee's application shows that the employer could have reasonably predicted they were hiring a lawsuit just waiting to happen.

By looking for the following ten danger signals, an employer can avoid hiring a problem employee in the first place—

1. **Applicant does not sign application.** An applicant with something to hide may purposely not sign the application form so the applicant later cannot be accused of falsification.

2. **Applicant does not sign consent for background screening.** When a firm uses an outside agency to perform screening, federal law requires a separate disclosure and signed consent from the applicant. A background consent form protects employers in two ways: 1) it discourages applicants with something to hide and 2) encourages candid interviews. If a candidate fails to sign the consent, it is not a good sign.

3. **Applicant leaves criminal questions blank.** An applicant with a past problem may simply skip the questions about criminal records. Every employment application should ask, in the broadest possible terms allowed by law, if the applicant has a criminal record. Most jurisdictions only permit questions about convictions and pending cases. A criminal record can be either a felony or a misdemeanor; employers make a big mistake if they only ask about felonies since misdemeanors can be extremely serious too. Although employment may not be denied automatically because of a criminal conviction, an employer may consider the nature and gravity of the offense, the nature of the job, and the age of the offense when evaluating whether there is a sound business reason not to employ someone with a criminal record. If an applicant lies about a criminal record, then the false application may be the reason to deny employment.

> **Author Tip** ➡ The first four points are sometimes referred to as the "honest criminal syndrome." A person may have had a criminal record in the past and does not want to be dishonest about it. On the other hand, the person may not want to be fully revealing either. That is why it is so critical to look at the application's criminal question carefully to ensure it is filled out. Self-reported offenses should be looked at extra carefully. For example, an applicant self-reported that he stole some beer from a store. He neglected to mention it was stolen at the point of a gun, which is robbery, a much more serious offense. Another applicant reported he was stopped by police when he was younger and some recreational drugs he had were found under the car seat. A review of the court records revealed it was actually two pounds of cocaine — which is a lot of recreation.

4. **Applicant self-reports a criminal violation**. Just because an applicant self-reports an offense does not eliminate the possibility other offenses exist, or the applicant may report it in a misleading way to lessen its seriousness. An employer is well-advised to check it out.

5. **Applicant fails to explain gaps in employment history**. There can be many reasons for a gap in employment. For example, an applicant may have been ill, gone back to school, or had difficulty finding a new job. However, if an applicant cannot account for the past seven to ten years, that can be a red flag. It could potentially mean he or she was in custody for a criminal offense. It is also important to know where a person has been because of the way criminal records are maintained in the United States. Contrary to popular belief, there is not a national criminal database available to most employers. Searches must be conducted at each relevant courthouse, and there are over 10,000 courthouses in the U.S. However, if an employer knows where an applicant has been, it increases the accuracy of a criminal search, and decreases the possibility that an applicant has served time for a serious offense. If there is an unexplained gap, an employer may not know where to search and can miss a criminal record.

6. **Explanations for employment gaps or reasons for leaving past jobs do not make sense**. If there were employment gaps reported by the applicant, do the reasons for the gaps make sense? A careful review of this section of the application is needed and anything that does not make sense must to be cleared up in the interview.

7. **Applicant fails to give sufficient information to identify a past employer for reference checks**. If an applicant does not give enough details about past employers, that can be a sign of trouble. Verifying past employment is a critical and important tool for safe hiring. Some employers make a costly mistake by not checking past employment because past employers historically tend not to give detailed information. However, even if a reference check only reveals dates of employment and job titles, this critical information eliminates employment gaps. In addition, documenting the fact that an effort was made will demonstrate due diligence.

8. **Applicant fails to explain reason for leaving past jobs.** Past job performance can be an important predictor of future success.

9. **Applicant fails to indicate or cannot recall the name of a former supervisor.** Another red flag. Past supervisors are important in order to conduct past employment checks.

10. **Excessive cross-outs and changes**. This can be an indication that an applicant is making it up as he or she goes along.

These ten danger signs all assume that an employer is using an application form, not a resume.

## Review the Form with the Applicant

One way to avoid making these mistakes is to go through the application with the jobseeker, checking to be certain that the applicant filled out the forms completely. Rehash the question with the applicant if he or she had shown questionable answers. The process is not intended to necessarily ensure accuracy, but to determine with certainty that the applicant stands behind what he or she has stated on the application form.

> **Author Tip** ➡ The author testified as an expert witness in a case where a school district hired a teacher who had been convicted in another state of a felony charge — sex with a minor. The offense made the person ineligible to teach. On the employment application, where it asked if the applicant had ever been convicted of a crime, the applicant put a slash mark in between the Yes and the No. The school district has a policy of reviewing the application with the applicant to clarify what the applicant meant. A school district employee asked the applicant which box he meant to check, and the applicant then clearly indicated "Yes." Unfortunately, after being on notice there was a criminal offense in the applicant's background, the school district failed to follow through and investigate the offense. After the applicant was hired, he was accused of inappropriate behavior with female students at the school. Under legal scrutiny, the failure to follow through after being put on notice of a past crime was found to be negligent hiring.

# Applications and the Disclosure of Criminal Records

One of the most effective uses of an effective application form is to enable an employer to directly ask an applicant if he or she has a criminal record. Unfortunately, many employers use language in their applications that is either too narrow, too broad, or too ambiguous. Each of these mistakes can put an employer in difficulty. Let us go over this language in detail—

## Too Narrow

An example of a question that is too narrow is to only ask about felonies and not misdemeanors. Misdemeanors can be very serious. Under California law, for example, most employers would want to know if an applicant had a conviction for offenses such as fighting with a police officer, illegal possession of weapons, spousal abuse or child abuse, commercial burglary, assault and many other offenses. Yet in California, these can all be misdemeanors. Many serious offenses are plea-bargained down to misdemeanor offenses as well. Without the proper language, an applicant can honestly answer he or she has not been convicted of a felony even though there may be serious misdemeanor convictions an employer *needs* to know about.

## Too Broad

On the other hand, some employers ask questions that are so broad that it improperly covers matters that are protected. There are a number of limitations under state and federal law concerning what an employer may legally ask about or "discover" concerning an applicant's or employee's criminal record. In fact, it can be a misdemeanor in California for an employer to knowingly violate some of these rules. Furthermore, if an applicant is placed in a position where he is forced to reveal information about himself that he is legally entitled not to disclose, an employer can actually be sued for "defamation by compelled self-publication" — in some states. In other words, if forced to say something defamatory about himself, an applicant may be able to file a lawsuit against the employer for defamation.

## Too Ambiguous

The third mistake is to ask an applicant, "*Have you ever been convicted of a felony or serious misdemeanor?*" or "*Have you ever been convicted of a crime of violence?*" or a similar question that calls for *an opinion*. The problem occurs when an applicant is called upon to make a judgment about his own offense. For example, if a misdemeanor is serious, this can call for a very complex legal and factual determination on which lawyers *and even judges* could disagree. By asking a question that is ambiguous and leaves waffle room, an applicant can argue that in his or her mind the offense was not serious and a "no" answer was truthful. That is why a question cannot contain any ambiguity.

At times an applicant is simply confused by court proceedings and may not understand the results or what they mean.

---

# A California Example

Here are some of the limitations involved in California. Although not every state has rules as restrictive as California, employers in all states should be careful to ensure that their applications are legally compliant.

- An employer may NOT ask about arrests or detentions that did not result in a conviction.

- An employer may only consider convictions or pending cases.

- There are certain limitations on misdemeanors, crimes that have been sealed or otherwise expunged, cases where a person participated in pre-trial diversion, or certain minor marijuana convictions.

- An employer should NOT automatically deny employment due to a criminal conviction, but should consider the nature and gravity of the offense, whether it is job related, and when it occurred.

Below are examples of language that a California employer should consider using. Again, keep in mind that every state has its own rules, and an employer should check with an attorney in regards to state law.

> *Have you ever been convicted for a crime? (Exclude convictions for marijuana-related offenses for personal use more than two years old; convictions that have been sealed, expunged or legally eradicated, and misdemeanor convictions for which probation was completed and the case was dismissed) Yes_____ No___*

An alternative wording that avoids the problems associated with certain minor convictions—

> *"Have you ever been convicted of a felony, or a misdemeanor involving any violent act, use or possession of a weapon or act of dishonesty for which the record has not been sealed or expunged?"*
>
> *If yes, please briefly describe the nature of the crime(s), the date and place of conviction and the legal disposition of the case.*
>
> *This company will not deny employment to any applicant solely because the person has been convicted of a crime. The company however, may consider the nature, date and circumstances of the offense as well as whether the offense is relevant to the duties of the position applied for.*
>
> *Are you currently out on bail, the subject of a current warrant for arrest, or released on your own recognizance pending trial? Yes ___ No ___*

As mentioned previously, it is normally recommended the application contain language saying "the conviction of a crime will not automatically result in a denial of employment." Automatic disqualification could be a violation of state and federal discrimination laws. However, an employer may deny employment if the employer can establish a business-related reason for the refusal to hire. See Chapter 5 for a detailed discussion on discrimination laws and safe hiring.

# Where to Find a Good Application Form

Application forms are available from a number of sources.

- The local or state Chamber of Commerce may have forms available.
- A firm's business or labor attorney will normally have a new employee package available with an application form
- Human resources consultants and HR organizations may have forms.
- Office supply stores sell basic business forms including application forms.
- Books about running a business are available from local book stores and may have sample forms.
- There are firms that specialize in selling employment related forms and products on the Internet.

Many firms design their own employment forms to reflect the particular needs of their firm or industry.

One word of caution — many states have unique rules regarding what can and cannot be on an application. Some of these rules concern what an employer may ask about past criminal convictions. It is beyond the scope of this book to review the requirements for all fifty states, however, an employer is well-advised to consult with a labor attorney for every state they hire within to review the legality of their application forms.

# Chapter 8

# The Interview Process

Interviews must be conducted in a manner that not only assures the employer of finding the best candidate for the position, but also is legal and does not put the employer in harm's way. In this chapter let us examine the job interview as in integral part of a Safe Hiring Program— the SHP.

## The Importance of Interviews

The interview is the first opportunity for an employer to meet face-to-face with applicants who may literally and figuratively hold the keys to future business success in their hands, and during the interview process an employer practicing safe hiring must take steps to protect the workforce and ensure that the best and most qualified candidates are hired.

Within a Safe Hiring Program, an interview can accomplish three goals—

1. **Convey critical information to the applicant in order to discourage bad applicants and to encourage honesty.** Applicants need to understand clearly that your firm has a Safe Hiring Program. Use the interview to convey the message to all applicants. Since at the same time an employer is recruiting qualified employees who will adopt the firm's values and become loyal and hardworking, the safe hiring process cannot be accomplished in an overbearing fashion. Think of the interview as an opportunity to reinforce the message already communicated in company application forms and job announcements— your firm practices safe hiring!

2. **Allow for the transfer of information from the applicant to the employer.** The interview is when an employer has an opportunity to fill in any gaps. Also, the employer has a chance to ask the additional penetrating questions if the candidate seems to have attempted to conceal or lie about unfavorable information.

3. **Permit an assessment of the candidate.** Even though a Safe Hiring Program is based upon the premise that instinct and intuition alone are not enough, the interview still provides the employer an opportunity to assess the knowledge, skills and abilities of the applicant in person. However, keep in mind that good candidates can come across poorly, and bad candidates can come across well. The assessment is just one of many tools used in the calculus of a hiring decision.

Given these three goals, how does an organization ensure that positive results happen? This chapter examines the needed tools.

# Advantages of a Structured Interview

An interview is typically accomplished using a written set of questions selected ahead of time by the employer and provided to the hiring managers conducting the interviews. There are literally thousands of potential interview questions that can be asked. Questions can also depend upon the particular industry, the needs of the firm, and the position being filled. An employer needs to review all potential questions and select a set of questions that would be the most useful for selecting the best employees. That does not mean that everyone is always asked the exact same question. Different positions may require that certain portions of an interview require customized questions. This can be done by a supplemental question set that is position-specific. However, the interview should assure all similarly situated candidates have the same question set.

A structured interview is defined as an interview format used across an organization. Structured interview questions are usually pre-printed on forms. The advantages for an employer using a structured interview are significant.

First, it ensures uniformity in the interview process and protects against claims of discrimination or disparate treatment.

Second, it helps to keep hiring managers on track by using legally defensible questions. By giving interviewers a script to follow, it helps an employer's efforts at training interviewers not to ask prohibited questions. A discussion and chart of permissible and impermissible questions is presented later in this chapter.

Third, and most critical from the aspect of a Safe Hiring Program, the structured interview ensures the employer that certain essential "integrity questions" are asked of all candidates. Some of these questions are covered below.

At the same time, the process does not mean the interviewers are simply clerical robots, going through the motions and recording responses in a rote fashion. Penetrating follow-up questions and keen observations of the applicants are still critical to make sure all required areas are covered.

> **Author Tip** ➡ Another helpful hiring tool is a preliminary telephone screen. After an employer has reviewed and narrowed down a possible list of candidates, doing a telephone screen will help narrow down the list even further and save an employer valuable time. A phone screen is accomplished by calling each potential candidate and asking the same list of questions. If the candidate appears to meet the initial criteria, then an interview can be immediately scheduled. If a message is left and the applicant does not call back, then that applicant can be eliminated from consideration. A sample telephone screen script can be found in Appendix 3. **Also keep in mind that in order to develop job-related interview questions, an employer first needs a written job description so that meaningful questions can be developed.**

## Behavior-Based Questions Should be Used

An essential part of a Safe Hiring Program is to question applicants carefully about their knowledge, skills, abilities, and experience. Part of the interview is designed to determine if the applicant will be a good fit, taking into account the work environment and the team the person will work with.

Interview techniques where the applicant is merely told to "tell me about yourself" have not proved altogether effective. In order to obtain more insight employers may ask hypothetical questions such as "what would you do if..." The "if" could be anything ranging from working with difficult people to completing assignments under deadlines. However, that still does not tell an employer about how the person actually did in the past.

**Behavior-based interviewing** is one of the newest and most effective methods for establishing if a person is a good fit for both the job and the organization. In a "behavior-based interview," a person is asked to accurately describe real situations they have encountered and what they did to resolve the issue or problem. The method is based on the concept that the most accurate predictor of how a candidate will perform in the future is how he or she performed in the past in a similar situation. The question could be about a time when a person faced a typical workforce problem. This type of interview question may typically start with the phrase, "Tell me about a time when..."

There are numerous books, resources and websites that offer suggestions on behavior-based interview questions. Here are sample questions to demonstrate the format—

- Tell me about a time when you had to coordinate several different people to achieve a goal. What were the challenges involved, and how did you overcome them?

- Tell me about the most difficult business related decisions you have had to make in the past six months. Describe the situation and what made it difficult. How did you resolve it?

- Give me an example of when you had to work with someone who was very difficult to get along with, and how you handled that situation.

# The Integrity Interview

For organizations that hire people for extremely sensitive or high-risk positions, the firm can conduct a full "integrity interview" to determine if a person is a good fit. Also, the same questions can be used to help detect if there is any reason NOT to hire the person.

Integrity questions are used to explore...

- Does the applicant really have the knowledge, skills, abilities, and experience claimed?

- Is the applicant really who he says he is, or she is?

- Has the applicant left any material out of the application process?

- Has the applicant misstated any qualifications in the application process?

- Is there any reason to think the applicant's moral rudder is not set straight? In other words, is the applicant an honest person?

A good interviewer creates a comfortable and professional environment but also stresses the need for complete honesty. Consider the following specific questions—

> *"It is not unusual to exaggerate in an application or resume. However, we need complete and accurate information concerning certain areas."*

> *"Is there anything in your employment application that you want to change or correct? This is the time."*

> *"If we checked with your former employers, would any of them report that you were asked to leave?"*

If the interviewer wished to cover potential security issues such as criminal record or drug and alcohol use, then this question could be asked—

> *"If we were to check court records, would we find any convictions or outstanding warrants?"*

> **Author Tip ➡** One way to accomplish an integrity interview is to retain the services of a professional interviewer from outside your office. This professional can conduct an in-depth interview covering a full employment history and also address security concerns such as terminations, drug and alcohol use, and criminal record. In the case of a large firm, the interview could be completed by another person within the organization such as personnel in security or loss prevention departments.

## Open-Ended Questions and Follow-Up Questions

A proven technique of an integrity interview is the use of "open-ended" and "follow-up" questions. A key to using this technique is for the interview not to rely upon information given beforehand.

Let us say the interviewer starts with questions about a person's job history. If the interviewer does not have a resume or application, every question is "open-ended," meaning the interviewee supplies all the information and no part of the answer is suggested by the question. This is the opposite of a "leading question" where the question itself suggests an answer.

For example, if an interviewer says, "I see you left Acme Industries due to a lay-off." That is a leading question. It suggests the answer, allowing the applicant to merely expand on that theme. An example of an open-ended question is "How long was your employment with Acme?" or "Why did that employment end?"

It is critical to ask follow-up questions when the answers do not make sense. If an applicant says something illogical, the interviewer should not hesitate to ask the applicant to review the answer. Sometimes it helps to ask the same question in a different way. For example, ask the applicant to describe in detail what occurred leading up to or after the event. If the applicant is making something up, that may be obvious. If an applicant gives a non-answer or an answer that is too fast and too pat, then a follow-up question would be helpful. For example, if an applicant says, "We already covered that," the interviewer, simply says, "I must have missed it. Can we review that again?"

As a practical matter, company managers and HR professionals are not expected to give every applicant the third degree. However, interviewers should be trained so they are not so glued to the questioning process that they do not pay attention to how the answers are given.

# The Five Questions That Should Be Asked In Every Interview

In order to help hiring managers have a better understanding of a candidate, and to weed out those who are unacceptable risks, it can be very effective to empower interviewers with some key "standard questions." Asking standard questions has several advantages. They allow for a consistent process, so that all applicants are subjected to the same questions. Standard questions create a more comfortable environment for the interviewers. They do not have the pressure of having to remember every question they asked because the questions are written out for them. If the questions on safe hiring issues feel uncomfortable, then the interviewer can simply indicate that these questions are asked of everyone and they are required due to standard company policy.

There are five suggested, critical interview questions every employer or hiring manager should be trained to ask. Of course, an employer would not want to get the interview off on the wrong foot with questions aimed at past criminal conduct or negative employment experiences. One of the goals of an interview is to help foster a talking environment where a potential employee understands and accepts the goals and direction of the organization. However, every interview does have a "housekeeping" portion where standard questions are asked. That would be a good time for the following five questions.

1. *Our firm has a standard policy of conducting background checks on all hires before an offer is made or finalized. You have already signed a release form. Do you have any concerns about that?*

   This is a general question about screening. Since the applicant has signed a release form, there is a powerful incentive to be honest and reveal any issues.

2. *We also check for criminal convictions for all finalists. Do you have any concerns about that?*

   This question goes from the general to the specific. Be sure to ask the question in a form that is legally permissible in your state. It is important NOT to ask a question that is so broadly worded that it may lead to an applicant revealing more information then allowed by law. Again, make sure the applicant understands that he or she has signed a release and this process is standard company policy.

3. *When we talk to your past employers, what do you think they will say?*

   Note the questions says, "<u>When</u> we contact your past employers…" indicating that they <u>will</u> be contacted. This general question again provides a powerful incentive to be very accurate.

4. *Will your past employers tell us that there was any issues with tardiness, meeting job requirements, etc.?*

This question goes again to a specific area. Ask detailed questions about matters that are expressly relevant to the job opening.

5.  *Tell me about any unexplained gaps in your employment history.*

    If there are any unexplained employment gaps, it is imperative to ask about them.

Since applicants have signed consent forms and believe the firm is doing checks, applicants have a powerful incentive to be truthful. These questions are the equivalent of a "New Age" lie detector test. Employers can no longer administer actual lie detector tests and probably would not want to even if they could. However, these questions serve a valuable function by providing a strong motivation for applicants to be self-revealing. It also takes advantage of the natural human trait to want to have some control over what others say about you. If an applicant believes a future employer may hear negative information from a past employer, the applicant may want to be able to set the record straight before the future employer has the chance to hear negative information from someone else.

Good applicants will shrug the questions off and applicants with something to hide may reveal vital information. Applicants with something to hide may react in a number of different ways. Some applicants may tough it out during the first question. However, the questions are designed to go from the general to the specific. By the second question, an applicant may well begin to express concerns or react in some way that raises a red flag. An applicant may object to the questions by asking if the questions invade their privacy rights. If an applicant raises such an objection, then simply indicate that these are standard job-related questions asked of all applicants.

# Why Are Employment Gaps So Important?

An employer related the following story. The applicant was just perfect for the computer job. He had all of the right qualifications. During the interview, the interviewer asked the usual questions. While taking a last look at the resume, the interviewer happened to notice a two–year gap in the employment and education history. Out of curiosity, the interviewer asked about the gap.

The applicant explained that he had decided to go back to go school and retrain so he could join the computer age. The interviewer was merely curious about the classes because he wanted to find some good classes for other employees. *Where was it?* Oh, it was a state-sponsored job-retraining program. *Where was the program based?*

With just a few questions it finally came out. The so-called computer school where the courses were taken was actually classes offered at a state prison. Of course, the applicant did have a perfect attendance record.

This story illustrates two key points—

*   Look at the resume or application for unexplained gaps.

- Use the interview to ask the applicant about any gaps.

Actually, the criminal record by itself would *not* have disqualified the computer technician. The real problem was that the job the applicant interviewed for required a person to go inside state prisons to fix computers — and prisons may not care to have former inmates come back in a professional capacity.

# The Questions Not to Ask — and Why

As mentioned at the outset of this chapter, a true Safe Hiring Program means the job interview process must be conducted in a legal manner. Just as there are troublesome, improper areas or questions to be avoided on an employment application, the same is true for job interviews. If certain questions are asked or if questions are asked in a certain way, then an employer can be exposed to a variety of discrimination charges and lawsuits.

## Pre-Employment Inquiry Guidelines

By Barbara S. de Oddone[1]

In order to avoid claims that you have not compared candidates equitably based solely on job-related criteria, you should have an outline of job-pertinent questions (open-ended, not "yes" or "no" questions) that you ask of every candidate seeking a particular position. In order to provide documentary evidence of your questions and the candidates' answers, you should make brief notes of the answers on your interview outline. Avoid keeping any notes that are not related to the job in question.

One particular category of pre-employment inquiries deserves special caution: inquiries that may reveal that the applicant is a person with a disability. It is impermissible to ask a question that will elicit information about a disability or medical condition, including workers' compensation history. See the Pre-Employment Inquiry Guidelines Chart on the following pages. On the other hand, if it is obvious that an applicant is a person with a disability, such as an applicant who uses a wheelchair, it is permissible to ask whether the applicant will need a reasonable accommodation to proceed through the application process and, if employed, to perform the essential functions of the job. The Federal Equal Employment Opportunity Commission states—

- [when] an employer could reasonably believe that an applicant will need reasonable accommodation to perform the functions of the job, the employer may ask that applicant certain limited questions. Specifically, the employer may ask whether s/he needs reasonable accommodation and what type of reasonable accommodation would be needed to perform the functions of the job.

---

[1] Barbara S. de Oddone, an attorney specializing in labor law.

The EEOC describes the permissible circumstances for this inquiry as follows—

- [when] the employer reasonably believes the applicant will need reasonable accommodation because of an obvious disability;

- [when] the employer reasonably believes the applicant will need reasonable accommodation because of a hidden disability the applicant has voluntarily disclosed to the employer; *or*

- [when] an applicant has voluntarily disclosed to the employer that s/he needs reasonable accommodation to perform the job.

Remember: keep all information gathered about applicants confidential. It is important to maintain all job applicant information in confidential locked files and refrain from disclosing information to any but those who need to know. The California Constitution, Article I, Section 1, protects the right to privacy, and courts have held that employees have privacy rights in their personnel information.

# Pre-Employment Inquiry Guidelines Chart[2]

Mr. Rod Fliegel, an attorney and shareholder with Littler Mendelson, P.C. , has graciously supplied us with the following chart, an excellent guide to use for protecting a Safe Hiring Program's application and interview processes.[3]

Mr. Fliegel also notes that the relationship between a screening firm and the employer is an "agency" relationship with legal ramifications. Both parties must be aware of this. Simply put, when an employer outsources aspects of its hiring process to a screening firm, such as pre-employment background or reference checks, the employer is trusting the screening firm to act on its behalf and in compliance with all applicable federal, state and local legal constraints. Take for sake of example pre-employment disability-related inquiries. The EEOC's "Technical Assistance Manual" or "TAM" expressly states: "If an employer uses an outside firm to conduct background checks, the employer should assure that this firm complies with the ADA's prohibitions on pre-employment inquiries. Such a firm is an agent of the employer. The employer is responsible for actions of its agents and may not do anything through a contractual relationship that it may not itself do directly." (The TAM is available at www.ada-infonet.org/documents/titleI/tech-assist-man.asp.)

---

[2] adapted from "Employment Inquiries," California Department of Fair Employment & Housing, www.dfeh.ca.gov/Publications/DFEH%20161.pdf

[3] Mr. Fliegel has extensive experience defending national and local employers in state, federal and administrative litigation, including high-stakes class actions. Mr. Fliegel has special compliance and litigation expertise concerning the intersection of the federal and state background check laws.

| | **You May Ask:** | **Do <u>Not</u> Ask:** |
|---|---|---|
| Name | "Have you ever used another name?"<br><br>"Is any additional information necessary to enable a check on your work and education record such as a name change, nickname or use of an assumed name? If yes, please explain." | "What is your maiden name?" |
| Address/ Residence | "Can you be reached at this address?"<br><br>"Can you be reached at these telephone numbers?" | "Do you own your home or rent?"<br><br>"Do you live with your spouse?"<br><br>"With whom do you live?" |
| Age | "If hired, can you show proof of age?"<br><br>"Are you over eighteen years of age?" | Any questions that tend to identify applicants over 40, e.g., birthdates, dates of attendance or completion of elementary or high school. |
| Citizenship | "Are you able, after employment, to present authorization to work in the United States?"<br><br>If this questions is asked, it should be asked of all applicants and not only of those with accents or who otherwise appear to have non-USA origins in order not to discriminate based on national origin, language, etc. | "Are you a United States citizen?"<br>(Note: In very limited circumstances involving national security, citizenship could be a qualification for employment.)<br><br>Any questions about birthplace of applicant or applicant's parents, spouse, or other relatives.<br><br>Any questions about requirements to produce naturalization or alien registration papers prior to a decision to hire. |
| Color or Race | | Any questions concerning race or color of skin, eyes, hair, etc.<br><br>Any requirement to provide a photograph. |
| Credit Report | | Any report that indicates information otherwise unlawful to ask such as marital status, age, residency, birthplace, and so on. "Have you ever had a bankruptcy?" |
| Criminal Records | You may ask applicants about misdemeanor or felony *convictions* <u>except</u> for those that have been sealed, expunged, or eradicated by statute, or convictions for certain mari-juana-related offenses over two years old.<br><br>You may ask whether the applicant has charges are pending and is awaiting trial.<br><br>Tell the applicant that a Yes answer will not necessarily be disqualifying. | Questions about arrests. Certain states have restrictions employers must follow.<br><br>Law enforcement and certain state agencies, school districts, businesses and other organizations that have a direct responsibility for the supervision, care or treatment of children, mentally ill or disabled persons, or other vulnerable adults, may have more latitude to make inquiries. |

| | **You May Ask:** | **Do Not Ask:** |
|---|---|---|
| Disability or AIDS or Medical Condition | "Are you currently able to perform the essential duties of the job for which you are applying?" <br> "Are you able to perform [specific task]?" <br> If the disability is obvious, or disclosed, you may ask about accommodations that would enable the applicant/employee to perform the essential duties of the job. <br> Statement that an offer may be made contingent on passing a physical exam. | "Are you disabled?" <br> "How much sick time or medical leave did you use at your last job?" <br> "Have you ever been hospitalized?" <br> "Have you ever been treated by a psychologist or psychiatrist?" <br> "Are you taking any prescription medications? If not, have you? <br> "Have you ever had treatment for drug or alcohol use or any other addiction?" <br> Any questions about health or medical conditions. An employer may *not* make any medical inquiry or conduct any medical examination prior to making a conditional offer of employment. In California, post-offer, pre-employment medical examinations also *must* be job-related and consistent with business necessity. <br> Any questions about an applicant's prior workers' compensation history. |
| Education | "Are you presently enrolled or do you intend to enroll in school?" <br> "What subjects did you excel in at school?" <br> "Did you participate in extracurricular activities that relate to the job you are seeking with us? In what ways?" <br> "What did you select as your major?" <br> "Did you work an outside job while attending school? Doing what? What did you like/dislike about your part-time job during school?" <br> "Are you interested in continuing your education? Why? When? Where?" <br> "Did your education prepare you for the job you are seeking with us? In what ways?" | Any questions about dates of schooling. <br> Privacy-related education issues— <br> "Who paid for your educational expenses while you were in school? <br> "Did you go to school on a scholarship?" <br> "Do you still owe on student loans taken out during school?" <br> "When did you graduate from high school?" |

| | You May Ask: | Do <u>Not</u> Ask: |
|---|---|---|
| Experience, Skills, and Activities | Questions about special skills or knowledge; when the applicant last *used* skills that are related to the position, and activities that have provided the applicant with experience, training, or skills that relate to the position for which the applicant is applying. | "Does your physical condition make you less skilled?"<br><br>"When did you acquire that skill?" |
| Family | Name and address of parent or guardian if applicant is a minor. | Questions that elicit any information on marital status.<br><br>"How many children do you have? How old are they?"<br><br>"Who takes care of your children while you are working?"<br><br>"Do your children go to day care?"<br><br>"What does your husband think about your working outside the home?"<br><br>"What does your spouse do?"<br><br>"What is your spouse's salary?" |
| Marital Status, Sexual Orientation | "Please state the names of any relatives already employed by our organization."<br><br>Employers may state the company policy regarding work assignment of employees who are related. | "Is it Mrs. or Miss?"<br><br>"Are you single? ...Married? ...Divorced? ...Separated? ...Engaged? ...Widowed?"<br><br>"Do you have a domestic partner?"<br><br>Any questions that elicit information related to marital status or sexual orientation. |
| Military Service | "Have you served in the U.S. military?"<br><br>"Did your military service and training provide you with skills you could put to use in this job? | "Have you served in the military of a foreign country?"<br><br>"What type of discharge did you receive from the U.S. military service?"<br><br>"When was your discharge from military service?"<br><br>"Can you provide discharge papers?" |

|  | **You May Ask:** | **Do <u>Not</u> Ask:** |
|---|---|---|
| National Origin | You may state that, after hire, verification of the legal right to work in the United States will be required in order to comply with the Federal Immigration Reform and Control Act of 1986. | Any questions regarding nationality, lineage, ancestry, national origin, descent or parentage of applicant or his/her parents or spouse.<br><br>"Where were you born?"<br><br>"What is the origin of your name?"<br><br>"What is your mother tongue?"<br><br>"What country do your ancestors come from?"<br><br>Any questions on how the applicant acquired the ability to read, write, or speak a foreign language. |
| Notify In Case Of Emergency | "Whom should we contact in case of an emergency?" | Name, address and/or relationship of relative in case of accident or emergency. |
| Organizations | "What organizations do you participate in that relate to the job for which you are applying? Please omit any organization that is not job-related or any organization that indicates your race, religious creed, color, national origin, ancestry, disability, medical condition, marital status, sex, sexual orientation, or age." | "List all organizations, clubs, societies, and lodges to which you belong." |
| Photographs | For identification purposes, ask for a photograph *after hiring*. | Ask applicant to submit a photograph whether mandatory or optional before hiring.<br><br>Any questions about physical characteristics such as height or weight.<br><br>Any applicant to submit to videotaping of the interview. |
| Pregnancy | "How long to you plan to stay on the job?"<br><br>"Are you currently able to perform the essential duties of the job for which you are applying?" | "Are you pregnant?"<br><br>"When was your most recent pregnancy terminated?"<br><br>"Do you plan to become pregnant?"<br><br>Any questions about pregnancy and related medical conditions.<br><br>Any questions about child bearing or birth control. |

| | You May Ask: | Do <u>Not</u> Ask: |
|---|---|---|
| Prior Employment | "How did you overcome problems you faced there?"<br><br>"Which problems frustrated you the most?"<br><br>"Of the jobs indicated on your application, which did you enjoy the most, and why?"<br><br>"What were your reasons for leaving your last job?"<br><br>"Have you ever been discharged from any position? If so, for what reason?" | "How many sick days did you have at your old job?"<br><br>"Did you file any types of claims?" |
| References | "By whom were you referred for a position here?" | Questions on the applicant's former employer or persons given as references that elicit information about the applicant's race, color, religious creed, national origin, ancestry, physical or mental disability, medical condition, sex, marital status, sexual orientation, or age. |
| Religion or Creed | You may make a statement about the regular days, hours and shifts that are required by the job. | "What is your religion?"<br><br>"What church do you go to?"<br><br>"What are your religious holidays?"<br><br>"Does your religion prevent you from working weekends or holidays?" |
| Sexual Orientation | | "Are you a homosexual?"<br><br>"Do you have a domestic partner?"<br><br>"What are your views of same-sex partner relations and benefits?" |

# Looking for Red Flag Behavior

A savvy interviewer will be able to spot red flags that indicate further questions may be needed. Many of these tip-offs are non-verbal in nature. Of course, a perfectly honest and capable candidate may exhibit these red flags, while a practiced liar may not exhibit any at all! Therefore, this standard list of non-verbal clues is certainly not to be used as a basis for a hiring decision, but could be used as a basis to ask more questions.

The list below is by no means complete, since many additional behaviors could be added.

- Non-responsive answers such as answering a question other than the question asked
- Answering your question with a question or repeating your question
- Answers do not make sense or are inconsistent
- Becoming defensive inappropriately
- Breaking eye contact
- Clearing throat, stuttering, voice changing pitch, speed, or volume
- Shifting body position or defensive body language such as crossing arms, shrugging shoulders
- Hesitation before answering
- Inability to remember dates and details
- Loss of previous cooperative behavior
- Making excuses before asked
- Nervous hand movements such as wringing or tightly gripping hands, repeated fluttering, brushing of lint, or moving documents
- Not remembering something when applicant has remembered other events in detail
- Protesting too much that they made the choice to leave a company

> **Author Tip** ➡ Where can employers locate interview questions? There are numerous books on the topic as well as resources on the web. One tool is the Interview Generator, a free utility created by the author where employers can construct a printed structured interview form using suggested questions or inserting their own questions. See www.esrcheck.com/Interviewgenerator.php.

Below is an interesting story by Dr. Marty Nemko. Dr. Nemko is co-author of *Cool Careers for Dummies*. He is a career and small business counselor in Oakland, California. His writings can be found at www.martynemko.com.

# How it Works — A Story by Dr. Marty Nemko

Chester the Molester is looking through the Chronicle's employment ads. He finds an ad that sounds good — assistant manager of Pooh's Corner Children's Bookstore. On the bottom of the ad he reads, "We conduct background checks." He thinks, "Whoops, better look elsewhere."

Then Chester figures, "Ah, what the heck. They probably don't really do background checks." So he applies, sending that resume and cover letter he so cleverly concocted. For example, "2000-2002: state-sponsored education program." Translation: Two years in San Quentin. "I mean, I did learn a lot there!" he rationalizes. His cover letter and resume make Chester sound like a cross between T. Berry Brazelton and Maria from The Sound of Music.

The ruse works and Chester gets a call from Happy Chappy. They want him to come in for an interview! In his Mr. Rogers get-up, Chester saunters in, but he is in for a surprise. The receptionist says, "Before your interview, would you complete this application form and sign at the bottom authorizing the background screening?" He replies, "Sure, no problem," but he is thinking, "Uh-oh."

Chester shows for the interview, handing the application to the interviewer, Sally Savvy. Most of the questions are those standard simulations. Chester is so slick at BS'ing questions such as "What would you do if a child throws a tantrum?" Then Sally asks, "Before offering you the position, we would do a background check. Any objection to that?" Chester's heart starts to race, but he forces himself to look calm. "Not at all," he lies.

Sally continues: "As part of that check, we look to see if you have a criminal record. I notice on the application form, you didn't answer the question, 'In the past seven years, have you been convicted of a crime?' " Chester responds, "Oh, I forgot. I'll answer it now." He writes "No." His heart pounds through his chest wall.

Sally is relentless: "Oh, and of course, we contact your previous employers. Is there anything negative they're likely to say about you?" Beads of sweat form above his upper lip, like Richard Nixon in the 1960 presidential debate. "Well, uh, no." Chester manages to keep his voice calm sounding but he cannot control his eyes and forehead. The perceptive Sally knows he is nervous.

"Oh, and one more question. Because this job will require you to handle customers' money, we will be conducting a credit check. Do you have any objections?" This is the last straw— Chester's debts greatly exceed the job's salary. Now he cannot even control his voice. "Be my guest," he squeaks.

The interview ends and Chester thinks, "I don't want this stupid job anyway." Sally thinks, "There's something wrong with this guy." Even if she had planned to offer him the position, she would have first done a background check using a firm such as Rosen's Employment Screening

Resources, Inc. (www.ESRcheck.com). That would likely have revealed Chester's criminal record and that his previous employer fired him for inappropriately touching children.

# Additional Integrity Questions

Below are additional questions that can be used during an in-depth integrity interview.

- Tell me every job you have had in the past 10 years, including start and end date, salary, job title when started and ended and supervisor, including names, addresses, and telephone numbers.
- Are there any falsifications on your application?
- Did you leave any jobs off your application?
- How will your previous employers describe your attendance? ...Excellent? ...O.K.? ...Poor?
- How many days have you missed in the last year?
- How many verbal/written reprimands for your attendance did you receive in the past 2 years?
- How many tardiness' were recorded in your personnel file in the last year / job?  Why?
- How many disciplinary actions in the past 3 years?
- Where have you been suspended?  Why?
- Where have you been fired or asked to resign?  Why?
- Will any of your previous employers say they let you go or fired you?
- Where will you receive your best evaluation?  The worst evaluation?
- Where have you suspected or had knowledge of co-workers or supervisors stealing?
- What have you taken?
- What will be found when your criminal record is checked? Note: convictions will not necessarily disqualify any applicant from employment.
- What does your current driving record show in the way of violations?
- Describe your best work related qualities
- What is the worst thing any former employer will say about you?
- Whom do you know at the place of employment you are applying at?
- When was the last time in possession of illegal drugs?
- Currently, or within the past six months, what is your use of any controlled substance? ...Marijuana? ...Cocaine? ...Speed? ...PCP? ...LSD? ...Hashish? ...Other?
- What is your current use of alcohol?
- Has the use of alcohol ever interfered with your work?
- To what extent do you gamble?  Has gambling ever been a problem for you?
- Have you ever been the subject of, or a witness in, any type of investigation at work?

# Chapter 9

# Legal and Effective Past Employment Checks

Before reading further, it is important to understand the distinction between some terms—

1. **Verification** of past employment refers to verifying **factual data** such as start date, end date, and job title.

2. **A Reference Check** of past employment means obtaining **qualitative information** about the person's performance such as how well the person did or where improvements are needed or if the person would be rehired.

3. Often, larger firms provide verifications through a Human Resources, staffing, or payroll department, or through someone else who does not actually know the applicant but is familiar with the firm. The verifier has the applicant's history of dates of employment and job titles. A reference, by comparison, is typically given by someone who actually knew the applicant, such as a former supervisor. That is referred to as a **Supervisor Reference**.

4. **A Personal Reference** comes from someone who is familiar with the applicant in a context other than employment.

The first part of this chapter examines the importance and use of the verification as part of a Safe Hiring Program.

## Even if All You Get Are Name, Rank and Serial Number, Verification Checks Are So Critical

> In the height of the Cold War, during negotiations with the Soviet Bloc on weapons reductions, a popular phase was "Trust, but Verify." Good advice, especially today!

It can be argued that verifying past employment is one of the most critical components an employer can undertake in the hiring process. Ideally, these checks provide specifics about past job performance that could be used as likely predictors of future success. Some employers make the costly error of not checking references. They know many organizations have policies against giving out detailed information about current or former employees. Employers might assume the effort is worthless because all they will get is "name, rank, and serial number," if anything at all.

However, here is the critical point—

> **Even if all you get is verification of dates of employment and job titles, past employer phone calls are still vital for safe hiring.**

Why is this so important? There are actually five essential reasons why a Safe Hiring Program requires calling past employers regardless of whether the past employer limits the information to start date, end date, and job title.

## 1. Eliminates Unexplained Employment Gaps

If you do *not* know where a person has been, then you are hiring a *stranger*. If you hire a stranger, then you have a substantial risk of being the victim of the legal and economic fallout of a bad hire.

As covered in previous chapters, if there are unexplained employment gaps in an application or resume, the employer cannot eliminate the possibility that the person's "absence" from the work force was involuntary, such as in being incarcerated for a criminal offense. By eliminating any gap in employment over the past five to ten years, it lessens the possibility the applicant spent time in custody for a significant criminal offense.

> **Author Tip ➡** The issue is not whether a person has gaps in his or her employment, but whether any gaps are *unexplained*. Not everyone has an uninterrupted employment history. Employment gaps can have very reasonable explanations, such as time off to go to school or for a sabbatical, or for personal and family reasons. Sometimes it can take a person time to find a new job. Gaps can indicate negative things too, such as a prison or jail stay.

Keep in mind that finding no gaps does not completely eliminate the possibility an applicant spent time in jail for some lesser offense. In many jurisdictions, a person convicted of a misdemeanor, such as a DUI, can fulfill a jail sentence in alternative ways — community service program, weekend custody, etc. In some jurisdictions, lesser offenders are eligible for a "bracelet" program, where they wear an electronic bracelet programmed to send a signal if they are not home by curfew. Also called the "commit a crime, go to your room program," this allows them to leave the house during specified hours to go to work.

Remember the story in Chapter 1 about the carpet cleaner? If the carpet cleaner had served time in a federal prison, the background check may not have revealed there was a criminal record. Therefore, the only way the employer could have uncovered the prison stay was to call the bogus past employers on the application or resume. A quick telephone call would have revealed a falsified application.

The importance of looking for unexplained gaps is underscored by the requirements imposed by the Federal Aviation Authority (FAA). When jobs fall under their authority, such as at airports and airlines, everyone hired must have a complete, validated ten-year history. If there is a gap, then the gap must be explained.

## 2. Indicates Where to Search for Criminal Records

There is no national database of criminal records that private employers can legally access. Criminal record searches must be conducted at each relevant courthouse, and there are over 10,000 courthouses covering some 3,500+ state and federal jurisdictions. However, when an employer knows where an applicant has been, then "the knowing where to look" increases the accuracy of a criminal search.

If an employer does not know where to search, then he can easily miss a court where an applicant had a significant criminal act, and thereby inadvertently hire a person with a serious criminal record. Details are discussed in Chapter 12 on Criminal Records.

## 3. Allows an Employer to Hire Based Upon Facts, Not Only Instinct

The pitfalls of using the "warm body theory" of hiring have been demonstrated in Chapters 1–3. Although the use of instinct is valuable in the hiring process, there is simply no substitute for factual verifications. Given the statistics that up to one-third of all resumes contain material falsehoods, the need to verify statements in a resume or application is critical. Just knowing with certainty that the applicant did in fact have the jobs and position claimed goes a long way towards a solid hiring decision.

## 4. Allows an Employer to Demonstrate Due Diligence

Here is the critical point—if something goes wrong, an employer needs to be able to convince a jury that the **employer made reasonable efforts,** given the situation, to engage in safe hiring. Documentation for each person hired shows that an employer made reasonable steps by contacting past employers to confirm job information and to ask questions. This is powerful evidence an employer was not negligent. As stated before, an employer is not expected to be 100% successful in their hiring. No one is. Any employer is expected to act in good faith and to take diligent efforts to hire safe and qualified people. This cannot be done without demonstrating that the employer made the effort, which means documenting that he or she picked up the phone and tried.

What constitutes a reasonable effort? Taking reasonable care means attempting to obtain employer references and documenting those attempts. To a degree, the level of reasonable inquiry depends upon the nature of the job and the risk to third parties. A higher standard of care may be required for hiring an executive than a food service worker. Regardless, every employer has a legal obligation to exercise appropriate care in the selection and retention of employees. The law does not require that an employer be successful in obtaining references. It is clear that an employer must at least try.

## 5. Potential Employer May Receive Valuable Information

Many employers assume that when they call a past employer they will get a "No comment," or "We do not give references." However, there is a significant percentage of time when both a verification and reference is possible. Sometimes this occurs when a firm has not been strongly counseled by their employment attorney not to give a reference. The overwhelming numbers of employers in the U.S. are small employers, who may not have been trained by a lawyer not to give references. Also, the previous employer may feel morally obliged to give references. Successful reference calls can also occur when the person calling has excellent communication skills, is professional, and is able to start some dialogue. There are many HR and security professionals who have developed the ability to obtain references, even from the most reluctant sources. Techniques on how to obtain references are given later in this chapter.

# The Importance of the Reference Check

As mentioned earlier, doing a reference check of past employment means obtaining **qualitative information** about the person's performance, including past performance, improvements needed, and recommendation for rehire.

Employers, HR, and security professionals seeking to obtain references face a substantial challenge. Sometimes it may not be possible to obtain references because the previous employer has an established policy against giving references. Other times the challenge may be how to locate an actual supervisor or former supervisor who is willing to talk about the applicant. Many firms refer all reference questions to payroll or accounting, where a staff member can only give the basic information. The new "900 number" reference services do not even allow for a discussion with a live human being — it is all completed by computer.

Here is a fundamental rule— when you need to know something, there is always someone who knows what you need. The old adage "when there is a will, there is a way" also applies to reference checking. The challenge is finding that person and convincing him or her to give you the information. Sometime, it requires more effort. Is it worth the additional effort of extensive attempts at checking? For an executive position, the extra effort may be worth it. For a position that can be more accurately described as "rank and file," or where there is a large scale hiring program, the real world limitation on time and budget may dictate setting up a program where a reasonable effort is made to satisfactorily demonstrate due diligence.

# How Far Back Should Reference Checks Go?

How far back should one go when checking previous employers? The answer can depend upon the applicant's relevant work history, the sensitivity of the position, and the availability of information. Some applicants may only have had one employer in the past ten years. Others may have had a large number. If a person is an hourly worker, then it is possible the person has held numerous past jobs. A young worker may not have a work history to check.

As a general guideline, employers should go back a minimum of five years, although seven to ten is much better. If the employer is in an industry where there is a great deal of turnover, then it may not be practical to go back even five years, if the five-year span represents a large number of previous employers. Employers should utilize a rule of reason, but also keep in mind that an employer should be internally consistent so that all similarly situated applicants are treated in a similar fashion. If an employer goes back five years for an administrative assistant, then all candidates who have reached the stage where references are conducted should also have their references checked going back five years.

# The Procedures Employers Need to Implement for Quality Reference Checking

A successful, in-house system of reference checking is possible. Here are ten important steps every employer should know about the mechanics of obtaining past references.

## 1. Set up a physical system to make and track calls, and monitor your progress by using a Past Employment Worksheet

Effective reference checking requires a system otherwise it is nearly impossible to track who has been called, the status of each call, and who else needs to be called.

This is especially true in a large company environment. In a typical large company reference-checking situation, a checker may be given a number of applicants to check references. Assume HR is given five applicants to check. Also assume that each applicant has on the average three past employers, making a total of 15 needed calls. Chances are that the percentage of successful first time calls will be limited. A successful call means getting through to the right person and getting as much information as the person can give you. The reality is most calls will result in an "incomplete," meaning that a call back is needed. Perhaps the caller had to leave a message on a voicemail, or the phone number did not work or is busy, or the past employer needs "a release" from the applicant. All of these situations require that HR note the outcome and schedule a follow-up. As the HR person is calling on the third candidate, past employers may be calling back in response to earlier messages. Sometimes a round or two of "phone-tag" is involved. Obviously, a tracking system is a necessity.

Here are suggestions to make the work flow easier—

a.  Have a prepared Past Employment Worksheet ready to go for each candidate. For each applicant, the reference checker needs to fill out the name and contact information for each past employer as well as any standard reference questions. A sample Past Employer Worksheet is found in Appendix 3.

b.  Use the Past Employer Worksheet to track all phone calls, including who was called, and the results. The information is worth its weight in gold should an employer ever be called upon to demonstrate due diligence in court. Even if the reference attempt was unsuccessful, a completed worksheet showing each call — including the date, time, phone number, person called, and the result — is the best possible proof that an employer exercised due diligence.

c.  In advance, it is helpful to place the essential information reported by the applicant on the Past Employment Worksheet. Now, during a call, the reference checker can write down what the past employer reports, providing an easy-to-read side-by-side comparison.

d. If specific job-related questions are being asked relevant to the knowledge, skill, and abilities related to a particular position, then make sure those questions are ready. This may mean having the application easily accessible for a quick reference.

e. Using a Past Employer Worksheet also insures you are asking the same questions for similarly situated candidates. A critical function of a reference-checking program is to treat all candidates fairly. Treat similarly situated candidates the same way!

## 2. Independently confirm the phone number for the past employer

It may not happen very often, but many HR and Security Professionals have heard of situations where an applicant set-up a fake reference on a resume by providing a friend's telephone number, with the friend standing by to answer, posing as a past employer. When the prospective employer makes the phone call, the friend gives a glowing and professorial reference. Or, an applicant bent on a "fake reference" can use other alternatives such as setting up a voicemail service, leaving a message indicating the voice mail box belongs to a supposed reference, and later have a friend return the call posing as a past supervisor. Cases are reported of applicants attempting to act as their own reference. With cell phones, call forwarding and internet phone services, such trickery is now easier than ever.

To avoid the possibility of a fake reference, it is recommended that a verifier independently locate the past employer's phone number by use of an internet service or local phone book. There are a number of websites where phone numbers can be found very quickly. They typically have the same data that dialing "411" information would have, except the internet services are free. Any legitimate firm will have a listed phone number. The chance of an applicant going to the trouble of creating a legal entity just to get a listed phone number is, well, not likely.

Here are some websites where employer phone numbers can be located—

- www.infousa.com
- www.city-yellowpages.com
- www.switchboard.com
- www.superpages.com
- www.infospace.com
- www.411.com

In addition, verifiers can also "Google" the past employer by running the name on the internet search engine at www.google.com.

There may be times when a firm is not listed. That can happen if the firm has moved, merged, changed names, or gone out of business. In that situation, the new employer may well have to talk further with the applicant to find someone who can verify an employment.

Of course, a verifier must also use good judgment. If the phone is not answered in a professional manner, or there are the sounds of traffic and children in the background, then something is not right.

Finally, if there is any suspicion of a set-up or fake reference, it may be necessary to verify if the person giving the reference was, in fact, employed by the past employer. That may even require, in some situations, calling HR or payroll to make sure the person the verifier is talking with was in fact employed there.

## 3. Be careful when contacting an applicant's *current* employer

A recurring issue in any past employment check is sensitivity about contacting the current employer. A current employer should NOT be contacted unless the applicant specifically gives permission.

The reason is there are some employers who, upon learning a current employee is looking to leave, will immediately take steps to terminate the employee. This is especially true for positions of greater responsibility where the applicant may have access to customer lists or trade secrets. In some industries, within minutes of learning an employee is actively looking for a new position, the current employer will have the Security Department box up the employee's personal items, confiscate all computers and disks, turn off all access to any computer systems, de-activate the parking permit and building access code, and have the person physically escorted off premises with a last paycheck.

If such a hasty departure is caused by a phone call by the prospective new employer, and the job offer does not come through, then the applicant is left without a job and free to contemplate whether they should visit a lawyer—

In order to avoid this, here is a simple two-step program—

    a.   On the application, in large letters, make sure there is a box someplace asking an applicant "May we contact your current employer?"

    b.   Do NOT call the current employer unless the applicant has clearly marked the "Yes" Box. If the applicant failed to check either box, then do not call until that is clarified. Anything other than a clear indication of YES can create problems.

If the employer still needs to verify current employment, there are three options for doing so—

    a.   Ask the applicant for the name of a past supervisor or co-worker who is no longer working with the applicant at the current place of employment. Again, if there is any question about the authenticity of the supplied name, the employer can call and verify the ex-employee did in fact work at the current workplace.

    b.   Ask the applicant to bring in W-2's for each year of work, or at least the full past year.

    c.   Wait until after the employee is hired before calling the past employer, providing the new hire is subject to a written offer letter that clearly states "continued employment is conditional upon a background screening report that is satisfactory to the employer." Once the new employee comes on broad there can be a final phone call. By making current employment part of the written offer letter, an applicant has a powerful incentive to be accurate about his or her current employment situation, since any false or misleading statements or omissions will have serious consequences. It is also important to say the screening report must be "satisfactory to the employer" in order to avoid a debate with an applicant/new hire about what is or is not a good screening report.

## 4. Use "Soft Sell Techniques"

If a verifier faces resistance to a reference, the best approach is usually a soft sale. Here are some techniques that may help convince a past employer to give the information you need—

a. Do not start right off asking for an employment reference. That will immediately make an employer defensive and create a barrier to effective communication.

b. Explain the purpose and try to convince the past employer to be of assistance. How? By finding a common ground. For example, explain that your applicant cannot be employed without some additional information, or that getting *some* information would be a great benefit.

c. Start with a non-controversial request, such as start date, end date, or job title.

d. Before asking reference questions, segue into the subject with non-controversial questions such as "What was the nature of the job?" If you are told the person's job title was "project manager," then ask the past employer what that job entails. It is then a short trip to ask "How did the applicant perform the job?"

e. If your state has a statute that protects an employer that gives an employment reference, then you may explain that to a reference.

f. Offer to send a release. A release gives a past employer a great comfort level. It demonstrates that the new employer, in fact, has a valid business reason for requesting the information, and that the past employer has *permission* to give it. Keep in mind, however, a release is not a blank check for the past employer to say anything they want. Even with a release, the past employer must be careful to limit the information to those items that are job-related and factual.

## 5. Be careful about the "Eligible for Rehire" question

If nothing else works, a firm can at least be asked if the previous employer would rehire the applicant, or whether the applicant is eligible for rehire. This has become a standard reference question. Even firms with a "name, rank, and serial number" policy are comfortable with answering this question. In reality, the past employer is being asked the ultimate question, which is, "knowing what you know about the person," and assuming you are also a highly trained, competent and motivated HR manager, "Would you want the person back?"

However, there are several problems with the "Eligible For Rehire" question. First, if a firm in fact has a no reference policy, then they are technically violating their policy if they answer. They are essentially giving a qualitative evaluation of the person. If they answer "No," that potentially could be a form of defamation.

Second, a real issue with the question is the answer is often meaningless. Here is why. Suppose a past employer is called and asked about "eligible for rehire" and the past employer says, "Yes." What does that mean? It could mean that technically the person is "eligible" to be rehired because there is no notation on the personnel file that indicates there is a prohibition against accepting that application. However, in truth and in fact, that past employer would never consider rehiring that person, they just won't say so.

Conversely, a "No" answer could mean the particular employer has a policy against rehiring anyone who left, even though the applicant was the best worker they could ever hope for.

The wording of the question that is most helpful is the following: "Knowing what you know about Mr. Smith, if you were in a position to rehire him for the same job he left, would you want him back?"

In order to interpret that answer, the verifier must understand the assumptions being made. They are assuming that the person who is giving the answer has a similar interest to the new employer and is capable of making a meaningful judgment. In other words, in order to give the answer meaning, the verifier has to make assumptions about the knowledge and judgment of the person giving the information.

If an HR professional, who the verifier happens to know, is giving the information and the verifier has respect for the experience and judgment of the HR professional, then the answer is extremely valuable. If the verifier is talking to a stranger, then it is really a judgment call as to the value of the information.

It really comes down to the old rule– information from a trusted source is the best information.

> **Author Tip ➡** If your organization has been instructed not to answer reference questions but to verify information only, then the "rehire question" is really a reference question. In fact, "Would you rehire?" is the ultimate reference question since employer 1 is asking employer 2's ultimate judgment about whether a new employer should hire their former employee.

## 6. Send a faxed request — It is harder to ignore than voicemail

Often times a verifier cannot get through to a live person and must leave a voicemail. As everyone knows in this busy world, it is easy to ignore voicemail. By the time the verifier leaves the third voicemail, it becomes less likely the past employer intends to respond. Assuming the verifier has verified that the reference person is not away on a leave or vacation, and it is the right person, the verifier needs a way to get through.

Short of physically going over to the past employers office and demanding time (not very practical, of course) the next best thing is to send a fax request. For some reasons, a piece of paper demands attention — people feel they need to do something with a piece of paper but they can ignore voicemail. A fax to a former employer can also include the information to be verified, along with a return fax number, of course.

If all else fails, a faxed request at least shows a due diligence effort to get the information. The fax to the past employer should be maintained in the file as proof of the efforts made.

Another technique is to mail a written request. This technique is only effective for verification of factual information. How much meaning should be put on past employers answers to faxed or mailed reference questions? That is difficult to say.

## 7. Use other sources such as former co-workers or supplied references

Depending on the importance of the position and the time and resources available, the verifier may attempt to talk with a professional reference the applicant has supplied. This is known as a "supplied reference."

One technique is to ask a supplied reference for another person who may know the applicant. This is known as talking with a developed reference. A "developed reference" is a source of information the verifier has developed on his or her own, without input from the candidate.

Talking to a developed reference can be a very valuable source of information. The verifier can get information from someone who was not told in advance he or she would be contacted, which increases the probability of a truly spontaneous and non-rehearsed conversation leading to additional insights about the candidate.

## 8. Use professional networking when possible

HR professionals can sometimes engage in <u>professional networking</u> to obtain reference information. Sometime just "reading between the lines" can be of assistance. A previous employer may be unwilling to give specific information, but may be willing to convey a sense about or opinion about the applicant, or communicate in some other "unofficial" manner.

It should be noted there is no such thing as an "off the record comment." Should a matter ever go to litigation and a deposition is taken, an HR manager or employer would have a legal obligation to reveal all the details of a conversation, if directly asked.

There is, however, an ethical issue to consider. If an HR or security professional knows that a colleague works at a firm that has a strict policy against giving references, then a request for information is really asking another professional to violate a firm's policy. The fact that such a conversation may be "off the record" may not help.

## 9. Use other procedures if the former employer is out of business, bankrupt, moved, merged, or cannot be located

For a number of reasons a previous employer may not be available for a past employment check. First, a verifier may have trouble obtaining information if a firm has merged or been acquired and no one can locate the personnel records. In this situation, a verifier has two options. One is to contact the applicant to locate a former co-worker or supervisor; however, that requires the verifier to confirm the credibility of the former employee, since there would be no way to verify the source of information from the former employer. The second option is to contact the applicant and request a copy of the W-2 (if the applicant was on the payroll) or a 1099 (if the applicant was a contractor). To help confirm employment, an employer can also "Google" the applicant or use a new service available at www.zoominfo.com to see if there are any references on the internet.

A verifier can also run into difficulties if given insufficient information about the past employer. It is critical to require any applicant to completely identify the past employer by name, city, and state in order to facilitate a telephone call. Using an applicant-supplied phone number can be a source of difficulty; not only must the verifier be alert to the possibility of a "fake or set-up reference," but often, the phone number an applicant recalls was the number for a division or branch, not the number needed for that firm's past employment verifications.

## 10. If a past employer says there is no record, then a verifier needs to go one step further

What if a past employer tells a verifier there is no record of an applicant having worked there? Before jumping to the conclusion the applicant has lied, a verifier should dig deeper. There can be reasonable explanations for apparent discrepancies. An applicant may have worked at the previous company as a temporary worker, under contract, or was actually employed by a third-party employer organization.

Many companies utilize the services of a Professional Employer Organization (PEO) to act as the employer of record although the work is performed at the company workplace under the company's direction and control. In these situations, the previous company's records will show that no such person worked there, though their facility was the physical location where the applicant worked. Since the applicant physically worked at the firm's premises, the applicant may well report that business as the employer. The applicant may not be certain who actually issued the check.

It is also important to ask the employer to double-check their records under the applicant's Social Security Number and any other names the applicant may have used.

Some employers utilize an outsourced service called The Work Number for Everyone found at www.talx.com. According to this website, "More than 1,000 employers outsource the verification process to The Work Number, including more than half of the Fortune 500." An employer or background firm attempting to verify past employment pays a fee to access a computerized phone message service which gives basic employment data about the applicant. If there is concern about the accuracy of data about an individual applicant, Talx provides an email address for questions.[1]

---

**Case in Point—**

An applicant reported a two-year employment history. However, a telephone call to the past employer showed the applicant only worked there for a year and a half. On the surface, it looked like the applicant lied about the time period of employment. Since honesty and integrity is integral to any employment relationship, the employer was about to terminate the hiring process and rescind the offer. However, the employer could not believe that such a good prospect actually lied. The employer took the extra step of asking the applicant about the apparent discrepancy. Upon further investigation, it turned out the applicant started off working for the past employer as an unpaid intern for six months, then was hired full-time. From the applicant's point of view, he had worked there for two years — employment records for the company reflected only a year and a half. If the employer had not gone the extra step, then all of the time, energy, and expense of recruiting the prospect would have been wasted. On the other hand, if the person had lied, the extra time spent confirming the facts would also have protected the employer in the event of any adverse legal action.

---

# Other Effective Reference Techniques

Appendix 3 has a list of sample reference questions.

Some suggestions made by experts include—

- Use of questions showing behavior – e.g. "Can you give me a specific example of how he (or she) was a great team player?"

- Ask a targeted question – e.g. "The candidate states he (or she) implemented a sales training program. Can you tell me about their contribution?"

- Read the candidate's resume to the past employer and ask for a reaction to the resume content.

- Use open-ended questions to inspire narrative answers.

Human Resources consultant and expert on hiring and reference questions Wendy Bliss gives the following tips on effective reference techniques. More information on this topic is available in her book *Legal, Effective References: How to Give and Get Them*, published by the Society for Human Resource Management in 2001.

---

[1] at print time, the e-mail address is dataquality@talx.com

# Mission Possible: 10 Tips for Effective Telephone Reference Checks[2]

By Wendy Bliss, J.D., SPHR

Author of *Legal, Effective References: How to Give and Get Them*

www.wendybliss.com

Due to the popularity of the "name, rank and serial number" approach to reference requests, it is often challenging to uncover useful, in-depth information about job applicants during telephone reference checks. However, it is by no means impossible! With practice and persistence, you can greatly increase the quantity and quality of information obtained in conversations with reference sources. On your next reference-checking mission, use the following tips—

1.      **Create a powerful script.**   Do not "wing it" when calling references. Develop a written outline that includes questions and comments that will enable you to: 1) establish rapport with reference contacts; 2) minimize potential opposition to your inquiries; 3) obtain relevant, detailed information about the applicant; and 4) follow up with the source as needed. Tips 2 through 9 below provide techniques for accomplishing each of these objectives. To build skill and consistency, use your reference check script for every reference check.

2.      **Open the door for effective communication in the first sixty seconds.**
When contacting a reference, your initial goal is to make a positive connection and set the stage for a candid conversation. Identify yourself by name and position. Share general information about your company and the specific opening there for which the applicant is being considered. Let the reference contact know that you have the applicant's permission to call, assuming that is the case. (If the applicant has not given your organization prior written consent to do so, it is inadvisable to conduct any reference checks.) After sharing this introductory information, making a complimentary statement about the source, such as "Betty made favorable comments about your guidance and supervision during her interviews with us," may predispose the source to sharing full and frank feedback with you.

3.      **Avoid the "R" word.**   The mere mention of the word "reference," particularly in the initial stage of a reference check call, may arouse worries about defamation and other legal claims in the mind of the person you have contacted. So, you should set the stage for cooperation. Explain the purpose for the call and the potential benefits of sharing candid information by taking a future focus. For instance, stating that "An important reason for my call is to gain information that will help our company most effectively supervise Richard in the event we hire him" emphasizes the developmental benefit of answering your questions fully.

**4.** **Ask the right questions, in the right order.** After establishing rapport with the source, climb the ladder of reference inquiries to gain a thorough understanding of the applicant's employment history, qualifications, job performance, and past problems on the job. Start by asking the most innocuous and easily answered questions first, including confirmation of dates of employment, positions held and salary history. Next, move up the ladder of inquiry to gather information about the applicant's job duties, performance, work habits, and his or her suitability for the open position at your company. Finally, inquire about the most sensitive topics including reasons for leaving, and incidents of misconduct or dangerous behaviors. This three-tiered approach to questioning — when you save the toughest topics for last — usually leads to at least partial cooperation from reference sources.

**5.** **Ask open-ended questions, and give prompters.** Questions about the applicant that begin with the words "what," "how," or "why" invite detailed responses. Other phrases that encourage full and specific disclosure begin with phrases such as "Give me an example of the applicant's ability to . . .,"or "Describe a time when the applicant . . ." Follow up questions or statements such as "Can you elaborate on that?" or "That's interesting. Please tell me more about that," prompt the source to give more details.

**6.** **Listen carefully for vocal clues.** Many reference sources who are reluctant to share negative information will often tip off reference checkers to potential problems with the applicant through a variety of signals. Is the source's tone of voice guarded? Does he or she sound cautious or reluctant to answer even basic fact verification questions? Reference checkers should also be on the alert for unusually long pauses, throat-clearing, or "umms" and "ahs" that may indicate hesitancy to give information candidly, particularly if these occur in response to a sensitive question.

**7.** **Dig deep when you get shallow responses.** When a reference source gives a vague answer, carefully rehearsed, or inconsistent, probe for more useful information. In such situations, politely ask for more details with remarks such as "I am not sure I understood what you meant when you said . . .; can you clarify that for me?" Another technique that may help you discover the truth when you are being stonewalled is to ask very direct questions that require a "yes" or "no" response. For example, ask "Was Pat fired?" or "Was Chris ever disciplined for poor performance or misconduct while employed at your company?" These questions forcefully probe non-answers about an applicant's reasons for leaving a prior job, or clues us in about his or her performance and conduct with the previous employer.

**8.** **Be prepared for reluctant references.** While the above techniques will increase your overall success in obtaining useful information during reference checks, you will undoubtedly still encounter stiff resistance from some reference sources. When this occurs, offer to fax the source a copy of the reference authorization form signed by the applicant. This will be particularly helpful if your reference authorization form includes a waiver of liability that protects anyone who provides a reference about the applicant. You can also explain that the applicant will not be hired without satisfactory information about the applicant's performance in past jobs, which is an effective way to encourage sources having positive information about the applicant to go ahead and do the right thing. Additionally, you can inquire as to whether the source's unwillingness to share information about the applicant is an indication of problems with the applicant. If all else fails, contact a different source at the same organization - such as a higher level manager, another supervisor, or even a colleague - anyone who worked directly with the applicant. It is very possible that a different source in the same organization will be willing to give you the information you seek.

**9.      When closing a call, leave the door open to get more information.**
At the end of your reference check discussions, thank the source for his or her time. Ask for permission to contact the source again if you have additional questions. Finally, ask if the source knows of any other people inside or outside the source's organization who would have knowledge of the applicant's background, job performance or others matters relevant to the applicant's suitability to work at your organization.

**10.     Use good form in documenting calls.**   All telephone reference check attempts and calls should be documented using a standardized form. This form can be developed internally, or can be obtained from books on reference checking such as my book *Legal Effective References: How to Give and Get Them.*[3]

# Use Reference Questions that are 100% Legal

Remember the same standards apply to reference checking that apply to interview questions. That is, all questions must be specifically job-related. Never ask any question of a reference that you would not ask the candidate face-to-face. Focus on skills and accomplishments as well as performance issues that apply specifically to your job opening, such as the ability to meet deadlines or to work well with others on a team project. See Chapter 8 for a list of questions that can and cannot be asked of an applicant in an interview. Again, these questions are also applicable when interviewing a past employer.

# Who Should Make the Past Employment Calls?

There are three different groups who can do past employment checks—

1.   The actual hiring managers

2.   Human Resources

3.   An outsourced third party, such as a background firm

Here are the pros and cons of each group—

---

[3] *Legal Effective References: How to Give and Get Them, by Wendy Bliss* can be purchased online from the Society for Human Resource Management at www.shrm.org/shrmstore

## Hiring Manager

**Advantages:** The manager knows the job and know what talents and skills are needed. Also, the hiring manager is the person who has to live with the decision. For sensitive or critical positions, the manager may want to receive input directly from previous employers. Even if the previous employer has a "no comment" policy, there may still be an advantage in talking personally to the previous employer and attempting to glean what information is available "between the lines."

**Disadvantages:** There is much less control over the process in terms of whether the hiring manager is asking legal questions, or treating candidates in a similar fashion. In addition, many hiring managers may be tempted to make fewer calls, and may settle for just one completed call before making a decision. Hiring managers may not be as concerned about the need to establish a full employment history or look for employment gaps. Although these drawbacks can be lessened with written procedures, training, and auditing of hiring files, they are still sources of concern.

## Human Resources

**Advantages:** Any reference check done by human resources more likely will be done thoroughly, properly, and legally with proper documentation and consistency.

**Disadvantages:** The human resources department does not know the job requirements nearly as well as the hiring manager. In addition, even for a firm with a fully staffed Human Resources department, employment reference checking is a time consuming task. The difficulty with performing employment reference checks in-house is not the time the actual interview takes; it is the constant interruptions of returned phone calls throughout the day, tracking the progress of each candidate, and making repeated attempts when there is not a callback. It can also take time to locate former employers and phone numbers as well.

## Background Checking Firm

**Advantages:** By outsourcing, a firm knows that nothing will fall through the cracks, since a background firm can be counted on to methodically contact all past employers. In addition, the fees charged by screening firms are typically very modest.

**Disadvantages:** A verifier employed by a screening firm typically knows little about the employer or the job. Screening firms often do employment checks in high volume and are unlikely to ask in-depth, pertinent questions. In addition, given the prices charged by screening firms, the verifiers are not HR professionals, but rather have skills that are closer to a professional call center.

## Who Makes the Call? — Conclusion

The answer is to recognize the difference between *reference checks used to determine if a person should be offered the position* in the first place, and *due diligence of past employment checks* utilized to ensure an employer has confirmed dates and details of past employment and subjected all finalists to the same process.

In order to make sure nothing falls through the cracks, HR or a background screening firm may be called upon to do a check, just to make sure all the bases have been covered. The worst that can happen is some former employer may be called twice — once by the hiring manager and again by HR or a background screening firm.

Many organizations encourage the hiring manager to make whatever employment checks are needed to help decide if the person is a good fit — to form an opinion as to whether or not to make a job offer in the first place. Of course, employers are well advised to make sure a hiring manager is trained, so that only legal and permissible questions are asked.

# Why Employers Won't Give References

The current system of employment reference checks makes no sense.

Even though everyone agrees that past employment checking is an essential part of the hiring process, many employers, on advice of legal counsel, have a "no comment policy," allowing only verification of basic information such as start and end dates, and job title. Some companies will not even release salary information — salaries coming under the heading of "competitive intelligence," thus protected — even when presented with a signed release.

The results are not only illogical but also run counter to the best interest of employers and well-deserving job applicants. Good prospects are sometimes unable to get the recommendations they deserve, while applicants with a negative history can go on to victimize new and unsuspecting employers, with their history safely hidden behind them. In fact, the only beneficiaries of this upside-down system are the very job applicants that employers want to avoid.

Adding to the confusion is the fact that oftentimes the very employer or HR professional who is attempting to get a reference will turn around on the same day and refuse to give out a reference on one of their own past employees. Despite the fact that employers, labor lawyers, HR, and security professionals all agree that past employment checks should be conducted, it is also a well-known fact that most employers will not give any information beyond "name, rank, and serial number."

What is happening here? What is the reason for this completely illogical system?

**It is the fear of being SUED!**

Employers who give negative references can be sued for defamation. When the defamation is in oral form (such as over the phone) it is called *slander*. If it is in written form (such as a negative letter of recommendation) it is called *libel*.

For example, what if a applicant had a history with previous employers that showed he was often late, did not get along with others, was not productive, did not meet goals or was disciplined for inappropriate workplace conduct? These are all critical items of information that a new employer would want and need to know.

Yet, few former employers are willing to convey this information. Labor lawyers repeatedly instruct employers NOT to give out anything but "name, rank, and serial number."

If there is no question that misconduct occurred, such as a criminal conviction, then the former employer is probably on safer grounds. However, in situations where the former employee can dispute the accusation, an employer should be concerned about a lawsuit. Suppose a former employee was accused of harassment and an internal company investigation indicated the harassment did occur. If the company reveals this about the applicant to the new employer, the previous employer could still face a lawsuit. An internal company investigation does not carry weight of law, thus it may be defamation.

To make matters even worse, employers can be sued, believe it or not, by giving a POSITIVE reference. This can happen where the employer gave a good reference letter, but withheld negative information for fear of being sued for defamation. If the resulting recommendation created a false impression, and as the result of the misrepresentation it is foreseeable that someone can be injured, the past employer can be sued. And why not? They lied.

---

### Liability for a False Positive Reference – the School District Case

In a 1997 California case, the State Supreme Court ruled that a school district could be liable for damages when it gave a very positive job recommendation and left out important negative information. A school administrator was accused of inappropriate sexual misconduct towards a 13-year-old girl. The named victim not only sued the administrator, but also sued former schools that gave him favorable employment recommendations even though the former schools were aware of similar allegations of sexual misconduct at previous schools. The favorable recommendations included statements such as—

- He had "genuine concern" for students and had "outstanding rapport" with everyone.

- "I wouldn't hesitate to recommend (him) for any position."

- He was "an upbeat, enthusiastic administrator who related well to the students."

- He was "in a large part" responsible for making the school "a safe, orderly and clean environment for students and staff."

The Court ruled that a former employer providing a recommendation owes a duty to protect employers and third parties, and cannot misrepresent the qualifications and character of an ex-employee where there is a substantial risk of physical injury. In other words, an employer could not portray a former employee in a false light by only giving the good and not the bad. Having written a letter that they knew would be used to gain employment at other schools where there were potential victims, the schools had an obligation tell the whole truth. See *Randi W vs. Muroc Joint Unified School District*, (14 Cal.4th 1066)(1997)

---

So, here is the situation. If a past employer gives a negative reference, the past employer can be sued for defamation by the applicant. If the employer gives a positive reference, a victim of misconduct can potentially sue the past employer for giving a false reference if negative information is left out.

The law arguably places employers who give recommendations in a "catch-22." If an employer fails to disclose an accusation because of insufficient credible evidence, then the employer risks being sued by third party victims. However, if the employer does mention an accusation, the ex-employee can arguably sue for defamation.

---

**Interesting Facts About Defamation Lawsuits—**

According to facts contained on the website for the National Workrights Institute, the threat of defamation lawsuits are grossly over-exaggerated.

"The reality of the threat of defamation from employer references is often well exaggerated. The truth is that very few employers are ever sued for defamation and almost none are found liable. In 1997 there were only 13 cases in the United States in which employees sued ex-employers for defamation in the context of reference giving. Of those cases, only four were successful and only once was a plaintiff's award of damages upheld. In 1998 there were four cases with not one successful plaintiff and in 1999 there were five case with only one plaintiff succeeding."[4]

---

Still, hesitation to give references exists despite protection given under many state laws. Forty states currently have some sort of employer immunity statute. These statutes are designed to promote good faith communication of job related information between employers.[5] For example, California Civil Code Section 47(c) was amended in 1994 to add a section to protect employers from defamation lawsuits when giving an employment reference to another employer. The code states—

> "This subdivision applies to and includes a communication concerning the job performance or qualifications of an applicant for employment, based upon credible evidence, made without malice, by a current or former employer of the applicant, to and upon request of the prospective employer."

What does this mean in plain English? Essentially it means that if a new prospective employer contacts a former employer, the former employer has a "qualified privilege" to give information, as long as the information is—

- Job related;
- Based upon credible evidence; and
- Made without malice.

Unfortunately, it is difficult to gauge whether these laws have actually encouraged employers to free up the flow of necessary information. For the most part, these laws merely put into a statute what has already been the case law, or "common law," in most jurisdictions — that good faith communication between interested parties has some protection. However, even with this protection, many legal sources argue that the risk of a defamation claim outweighs any benefit to an employer from giving reference

---

[4] see www.workrights.org/issue_other/oi_reference_check.html

[5] a list of many of these state laws is found at www.esrcheck.com/safehireupdates.php

information. For one thing, applicants can still sue for defamation if they contend the reference was given in "bad faith." Further, what constitutes, "credible evidence," or what is "job related," can be open to interpretation.

One more consideration must be added to the mix. Generally, an employer has no obligation to say anything at all. If a firm was considering the application of Jack D. Ripper, and called up a past employer, that past employer can legally say "No comment." In other words, past employers have **no duty to warn**. The exception of course may be if the employer only gives the "good stuff" and leaves out the bad, as in the California School case.

If employers had a duty to warn, it would potentially put an impossible task on employers. Why? Because employers would be placed in the untenable position of being sued every time one of their ex-employees would get a new position. It would create an incredible burden if every time an employer was called up for a reference, they had to choose between being sued by the applicant for defamation, or being sued by the new employer or a victim for failure to warn or for giving a negligent reference.

### Past Employer References— Conclusion

Because of these complications, and the fact that an employer has no obligation to give a reference, many lawyers advise the "no comment" policy. That is the reason why many employers will only give "name, rank, and serial number."

Unfortunately, if everyone followed this policy, then all companies would be placed in jeopardy because it becomes very difficult to know whom you are hiring.

# Suggestions on How to Deal with Requests for References

Employers who are concerned about obtaining references will undoubtedly find themselves in the position of being asked for references. Employers and Human Resource professionals have responded in various ways.

Many firms have a rigid policy of not giving any information beyond the basics, such as start and stop date and job titles. Requests for references are often referred to payroll or accounting departments. That gives the maximum legal protection because it limits situations where a manger may give a reference *against* company policy.

A number of large firms have signed up for a "900 number" telephone service where employment verifications are conducted by a computerized voice only. Other firms are willing to indicate only that a person is eligible for rehire. However, some companies are concerned that even stating an employee is not eligible for rehiring could cause legal exposure.

One possible solution is to follow the old adage that unless you have something nice to say about someone, then do not say anything at all. Some companies have a policy of only giving reference information when they can do so without reservation. The downside is that an ex-employee can complain that by implication of a no response, he or she is receiving a negative reference.

Companies who would like to give negative information often do so **"between the lines."** One example is to suggest the new potential employer ask their applicant to send a release of performance appraisal files because "that would make interesting reading." That implies enough to raise a **red flag**.

Keep in mind there is no such thing as comments **"off the record."** If litigation should ever occur, and a human resources staff member is asked to give a deposition under oath, there is no privilege not to reveal information given "off the record."

Other companies, as a matter of their own corporate philosophy, are willing to disclose negative information as well as positive information in order to protect other employers and the public. In those situations, it is important to take steps to document the sources of the information, and document to whom it is given.

## The Following Guidelines Should be Considered When Giving Reference Information

- A firm should have a written policy and procedure for giving references.

- All information should go through a central source. This gives a firm consistency and reduces the chances that a manager may give out information that is contrary to company policy.[6]

- Clearly document who is requesting the information and for what purpose. Former employees have been known to have friends or paid "reference checkers" contact previous employers. Also document exactly what is provided.

- Clearly document who in the company is giving the information because this can be important in order to trace who-exactly-said-what in a reference check. Keep in mind that staff members may leave a company and, without a written record of a staffer's account, an employer may not be able to defend their reference actions.

- If the information requested goes beyond dates and job title, a company may ask for a copy of a written release. This also provides some protection against defamation lawsuits.

- If an ex-employee has filed a discrimination charge or lawsuit against the company, then <u>no information</u> should be given beyond job dates and job title without contacting your legal department.

If the employer intends to give negative information, the following may be helpful—

- Remember that employees most often seek the advice of an attorney when they are surprised and imagine an applicant's surprise when he or she hears for the first time from some new potential employer they are getting a negative reference from a past employer. If negative references may be an issue, what the past employer intends to say should be handled and documented at the time the employee leaves during the exit interview.

---

[6] As a practical matter, many organizations understand that even though there may be such a policy, there is in reality a practice of individual managers giving information. When that is the case, an alternative policy is to allow managers to do so under a strict program where there are procedures, training, and consequences for failing to follow procedures.

- Disclose only factual information. Make sure everything has been documented. For example, if the former employee was convicted of a crime, a past employer can simply report the public record. A past employer's evaluations of the employee can be a good source of information. The employee has already seen the performance evaluations and in most cases signed them.

- Avoid conclusions and give facts instead. For example, avoid saying a former employee "had a bad attitude." Instead, convey facts showing a failure to get along with team members. Let the facts speak for themselves.

- Include favorable facts about the employee. That demonstrates an employer is even-handed.

- Make sure the personnel file is factually correct. That is something HR may do when an employee leaves.

In the event the former employee has a pending claim against the company for any reason (e.g. workers compensation, lawsuit), an employer should strictly limit any comment to only the basic data such as start date, end date, and job title.

---

**Author Tip** ➡ There is another reason to be very careful about giving references. There are a number of firms that offer private references checking services on behalf of job applicants who want to find out **if a past employer is giving a negative reference.** In fact, there is one firm that hires court reporters to call past employers on behalf of job applicants. The court reporters transcribe the conversation exactly as it occurs. In many states a tape recording would be illegal, but a court always accepts a court reporter's transcript as accurate. The court reporter calls a past employer and tells them they are doing an employment reference. They just don't happen to mention that it is on behalf of the past employee fishing for material for a defamation lawsuit.

# Section 3

# Employer & Vendor Guidelines to Background Screening Tools

Your Safe Hiring Program — and how to perform all the components used in a background check.

Chapter 10 examines the pre-employment screening process and when to outsource screening to vendors.

Chapters 11 through 16 emphasize the correct and legal way to access criminal records, Social Security traces, educational verifications, and the myriad of other records needed in the screening process.

Chapter 17 examines privacy and identity theft issues.

Chapter 18 demonstrates how to continue the Safe Hiring Program for the entire term of employment.

# Chapter 10

# Pre-Employment Screening: What Is It and Who Does It

A core component of a Safe Hiring Program is performing in-depth screening of applicants. A number of procedures and tools are used to screen applicants before these applicants come on the premise as employees. Consider the following definition—

> *Pre-employment screening is an assessment of a group of applicants for employment by means of methodically assembling standardized types of information concerning qualifications and behavior that when obtained and applied in a legal fashion is considered relevant to the potential job, in order to reasonably detect those applicants that are either not qualified or have risk factors that need further consideration.*

## The Pre-employment Screening Process

In the broadest sense, the term "pre-employment screening" is shorthand for the process of assessing applicants for an employer's particular job or category of job.

The assessment is performed according to employer policies, based upon the nature of the job category and applicable laws, all designed to reveal fully-qualified applicants.

These policies are implemented according to practices which are designed to reasonably separate those applicants who are qualified for the particular job from those who may not be qualified due to (1) lack of experience or credentials, or (2) other personal factors that may pose an unacceptable risk to the employer, other employees, or those using the employer's services.

Practices are documented through procedures that methodically assemble standardized types of information concerning applicants.

Above all, the approach and assessment a firm takes to implement these pre-employment screening practices are integral to the success of a firm's Safe Hiring Program. The ultimate purpose of a Safe Hiring Program? 1. Get the best person for the job so that the company can prosper, 2. do not get sued.

## What Are These Tools and Procedures?

The next several chapters discuss in detail elements involved in the screening process, including proper procedures, documentation, and related legal compliance issues. Below is a partial list of these elements. Keep in mind that a few of these elements may be optional in your Safe Hiring Program—

- Education and Credentials Verification
- Past Employment References
- Criminal History
- Motor Vehicle Report (driving record)
- Social Security Number Trace
- Credit Report

- Worker's Compensation Records
- Civil Lawsuits, Judgments, Liens
- Security Clearances
- International searches
- Merchant Databases

It is important to note that a background screen is NOT the same thing as an in-depth investigation of each applicant. The term "investigation" refers to a more focused look at each candidate and can include seeking to develop information unknown to the investigator. For example, in an investigation, the investigator may not know the past employers and schools and may have to locate that information. In a background screening, the employer is seeking to *verify* the past employment and school information given. In addition, an investigator may look for all property and assets owned by a subject, and this detailed of an approach is normally not appropriate for pre-employment screening.

Screening is not going to detect *every potential problem* of an applicant, and neither may an investigation. Given that a background check is performed on a number of applicants and that cost considerations are always present, even the best screening program can result in a "bad apple" getting through. However, reasonable steps are taken to try to limit and discourage bad hires and to demonstrate due diligence.

# Screening Versus Investigation—Not the Same Thing

The difference between "screening" and "investigations" is analogous to the difference between giving cholesterol tests to a large number of consumers for a medical risk factor for heart disease, versus doing an exploratory surgical procedure one patient at a time. Obviously an exploratory procedure is much more reliable, but it is also intrusive, time consuming, and expensive. On the other hand, when giving merely a cholesterol test instead of performing exploratory surgery, it is possible that someone with a serious condition might slip through the cracks and have a more serious condition than indicated. However, the cost must be weighed against the benefit of faster, less-expensive and less-intrusive procedures that have an excellent detection rate on a greater number of people.

Think of *screening* as working with what you see. *Investigation* is digging for what is not seen.

## Importance of Consistency and Scope

Critical in nearly every area of employee screening, similarly situated people should be treated in a similar fashion. Proper pre-employment screening does not mean all applicants must be screened exactly the same. What it does mean is that all applicants who are finalists for a particular job opening should receive the same level of scrutiny. A firm may choose to screen in more detail candidates for a vice president's position than those applying to be on the maintenance crew. All vice presidential applicants should be screened in the same way, while all maintenance worker candidates should be screened like all other maintenance worker candidates.

All applicants do not have to be submitted for review by an outside agency performing background screening. An employer might elect only to utilize those services for a finalist or finalists. Regardless, each similarly situated finalist should be screened in the same fashion. Similarly, if background checks are handled in-house, it is acceptable only to perform the courthouse searches for those individuals that you have narrowed down to be potential new hires, acceptable as long as it is done consistently.

The degree of scrutiny for any particular category of jobs is determined by a number of factors, such as access to money or assets, the level of authority over others that the position carries, or access to the public or co-workers. Also, employers should take into account the difficulty faced in replacing the new hire if he or she does not work out, or the damage that could be done to the organization's productivity if an incompetent person is hired in that position.

Once an employer has determined how intensively the position should be researched, then all finalists for this job level should receive consistent treatment. There are laws working against you if you don't.

# Survey Shows Employment Screening on the Rise

A 2004 study released by the Society for Human Resources Management (SHRM), revealed a significant increase in the number of firms that conduct pre-employment screening. The "Workplace Violence Survey" is found at www.shrm.org

According to the study, 82% of the respondents in 2003 indicated they conduct some degree of screening of potential employees, up from 66% in 1996 survey. Reference checks (80%), past criminal checks (80%), and work history (79%) were the most widely used tools. The remaining tools were education records (55%), motor vehicle records (44%), credit checks (35%), and military discharge information (21%). The survey also broke down the use of screening tools by the size of firms. Large firms with 500 or more employees were more likely to check education than the small firms. Overall, the larger the firm, the more pre-employment tools were used.

The two screening tools that had the largest increase in usage were criminal records (80% in 2003 compared to 51% in 1996) and credit reports (35% in 2003 compared to 19% in 1996).

The statistics do bear out the experience of HR and security professionals — employment screening has risen dramatically since the events of 9/11/2001.

Each of these tools has its pros and cons. For example, credit reports should be approached with caution to ensure they are used fairly and do not invade privacy.

The findings are in line with a survey reported in the September, 2004 edition of *HR Executive* magazine. According to this survey of 322 HR professionals, there has been a 64% increase or enhancement of background screening requirements over the past three years. 34% reported no change while just 2% indicated they had decreased screening.

# Pros and Cons of— 1) Employers Performing the Background Screen, or 2) Outsourcing!

Every employer faces an important choice in their Safe Hiring Program — what services should be performed in-house and what services should be outsourced?

There are numerous tasks an employer could certainly perform in-house — verifying professional licenses or contacting past employers. In fact, as discussed in Chapter 9, there are advantages to employers doing the initial reference phone calls in-house because only the employer can determine if an applicant is an appropriate fit.

However, some employers find it more efficient to outsource certain screening tasks even if they have sufficient staffing to do it themselves. Most employers do not clean their own office windows or build their own office furniture just because they can. Deciding who will do screening tasks — in-house or outsource — comes down to economics and "focus on core competency."

There are six points to consider when deciding what part of the screening program an employer should perform in-house and what should be outsourced to a professional screening firm.

### 1. Is it a better use of time and energy to outsource?

Human resources and security departments realize there are only so many functions an in-house department can provide, and it makes sense to identify those tasks that can be efficiently outsourced to a third party. Many firms are finding it is an inefficient use of their time and energy to attempt to perform services that a third-party specialist can provide efficiently and cost-effectively. As a result, many firms have found that outsourcing their screening tasks to a professional pre-employment screening firms allows HR and security departments to devote more time and resources to the function of managing people and delivery of vital HR services to employees.

### 2. Does the employer have the required expertise to perform background screening in-house?

Sometimes it is not practical for an employer to attempt to perform many of the tasks involved in pre-employment screening because of the highly specialized knowledge and resources required. To do pre-screening in-house, an employer would have to learn how professional applicant screening is accomplished. The employer would have to learn the many complicated state and federal laws governing what information they can and cannot access. Furthermore, the employer would have to find cost-effective sources for the information such as criminal record checks.

**3. Is outsourcing more cost-effective than in-house processing?**

Consider the cost to devote staff time and resources to the physical management of the process, including computers and implementing a software solution to manage and track all applicants being screened including each applicant's current status. *A typical report from a screening firm should cost less than the first day's salary paid to the new employee.* This is called the "Less Than One Day's Pay Rule." Considering the cost of a bad hire, this is a very minimal investment. Of course, firms may do more in-depth screening for higher paying positions. However, even if the position is paid more, the "Less Than One Day's Pay Rule" usually holds true.

For larger employers, deep discounts from screening vendors are often available with volume. Even with such discounts, some employers look at the total spent on screening as a line item on the budget and are concerned with the total amount. However, even for large firms hiring thousands of employees, screening costs are still likely to be less than the cost of just one lawsuit.

Let us add up real in-house screening costs, including "soft-costs" and associated overhead costs. Take the employer who feels it is less costly to do educational verifications in-house than to pay a screening firm, but this logic fails to take into account all the associated costs including training, supervision, the infrastructure costs; the administrative cost of maintaining employees; the cost of other tasks not being done; and all of the other costs associated with *employees*. One reality is verification phone calls are typically not completed on the first attempt; chances are an employer makes four calls but only one will get through. Leave a message? Quite often those verification targets call back up to 48 hours later. During the day, the employer will be continually interrupted with return calls. In the end, the true cost of an in-house verification process is usually much higher than most employers' first estimates.

**4. Can the employer effectively manage the outsource process in terms of quality and performance levels?**

When using a software/internet-bases system, does the employer have appropriate and prioritized controls over the outsourced work? If an employer retains the services of a firm that utilizes an internet software tracking system, then employers have a high degree of control over timeliness and quality since these systems usually allow the employer to privately monitor in real-time the exact status of all reports. Will an employer have an in-house system with the same performance benefits? Perhaps, but it may be costly to set up.

**5. Are there legal advantages to outsourcing?**

The fifth consideration is legal compliance. By outsourcing screening tasks, employers enjoy the protection of the Fair Credit Reporting Act (FCRA). As explained in Chapter 6, this federal law governs the activities of screening companies and third party agencies. By following FCRA law, both employers and job applicants enjoy significant legal protection.

When an employer performs these services in-house, care must be taken to not unduly invade an applicant's privacy. Employers that do perform any screening in-house are well advised to conduct the program under the rules of the FCRA, which includes 1) a disclosure to the applicant that a screening is being conducted, 2) obtaining a written consent, and 3) giving an applicant an opportunity to correct any information before it is used as a basis not to hire.

There are additional special circumstances employers needs to be aware of. In states where there is a seven-year limitation on a background firm reporting criminal information, an employer who does their own criminal investigation is not subject to the limitation.

**6. Are there organizational advantages to outsourcing?**

As a matter of corporate culture, many organizations do not want new applicants to feel as though the other company employees are conducting an investigation into their background. By outsourcing the task to an independent third party, there is a greater sense of privacy. Job applicants understand that background screening is a necessary business practice, but many feel relieved if others in the same organization are not doing the investigation. In addition, why should an applicant's first contact with the HR Department be a background screening? That is a negative. Human resource managers have found there is a substantial advantage to advising applicants that a professional outside agency conducts the screening.

## The Advantages of a Management Fee Model

For organizations that do substantial hiring, there are advantages to using a **management fee model**. In this program, management retains a screening firm as a management consultant. For a fixed percentage fee, the screening firm helps set-up procedures, provides software, and negotiates prices with information provider sources. This gives the large enterprise employers the same economic advantages enjoyed by an outside screening firm. Instead of the employer paying the screening firm for data, the employer pays for information services at a wholesale level. Of course, the employer pays all overhead and labor when using its own employees and facilities. The big advantage for the employer is the total control over the process and the fact there is complete transparency in the pricing model. With a standard vendor relationship, the employer has no idea as to the mark-up of data or the profit level. The employer has no control over what profit margin the screening firm is taking or how much the screening firm is spending on qualified labor. Conversely, under the management fee model, the employer has direct control over all costs and is only paying for expertise.

When deciding if a management fee model is right for them, the employer should consider the following factors—

1. The employer's hiring volume is so large there is significant cost savings by setting up its own screening program.

2. Safe hiring is such an integral part of its business that having *internal control* is a crucial business need.

3. The firm operates in a number of states and jurisdictions, so a centralized office can contend with each jurisdiction, helping the firm to meet national screening and hiring standards.

# How to Choose A Background Screening Firm

Since there are scores of companies that offer similar employment prescreening services, some cautionary advice is in order with respect to choosing one screening firm from among competing companies. First, an employer should look for a professional partner and not just an information vendor selling data at the lowest price. Second, an employer should apply the same criteria that it would use in selecting any other provider of critical professional services. For example, if an employer were choosing a law firm for legal representation, the employer would clearly want to know it is selecting a law firm that is competent, experienced and knowledgeable, reputable and reasonably priced. Above all, an employer would want to know that it is dealing with a firm that possesses integrity. This same criteria should be used for selecting any provider of a professional services.

The following specific suggestions are offered for any organization that chooses to use a pre-employment screening firm.[1]

## Consider a Screener's Overall Expertise

A screening service must have the proven ability and knowledge to provide this professional service. A review of the company's website and materials as well as contacting the firm's current clients for a professional reference should be helpful in establishing the firm's qualifications.

> **Author Tip ➡** An employer should look to see if a firm has joined the National Association of Professional Background Screeners (NAPBS).[2] Membership in NAPBS demonstrates a commitment to professionalism and an industry-wide code of conduct. Employers should carefully consider if they want to utilize the services of a firm that has not joined their respective industry association.

Another aspect of a firm's expertise concerns representations made on the firm's website and literature. Here are some examples of "red flags."

- Does the firm discuss applicable federal and state law such as the Fair Credit Reporting Act and discrimination laws? If not, an employer should be very concerned with the issue of legal compliance.

- Does a firm express an understanding that a so-called "national criminal" database search is "only a secondary screening tool and cannot be relied upon generally as a primary source of information"? If not, that is a red flag!

- If a firm advertises a bankruptcy search as a tool for hiring, then an employer may be concerned since bankruptcy is generally impermissible for employment purposes.

---

[1] a sample Request for Proposal (RFP) is attached in Appendix 3 to assist employers in selecting a screening firm

[2] NAPBS members are listed at www.napbs.com

- If a firm offers to provide employers other records such as property ownership, or reveal the names of friends and associates, then the employer needs to question it that firm understands screening and employment law. Those two searches are not likely to be a valid predictor of job performance, and that can be discriminatory.

- Another danger signal occurs if a screening firm represents that a Social Security trace "verifies" a person's Social Security Number. Although a valuable tool, a Social Security *trace is not* an official government record.

A discussion of each of these "red flags" follows in later chapters, particularly at the end of Chapter 12.

## Legal Compliance Expertise

It is imperative that a screening service understand the laws surrounding pre-employment screening and hiring, and they make a commitment to provide an employer with only the information the employer may legally possess.

As mentioned previously, the Federal Fair Credit Reporting Act (FCRA) defines a background screening company as a Consumer Reporting Agency (CRA). There are four levels of inquiry an employer needs to make when it comes to analyzing a CRA's legal compliance abilities.

1. Does the CRA clearly understand which laws regulate what a CRA must do and cannot do? A CRA must have a deep understanding of the FCRA *and* applicable state laws that control everything from the forms needed and what is legal to report, to how to respond to a consumer inquiry or complaint. It is not enough that a CRA understands the federal law; does the CRA understand the laws in all fifty states?

2. Does the CRA have a commitment to keep its clients posted on all of the rules and regulatory changes of concern? As discussed throughout this book, there are numerous regulations affecting employers. For keeping up to date on legal matters, an employer should determine how much assistance to expect from their CRA.

3. Does the CRA have fifty state legal knowledge since state laws are as critical as federal law?

4. In order to protect the employer from having impermissible data, does the CRA make any effort to review specific reports or data before handing them over to the employer? Some CRA's will make the commitment to review all reports to make sure that clients only receive what they can legally possess. For example, in California there are numerous rules, regulations, and restrictions on the employer's use of criminal records. Some CRA's take the position that this is not their department and just forward whatever they find. The result is that employers can very quickly find themselves in legal hot water. Other CRA's make it part of their service to review all negative data and scrub out anything that is clearly not reportable per state regulations.[3]

---

[3] Although a screening firm is not giving legal advice, a firm can follow standard industry guidelines and practices in making these determinations. There are some CRA's that actually have their field researchers write the "hit reports" when a criminal record is located and forward the reports directly to an employer. The difficulty, of course. is that field

# Focus on Legal Compliance

Because of the mosaic of overlapping federal and state laws, employment screening is increasingly becoming a legal compliance industry. Not only are there specific laws intended to regulate the activities of screening firms but screening also intersects with the immense complexities of federal and state employment and discrimination laws. KPMG Corporate Finance LLC,[4] a leading provider of investment banking and strategic advisory services globally, closely follows the screening industry, and in an industry report released in Fall, 2003, KPMG observed—

> **"There is likely to be an increased focus on compliance and legal issues in background screening.** Compliance with the constantly evolving maze of state and federal regulations covering consumer information and background screening is challenging. Many employers and background screening companies are not focused on the issue, cannot afford the investment required to stay compliant, or choose not to make the investment as a calculated risk of doing business. We believe that the increased visibility of background screening and the sensitivity of the information involved are likely to lead to increased litigation and scrutiny of the process. The burden of compliance will continue to emerge as an important barrier to entry for the industry, and it is another factor that favors larger firms that can better leverage the required investment."[5]

## A Screening Firm's Personal Service, Consulting, Training

It is critical to keep in mind that pre-employment screening is much more than just providing raw data. The HR department should expect immediate assistance on any special situations that arise or if further applicant background investigation is required. A service provider should be able to work directly with the human resources department and conduct whatever training and orientation is necessary.

It is important to choose a firm that is familiar with any special needs of your industry. For example, the health care industry has special concerns and requirements — unique licensing standards and disciplinary actions — so a health provider should ensure that their screening firm is familiar with those needs.

---

researchers are seldom lawyers or HR professionals. Field researchers are court runners that come from all walks of life, but generally have no training in determining what is or is not reportable. An employer needs to know who actually fills out the hit reports, be it a knowledgeable background specialist that works for the CRA, or some anonymous file retriever. An employer must be clear on this when retaining the services of a data vendor or any firm that provides professional document retrieval or screening services.

[4] KPMG Corporate Finance LLC is online at www.kpmgcorporatefinance.com/us

[5] the full report is available at www.kpmgcorporatefinance.com/us/pdf/bkgd_screen.pdf

## Screening Firm Pricing

Although it is important to obtain competitive pricing, it is usually not advisable to choose the lowest cost provider. As the old saying goes, you get what you pay for.

# What Does Screening Cost?

Since there are many screening firms, some even advertising their pricing on the internet, there are a wide variety of pricing options available to employers. As a general rule, an employer should expect to pay no more than the new hire's first day salary. The reason this rule works is that the higher the position, the more screening an employer may do. A lower position in terms of salary would likely require less screening.

Some firms offer packages with bundled services, but many screening firms also sell services a la carte. Essentially, data is a commodity. Many employers base their cost comparisons on the price of a criminal record searched at the county level. Looking at internet advertisers, the average cost of a one-county criminal search is in the $18-22 range, although some firms advertise as low as $15 per county. Pricing also depends greatly on volume. Generally speaking, background screening is a low-margin, high-volume business. Larger employers would expect to receive substantially lower prices, and usually do.

Within a relatively narrow range, most firms have similar costs of data. The real price differential is the cost of labor and business efficiencies. Firms can offer low cost by utilizing cheap labor to process background reports. The disadvantage to an employer is that they are not dealing with knowledgeable people. Firms can lower costs by sheer economies of scales or technology. A low quote could also be the result of a firm trying to "buy" market share by undercutting market costs, or using screening services as a "loss leader" to sell other services.

Employers always need to make certain they are comparing "apples to apples." For example, if a bid for a criminal record check is extremely low, the employer needs to be certain they are getting a search for both felonies and misdemeanors, and not just a felony search. An employer also needs to confirm if criminal searches are being conducted at the courthouses, or if low-cost database-only searches are actually being used instead of the real thing — a courthouse search. Although databases are a valuable secondary tool, they are subject to limitations described in Chapter 12.

## Performance Criteria for Information Providers

Keep in mind that no screening firm can ever guarantee when information will be available. In fact, there are times when information is simply not available, even if the employer were to hire Sam Spade and money were no object.

Examples of situations where there can be delays beyond one's control are—

a. **Criminal records.** Records are generally returned in 72 hours. There can be a delay if there is a possible match and the researcher asks a court clerk to pull the file for verification. A screening firm has no control whatsoever when the court clerk will make the information available. In some counties, budgets and staffing can cause delays.

b. **Education.** The school can be closed during holidays or vacations. If an employer wants to verify a degree over Winter or Spring break, then short of breaking into the school or hacking their computer, there is no physical way for that search to be completed until school is back in session. More and more schools are making verification available via internet inquiry, particularly if you have a student's username and password.

c. **Past employment.** As noted in Chapter 9, there are a number of instances when the most conscientious background firm will not be able to obtain a timely employment verification. This can happen if an employer refuses to call back, or is out of business, or has moved or merged or has not retained employment records. If an employer refuses to call back despite repeated attempts, there is little that can be done short of sending a "bouncer-type" to physically sit in the employer's office until the past employer complies.

## Software and Internet Options

A service provider should also be able to provide reports and related services with an internet access option in addition to conventional media methods of fax, email, mail. One big advantage to internet software is the ability to track a report, seeing when the various screening components are completed.

# Beware of Whistles and Bells

How critical is technology in selecting a service provider? During the dot.com boom, some background firms touted all sorts of internet-based features as significant advantages for employers. Now, when selecting a background screening firm, technology is a given. The differentiators between screening companies today is the value added by knowledge and service. Although a firm may devise new features and tout them as unique, it is not difficult for other firms to eventually match those.

With the evolution of the hr-xml standard and ASP (Application Service Providers) software[6], even small local screening firms have access to technology that is every bit as good as the larger national players. Large firms may have more resources to provide customized solutions for employers at the enterprise level, however, this advantage is quickly dissipating as technology advances. Employers should question the screener's investment of time and energy in developing the knowledge, experience, and customer service needed to help employers navigate

[6] see Chapter 20 for an in-depth discussion of the hr-xml standard and applicant tracking systems

the various ins and outs of safe hiring. Screening firms must react quickly to assist employers in responding to a criminal "hit" or to applicants who claims their report is wrong.

For screening firms that focus on the "enterprise" or Fortune 500 level, their investment in technology gives them a distinct advantage when it comes to a seamless interface with a current HR system. In addition, some of the larger screening firms can provide interfaces to related services such as drug testing or various pre-employment assessment tools. Such integration will be commonplace in the near future among all sizes of background screening firms. If every screening firm has similar technology, then the issues for employers once again become service and knowledge.

For most employers, screening and safe hiring is ultimately a professional service and not just a commodity where screening firms merely compete to sell data cheaper. Although one may predict a few large national screening firms will emerge in the future, a substantial number of regional screening firms will likely thrive. The regional firms can provide greater levels of customer service, support and knowledge that large enterprise-level screening firms are traditionally not able to deliver.

## Safeguarding Privacy

Although the information in a background report is not secret, the reports by their nature are sensitive and confidential. By law, the reports must be restricted to those individuals who are directly involved in the hiring process. To preserve confidentiality, a screening firm should have policies and procedures in place to ensure confidentiality — and should work with an employer to assist in keeping these matters private.

Here are suggested practical guidelines to maximize confidentiality—

1. Look for a privacy and security policy on the screening firm's website or in their literature.

2. Ask about how information is gathered. For example, if a firm uses home operators, that is a potential red flag. Unsupervised home operators create quality control issues, as will as privacy concerns. Employers may want to think carefully before utilizing a service that sends an applicant's personal data such as a Social Security Number or data of birth, to home workers in an unsupervised environment.

3. If a report is to be faxed, the screening firm must clearly determine if the fax machine is a private or secured machine. If not, the screening company needs to have a "call before fax" policy so only the intended recipient will receive the report.

4. The front page of a printed version of a screening report should not contain any confidential information, and should clearly establish that the report is a confidential matter only.

5. A screening company should advise an employer to set up the following procedure to safeguard privacy. These can include—

   a. All reports go directly to the designated HR or security manager that is in charge of the program and will remain only in that person's possession.

   b. If a report raises issues that need to be discussed with others in the company, the person in charge of the background program should maintain physical custody of the actual report, unless there are more appropriate measures aimed at maintaining confidentiality. Background reports should not be sent through the office mail, or left lying on a supervisor's desk.

6. Reports should be maintained securely and separately from an employee's personnel file. After someone is hired, there is no reason why a supervisor or anyone else should have access to the report. For example, an employer would not want a supervisor reviewing a confidential report that might bias an individual's routine performance appraisal.

7. If the report is transmitted through an internet or Intranet system or by email, then the employer should ask for assurance from a background firm that they are following appropriate security procedures for maintaining confidentiality.

    a. Does the firm have appropriate firewalls and internet security in place, with reports being sent in a secured and encrypted manner?

    b. Are there adequate password protection and policies in place to allow only the appropriate individuals to order and view reports?

8. Adapt other appropriate measures to ensure that only authorized individuals will receive information — periodically change passwords, or audit who has access to the company Intranet system.

9. Firms with advanced technology are able to provide employers with a completely paperless system, so screening reports need not be printed. That saves the employer from having to download or print reports. That lessens the possibility of paper reports being viewed by individuals who do not have a permissible purpose. Some screening firms are able to retain reports for employers indefinitely.

## Internal Controls

A screening company should also be evaluated on their internal controls over their information providers and sources. For example, if a screening firm utilizes courthouse researchers to obtain court records, how does the screening company select such researchers, and how do they audit the process? An employer may also want to be made familiar with processes used by the screening company for each type of service performed

## References

As with any provider of a professional service, an employer want to check the provider's references. Just as a screening company should advise an employer to carefully screen each applicant before he or she is hired, an employer should exercise the same due diligence when retaining a screening company.

# Private Investigator or Screening Company?

As mentioned earlier in this chapter, screening and investigation are two separate endeavors. A number of states have statutes to license private investigators. Whether screening firms also need to have a PI license is unclear in many states. State statutes that regulate private investigators normally exempt those other entities that regularly examine public records, otherwise anyone who utilized public records — from real estate agents to genealogists — would be in violation of state PI laws. Some confusion has been caused by the fact that the FCRA labels certain screening activity as an "Investigative Consumer Report." This applies when a Consumer Reporting Agency calls a past employer and asks about past job performance. Because the word "Investigative" is used, the argument has been made that when a screening firm does an "investigative consumer report," a PI license is necessary. On the other hand, many professional investigators do not consider making routines phone calls from a call-center environment to past employers an investigation, and many pre-employment screening firms do not possess PI licenses because they do not consider their work to be investigative.

The best advice is— an employer should determine if, in their state, a private investigator license is required for employment screening firms.

For more information on pre-employment background checks, see the following resources:

- The National Association of Professional Background Screeners website; www.napbs.com
- The LPA Background Check Protocol by the Labor Policy Association (2003)
- The ASIS Pre-employment Background Screening Guidelines -2006; www.asisonline.org/guidelines/guidelinespreemploy.pdf

## No One Definition of a Background Check

The term "background check" has become a common phrase in today's business vocabulary. There are numerous news stories about the need for background checks or efforts made by various organizations, such as churches, charities, or businesses to obtain "background checks." However, there is one significant problem: There is simply no one definition as to what constitutes a background check.

A "background check" can vary from a one county criminal check, all the way to an in-depth FBI-type investigation that costs thousands of dollars. Employers and consumers can be misled into making certain assumptions about a person because they have been the subject of a "background check." The biggest assumption— that the person must be safe or qualified because they passed a "background check."

Unfortunately, nothing may be further from the truth. Employers, consumers and online daters should not be lulled into a **false sense of security** just because some site has performed a "background check," unless you know exactly what was checked, how it was checked and when.

For additional information on this issue, see www.ESRcheck.com/safehiringupdates.php

# Chapter 11

# The Role and Legal Use of Criminal Records in Safe Hiring

> It is a statistical certainty that unless an employer checks for criminal records, the employer will eventually hire someone with an unsuitable criminal record.

## Why Criminal Records Are Important Indicators

An essential element of a Safe Hiring Program is performing a criminal record check. An unsuitable criminal record may be evidence of past behavior that may be inappropriate for a particular job. Consider these true stories taken from the files of background screening companies—

**True Story 1:** An applicant for a manufacturing job looks good in the interview, and the hiring manager is prepared to make an offer. The Human Resources Department sends the background package to a screening service for a standard background check. The background check indicates the applicant has over ten criminal convictions. The convictions range from assaulting police officers, to selling drugs, to possessing weapons, to assault on girlfriends. Except for a background check that person would have been a member of that company's workforce. What a nightmare.

**True Story 2:** A healthcare facility makes a job offer to a health worker. The job includes access to drugs. A standard criminal check on the worker discloses two serious drug-related convictions. That person came within an inch of having a key to the drug locker.

**True Story 3:** A driver for an airport pick-up service takes a female passenger to a remote location and sexually assaults her. Later it is discovered the driver had recently been released from prison for a sex crime. The company claims it had done everything it could to perform a background check. In order to test that claim, a screening firm does a background check based upon the limited information in the newspaper. Within six hours, the screening company has the full story on the driver's background. For a very small amount of money – the cost of a background check – disaster would have been avoided.

These examples show why employers need the protection of a pre-employment background check that includes a criminal record check. Newspapers and law books are full of cases of employers sued for negligent hiring because a criminal record check was not performed. Failure to do even most rudimentary background checks has lead to innocent people being the victims of crimes in their home or workplace, including murder, robbery, theft, child molestation, sexual assaults, and more.

In addition, an employer has a continuing responsibility after a person is hired even if there is not a criminal record. An employer should have policies and procedures to govern post-hire workplace situations. Timely and attentive management of potential problem situations along with appropriate follow-through and documentation are the keys to avoiding legal claims of negligent retention and negligent supervision.

## Criminal Records and Repeat Offenders

In employment law, the fundamental basis of negligent hiring lawsuits is the assumption that a person with proven dangerous propensities in the past may well exhibit those in the future.

Statistics seem to bear that out. The 2002 Federal Department of Justice on recidivism suggests recidivism within three years of release from a prison is as high as 67 percent.[1] The data is from the largest recidivism study ever conducted in the United States, tracking prisoners discharged in fifteen states, representing two-thirds of all state prisoners released in 1994.

The study found that—

- Most former convicts were re-arrested shortly after getting out of prison — 30 percent within six months, 44 percent within a year, 59 percent within two years, and 67 percent by the end of three years.

- Post-prison recidivism was strongly related to arrest history. Among prisoners with one arrest prior to their release, 41 percent were re-arrested. Of those with two prior arrests, 47 percent were re-arrested. Of those with three earlier arrests, 55 percent were re-arrested. Among those with more than 15 prior arrests (about 18 percent of all released prisoners), 82 percent were re-arrested within the three-year period.

- The 272,111 inmates had accumulated more than 4.1 million arrest charges prior to their current imprisonment and acquired an additional 744,000 arrest charges in the 3 years following their discharge in 1994 – an average of about 18 criminal arrest charges per offender during their criminal careers. These charges included almost 21,000 homicides, 200,000 robberies, 50,000 rapes and sexual assaults, and almost 300,000 other assaults.

Screening industry statistics also strongly suggest that without doing a screen for criminal records, there is a **statistical certainty** that an employer will hire a person with a criminal record that is inconsistent with safe hiring. Screening firms report a criminal "hit rate" up to ten percent. Keep in mind this hit ratio represents applicants who signed a background screening form telling them that background checks would be conducted.

---

[1] see www.ojp.usdoj.gov/bjs/pub/press/rpr94pr.htm

Of course, all statistics need to be examined carefully. The "hit" statistic may include lesser offenses that are not disqualifying, or offenses that the applicant may have revealed. However, a ten percent hit rate is still an astounding number.

The "hit rate" statistic is not that surprising in view of government studies concerning the rate of criminal convictions and incarceration in America. According to a Justice Department Bureau of Justice Statistics report issued in August, 2003, about one in every 37 U.S. adults was either imprisoned at the end of 2001 or had been incarcerated at one time. The government reported that 5.6 million people had "prison experience" that represented about 2.7 percent of the adult population of 210 million as of December 31, 2001. The study looked at people who served a sentence in state or federal prison. The study did not include those who served time in local county jails for misdemeanor violations or felony offenses where they received probation and a county-time jail sentence.

The full study is available at www.ojp.usdoj.gov/bjs/pub/press/piusp01pr.htm. Also, numerous criminal justice statistics are available at www.ojp.usdoj.gov/bjs.

Based upon the numbers, it is no wonder that employers face increased exposure from negligent hiring. However, there is also research to suggest that the longer an offender is able to stay out of jail, the less likely they are to re-offend, and after three years, the risk may fall off rapidly. Issues concerning the use of criminal records as a valid predictor of future criminal behavior as well as concerns over giving ex-offenders an opportunity to re-enter society are reviewed in a report to the American Bar Association in 2007. See:

http://meetings.abanet.org/webupload/commupload/CR209800/newsletterpubs/SealRescleanRC6507alfsasFINAL.pdf

## Courts and the Relevancy of Repeat Offenders

If a person is charged with driving under the influence of alcohol, and the person has been convicted in the past of the same offense, chances are the jury will never be told about the first conviction. Why is that information kept from the jury? Is it because evidence of prior bad conduct is not relevant?

Actually, prior criminal behavior is often kept from juries because experience demonstrates it is **too relevant**. Courts all across the U.S. have recognized the basic principle that evidence of a prior criminal conviction is so powerful that it overwhelms the jury's decision-making process — that human beings jump to the conclusion the accused did it again regardless of the evidence of the actual crime in the new case. Courts recognize part of the human make-up is to assume what a person has done in the past is what they will do in the future. For that reason, in criminal cases, evidence of past misconduct is admitted under very limited circumstances, for instance, when the past arrest is specifically relevant to some disputed fact in the case. However, a prosecutor may not introduce evidence of prior criminal behavior just to show the defendant is a "bad" person; if he did it before, then he did it again.[2]

---

[2] There are reasons why a prosecutor can argue that evidence of a past crime is admissible. However, because the evidence is considered so prejudicial against a defendant, there must be a justification to introduce the past bad acts. The probative value must exceed the prejudicial impact. Reasons to introduce the evidence of past crimes can include: (1) The past crime proves some element of the new case, such as a unique method of committing a crime that it provides proof of identity, motive, or means;  (2) The defendant testifies and the past act is used to impeach the

# Mandatory Criminal Record Checks

In some regulated industries, state or federal law mandates criminal record checks. It is not a matter of criminal propensities or statistics — it is the law.

All states have regulations requiring criminal background checks for jobs that involve contact with populations who are vulnerable or at risk. This may include teachers, childcare workers, health care professionals, workers who care for the elderly or populations at risk. Another example is a professional licensing board. Per state law, these boards are state agencies that oversee the certification of certain professions. Those employees subject to such regulations are normally aware of it through licensing procedures or industry contacts. Typical professions that require a criminal record background check include private investigators, security guards, security brokers, insurance agents, bail bondsmen, jockeys, casino workers, and so forth.

Mandatory criminal record checks are typically done with a fingerprint check of state and federal criminal records. Usually the checks are arranged for the employer directly through the specific state licensing agency rather than using the services of a professional background screening company.

There are also federal rules for certain industries. For example, the Federal Aviation Administration (FAA) has rules for mandatory background checks for workers employed by airport operators as well as employees having unescorted access to restricted areas. Similarly, the banking industry has certain mandatory background checks.

Given the news stories surrounding negligent hiring or child abductions and child abuse in volunteer and community organizations, new laws are proposed in nearly every state every year. These laws seek to expand the number of occupations that are subject to mandatory checks. For example, in Pennsylvania, in response to the horrific murder of a guest by a hotel worker with a criminal record, efforts are under way to require hotels to conduct background checks on all employees.[3] The clear trend is towards the government getting into the background checking business by making criminal record checks mandatory.

## Post 9/11 and Homeland Security concerns

There has also been a new impetus behind mandatory screening as a result of the Homeland Security efforts. These are touched upon in Chapter 22.

---

defendant's credibility or to contradict the claim of defendant while testifying; (3) The defense presents evidence of good character, and the past acts are used to impact the character witness under cross-examination; (4) The past crime is an element of the new crime, such as a charge of a felon in possession of a gun, so that the past felony is part of the new offense; (5) The past crime is considered by the jury as part of the penalty such as in a death penalty case.
[3] see www.nanslaw.org

# EEOC and Use of "Arrest Only Records"

A critical point is the **difference between an arrest and a conviction**. An arrest is the process by which a criminal case is initiated by means of a police officer taking some action to initiate criminal charges. It can be a physical arrest, where the person is taken into custody, or some alternative form of custody such as a citation or order to appear in court. However, if NO CONVICTION occurs as a result of the arrest, then in terms of pre-employment screening, this action or record is considered to be an "arrest only."

If there are limitations for convictions, then it stands to reason there would be even more stringent limitations when it comes to an arrest. Why? Because an arrest itself is only a police officer's opinion. An arrest only does not prove underlying conduct, and only underlying conduct may be considered.

There are many reasons an arrest may not turn into a conviction, including—

1.  A prosecuting attorney may determine there is insufficient evidence to file the charges, and a criminal charge is never filed in the courthouse.

2.  In some jurisdictions, arrestees for certain offenses are taken before a magistrate for a probable cause determination or a grand jury. At that point in the system, charges may not be filed or are dropped.

3.  In some instances, even after the charges are filed, a District Attorney may end up dropping the charges for any number of reasons, such as insufficiency of the evidence or inability to obtain witnesses.

4.  In some cases, the criminal charges may be dismissed by a court based upon motions brought by the defendant, alleging such things as illegal search and seizure or some other deficiency.

5.  Finally, a person could be found not guilty as a result of a court trial or jury trial, meaning the underlying facts of the arrest were insufficient for a determination of guilt.

In each of the first four instances, the end result was never a judicial determination on the guilt or innocence to the person arrested. Therefore, the arrest itself is only an opinion of the police officer and not facts of any conduct or behaviors. As the United States Supreme Court has ruled, "the mere fact that a (person) has been arrested has very little, if any, probative value in showing that he has engaged in misconduct." *Schware vs. Board of Bar Examiners*, 353 US 232, 241 (1957)

What about a **Pending Case?** A criminal case can also be in the gray area between an arrest and a conviction. This occurs in a case where an arrest has been made, a court case has been filed and a public record as been created, but the case is still in court pending a resolution. There has been no factual determination of the truth of the charges, nor have they been dismissed. Since a case has been filed, a search of courthouse records *may* uncover the pending case. In one state, California, an employer is specifically not prohibited from asking an applicant about an arrest for which the employee or applicant is out on bail or on his or her own recognizance pending trial.[4] In addition, since showing up for work

---

[4] see California Labor code section 432.7

is normally an essential function of any job, a pending court case may have relevance since an applicant may miss work to go to court and if convicted, may not be able to come to work. There are other criminal dispositions as well that can fall into a gray area such as a deferred adjudications or diversion programs. It is up to the rule of each state as to whether such matters can be considered.[5]

## EEOC Rules on Arrest Records

Under the Federal Equal Employment Opportunities Commission rules, when making employment decisions, there are strict limitations on using the fact an applicant has been arrested. In addition, many states have similar limitations. We already reviewed the fact the EEOC requires a business justification before using a *conviction* as the basis of an employment decision.

# Read It Yourself— What is the EEOC Position on Arrests?

Excerpts from EEOC Notice N-915-061 (9/1990) deals specifically with the use of arrest records in employment.[6]

The question addressed in this policy guidance is "…to what extent may **arrest records** be used in making employment decisions?" The Commission concludes that since the use of arrest records as an absolute bar to employment has a disparate impact on some protected groups, such *records alone cannot be used to routinely exclude persons from employment.* However, conduct which indicates unsuitability for a particular position is a basis for exclusion. Where it appears that the applicant or employee engaged in the conduct for which he was arrested and the conduct is job-related and relatively recent, exclusion is justified.

> "…**Conviction records** constitute reliable evidence that a person engaged in the conduct alleged since the criminal justice system requires the highest degree of proof ("beyond a reasonable doubt") for a conviction. In contrast, arrests alone are not reliable evidence that a person has actually committed a crime." Schware v. Board of Bar Examiners, 353 U.S. 232, 241 (1957) ("[t]he mere fact that a [person] has been arrested has very little, if any, probative value in showing that he has engaged in misconduct.")

Thus, the Commission concludes that to justify the use of arrest records, an additional inquiry must be made. Even where the conduct alleged in the arrest record is related to the job at issue, the employer must evaluate whether the arrest record reflects the applicant's conduct. It should, therefore, examine the surrounding circumstances, offer the applicant or employee an opportunity to explain, and, if he or she denies engaging in the conduct, make the follow-up inquiries necessary to evaluate his/her credibility. Since using arrests as a disqualifying criteria can only be justified where it appears that the applicant actually engaged in the conduct for which he/she was arrested and that conduct is job related, the commission further concludes that

---

[5] see chapter 26 for a discussion of criminal disposition other then a conviction that can be subject to special state rules
[6] the full EEOC notice is reprinted in the Appendix 2

an employer will seldom be able to justify making broad general inquiries about an employee's or applicant's arrests."

"... As with conviction records, arrest records may be considered in the employment decision as evidence of conduct that may render an applicant unsuitable for a particular position. However, in the case of arrests, not only must the employer consider the relationship of the charges to the position sought, but also the likelihood that the applicant actually committed the conduct alleged in the charges."

"...Where the position sought is security sensitive, particularly where it involves enforcing the law or preventing crime, courts tend to closely scrutinize evidence of prior criminal conduct of applicants."

"...Even where the employment at issue is not a law enforcement position or one which gives the employee easy access to the possessions of others, close scrutiny of an applicant's character and prior conduct is appropriate where an employer is responsible for the safety and/or well being of other persons. (Citations omitted.) In these instances, the facts would have to be examined closely in order to determine the probability that an applicant would pose a threat to the safety and well being of others."

"...An arrest record does no more than raise a suspicion that an applicant may have engaged in a particular type of conduct. Thus, the investigator must determine whether the applicant is likely to have committed the conduct alleged. This is the most difficult step because it requires the employer either to accept the employee's denial or to attempt to obtain additional information and evaluate his/her credibility. An employer need not conduct an informal "trial" or an extensive investigation to determine an applicant's or employee's guilt or innocence. However, the employer may not perfunctorily allow the person an opportunity to explain and ignore the explanation where the person's claims could easily be verified by a phone call, i.e., to a previous employer or a police department. The employer is required to allow the person a meaningful opportunity to explain the circumstances of the arrest(s) and to make a reasonable effort to determine whether the explanation is credible before eliminating him/her from employment opportunities."

## The EEOC Obligates Employers to Determine the Facts of Arrests

For employers, the following considerations are important—

- An employer must look beyond the arrest and determine what actually happened.
- After determining what actually happened, the employer must then determine whether the conduct is relevant to an employment decision.

If an employer locates an arrest, then it can be very difficult to determine the underlying conduct. It may well require phone calls to the local police or prosecutor, and they may not be willing to cooperate. Under the EEOC rules, the inquiry does not require an "informal 'trial' or extensive investigation," but more must be done than to simply ask the applicant to give his or her side and then ignore it without some reasonable effort to determine if there was a credible explanation. As a practical matter, many employers find that it is just not practical to try to consider the underlying facts. What if the applicant went to trial and was found not guilty?

Because of the difficulties, the EEOC concluded—

> *Since using arrests as a disqualifying criteria can only be justified where it appears that the applicant actually engaged in the conduct for which he/she was arrested and that conduct is job-related, the commission further concludes that an employer will seldom be able to justify making broad general inquiries about an employee's or applicant's arrests.*

Even if the employer is able to establish the underlying conduct, the employer must then go through an analysis to determine if there is a business justification to deny the employment similar to the analysis used for a conviction. However, the EEOC notes that where the position involves security, or "…which gives the employee easy access to the possessions of others, close scrutiny of an applicant's character and prior conduct is appropriate where an employer is responsible for the safety and/or well being of other persons."

As a practical matter, employers need to think long and hard before using information from an arrest in the view of clear EEOC rules.

## FCRA Considerations When Obtaining Underlying Facts About an Arrest

If a third party is used, employers need to make sure that the criminal information is used in accordance with the Federal Fair Credit Reporting Act. *What if an employer obtains the information themselves without the use of outside third parties?* This procedure can trigger the FCRA even if an employer does not intend to. The FCRA considerations, as well as state laws similar to the FCRA, are discussed in detail in Chapter 6.

## Time Limits on Use of Criminal Records and Arrest Records

The age of the conviction or an arrest can be a critical issue. Under the FCRA, as amended effective November 1998, there is no limit on how far back a background screening firm can go in obtaining criminal records. Prior to that amendment, there was a seven-year limitation unless a new hire is expected to have income over $75,000 a year. There are a number of states that still have a seven year limit; see 'Special State Rules About Using Records' later in this chapter. State law also may limit employers who do the research themselves. Keep in mind there is still a FCRA seven-year limitation on arrest only records.

Even the EEOC has some bearing on time limits. If employers go back further than seven years, recall the EEOC position that the older the conviction or arrest, the less relevant it may be.

# Importance of When a Criminal Record is Discovered

As has been shown, federal and state laws associated with obtaining and using a criminal record are not only overwhelming, but also very confusing. What is legal in one state to utilize for employment purposes may not be legal in another state. Employers and professional screening companies must pay strict heed to the Federal Fair Credit Reporting Act (FCRA) and the requirements of the Equal Employment Opportunity Commission (EEOC). Certain portions of these laws can apply depending on "when" the record was discovered.

An employer may uncover a criminal record at one of three different stages of the hiring or employment cycle. In each stage there are a number of considerations to what an employer legally can or should do in response to this information. Each stage invokes a different set of compliance rules.

1. **When an applicant accurately self-reveals a criminal record.**

   This may occur if an applicant accurately self-reports a criminal matter in the application, resume, or during an interview.

2. **When an applicant is not truthful about the past criminal record, either by denying it or by reporting it inaccurately.**

   This discovery may occur in a variety of ways. During the hiring process an employer may discover the criminal record through a past employer reference check or from the background report. A past criminal record may also come to the employer's attention after the applicant has been hired. For example, a worker may tell a co-worker about his or her criminal past and the conversation is reported to management, or an applicant may misrepresent a criminal record such as disclosing a petty theft that was in fact a robbery.

3. **When an employee commits an offense after being hired.**

   How the employer discovers a new criminal matter can occur in a variety of ways. Perhaps an employer may first hear about an arrest or conviction from the news media, or as a result of investigating absenteeism, or even after being contacted by the local probation office to arrange for an employee's participation in some sort of jail-release program.

# 1) Legal Compliance When the Applicant Accurately Self-Reveals a Criminal Record

When the applicant accurately tells an employer about a criminal record, and there is no element of dishonesty, then the issue arises as to what an employer can legally do and should do.

Following are the crucial considerations.

## Discrimination and the No Automatic Disqualification Rule

This is a critical rule when it comes to the use of criminal records— you cannot deny employment *automatically*. An employer needs a business justification not to hire based upon a criminal past. The United States Supreme Court ruled in *Griggs v. Duke Powe*r, 401 U.S. 424 (1971) that a plaintiff can allege employment discrimination without a proving a discriminatory intent.

As a result of *Griggs* and ensuing cases, the Equal Employment Opportunity Commission (EEOC) has made it clear the automatic use of a criminal record without showing a business necessity can have discriminatory impact by disqualifying a disproportionate number of members of minority groups.[7] The key term is of course business necessity.[8]

Here is the EEOC's position when it comes to the use of criminal records—

> *"(a)n employer's policy or practice of excluding from employment on the basis of their conviction records has an adverse impact on Blacks and Hispanics in light of statistics showing that they are convicted at a rate disproportionately greater than their representation in the population. Consequently, the Commission has held and continues to hold that such a policy or practice is unlawful under Title VII (*the Equal Employment Opportunity law*) in the absence of a justifying business necessity."* [9]

The key term is of course *business necessity*. The EEOC defines *business necessity* in its 2/4/87 Notice–

> *"The (employer) must show that it considered these three factors to determine whether its decision was justified by business necessity:*
> - *The nature and gravity of the offense or offenses,*
> - *The time that has passed since the conviction and/or completion of the sentence, and,*
> - *The nature of the job held or sought."* [10]

What does this mean in plain English? An employer cannot simply say, "No one with a criminal record need apply." That statistically could end up having an unfair impact on certain groups. Instead, if an applicant has a criminal record, the employer must determine if there is a rational, job-related reason why that person is unfit for that job. In other words, an employer must show that the consideration of the applicant's criminal record is job-related and consistent with business necessity.

---

[7] see Chapter 5 for a general discussion on the impact of the EEOC and the use of screening tools

[8] Important court cases on the subject were summarized recently in El v. Southeastern Pennsylvania Transportation Authority, 479 F.3d 232 (3d. Cir. 2007)

[9] see EEOC Notice N-915 (2/4/87) attached in Appendix 2

[10] Long time employers, HR, and security professionals involved in employment decisions may recall a different set of rules. The EEOC changed the earlier rule in the 2/4/87 notice. Prior to that, business necessity was established by a two-step process. The first step involved showing the conviction was job-related. If it was job-related, then the employer had to demonstrate that the applicant could not safely and efficiently perform the job based upon: (1) number of offenses and the circumstances of each offense; (2) length of time between the offense and the employment decision; (3) applicant's employment history; and (4) efforts at rehabilitation. The revised 2/4/87 standard eliminated the need to consider an individual's employment history or efforts at rehabilitation, however, as a practical matter, an employer may wish to consider these points if they intend to hire a person with a criminal record.

How do you apply this test? Each element of the test has a different meaning.

1. **The nature and gravity of the offense or offenses.**

   a. **The nature of the offense** generally means the characteristics that underlie that type of offense. For example, a theft offense has character traits of dishonesty. Robbery, which involves theft as well as an element of threatened violence or actual violence, has the character traits of both theft and violence. These are both offenses of moral turpitude, which are acts or behavior that gravely violate the accepted standard of the community.

   b. **The gravity of the offense** generally refers to the seriousness of a crime, or the degree of harm it causes. For example, a crime that involved great bodily injury or risk of death is likely very grave, as are most sexual offenses. On the other hand, a one-time driving under the influence charge, where the applicant has no prior offenses and in fact did not hurt anyone, may not be as grave.

2. **The time passed since the conviction and/or completion of the sentence.**
   Age of the offense is another way of saying as an event recedes in time, it becomes less important. In addition, an employer may wish to consider what a person has done since the criminal conviction.

3. **The nature of the job held or sought.**
   This refers to the characteristics needed to safely and efficiently perform that job, such as a person working with children or the aged, or going into the homes of a vulnerable population certainly requires someone who is honest and law-abiding. The same considerations apply for positions that involve handling money. On the other hand, for a worker on an assembly line who is supervised, a past theft conviction may certainly not be as relevant.

Let us take these criteria and apply them to different facts in order to illustrate how an employer may analyze a disclosed criminal record in the hiring process. This following example is meant to show how the criteria may apply only—

Assume a person had a robbery conviction four years ago. He is applying to work in the warehouse of a furniture store where the duties include furniture delivery to customers. Under these facts, an employer could find a business necessity not to hire. The nature of a robbery is that it is a violent crime showing theft, dishonesty, and violence. In addition, any offense involving use of a weapon can be considered very grave. When analyzing an event that occurred just four years ago, an employer might be concerned that the behavior was too recent, and there have not been any intervening events to show the applicant does not still possess the character traits showing a propensity to re-offend. In addition, any position that involves sending someone into a home requires extra sensitivity.

However, assume the crime occurred ten years ago, and in the intervening years the person has successfully held jobs and has good recommendations. Also, assume the job involves working on a supervised roofing crew. Under those facts, an employer may come to a different conclusion.

Because there are so many different possible crimes covered by the criminal codes of the fifty states as well as federal law, it is impossible to create an exact table that outlines for employers what particular crime is disqualifying and what crime is not. There would also be EEOC and state discrimination law considerations, even if such a table were possible. See the section to follow regarding "Written Employer Policies on Criminal Records."

In fact, even if there were an overall table of crimes, it still would not tell employers in all instances what crimes are disqualifying because each particular event and person is unique. For example, a one time battery during the course of an argument with a neighbor by someone with no criminal record and an excellent work history may well be treated differently than a battery by a person with a history of violent criminal acts and a very poor work history. The very point is to give an applicant individualized consideration

Instead, have a policy that says, as an employer, you maintain a safe work place and will conduct a strict review of any applicant with a criminal record, without automatic disqualification. If you decide to hire someone with a criminal record, then document the reasons for your decision. This documentation will be important in case a third party later sues you for injury caused by this applicant, or in case a future applicant with a similar record is not hired and sues.

## Be Aware of State Discrimination Laws

The states listed below have discrimination restrictions on the use of criminal records, including convictions and arrests law similar to the EEOC rules. Some states impose rules that are more stringent than the EEOC. Even in states without a separate set of rules in this area, the federal rules would apply. Employers in the states listed below[11] should check with their employment lawyer. Employers in states NOT listed should probably check as well in order to ensure there are no restrictions.

> Alaska, Arizona, California, Colorado, Connecticut, Delaware, District of Columbia, Florida, Georgia, Hawaii, Idaho, Illinois, Iowa, Kansas, Louisiana, Maine, Maryland, Massachusetts, Michigan, Minnesota, Missouri, Nebraska, Nevada, New Hampshire, New Jersey, New York, North Dakota, Ohio, Oklahoma, Oregon, Pennsylvania, Rhode Island, South Dakota, Texas, Utah, Vermont, Virginia, Washington, West Virginia, Wisconsin.

As an example of how complex discrimination issues can be, there is a study released November, 2006 that suggests that criminal background checks actually result in more minority hires. The gist of the study is that once employers confirm there is no criminal record, this can overcome certain assumptions employers may otherwise make. For more details, see: www.ESRcheck.com/safehiringupdates.php.

# 2) Legal Compliance When the Applicant Lied and Did Not Reveal a Criminal Record

If a background check locates criminal matters that an applicant misrepresented, then the dishonesty can be the grounds to deny employment. Employment applications should ask about criminal records in broad, clear language, and inform applicants that *dishonesty is a basis to deny employment.*

Here is a common scenario to watch out for. An employer uses an application form that only asks about *felonies.*[12] The applicant's background report comes back and reveals convictions on serious

---

[11] the list of states is provided for educational purposes only, and no representation is made that this list is accurate or current.

[12] see Chapter 7 for three common mistakes employers make regarding the criminal question on an application form

misdemeanors. The employer's first reaction is to deny employment because the person lied. The applicant did not lie — the question was answered truthfully. As a result the employer must make a decision based upon the three-part EEOC test discussed earlier — are the crimes job-related?

If the question on the application was worded properly and the employer caught the applicant in a lie, then it is the LIE that forms the basis for the termination of the hiring process. *Dishonesty is always a basis not to hire.*

# 3) Arrests and Convictions That Occur After Employment

An employer should review their employee manual on the subject of arrests. In Chapter 4, suggested language was offered on employment screening and safe hiring. The language below covers employees who are on the job and are arrested for a criminal act AFTER being hired.

> *In addition, in order to ensure a safe and profitable workplace, all employees are required to report to their supervisor if they are arrested, charged or convicted for any criminal offense, with the exception of minor traffic offenses unless the employee is in driving position.[13]*

> *If an employee is arrested, charged, or convicted for any offense, then the employee must report the matter to their direct supervisor and submit a police report or other documentation concerning the arrest and/or charges. The report must occur within two business days of the arrest.*

> *The employer will review the underlying facts of the matter. The employer will not take any adverse action based only upon the fact of an arrest. Any action will be based upon the underlying facts of the arrest. Any action will be considered on a case-by-case basis taking into account the underlying facts and the totality of all the circumstances. At the employer's discretion actions may range from no action, to leave with or without pay, to termination.*

> *Noncompliance with the above stated requirement constitutes grounds for termination. Furthermore, misrepresentation of the circumstances of the events can serve as grounds for termination. Employees that are unavailable to report for work due to incarceration are subject to suspension or termination in accordance with the terms of the employee manual.*

Before implementing this policy, employers should contact their legal counsel concerning the laws in their state. It is important to note that the employer should not take action due to the mere fact of the arrest. That could violate the EEOC policy. The employer needs to base any decision on the underlying facts of the arrest or on the conviction. If, as a result of an arrest, a person is incarcerated, the inability to come to work may give grounds for an employer to terminate employment.

---

[13] driving position is any position where the employee drives on company time or for the benefit of the company

# Special State Rules For Using Records

Many states have their own procedural rules on the proper use of criminal records that employers and screeners must follow when obtaining background reports. These rules are aimed generally at not shutting out ex-offenders from job opportunities and allowing for an opportunity at rehabilitation by not being draconically saddled with a criminal record. Many states have limits on what information an employer can use or whether an employer can utilize an arrest not resulting in a conviction.

Brief summaries of some of the state rules is listed below. The listing is for general information only. These materials contain generalizations and do not constitute legal advice. Specific factual situations should be discussed with your legal counsel. Laws can also change. In addition, there is another set of separate state rules when using a third party background-checking firm, discussed in Chapter 6.

**States with some sort of prohibition against employers using arrest only records—**

California, Hawaii, Illinois, Massachusetts, Michigan, Nevada, New York, Pennsylvania, Rhode Island, Utah, Virginia, Washington, Wisconsin (unless position is bondable).[14]

**States that prohibit or restrict consideration of misdemeanors in some way—**

California, Hawaii, Massachusetts.

**States that prohibit or limit the use of Expunged or Sealed Records—**

California, Colorado, Hawaii, Illinois, Ohio, Oklahoma, Oregon, Rhode Island, Texas, Virginia, Louisiana, Maryland, New Jersey, South Dakota, Utah, Virginia.

**States that limit the use of "First Offense Records"—**

Georgia, Massachusetts.

**States that prohibit employers from using certain records based upon age of record—**

Hawaii, Massachusetts.

Note that a court record by itself may be insufficient to determine the true nature of the offense since the final outcome may be influenced by a plea bargain or some other resolution not reflecting the true offense. A firm may need to attempt to verify the true nature of the offense by contacting, or at least attempting to contact, a person in authority such as a parole or probation officer, a police officer, or a prosecuting attorney. Again, documentation is a must.

> **Author Tip** ➡ Employers need to proceed with caution before utilizing "non-criminal" offense records. Some states, such as New York and New Jersey, have created categories of minor offenses that are specifically deemed to be "non-criminal." See **Non-Criminal Offenses And Violations Can Trip Up Employers** online at www.ESRcheck.com/safehiringupdates.php
>
> An excellent source of citations and explanations of all the states' laws regarding the access and use of state criminal records is found in Derek Hinton's book *The Criminal Records Manual*.[15]

---

[14] note that even in states without prohibitions, arrest only records are subject to EEOC limitations

# Written Employer Policies on Criminal Records

Given all the EEOC, FCRA, and state restrictions, what **policy** should an employer have regarding the use of criminal records? In their policies, employers make three common mistakes—

1.  **Having a policy that flatly prohibits employment of an applicant with a criminal record or employment for persons with certain crimes.**

    According to the EEOC, a flat policy against anyone with a criminal conviction is likely to have an adverse impact on members of a protected class, and therefore could be contrary to the rules of the EEOC. The EEOC covers this topic in Notice N-915 (7/29/87), found in Appendix 2. If challenged, the employer has a duty to present statistical data concerning applicant data flow to demonstrate that a flat policy against hiring anyone with a conviction would not have an adverse impact. However, the EEOC also cautions that such data could also be challenged if the applicant pool artificially limits members of the protected groups from applying in the first place. According to the EEOC notice, "if many Blacks with conviction records did not apply for a particular job because they knew of the employer's policy and they therefore expected to be rejected, then applicant flow data would not be an accurate reflection of the convictions' policy actual effect." Notice N-915 (7/29/87).

    Unless an employer plans to hire a professional statistician and a team of labor lawyers and demographics experts, the best policy is to not have a flat and automatic prohibition on applicants with criminal records.

2.  **Having a scoring policy, where a conviction of certain crimes automatically eliminates an applicant.**

    Another potential mistake employers make is to have a flat prohibition on certain crimes. For example, an employer may have a flat and automatic prohibition against hiring someone with certain convictions such as theft, robbery, violence, or drugs.

    Some employers go even further and have a "scoring" system whereby an employer uses the services of a screening firm to automatically eliminate an applicant. Some employers use a "traffic light system." If the applicant has no criminal records, then he or she is given a "green light." If the applicant has a disqualifying criminal record, such as a violent crime, the screening company gives the applicant a "red light." If there is a crime that is not on the employer's automatic elimination list, that person receives a "yellow" or "caution light" so that the crime can be reviewed with the employer.

    The same EEOC Notice mentioned above also addresses this issue. According to the Commission, past decisions were based upon national or regional statistics for crime as a whole. However, if the employer can present more narrow regional or local data on conviction rates for all crime or the specific crime showing that protected groups are not convicted at disproportionably higher rates, then the employer may be able to justify such a policy. In

[15] *Criminal Records Manual*, ©2004 by BRB Publications, PO Box 27869, Tempe, AZ 85285; www.brbpub.com

addition, the employer can show that the policies in fact did not result in disproportionately higher rates of exclusion. This is a tough sell for an employer.

In view of the legal exposure for discrimination and the potential high cost of defending the process, employers may consider changing the "red flag" from automatic disqualification to a policy of "strict scrutiny of the offense" pursuant to the EEOC three-part test. Now the red-flagged person will go through a special process whereby the employer reviews the details of the past offense, the applicant, the job, then reaches an individualized, documented decision.

3. **Having no policy.**

As a general rule, it is a *best practice* for employers to have *written policies* on important issues. Without a policy, an employer's actions in denying employment may become harder to defend. Having no policy also subjects an employer to claims of a discriminatory practice.

---

# Flat Polices Are Inherently Unfair

Some Security and HR professionals have suggested that a flat policy against criminal offenders is inherently fairer because an employer is not required to make a distinction between candidates. A flat policy is fair, they suggest, because it is applied regardless of the person. In fact, the opposite is true. A flat policy that judges a person by his or her status or membership in a category (i.e. criminal offender) is inherently prejudicial because it denies individualized consideration. In other words, a person is being pre-judged not based upon who they are, but upon the label attached to them. The root of the word prejudice is to "pre-judge."

Of course, this means that an employer could be placed in a situation where they have two applicants with identical criminal records, but one gets a job offer and the other does not. That can happen because one applicant has engaged in substantial rehabilitation and has great references. In this decision, an employers needs to document why the two individuals are being treated differently. The answer is simple— although they committed the same crime, they are different people with different qualifications.

---

## Suggested Policy Language on Criminal Records

Here is sample policy language for an employer's policy on criminal records. The sample is offered for the purpose of illustration only and should be reviewed by legal counsel before utilizing any language.[16]

---

**Suggested Employer Policy on Use of Criminal Records**

To ensure that individuals who join this firm are well qualified and have a strong potential to be productive and successful, and to further ensure that this firm maintains a safe and productive work environment that is free of any form of violence, harassment, or misconduct, it is the policy

---

[16] a complete sample policy regarding all aspects of safe hiring and pre-employment screening is provided in Chapter 4

of this company to perform pre-employment screening and credentials verification on applicants who are offered and accept employment. A pre-employment background check is a sound business practice that benefits everyone. It is not a reflection on a particular job applicant.

The background check may also include a criminal record check. If a conviction is discovered, then the criminal offense will be closely scrutinized to determine if the conviction is related to the position for which the individual is applying or would present safety or security risks before an employment decision is made. The employer will take into account the nature and gravity of the offense, the nature of the position applied for, and the age of the criminal conduct. A criminal conviction does not necessarily automatically bar an applicant from employment.

## Using a Conditional Offer of Employment

A criminal background check can take a little time — several days or weeks — depending on the government agencies involved and who is doing the check. Meanwhile, an employer may have a difficult position to fill, or have concerns about losing a good candidate who has cleared the earlier safe hiring steps and seems to be a good fit for the job. The employer may choose to make a contingent offer of employment based upon the receipt of an acceptable background report.

If a contingent offer is made, then the following language is recommended for the offer letter—

> *This offer of employment is conditional upon the employer's receipt of a pre-employment background screening investigation that is acceptable to the employer at the employer's sole discretion.*

This suggested language specifies the report must meet the **employer's satisfaction**, so there can be no debate over what constitutes a satisfactory report. If candidates have not been forthcoming up to this point, many will self-elect to decline an offer letter that is tentative, pending results.

# Criminal Records and Safe Hiring Checklist

If negative information is located, is there a company policy in place or procedure to follow? What are the important considerations? Below is a quick checklist guide—

1. **Policies**— Are there written guidelines to follow?

2. **Documentation**— Are all procedures and decisions documented to file?

3. **Review**— Is there a review process, with a particular person in the organization in charge of the process?

4. **Uniformity**— Are similarly situated applicants treated the same?

5. **Privacy**— Is there a mechanism to ensure that information remains private and secured, and only appropriate decision makers view the information? (e.g., reports with negative information are not sent through office mail to a hiring manager's desk).

6. **Legal compliance FCRA**— If a third party obtains information under the FCRA, is there a procedure to ensure pre-adverse action and post-adverse letters are handled as required by law?

7. **Legal Compliance EEOC**— If the negative information is a criminal record, does the firm understand and follow the Equal Employment Opportunity Commission rules concerning the use of criminal records? Under EEOC rules, an employer may not deny employment to an ex-offender unless it is a business necessity, determined by reviewing the following three factors—

    a. The nature and gravity of the offense;

    b. The nature of the job being held or sought; and

    c. The amount of time that has passed since the conviction or completion of sentence.

# With All of These Rules, Are Criminal Records Still Worth Accessing?

By this time, an employer may well be scratching his or her head wondering if it is worth the trouble to do a criminal records check given all the rules and procedures involved. If the employer makes a mistake, then they risk a lawsuit from a disgruntled applicant accusing them of violating their rights. Or, an employer may be concerned about the EEOC or a state authority becoming involved if an applicant complains of discriminatory practices.

Even with these complications, experts agree that it is incumbent upon employers to check for criminal records. Here is why: The chance of being sued, much less being sued successfully by a person with a serious criminal record, is remote. As long as the employer does not engage in the automatic disqualification of applicants with criminal records and treats every applicant fairly, the chance of a lawsuit is remote.

On the other hand, according to all of the available statistics, there is a statistical certainty that unless a firm exercised due diligence, they will hire a person who is dangerous or unfit for the job. As discussed in Chapter 1, The Parade of Horribles, the legal and financial fallout can be a never-ending nightmare.

To put it another way, *the number of lawsuits from disgruntled applicants with criminal records is minimal. The potential lawsuits or harm from not doing a criminal check is enormous.*

## Can They Sue?

Attorneys are often asked by employers, "Can they sue me?" The answer is always "YES." Anyone in the U.S., for a modest filing fee, can sue anyone else for nearly anything they want.[17] Of course, the key term is a "successful" lawsuit. So, there is never a guarantee that a lawsuit will not be filed.

The question is— "What risk is there of a successful lawsuit?

---

[17] the exception is certain people who have abused the system by filing multiple lawsuits of doubtful validity can be declared a "vexatious litigant" and not be allowed to sue without court approval

Whether or not to use criminal records ultimately comes down to a risk management decision where an employer has to weigh the cost versus the benefit.

- **Costs:** Overall costs include the time, money, and effort spent in obtaining the criminal report, as well as the potential, though not very realistic, risks of a lawsuit from a disgruntled applicant.

- **Benefits:** The benefits can range from merely avoiding an unpleasant situation to avoiding the loss of life and the loss of the business.

*On a cost-benefit basis, employers are clearly ahead by doing criminal checks.*

# If a Person With a Criminal Record is Hired...

If a firm decides to hire an individual with a criminal record, then it is crucial to document the reasons for the decision and the processes the firm went through leading up to the decision. Employers should insure that the applicant is reasonably-suited for the job. Employers should also note any considerations made as to whether these individuals need special supervision or assistance to help them succeed — and maintain workplace safety.

## Persons With Criminal Records Should Still Be Able to Find a Job

As always, there are two sides to any story. On one hand, employers have an incentive to conduct background checks because of the overwhelming evidence of the importance of criminal records in anticipating future behavior.

However, as we review criminal records, it is important to keep in mind that no one is suggesting that just because a person has a criminal past, he or she can never be hired. Unless our society wishes to create a permanent criminal class, it is critical for ex-offenders who have paid the price to society to be able to get a J-O-B. Without a job, ex-offenders can never become tax paying, law-abiding, productive citizens. Logic and statistics suggest that ex-offenders who are not able to find and keep gainful employment are likely to re-offend. Unless our society wants to spend an inordinate amount of tax money on building prisons, ex-offenders need a chance at a decent career. In fact, the law provides that a criminal record cannot be used to automatically deny a job. This is discussed in detail in the next chapter.

A person with a criminal record does not have a big scarlet C for criminal emblazoned on their forehead so that they can never rejoin society. There are certain jobs that are just inappropriate for individuals with certain backgrounds. For example, a person with an embezzlement record may not be a good candidate to be a bookkeeper. However, such a person may do perfectly well in other jobs. There is a job for everyone, but not everyone is suitable for every job.

# Recent Actions by State & City Governments

The concern over giving ex-offenders a second chance in order to re-enter society is so acute that a number of city governments have instituted a new policy to help ex-offenders re-enter the workforce by taking out questions about past criminal conduct from the employment application. Cities such as Boston, Chicago, Minneapolis, San Francisco and St. Paul have taken the lead in trying to get ex-offenders into the workforce by not asking questions about past offenses in the initial application process that would limit ex-offenders from applying in the first place. Other jurisdictions, such as Indianapolis, Los Angeles, Newark and Philadelphia are considering such legislation. In Boston, the law has gone further and applies to an estimated 50,000 vendors who do business with the city.

The logic behind the law is to ensure that applicants are considered for jobs based upon their qualifications and experience before the employer searches out criminal records. In addition, such protection also encourages ex-offenders to apply in the first place. The law is designed to address the problems faced by ex-offenders who are unable to obtain the employment necessary to become tax paying and law-abiding citizens, and to reduce the high recidivism rate of ex-offenders. It can cost taxpayers over $30,000 per year to incarcerate an individual, so society has a vested interest in having ex-offenders succeed.

These laws do not mean that convicted child molesters will be getting jobs as playground supervisors. The cities and counties passing such laws allow for background checks on finalists, consistent with the EEOC guidelines on the permissible use of criminal records for employment.

In November, 2004, the Illinois legislature passed a bill effective 2005 that allows for the sealing of certain non-violent felonies in order to ease ex-offender's re-entry into society by helping them get jobs without being hindered by a criminal record. According to one legislator quoted in a press story: "It costs us more than $25,000 a year to send someone to prison. Helping people re-integrate into society doesn't just help the individuals. It helps the state. People with jobs will be less likely to turn to crime, which means fewer people in prison."

Another supporter noted that, "Most Chicago ex-offenders return to high-crime and low-employment communities. This leads to difficulties not only for the ex-offender themselves but contributes to neighborhood deterioration. Easing their transition back to pubic life will improve neighborhoods and the city as a whole."

Supporters also noted that although Illinois African-American are 15 percent of the illicit drug users, they are 37% of those arrested for drug offenses and more than 75% of the total drug prisoners in Illinois.

The logic here is sealing certain criminal records will drop one of the most significant barriers in finding work. The new law allows law enforcement to access the records, and the records can still be utilized for certain high-risk occupations such a childcare or driving a school bus. The law also calls for study of recidivism rates among those with their records sealed.

See Chapter 30 for advice to job applicants with criminal records.

# Chapter 12

# Where and How Employers Legally Obtain Criminal Records

So, where *do* employers and screening firms search for criminal records? This chapter examines the "where and how" to properly access criminal records as part of any employer's Safe Hiring Program.

## Core Concept – There is NO Central Location for All U.S. Criminal Records

Contrary to popular belief, obtaining a criminal record is not as easy as going on a computer and getting a thumbs up or a thumbs down. There are over 10,000 state and federal courthouses in the United States, spread out over some 3,300 jurisdictions, each with its own records file. There is simply no national computer database of *all* criminal records available to private employers. Period. *End of story*.

Yes, the FBI and state law enforcement have access to a national computer database called the National Crime Information Center (NCIC). The NCIC is a computerized index of criminal justice information such as criminal record history information, fugitives, stolen properties, and missing persons maintained by the FBI's Criminal Justice Information Services Division in Clarksburg, West Virginia. However, it is absolutely illegal for most private companies to obtain criminal information from law enforcement computer databases *without specific legal authorization*.[1]

> To learn more about some of the basics of criminal records, including terminology and an overview of where records are located, turn to Chapter 26, A Criminal Records Primer.

---

[1] There are three situations where information from the FBI records is provided to private employers. First, a state may pass legislation authorizing such a check. Examples are school teachers, child care and water-treatment plant workers. Second, the federal government may require an FBI criminal check. Examples are nuclear plant workers, aviation or certain other positions in transportation. Third, some types of employers have been given direct access to the FBI, such as banking institutions through the American Banking Association (ABA). One difficulty for employers – if there is "hit" on the FBI rapsheet – the report can be very confusing and it can be difficult to determine the nature and current status of the record without going to the courthouse and examining underlying court documents. The U.S. Congress requested in 2004 that Justice Department conduct a study on the feasibility of opening up the FBI database to private employers directly. A report was issued by the Justice Department that examined a host of issues involved with opening up direct employer access to all private employers to the FBI criminal records. As of the printing of this book, there is still not direct employer access to the FBI criminal records to all private employers. The report, *The Attorney General's Report on Criminal History Background Checks* can be found at: www.usdoj.gov/olp/ag_bgchecks_report.pdf

The following text is taken from Derek Hinton's *The Criminal Records Manual*[2] —

# The Real Story About the FBI's Criminal Records Database

The FBI database's formal name is the National Crime Information Center (NCIC) and is an automated database of criminal justice and justice-related records maintained by the FBI. The sources of the FBI's information are the counties and states that contribute information as well as the federal justice agencies. Two important points about the NCIC are—

1. The NCIC is not nearly as complete as portrayed in the movies. Because of the chain of events that must happen in multiple jurisdictions in order for a crime to appear in NCIC, many records of crime do not make it into the system.

2. The information the NCIC does have is predominantly arrest-related. The disposition of most crimes in NCIC must be obtained by searching at the adjudicating jurisdiction. Dispositions are important issue for employers.[3]

Occasionally an employer happens upon a "good deal." This good deal usually consists of a friend in law enforcement that obtains criminal records from NCIC and provides them free or sells them to the employer. The problem is that this is illegal, and the Feds have been targeting and prosecuting violators.

# The First Step— Determine Where to Search

## County Courthouses

For employment purposes, the **access method most often used** is to **physically visit each relevant county courthouse and look up the record**. That is done for two good reasons. First, it is reliable and usually the fastest method. Indexes and records cans be viewed immediately. Second, if there is a potential match, the researcher can make arrangements to view the file, look at case details, finding identifiers to be certain it is indeed their person, on the spot.

---

[2] Derek Hinton's *The Criminal Records Manual*, published by Facts on Demand Press. This publication is the leading authoritative on about criminal records in the U.S.

[3] Another issue with the NCIC is that it depends upon the states to report, and there is a wide range of practices in how and when the states report. For detailed information on the drawbacks to the NCIC, see a report sponsored by the National Association of Professional Background Screeners (NAPBS), written by Prof. Craig M Winston and directed by Les Rosen and Michael Sankey, at www.napbs.com. The report name is The National Crime Information Center - A Review and Analysis; its stated purpose is to review the NCIC and IIS in order to evaluate its effectiveness in maintaining accurate and complete criminal records. An authorized organization or entity will receive an Originating Agency Identification (ORI) number from the FBI.

Since you cannot search every county courthouse, the key is to choose which counties are relevant. Here are some guidelines—

- **County of Residence:**  At a minimum, employers should search the county of residence or the last place where the applicant spent the most time. Although there are no conclusive studies to prove the point, many criminal justice professionals have observed that the county of residence is the most likely location for a criminal to commit a crime. Many background screening firms have found that employers get the "biggest bang for the buck" by searching the county of residence – assuming a person has not moved there recently.

- **Last Three Counties:**  Some employers have a policy to search the last three counties lived in. "Three" is not based upon any court case or official government recommendation; rather, it is based upon the experience of screening firms showing that most applicants have lived in an average of 2-3 counties in a seven-year period.

- **Seven-Year Search:**  A much higher degree of protection is a seven-year county search of all places where the applicant lived, worked, or studied based on his or her application. The county names can be determined as a result of verification of past employment and all past addresses provided as part of a **Social Security Trace**. The Social Security Trace is discussed in detail in the next chapter.

- **Adjacent County or Metro Searches:**  An employer can go to an even higher level by also searching metro areas of adjacent counties. This search recognizes the fact that there is nothing to prevent a person with a criminal record from crossing county lines. For example, if an employer wanted to search for criminal records for a person who lived in Boston, the employer would likely check Suffolk County. However, a metro search would include Norfolk, Middlesex, and Essex Counties.

  Here are other examples (the first county named is where the city is located)– [4]

  - **San Francisco -** San Francisco, Alameda, Contra Costa, Marin, San Mateo
  - **San Jose -** Santa Clara, Alameda, San Benito, San Mateo, Santa Cruz, Stanislaus
  - **Atlanta -** Fulton, Clayton, Cobb, Dekalb, Douglas
  - **Chicago -** Cook, Dupage, Kane, Lake, Will
  - **Baltimore -** City of Baltimore, Anne Arundel, Baltimore, Howard
  - **Detroit -** Wayne, Macomb, Monroe, Oakland, Washtenaw
  - **Dallas -** Dallas, Collin, Ellis, Kaufman, Tarrant

There are two other potential sources for employers to obtain criminal data. However, these are not as useful when it comes to employment decisions.

## Statewide Court Databases and Websites

For the reasons discussed below, these sources must be approached with caution and are typically not a primary source of information for employers. First, consider: many statewide systems are only

---

[4] A database of all adjoining counties in the U.S. is available through BRB Publications. The adjoining county data is available as a CD-rom product and as part of an online subscription service. See www.brbpub.com

clearinghouses for those counties that choose to deposit records. There are no guarantees that all counties are up-to-date or even participating. Also, other statewide databases might put together by correctional authorities and are not complete. There are some counties that have their records online, and some states that have online records directly from the state court – but not all.

In the event of a "hit" during a database search or online search, the physical files still need to be pulled for inspection, and there are a number of traps for the unwary.

## State Criminal Record Agencies

Many states have a central criminal justice agency such as the Department of Public Safety or Department of Justice where an employer can obtain a state criminal record. According to criminal records expert Derek Hinton, approximately 21 states will release information to the public without restriction, and another 15 states[5] require some sort of release, often including a notarized signature. The remaining 15 states restrict access to employers with some sort of statutory access.[6] An in-depth profile of each state agency's access restrictions and procedures can be found in Derek Hinton's *Criminal Record Manual*.[7]

For employment purposes, accessing state records may not be very useful as we might expect due to the time factor involved. In nearly every state offering a criminal records service there can be substantial time delays. Complicating matters, the employer must make sure they utilize the appropriate form, and send the required means of fee payment. Often, a release form signed by the applicant and even fingerprints are required. There is a bureaucratic delay as someone in the appropriate state office physically processes and responds to each request. If the request form is not filled out correctly, the request may be sent back.

If there is a potential "hit," then delays can be even longer since someone at the state agency may be required to conduct a physical review of the material to determine if it is eligible for release. Reviewing criminal files quickly may not be a state employee's number one priority. If the state is willing to release information, the data in their computer system may be only a summary of the charges, or incomplete. Then the employer may need to request and view the actual file to determine what the case is about.

**Criminal Records Alternatives and Resources** Employers and screening companies are free to use a combination of resources. In some states it may make sense to do a criminal record at both the county level and at the state level. Other employers may enhance their search results when they do a name search at the county level and also a search through PACER, which is the federal court records online system. There are also private vendor databases, state drivers' records, and jail and prison records.

Employers who use the services of pre-employment screening firms will find these screening experts will have plenty of good suggestions on which sources to search for criminal records.

---

[5] including the District of Columbia
[6] this adds up to 51 states because the state data includes the District of Columbia
[7] *The Criminal Records Manual*, 2004© BRB Publications and Facts on Demand Press, Tempe, AZ www.brbpub.com

## Finally, Is the Search Compliant with Regulations?

Unless an industry is controlled by a federal or state regulation, there are no national standards for conducting criminal record checks by private employers. When there is a lawsuit involving wrongful use of criminal records, a jury decides whether an employer was negligent or not. Two states, Florida and Texas, have passed some laws setting criminal records use standards. In Florida, an employer that uses the official Florida online database is presumed not to be negligent, although NOT using an official state databases does not result in an employer being presumed to be negligent. Texas now requires criminal record checks on in-home workers.

Of course, the search must also comply with FCRA requirements, discussed in Chapter 6.

# How To Do A County Courthouse Search

Since the most accurate and least complicated search is at the courthouse, employers should have an understanding of how this type of search is performed. For employment purposes, state court searches are performed at the actual courthouse, in the clerk's records office, by human beings. Keep in mind the methods of storage and retrieval of criminal records can vary from court to court. Who performs that actual search? Some courts require that the names to be search for be handed over to the court clerk who performs the actual search. Some courts have computer terminals that a researcher can view in person; the researcher may have to type in each name, or the researcher views a list of names to see if the applicant's name appears. Some courts index names in other searchable formats such as ledgers, microfiche, or microfilm. How far back should a search go? For additional tips, see www.ESRcheck.com/safehiringupdates.com.

## Start by Doing a Name Search

The first step involves the researcher looking on an index for the applicant's name, or the absence of it. If the name is not shown, then the search is marked "clear." When the name is found, there are additional steps to follow...

The critical point in doing a name search depends upon a human being either entering data in a computer or visually reviewing a list of names. As with any human endeavor, errors are possible. Any human error in data input, or when looking at a list of names, can result in a "false negative," meaning a person who in fact has a criminal record is reported as "clear" when in fact they are not.

Names can also be missed if the applicant used a variation of his or her first name. For example, if looking for "Robert Smith" a researcher must also look for a "Rob Smith" or a "Bob Smith." If a researcher was looking for a "James Evans" and the person was arrested under "Jim" Evans," then the name could be missed. If the applicant is a "Junior," a court index may list that at the very end instead of in alphabetical order. If an applicant was arrested under the name "Joe Smith, Jr," a search under the "S" category may miss it.

A researcher also faces cultural complications when it comes to naming conventions. In some cultures, a person uses both the maiden name and the family surname. For example, Spanish names are often based upon a first name, the mother's maiden name and the family name. However, if an applicant only goes by the mother's name, a completely different search strategy is needed. If a search is conducted for the name Juan Garcia Hernandez, and a person was arrested under the name Juan Garcia, then there is a strong likelihood the record will be missed.

A similar problem exists with former names or aliases. A common former name issue is with a female applicant who has changed her last name as a result of marriage. An employment application or screening form should ask for previous names. It should also ask for the DATE of the name change. For example, if a name change was 20 years ago and a employer is only searching back seven years, there is no reason to search under the former name. It is also important to remember that an alias search is a separate search. If an applicant now has the name of Susan Jones and she changed her name three years ago from Susan Barry, then both names should be searched. As far as court records are concerned, Susan Jones and Susan Berry are two entirely separate people. If the court is doing the search, two fees will be involved because two names are searched. The same holds true if a screening firm conducts the search. There is normally an extra charge for the second name or alias search since the court researcher is looking for two entirely different names in the court records.

> **Author Tip ➡** A second name search should *not* be referred to as a "maiden name" search since that clearly indicates that an employer is obtaining information on martial status, which is a prohibited basis upon which to make an employment decision. The second name search should be referred to as a "previous name search." More about this trap and other legal concerns stemming from discrimination laws are reviewed in Chapter 5.

The idiosyncrasies surrounding the name search make it critical for employers to understand that criminal record searching is not perfect, and should only be considered as only one of many tools that are part of an overlapping system of checks. The fact that a criminal record can be missed also serves to underscore the importance of getting the applicant to be honest on his or her application and in interviews. Employers who utilize the AIR Process find there is a much-reduced likelihood of hiring a criminal.

## Court Access Fees

Keep in mind that many county courts charge an **access fee** or **search fee**. This court fee can range from $1.00 to $15.00, but some jurisdictions, such as courts in New York, charge as much as $52.00 for a court access search fee.[8] A court may also charge a copy fee for documents, and a certification fee if that document needs to be certified. A note of caution — background firms add the court fees as a surcharge to all searches since the fee represents an actual out-of-pocket cost. Since the fees vary by courts, some background screening firms add the surcharge automatically when an employer orders a search from a particular court. This method is fair to employers since each employer is only paying for

---

[8] although New York authorities claim that is for an entire statewide search, it is not clear that all relevant courts or all potential offense are covered

what they order. Other screening firms may average in the cost of the court fees on the theory that flat fees makes accounting easier. Either way, it is a real cost that is eventually passed on to employers. An employer should make sure they understand which billing/fee approach a background firm utilizes.

## How to Do it Yourself

If an employer is hiring locally, the employer can go to the local courthouse, talk to the court clerk, learn the system, and search the records. Of course, the court clerk cannot give an employer legal advice, but he or she may be helpful in showing the employer the local record keeping system.

> **Author Tip** ➡ Most court clerk's offices have signs that say they do not give legal advice. Court clerks are generally prohibited by law from giving legal advice. Not only that, but free legal advice is worth exactly what you pay for it.

Suppose you have an applicant from one county away, or from the other side of the state, or even in another state? Record checking becomes a very different process. Presumably, an employer does not want to drive everywhere to check records, not to mention the value of the employer's time.

There are two alternatives. The first is to contact the far away court by phone, fax, or letter. The employer first needs to figure out which court is relevant to which past address. If an applicant lived in a town in Kansas, then the employer needs to locate the county for that town. The employer then needs to locate the courthouse for that county. Since every court is different, the employer then needs to contact the court ahead of time to find out exactly what procedures they use. The court may require a letter or fax, a consent form, or a fee. Then there is the issue of turnaround time. By the time the request is mailed, processed and returned, weeks may have passed. If there is a potential match – a "hit" – then further communication is needed to arrange getting a copy of the file. Courts typically charge a per-page copy fee, and usually require any fees to be paid in advance. However, many courts will not do a name search of criminal records, ignoring requests sent by mail or telephoned. That is where the second alternative is advantageous…

The second alternative is to retain the services of an outside vendor. The most obvious choice is a firm that specializes in pre-employment background screening. For much less than an employer's cost to drive there, screening firms have networks of researchers set-up who can access any U.S. court within a day or so. As mentioned throughout this book, when working with a screening firm the employer is protected by the FCRA.

Another option is to find a firm or individual that specializes in doing only court record searching. These entities usually work for only ongoing business customers, such as attorneys or screening firms. A county-by-county list of a select group of these retrievers who abide by a code of professional conduct is found at www.brbpub.com/prrn.

Internet services and also available, but employers need to be very wary of them. See Chapter 10 on Pre-employment Screening, What Is It and Who Does It.

# If There Is a "Hit," a Researcher Must Pull a Court File to Confirm Identity

If a researcher finds a criminal record in the name of the applicant, does that mean the applicant cannot be employed? The answer is an emphatic NO. The location of a criminal record by a name match is just the **start of the process**. If there is a "hit" (a name match), then the researcher needs to determine if the person located is truly the applicant.

A researcher needs to locate an identifier in order to match the court record to the applicant. Examples of commonly used identifiers are—

- Date of birth
- Driver's license number
- Social Security Number

Some records may track by race. However, for reasons discussed in Chapter 5 concerning discrimination laws, race is not a helpful criteria category for private employers to use.

### Where are the identifiers located?

That depends upon the court and the way the records are kept. In some courthouses, identifiers may be part of the index system. An identifier may be on the computerized index, microfiches, or whatever system the court uses to provide a record index. In some courts, there are limitations on identifiers in order to protect privacy. In courts that limit identifiers, criminal case research is made more difficult because a researcher only has a name match.

> **Author Tip** ➡ If there is a name match on an index without identifiers, then the researcher must review each possible court file that bears the same name of the applicant, in order to determine if there is a matching identifier. If it is a common name, this can become a very laborious procedure.

### What does a researcher look at in the court files?

- The **charging document** specifies the exact law, by section, that the defendant is charged with, along with other details such as the name and location of the court and the prosecution who brings the case. It may contain identifiers about the defendant.

- The **court docket** and/or **clerk minutes** contain the events that occurred at each court appearance. It is essentially the history of the case. The **docket** will include such items as the plea entered by the defendant, and in the event the defendant either pleads guilty or is found guilty, it will contain the sentence imposed as well as the exact charges for which the defendant was convicted. This file may also contain identifiers.

In order to review the case file to look for identifiers, a court researcher must typically ask court personnel to find – or pull – files. In some courts, there are limits to how many files a court clerk can pull. Further delays are possible if the file is placed in storage. Although citizens generally have a right to access public files, the speed at which a court clerk chooses to obtain the files is up to that court clerk. Even when an employer performs background checks in person, there can be delays.

# Why Do Some Government Agencies Feel Compelled to Shoot Themselves in the Foot?

In some jurisdictions, court clerks have taken the position that identifiers should be masked or not be made public in order to protect privacy and to guard against identity theft. When this occurs, several things happens. First, employers and job applicants are immediately penalized because background checks take much longer. Second, criminals and terrorists are arguably the primary beneficiaries since they have a better chance of avoiding detection. Finally, the courts end up becoming over-burdened because suddenly there is a much-increased workload, as employers and researchers have a greater need to pull files to search for identifiers. If a researcher finds a match for common names in the court index, the researcher will need to request and review every file to look at identifiers in an effort to determine if the case belongs to the applicant in question. That substantially increases the workload on county clerks.

Although protecting privacy and combating identity theft are important considerations, courts need to balance privacy versus public access and the public good. Perhaps the best way to achieve the balance is to leave in the date of birth identifier needed to perform an accurate check and mask out the Social Security Number.[9] This way, researchers have access to date of birth, which is the primary identifier. Privacy is protected, since typically the Social Security Number is the tool used for identity theft. Leaving a date of birth on a court record presents a small privacy risk since little harm occurs to an individual if the date of birth is used.

However, nothing is ever as simple as it seems. As discussed in Chapter 5 under the topic of age discrimination, there is a growing trend among employers to not request date of birth from applicants. On the other hand, employers universally collect the Social Security Numbers. The result is that the most valuable identifier – the Social Security Number – is precisely the one identifier that can cause the most trouble if left available on public records.

The evolving solution is – whether employers who do in-house criminal searches or hire background firms – to devise a way to obtain a date of birth without running afoul of age discrimination rules.

## The Researcher Must Confirm Case Details

Assuming the criminal file is examined and identifiers are located, that still does not mean the criminal matter can be used in the consideration of the applicant's employment. There are a number of reasons a criminal record may not be legal to use — there are a number of regulatory considerations to weigh *before* using a criminal record.

---

[9] as discussed in Chapter 17 on identity theft, the Social Security Number is the root to many the I.D. theft problems

In order to determine if the record may be used, a researcher must obtain details about the case — the nature of the offense, the offense date, future court dates, sentencing; probation terms, and whether the case is a *felony* or a *misdemeanor.*

One note of caution— in most jurisdictions, the actual **police reports** are typically not **public records** and therefore not available in the file. Police reports typically contain witness statements, a description of the offense or crime scene, the statement of the defendant if one was made, and facts upon which a prosecution is based. This information is generally not available in the court file open to the public.

Still, searching the court file is helpful. First, there may be documents in the file pertaining to some legal process of interest. For example, in a criminal case a defendant has the opportunity to file various motions, such as a motion to suppress evidence, or a statement, or to request some other legal remedy, such as a dismissal of charges. Also, in the legal papers filed by both sides, critical facts of the case may be revealed.

Information can be gleaned just from the public documents, typically a complaint, indictment, or some sort of charging document that would normally state the basis of the charges and may reveal the victim or additional case details. The court may state certain terms and conditions in the sentencing that may shed light on the case. If the defendant was convicted of assault, and the court orders the defendant to attend a drug program, that may indicate drugs were involved.

## It Can Be a Big Mistake Not to Look for Misdemeanors

One of the biggest mistakes an employer can make is to only ask about or search for felonies, or the job application only asks about felonies. This practice is partly because in many states there are limitations on asking about misdemeanors. However, in some states, misdemeanors can be very serious.

An employer certainly wants to know if an applicant has been convicted of—

- Resisting arrest
- Battery on a police officer
- Possession of drug paraphernalia
- Illegal gun possession
- Commercial burglary
- Assaulting a child or spouse

In many states, these violations are misdemeanors, not felonies.

In some instances, a misdemeanor case can be extremely relevant to a job, and even more relevant than a felony. For example, petty theft may be a misdemeanor, but if an applicant was being considered for a bookkeeping position, that would be good information to have. Another example: a driving under the influence can be a misdemeanor, but a very relevant one to any position involving driving.

It is not unusual for felony charges to be reduced to a misdemeanor through a plea bargain. Where some element of the case may be hard to prove, the felony charge can be reduced to a misdemeanor by plea-bargaining. There may have been mitigating circumstances in either the crime itself or in the life of the perpetrator, so that a prosecutor feels a misdemeanor is appropriate under the circumstances. Sometimes one "bad actor" commits a crime against another "bad actor," leading to one person with a criminal record is testifying against another with a criminal record after having bargained for a lesser penalty in exchange for cooperating with authorities. In large jurisdictions with more crimes to prosecute than there are resources, there may be more pressure to plea-bargain cases out of the system.

**The bottom line**— because a misdemeanor can be the result of behavior that may otherwise have been serious enough to be considered a felony, and is only a misdemeanor due to a plea bargain, employers cannot afford to ignore misdemeanors.

In order to ask about misdemeanors, it is important to first be aware of the rules in your state.

## Looking for Criminal Offenses in Counties with Multiple Courts

While most counties have a central court where all felony records can be reviewed, some jurisdictions have multiple lower level courts such as municipal courts or justice of the peace courts. Local courts may not report all convictions to a central court. The good news, however, is that these outlying lower courts usually handle minor cases. If these cases were more serious, then they would typically be sent to the central court. Therefore, it is not likely an employer is missing much if they fail to check the small courts. In addition, these local courts can be difficult to search, have irregular hours of operation, or may be located in remote areas. One plus is that if the offense is driving-related, such as a driving under the influence case, it should be reported to the state motor vehicle department and should show up in a driving record.

For example, in Darlington County, SC, there is a central circuit court where felonies and most misdemeanors are available. There are also four magistrate courts with minor case offenses. It is not practical for employers to go driving all over the county in case there is a minor record in a remote lower court not reported to that central circuit court.

When using the services of background screening firms, they typically only provide court records by searching the central courthouse.

The bottom line is that once again criminal record searches are not perfect and some offenses can still slip through the cracks.

# Federal Courts Are A Separate System

There are two entirely separate court systems in the United States – federal courts and state courts. A search of one system does not include a search of the other system, and each system operates under its own sets of rules, has its own courthouses, clerk's offices, indexes, and judges.

Based on the fact that the overwhelming numbers of prosecutions are in state courts, many feel that federal searches have a relatively low rate of return.

For example, in 2001, only 68,533 people were convicted and sentenced in federal court. As of September 30, 2001, 136,395 sentenced offenders were under the jurisdiction of the Federal Bureau of

Prisons — approximately 55% of sentenced federal prisoner are there on drug charges. Another 103,794 offenders convicted of a federal offense were on community supervision.[10]

Compare those numbers to the number of people that are currently under the jurisdiction of state criminal justice systems. As of January 2003, 2,033,331 prisoners were held in federal or state prisons or in local jails. Subtracting the number of federal prisoners means that state prisons and local jails have nearly 2 million prisoners.[11]

The decision to include a federal search, especially when hiring for a lower paid position, should take into account two other factors—

1.  **The Nature of Federal Prosecutions.** The old saying, "Don't make a federal case out of it" has some relevance to the type of cases employers might find in federal court. By definition, federal courts are the place where violations of federal law are prosecuted. Although in recent years there has been a trend in congress toward "federalizing" more offenses that have traditionally been associated with state courts, federal crimes still tend to be slanted toward more serious cases, such as large drug cases, financial fraud, bank robbery, kidnappings, and interstate crimes. The majority of criminal cases in federal court are for drug violations. In 2001, of the 82, 614 cases commended in federal court by the U.S. Attorneys office, 86% were for felonies. Of those, 43% were drug related. Another 14% involved immigration offenses.

2.  **Federal Sentencing Procedures.** In federal courts, defendants are sentenced according to mechanical procedures set forth in the *U.S. Sentencing Guidelines.* This procedure has produced very long sentences, especially for drug offenders and those who commit acts of violence or crimes with weapons. In 2001 the average federal prison sentence was 57 months, with the highest sentences going to defendants convicted of violent felonies (91 months), weapons felonies (87 months), and drug felonies (74 months).

In many instances, the tip-off to a federal violation is not a court record search, but a large unexplained gap in the employment history. This underscores a key point made previously — that a past employment check can be just as critical as a criminal record check

Because of the nature of federal crimes and sentences, many employers have seen less relevance in doing federal searches. Another reason for the lack of enthusiasm for federal record searches is the fact that a federal offense by definition can occur anywhere in the U.S. Thus, it is harder to select which jurisdictions to search, unless an employer uses the PACER system described below.

## The Good, the Bad and the Ugly about Federal Criminal Record Checks

### The "Good"

Federal District Courts are the trial courts that oversee criminal law cases and therefore these court records can be a critical search resource for employers. The federal courts use a centralized online system called PACER that provides record searches for the public for most U.S. courts.

---

[10] for data breaking down federal crimes, see www.ojp.usdoj.gov/bjs/fed.htm

[11] for prisoner number data, see www.ojp.usdoj.gov/bjs/prisons.htm

PACER stands for **P**ublic **A**ccess to **C**ourt **E**lectronic **R**ecords. Through PACER, a user accesses the "U.S. Party/Case Index." This index contains certain information from the court files — case numbers and the names of those involved in the case. For an employer trying to determine if an applicant has a federal criminal record, the system is beneficial since it allows one to search by name.

The PACER website is http://pacer.psc.uscourts.gov. Note that there is no "www" in this address.

### The "Bad"

There are two "bads" about PACER. The first is that not every district court in online with PACER. The PACER website lists the exceptions and updates them nightly. However, the courts not available through PACER need to be searched through their own electronic access. That means as a practical matter that as long as there are exceptions, it is not possible to perform a true "nationwide" federal search without identifying the courts not on PACER and then searching those courts one by one.

The second "bad" is that PACER typically does not provide enough identifiers to do a proper name match. If the applicant has a common name, identification can be very difficult. Often additional documents are needed and, depending upon the court, documents may have to be pulled directly from the courthouse.

### The "Ugly"

Even if a federal court document is pulled, identifiers are typically hard to find, unlike the county level courts where there is often a date of birth. If there is a name match only, then other means must be used to determine if that case relates to a particular applicant. For example, if a person was found guilty of a serious offense and the court files indicate a substantial prison sentence, but the applicant in question was employed during that time period, then the case was probably not the same person. If a conclusion cannot be reached by comparing information in the court file to information that has been confirmed by the employer, then it may be necessary to roll up your sleeves and do some sleuthing, perhaps with a phone call to the AUSA (an Assistant United States Attorney who acts as the prosecutor in federal court cases) or the criminal defense attorney. Case materials will typically reveal the attorneys for both sides.

# Additional Databases To Search For Criminal Records

In addition to the sources already mentioned, there are other search resources available to employers. These include driving records, the local prison system, the Federal Bureau of Prisons (BOP), and sexual offender databases.

What each of these searches has in common is that, in theory, the records should have already been found. For example, a search of state and federal prisons should indicate the same record found during a court search. The driving records and sexual offender databases are compilations of a particular category of conviction that also would have generated a criminal record in the first place.

Given the limitations inherent in criminal records, checking these "secondary sources" provides an extra layer of protection. However, each of the searches has a drawback.

## State Motor Vehicle Records – MVR's

For purposes of criminal records, it should be noted that the matters reported on driving records are driving related only, thus not nearly a complete resource of criminal records. On the plus side, an MVR search is a true statewide search. These records are discussed in more detail in Chapter 16.

## State Sexual Offender Registers

State sexual registration requirements became mandatory on May 17, 1996 when a law, popularly now known as Megan's Law, was signed by President Clinton. This law had two primary goals: (1) to require each state and the federal government to register sexual predators; (2) to provide for community notifications.

A more detailed discussion of the uses and limitations of these sex offender searches is provided in Chapter 15.

## Federal Prison Locator

The Federal Bureau of Prisons (BOP) has an inmate locater on its website www.BOP.gov. The site contains information about inmates going back to 1982. However, as a research tool, the database has the same drawbacks as most other large databases of names. If an employer already has the inmate's prison number — or another government number, such as the FBI or INS number — then the look-up is easy. However, for a pre-employment inquiry, an employer presumably would not have that number. There may be a additional look-up options that allow lookup by other factors such as race, sex, and age usually within two years. Due to rules concerning the use of race as a factor in employment, it is unlikely that any employer will use that search option. In addition, many employers have the same sensitivity about age. This leaves only a name search. Any database that depends upon a name look-up inherently has problems, plus, when information is entered into a database from numerous sources, there is increased likelihood of discrepancies. As a result, this is another database that requires a researcher to run all sorts of first name variations, including just the first letter of the target's first name.

## State Prison Records

A number of states have state prisoner locator services on the Internet. Each state with a locator operates differently. Some sites contain only current prisoners, some contain those on parole, and others contain historical information. Again, as with any database, a researcher needs to fully understand the look-up logic and be prepared to run a number of name variations.

There are two excellent resources to find these websites.

- www.corrections.com/links/index.asp (go to "Inmate Locator")
- www.brbpub.com/pubrecsites.asp

Many of the state correctional databases are included in proprietary databases compiled by vendors, as described in the next section.

# Take Caution When Using Public Databases

A public database is a database maintained by an official government body, such as a court, where records are available online to the public for name look-ups. An example is the Federal PACER system. Some public databases are free to search, while others are commercial systems operated by third parties with fees and access restrictions involved.

> **Author Tip** ➡ One of the most comprehensive and up-to-date lists of free searchable public databases is located at www.brbpub.com/pubrecsites.asp. The site shows over 5,000 county, state, and federal websites where any member of the public can access information for free. In addition, BRB has a subscription service that profiles over 20,000 government agencies, indicating all the details searchers need to know to access both fee and free sites.

It has been estimated that upwards of 35% of the courts in the U.S. have some sort of online access capability and the number is growing, However, just as with PACER, there is good news and bad news when it comes to obtaining information online.

**The Good News**

With online access, employers can go to the court website and do name searches to see if their candidate is listed on any index of criminal cases.

**The Bad News**

Unfortunately there is much more bad news about online court websites—

- Typically, court website searches are only of a record index. If there is an index "hit," the site does not give the searcher the full case file information. This means that arrangements must be made to retrieve actual court records. That may require some back-and-forth correspondence with the court, plus fees, release forms, etc., as described earlier.

- Online searches also have limitations when it comes to first names. For example, in 2003, Los Angeles County introduced an online access system. Unfortunately, the system only searches on the basis of the exact information input. So, if you have a Robert Smith who was charged under the name "Rob Smith" or "Bob Smith," an employer can get a "false negative." This means the person will come back "clear" and, in fact, he or she could have a criminal record. The alternative is to pay to search for each permutation of the first name.

- Identifiers are an issue for online services. Many court online systems require a requester to submit a date of birth. As discussed earlier, there can be a problem for the employer to obtain the DOB. A related problem is that the online index may contain only names with no identifiers. If the name does not appear (assuming you ran the right first name), then the person is clear. If you run a common name and get matches, someone is then required to go to the courthouse and pull files to determine the proper identity.

- For various reasons, most of the state databases can have "gaps." For example, Florida has the Florida Department of Law Enforcement (FDLE) database online is dependent upon courts submitting case information to them, which takes place per the courts' schedule. States that take records directly from the courts have the more accurate databases. North Carolina draws its data online directly from every court on a real-time basis. That is the safest type of database to use, assuming the researcher knows the ins and outs of the database.

- Remember those TV shows where a professional stunt person would perform, and the announcer would say, **"Remember, we are professionals. Do not try this at home."** To avoid getting false results, there is an element of training and experience needed when using some databases. For example, there are at least two states with two sets of statewide databases. Unless a researcher knows this, searches will be incomplete.

An employer or researcher without expertise in using databases can easily error and miss a record.

---

**A Graphic Illustration of the Need for Caution in Using Court Databases**

During the 2003 California recall elections, an individual made allegations of misconduct against one of the candidates. A supporter of an opposing candidate apparently went online to the Los Angeles County court system and ran the name, finding serious criminal records that certainly raised questions about the character of the accuser. The problem was, according to news accounts that came out later, the criminal record belonged to someone else. So, defamation lawsuits were contemplated. This is a graphic reminder of the pitfalls of using court indexes without pulling files to look for all possible identifiers *before* making conclusions.

---

# Take Caution When Using Private Databases

A new tool being touted to employers is a "national database search" of criminal records. A number of vendors advertise they have, or have access to, a "national database of criminal record information." These services typically talk about having over 160 million records from 38 or more states. When sexual offender data is added, these services claim even more states and records are covered. Unfortunately, this form of advertising can create an impression in an employer's mind that they are getting the real thing — access to the nation's criminal records. Nothing could be further from the truth.

These databases are compiled from a number of various state repositories, correctional, and county sources. There are a number of reasons why this database information may not be accurate or complete. It is critical to understand that these multi-state database searches represent a **research tool only, and under no circumstances are they a substitute for a hands-on search at the county level**.

The bottom line— just because a person's name appears in one of these databases it does not mean the subject is a criminal. On the other hand, if a person's name does not appear, this likewise should not be taken as conclusive the person is not a criminal. In other words, these databases can result in "false negatives" or "false positives;" and an over-reliance can cause one to develop a false sense of security.

Our discussion of these databases will focus on two areas — VALUE and LIMITATIONS.

## Database Value

These database searches are of value because they cover a much larger geographical area than traditional county-level searches. By casting a much wider net, a researcher may pick up information that might be missed. The firms that sell database information can show test names of subjects that were "cleared" by a traditional county search, but criminal records were found in other counties through their searchable databases. In fact, it could be argued that failure to utilize such a database demonstrates a failure to exercise due diligence given the widespread coverage and low price.

Overall, the best use of these databases is as a secondary or supplemental research tool, or "lead generator" which tells a researcher where else to look.

## Database Limitations

The compiled data typically comes from a mix of state repositories, correctional institutions, courts and any number of other counties agencies. The limitations of searching a private database are the inherent issues about completeness, name variations, timeliness, and legal compliance.

### Completeness Issues

The various databases that vendors collect may not be the equivalent of a true all-encompassing multi-state database. First, the databases may not contain complete records from all jurisdictions — not all state court record systems contain updated records from all counties. Second, for reporting purposes, the records that are actually reported may be incomplete or lack sufficient detail about the offense or the subject. Third, some databases contain only felonies or contain only offenses where a state corrections unit is involved. Fourth, the database may not carry subsequent information or other matter that could render the results not reportable, or result in a state law violation concerning criminal records use.[12]

The result is a crazy quilt patchwork of data from various sources, and lack of reliability. These databases can be more accurately described as "multi-jurisdictional databases."

### Name and Date of Birth Issues

An electronic search of a vendor's database may not be able to recognize variations in a subject name, which a person may potentially notice if manually looking at the index. The applicant may have been arrested under a different first name or some variation of first and middle name. A female applicant may have a record under a previous name. Some database vendors have attempted to resolve this problem with a wild card first name search (i.e. instead of Robert, use Rob* so that any variations of ROB will come up). However, there are still too many different first and middle name variations. There is also the chance of name confusion for names where a combination of mother and father's name is used. In addition, some vendors require the use of date of birth in order to prevent too many records from being returned. Also, if an applicant uses a different date of birth it can cause errors.

Finally, there are some states where a date of birth is not in the court records. Since databases match records by date of birth, search when no DOB exists is of little value since no "hits" will be reported. In those situations, it is necessary to run a search in just the state in question and then individually review each name match. That can be tedious, especially if a common name is being searched.[13]

---

[12] also see the two studies cited on page 312 concerning database searches

[13] Technically, the issue comes down to how broad or how narrow the database provider sets the search parameters. If a database sets the search parameters on a narrow basis, so it only locates records based upon exact date of birth and last name, then the number of records located not related to the applicant would be reduced. In other words, there will be less "false positives." However, it can also lead to record being missed, either because of name variations or because some states do not provide date of birth in the records. That can lead to "false negatives." Conversely, if the parameters are set broadly to avoid missing relevant records, then there is a greater likelihood of finding criminal records relating to the applicant, but at the same time, there are likely to be a number of records that do not belong to

### Timeliness Issues

Records in a vendor's database may be stale to some extent. These records are normally updated monthly, at best. Even after a vendor receives new data, there can be lag time before the new data is downloaded into the vendor database. Generally the most current offenses are the ones less likely to come up in a database search.

### Legal Compliance Issues

When there is a "hit" an employer must be concerned about legal compliance. If an employer uses a commercial database via the Internet, the employer must have an understanding of the proper use of criminal records in that state. If the employer acts on face value results without any additional due diligence research, potentially the applicant could sue the employer if the record was not about them.

If a screening firm locates a criminal hit, then the screening firm has an obligation under the FCRA Section 613 (a)(2) to send researchers to the court to pull the actual court records. This section requires that a background-screening firm must—

> …maintain strict procedures designed to insure that whenever public record information, which is likely to have an adverse effect on a consumer's ability to obtain employment, is reported, it is complete and up-to-date. For purposes of this paragraph, items of public record relating to arrests, indictments, convictions, suits, tax liens, and outstanding judgments shall be considered up-to-date if the current public record status of the item at the time of the report is reported.

As discussed in Chapter 6, FCRA section 613(a)(1) provides an alternative procedure. Instead of going to the courthouse, a CRA can notify the consumer that public record information is being reported by the consumer reporting, and give name and address of the requester. However, some states arguably do not permit this alternative procedure.[14] This is a potential compliance issue for employers who operate in states that do not allow the "notification" procedure to be used instead of the "strict procedure" method of double-checking at the courthouse.

The best approach for an employer is to insist that a CRA always confirm the details of a database search by going to the courthouse to review the actual records.[15] Additional information about the FCRA and databases is covered in Chapters 6 and 10.

## Conclusion About Private Databases—

Criminal record vendors and background firms should make clear, and employers need to understand, the exact nature and limitations of any database they access. These private database searches are ancillary and can be very useful, but proceed with caution. In other words, it cannot be assumed that a search of a proprietary criminal database by itself will show if a person is or is not a criminal, but these databases are outstanding secondary or supplemental tools with which to do a much wider search.

---

the applicant. That can happen for example in a state where no date of birth is provide, and the database is run on a "name match only basis. The bottom-line: with use of databases, employers need to understand there is the possibility of both "false negatives" and "false positives," depending upon how the particular background firm runs the databases.

[14] for a list of states that currently have their own requirements for accuracy as well as the text of the state statues, see www.ERcheck.com/safehiringupdates/php

[15] for a detailed discussion about the legal uses of a database, see an article co-authored by Les Rosen and national FCRA expert Carl Ernst called *"National" Criminal History Databases,* at www.brbpub.com/CriminalHistoryDB.pdf

# Chapter 13

# Using Credit Reports and Social Security Traces

## Employers and Credit Reports

Many job applicants are discovering that employers require pre-employment credit reports before they hire. For many companies, a credit report has become a screening tool to evaluate a candidate and to exercise due diligence in the hiring process. For job applicants, a credit report can feel like an invasion of privacy or a violation of their rights. Of all the potential tools available to the employer to make safe hiring decisions, a credit report comes closest to invading a perceived zone of privacy since it directly reflects where and how we spend money in our personal lives. A credit report can indicate where you shop and the amount you spend.

However, job applicants have substantial legal protection concerning the use of credit reports for employment. In fact, an employer cannot obtain a credit report without an applicant's written permission and cannot use it to deny a job until the applicant has had the chance to review the report. Therefore, employers should approach credit reports with caution, making sure they are used only for valid business-related reasons and that employers are only using information that is fair, recent and relevant.

### What is a Credit Report?

A personal **credit report used for employment purposes** typically contains four types of information.

1. Identifying data such as name, Social Security Number, and past addresses.

2. Payment and credit data that shows how persons pay their debts such as credit cards and personal loans, and indicates if there are car payments, student loans, and mortgage payments. It also shows how much credit a person has been given, how much they currently owe, and whether debts have been paid late, were delinquent, or sent for collection.

3. Records of others who have requested the credit report. When used for employment, requesting a credit report does not NOT affect a person's credit score.

4. Public records are reported such as court judgments, liens, and bankruptcies. Negative information will stay on a report for seven years, and bankruptcies for 10 years.[1]

A common misperception is that "credit scores" are used for employment purposes. Credit reports for employment purposes will have a credit history that will show, for example, if a person misses payments. But an employment credit report does NOT contain a credit score and the three major credit bureaus use a special reporting format that leaves out actual credit card account numbers, credit risk scoring, and age. Even though there is research suggesting that credit scores can have a discriminatory impact, credit scores are simply NOT used for employment purposes.

## How is Credit Information Accumulated?

Credit reports are based upon millions of records being gathered in a variety of methods all over the United States. Records are obtained directly from furnishers of credit such as credit card companies, gas companies, or department stores that issue credit cards. Data is also obtained from court runner services that go to courts daily across the U.S. to obtain public records, including judgments, liens, and bankruptcies. Add to the mixture the fact there are a number of competing credit organizations in the U.S. There are the three major national credit bureaus, as well as local or regional organizations that gather credit data and may be associated with one of these national bureaus.

## What Should Employers Take Into Account Before Using a Credit Report?

Employers should approach the use of credit reports with caution, having polices and procedures in place to ensure the use of credit information is both relevant and fair. An employer should first determine if there is a sound business reason to obtain a credit report. Many employers limit credit reports to management and executive positions, or to positions that have access to cash, assets, company credit cards, or confidential information. Employers are well advised to run credit reports on bookkeepers or others who handle significant amounts of cash.

Unless the information in a credit report is directly job related, its use can be considered discriminatory. For example, running a credit report for an entry-level person with low levels of responsibility or no access to cash is probably not a good practice. Unnecessary credit reports can discourage applicants from applying, and running mass credit reports on all applicants, regardless of the position, can have the effect of discriminating against certain protected classes. Although an employer may want to run credit reports on perspective cashiers, for example, most employers do a drawer count at night, and if money is missing, an employer will know almost immediately.

In addition, employers should avoid making negative hiring decisions on credit report information that is old, relatively minor or has no relevance to job performance. For example, poor credit caused by medical bills may have noting to do with employment.[2] Finally an employer needs to ensure that the information is accurate. In order to protect a consumer's rights, and guard against error, an employer

---

[1] there are limitations to using a bankruptcy in an employment decision
[2] A 2007 study showed the use of credit cards for medical payments is on the rise. For more details, see www.esrcheck.com/safehiringupdates.php.

must carefully follow the requirements of the federal Fair Credit Reporting Act, and any applicable specific state rules.

## Are There Mistakes in Credit Reports?

Mistakes are always possible. Although credit bureaus make efforts to be accurate, credit reports are based upon millions of pieces of data assembled by human beings and computers.

According to screening expert Dennis L. DeMey, author of *Don't Hire a Crook—*

> "Keep in mind that there may be mistakes. Also, different credit bureaus can have different information. One credit bureau may have extensive information on the subject whereas another may have very little. Lenders do not necessarily utilize and/or communicate with every bureau. Consequently, one bureau may be more up-to-date than another in a specific region. In instances where such a search is critical, it is wise to verify using more than one bureau."

## How Frequently are Mistakes Made?

A 2003 study released by the Consumer Federation of America and the National Credit Reporting Association demonstrates why employers need to be careful using credit reports. The study found discrepancies in more than one-third of consumer reports. Any inaccuracies in a credit report could adversely affect employment for those employers who utilize credit reports in making employment decisions. The study also dealt with consumer credit scoring, which does not appear in a credit report used for employment purposes. In response to the study, the credit bureaus countered that the discrepancies were not errors, but only a reflection of the fact that the three major bureaus may report items differently. Perhaps, but not always. This report underscores the fact that use of credit reports must be approached with caution.

This possibility of error is a big reason why employers need to move cautiously when it comes to the use and analysis of credit reports.

## Why Do Employers Use Credit Reports in Employment Decisions?

Employers seek credit reports on job applicants for a variety of reasons. However, there is currently no mathematical model that attempts to "score" a credit report for employment purposes. Such a scoring would face substantial challenges to prove it is a valid and non-discriminatory predictor of job performance. As a result, the use of credit reports tend to be "judgment calls," where the credit report is utilized in conjunction with all other available information.

Some employers take the position that a credit report shows whether an applicant is responsible and reliable by looking at the way that applicant handles his or her personal affairs. The logic is that a person who cannot pay their own bills on time or make responsible personal financial decisions may not be the best fit for a job that requires handling the company's funds or making meaningful decisions.

Employers may request credit reports to alert them to applicants whose monthly debt payments are too high for the salary involved. The concern is if a person is under financial stress due to a monthly debt that is beyond their salary, then that can be a "red flag." One of the common denominators in cases of embezzlement is a perpetrator in debt beyond his or her means, or had excessive financial pressure due to personal debt. See Chapter 23 on Dealing With Fraud, Embezzlement, and Integrity.

Employers hiring sales positions may require that a salesperson utilize a personal credit card. A credit report may help to indicate a potential candidate's ability to use a credit card wisely. There have been employers who discovered months into the employment relationship the reason a salesperson was not making their quota was the person was not able to fly or travel due to an inability to cover advance travel expenses.

Credit reports also help verify identity. The top part of a credit report, often referred to as the "credit header," contains personal data about the applicant such as past addresses. However, an employer does not order an entire credit report just to obtain the credit header.

A separate search called a "Social Security Trace" provides an employer with information to help confirm identity. A discussion on this important tool for employers follows later in this chapter.

---

# You Never Know What You Will Find...

An interesting story is told by a private investigator who obtained a credit report during an in-depth background investigation. In reviewing the credit report, the investigator looked at the section concerning inquiries. This is the list of entities that previously requested a credit report on the individual. One requestor was the United States Probation Office. A little further research revealed that the U.S. Probation Office requested a credit report because the applicant was in fact on federal probation for a federal crime and had been ordered to pay restitution. This story demonstrates that doing a background investigation sometimes requires more effort than merely buying data. It is important to look at the whole person and to "connect the dots" by looking at a number of factors and performing appropriate follow-ups.

---

## What Exactly Does an Employer Look for in a Credit Report?

In reviewing a credit report, an employer is typically looking at the following—

- What are the person's total monthly payments? How does it compare to the projected salary and benefits?

- How many negative items are listed, such as late payments, collection actions, defaults, or accounts closed?

- Are there negative public records and are they related to employment? For example a tax lien may indicate someone has not paid attention to their affairs or is under financial stress. If there is a bankruptcy in the credit report, then the employer should NOT utilize the bankruptcy without talking to the attorney. It can be a form of discrimination to deny employment based upon an applicant taking advantage of their legal right to start over and get a fresh start through bankruptcy proceedings. Federal law expressly prohibits a private employer from discrimination solely on the basis of a person exercising their rights under the bankruptcy laws.[3]

- Are there any alerts from the credit agencies? Some bureaus issue fraud alerts based upon a variety of criteria — if there is suspicion of fraud or abuse.

# Credit Reports and EEOC Consideration

If the use of credit reports for employment decisions results in the unfair exclusions of applicants with poor credit, it may have EEOC implications. Even though a credit report may appear neutral on its face, if its use results in a "disparate impact" upon members of protected groups, a claim can be made that the use of credit reports is in fact discriminatory.

The EEOC has launched a new initiative called E-RACE (Eradicating Racism and Colorism From Employment.) According to the EEOC, the use of credit, although it appears facially neutral, can have a discriminatory impact. See: www.eeoc.gov/initiatives/e-race/why_e-race.html. According to an interview with SHRM magazine in April 2007 with an EEOC official, unnecessary credit reports can end up being a subtle from of discrimination and are best utilized when there is a legitimate business need.
www.shrm.org/hrnews_published/archives/CMS_020975.asp

Statistics by the Texas Department of Insurance seemed to suggest that members of protected groups do have lower credit scores. Even though an employment credit report does not provide a credit score, the credit history is included.

The state of Washington has addressed these concerns through a new law passed in 2007 that prohibits employers from obtaining a credit report as part of a background check unless the information is: substantially job related and the employer's reasons for the use of such information are disclosed to the consumer in writing; or required by law. (See: RCW 19.182.020)

A recent study reported by the Society for Industrial and Organizational Psychology (SIOP) questioned whether credit checks have any validity in predicting the job performance of employees. According to the report, two Eastern Kentucky University researchers studied credit reports of nearly 200 current and former employees working in the financial service areas of six companies. The results suggested that a person's credit history is not a good predictor of job performance or turnover. The full report is found at: www.newswise.com/articles/view/502792/

---

[3] see 11 USC 525

Before utilizing negative information found in a credit report, the employer should consider—

- Is the negative information a valid predictor of job performance?
- Is the information current and correct?
- Is there negative information reported outside the applicant's control such as the result of a disputed bill, medical bills, dissolution of marriage or some other problem?
- Is there any reason not to consider the negative information? (For example, an employer generally should not consider a bankruptcy.)
- Is the employer consistent in the use of negative information? i.e.: have other applicants been hired with the same type of negative information and, if so, is there a rational reason why it was overlooked for others? Is there a company hiring policy or some documentation put in the file to demonstrate that the employer is consistent? )
- Has any decision or conclusion been documented?
- Is the applicant being afforded all for his or her legal rights?

> **Author Tip** ➡ To prevent the misuse of credit reports, the credit bureaus have significantly increased safeguards. Before a background firm may issue a credit report to an employer, the background firm must essentially conduct a background check on the employer. This includes an on-site inspection to ensure the employer is a legitimate business with a proper and permissible purpose for using an employment credit report.

## What are the Legal Limits in Obtaining a Credit Report?

The job applicant must provide written authorization before an employer can request a credit report. Under the Federal Fair Credit Reporting Act, an applicant has a series of additional rights. If an employer intends not to hire someone based upon information in the credit report, then the applicant must first receive a copy of the report and a statement of rights. The applicant has a right to review the credit report and to dispute any information believed to be inaccurate or incomplete. This right applies even if the employer has additional reasons not to hire the person or even if an applicant has excellent credit, and even if there are other concerns such as a reported high debt level. For example, an employer may be concerned that an applicant's debt level is higher then the job pays even though the applicant has a perfect payment record. It may be that the applicant has refinanced their home and the credit report is erroneously showing the old mortgage to still be outstanding. If the employer did not give the applicant their right under the FCRA to review the credit report for errors, then the applicant would have been unfairly eliminated. If a final decision is made, then an applicant is entitled to a second confirming letter. In California and certain other states, job applicants must also be given the opportunity to request a free copy of a report originally obtained by an employer.[4]

The Federal Trade Commission (FTC) published an article for employers on the proper use of credit reports. Here is an excerpt every employer should read if they use credit reports for employment decisions—

> **In Practice...**
>
> ...You advertise vacancies for cashiers and receive 100 applications. You want just credit reports on each applicant because you plan to eliminate those with poor credit histories. What are your obligations?
>
> - You can get credit reports — one type of consumer report — if you notify each applicant in writing that a credit report may be requested and if you receive the applicant's written consent. Before you reject an applicant based on credit report information, you must make a pre-adverse action disclosure that includes a copy of the credit report and the summary of consumer rights under the FCRA. Once you have rejected an applicant, you must provide an adverse action notice if credit report information affected your decision.
>
> ...You are considering a number of your long-term employees for a major promotion. You want to check their consumer reports to ensure that only responsible individuals are considered for the position. What are your obligations?
>
> - You cannot get consumer reports unless the employees have been notified that reports may be obtained and each has given their written permission. If the employees gave you written permission in the past, then you need only make sure that the employees receive or have received a 'separate document notice' that states "reports may be obtained during the course of their employment." No more notice or permission is required. If your employees have not received notice or have not given you permission, then you must notify the employees and get their written permission before you request their reports.
>
> In each case where information in the report influences your decision to deny promotion, you must provide the employee with a pre-adverse action disclosure. The employee also must receive an adverse action notice once you have selected another individual for the job.
>
> ...A job applicant gives you the okay to get a consumer report. Although the credit history is poor and that's a negative factor, the applicant's lack of relevant experience carries even more weight in your decision not to hire that applicant. What is your legal responsibility?
>
> - In any case where information in a consumer report is a factor in your decision — even if the report information is not a major consideration — you must follow the procedures mandated by the FCRA. In this case you would be required to provide the applicant a pre-

---

[4] under the FACT Act passed in 2003, consumers now have the right to request a free copy of their credit report every year, see www.ftc.gov/bcp/conline/edcams/credit/ycr_free_reports.htm for information

adverse action disclosure before you reject his or her application. When you formally reject the applicant, you would be required to provide an adverse action notice.

...The applicants for a sensitive financial position have authorized you to obtain their credit reports. You reject one applicant whose credit report shows a debt load that may be too high for the proposed salary even though the report shows a good repayment history. You turn down another whose credit report shows only one credit account because you want someone who has shown more financial responsibility. Are you obliged to provide any notices to these applicants?

- Both applicants are entitled to a pre-adverse action disclosure and an adverse action notice. If any information in the credit report influences an adverse decision, then the applicant is entitled to the notices — even when the information isn't negative.

**Non-compliance**

There are legal consequences for employers who fail to get an applicant's permission before requesting a consumer report, or who fail to provide pre-adverse action disclosures and adverse action notices to unsuccessful job applicants. The FCRA allows individuals to sue employers for damages in federal court. A person who successfully sues is entitled to recover court costs and reasonable legal fees. The law also allows individuals to seek punitive damages for deliberate violations. In addition, the Federal Trade Commission, other federal agencies, and the states may sue employers for noncompliance and obtain civil penalties.

For the entire article, including a summary of how to comply with the FCRA, see: www.ftc.gov/bcp/conline/pubs/buspubs/credempl.htm

# What Other Rights do Job Applicants Have?

Because of the potential for errors on credit reports, applicants have a right to review a report before it is used to affect his or her employment adversely.

If job applicants are concerned about their credit reports, then they should first contact all three major credit bureaus and request a copy. Typically, there is a fee not exceeding $8.00, but in some circumstances reports are free. Under new federal law that took effect in 2004, applicants have a right to a free credit report once a year.[5] Credit reports, as well as information on costs and procedures to dispute information, can be obtained from the following sources—

- Trans Union   www.transunion.com - 800-888-4213.
- Equifax      www.econsumer.equifax.com - 888-532-0179
- Experian     www.experian.com - 800-972-0322

If there is an error or explanation the applicant cannot resolve with the creditor, then the applicant should write a detailed letter to the three credit bureaus, which have thirty days to investigate and resolve the dispute. If the report is corrected, the applicant may request the agencies to notify anyone

---

[5] in some states, this right for a consumer to receive a free credit report already existed

who has received the report for employment in the past two years. If the dispute is not resolved to the applicant's satisfaction, the applicant has a right to place a brief statement on his or her credit report. All of these rights are explained in detail on the Federal Trade Commission website at www.ftc.gov/bcp/menu-credit.htm which oversees the credit industry.

If a job applicant has bad credit and wants to clear it up, there are excellent credit-counseling services available. The National Foundation for Consumer Credit is a non-profit organization that has over 1,400 affiliates throughout the United States that provide this service, see www.nfcc.org. Unfortunately, there also are scam artists who make false or misleading claims; the Federal Trade Commission issues warnings about these scams and provides information for consumers on the FTC website.

It is worthwhile to take steps to maintain good credit because it can affect a job application.

# The Social Security Trace

A standard tool used by nearly every pre-employment screening firm is a "Social Security Trace." In cases where an employer does not have a sound business reason to obtain a credit report, obtaining the Social Security Trace can give information about a person's past addresses and will help to discover any identity fraud issues.

## The Social Security Trace is a "Credit Header"

The Social Security Trace report contains the same information as does a credit report about names and addresses associated with a Social Security Number, but the Social Security Trace does not include any of the financial information.

The information is taken from the top portion of a credit report, ergo this report is referred to as a "credit header." The top portion of a credit report is compiled from identifying information obtained by credit bureaus when individuals apply for credit cards, provide a change of address to a credit card company, or engage in any transaction that is credit-related. For example, anytime a person applies for a credit card, the data (including the person's SSN as well as a name and address) goes into large computer databanks kept by the major credit bureaus. If two years later a person moves and submits a change of address card, then that new data also goes into the computer memory.

## The Social Security Trace Helps Verifies Social Security Numbers

A Social Security Trace report will assist an employer in determining if their applicant is in fact associated with the Social Security Number submitted. It can also reveal other data such as state and approximate date of issue. Remember, though: not all employers want date of issue or date of birth due to discrimination problems associated with knowing an applicant's age.[6]

---

[6] discrimination and age issues are discussed in Chapter 5

**About the Social Security Number**

A Social Security Number (SSN) is a nine-digit number issued by the U.S. Social Security Administration, the federal agency with responsibility to administer various Social Security programs. Although the intent was never to be used as a national identification number, the SSN has become a critical pre-employment screening tool for employers.[7]

This is how the make-up of a SSN works. The first three digits of the SSN relate to the state of issue. The middle two digits are the "group numbers" which indicate the range of years when the SSN was issued. By understanding the methodology behind these two sets of numbers, an employer can determine the state of issue and the approximate year of issue. The last four numbers are unique to the individual who received the SSN. For example a Social Security Number 548-72-xxxx was a California number. The '548' is associated with California. The '72' is the group number that helps to determine when it was issued. The last four digits belong uniquely to the individual.

Attached at the end of this chapter is a list of the first three digits showing which Social Security Numbers are associated with each state.

## The Social Security Trace Shows Past Addresses

Past addresses are critical because it helps employers determine where to search for criminal records. Since there is no true national criminal database available for private employers, and there are over 10,000 courthouses in America, a social trace can help employers narrow down which courts to search.

In addition, there may be occasion when there are names or addresses incorrectly associated with a SSN. This can occur for a variety of reasons. For example, if a data entry clerk for a credit card company accidentally switched two numbers in a Social Security Number while entering a change of address form, the credit bureau records may link the wrong name and addresses to a Social Security Number. Sometimes, members of the same family may have their credit history intertwined. For example, if a father and son have similar names, the databases can end up "merging" their data, causing confusion. Also, with the increase in identity theft, confusing numbers can also cause confusing results.

## What a Social Security Trace is Not

Many employers mistakenly believe these searches are an "official review" of government records. The Social Security Trace information is NOT being accessed directly from government records, and is therefore not an official verification of a Social Security Number. A Trace report may contain data from the Social Security Administration's list of deceased individuals, but usually the report is created from data found in the databases created by private firms, and in credit headers.

In addition, it is critical to understand that a Social Security Trace report is NOT an official registry of current or past addressees. For a number of reasons, current and past addresses will not appear on a trace report if the applicant never used those addresses in any dealings of interest to the major credit bureaus. On occasion, there may be no names or addresses associated with an SSN. This can occur

---

[7] see discussion on verification of identity in Chapter 17

when a person has never applied for credit, either they are too young to be in the credit bureau records, or they are new to this country and have recently obtained a Social Security Number.

An employer should never make a direct hiring decision based upon the absence of an address in a Social Security Trace. Although Trace reports can be helpful for identity purposes and for determining where to search for criminal records, they are not positive proof of identify or the validity of a Social Security Number. However, the information in a trace report can be the basis for further research of an applicant.

# Do Only Dangerous and Nefarious People Have AKA's?

The author went into a major department store to purchase some items and was told the store had a promotion whereby the author could get a 10% discount on purchases if he signed up that very day. It only required a SSN and driver's license to get an instant credit card and the discount. Seeing no downside, he went ahead and did it.

It turned out that the young employee behind the cash register was not very experienced, and managed to misspell the author's first name as "Lesler" instead of Lester. Signing up for a credit card is a "credit event" since the Social Security Number is involved. The usual procedure is for the SSN used in the credit application, along with the name and address associated with the number, to be forwarded by the store to one or more national credit bureaus. Because of the clerical error, the author's name in some reports could read that he has an AKA, in that he sometimes goes by the alternate name of "Lesler." Of course, only dangerous and nefarious people trying to hide something have "AKA's."

This story shows the margin for error when millions of SSN's are being recorded every day into credit bureau databases and public record databases.

Because of the possibility of human error, a Social Security Trace is used as a helpful tool in a background report but is not considered an "official report." If an applicant is concerned about any such discrepancy, then they can contact all three major credit bureaus to review their files.

## Where to Obtain a Social Security Trace

With the applicant's signed release, the Social Security Trace can be obtained directly from major credit bureaus or through pre-employment screening firms. Background screening firms have recently introduced new searches that enhance the Social Security Trace search with name and address information gathered from a number of additional sources; the information is gathered by private organizations and comes from multiple sources, including billions of public and private records.

# How to Verify a Social Security Number After an Employee is Hired

The method for employers to officially verify a Social Security Number (SSN) **after** employment is to contact the Social Security Administration (SSA). They will verify SSN's to ensure the records of employees are correct for the purpose of completing Internal Revenue Service Form W-2 – the employee Wage and Tax Statement. A background screening firm or employer cannot use this service – now known as SSNVS – prior to an offer of employment being made. Employers typically call later as part of the new hire paperwork and during the I-9 process – the process employers undergo to confirm an applicant has a legal right to work in the United States.

The Social Security Administration has also posted a Legal Use Policy, as shown below.

---

**Legal Policy – Don't Discriminate or Misuse SSNVS**

"SSA will advise you if a name/SSN you submitted does not match our records. This does not imply that you or your employee intentionally provided incorrect information about the employee's name or SSN. It is not a basis, in and of itself, for you to take any adverse action against the employee, such as termination, suspending, firing, or discriminating against an individual who appears on the list. SSNVS should only be used to verify currently or previously employed workers. Company policy concerning the use of EVS should be applied consistently to all workers, e.g. if used for newly hired employees, verify all newly hired employees; if used to verify your database, verify the entire database. Any employer that uses the information SSA provides regarding name/SSN verification to justify taking adverse action against an employee may violate state or federal law and be subject to legal consequences. Moreover, this makes no statement about your employee's immigration status."

---

The toll-free Social Security Administration telephone number is 1-800-772-6270 and is open weekdays from 7:00 a.m. to 7:00 p.m. EST. An employer will also be asked for the company name and EIN.[8] More information is available at www.ssa.gov/employer/ssnv.htm

# Privacy and the Social Security Number

The Social Security Number has been getting a great deal of attention in the media recently due to the growing problems involved in identity theft. The ability of identity thieves to obtain Social Security Numbers in order to commit fraud has become a national issue.[9] The issue of privacy and Social Security Numbers is being looked at carefully in Washington DC, as well as in various states. Part of the concern expressed by privacy advocates is the proliferation of internet websites that sell data on consumers.

---

[8] federal Employer Identification Number
[9] see Chapter 17 on Identity Theft

For the purposes of a Safe Hiring Program, any time information is obtained by an employer or a screening firm, it is always done with the expressed consent of the applicant for the expressed purpose of employment. In addition, if a third party firm is used, such as a background screening firm, then the requirements of the Fair Credit Reporting Act kicks in as well, adding additional layers of protection and privacy for the applicant.

Recent changes to the FCRA effective in 2004 also address privacy concerns and the use of the Social Security Number. The FCRA requires that screening firms, upon request from a consumer, must truncate the Social Security Number on a background report. When a Social Security Number is truncated, only the last four digits display. A truncated SSN may look like: xxx-xx-1234. The reason for the truncation requirement is that, often, identity theft occurs at the consumer's mailbox, where background reports mailed to the consumer can be stolen. By truncating the SSN, the consumer has some protection if the screening report falls into the wrong hands.

At least one state, California, has already passed strong legislation to protect the confidentiality of Social Security Numbers, which includes controlling the use of SSN's by employers. California Civil Code 1798.85 places numerous limitations on the use of SSN's including restrictions on anything mailed to the consumer. There is an exception in the law for any document whereby state or federal law requires the SSN to be on the document. Another California law also requires that California residents have an opportunity to check a box so they can receive a copy of any screening report, which is typically sent by mail. They are entitled to the same report the employer receives, which includes the applicant's SSN. To comply with these various California requirements, some screening firms have take the position that the best practice it is to truncate the SSN on any report sent to a California resident, revealing only the SSN's last four digits.

---

**Author Tip ➡** Identity theft is also a significant issue in the workplace. Employers who obtain background reports may wish to consider having a paperless system. Background reports can be electronically restricted only to those with a need-to-know and it prevents the possibility of paper reports "floating" around the office or sitting on desks. Another solution is to require a screening firm to put a security page on the front of each report with only the applicant's name and no identifiable data. Another option is to truncate the SSN on any printed version of a screening report.

---

Another attempt by the federal government to protect the privacy of a Social Security Number is the Financial Modernization Act of 1999, also known as the "Gramm-Leach Bliley Act" or GLB Act. That law was passed in order to protect consumers' personal financial information held by financial institutions. However, since pre-employment screening is done in a consensual matter, the GLB has not had an impact on the use of the Social Security Number for safe hiring purposes, especially when screening is conducted by an outside agency under the Fair Credit Reporting Act.[10]

---

[10] more information is available at the Federal Trade Commission website at www.ftc.gov/privacy/glbact

# Using the Social Security Number To Cross Check Your Applicant

The Social Security Number is a valuable tool in cross checking the identity and history of an applicant. Employers, human resources professionals, hiring managers or security professional should spend time studying what is contained in a Social Security Trace in order to spot red flags and areas of further investigation.[11]

The following checklist of what to look for in the results of a Social Security Trace has been provided to us by Dennis DeMey, author of *Don't Hire a Crook* and *25 Essential Lessons for Employee Management.*

## Social Security Trace Checklist

__ **Does the Social Security Number provided match the subject?**

If not, verify that the number provided was entered correctly by the credit bureau as well as by your company staff.

Also, ask the applicant to provide proof of their Social Security Number.

__ **Does the name in the Social Security Number Trace result match that of the subject?**

The middle name, initials and suffix are important for proper identification, especially if the subject has a relatively common name.

The subject may have the same name as a relative, with only a suffix to distinguish between them, i.e. Jr. (junior), Sr. (senior) or I (the first), II (the second), etc.

An individual's proper name may be George David Smith, but the subject prefers to go by the name David Smith. He or she may also have used a shortened version of his or her name as a matter of convenience, and that may or may not show up in the SSN Trace report.

__ **Have additional names been revealed?**

Perhaps a maiden name has been identified but was not provided by the subject. If the subject is recently married, then most of that person's information may appear under the maiden name, suggesting an additional search is necessary.

Also, the subject may have divorced and resumed the use of her maiden name. The subject may even have another name from a previous marriage.

Regardless, to enable proper identification and facilitate subsequent searches, it is important to determine why variations of the name exist.

---

[11] Chapter 22 has add'l discussions on how the Social Security Trace is a critical tool in protecting a workplace

Keep in mind that other names can appear for any number of reasons that have nothing to do with the applicant. It may not be possible to investigate or to even determine why information not associated with the applicant is appearing. The existence of extra names can be an early indicator of identity theft. It can also be clerical data entry errors. A simple error in the entry of a person's SSN may result in total strangers being linked in Social Security Trace reports.

### __ Has the Social Security Number been issued by the Social Security Administration?

When faking an identity, people frequently use numbers that have not yet been issued by the Social Security Administration. To see if the first three numbers have been truly issued, check the Social Security Number Allocations Table to follow.

If the results of the verification indicate the number has not been issued, then ask the applicant to provide proof of his or her Social Security Number.

### __ Was the number used to file a death claim?

Numbers used to file a death claim are also utilized to falsify an identity. If the SSN Trace results indicate the number is shown on a death claim, ask the applicant for proof that he or she is truly entitled to the use of that number.

Be aware that it may appear that someone is using the Social Security Number of a deceased person, when in reality he or she has only collected Social Security benefits as a relative of the deceased person.

### __ In what state was the number issued?

It is entirely possible the number was issued in a state other than the state in which the applicant now resides, and is not, in itself, cause for alarm.

However, such information can indicate other areas of the application should be reviewed. Perhaps it hasn't been that long since the applicant moved from the state of origin, in which case he or she should have listed the previous addresses from that state.

### __ In what year was the Social Security Number issued?

A Social Security Trace can indicate the year the SSN was issued. Comparing the year of issue of the SSN to the applicant's date of birth can be helpful.

Around 1984, it became mandatory to obtain a Social Security Number for a child at birth. Prior to this, there was no time limitation. However, most individuals acquired a Social Security Number at a fairly early age, generally no later than the time they entered the work force.

Some employers will obtain a version of the Social Security Trace from a screening firm that omits the year of issue. The concern is that having the year of issue may tend to reveal age, and some employers are sensitive to have anything reflecting ages in their files.

Immigrants should obtain a Social Security Number upon accepting employment in the U.S.

\_\_ **Do addresses and the corresponding time frames provided by the subject concur with those obtained from the verification?**

If the SSN provides information that does not match the addresses provided by the subject, then the employer should question the applicant about these findings. The omission of addresses may be intentional, and therefore, further investigation is warranted.

However, the absence of an address may merely be an oversight. The subject may have resided at the location for only a short time or may have used the address of a friend or relative while between residences. Many individuals, particularly those who are single, will use a parent's address as their permanent address rather than their actual place of residence, which is more likely to fluctuate.

[**Warning**: The Social Security Number Trace is not meant as an official registry of past addresses. It only contains those addresses that have come up in a Trace report. An employer should NEVER use the fact that a claimed current address does not appear on a Trace report as any sort of indication that a person gave a false address. There can be multiple reasons why a valid current address would not appear. That also means a SSN Trace should not be confused with current address verification. ]

\_\_ **Do past employers (and the corresponding time frames) given by the subject coincide with those revealed by the SSN verification?**

If additional employers are identified, then they should be contacted to verify the validity of previous employment.

[**Warning:** Past employment does not appear routinely in credit reports or Social Security Trace reports. The lack of past employers listed on credit or trace reports should not be the basis of an employment decision.]

\_\_ **Is the subject using and/or associated with more than one Social Security Number?**

All additional Social Security Numbers should be examined. However, the extra numbers may actually be very similar to that of the subject and potentially the result of a data-entry error. Also, the number may belong to a spouse, relative, or friend who applied for credit jointly with the subject.

\_\_ **Does the date/year-of-birth and/or age match that provided by the subject?**

In some instances, the age or year of birth may be off by a year or two. This may be due to computer or typographical error.

If there is a great difference, say, greater than seven years, that could be a matter of concern.

[**Warning:** Some employers do not want to view a date of birth or year issued due to legal considerations concerning age discrimination. Background screening firms have the ability to leave out date of birth and year of issue for clients who have sensitivity to that issue. ]

___ **Are additional individuals using the same Social Security Number?**

Doing a Trace search may reveal more than one individual is using the same SSN. There are several legitimate reasons why.

The additional individual may be a friend or relative who has applied for joint credit with the applicant, or there may have been a typographical error if the additional individual happens to have a Social Security Number very similar to that of the applicant.

If the applicant claims to have no knowledge of the additional individuals, then he or she should be advised to contact the credit bureau from which the information was obtained. He or she should start by contacting all three credit bureaus. See Chapter 17 on Identity Theft.

A Social Security Trace report or verification showing numerous different names can indicate the applicant is using a fraudulent SSN. Clarify this by asking the applicant to contact the Social Security Administration to demonstrate it is genuinely his or her number. Alternatively, an employer can contact the Social Security Administration *after* a tentative employment offer is made.

# Social Security Number Table – First 3 Digits

The chart below shows the first 3 digits of the Social Security Numbers assigned throughout the United States and its possessions. See the "Notes" at the end of the list.

For online information on employment and SSNs, visit www.ssa.gov/employer/stateweb.htm.

THIS FOLLOWING DATA IS FOR INFORMATIONAL PURPOSES ONLY.

| | | | | |
|---|---|---|---|---|
| 001-003 | New Hampshire | | 247-251 | South Carolina |
| 004-007 | Maine | | 654-658 | |
| 008-009 | Vermont | | 252-260 | Georgia |
| 010-034 | Massachusetts | | 667-675 | |
| 035-039 | Rhode Island | | 261-267 | Florida |
| 040-049 | Connecticut | | 589-595 | |
| 050-134 | New York | | 766-772 | |
| 135-158 | New Jersey | | 268-302 | Ohio |
| 159-211 | Pennsylvania | | 303-317 | Indiana |
| 212-220 | Maryland | | 318-361 | Illinois |
| 221-222 | Delaware | | 362-386 | Michigan |
| 223-231 | Virginia | | 387-399 | Wisconsin |
| 691-698 | | | 400-407 | Kentucky |
| 699* | | | 408-415 | Tennessee |
| 232-236 | West Virginia | | 756-763* | |
| 232 | North Carolina | | 416-424 | Alabama |
| 237-246 | | | 425-428 | Mississippi |
| 681-690 | | | 587-588 | |

| | | | | |
|---|---|---|---|---|
| 752-755* | | | 600-601 | |
| 429-432 | Arkansas | | 764-765 | |
| 676-679 | | | 528-529 | Utah |
| 433-439 | Louisiana | | 646-647 | |
| 659-665 | | | 530 | Nevada |
| 440-448 | Oklahoma | | 680 | |
| 449-467 | Texas | | 531-539 | Washington |
| 627-645 | | | 540-544 | Oregon |
| 468-477 | Minnesota | | 545-573 | California |
| 478-485 | Iowa | | 602-626 | |
| 486-500 | Missouri | | 574 | Alaska |
| 501-502 | North Dakota | | 575-576 | Hawaii |
| 503-504 | South Dakota | | 750-751 | |
| 505-508 | Nebraska | | 577-579 | District of Columbia |
| 509-515 | Kansas | | 580 | Virgin Islands |
| 516-517 | Montana | | 580-584 | Puerto Rico |
| 518-519 | Idaho | | 596-599 | |
| 520 | Wyoming | | 586 | Guam |
| 521-524 | Colorado | | 586 | American Samoa |
| 650-653 | | | 586 | Philippine Islands |
| 525, 585 | New Mexico | | 700-728 | Railroad Board** |
| 648-649 | | | 729-733 | Enumeration at Entry |
| 526-527 | Arizona | | | |

* = New areas allocated, but not yet issued

** 700-728 Issuance of these numbers to railroad employees was discontinued July 1, 1963.

## Notes:

The same area, when shown more than once, means that certain numbers have been transferred from one state to another, or that an area has been divided for use among certain geographic locations.

Any number beginning with 000 or ending with 0000 will NEVER be a valid SSN.

Information in SSA records about an individual is confidential by law and cannot be disclosed except in certain very restricted cases permitted by regulations.

# Chapter 14

# Education and Credentials Verifications

## Education Verification

Educational credentials can be an important part of an employer's decision making process in hiring. Educational achievement tells an employer a great deal about an applicant's ability, qualifications, and motivation. Many employers feel that educational qualifications are a critical factor in predicting success on the job. For many positions, education is a prerequisite in terms of subject matter knowledge or for obtaining the appropriate license for the position.

Studies that examined resumes and application forms have shown that as many as 30% of all job applicants falsify information about their educational backgrounds. The falsifications can include outright fabrications such as making up degrees from legitimate schools the applicant never attended or valueless degrees from diploma mills.

An applicant can falsify his or her educational achievements based upon some semblance of fact, such as claiming degrees from schools the applicant actually attended but did not obtain the degree claimed. Typically a candidate turns their months or weeks of attendance into an AA degree, or claims a BA or an advanced degree even if they did not complete the course work or fulfill all graduation requirements.

The incidence of fraud underscores the need to do research on the educational qualifications of candidates. Confirming diplomas, degrees, or certificates, along with dates of attendance, verifies applicants' education and skills as an indication of their ability to do the job. Confirmation also supports their honesty by substantiating claims made on an application. To the employer, the value of diplomas, degrees, or certificates also depends upon the quality of the degree-granting institution. The issue of accreditation is important for employers attempting to determine if a degree translate into knowledge, skills or experience that will be of benefit in the workplace.

Colleges and universities also have a vested interest in confirming educational accomplishments. Confirming an applicant received a degree from their school helps their graduates and promotes the reputation of their school. Conversely, uncovering the fraudulent use of the school's good name helps to preserve and protect the school's reputation.

Under the Federal Family Educational Rights and Privacy Act (FERPA) — if a school has received funds from an applicable program from the U.S. Department of Education — there are limits to what student information a school may make available to an employer. Schools cannot provide confidential information such as actual grade point average. A school will normally provide dates of attendance and degrees and honors awarded. If an employer has a need to obtain the actual listing of course work and grade point average, then a signed release is required. For employment purposes, many employers simply want to verify dates of attendance and any degree awarded, but some employers will ask the applicant to contact the school and obtain the transcript, which typically requires the applicant to contact the school to obtain the appropriate record access procedures. Schools normally charge a fee for a transcript; a well-prepared job applicant may already have a transcript copy in hand.

# How Third Parties Perform Verifications

Employers have two methods to verify education. First, the employer can call the school themselves. The alternative is to outsource the process to a third party firm, typically an employment screening firm.[1]

For employers that verify education in-house, the first step is to locate the school. Schools normally verify information through the Registrar's office. Schools and universities can often be located through directory assistance or by use of an internet search engine.

An excellent source of information on the locations and contact information for schools is the *National Directory to College and University Student Records*, published by BRB Publications, Inc. The current edition published in 2004 lists detailed contact information for over 4,750 U.S. and Canadian Universities.[2]

Here is a sample contact for the author's alma mater—

> **University of California-Los Angeles.** Office of the Registrar, Box 951429 (1105 Murphy Hall). Los Angeles, CA 90095-1429: 310-825-3801; fax-310-825-6299, 9AM-5PM. Enrollment: 33,277. Records go back to 1898. www.ucla.com
>
> Verifications made by telephone are free.
>
> **Awards: Bachelors, Masters, Doctorate.**
>
> Attendance and degree information available by phone, fax, mail. Search requires name plus SSN, DOB. Also helpful: approximate years attended. Mail back fee is $5.00.
>
> Transcript available by fax, mail. Search requires name plus SSN, DOB, exact years attended, signed release. Also helpful: approximate years attended. Fee is $5.00
>
> Your phone number is required. International fax fee $10.00 per document. Services can be billed. Mail requests: SASE is required. Adverse incident report source: Student Affairs. Alumni Association phone: 310-825-2586.

---

[1] At an increasing number of colleges and universities schools, students may access their information online, direct from the school's computerized database. Access is password protected, and the student's ID or username is required.

[2] see www.brbpub.com

This entry gives the contact information for UCLA, the number of enrolled students, how far back records go, and the website. It also tells the employer that they can obtain a telephonic verification at no cost at the phone number provided. The degrees offered by UCLA are also listed so that an employer can instantly tell if the degree claimed matches what the school awards. If an employer wants something mailed back, they will need to send a check for $5.00 and send a self-addressed stamped envelope (SASE) along with identifying data such as the applicant's Social Security Number (SSN) and date of birth (DOB). If the employer wants a transcript, then the requirements at UCLA, like most schools, are more stringent, perhaps requiring the exact year of attendance and a signed release. On all requests other than by phone, the requestor's phone number is apparently required. If UCLA is asked to fax internationally, then there will be a fee, presumably required in advance.

Two other resources — the school's office that handles adverse incident reports, and alumni association records — may supply employers with more detailed information about the student's history. A release would likely be necessary.

## Typical Verification Problems

There are some practical issues an employer may experience when verifying past education.

### Name of Institution

The popular name for a school may not match the "official" name. That may throw off employers when searching for a school. A person may report that he or she went to school at Michigan— the actual school name is the University of Michigan, which means looking up the school name under "U" for university rather than "M" for Michigan.

Also, given the number of schools in the U.S., there can be name matches. For example, there are Gateway Community Colleges in both New Haven, Connecticut and Phoenix, Arizona.

### Different Campuses

Many state university systems have a number of campuses. The employer must be certain to call the right division or campus. For some state systems, there may be a central Registrar's office for the entire system. In other cases, each campus maintains its own records.

### Use of Fax Numbers

Some schools, not all, allow an employer to fax a form asking for the information. A blank request form may be found online on the Registrar's webpage, or a "forms" page.[3] Employers ask for results to be returned by fax, though some schools will not fax back the results unless it is to a local number or toll-free number, or they only mail back results.

---

[3] BRB Publication's *National Directory to College and University Student Records* online or CD gives registrar office access information, see www.brbpub.com

# Private Repositories of Information

There is an increasing trend for schools to provide their information to private firms that gather degree information from schools, thus act as the schools' agents. A school may refer the requester to a website where the degree verification must be purchased from the private party.

The two largest services that host school information and provide employers with a primary source of data are—

1. National Student Clearinghouse  www.nslc.com
2. Credentials, Inc.  www.degreechk.com

> **Author Tip** ➡ Schools do not operate on the same schedule as Corporate America. One of the great advantages of academic life is the academic calendar. Traditionally, schools are off during the Summer as well as breaks over Thanksgiving, Winter, Spring, and even ski-week. Due to an urgent hiring need, one corporation asked a pre-employment screening firm to verify a degree in 24 hours, no matter what. However, the request occurred over the Winter break in late December, and everyone from the school had gone home. Short of breaking and entering into the school administration building or hacking the school's computers, it simply was not possible to get the verification any sooner then January 2. The employer was very upset and ordered in no uncertain terms the background firm to "do its job and get it done tomorrow," but to no avail. The moral of this story is employers must keep in mind there can be delays if hiring is done during summer or over holiday periods. When a business needs go up against the academic schedule, the school wins.

When performing educational verifications, there are occasions when it may appear the person has falsified a credential. This can occur when a school apparently has no record of the applicant attending. In that situation, the employer must ask the school to search records under the Social Security Number to guard against an error caused by a variation in name. Many institutions of higher learning have different campuses, or different colleges that may maintain different records, so the employer needs to double check to be certain they are calling the right school and the right campus. One screening firm reports that a major university did not verify an applicant with the first name "Thomas." It turned out that in his college days "Thomas" went by "Tommy," and that university recorded by exact name only. Under the name "Tommy," the applicant had the degree claimed.

If an employer suspects a phony academic credential, a good practice is to give the applicant a reasonable opportunity to prove his or her claim. Jumping the gun can lead to a perfectly qualified applicant being wrongfully eliminated from consideration.

# Do Not Jump to Any Conclusions...

Case in point: *USA Today* (Feb. 20, 2004) reports the case of Louisville womens' basketball coach Tom Collen. Collen was a successful coach at Colorado State. On May 1, 2002, Vanderbilt hired him away, but he was forced to resign the very next day because of allegations he misrepresented that he had two masters degrees from Miami University (Ohio), and Miami reported he had just one. At the time, the story about Notre Dame's problems with its football coach and a false resume was very much in the news, so resume fraud was a hot topic in college sports.

It turned out that Collen did in fact have the credentials he had listed. Events moved so fast that he had no time to make heads or tails out of the discrepancy and set things straight. By the time the dust settled, Miami University discovered they made an error in their communication to Vanderbilt. Because of a clerical error and everyone being in a rush, a highly regarded coach was falsely maligned. The good news is that Collen reportedly received a financial settlement and is continuing his career at Louisville.

The moral of this story is things are not always what they seem at first blush. The applicant should have a meaningful opportunity to review, reflect and respond to any allegations of educational dishonesty.

If all else fails, then ask the applicant for a copy of the degree. However, there is a critical next step. An employer should never take a diploma at face value. The employer should fax the copy to the registrar's office. The registrar will know immediately if it is a legitimate degree issued to one of their graduates. However, a degree all by itself cannot be accepted as positive proof at face value since they are easily faked.

## "Genuine" Fake Diplomas on the Rise

Getting a college diploma apparently no longer requires years of hard work, taking tests, paying tuition or even reading a book. Why bother going though the formalities when all a person needs is a credit card and a web browser in order to buy an authentic looking diploma that mimics real colleges, universities and even high schools across the U.S. Go to any search engine and run keywords such as "fake Diploma" and anyone can instantly "graduate" from nearly any school in America with a very handsome and authentic looking diploma suitable for hanging.

One such website advertises that it creates, "very realistic diplomas/transcripts. These diplomas/ transcripts are extremely high quality printed on official parchment quality paper. You can show your employer and they will never doubt that you indeed attended college. You will not find better quality anywhere!!!"

Some of these sites "officially" caution that the diplomas and transcripts are intended for "Novelty and Entertainment Use Only." However, the fake documents you receive do not have a disclaimer written any place on them.

With statistics showing that resume fraud is a significant issue, employers must be very cautious about accepting a physical diploma as proof of a degree. When presented with a physical diploma or transcripts, employers should fax a copy to the school to confirm its authenticity. Most background firms can tell stories of faxing copies of degrees, supplied by the applicant, to high schools and colleges only to be told the degree is a fake.

These fakes have not entirely escaped official attention. In Illinois, the legislature passed a law in 2004 aimed at addressing educational fraud. It is now a Class A Misdemeanor to knowingly manufacture or produce for profit or for sale a false academic degree, unless the degree explicitly states "for novelty purposes only."

# How To Recognize Diploma Mills and Worthless Degrees

In 2004, the United States Department of Education announced that it was moving toward developing a "positive list" of accredited institutions of higher education. This announcement was in response to a series of incidents of federal workers found holding worthless credentials issued by "diploma mills." The government became concerned about diploma mills when a senior director in the Department of Homeland Security was placed on administrative leave following an allegation that his degree came from Hamilton University, allegedly a diploma mill that operated out of a refurbished hotel in Evanston, Wyoming. A memo issued April 2004, by the Federal Office of Personnel Management (OPM) reported other abuses including a computer specialist who claimed both a bachelors and masters degree in computers obtained only four months apart, and a police officer who submitted his resume online to a diploma mill and received a degree based upon life experiences. One convenient place to check colleges and universities lists is the federal Office of Postsecondary Education website at www.ope.ed.gov/accreditation/search.asp which provides searching by accreditation agency.

Here is another alarming story. In April, 2004, Ronald Pellar (aka Ronald Dante), 75, was sentenced to eight months in prison for his role in running a diploma mill called Columbia State University. According to a news release from the Department of Justice—

> "According to court documents, Pellar set up Columbia State University in 1996 at a business office in San Clemente. CSU falsely represented itself to be a government-approved university in Louisiana and it falsely claimed to have faculty and accreditation sufficient to confer bachelor's, master's, and doctoral degrees by correspondence in as little as one month. Pellar created promotional materials, including a university catalog, that falsely told prospective students that CSU had an administration composed of PhDs and medical doctors and that it had received full accreditation from legitimate accreditation agencies. The catalog cover featured a photograph of a building that bore no relation to the fictitious CSU or its San Clemente office. The mailing address was in Metairie, Louisiana, but in reality that was only a mail forwarding service that simply resent all correspondence to CSU's addresses in Southern California. The indictment

alleges that, in November 1997, Pellar fled the U.S. and continued to direct the activities of CSU from Mexico through subordinates.

The indictment alleges that CSU took in more than $10 million from students around the country in tuition fees during the scheme. The indictment alleges that students around the country were defrauded because CSU gave them the impression that it was a legitimate academic institution, but in reality it was nothing more than a diploma mill."

## A Great Degree Verifying Website From Oregon

The State of Oregon has an Office of Degree Authorization that tracks the authenticity of college degrees. According to this office—

> Diploma mills – or degree mills – are substandard or fraudulent "colleges" that offer potential students degrees with little or no serious work. Some are simple frauds, a mailbox to which people send money in exchange for paper that purports to be a college degree. Others require some nominal work from the student but do not require college-level course work that is normally required for a degree.[4]

In fact, Oregon's website contains an extensive list of schools that are not recognized as legitimate in Oregon. See www.osac.state.or.us/oda/unaccredited.html.

State of Michigan offers its list at www.michigan.gov/documents/Non-accreditedSchools_78090_7.pdf.

> **Author Tip** ➡ Diploma mills should not be confused with legitimate schools that offer valuable distance-learning programs over the internet. If an employer is not familiar with a school, the employer should review the school's website to check out the its accreditation, curriculum, faculty, and graduation requirements.

## Waging War Against Diploma Mills and False School Credentials

The problem with these lists of diploma mills is that the mills are moving targets. They can change their names overnight and new ones can sprout up as easily as a scam artist can put up a new internet site. There are literally hundreds of websites that offer fake degrees, diplomas, or certificates.

Here are some of the spins used in their advertisements—

- *Here is an opportunity to get ahead*
- *University diplomas*
- *Obtain a prosperous future, money earning power, and the admiration of all*
- *Diplomas from a prestigious university*
- *Based upon your present knowledge and life experience*
- *No required tests, classes, book or interview*

---

[4] State of Oregon Office of Degree Authorization located online at www.osac.state.or.us/oda/

- *Bachelors, masters, MBA, and doctorate (PhD) diplomas available in your field of choice*
- *No one is turned down*
- *Confidentiality assured. Call now to receive your diploma within days*

Of course, these schools have no classes, no faculty, no course catalog, and typically a single point of contact such as email address or P.O. Box, but these schools typically do have really impressive websites with outstanding testimonials and wonderful pictures of campus life. They also provide wonderful looking diplomas, which any good graphic artist and print shop can produce.

The following excerpt comes from an article by Mr. John Bear, who has written on educational issues—

"There are more than 300 unaccredited universities now operating. While a few are genuine start-ups or online ventures, the great majority range from merely dreadful to out-and-out diploma mills — fake schools that will sell people any degree they want at prices from $3,000 to $5,000.

"It is not uncommon for a large fake school to "award" as many as 500 Ph.D.s every month.

"The aggregate income of the bad guys is easily in excess of $200 million a year. Data show that a single phony school can earn between $10 million and $20 million annually.

With the closure of the FBI's diploma mill task force, the indifference of most state law enforcement agencies, the minimal interest of the news media, and the growing ease of using the internet to start and run a fake university, things are rapidly growing worse."

Mr. Bear's web page is at www.degree.net/html/diploma_mills.html. His book, *Bears' Guide to Earning Degrees by Distance Learning,* is also a resource for employers and is available from that site.

---

**Author Tip** ➡  One suggestion to help employers is to include the following language on the employment application:

*"Please list all degrees or educational accomplishments that you wish to be considered by the employer in the employment decision."*

This statement has the advantage of putting the burden on the applicant to determine if they want to report a degree or educational accomplishment. The applicant is on notice that any degree they report can be used by the employer for the employment decision. If the applicant chooses to report a worthless degree, or a degree not earned, they can hardly complain if an employer uses that to deny employment, even if the degree was not a requirement of the job.

---

# Complexities of Academic Accreditation

How are employers supposed to avoid diploma mills or worthless degrees? The first line of defense is to see if a school is accredited by a **recognized accrediting agency.**

Accreditation is a complicated process of peer and self-assessment aimed at improving academic quality and demonstrating the quality of an institution to the public. A legitimate accreditation can give the employer a greater comfort level in the legitimacy and quality of an applicant's degree.

Unlike most of the rest of the world however, accreditation in the United States is not done directly by the government. In the United States, numerous private organizations can provide accreditation to a school. The recognized U.S. accrediting organizations all have one thing in common— the accrediting agencies are in turn accredited by one of two nationally recognized agencies.

1.  **The U.S. Department of Education.** According to the Department of Education, "The goal of accreditation is to ensure that education provided by institutions of higher education meets acceptable levels of quality." For an overview, see the website at
    www.ed.gov/admins/finaid/accred/accreditation.html#Overview

    The Department of Education limits their accreditation activities to institutions that receive federal money such as financial aid. The U.S. Department of Education has provided an internet listing of organizations that it has accredited to be an accrediting agency. See
    www.ed.gov/admins/finaid/accred/accreditation_pg4.html

2.  The other accepted organization that can accredit the accreditors is the **Council for Higher Education Accreditation (CHEA)** found at www.chea.org, CHEA is a successor to two previous organizations that also fulfilled this function — the Commission on Recognition of Postsecondary Accreditation (CORPA) and the Council on Postsecondary Accreditation (COPA). At the CHEA website, employers can find not only the names and contact information for each recognized organization, but can also do a look-up by state that gives a link to every school accredited. The Department of Education website states, "CHEA is currently the entity that carries out a recognition function in the private, nongovernmental sector."[5]

CHEA and the U.S. Department of Education **classify accrediting institutions** into three types of organizations—

1.  **Regional accreditation organizations.** There are six regional associations that accredit public and private schools, colleges, and universities in the United States. In the list at the end of this chapter, eight such organizations are listed. Two have two branches reflecting a division for "colleges and universities" and a division for "other types of institutions." A list with details about these regional accreditations organizations is located at—

    *   www.chea.org/Directories/regional.asp
    *   www.ed.gov/admins/finaid/accred/accreditation_pg5.html.

---

[5] for more information on the function of CEHEA, see www.ed.gov/admins/finaid/accred/accreditati on_pg2.html

2. **Single purpose national accreditation organizations.** These organizations accredit a particular type of school. At the end of the chapter are the names of eleven such national organizations, of which only six are recognized by CHEA. All are recognized by the U.S. Department of Education. The six national accreditation agencies recognized by CHEA are located at www.chea.org/Directories/national.asp. Additional ones accredited by the U.S. Department of Education listed at www.ed.gov/admins/finaid/accred/accreditation_pg6.html

3. **Specialized and professional accrediting organizations.** These academic programs are administratively located in degree or non-degree granting institutions. These bodies range from acupuncture (Accreditation Commission for Acupuncture and Oriental Medicine) to veterinary medicine (American Veterinary Medical Association, Council on Education). For lists, see—

   - www.chea.org/Directories/special.asp
   - www.ed.gov/admins/finaid/accred/accreditation_pg6.html#aom

## Tips on How to Verify That a School is Accredited

Given this framework, how should an employer attempt to verify if an institution that grants a degree can legitimately do so?

One way is to ask the school directly. Another is to search the school website to find the name of the accrediting organization, then utilize the web pages for the Department of Education or CHEA to confirm if the accreditation agency is real and to locate that agency's website. At the accreditation agency's website you may confirm that the school is on the list of accredited institutions.

When contacting a college or university degree, look for the word "Accreditation." Do not be satisfied if a school uses terms such as "pursuing accreditation," "chartered," "licensed," "registered," "recognized," "approved," or "accredited faculty" — these words may have some meaning is some states, but our concern is accreditation by a "recognized" accreditation agency, and these legitimate agencies are listed at the end of this chapter. A claim by a college or university to have been issued a state license as a condition "to do business" is *not* an indication that school is legitimate.

Another approach is to go to www.CHEA.org and click on the link for "Institution Database." This link takes the user to an agreement page. After agreeing to the terms of use you will be linked to a page offering various lookups. An employer can do a look-up by state and view every accredited school in a state, regardless of whether the accreditation agency is CHEA or Department of Education approved. An employer can review the list, find the institution, then click on its link. An employer can use the Department of Education schools list as well; see www.ope.ed.gov/accreditation/search.asp.

## Database of Institutions Accredited By Recognized United States Accrediting Organizations

A listing of all recognized CHEA accreditation bodies is at www.chea.org/pdf/CHEADirectory.pdf

Keep in mind that even if an employer reviews the accreditation resources, things can still slip through the cracks. Here is why—

- A school may have changed names
- A website may not have been updated
- A school may have lost accreditation
- A school may be accredited, but since the last accreditation, the quality has fallen, or
- The so-called accreditation was by a non-accredited accreditation agency, see below.

# Fake Accreditation Scams

The scam artists that sell fake credentials have figured out that it helps to be accredited. Therefore, the diploma mill and fake diploma industry has developed a fake accreditation industry. There are even fake agencies with names similar to authenticated agencies.

The bottom line— just because a school says they are accredited does not mean they are.

According to the State of Oregon, here are some "fake" accreditation agencies—

- Accrediting Commission International
- American Association of International Medical Graduates
- Association for Online Academic Excellence
- Association of Christian Colleges and Theological Schools
- Central States Council on Distance Education
- Distance Graduation Accrediting Association
- Distance Learning Council of Europe
- European Council for Distance & Open Learning
- International Association of Universities and Schools
- International University Accrediting Association
- Office of Degree Authorization
- Southern Accrediting Association of Bible Institutes and Colleges
- United Congress of Colleges
- US-DETC[6]
- Virtual University Accrediting Association
- World Association of Universities and Colleges

---

[6] US-DETC is not to be confused with the legitimate DETC or **Distance Education and Training Council**, based in Washington DC. DETC is recognized by both the Department of Education and CHEA.

# High Schools, Trade Schools, and Distance Learning Programs

**Verifying high school degrees.** This is easily done if the employer is hiring from a local familiar area, provided the employer understands that during summer vacation and school breaks there may not be anyone at school offices to answer the phone. When employers hire from outside their locale, there are practical problems. First, it is not always easy to locate a particular high school. For the most part, each state will have a website or an office that provides school lists. If a student received his or her high school degree by testing, such as GED, then there can be delays in obtaining those through the appropriate state or district office.

**Verifying post-secondary school, vocational school, or trade school awards or Distance Learning Programs.** Not all vocational or trade schools are accredited by recognized accrediting organizations. Each state has an agency in charge of certifying state-approved educational programs. If there are questions about the legitimacy of a vocational or trade school, then an employer should contact the appropriate authority in their state. There are numerous distance learning programs available on the internet as well. The same verification rules apply. An employer should determine what accreditation or recognition they have, then evaluate the value of the degree. It is the employer's job to evaluate how a degree or coursework from a vocational or trade school or distance learning program translates into a person's ability to perform a given job. An employer needs to view the school's literature or website to find out about the quality of the facilities and faculty, the course of study required, and other factors that go into determining the value of the education to the job position.

For more information about post secondary vocational and trade schools, see—

- www.ftc.gov/bcp/conline/pubs/services/votech.htm
- www.ed.gov/students/prep/college/consumerinfo/pubsresources.html
- www.ed.gov/students/prep/college/consumerinfo/index.html

# Credentials Verifications

For confirming the status of a license or credential needed to legally practice a profession there are literally thousands of governmental boards that have control over licenses and professional certification. There are also private organizations that issue certifications.

Examples? Hospitals may need to verify the license status of a doctor, nurse, radiologist, or physical therapist. An employer may want to confirm that a person claiming to be an accountant is, in fact, licensed by the state board that licenses accountants. In order to verify a license an employer needs to require that the applicant provide key information—

- The name or type of license
- The issuing agency
- The state AND date of issuance
- Current status and date of expiration

Nearly every governmental licensing organization can be contacted by telephone. Many agencies have internet sites where verifications can be done immediately. An extensive listing of agency websites that offer some type of free search of a licensee list is available at www.searchsystems.net/freepub.php. For the professional, BRB Publications, Inc. at www.brbpub.com has several products including *The Public Record Research System* that lists all 7,800+ licensing boards in the U.S., with details on how to verify a licensee by phone, fax, or online.

> **Author Tip ➡** During the verification process, an employer will also want to know if the agency reports any actions against the license or derogatory information about the applicant. That helps to determine if the applicant's license is in good standing.

**Confirmation of certifications issued by private organizations.** Certificates issued by private organizations are typically difficult to verify. Unless the certification was conducted through an accredited school, such as a community college, it is a substantial challenge to verify it. These can include items such as any kind of "Certificate of Good Work," and a number of different computer and software-related certificates provided by a number of organizations, legitimate or otherwise.

# Conclusion— Educational Credentials Checking

When it comes to education credentials — employers beware! If an employer is not familiar with the school, check it out. Do not be fooled by a slick looking website with pretty pictures of a campus and academic scenes and glowing testimonials. The existence of a very academic looking diploma does not mean anything; fake schools are capable of producing some very convincing worthless diplomas. A common sense approach is a valuable tool in evaluating the worth of a degree. Look first to see if it is accredited by a recognized accreditation agency, then take reasonable steps as necessary to confirm the value of the degree such as examining the curriculum, the qualifications and reputation of the faculty members, the facilities, the qualifications of the institution's president, or graduation requirements.

## List of Regional Accrediting Organizations

The following Regional Accrediting Organizations are recognized by both CHEA and DOE.

**Middle States Association of Colleges and Schools** www.msache.org

Delaware, the District of Columbia, Maryland, New Jersey, New York, Pennsylvania, Puerto Rico, and the U.S. Virgin Islands, including distance education programs offered at those institutions.

**New England Association of Schools and Colleges** www.neasc.org

Connecticut, Maine, Massachusetts, New Hampshire, Rhode Island, and Vermont.

**North Central Association of Colleges and Schools** www.ncahigherlearningcommission.org

Arizona, Arkansas, Colorado, Illinois, Indiana, Iowa, Kansas, Michigan, Minnesota, Missouri, Nebraska, New Mexico, North Dakota, Ohio, Oklahoma, South Dakota, West Virginia, Wisconsin, and Wyoming.

**Northwest Commission on Colleges and Universities**  www.nwccu.org

Alaska, Idaho, Montana, Nevada, Oregon, Utah, and Washington.

**Southern Association of Colleges and Schools**  www.sacscoc.org

Alabama, Florida, Georgia, Kentucky, Louisiana, Mississippi, North Carolina, South Carolina, Tennessee, Texas, and Virginia.

**Western Association of Schools and Colleges, Accrediting Commission for Senior Colleges and Universities**  www.wascweb.org

California, Hawaii, the United States territories of Guam and American Samoa, the Republic of Palau, the Federated States of Micronesia, the Commonwealth of the Northern Mariana Islands and the Republic of the Marshall Islands.

# National Accrediting Organizations

The following National Accrediting Organizations are recognized by both CHEA and the DOE—

**Accrediting Association of Bible Colleges (AABC) Commission on Accreditation**

www.aabc.org

**Accrediting Commission of the Distance Education and Training Council (DETC)**

www.detc.org

**Accrediting Council for Independent Colleges and Schools (ACICS)**

www.acics.org

**Association of Advanced Rabbinical and Talmudic Schools (AARTS)**

212-363-1991  (Web: N/A)

**Association of Theological Schools in the United States and Canada (ATS)**

www.ats.edu

**Transnational Association of Christian Colleges and Schools Accreditation Commission (TRACS)**

www.tracs.org

The following National Accrediting Organizations are recognized only by the DOE—

**Accrediting Bureau of Health Education Schools**

**Accrediting Commission of Career Schools and Colleges of Technology**

**Accrediting Council for Continuing Education and Training**

**Council on Occupational Education**

**National Accrediting Commission of Cosmetology Arts and Sciences, Inc.**

For listings of Specialized and Professional Accrediting Organizations, see—

www.ed.gov/admins/finaid/accred/accreditation_pg4.html

www.chea.org/Directories/special.asp

**Chapter 15**

# Other Important Screening Tools for Employers

An employer may consider any number of sources of information on applicants. This chapter examines driving records, workers' compensation records, civil court records, judgments, liens, bankruptcies, sex offender registries, security clearances, military records, merchant databases, and the National Wants and Warrants list.[1]

## Driving Records

The employment screening industry refers to driving records as "MVRs" Many employers simply call them driver records and utilize them as a safe hiring tool whether the position applied for involves driving America's highways and byways or not.

It is important to note that each state has its own database of drivers' records — there is no national database. Typical information on an MVR might include full name, address, Social Security Number, physical description, and date of birth along with conviction and accident history. Also, there is license type, restrictions, and endorsements which can provide useful background data on an individual. However, while there is some consistency, what appears on a MVR record varies from state-to-state. Also, the specific access requirements will vary by state, depending on individual state privacy laws and administrative rules. Sometimes the version of the MVR provided to employers by a background screening firm will contain the applicant's name and driving record, but with personal data — date of birth, address, physical characteristics, etc. — removed.

### Driving Occupations

For a person who is driving a company vehicle or is in a "driving position" for the company, such a check is a necessity. However, in most jurisdictions, "driving for work" is very broadly defined. The question is, *when* is an employee driving for work? The term "driving for work" can cover *any* employee behind the wheel of a vehicle for the employer's benefit.

---

[1] A new tool for employers is the use of Internet searches of applicants, or utilizing social networking sites such as Facebook or MySpace. For more information, see www.esrcheck.com/safehiringupdates.php

For example, an employee who drives to the office supply store during lunch or between branches of the same firm, or attends classes that are paid for by the company, can be considered "driving for work." If an accident occurs in any of those situations, an employer may be sued.

The one time an employer likely has no responsibility for an employee's driving is for an employee who only drives to work and drives home. This is referred to as the "Going and Coming Rule" — a worker driving to work and driving home does not drive for the employer in-between work and home.

For positions that involve driving, an employer can review the applicant's driving history and verify a license's status. A check of the driving record may also give insight into the applicant's level of responsibility. Just having moving violations may not relate to the ability to perform the job, but if an applicant has a history of failing to appear in court or pay fines, that can be a telling indicator about their level of responsibility.

Statewide driving records databases may be the first place where difficulties with drugs or alcohol are revealed — there may be "driving while impaired" violations. However, there are restrictions on the use of this information under the federal Americans with Disabilities Act (ADA), plus anti-discrimination law in certain states. The employer must determine whether the information is job-related and should exercise discretion when using it to the detriment of the applicant.

## Record Access Restrictions and Signed Releases

In recent years there have been major changes regarding the release of motor vehicle data to the public and to employers. These changes are a direct result of the Driver's Privacy Protection Act (DPPA), which was signed into law by President Clinton in 1997. States now differentiate between who are *permissible* users (14 permissible *uses* are designated in DPPA) and who are *casual requesters* to determine who may receive a record and/or how much personal information is reported on the record. For example, if a state DMV chooses to sell a record to a "casual requester," the record can only contain personal information (address, gender, etc.) with the written consent of the subject.

Does the *permissible use* designation apply to employers obtaining driving records on applicants? **No,** unless the employer is hiring a licensed commercial driver such as truckers of 18-wheelers, etc. This means that **employers must obtain a signed release** from a prospective applicant before access to the record is granted.[2]

Here are the advantages—

Employers usually obtain MVRs through the services of an employment-screening firm. A screening firm can typically obtain a driving record in one or two business days. Most states permit the release forms to be on file with the screening company rather than require a paper release submitted with each request.

Screening companies, in turn, usually utilize the services of an MVR vendor. MVR vendors obtain and supply records nationwide in a timely manner for a very low service fee. The MVRs are delivered electronically, are uniform in appearance and are reliable in content. There are a limited number of national and regional driving record vendors. Many of the national vendors limit their clientele to

---

[2] except for commercial drivers' records

permissible users, such as the insurance industry, but there are vendors who will process requests from employers and background screening companies, *providing* the employer or company complies with state regulations.

Some states' DMVs offer a notification program for employers who hire a large number of drivers. The employer is notified if a driver has activity or a moving violation. There is typically a modest fee paid to register each driver, then a fee when activity is shown. More information about these programs can be obtained from state DMVs.

# Idea! Have Applicants Obtain Their Own Records

Some employers who hire for a position that requires a driver's license require all applicants to bring a certified driving record to the job interview. Applicants must visit their local DMV office and request an official copy of their own license, with a "certification" stamp showing it is authentic. To obtain your own records, there is usually a minimal fee charged by the DMV

There are two reasons that employers engage in this process. First it makes the application process go more efficiently by eliminating those without a satisfactory driving record.

Secondly, some employers feel that by requiring an applicant bring in a certified license, an employer can eliminate from consideration applicants who are unable or unwilling to accomplish that small task. By requiring an applicant to jump through a "small hoop" the employer eliminates anyone who is unable or unwilling to compete a simple task.

At least one employer has reported a potential "scam" in the process. An applicant with a poor driving record found a friend with a "clean record." Both the applicant and the friend went to the DMV and got their records. The applicant then took the bottom half off the friend's clean record, added the top part of his record with his name, then copied the fake record. He then presented what looked like a clean record to the employer. Fortunately, the applicant's ingenuity was not matched by his artistic skills. He created a suspicious document that caused the employer to look deeper and uncover the deception.

Readers interested in extensive, detailed information about state driving records, access restrictions and procedures, and violation codes, may refer to BRB Publications' *The MVR Book* and the *MVR Decoder Digest*, see www.brbpub.com/books/

# Workers' Compensation Records

Employers have become very aware of the high costs of compensation claims. The loss to American business from both fraudulent claims and re-injury causes many employers to want to know whether a job applicant has a history of filing workers' compensation claims.

At the same time, the Federal Americans with Disabilities Act (ADA) as well as numerous state law, seek to protect job seekers from discrimination in hiring as a result of filing valid claims. The ADA also seeks to prevent the discrimination against workers who, although suffering from a disability, are nevertheless able to perform essential job functions as long as there are reasonable accommodations.

Before the ADA was introduced in 1990, employers had little legal limitations when it came to asking job applicants about their medical history or past workers' compensation claims. Now there are numerous legal restrictions that must be observed closely. The bottom line is that an employer cannot request workers' compensation records in order to have a policy of not hiring anyone who has made a claim. It is discriminatory to penalize a person who has exercised a lawful right and filed a valid claim.

Employers are well-advised to contact a labor lawyer before seeking to obtain workers' compensation records. A labor law expert can assist an employer in preparing company policies, job descriptions, and forms and procedures necessary to comply with the ADA, such as a **conditional job offer** and **medical review form.**

## Obtaining and Using Workers' Compensation Records

The following brief summary describes the major points involved in obtaining and using workers' compensation records.

1. There are wide variations between the states in the availability of these records. In a few states, the records are not available to the public, period. In other states, it can take two to three weeks to obtain a record. In some states, there are special requirements before obtaining the records such as a notarized release. Because they are familiar with state regulations, background screening firms can assist employers in obtaining these records.

2. Under the ADA, an employer may not inquire about an applicant's medical condition or past workers' compensation claims until a **conditional job offer** has been extended. A conditional job offer means that a person had been made an offer of employment, subject to certain conditions such as a job-related medical review. The conditions must be fulfilled prior to coming on-site for employment.

3. Any questioning in a job interview must be restricted to whether the person can perform the essential job functions *with or without* reasonable accommodation.

4. If a candidate discloses a disability, then there should not be any follow-up. Questioning should be limited to whether that applicant can perform the job.

5. Only after a **conditional job offer** has been extended may an employer inquire about past medical history, require a medical exam, or inquire about workers' compensation claims.

6. The better procedure is to have an applicant fill out a written **medical review form** that reviews their medical condition and workers' compensation claims history, and provides consent as well. Firms that utilize medical examinations as part of their procedures should have a written medical review policy.

7. The procedure should be administered uniformly. If one worker in a job category is the subject of such an investigation, then all applicants must be treated the same. However, an employer

may treat different job categories differently. Not all employees must be sent for a medical exam.

8. If a history of filing workers' compensation claims is found, then the offer may only be rescinded under very limited circumstances:

    a. The applicant has lied about a workers' compensation history or medical condition, usually during a medical examination;

    b. The applicant has a history of filing false claims;

    c. The past claims demonstrate the applicant is a safety or health threat to himself or others in the opinion of a medical expert;

    d. The past claims demonstrate the applicant is unable to perform the essential functions of the job even with a reasonable accommodation.

9. If the applicant has lied on the medical questionnaire, then the employer may be justified in rescinding the job offer based upon dishonesty. If an applicant has a history of multiple claims that have been denied, then an employer may be justified in rescinding the offer. The recession is based upon an inference of fraud, not disability. However, even individuals with false claims will usually not have multiple false claims. Rescinding the job offer based upon reasons (b) and (c), however, does require a medical opinion.

Some firms content that a workers' compensation record may also be used to determine the truthfulness of information on a job application on the theory that an applicant may try to hide a past employer where a claim was filed. However, even with this justification, if used, the best practice may be to review the records post-hire only.

# Civil Lawsuits

Another screening tool for employers involves using civil court records. A civil case occurs when one party sues another. Unlike a criminal case, which is brought by the government and a defendant can face jail time, a civil case is typically about money.[3] Civil cases can be for torts or contracts.

A contract case is when one party sues another for a violation or enforcement of an agreement. A tort case is when one party sues another for an injury in civil court for actions other than breech of contract. Tort cases can involve both intentional conduct and unintentional conduct. An unintentional tort is typically a negligence action, such as an auto accident. An intentional tort can be such causes of action as assault, intentional infliction of emotional distress, or some intentional wrong. Although the same conduct could also form the basis of a criminal case as well, a criminal case is only brought by the government. Tort cases can involve injury to the person (assault and battery or infliction of emotional distress), injury to property (trespass, theft, conversion), injury to reputation or some business advantage (slander and liable).

---

[3] There are some lawsuits that seek remedies other than money, such as a request for an injunction, which is where a party seeks to have another party ordered to do or not do some physical act. Lawsuits brought in family court or probate courts are also considered civil lawsuits.

---

**A Familiar Illustration of Civil and Criminal Cases—**

When O.J. Simpson was prosecuted for murder, that case was brought in the criminal courts by a prosecuting attorney. That case was called, *"The People vs. Simpson."* However, Simpson was also sued in civil court by private attorneys hired by plaintiffs who were the family members of the victims. That case had the title of the parties to the case— *Sharon Ruffo, et al. vs. Simpson.*

---

The fact that Simpson was found not guilty in the criminal case but guilty in the civil court also illustrated the difference between civil and criminal cases. In a criminal case, a prosecutor must convince all twelve jurors unanimously, beyond a reasonable doubt, the defendant is guilty. On the other hand, in a civil case, a plaintiff only needs to prove the case by a preponderance of the evidence, which is a much lesser standard. That standard means that it is more likely than not the plaintiff proved the case. Sometimes it is described as a standard whereby the plaintiff must prove the case by 51%. In civil cases, a plaintiff only needs nine jurors to agree, not all twelve.

The following table illustrates the differences between civil and criminal cases.

| Subject | Criminal Case | Civil Case |
|---|---|---|
| Who brings the case | A government prosecutor | A private party normally though their attorney |
| Name of case | People vs. Smith (if state court) or the United States of America vs. Smith (if federal court) | Adams vs. Smith (the names of the parties) |
| Outcome if Plaintiff successful | Criminal sanctions including imprisonment, fine, and probation terms | Monetary damages. In some lawsuits the plaintiff may be seeking injunctive relief. |
| Jurors who must agree with the plaintiff | All twelve-unanimous verdict | Nine jurors out of 12 |
| Standard of proof | Government must overcome the presumption of innocence by proving guilt beyond a reasonable doubt. | Plaintiff only needs to show their side is more convincing, so that it is more probable they are right. |

## Obtaining Civil Case Records

Obtaining civil records is similar to obtaining criminal records, but with many more complications. Similar to criminal records, civil records are located at the county courthouse level in state court. Researchers locate records for civil lawsuits in the same fashion they search for criminal records. However, unlike criminal records that have a connection to where a defendant has lived or worked, civil records can be more diverse geographically. The rules for jurisdictions are somewhat broader for civil cases. For example, in a lawsuit for breach of contract, the suit can be brought where the contract was formed or breached. An applicant may not have lived in any of those places. Therefore, civil record searches can take on a "needle in a haystack" quality. Published appellate cases where the lawsuit was appealed can also be searched. However, published appellate opinions represent an extremely small fraction of all civil cases.

## Locating Identifiers

The next big problem is that civil records have very few identifiers. The initial search is by name match only, a similar problem to searching for federal criminal records, as explained previously. For example, if an Adam Smith is prosecuted for a crime in state court, there is likely going to be a date of birth, a Social Security Number, or a driver's license somewhere in the court file. However, if Adam Smith is involved in a civil lawsuit as either a defendant or a plaintiff, there are no reasons that any identifiers are necessarily present in the file.

In order to determine if a civil record belongs to the job applicant, it is necessary to look for clues in the files. In most civil lawsuits, the allegation will contain a description of the party that is related to the reason for the legal action. So, if there is a lawsuit for medical malpractice, and the applicant is not a doctor, it is not likely a legal action involving your applicant. The complication occurs when a court researcher goes to the courthouse; the researcher normally does not have the knowledge to determine from the lawsuit or other information in the file if the lawsuit pertains to your applicant. The researcher normally must ask the court clerk for a copy of the file. However, civil files can be very large and also very expensive to copy. Before getting surprised with a large bill for court clerk copies, an employer needs to determine how many pages are necessary. Usually the first five or so pages will set out the identities and relationship of the parties. There may be other means in the court file to identify the parties, such as information on a summons or proof of service of the lawsuit, reference to employment, or data found in exhibits attached to the civil complaint.

## Utilizing Civil Records in Employment Decisions

The third issue is to determine if a civil lawsuit has any relevance to the position. Many civil lawsuits are clearly not job related. For example, if an applicant is a plaintiff (the person bringing the action against the defendant) in a personal injury lawsuit, this would not likely have bearing on job performance (unless the applicant was suing a past employer and had a custom and practice of doing that). A civil search may uncover a case of dissolution of marriage. Often such lawsuits will have a detailed description where the parties are bringing out all the dirty laundry. As interesting as that might be to read from a human-interest point of view, it likely to have little bearing upon employment.

Employers are likely looking for lawsuits that have some rational relationship to the job or workplace performance. These lawsuits can be directly job-related, such as an harassment suit by a former employee or character traits that may be involved in workplace behavior, such as lawsuits for violence or dishonest behavior.

Of course, as we have seen over and over again, nothing is as simple as it seems when it comes to public records. Every lawsuit has some sort of caption that indicates the court where it is filed, the parties involved and the type of lawsuit. However, lawsuits in state or federal courts usually only have a rather cursory description of the nature of the action in the caption. The lawsuit may only be described as a "Suit for Damages." That tells a researcher nothing at all. In order to determine the underlying nature of the litigation, it is again necessary for the court researcher to request that the court clerk copy the first few pages where the essential thrust of the allegations of the lawsuit are usually recounted. The file could indicate, for example, that if a person was being sued for harassment in the workplace, the defendant was the employer or manager.

# Judgments, Liens, and Bankruptcies

Another source of data about job applications are the judgment, liens, and bankruptcy databases.

**Judgments** are typically a final decision in court cases where the judge or jury awards monetary damages against the defendant. Often, the party who wins the judgment will record the judgment with the county records clerk. Information provider firms have assembled national databases consisting of these judgments. The purpose is to allow employers to know an applicant has been sued. As with civil records, employers must approach this type of information with caution when using the records for employment purposes. First, the employer must make sure the judgment is valid. Next, the employer needs sufficient data to conclude that the judgment pertains to their applicant. Third, the employer must determine if the judgment is relevant to a job. Another problem is that judgment databases can have errors and be missing judgment records. In addition, the great majority of civil lawsuits are settled out-of-court, so there may not be a judgment entered.

Another search that some employers use is a search for **tax liens**. These searches are typically combined with a judgment database search. When a person or business owes delinquent, unpaid taxes to a government agency, the agency can *record* a tax lien that gives the government priority to collect upon the proceeds from the sale of real property. Like judgments, tax liens must be taken with a grain of salt. An employer must determine 1) if that tax lien data applies to the applicant, 2) if the data is accurate, and 3) if used for employment purposes, is it relevant and fair? Tax liens are generally found in the same state database that records Uniform Commercial Code (UCC) filings.

The third category is **bankruptcies**. All bankruptcy cases are heard in a federal court. The information is easily accessible, however, employers should exercise extreme caution in attempting to utilize these records. A private employer *may not discriminate* with respect to employment if the discrimination is based solely upon the bankruptcy filing.[4] Federal law makes it very clear that using a bankruptcy against a job applicant can be a form of discrimination. A person cannot be penalized for the lawful exercise of a legal right. Under the "fresh start rule," a consumer is entitled to start over again; if a person went into bankruptcy to re-arrange a life, but cannot get a job because of the bankruptcy, then that person could never get ahead. He or she would be placed in a new form of debtors' prison, unable to break the debt cycle. If for any reason an employer feels that bankruptcy is relevant to the job, then the employer should consult his/her attorney to determine if there is a bona fide occupational reason to justify consideration of a bankruptcy search.

---

[4] see 11 USC 525 regarding bankruptcy record use

# Sexual Offender Databases

Another tool available to employers is the use of sexual offender databases. These state sexual registration requirements, popularly known as Megan's Law, were signed into law by President Clinton on May 17, 1996. The law had two primary goals. The first goal was to require each state and the federal government to register sexual predators. The second goal provided for community notifications by the local police.

Although a potentially valuable tool, these databases were the subject of a news story in 2003. The story centered on a survey of the fifty states by a child advocacy group that found literally tens of thousands of offenders who should have been registered but were "lost" in the system. Either the sexual offenders did not register or the state did not know where the registrants were located.

The group – Parents for Megan's Law – contacted all fifty states by telephone. According to news accounts, the study showed that states, on average, were unable to account for twenty-four percent of sex offenders who were supposed to be in the databases. Eighteen states said they were unable to track how many sex offenders were failing to register, or simply did not know.

---

**According to ABCnews.com   (October, 2003)**

"The extent of the problem was dramatized this summer in California when a state audit of the sex offender registry found that some 23,000 people on the list were unaccounted for because their records had not been updated in at least one year. The records of 14,000 of those had not been updated in at least five years.

"That audit was carried out after the state had mounted a concerted effort to locate missing sex offenders, after a report in January by The Associated Press that California law enforcement had lost track of about 39 percent of the more than 70,000 people on the list."

---

## FAQ's about Sexual Offender Registration Searches

### How does a sexual offender search differ from a criminal search?

Both searches are looking for criminal records but a sexual offender search is limited to violations that require a person to register with a central authority. The state registry is a compilation of records of offenses that are sexual in nature, taken from counties across the state. Of course, a criminal search is looking at all criminal records regardless of nature or gravity.

### How does an employer locate sexual offender records?

Three sources for sexual offenders lists exist. The most accurate sources are the lists maintained directly by states and counties. However, not all jurisdictions provide sufficient detail to identity or locate an offender.

Below are four helpful URLS with links to the state and county sites currently available.

- www.sexoffender.com
- www.sexualoffenders.com/sexoffenders.htm

- www.prevent-abuse-now.com/register.htm
- www.brbpub.com/pubrecsites.asp

In addition, there are information provider firms that have assembled large national databases composed of data from various state and local sources. These national sexual offender databases are an excellent secondary or supplemental tool to perform a broader search that is national in nature. However, some of the national database providers are unable to produce a date of birth or other identifier for all states, so an employer can be stuck with a name match only, which would have to be confirmed by going to a more specific state database or pulling a court record. Finally, the U.S. Department of Justice announced its searchable website in 2005 at www.nsopr.gov. The database supplies what each state reports to it.[5]

### What are the advantages of a sexual offender search?

In theory, a sexual offender search includes the entire state, so that it is less subject to the limitations of a county search. A person may have been convicted of a sexual offense in a county where an employer or background firm may not know to look. For example, a person may not list the county where the sexual offense occurred, and it may not come up on a SSN Trace.

### Are sexual offender searches subject to accuracy issues?

Yes. There are a number of problems with the accuracy and completeness of the data, similar to the issues described in Chapter 12 for criminal databases. There can be both false positives and false negatives. A "false positive" is where there is a match, but upon further research it is not the same person as the job candidate. A "false negative" is where a sexual offender is not located, but in fact the person is a sexual offender. That is one reason why searchable websites, including those maintained by states, have disclaimers warning that records can be missed.

### What are the reasons for a "false negative?"

False negatives can occur for several reasons. First, if the person should have registered but did not, and the state did not track him or her down, then the current information may not be on the list. Second, if a sexual offender leaves a jurisdiction and goes elsewhere and does not register, the offender will not show up on the appropriate sex offender registry. That person may roam free unless a law enforcement agency happens to encounter them and runs them through a computer that identifies them as a sex offender. Some jurisdictions are discussing ways to monitor the movements of sex offenders, such as electronic bracelets, which can be an expensive proposition if it works at all.

The difficulty with these registries is that each state does things its own way, and not all states do it as well as others. As seen from the ABC News stories above, many states have large holes in their databases. It is an immense task, requiring substantial resources, to track all offenders, and a difficult challenge when law enforcement budgets are tight. Perhaps a person may have committed

---

[5] The use notes for each state should be carefully reviewed. In addition, unlike commercial databases, the state lists that are reported through the U.S. Department of Justice database may drop an offender's name when the registration period is over.

a number of crimes, including a sex crime, and pursuant to a plea bargain, the sex crime may have been dismissed, resulting in the person not being required to report.

A false negative can also occur because less severe offenses may not be reportable. Nearly all states place some access limits based on the severity of the offense. For example, most states divide offenses into three levels and will only report the more serious offenses, such as level 3 only, or levels 2 and 3.

Also, the date the database "began" can affect a search. Many states began their databases after 1997. In reviewing state databases, it is important to know when the database was started. Another reason for false negatives is that registration is not necessarily permanent. Depending upon the state, the offense and the offender, registration requirements can be removed.

The manner in which records are kept by the state can also contribute to an error rate. Each state's central repository must collect data from local courts. If a county is late or inaccurate, then there can be errors. Also, not every state makes their central repository available to the public — a researcher would need to check county by county for a complete sex offender record search.

These reasons underscore the basic message— searches, although valuable, are far from perfect and should just be one element in the background screening process.

**What are the reasons for "false positives?"**

As in all public records, identifiers are critical before assuming that a criminal record belongs to a particular applicant. With approximately 300 million people packed into 50 states in the U.S., the statistical likelihood of people with the same name and same date of birth is higher than one might imagine. For this reason, an employer should never assume that an applicant is a sexual offender without the positive proof of an ID match or pulling the underlying court record.

**What should an employer do if a sexual record is located?**

The same rules apply as to any criminal records. First, the employer must ensure that they have positive ID so that they know the record belongs to their applicant. Next, the employer needs to determine if the applicant lied about a criminal record by reviewing the application and what was said in the interview. This is where the AIR Process discussed in Section 2 proves so valuable. Third, the employer or volunteer group should pull a copy of the court file from the courthouse to ensure that the information is accurate and up to date and to ascertain the details. Finally, the employer must also consider if, under EEOC rules, there is a "business justification" for disqualifying the applicant based on the criminal conviction. For example, in California it is illegal to use the sexual offender information unless there is an identifiable group at risk, meaning that there must be a job-related reason to utilize sexual offender data.

# Sex Offender Records— Conclusion

A sexual offender database search, both nationwide and using state and local websites, is an extremely valuable tool. It is especially valuable when the position involves access to a group-at-risk such as children or the elderly. However, employers and volunteer groups need to understand that these databases are not primary tools, but supplemental tools subject to some degree of error and should be utilized with some caution and in conjunction with other safe hiring procedures.

# Military Records

Another record that some employers may want to verify is a military service record. With the national focus on the military after the events in Iraq, it is likely that employers will receive applications from those with military experience. Many employers find that applicants with military service provide critical skills and training that are extremely valuable in the workforce.

The standard way to verify military records is to ask an applicant for a copy of his or her DD-214. This is the common term for the document given to all members of the military who are discharged from the U.S. Navy, Army, Air Force, Marine Corp, or Coast Guard. The "DD" stand for Department of Defense. The short name is "discharge papers."

For employers who want more than a cursory confirmation of military service, the story goes much deeper. There are actually a number of different copies of the DD-214 with different pieces of information. A discharged service person receives copy 1, which has the least information. The copy with the codes that gives the nature of the discharge, i.e. General, Honorable, Dishonorable, etc. – and details of service is actually on copy 4. The codes characterize the service record of a veteran. The codes are known as SPD (Separation Program Designator), SPN (Separation Program Number) and RE (Re-Entry) codes. Other issues with access and use of the DD-214 are listed below.

1. For a discharged service person to get copy 4, the person must actually ask for it.

2. If a person did not ask for the copy 4, or wants to hide some embarrassing fact, then the person may only present copy 1 to an employer.

3. If the employer wants copy 4 and the applicant does not have it, then there can be a problem acquiring and understanding the copy. The employer can have the applicant sign a Form 180 and send it to the National Personnel Records Center (NPRC) in St. Louis, Missouri. However, there can be a wait — up to six months. Some records are no longer available due to a very destructive fire at the St. Louis facility in 1973.[6]

4. A note of caution. Even after getting a copy 4, there is the issue of translating the military codes. There are websites that provide a complete list of the codes and definitions. However, should civilian employers use these codes for hiring decisions, since the codes were meant for internal military use only? The various codes may represent items that have no foundation or were the result of clerical errors, or are simply not related to job performance.

When making hiring decisions, employers should be very careful before attempting to draw conclusions from various codes on the DD-214. Using the codes on the DD-214 to infer conduct in order to make hiring decisions could result in claims of discrimination, or decisions being made based upon irrelevant or unsubstantiated criteria. The situation can be further complicated if the employers insist that an applicant first obtains a complete DD-214 and then rejects the applicant. That record request could potentially be viewed as evidence of discrimination.

---

[6] although the government has reconstructed some of the records by use of other military documents. For details about these military records, see www.archives.gov/research_room/obtain_copies/veterans_service_records.html

An employer should also exercise caution in using a discharge as a basis of an employment decision. There are four common types of military discharges: honorable, general, undesirable, and dishonorable. Of these, only a dishonorable discharge is given as a result of a factual adjudication equivalent to a criminal trial. In order to avoid potential EEOC claims, an employer should treat a dishonorable discharge in the same fashion as a criminal conviction, taking into account the various factors reviewed in Chapter 11. A general discharge or undesirable discharge may or may not have any bearing on employment and generally should not be the basis of an employment decision.

The best advice may be to use the basic DD-214 to confirm a person was in fact in the military, then ask for the names of references from their military service to obtain job-related information that would be relevant to an employment decision.

# Security Clearances

On occasion an employer may want to verify that a person had a security clearance in the past. This will occur when an employer receives a resume from an applicant indicating, as part of past qualifications, he or she had a security clearance. The employer wants to confirm that the person is being truthful. Some employers will ask if a person has ever had a security clearance, if they had been refused one, and details about the last clearance held, including granting agent, level, date granted and date expired.

If the current job requires a security clearance, then there is already an established process in place. Entities who have security clearance needs, such as private employers used by government, will have an authorized designatee in charge of a process called the Special Security Officer (SSO). Security clearances stay with the entity and do not travel with the individual. If the individual leaves a position, the person no longer has a clearance. When a person leaves one employer that requires a clearance to go to another position that also requires a clearance, then the SSO at each entity arranges for the appropriate transfers.

If an applicant is applying for a job that does not require a security clearance, and the employer wants to verify the past claim, then the best procedure is for the employer or screening firm to contact the past employer and request the name and mailing address of the SSO. If a copy of a release is provided, then the SSO may verify that there was some level of clearance, but may not go into detail.

Another source of information is various sanctions and disbarment databases. These are typically lists of governmental actions or sanctions relating to some sort of license, qualifications, governmental sanctions or the ability to do business with the government. For further discussion and examples, see www.ercheck.com/safehiringupdates.php or visit the free public record links at www.brbpub.com.

# Merchant Databases

Some firms offer a product commonly referred to as a merchant database, typically used by large retailers who hire a large sales staff. They are databases in which retail stores contribute information about employees who have admitted to theft, whether or not a criminal case occurred. The database may also contain other information such as records from various state criminal databases and Social Security Number information. These searches are relatively inexpensive, which is an advantage for employers. Since retail positions are often filled by lower-paid employees with high turnover rates, there is pressure on retailers to keep background screening as low cost as possible.

The difficulty with using these databases is the underlying reliability of the data. The database includes information on individuals who were never prosecuted. The information is often based upon a report from a store loss-prevention professional concerning an interrogation where a person admitted they committed the theft in exchange for not being prosecuted. Since the matter did not go to court, there would not be a court file, police report, or any sort of adjudication in any factual matter.

Given the nature of these databases, there are two obvious problems with their use. First, use of such a database may run contrary to the EEOC rules, as explained in Chapter 5. An applicant may be the victim of a negative decision without any underlying factual determination. Considering the EEOC is concerned about the use of arrest records on the basis that an arrest is not a factual determination, unsubstantiated reports of a confession to store personnel are potentially troublesome.

The second issue is whether these databases are in fact FCRA compliant. Under the FCRA, a Consumer Reporting Agency (CRA) must take reasonable procedures to ensure accuracy. If information from a merchant database is a reported confession with no judicial findings, a CRA may have difficulty justifying the negative information unless it independently contacts the person performing the interview to confirm the facts. Otherwise, a person denied a job on the basis of a merchant database could claim a lack of reasonable procedures. The difficulty with relying upon confessions is that there is a large body of research that shows that false confessions are a significant issue in interrogations. Without other evidence such as recovery of stolen items or eyewitness confirmation, relying on confessions of theft as a basis for entry into a merchant theft database can be problematic.[7]

# National Wants and Warrants

Until 2001, there was one portion of the National Crime Information Center (NCIC) database that was available to employers through pre-employment screening firms. The NCIC is the FBI's automated "national" criminal record database described in Chapter 12. The portion of the database available to employers was known as the National Wants and Warrants. The data contained information on fugitives wanted on federal warrants, also state warrants when a state was willing to extradite an offender back to the issuing state. However, in 2001 the FBI decided to close access to background screening firms who in turn provided this useful information to employers.[8]

From the point of view of both law enforcement and the public, making this database available to background screening firms was a tremendous advantage to public safety. Background firms would routinely run numerous names through this database that law enforcement and the FBI would not have the tracking resources to do. In addition, when an employer ran the name through the screening firm, the screening firm had the current address for the person being run. If there was a "hit," then law enforcement had the opportunity of getting a wanted and potentially dangerous person off the street.

Given the Justice Department statistic that the recidivism rate can be a high as 67% for a person released from prison within three years,[9] it would seem that executing arrest warrants would be a big

---

[7] See: "Dangerous Confessions: The Psychology Behind False Confessions," by Susan Davis, *California Lawyer*, April, 2005

[8] Although the NCIC is not available, some private firms gather extensive wants and warrants information directly from various local and state jurisdictions and make those available. In addition, as of the printing of this book, at least one state will provide the names of jurisdictions where wants and warrants may be outstanding, but no other details.

[9] see the section on Criminal Records and Repeat Offenders in Chapter 11

public safety priority. A screening firm's use of the "Wants database" would certainly seem to further the goals intended of the NCIC database.

According to the website for the FBI Criminal Justice Information Services (CJIS), the organization with responsibility for the NCIC database, part of the CJIS mission is to—

> "Reduce terrorist and criminal activities by maximizing the ability to provide timely and relevant criminal justice information to the FBI and to qualified law enforcement, criminal justice, civilian, academic, employment, and licensing agencies concerning individuals, stolen property, criminal organizations and activities, and other law enforcement related data."[10]

By allowing access to this database, law enforcement did not have to rely entirely on the strategy of "chance encounter" to apprehend wanted individuals. The primary method for apprehending wanted individuals in the United States is this strategy of **"chance encounter."** Most warrants set patiently in the system in the hope that someday the wanted person will come back into the grips of law enforcement on some chance encounter such as a traffic stop. Unfortunately, it is also possible the person will come to the attention of law enforcement for a new crime. Because of budget restrictions and a host of other priorities, very little law enforcement resources are spent looking for individuals who are the subject of an arrest warrant.

Even though public safety is their mission and there is a crisis in American law enforcement when it comes to warrants, the FBI decided in 2001 to deny private employers one of the most potent weapons they had to protect the workplace and citizens by denying screening firms' access to the this database.

According to Version 2.0 of the CJIS Security Policy issued in 2001, under the section title "Dissemination of State or Federal Hot File Records," and with the subject "Commercial Dissemination," the FBI Policy is as follows—

> "The commercial dissemination of state or federal hot file records obtained from NCIC (CJIS Systems) is prohibited. Information derived for other than law enforcement purposes from national hot file records can be used by authorized criminal justice personnel only to confirm the status of a person or article, i.e., wanted or stolen. Any advertising of services providing 'data for dollars' is prohibited. The request for bulk data is prohibited. Authorized agencies are allowed to charge a processing fee for disseminating data for authorized purposes."

Then, under Commentary Section, the CJIS Security Policy further states—

> "The wholesale marketing of data for profit is not permitted, as in the example of a pre-employment screening or background checking company requesting that wanted person checks from NCIC be conducted on individuals for various non-criminal justice employments."

By shutting down access to wants and warrants, the "chance encounter approach" is more institutionalized then ever. However, according to a June, 1999 investigative report by the *San Francisco Chronicle* this chance approach is very troubling. The article indicated there was backlog of 2.5 million warrants in California alone. The article noted a number of drawbacks to the "chance encounter" methodology of serving warrants—

---

[10] see additional CJIS information at www.fbi.gov/hq/cjisd/about.htm

1.  The current system has cost the lives of police officers who had "chance encounters" with felons having no intention of risking custody. For example, one of the most potentially dangerous situations for a police officer is making a routine traffic stop or having some other sort of contact with a person who has an outstanding warrant. The felon does not know if the police officer knows about the warrant, leading to instances where felons not wanting to take a chance of going back to prison will shoot police officers.

2.  An individual who ... remains at large subjects the public to the risk of new offenses. A significant amount of crime is committed by criminals-at-large with outstanding warrants.

3.  The chance encounter may never occur, leaving the wanted person at large.

4.  Even if there is a chance encounter, the individual may be using a false identity, or the computer check may not reveal the warrant.

5.  The criminal justice system is downgraded, since accused offenders know if they ignore a want or warrant, there is a significant chance nothing will ever happen to them.

According to the article, one judge familiar with the crisis described it as a "Cataclysmic breakdown of the law enforcement system."

Allowing screening firms access to the wants and warrants would seem to be a much better solution than relying on "chance encounters."

## A Few Thoughts from Author Les Rosen...

The unintended consequences of this governmental policy to deny private screening firms access to the Wants and Warrants database unfortunately are to favor criminals and terrorists at the expense of employers, employees, and the American public. The government continues this position even after the events of 9/11/2001, when the government learned the harm in not sharing information.

Concerned instead with a "data for profit" issue, the government position ignores the fact the screening industry is an essential part of the U.S. homeland security and law enforcement effort, efficiently accomplishing tasks the government is either unable or not authorized to perform. The screening industry, pursuant to consents under the FCRA, has the opportunity to review the criminal histories of literally millions of job applicants every year and has current address information as well. It is true the screening firms do not provide this service for free. There is a cost to everything. On the other hand, the competitive nature of the screening industry prevents any firm from making an undue profit. From a cost-benefit point of view, the amount that employers are charged for this service from screening firms is small compared to the enormous benefit to society and law enforcement. It is not likely that a new government bureaucracy can provide the same data any faster, cheaper, or more efficiently. Additionally, since the data from the NCIC can be distributed by state agencies, screening provides a revenue source for those state and local agencies that process the data. The bottom line is that the old system benefited everyone, and the new restrictions simply makes it easier for those persons who have wants and warrants to avoid detection, endangering the lives of law enforcements officers and public.

# Chapter 16

# Screening Essential Non-Employees

## Screening Vendors and Independent Contractors

Up to this point *The Safe Hiring Manual* has emphasized that employers are sitting ducks for expensive litigation, workplace violence, negative national publicity, and economic loss if they do not take measures to conduct pre-employment screening and exercise due diligence in hiring.

However, many employers do not realize they potentially face the same exposure from vendors, independent contractors, or temporary employees from staffing firms. Employers' risk management controls often do not take into account the "need to know" about these workers who are on not on their payroll but are on their premises, with access to computer systems, clients, co-workers and assets.

The law is absolutely clear that if a vendor or independent contractor harms a member of the public or a co-worker, the employer can be just as liable as if the person were on the employer's payroll. All of the rules of due diligence discussed in Chapter 3 apply with equal force to vendors, temporary workers, or independent contractors. A business can be liable if, in the exercise of reasonable care, the business should have known that a vendor, temporary worker or independent contractor was dangerous, unqualified or otherwise unfit for employment. An employer has an absolute obligation to exercise due diligence not only in whom they hire on payroll, but in whom they allow on premises to perform work.[1]

In addition, many employers have found out the hard way that unscreened workers from a vendor or staffing firm or hired as an independent contractor can also cause damage. When an employer is the victim of theft, embezzlement, or resume fraud, the harm is just as bad regardless of whether the worker is on their payroll or someone else's payroll. No employer would dream of walking down the street and handing the keys to the business to a total stranger, yet many employers across America essentially do exactly that everyday when engaging the services of vendors and temporary workers.

For example, firms routinely hire nighttime janitorial services without appropriate due diligence. The fast food industry routinely hires suppliers and service firms that come into their restaurants to clean or deliver supplies. Without knowing who has the keys to facilities, an employer is giving total strangers unfettered access to his or her business — and is totally exposed to the risk of theft of property, trade secrets or damages.

Employers do have difficulty ensuring they have exercised due diligence regarding vendors and independent contractors. There is not a direct employer-employee relationship. However, an employer still has liability issues if a vendor or independent contractor causes harm to third parties. Case law

---

[1] see e.g. a compilation of cases throughout the U.S. annotated in 78 ALR3d 910

from courts throughout the United States is clear that businesses have liability for acts of independent contractors. The duty of care must be exercised in all aspects of hiring, and it applies to retaining the services of a vendor or independent contractor.

# Employment-like Nature of the Relationship

Another issue for an employer is that an independent contractor may be misclassified and is, in fact, an employee. A business may have an incentive to classify a worker as an independent contactor in order to avoid putting the worker on payroll, avoid paying benefits or overtime, avoid paying employer taxes like withholding, nor paying into state funds for workers' compensation or unemployment insurance. As discussed in chapter 3 on negligent hiring, the IRS along with state agencies and courts look closely at the true nature of the labor relationship, and not what the parties choose to call it. IRS' 20-point guideline is the most-often used determiner of the true nature of the relationship. As example guidelines, a true independent contractor may have business cards, insurance, and yellow page advertising. A true independent contractor would probably provide their services to multiple businesses. However, a firm that hires a so-called independent contractor that works under the firm's direction and control — and the so-called contractor does not provide the same services to other firms, and does not have insurance, a business license, or other typical attributes of a true independent business — is likely to be considered an employee in disguise. Proper classification is an important issue for a business, especially if an event occurs that triggers an audit such as an "independent contractor" filing a workers' compensation claim or seeking unemployment insurance payments. If an employer is found to have misclassified workers as independent contractors instead of payroll employees, the business can be held accountable for back taxes and all payments to state programs that should have been made, as well as large fines and penalties.

In addition, the Federal Trade Commission (FTC) has suggested that the FCRA applies to situation where a consumer has an employment-like relationship regardless of the label. FTC staff-issued letters of opinion following the 1997 amendment to the FCRA — although the letters do not have the force of law — are considered highly persuasive. In the Mr. Herman L. Allison letter dated February 23, 1998, the FTC staff was asked if the FCRA rules concerning disclosures and releases applied in the case of a certain trucking company who employed independent owner-operators. The truck drivers were not on the payroll as employees, but "owned and operated their own vehicles." The FTC rejected the position that there was not an employment relationship. The FTC cited a Fourth Circuit Court of Appeals case[2] that the broad purposes of the FCRA required that "employment" not be strictly defined in traditional terms, but would include independent contractor relationships. As a result, the application of the FCRA does not depend upon whether a worker receives a W-2 tax form as an employee or a 1099 as an independent contractor. The essential factor is the **employment like nature of the relationship**. Keep in mind, if an employer has classified a worker as an independent contractor, it is critical to adjust the background screening consent form to take out any reference to employment in order to not change the independent contractor status. An employer can utilize wording referring to an "engagement" instead.

---

[2] *Hoke v. Retail Credit Corporation,* 521 F.2d 1079, 1082 (4th Cir. 1975), *cert. denied,* 423 U.S. 1087 (1976)

# What Are The Employer's Screening Duties?

The practical issue for employers is how they ensure that vendors or workers hired by third parties are safe and qualified. Fortunately, there are a number of cost-effective avenues available to employers to protect their businesses, their workers, and the public. Employers can insist in any contract for any service that any time a worker comes on premises, that worker has been the subject of a background screening. This has become a practice gaining widespread acceptance in American businesses. An employer *must* have a hard and fast rule — no worker supplied by a third party is allowed to work unless the worker has a background check.

The following steps can help in administering the process—

1. Make it clear to all current service providers and independent contractors that the business has a background checking policy for its own employees, and the same policies apply to all workers supplied by a vendor or work performed by third party vendors.

2. Subject independent contractors to the same screening and safe hiring practices as would be done with a W-2 employee. Some employers may wish to alter the consent form in order to clarify that the individual being screened is an independent contractor, and that the screening procedure does not alter the nature of the relationship.

3. When using a temporary worker from a staffing firm, require the staffing agency or Professional Employer Organization (PEO) to conduct a background check. As an extra precaution, an employer can request that the FCRA release extend to the employer's workplace. Under the FCRA, as long as the applicant consents to this, it is perfectly acceptable for both the staffing firm and the employer of the workplace to review the background report.

4. A vendor must certify there has been a background check that is acceptable under the employer's criteria.

5. The vendor must provide the employer with the name and identity of the firm performing the background check, and a statement that the firm performing the background checks is experienced and suitable for the assignment.

6. For extra precaution, require the vendor to provide the employer with a "Certification of Compliance." This certification should indicate the following—

   - The name, identity and qualifications of the firm that provided the vendor's background checks.

   - A statement that vendor has advised their background service of the criteria required.

   - Only workers who pass the background check are allowed on your premises.

   - In the event there is something negative in the worker's background, the vendor has thoroughly investigated the issue, and has determined the matter does not otherwise disqualify the worker from going onto your premises.

   - In the event there is negative material, then the business may ask to review it as well to determine if the worker meets the business's criteria. The best practice is to require the vendor to have the worker sign a release permitting that process.

Employers often ask if these policies are illegal and will make it more difficult to find vendors and suppliers of services. The answer is a resounding NO to both questions. An employer has an absolute right to exercise the same due diligence in selecting vendors that they would use in selecting their own employees. As long as the screening requirements are fair, non-discriminatory and validly job-related, there is no legal reason why an employer cannot protect himself/herself.

In this way, vendors and suppliers also demonstrate that safe hiring and due diligence are critical parts of their business as well as their commitment to supplying quality workers. Any vendor not willing to engage in pre-employment screening is not likely to be a good choice anyway. Although there may be a slight increase to the vendor in terms of expenses, a vendor should be willing to pay necessary costs to obtain good workers and to satisfy the needs of the employer-clients.

The bottom line— there is no reason for employers not to require that vendors and independent contractors undergo background checks.

> **Author Tip** ➡ Employers need to be careful to make sure the vendor, staffing firm, or PEO does more than go through the motions. Reports must be ordered, tracked, documented. The employer must require that the vendor certify that they have reviewed the screening reports looking for any red flags, and that they took appropriate steps. Although this may seem obvious, it is worth clarifying who has the responsibility to review background reports and determine eligibility to work.

# Staffing Firms and Temporary Workers

One area where employers can be blindsided is working with temporary or staffing agencies. Employer would not intentionally bring people on the premises with criminal records, unsuitable for a particular job. Yet employers consistently hire temporary workers and independent contractors from staffing agencies with no idea who these people are. Employers hire temporary workers from agencies often without any assurance as to their background or qualifications. Given the sensitive information found on business computer systems, even one bad temp could do substantial damage.

Most staffing firms do not routinely perform due diligence checks before supplying workers. Staffing firms often do not want to incur the costs associated with doing background checks on workers they place. That reluctance is for two reasons. First, staffing firms are exceptionally cost conscious and given the large volume of workers they handle, the cost of background checks, such as criminal checks, has a significant impact on their bottom line. Second, staffing firms must work on an extremely tight time line. Staffing firms need to place workers as soon as possible. Every hour of delay is lost revenue to a staffing firm. In addition, if a potential worker is told to wait a day or two for a background check, that worker may go down the street to another staffing firm.

Staffing firms often advertise that they carefully "screen" all applicants, but without stating the extent of the screening. A business utilizing staffing services needs to be very specific when asking a staffing firm exactly what screening is done. Unless the staffing firm specifically tells the employer a criminal check is being done, an employer should assume that no criminal check is being conducted. An employer is well advised to require some of the steps suggested in the previous pages in order to confirm exactly what is being done in terms of a criminal background check. Issues regarding screening and criteria should be specifically addressed in any contract between a business and the staffing vendor.

An employer needs to carefully document what a staffing firm is doing because employers can have a "co-employment relationship" with temporary workers. Co-employment has been defined as a legal relationship in which more than one employer has legal rights and obligations with respect to the same employee or group of employees. Both the Internal Revenue Service and various courts have found that a temporary worker of a supplier working at the customer's work site — even though paid and treated as an employee of the supplier — may still be considered an employee of both the supplier and the customer for legal purposes. The employer sets the specific duties, the duration of the assignment, and the level and types of skills required even though the staffing firm is responsible for recruitment, placement, and pay rates.

Remember— even though workers may be on the payroll of a staffing agency, since the workers perform duties at an employer's place of business, the employer can be liable for harm a worker causes.

---

## Screening From the Staffing Firm's Point of View

Today, more and more staffing firms are conducting background checks on applicants before sending them to client locations. Some staffing firms have learned the hard way that failure to spend a few dollars to conduct due diligence can result in millions of dollars spent, should a dangerous criminal or imposter be sent to work for a client. Every worker sent by a staffing firm, PEO, or recruiter into a client's workplace has the potential to put the staffing vendor out of business. Solutions? Staffing firms need to be open with clients about disclosing the nature and scope of their background checks. It is critical for any staffing firm or recruiter to be very clear with a client on the issue of background checks, including if background checks are performed, who pays for it, what criteria is used, and who reviews the reports. If a business wants to review the background report, the staffing firm should ensure that the worker has signed an appropriate release.

---

Staffing vendors and third party recruiters may want to consider the following—

1. Carefully consider the cost of doing background checks versus the risk of not performing them. Preventing even one embezzler or violent offender from being sent to a client can be worth the cost in the long run in terms of avoiding litigation, lost clients, and a loss of professional reputation.
2. Carefully review any marketing materials and sales presentation to ensure that clients are accurately informed about your practices. Do not imply that your firm "carefully screens" or only "sends the best" if in fact you are not doing adequate background checks.
3. Be careful doing in-house criminal record checks. That can trigger application of the FCRA
4. Be careful of using commercial low-cost databases for all of the reason described Chapter 12. The use of databases may also trigger the FCRA.
5. Utilize the Safe Hiring Program outlined in this book and document all steps taken.

6. Make sure that your contracts with clients accurately describe what if any background checks you will be doing. Consider—

- Depth and level of screening
- Who reviews reports, what criteria is used, and who makes decisions on eligibility
- Who selects the screening firms
- Adequacy of consent issue – the consent form needs to release information to both the staffing firm and employer where the worker may being sent.

# Screening of Volunteers

Over the past few years, there has been a substantial increase in volunteer groups, youth organizations and churches performing background checks. Checks for criminal records have become standard procedures for organizations like the Little League or Scouts. The increased emphasis on these checks has been fueled by numerous news stories and lawsuits about children being the victim of criminal conduct, especially sexual abuse. Unfortunately, in today's world, the fact remains that sex offenders and deviants exploit volunteer, youth, and faith-based organizations to gain access to potential victims. Doing background checks help protect children and the vulnerable from criminals.

Certain states have legislation permitting organizations to take advantage of state fingerprinting or criminal record programs. On October 9, 1998, President Clinton signed the **Volunteers for Children Act** into law – Public Law 105-251 – amending the Nat'l Child Protection Act of 1993. Organizations and businesses dealing with children, elderly, or the disabled may now use national fingerprint-based criminal history checks to screen out volunteers and employees with relevant criminal records.

The Wisconsin Attorney General's Office has produced an excellent brochure describing not only their state program, but also the Federal Act and how to obtain FBI background checks; see the online version at www.doj.state.wi.us/dles/cib/forms/brochures/vol_children.pdf

The same office also provides a website listing state sites where volunteer organization can obtain fingerprint information.; see www.doj.state.wi.us/dles/cib/sclist.asp.

> **Author Tip ➡** One question that arises is whether a screening on a volunteer needs to be conducted under the Fair Credit Reporting Act (FCRA), since the volunteer is not paid. The best practice is to still operate under the FCRA, even for volunteers. There is no requirement under the FCRA that a person is only employed if they are paid in monetary form. Also, as noted earlier, the FTC takes the position that the FCRA is given broad interpretation to protect consumer's rights. Conclusion— an organization should not assume the FCRA does not apply just because a person is a volunteer.

One beneficial idea for volunteer organizations is to use the services of private firms for fast, low-cost background checks. Also, using the criminal offender databases described in Chapter 12 provides low-cost and instant searches of some sexual offender database information. Although a very valuable tool, these "offender databases" should be used with caution since they do not cover all states and they are not exhaustive, meaning that volunteers and individuals with criminal records can escape detection. Any organization planning to perform background checks must very carefully review their own situation, including resources available in their state, to develop a cost-effective program. In addition, organizations should consider no-cost tools, such as reference checking, to weed out potential problems.

# Workers in the Home

There are numerous horror stories about innocent and unsuspecting people who opened their doors to home service providers or workers, and became the victims of serious crimes, including murder, right in their own homes. Routinely, many people casually allow workers in their homes to deliver appliances or furniture, act as nannies or caregivers, clean carpets, make home improvements, perform household repairs such as plumbing or electrical, kill pests, and a multitude of other tasks.

Unfortunately, people are particularly vulnerable in their own homes. Good help is harder to get, and if there are children, senior citizens, or a disabled person at home, the risks are even greater. Yet, no state except Texas currently requires background checks on workers who enter homes. Results are tragic.

U.S. Courts have held employers liable for negligence when their workers committed crimes in the home. An employer obviously does not send a worker into the home in order to steal, murder, or sexually assault. Certainly, criminal action was not in the scope and course of the employee's duties, however, employers are held to a higher standard of care in view of the inherent risks involved in sending workers into homes. Employers can be found negligent for not only hiring someone who they should have known was dangerous, unqualified or unfit, but also for failure to supervise, train, or properly assign workers. If an employer was on notice that a current worker was unsafe, and retained the person anyway, then that employer can be sued for negligent retention.[3]

## The Nine Million Dollar Service Call

According to a news article by the *Daytona Beach News-Journal Online*, a civil case was settled for nine million dollars when a well-know air conditioner repair firm sent a worker who was a twice convicted sex offender to a home and he killed the home owner. According to the June 1, 2004 article, the repairman cleaned the air ducts and then returned six months later and raped and murdered the victim. According to the news study, a criminal background check would have revealed the repairman's criminal past. The victim's family has started an organization called the Sue Weaver CAUSE (Consumer Awareness of Unsafe Service Employment) to raise awareness that not all contractors can be trusted. The case underscores the heightened responsibilities of employers who send workers into people's homes.

If you hire employees to work in peoples' homes, do not skimp on background checks!

---

[3] see ALR5th 21 for an article entitled, *Employer's Liability for Assaults, Theft or Similar Intentional Wrong Committed by Employee at Home or Business of Customer*

# Health Care and Other High-Risk Occupations

Health care and physician recruitment has become more challenging in recent years due to increasing concerns over the qualifications and backgrounds of health workers. Financial liability for acts and misconduct of employees is becoming one of the most significant areas of exposure for health care organizations. The exposure occurs because a health care provider can be held liable for injuries resulting from failure to adequately screen physicians, aides, or hospital staff hired. Hospitals have a special duty of care toward patients, especially those who, because of their illness or condition, are particularly vulnerable to violence, abuse, theft, and other adverse acts. Recently there have been well-publicized cases where efforts to maintain standards have fallen through the cracks when physicians and nurses, or imposters, have caused damage. Courtrooms, state medical boards, and the popular media are increasingly becoming the venues where unfortunate, tragic stories of health care providers failing to exercise due diligence are played out. The economic cost to the medical profession is staggering and there is no way to calculate the cost in terms of negative publicity and loss of trust, the pain and suffering to the victims and their families.

These dangers in physician hiring for example, are underscored by some startling statistics—

- According to the Federation of State Medical Boards (FSMB), the representative organization for state licensing agencies, 4,569 actions were reported by the medical boards in 1999. Of the 4,520 total actions taken, 3,838 were prejudicial to the physician and were taken for violations such as quality of care, sexual misconduct, insurance fraud, alcohol/substance abuse, or inappropriate prescribing of controlled substances.

- According to the Public Health Citizen's Research Group in Washington, D.C., between 1984 and 1999, some 20,125 physicians were subjects of disciplinary action by a state medical board or other governmental agency, resulting in nearly 39,000 disciplinary actions. Equally of concern is the fact that more than 3,000 physicians were guilty of felony offenses. There is, of course, no way to calculate how many criminal violations were never reported.

Because of the vulnerability of patience in the health care system, there are numerous requirements in all states concerning background checks on health care workers. In addition hospital and health care organizations are increasingly being required to perform screening and credential verification as part of their accreditation process. The Joint Commission (formerly the Joint Commission on Accreditation of Healthcare Organizations or JCAHO) has announced a new standard effective in 2006 that hospitals must maintain *primary source verification* on the licenses of all employees and contract staff.[4]

Similar concerns extend to other high risk occupations such as childcare workers on in-home care providers. At a minimum, employers need to understand state licensing requirements, and any accreditation requirement or industry practices must also be followed. Finally, an employer involved in high-risk occupations must carefully review their entire hiring process and screening program, keeping in mind that, due to the nature of their business, they can be held to a higher standard of care based upon the higher risk of foreseeable harm.

---

[4] Healthcare providers must also review certain sanctions or disbarment lists. The federal Office of Inspector General (OIG) maintains a list of individuals and entities excluded from doing business with the federal government. See: http://oig.hhs.gov/fraud/exclusions.html.The General Services Administration (GSA) Excluded Parities List. See: www.epls.gov/epls/jsp/. There are other federal agency lists as well as licensing and certification agencies in all 50 states that are available as well.

## Chapter 17

# Employer Issues with IDs, ID Theft, and Privacy

## The Problem of Who is Really Who

America is undergoing an identity crisis. Identity theft is one of the fastest growing crimes in the United States.

For employers however, the difficulties associated with ID theft goes well beyond credit card fraud and other financial losses. Firms can be the victims of ID theft by hiring someone with a false or fraudulent identity, with serious consequences. Employers do need to be concerned about who they are really hiring since criminals and terrorists have been known to fake their identities.

Since 9/11/2001 there have been a number of initiatives to use modern technology to firmly establish who is who in our society. However, there is still a widespread ability for one person to steal the identity of another — or create a new identity — and masquerade as someone else. Numerous agencies and private firms are working on biometric identifiers, for a variety of reasons. The use of biometric data has become a critical element in Homeland Security efforts, particularly at airports and essential industries and services. There is a national debate over National ID cards, the privacy and social implications of the government assigning every individual a unique number or identity. Should we collect biometric data and continue building large information databases?

These issues affect the lives of every American and should be the topic of discussion in a free citizenry. Let us review what employers need to know, and what to do in our current environment to protect the workplace.

## Identity in America

What is a person's identity? Identity has many different meanings. Use of the word by a psychologist would be very different than use by a teenager, a philosopher, a police officer, a scientist, or a privacy advocate. A popular dictionary, gives this definition of *identity*—

1.  The collective aspect of the set of characteristics by which a thing is definitively recognizable or known.

2.  The set of behavioral or personal characteristics by which an individual is recognizable as a member of a group.

3.  The quality or condition of being the same as something else.

4.  The distinct personality of an individual regarded as a persisting entity; individuality.

For our purposes, we are looking at identity in the bureaucratic sense of the word, utilizing the third definition — *the quality or condition of being the same as something else.*

## Real Identity

Society has an interest in keeping everyone straight when it comes to financial transactions between each other, transactions with various levels of government from the IRS all the way down to getting a speeding ticket, and especially employment. These are a person's "real identity." Putting aside any philosophical implications — and for the purpose of safe hiring — real identity is the process of matching up the past history with the present.

A key element of a Safe Hiring Program is to know what a person has done in the past. That is not to say that a person is defined solely by the past, or that every past act can be, or legally should be, considered relevant to employment decisions. However, past acts that are in the public domain for the world to see are what an employer needs to have. Now the employer needs to verify the public history of the applicant is not only factual, but also is the history that belongs to that person. By knowing a person's real identity, an employer can match up the employment history, education, credentials, or past court records. The real identity is also needed for a number of governmental functions effecting labor regulation such as various tax withholdings.

## Positive Identity

Employers are less concerned with the concept of "Positive Identity." Positive identity means that you are the same person that was part of an original transaction, so that you have the right to be a part of the new transaction. For example, if you went to a website in the past and signed up for a service, the site would need positive ID that you are the same person coming back for another transaction. It is irrelevant to the website that you may have initially used a different or even a false identity. As far as the website is concerned — provided there is no fraudulent financial transaction — you *are* you as long as you now know the password, i.e. you have the unique identifier that only you would know.

Consider this— a person creates or steals an identity and is hired by a firm under the false name. If that firm engages in some biometric identification procedures, such as identity badges, then each time the person comes into the workplace, his or her positive identity is confirmed. The employer knows this is the person presenting the badge. However, there is the possibility that the badge was gained because of a false "real" identity in the first place.

## Negative Identity

Another type of identity is "Negative Identity." This means that you are NOT a particular someone. For example, when you get on an airplane, an important consideration is that you are not a terrorist or a wanted criminal. However, as a practical matter, the most efficient way of showing you are not someone is to show who you really are.

## In the Employee/Employer Relationship, Correct Identity is the Employer's First Concern

For employers, the primary concern is real identity. The problem is to accurately track, in a cost-effective manner that does not unduly invade our privacy, the identities of not only 300 million U.S. citizens, but also the people from around the world who apply for jobs here.

# Identification Criteria Used by Employers

There are different identification criteria possible, each with their own set of considerations—

## Name

**A person's name** is only one part of one's identity. Under English Common Law, people can change their name and be known by anything they want as long as they are not trying to deceive. Not only can people change names, but also they can use all sorts of variations of their first, middle or last names. In some traditional cultures, a woman may, upon marriage, take the family name of the husband. Many cultures have different protocols with names, such as variations of the family name or mother's maiden name. There is also an issue of non-English names, especially in those countries where a non-familiar alphabet is used and there are numerous English variations of the same name.

Finally, in any large database of people, there is bound to be a great many duplicate names. It is surprising for people who believe their names are unique to go on an internet phone directory and find many others across North America with identical matching first and last names.

The bottom line— name identification by itself is practically worthless for the purpose of real identification. It is necessary to have other identifiers as well. As a matter of both math and logic, the more identifiers associated with an individual, the more likely a job applicant can be identified as a "real identity."

## Date of Birth

**Date of birth** is probably the next most used identifier. The initial date used for date of birth comes from the applicant. However, if an applicant gives a different date of birth, a search for criminal records could be thrown off. To guard against this, a screening firm or investigator should review the records for all name matches even if the date of birth does not match. However, this creates a significant issue for a court researcher if the name is common.

Date of birth is subject to regulation due to laws concerning age discrimination, discussed in Chapter 5. These laws present barriers for employers or screening firms from requesting the date of birth.

Another difficulty, given the sheer size of the American population, is just name and date of birth can result in "computer twins." A "computer twin" is two people with identical names and dates of birth. The problem is created when two different people are possibly identified as the same person.

## Social Security Number (SSN)

The nine digit Social Security Number is an assigned number developed for the purpose of administering the U.S. Social Security program. As a practical matter, the **SSN** is treated as a de facto national identification number. It is widely used as a unique identifier and is commonly required for any number of transactions — practically any financial transaction will require the Social Security Number.

The first three numbers represent the state of issue. The second set of numbers is related to the date the card was issued. The final set of four numbers is issued randomly from a regional office. As a result, it is possible to tell the state and date of issue from the SSN.

As discussed in Chapter 13, an employer will typically obtain a Social Security Trace Report, also known as a "credit header." The report gives the employer additional information such as other names and addresses associated with the SSN, and possibly the date of birth.

There are problems with using the Social Security Number as an identifier. The biggest issue is that local Social Security Offices issue the numbers, and there is no effort made to uniquely attach a particular number to a particular person at the time of issuance. There is no fingerprint or other definite biometric measurement that is permanently associated with a particular SSN. On the other hand, government computers can eventually track if a number is being misused. For example, if an identity thief steals a Social Security Number and uses it for employment, the government may eventually note another use of the same number for tax withholding purposes.

## Motor Vehicle Driver's License

Each state issues its own **driver's license** (DL) that entitles the name on the card to legally operate a motor vehicle. In fact, the driver's license has become a national identification card since it is the only widespread and easily recognized official government card issued with a photo for identification. The DL is used for such purposes as cashing checks, entering the security area in an airport, and anything else that requires a proof of identify. Among the 50 states, there are not necessarily strict security controls over the issuance of the license. There have been instances of criminals using false identity papers to obtain a driver's license under a false name. In addition, a search on Google of a "fake driver's license" reveals a number of websites that sell books and resources on how to make a fake driver's license and other ID's. A person on the East Coast could potentially create a fake driver's license from a state in the West and hope that a lack of familiarity will allow the document to pass.

## Physical Characteristics

Identifying **physical characteristics** may be reported on a government identity form such as a driver's license. The most common physical features are height, weight, sex, hair and eye color. When photo identification is used, a physical identifier will also include facial features depicted in a photograph. It can also refer to race, although that is typically not used as an identifier because of concerns over discrimination.

There are two immediate problems with these physical identifiers. First, the identifiers can change. The weight or hair color shown on a driver's license tends to become inaccurate as time goes by. Second, there can be a question as to the integrity of the data in the first place. When the data appears on a driver's license, for example, there is an assumption that a government official verified the data, so the data has verified authenticity. However, the situation is different if the document was forged or obtained under false pretense, discussion below.

## Unique Biometric Characteristics

**Biometric characteristics** are a biological measurements. The notion behind biometrics is to provide a basis for personal authentication. Methods of recognizing a person are based upon physical characteristics such as fingerprints, eye scans of the iris, or retinal scans. Other types of measurements being studied are based upon the physical features of the face or geometric features of the human hand and voice print. There is also a study of biometrics based upon handwriting. A biometric measure relates to a particular individual as opposed to a password or a document that someone carries.

The challenge with a biometric identification is to ensure that the biometric identity is properly associated with the appropriate person when the measurement is first made. Unless the original identification can be trusted, subsequent identifications based upon the biometric have little value. If a criminal, terrorist, or imposter successfully obtains a false biometric identity, then that person essentially has a future "free pass" — unless the error is somehow detected and corrected.

With its U.S.-VISIT program, the United States has introduced biometric measurements at airports and seaports for visitors from certain countries. The biometric measurements include digital imaging of a visitor's face and a digital fingerprint.[1]

## Other Government-issued Documents

Identification can also be based upon other documents issued by state or local governments. A United States passport can be the basis for identification. Various governmental agencies may also issue identification of workers, for those in law enforcement or public safety identification. Other government issued identities can involve the issuance of "smart cards" that workers performing certain duties may be required to carry. These cards can contain embedded computer chips that allow identity verification and authorization to perform certain tasks, or allow access to certain areas.

## Past Data Associated with an Applicant

Another means of identification is to compare the applicant to public records contained in large information databases. There are a number of companies with access to literally billons of public records. One company claims that it has information on nearly 98% of the adult population and data entries relating to approximately 205 million individuals in the United States. Of course, access to the

---

[1] see www.dhs.gov/dhspublic/interapp/content_multi_image/content_multi_image_0006.xml

most extensive databases will cost money. There are two excellent websites that list links to literally thousands of free searchable public records databases; see www.searchsystems.net and www.brbpub.com/pubrecsites.asp.

In addition to the criminal records databases discussed in Chapter 12 and the Social Security Trace information discussed in Chapter 13, there are numerous other records maintained in proprietary databases. Available record types can include—

- Property ownership records
- Bankruptcies, liens, and judgments
- UCC filings
- Ownership of boats or planes
- Professional licenses

## Use of Private Documents for Identifying

Another source of identity documents are those issued by private firms. Examples are credit cards and membership cards. These documents are far from ideal identifiers. Applicants with something to hide can attempt to manipulate the drawbacks on these forms of identities, and create false identities. Who would want to do that? Individuals who do not want their true names or intentions divulged! These may be people simply wanting privacy, or they may be criminals or even terrorists.

# Tools Employers Can Use to Avoid Fraudulent Identification in the Workplace

While it may be beyond our purpose here to review the many ways that identity can be stolen or created, employers do need to be aware there are a great many ways a determined criminal or terrorist can steal or create an identity for the purpose of entering the workplace under false pretenses. Identity theft can run from simple and amateurish attempts such as simply using another name, to attempting to obtain false identification such as a Social Security Number or driver's license, all the way to sophisticated schemes involving document forgery and creation of an entirely fictitious person.

It can be a challenge for employers to identify a well-financed and sophisticated scheme to create a false identity. Although not impossible to do, it is still difficult to create a false identity. Employers do have substantial protections by taking some common sense precautions, mainly by conducting a background check.

To help prevent someone with a stolen identity from coming to your workplace, use the following tools. Keep in mind that use of these tools by themselves or even in combination are not guaranteed to protect an employer. Use of these tools go a substantial way to discouraging applicants with something to hide. These tools demonstrate due diligence in the workplace.

## Screening Discourages False Applicants

The best protection for an employer is to not have the issue of a false ID arise in the first place. Perhaps the first and best approach is to make it very clear to all job applicants that your firm *does engage* in a Safe Hiring Program. All finalists are subject to background checks. As a general rule, criminals and terrorists are looking for "soft" and easy targets. Why risk exposure at a firm that will perform a background check if they can go down the block to some organization who is not as particular about whom they hire? An applicant with a false identity may not know the extent of the employer's background checks, *but an imposter may not be willing to take the risk.*

An employer can take the following steps—

1. In the newspaper ad or job announcement, indicate that the employer does background checks. In looking at the "classified' section in any newspaper, it is common to see employers state that applicants must undergo drug testing and background checks.

2. Clearly state that the application process that a screening will occur, and obtain consent for it.

3. Utilize the five critical questions outlined on page 115 of Chapter 8 that demonstrate the employer's commitment to safe hiring.

As the hiring process begins, some employers utilize a Social Security trace tool as an initial identity tool. If the applicant's identity does not check out then the time and effort of a further background check is saved. However, a Social Security trace is only a limited tool, and the entire screening process is helpful to verify identity, along with post-hire procedures discussed later in this chapter.

## The Trusted Source Rule — Third Party Verification

When America was made up of small towns, farms and villages, everyone knew each other. There was no question who was who. This is obviously no longer the case. The best method for knowing what we know is still based on what people we know say, assuming we give those people credibility. Google, a leading internet search engine, works in a similar manner. It does not matter to Google what a website says about itself as much as what others say about it, in terms of linking to it. The more third party sites that validate a website by linking to it, the higher the rating. It is a form of third party verification. The same rule applies to safe hiring as well. As we have seen throughout this book, what is important is not what an applicant states, but what can be independently verified.

In employment, the old adage "it is not what you know but who you know" reflects the obvious truth— that employers would prefer to hire a known quantity. If an employer actually knows the applicant, that applicant stands a better chance of being hired. The next best thing is to have a hiring manager or current worker recommend you. That is why firms place so much emphasis on employee-based recruiting. These are all variations of the basic premise of this chapter— that employers prefer to use a trusted source of information.

If every business owner could only hire candidates they either knew personally, or were known personally by people they knew, then there would be less time and effort spent managing and dealing with employee problems. When a firm opens, it can easily hire known people. No doubt firms like Yahoo!, Apple, Microsoft, FedEx, HP, Intel did not worry about background checks on their first few employees. However, for every employer there comes a time when they realize their workers are strangers, and unless you want a stranger to have the ability to control your destiny, then it is a good idea to know whom you are hiring.

When it comes to preventing a person with a false identity from entering your workforce, at some point, your knowledge of an applicant must be tied to a trusted source. The trusted source may be another HR manager or a security professional you know and trust.

As seen throughout this book, reliance on public data or criminal databases alone is not advisable. A determined criminal, terrorist, or imposter may be able to steal an identity and pass such a test, or a database may give a "false negative," meaning the person is erroneously cleared when they should not be. Furthermore, just trusting a person's word for who they are is obviously insufficient.

The key is a trusted source that can independently verify that the person sitting in front of you for an interview is the same person who has the history they claim. This is best done by **past employment verification**. Verifying past employment allows the employer to detect and hopefully eliminate any red flags caused by unexplained employment history gaps, or discover the resume/application is false. Thus the employer breaks the chain of relying upon what people say about themselves, or relying upon documents that can easily be forged, or relying on databases that can contain errors.

If an employer is contacting someone they do not know, then the trusted source may turn out to be the telephone book. By using a phone book, directory assistance or some similar online service to validate the authenticity of a past employer's telephone number, an employer can independently confirm the validity of a previous employer. By having a listed telephone number, there is at last some assurance that the past employer is a legitimate business that qualified for a phone number and directory assistance. Past employers can also be "Googled" or researched from other databases.

A warning— there is a number of well-meaning attempts being made to create databases, cards, or other schemes to validate identity. The basis of these efforts is some mechanism to perform some sort of "clearance," then the individual is tied into some sort of biometric measure. However, the so-called "clearance" appears to be based upon simply searching pubic records and government databases. Any reliance on any database is problematic. The drawbacks are multiplied when a criminal, terrorist, or imposter manages to obtain such a card, then it can be used to help conceal their identity in the future.

The best practice in order to validate identity for purposes of employment, safety, or other type of security concern is to include an element of third party verification from a trusted source. Although contacting a trusted source is a manual task, and not nearly as quick or inexpressive as using databases, it is critical if there is to be any confidence in an identity validation or "clearance" program.

If the applicant claims self-employment, that can make it more difficult to find an independent verification source. In the case of self-employment, the approach is to ascertain from the applicant the names of past clients and then verify through directory assistance or some trusted source that the client is for real.

As discussed in previous chapters, verifying past employment is a critical factor for knowing who a person really is and to know where to search for past criminal records. If an employer can verify where a person has been for the past 5-10 years or longer, then the employer has a tremendous advantage.

## Confirmation of Facts

Confirming of facts is covered in a number of previous chapters. As the old saying goes, "trust but verify." Using the tools in this book, it is critical to verify facts and to utilize the various screening tools available, including a Social Security trace, past employment checks, verifying education and professional licenses, and a criminal records check.

## Look for Internal Consistency or Inconsistency

Another tool that goes hand-in-hand with the trusted source rule is looking to see if there is a pattern of consistency — or "applicant congruence." Congruence means "agreement, harmony, conformity, or correspondence."

Employers, hiring managers, human resources professionals or security professionals must ask themselves, "Does the total package make sense?" An employer needs to look at the applicant as a whole and, based upon the application and interview, be sensitive to anything that does not add up or make sense. For example—

- If a person claims to have a degree in computer science, does the person appear to have the appropriate knowledge in their interview?
- Does the employment history make sense for what the person did, where, and for how long?
- Are the educational accomplishments and past employment consistent with the person's knowledge, skills, and abilities?
- Are the job descriptions consistent with the person's knowledge, skills, and abilities?
- Are there unexplained gaps in employment?
- Did the applicant give specifics in the interview when discussing past jobs and knowledge, skills and experience, or did the person only give vague generalities?

In other words, does the person at the interview seem to match the history shown on the application? If something does not "add up," red flag!

## Cross-referencing Accumulated Data

Based upon all the data the employer obtains, the next step is to cross reference the known facts to determine if everything makes sense. For our purposes, cross-referencing is a process of not relying upon just one fact, but on a combination of accumulated facts obtained both from the applicant and other sources. Information from one source is compared to others to determine if the applicant is factual about their claimed identity and history. Keep in mind that use of massive databases for employment purposes does have some legal limitations as discussed in Chapter 12. Another issue is how to effectively utilize large databases containing literally billions of records. Data mining of large databases and specialized software to "connect the dots" to see trends and connections is a developing technology.

Again, one valuable tool is the Social Security trace. As described in Chapter 13, the Social Security trace is based upon information obtained by the three major credit bureaus — names and addresses associated with a particular Social Security Number. If an employer is working with a screening firm, then the employer *may* receive data that is also based upon a number of other public record databases. This should help you create a useful address history. It is important to understand that these reports are not an official list of past residences, and there can be errors and variation. However, for purposes of cross-referencing, it is a tool that employers should use. For example, if a person claimed employment as a production supervisor in Chicago from 1998-2002, but the trace report indicated two different addresses in Los Angeles during the same time period, that would be a red flag.

# I-9 Form "Right to Work" Compliance and Contacting the Social Security Administration

Every employer is obligated to utilize a procedure to insure that a person has a right to work in the U.S. This is done after a person is hired. The process is another layer of protect against employing a person with a false identity. The program is under the authority of the U.S. Citizenship and Immigration Services (USCIS) within the Department of Homeland Security (DHS). That department was formerly known as the Immigration and Naturalization Service (INS). The form used in this procedure is called a Form I-9. The basics for compliance can be found in a government publication called *THE FORM I-9 PROCESS IN A NUTSHELL* found at www.uscis.gov/files/article/EIB102.pdf. The I-9 Form is being revised as of the printing of this book, but the USCSI has indicated employers should use the most recent form available, even if expired. At print time, the most recent version, which expired March, 2007, is OMB No. 1615-0047.

This I-9 procedure is a valuable last step in the hiring process because the employer is required to physically view documents concerning identity and list eligibility. The I-9 process defines and utilizes three classes or lists of documents—A, B and C.

The A list includes documents that confirm both identity and the right to work. For U.S. citizens, the easiest means of proof is a U.S. passport. For individuals who are citizens of other countries, there are various documents they can provide, such as cards issued by the USCIS. If a person does not have an A list document, then one document from the B list and one from the C list must be provided.

List B includes documents that show identity, such a driver's license or various other government ID cards. List C are documents that show an eligibility to work, and can include a certified birth certificate or a card issued by the Social Security Administration.

Of course, a determined individual may find a way around this procedure. As reported on the official USCIS website, "Employers are not required to be document experts. In reviewing the genuineness of the documents presented by employees, employers are held to a reasonableness standard."

However, the I-9 verification process is one of the most powerful tools an employer has. At a minimum, it puts up roadblocks that may deter, or detect persons using fraudulent identification.

In addition to filling out the paper I-9, employers can also utilize the E-Verify Program, a voluntary program that allows employers to verify the employment eligibility of prospective employees through the Social Security Administration and the DHS. (**Note: As this book goes to press, the DHS changed the name from the Basic Pilot Program to E-Verify and added a number of enhancements. See www.dhs.gov/ximgtn/programs/go_1185221678150.shim.**) As of 09/2007, the program was still voluntary even though bills introduced in Congress would have made it mandatory. An employer must execute a Memorandum of Understanding (MOU) to participate in the program run by the (DHS), the Social Security Administration (SSA) and the U.S. Citizenship and Immigration Service (SAVE). Background screening firms may also act as an employers authorized agent. One state, Arizona, requires employers to utilize the E-Verify Program starting in 2008. There has been much debate as to the accuracy and completeness of the databases used, and if a worker is not verified then there are a number of steps an employer must go through to complete the process. Note that also in early 2007, the federal government significantly increased the penalty **on employers who employ workers with fake Social Security Numbers.**

# U.S. Citizenship and Immigration Services Procedures

Here is a description of the procedures taken from the website at www.uscis.gov/

### Employee's Responsibility Regarding Form I-9

A new employee must complete Section 1 of a Form I-9 no later than close of business on his/her first day of work. The employee's signature holds him/her responsible for the accuracy of the information provided. The employer is responsible for ensuring that the employee completes Section 1 in full. No documentation from the employer is required to substantiate Section 1 information provided by the employee.

### Employer's Responsibility Regarding Form I-9

The employer is responsible ensuring completion of the entire form. No later than close of business on the employee's third day of employment services, the employer must complete section 2 of the Form I-9. The employer must review documentation presented by the employee and record document information of the form. Proper documentation establishes both that the employee is authorized to work in the U.S. and that the employee who presents the employment authorization document is the person to whom it was issued. The employer should supply to the employee the official list of acceptable documents for establishing identity and work eligibility. The employer may accept any List A document, establishing both identity and work eligibility, or combination of a List B document (establishing identity) and List C document (establishing work eligibility), that the employee chooses from the list to present (the documentation presented is not required to substantiate information provided in Section 1). The employer must examine the document(s) and accept them if they reasonably appear to be genuine and to relate to the employee who presents them. Requesting more or different documentation than the minimum necessary to meet this requirement may constitute an unfair immigration-related employment practice. If the documentation presented by an employee does not reasonably appear to be genuine or relate to the employee who presents them, employers must refuse acceptance and ask for other documentation from the list of acceptable documents that meets the requirements. An employer should not continue to employ an employee who cannot present documentation that meets the requirements.

## Questions About Genuineness of Documents

Employers are not required to be document experts. In reviewing the genuineness of the documents presented by employees, employers are held to a reasonableness standard. Since no employer which is not participating in one of the employment verification pilots has access to receive confirmation of information contained in a document presented by an employee to demonstrate employment eligibility, it may happen that an employer will accept a document that is not in fact genuine – or is genuine but does not belong to the person who presented it. Such an employer will not be held responsible if the document reasonably appeared to be genuine or to relate to the person presenting it. An employer who receives a document that appears not to be genuine may request assistance from the nearest Immigration field office or contact the Office of Business Liaison.

## Discovering Unauthorized Employees

It occasionally happens that an employer learns that an employee whose documentation appeared to be in order for Form I-9 purposes is not actually authorized to work. In such case, the employer should question the employee and provide another opportunity for review of proper Form I-9 documentation. If the employee is unable to provide satisfactory documentation, then employment should be discontinued. Alien employees who question the employer's determination may be referred to an Immigration field office for assistance.

## Discovering False Documentation

False documentation includes documents that are counterfeit or those that belong to someone other than the employee who presented them. It occasionally happens that an employee who initially presented false documentation to gain employment subsequently obtains proper work authorization and presents documentation of this work authorization. In such a case, U.S. immigration law does not require the employer to terminate the employee's services. However, an employer's personnel policies regarding provision of false information to the employer may apply. The employer should correct the relevant information on the Form I-9.

## Photocopies of Documents

There are two separate and unrelated photocopy issues in the employment eligibility verification process. First is whether an employer may accept photocopies of identity or employment eligibility documents to fulfill I-9 requirements. The answer is that only original documents (not necessarily the first document of its kind ever issued to the employee, but an actual document issued by the issuing authority) are satisfactory, with the single exception of a certified photocopy of a birth certificate. Second is whether the employer may or must attach photocopies of documentation submitted to satisfy Form I-9 requirements to the employee's Form I-9. The answer is that this is permissible, but not required. Where this practice is undertaken by an employer, it must be consistently applied to every employee, without regard to citizenship or national origin.

## Another Option— Contact the Social Security Administration

Another option open to employers as part of the new employee in-take procedures is to contact the Social Security Administration (SSA) to officially verify a Social Security Number **after** the hire. Call the SSA weekdays from 7am to 7pm EST at 1-800-772-6270. An employer will be asked for the company name and EIN. More information is available at www.ssa.gov/employer/ssnv.htm

# Employee Privacy Rights

Beth Givens, Director of the Privacy Rights Clearinghouse at www.privacyrights.org has prepared the following summary of what an employer *should* and *must do* to protect identity.[2] For resources on responsible information handling practices, see www.privacyrights.org/ar/PreventITWorkplace.htm.

## What Employers Can Do to Protect the Privacy Rights of Employees

By Beth Givens

Experts in identity theft report that an increasing number of cases can be traced back to dishonest employees in the workplace or computer hackers who obtain Social Security numbers (SSNs) of employees and customers, then disclose that information to individuals involved in crime rings or other identity theft schemes.

One of the keys to preventing identity theft, therefore, is to safeguard sensitive personal information *within the workplace*, whether that workplace is a government agency, private business, or nonprofit organization. *Everyone* must get involved in protecting personal information such as SSNs, financial account numbers, dates of birth – in other words, any information used by identity thieves to impersonate individuals in the marketplace.

### Workplace Information-Handling Practices

The Privacy Rights organization makes these suggestions for the responsible handling of information. Although these recommendations are based upon California law, they comprise "best practices" for employers and institutions in all states.

---

[2] Reprinted here with permission. The original article is available at the Privacy Rights Clearinghouse website at www.privacyrights.org/ar/SDCountyIT.htm.

- **Adopt a comprehensive privacy policy** that includes responsible information-handling practices. Appoint an individual and/or department to be responsible for the privacy policy, one who can be contacted by employees and customers with questions and complaints.

- **Store sensitive personal data in secure computer systems**. Store physical documents in secure spaces such as locked file cabinets. Data should only be available to qualified persons.

- **Dispose of documents properly**, including shredding paper with a cross-cut shredder, "wiping" electronic files, destroying computer diskettes and CD-ROMs, and so on.[3] Comply with California's document destruction law, Civil Code 1798.80-1798.84.

- **Build document destruction capabilities into the office infrastructure.** Place shredders around the office, near printers and fax machines, and near waste baskets. Make sure dumpsters are locked and inaccessible to the public.

- **Conduct regular staff training**, including new employees, temporary employees, and contractors.

- **Conduct privacy "walk-throughs"** and make spot checks on proper information handling. Reward employees and departments for maintaining "best practices."

- **Put limits on data collection** to the minimum information needed. For example, is SSN really required? Is complete date of birth needed, or would year and month be sufficient?

- **Put limits on data display and disclosure of SSN**. Do not print full SSNs on paychecks, parking permits, staff badges, time sheets, training program rosters, lists of who got promoted, on monthly account statements, on customer reports, etc. Unless allowed by law, do not print SSN on mailed documents or require that it be transmitted via the internet. In compliance with California law, do not use SSN as customer number, employee ID number, health insurance ID card, etc. Comply with California Civil Code 1798.85-86 and 1786.6.

- **Restrict data access to staff** with a legitimate need to know. Implement electronic audit trail procedures to monitor who is accessing what. Enforce strict penalties for illegitimate browsing and access.

- **Conduct employee background checks**, especially for individuals who have access to sensitive personal information. Screen cleaning services, temp services, contractors, etc.

- **Safeguard mobile computers,** laptops, PDAs that contain files with sensitive personal data.

- **Notify customers and/or employees of computer security breaches** involving sensitive personal information, in compliance with California law Civil Code 1798.29 and 1798.82-1798.84, including security breaches involving paper records.

---

[3] The FACT Act passed in 2003 also added provisions in section 628 about the proper manner to dispose of consumer reports under the FCRA. The FTC has prepared regulations. A summary may be found at www.ftc.gov/bcp/conline/pubs/alerts/disposalalrt.shtm. Also, see chapter 18 on "After the Hire" issues.

# Chapter 18

# Important "After the Hire" Issues

A Safe Hiring Program does not stop once the candidate goes on the payroll. Lawsuits for negligent retention have put employers on notice that due diligence extends well beyond the hiring stage. In fact, employers have a continuing obligation during the entire employment relationship to exercise due diligence when it comes to protecting co-workers, the public, customers, and investors.

The laws governing employment relationship are complicated and involved and covered by scores of outstanding books and resources. The purpose of this chapter is to focus on areas unique to safe hiring and due diligence.

## The Offer Letter

Making a formal offer letter in writing is generally considered a best practice. The offer letter will verify the basic terms agreed upon by the employer and the applicant — the salary, job title, start date, and benefits.

If the employer makes the offer prior to the completion of the background report, then the offer letter serves another vital purpose: it explains to the applicant that the hiring decision is conditioned upon the employer's receipt of "a background screening report that is satisfactory to the employer." This is important language. First, the offer letter protects the employer in the event the screening is not yet completed, and by specifying the background report must be satisfactory to the employer, it limits a future debate over what is or is not an objectively satisfactory report.

### Importance of Well-Written Job Description

A well-written and detailed job description is normally the basis of any effort to recruit new employees. An employer needs to define *precisely* what the job requires and what reasonable accommodation will help the employee carry out the job. Job descriptions are used to determine the requirements for the position, identifying responsibilities, and setting compensation. While an offer letter will set out the knowledge, skills, and abilities needed to be successful on the job, a well-written job description will specify the essential functions of the job. This is critical in the event an applicant files a claim under the Americans With Disabilities Act (ADA). From a legal perspective, a well-written job description also assists an employer in defending against claims of discrimination. For the purposes of a Safe Hiring Program, the specification of qualifications is critical. See Chapter 7 for a detailed discussion on job descriptions and other hiring preparations.

# New Employee Orientations

Another critical step for new hires is the new employee orientation. The orientation starts the employment relationship off on the right track by letting new employees know what role they play in the company and how their contributions are important. Typically, the first few days on the job are stressful for any new employee. Experienced managers know that taking the time to go though a well-planned orientation can lessen the anxiety considerably and contribute to a new employee's success. As a practical matter, the new employee orientation also serves as an opportunity to convey necessary information to that employee on such practical matters as the physical layout of the premises and introduction to co-workers, and to a review of employment terms such as compensation and benefits.

From a Safe Hiring Program perspective, the new employee orientation also serves as a valuable opportunity to impress upon new employees the importance the firm places on safety and employees. It is an opportunity to underscore the firm's commitment to a workplace with zero tolerance for drugs, dishonesty, or violence.

# Employee Manual

An employee manual is a mission critical item for any organization. A manual spells out the terms and conditions of employment so there is no misunderstanding. From a legal viewpoint, labor lawyers have long taught employers that a manual is one of the most effective defenses an employer has for defending themselves against employment lawsuits. For example, if an employee violates a work rule, an employer has a much better chance of defending discipline or termination if the work rule was in a manual that the employee received and signed. If an employer has a sexual harassment or discrimination policy in their manual, this also gives increased protection.

From the perspective of a Safe Hiring Program, an employee manual is invaluable because it sets out policies in several important areas—

1.  **Workplace Violence**— It is a critical part of any effort to prevent workplace violence to clearly set out a policy that states the employer maintains a safe workplace; that there is a zero-tolerance policy for violence, threats, or intimidation; that all employees are expected to assist in the effort.

2.  **Drugs**— As discussed in Chapter 25 on drugs in the workplace, an employee manual is an essential aspect of any program to deal with employment related drug abuse.

3.  **Screening**— A best practice is to have information about safe hiring and references about screening in the employee manual.

4.  The employment is **"at will."** (See next section)

# Employment at Will and Probationary Periods

A critical issue for employers is the nature of the employee-employer relationship. Employers typically hire on an "at will" basis, meaning there is no employment contract and either side can terminate the relationship. Of course, nothing is that simple. Employers are normally advised to be very clear in all stages of the recruiting, interviewing, and hiring procedure that no promises or contracts are made, either expressed or implied, that modify the at-will arrangement. Again, nothing is that smooth. An applicant may argue that, by certain employer's actions or deeds, there is an implied promise of future employment that can only be terminated "for cause" as opposed to "at will." Examples of instances where an employee may argue they are no longer "at will" are listed below—

- Language in an interview that says "if a person does well, the company will take care of them," or other similar promise of special treatment on the part of the employer.

- Language in the employee manual that creates a "probationary period." The implication is that if a person passes the probationary period, they have vested or obtained a more secure status and there must be "good cause" to terminate rather than a right to terminate "at will."

- Employee manual language that sets out a series of progressive disciplinary steps where an employee has a chance to improve performance. The implication is if they meet the standards, then the person is no longer "at will."

- A listing of actions or omissions that are grounds for discipline or termination. The argument is if one of these enumerated acts or omissions is not committed, then the employer needs cause to terminate.

- When an employee has been with the employer for a period of time and has received promotions, regular pay increases and good performance reviews, the employee can argue he or she is no longer at will.

Along with appropriate statements in the application, the employee manual is also a critical tool to reinforce the "at will" nature of employment.

It is also necessary to insure that everyone with hiring responsibilities is trained not to make statements that imply a commitment beyond "at will." There are also other exceptions to the "at will" status, such as civil service employment, collective bargaining agreements, or public policy exceptions to "at will" status.

From the perspective of a Safe Hiring Program, maintaining the "at will" relationship can be vital to an employer in the event issues arise related to workplace violence or misconduct, or it is later discovered the employee made material misstatements or omissions during the hiring process. Even though an employer may have grounds to terminate based upon the misconduct or misrepresentation, the "at will" status will assist the employer's position.

# Confidentiality Agreements and Ethics Policy

Another best practice is to obtain a confidentiality and ethics agreement as part of the employment relationship. Some firms place the language in the employee manual. However, having it as separate document may give additional emphasis. Although the specific language may vary for a particular industry, the essential thrust is to establish that honest and ethical dealings are part of the firm's culture, and an essential element of the duties and responsibilities of every employee. Although some employers may assume that some truths are self-evident and that it goes without saying that honest and ethical behavior is required, saying so serves as a valuable reminder.

# Maintaining Your Employment Screening Records

For any employer, record keeping and personnel files are always an important issue. Files should contain information regarding the employment application, and qualifications for employment, as well as all personnel actions such as compensation, promotions, transfers, demotions, discipline, and terminations.

In reality, an employer maintains multiple files on an employee. In addition to the "official" personnel file, supervisors or managers may maintain files. In addition there are matters normally kept in a separate and secured file. These files are normally stored in an area only accessible to human resources personnel or the authorized. These files contain matters that are confidential or sensitive in nature, thus widespread publication could constitute an invasion of personal privacy. These files should NOT be accessible by supervisors during performance appraisals.

Confidential matters contained in these files can include—

- Background reports
- Letter of reference
- Verification of right to work (I-9 form)
- Workers comp claims
- Medical information
- Documents concerning employee status as a disabled person, veteran, or other status
- Defamatory information
- Information unrelated to the job

Supervisors may also keep files reflecting such things as notes or memos of discussions for issues or problems that have arisen. These notes may indicate what was discussed, when and who was present. These notes may be used during performance evaluations.

# Employees May Have the Right to Inspect Their Personnel Files

Keep in mind that, in many states, employees have a right to inspect their own personnel file. In California, Labor Code Sec. 1198.5(a) provides that every public and private employee has a right to inspect his or her personnel files except for public safety offenses and certain employees' subject to the Information Practices Act of 1977. The right to inspect includes files with information used to determine employee qualifications, promotion, compensation, termination or other disciplinary action. Failure to allow inspection is a misdemeanor, punishable by a fine up to $100 and imprisonment for 30 days.

Files should be maintained where the employee reports to work. Employers may impose reasonable restrictions such as setting up appointments during regular business hours or on the employee's own time or limiting the frequency, or require an employer representative to be present, but the employer cannot set arbitrary time limits. If there is an inspection, then the employer should keep a history of the request and the response.

The right to inspection does not include—

- A record of investigation of possible criminal offense.
- Letters of reference, unless steps are taken to safeguard the identity of the authors.
- If a file contains other confidential data, then the identity of persons can be removed, i.e. the employer should protect the privacy of third persons.

The right extends to current employees, employees on leave, and terminated employees unless the statue of limitations has run out. The right does not extend to job applicants, union officials, or designated agents.

# Screening Current Employees

Since the events of 9/11/2001, many organizations have revisiting their policies concerning pre-employment background checks and safe hiring. When reviewing background-checking policies, a question often arises about whether current employees should be screened, or whether the background check policy should apply to new applicants only.

The need to screen current employees can be necessitated by a new contract with a customer who requires all workers performing the contract have a background check. It can also occur when a firm "acquires" another workforce through a merger or acquisition. There can also be situations where an employer is concerned about some type of workplace misconduct such as theft or harassment.

There are two factors to consider in screening current employees— legal and practical.

It is perfectly legal to screen current employees as long as all their rights are respected. A current employee is entitled to the same legal rights as a new applicant, and if there is a union involved, perhaps even more rights. Under the Federal Fair Credit Reporting Act, if the background check is performed by a third party service provider, then current employees are entitled to the same rights as new applicants, which includes a disclosure of rights and written consent. Some states have additional rules that employers must be mindful to follow. Keep in mind if an existing employee is screened for allegations of wrongdoing or misconduct, then his or her consent may not be needed under the FACT Act amendment to the FCRA; see Chapter 6.

**The practical consideration** is whether the employer wants to ask existing employees to consent to a background check. The issue is one of corporate culture—not alienating employees that have been hardworking and loyal by performing background checks.

If an employer decides it is necessary to screen current employees, it is recommended that HR explain screening is "a business necessity for the good of the entire organization" and not directed to any employee. This will increase employee "buy-in." Equally critical is for employees to understand all their rights are being respected and nothing will occur as a result of a background check until the employee has an opportunity to discuss any negative findings with the employer. Problems can arise if an employee feels powerless in the process, concerned about an adverse action without an opportunity to be heard. It is crucial to tell all employees they may come to Human Resources to privately discuss the procedure. An employee may start off talking about *privacy concerns*, when in fact there is something of concern in the person's background.

Another consideration occurs when an employer is concerned that an existing employee may not sign a consent form. That has not proved to be an issue of a practical matter. If employees have a clear understanding of how this policy helps both the employer and the employee, then there is typically good employee "buy-in." However, in a worst case scenario where an employee absolutely refuses to consent, an employer can take the following tack – let the employee know that they have the right not to consent. On the other hand, just as the employee has a right not to consent, the next time the employee is up for a pay raise or promotion, the employer equally has the right not to promote or give a raise. This tactic may be considered if a current employee refuses to sign a consent form before the employer takes the more difficult track of termination.

---

### Kelchner v. Sycamore Manor Health Center

In the first court case to address the issue of an employee not consenting, a Federal District Court in Pennsylvania decided that an employer can terminate a current employee who refused to sign a consent for a background check. In Kelchner v. Sycamore Manor Health Center, 2004 U.S. Dist. Lexis 2942 (M.D. Pa. 2004), the employer required all employees to sign a consent to a consumer report. A worker with 19 years on the job refused to sign and was terminated. The Court held that the plain language of the statute as well as Congressional intent demonstrated that employers had the right to require such a consent and could terminate if an employee refused, just as an employer could refuse to hire an applicant who did not consent in the first place.

# If Screening Results Lead to Possible Termination Issues

What if the screening of a current employee results in a decision to terminate? If the screening reveals the applicant had a criminal conviction not indicated on the application, then an employer could choose to terminate for dishonesty. However, keep in mind that the exact wording of the criminal question on the employment application is critical. If the employer only asked about felonies, then an undisclosed misdemeanor — even a serious misdemeanor — may not be grounds to terminate for dishonesty. An employee may give other reasons why failure to disclose was not an act of dishonesty. An employee may claim that they did not realize it was a conviction or claim they did not understand what the judge or their lawyer told them. Some defendants enter a pea of "nolo" or "no contest." Although that may give a criminal defendant some protection if they are later sued in a civil court, a "nolo" or "no contest" plea has the same effect as pleading guilty.

Suppose the screening of existing employees reveals a criminal record that was not mentioned in the application or interview process. This is potential grounds for termination, providing the employer's application form put an applicant on notice that any material misstatement or omission is grounds for termination no matter when discovered. See the discussion about application forms in Chapter 7. The situation becomes difficult when the employee claims he/she did inform the manager of past difficulties, but the manager failed to inform human resources. The solution is to ensure that all pre-hire procedures are followed and documented, and all managers are trained in the hiring procedures.

In addition, if the screening discloses an offense that occurs AFTER employment, the employer may decide to take action. However, the EEOC rules outlined in Chapter 5 apply. The employer must take into account the nature and gravity of the offense, how long ago it occurred, and whether it is job-related in order to determine if there is a business necessity to deny continued employment.

An employer should also document any decision NOT to terminate in case the employer has to defend a decision to terminate some employees with criminal records and not others. If the employer has a written policy that requires employees to inform the employer if a criminal conviction occurs after employment begins, then an employer can take position that the termination is a result of a violation of a written company policy. As a practical matter, an employer would likely be aware of any serious criminal matter after employment commences, since an employee may not show up to work or need time off for court appearances. If an employee is arrested and not able to come to work, then an employer should examine the employee manual to determine the company's rule for unexcused absences.

If termination is considered, then the employer needs to be mindful of the FCRA requirements for pre-adverse action. An employee cannot simply be brought into the office and given their final check. The FCRA requires a **pre-adverse action notice**, giving the employee has a meaningful opportunity to review, reflect, and respond to the consumer report if the employee feels it is inaccurate or incomplete. One method is to meet with the employee, explain that a matter of concern came up in the screening report, and to provide the employee with a copy of the report and a statement of their rights prepared by the FTC, which the screening firm can provide. The employee should also be provided a letter advising that her or she should respond to the employer or the screening firm as soon as possible if there is anything the employee wishes to challenge or explain.

Since by definition the employer notice is pre-adverse action, an employer may consider placing the employee on three days paid administrative leave with instructions to either contact the employer in three days if the employee plans to contest the consumer report, or the leave turns into a termination. If the employer does not hear back, then the employee is terminated. See the Termination Procedures section below for special considerations on terminations.

If the applicant notifies the employer of plans to contest the report, then the employer can make a case-by-case judgment to either continue the employment, or place on unpaid leave, or terminate pending resolution of the re-investigation with a right to reapply. The FCRA does not require the employer keep a job open or keep an employee on paid leave during the re-investigation period, but only requires a meaningful opportunity to receive notice of pre-adverse action and deal with the report before the adverse action is taken. If the decision to terminate becomes final, then the employee is entitled to the second FCRA post-adverse action letter. The decision to place on leave can also be affected by the provisions of the employee manual or the existence of union contracts.

## Employee Misconduct Issues

Another situation where a background check may be warranted involves workplace misconduct, such as theft, harassment, or threats of violence. Prior to the 2003 amendments to the FCRA, these types of investigations presented substantial legal issues when background checks were conducted by professional third party investigators. Third party investigations had advantages when a firm did not have the resources to conduct an investigation, or in cases such as sexual harassment where outside and independent investigations helped to prove fairness. The difficulties were created by the 1999 "Vail" letter, where the FTC staff responded to an inquiry if sexual harassment investigations by a third party were covered by the FCRA. The FTC staff indicated that third party investigation of misconduct was covered by all of the provisions of the FCRA, including the various provisions providing for notice and disclosure. This created a number of difficulties. For example, if the investigation centered on suspected criminal activities such as theft, drug dealing, or workplace violence, it would be difficult to conduct an undercover investigation and obtain witness identities if consent had to be obtained first. A number of court decisions undercut the FTC's position. The matter was finally laid to rest with the passage of the Fair and Accurate Credit Transactions Act (FACT) in 2003, with amendments to the FCRA becoming effective in 2004. The amendments appear to allow investigation of current employees to take place without FCRA consents, subject to some requirements, such as if an adverse action was taken that there be disclosure. See Chapter 6 for further FCRA information.

# Ongoing Training

Ongoing training is also another critical aspect to employers. Training can cover a wide variety of topics; an employer should include issues related to safety and security.

Training should have an emphasis on supervisors, having them trained to recognize, report, and deal appropriately with workplace misconduct. In addition, supervisors must be properly trained and educated regarding the employer's liability for negligent hiring, supervision, retention and promotion.

# Performance Reviews and Ongoing Monitoring

Periodic performance appraisals as well as ongoing review of performances are additional mission critical tasks for employers. For purposes of ongoing safe hiring, the concern is whether the firm conducts periodic performance reviews of workers that include issues related to workplace conduct.

It is especially important that supervisors be evaluated on compliance with the duty to record, report, and address workplace misconduct. Supervisors must also understand they are evaluated in part upon monitoring workplace misconduct. Without proper documentation an employer may lack evidence later.

## Advantages of Performance Reviews

According to Dennis L. DeMey in his book *Don't Hire a Crook[1]*, performance reviews are an excellent way to maintain quality employment. As mentioned earlier, the job description informs the employee of the company's expectations of him or her. The performance review is the follow-up.

Performance reviews give employers the opportunity to examine employee performance and let them know areas where they need to improve. Oftentimes, a performance evaluation is conducted in conjunction with a salary review, then used to determine if a pay increase should be given and, if so, how much.

There are many times when a review may be conducted. Here are a few reasons—

- The employee has reached the end of his or her probationary period.

- The employee is being considered for promotion.

- The employee has exhibited unsatisfactory performance.

- Company policy requires that a review be documented annually.

- The employee has performed exceptionally well.

Performance reviews are yet another means of good communication between employee and employer. Likewise, it is a step that should be documented. By documenting performance reviews, two goals are accomplished: 1) The employee has a written copy of areas that need improvement, and therefore may refer back to it; and 2) the employer has a document that can be used to illustrate a history of problems, if that is the case.

---

[1] *Don't Hire a Crook* ©2001 BRB Publications, Tempe, AZ.

# Responding to Employee Complaints

Employees concerned about violence, dishonesty, or fraud should have the opportunity to lodge complaints.

For employers, timely and attentive management of potential problem situations along with appropriate follow-through and documentation are the keys to avoiding legal claims of negligent hiring/supervision.

To accomplish these goals, employers must have a mechanism for employees to report instances of workplace misconduct, such as violence, dishonesty, or fraud. The mechanism should also include the ability to report acts of harassment, discrimination, or other incidents that create a hostile work environment, but without fear of retaliation or reprisals, especially if the subject of the complaint is a supervisor or someone in authority. Under Sarbanes-Oxley, a whistleblower hotline may also be established. See Chapter 23 for more details on Sarbanes-Oxley.

In fact, in the employee policy manual an employer can even require that in the event of harassment or other misconduct, there is a duty to report it to management so the employer can investigate and take remedial action.

Also, the employer must have a mechanism in place to fairly and promptly investigate complaints, and to have demonstrated a commitment to take appropriate actions in response to the results of the investigation. Being able to document these procedures is critical should an employer be sued for negligent retention, or supervision.

# Termination Procedures

Termination of employees presents numerous challenges and consideration for any organization. Numerous legal and human resources materials are available to employers on dealing with termination. The fear of being sued over a termination is always a key consideration.

However, employers should also consider the possibility of being sued over *the failure to terminate.* Employers who fail to take action, including termination, where they have actual or constructive knowledge that a current employee is dangerous or unqualified for a position, can risk litigation for negligent retention, negligent supervision, or even negligent promotion.

## Method of Termination

The method of termination is very critical and there exists numerous resources and checklists of how to go about the process. The reason an employee seeks the assistance of a lawyer in order to explore bringing legal action is often because, at some fundamental level, the employee feels mistreated or somehow demeaned as an individual. Therefore it is critical that an employee be treated in a fair, impartial, and dignified way in the termination process. At the same time, the employer needs to protect the organization and co-workers. Below are some points to consider—

- When an employee is called in for the meeting with human resources or security about a consumer report or termination, a best practice is to do so at the end of the day to minimize embarrassment to the employee and disruption in the workplace. Many employers prefer to terminate at the beginning of the week rather than a Friday. Thus a terminated employment does not stew while still on the job and the workweek does not end on a sour note.

- A best practice is to have two employer representatives at the meeting so there is no question afterwards as to what was said.

- When the employee leaves the meeting, often a manager will accompany the employee to the employee's desk or to the exit in order to avoid disruption and to keep the situation calm.

- Depending upon the potential for violence or disruptions, some firms will have security service available for assistance.

- As part of the termination process, the employer must arrange to block passwords and access to the computer system and to change building entrance codes. If the employee has business material at his desk such as customer lists or phone numbers, then the material should also be secured by the employer.

- There are wage requirements to meet, such as giving the terminated employee a final paycheck that accounts for all wages, vacations, and any other time that is owed.

- The manner in which a termination occurs, when the person is escorted off premises or to their work areas to retrieve personal items, is also important. Employers have been sued for causing undue embarrassment and emotional distress in the way termination was handled.

- Many employers will take appropriate precautions to ensure that the reasons for the termination remain confidential.

- Consider if an offer of a severance agreement is appropriate. Such an agreement typically provides an employee with severance pay (such as two weeks) in exchange for a waiver of any claims the employee may feel he or she has against the employer. An employer should contact an attorney to determine what rules apply in their state. Some of the critical aspects include a fair payment to the employee ("adequate consideration" in legal terms), adequate time for the employee to consider all options, a very clearly drafted agreement so the employee cannot later claim a lack of understanding to any rights given up, and the ability to rescind the agreement within a certain time period.

## Exit Interviews

Exit interviews are an often overlooked opportunity for employers to exercise due diligence in protecting their workplace and third parties — an opportunity to locate potential landmines in an organization. Employees may have more information on what is actually occurring in an organization than managers and supervisors. An employee who is leaving may be willing to tell an employer what is really going on in the organization. For example, employees who have been terminated may be a source of information for acts of misconduct they have witnessed.

If the separation is involuntary, then the employer should still attempt an exit interview. There have been occasions, for example, where terminated employees used the exit interview to talk about how unfair the termination was in light of what others are doing who have not been terminated.

A sample Exit Interview Form is provided in the Appendix.

## Maintaining Documents After Separation

The question arises as to how long records and documents should be maintained after separation. There are a number of state and federal laws that control document retention, and labor attorneys will typically advise employers on how long various documents must be retained. However, for purposes involving safe hiring and background screening, the recommendation is six years. The FCRA was amended in 2003 to lengthen the statue of limitations under the act to five years. In addition, state laws often allow a one-year period to file and serve a lawsuit. As a workable general rule, a six-year retention period should serve employers — the six years run from the termination of employment or, if not hired, from the time the decision was made not to hire the applicant.

If disposing of any information in a consumer report, it is important to follow regulations set out by the FTC pursuant to FCRA Section 628. Paper or electronic reports must be destroyed, pulverized or erased so it cannot be read or reconstructed. an employer must show due diligence when a shredding firm is hired. See: www.ftc.gov/bcp/conline/pubs/alerts/disposalalrt.shtm.

> **Author Tip** ➡ Employers, HR professionals, and security professionals are not finished with their due diligence obligations when an offer of employment is made. Considerations exist during the entire employment relationship and even after the employment relationship has ended, thus the need for maintaining accurate employment and hiring history records.

## Continuous Screening

A new evolving practice called "Continuous Screening" is aimed at running periodic criminal records checks, such as every two weeks or monthly, on employees. These periodic checks have the potential to identify criminal cases that occur after the person was hired. Although such continuous searches can be a valuable risk-management tool, an employer needs consider a number of factors–

- False Sense of Security
- Consent Issue
- What to do if a Record is Found
- EEOC Considerations
- Impact on Workforce

One possible solution for employers considering continuous screening is to use a random pool similar to drug testing and perform searches at the local courthouse. For a more detailed discussion, see www.esrcheck.com/safehiringupdates.php.

## Handling Calls from Prospective Employers on Ex-employees

Because of the possibility of future employment reference checks, employers must still be concerned about past employees for many years after a person is no longer employed. This topic is addressed in Chapter 9.

# Section 4

# A Crucial Safe Hiring Program Reference Library

Section 4 is a resource for guidance on a variety of topics and issues important to today's employers.

Topics include international background checks, terrorist databases, drug testing, workplace violence.

Chapters 29 and 30 — to assist job applicants

Chapter 19 — a test for employers to audit their existing hiring programs

Chapter 20 — Special Issues and Trends for Employers — an important chapter for HR professionals wanting to know what is on the horizon for employers and the hiring process

# Chapter 19

# The Safe Hiring Report Card – Take the Test

## Employee Problems, Problem Employees

Everything covered in this book comes down to one sentence—

*Employee problems are caused by problem employees,*
*and those problems can be avoided in the first place with a Safe Hiring Program.*

If a firm does not practice a Safe Hiring program, then they can suffer what lawyers like to call the "Parade of Horribles." These "Horribles" are examples of the bad things that an employer may encounter, and let us hope you will not encounter many of these situations. In fact, through luck or good fortune some employer may not *as of yet* have encountered any. However, without a Safe Hiring Program, eventually a problem will occur.

### If Your Firm is Sued, Can You Show Due Diligence?

If your firm is sued, the question before a jury is "did your firm take appropriate steps in your hiring practices to protect the public, co-workers, or others at risk?"

Every employer has a legal duty to exercise due diligence in hiring. Firms that fail to exercise due diligence in their hiring also have a litigation exposure. An employer can be sued for negligence if they hire someone who they **knew, or in the exercise of reasonable care should have known,** was dangerous or unfit for that particular job.

Employers are at a disadvantage in litigation. A lawsuit for negligent hiring is typically brought as a result of serious injury to an employee or member of the public. In an extreme case involving a murder in the workplace, it can be the surviving spouse or family members who may be suing, claiming essentially that you were responsible. Not only is the jury hearing evidence of a serious loss, but also in these cases, the evidence will show that the employer had greater ability and resources to prevent harm through safe hiring. After all, it is the employer who has a legal duty of care as well as the resources to have prevented a hiring mistake.

A jury decides if an employer is negligent by using the mythical "reasonable person" standard. That standard leaves a great deal of latitude for a jury to decide that with a little more effort, an employer could have prevented the harm. Jurors are often employees themselves. They may be more likely to identify with an injured victim or family than an employer who was too lazy, cheap, or unconcerned to exercise due diligence procedures. Unless an employer has a really good reason why the injury, sexual assault or other harm was not their fault, employers lose the majority of cases

So, for employers, here is the Big Question. If your firm is sued, can you demonstrate due diligence?

# Audit Your Hiring Program

Below is a two-part test for employers – a Safe Hiring Report Card. This exercise allows you to see how your organization measures up in case you have to defend your firm's hiring practices in court or in a deposition before trial.[1]

## Start with a Benchmark Exercise

Trial attorneys often take a "test drive" to identify the fundamental thrust of case. A test drive can range from something as sophisticated as presenting their case to a "mock jury" to simply running the facts by non-lawyers to get their response. To determine how your firm may do in a negligent hiring lawsuit, let us create a hypothetical scenario and ask what you would tell a jury when called upon to defend your firm's safe hiring procedures. This "test drive" will establish a benchmark and you will be auditing your firm's hiring program.

Assume your organization hired an accounting clerk who falsified his or her credentials and later attacked and injured a co-worker during an argument over the clerk's numerous professional errors. The co-worker was hurt and cannot work, and consequently sues your firm for negligent hiring. Describe—

- What your firm did to exercise due diligence.
  To merely say you had a background screening firm do a check is not sufficient.

- What due diligence was exercised in selecting the background firm.
  Include pre-hire steps taken in the application, interview, and reference checking process before the background check.

After you have compiled and written your response to this exercise, take the Safe Hiring Audit that begins on the following page.

---

[1] A deposition is a device used in a civil lawsuit where each side is allowed to question potential witnesses under oath. All information is recorded by a court reporter. This is part of what is called the "Discovery Process." In the discovery process, each side is allowed to discover facts that may be relevant to the case before the trial. A witness is put under oath by the court reporter and testifies as though the person was in court, but there is no judge or jury. Whatever a witness says is transcribed into a written booklet and can be referred to in court. There are other discovery devices as well, depending upon the jurisdiction (state or federal). For example, each side can send written questions to each other that must be answered. They are called "Interrogatories." Parties can also send a demand to each other requesting they admit or deny certain items of information, called a "Request for Admission." Demands can also be made to provide documents, or to allow an inspection of premises.

The goal is to perform a self-assessment audit of procedures found in the hiring process. The audit is used to identify your present hiring program's strengths and weaknesses — to find areas that need improvement or where your compliance may be weak.

**Note of caution**– The Safe Hiring Audit is for educational purposes only. Do not create a document that could be construed as a company policy analysis; it could be used against your organization in court. If your organization decides to conduct a formal audit, a best practice would be to have an attorney perform the audit so it would be protected by work product or attorney-client privilege.

---

**Author Tip ➡** When performing the audit, it is worth recalling the discussion on Policies, Practices and Procedures...

...A **Policy** is a general statement of a principle according to which a company performs business functions.

...A **Practice** is a general statement of the way the company implements a policy. Best practices support policy.

...A **Procedure** documents an established practice. Documentation is the KEY. In a lawsuit, documentation is a very critical factor. For example, it is not sufficient to simply have a training session. Can you document who attended, when, if they stayed for the entire time, what was taught, if there was any follow-up or testing of skills learned? Everything needs to be documented in writing.

A firm cannot score high on this audit without documentation.

---

# The Safe Hiring Audit

For each of the 25 steps that follow, measure your organization on a 0-4 scale.

> 0 = doing nothing or out of compliance (equivalent to an F on a report card)
>
> 1 = taking some steps but falling short of what an employer should do (D)
>
> 2 = taking some measures but need to improve (C)
>
> 3 = taking strong measures; have some but not all documentation (B)
>
> 4 = your operation could be a model for other firms; all documentation is verified as legal (A)

Once your have completed all 25 questions, add the scores and then divide by 25. For instance, if the total is 78, the result would be 3.1. This will give you a general idea of the quality of the Safe Hiring Program. There are 100 possible points on a perfect audit.

## 1. Written Policies, Practices and Procedures __

**Best Practice:**

- How would you rate your company's **written policies** as far as demonstrating a commitment to safe hiring, such as found in your employee manuals or operations manuals?
- How accurately are specific **practices** documented?
- How well will **written forms** and **procedures** stand up to an **audit**?

**Case in Point:**

Although a firm had an "understanding" between managers to hire safe, qualified workers, the hiring procedure is done on the basis of "oral tradition." This would be a "0" – not compliant.

## 2. Policies/Practices Reviewed for Legal Compliance __

**Best Practice:**

- Review your Policies, Practices and Procedures for legal compliance.
  - o   Federal Fair Credit Reporting Act (FCRA) followed if third party firms involved.
  - o   In compliance with EEOC and state equivalent.
  - o   ADA and state ADA rules followed.
  - o   Specific state laws obeyed (i.e., California regulates both third-party screening AND internal employer investigations through the Investigative Consumer Reporting Agencies Act).
  - o   Privacy Protection and Defamation-avoidance procedures in place.

## 3. Communication of Policies and Practices __

**Best Practice:**

- Are the company's policies and procedures on safe hiring communicated effectively to the workforce and managers?

**Procedures:**

- Can you document how frequently policies and procedures are communicated?
- If you are in a deposition, how can you document communication of your policies? If so, what are the details? Hint— written documentation detailing dates and times works best.

## 4. Organizational Responsibility for Safe Hiring __

**Best Practice:**

- Is there a position specifically responsible for safe-hiring practices; i.e. are safe hiring responsibilities in someone's job description?
- If safe hiring is decentralized in hiring departments, are there documented procedures in place across the organization, including training and audit of performance?

## 5. Tools and Training to Ensure Hiring Managers Follow Plan __

**Best Practice:**

- Is there training for hiring managers, HR, etc.?

**Procedures:**

- How is the training conducted?
- Frequency of training?
- How is training success monitored and measured?
- Is an identifiable person responsible to analyze, implement, and evaluate the training program?
- How is compliance documented?

**Case in Point:**

- The school district had great policies but managers failed to follow practice guidelines, which permitted a teacher with a questionable history to be hired. Also, the managers failed to document the results of background checking done on the teacher.

## 6. Auditing of Safe-Hiring Practices __

**Best Practice:**

- Is there a documented audit procedure to ensure safe-hiring practices are followed? …i.e. can you prove someone was auditing procedures to see if it was followed?

**Procedures:**

- How is the completed audit information maintained?
- How frequently does auditing occur?
- Who conducts the audit process?
- Does the audit trail go to the TOP; i.e. local managers checked by regional managers, etc.

## 7. Consequences of Not Following Program __

**Best Practice:**

- Are there consequences/penalties if the hiring manager, HR personnel, etc. fail to implement or follow the plan?

**Procedures:**

- Can employer document that anyone not following procedures is adversely impacted?

## 8. Procedure to Place Applicants on Notice __

**Best Practice:**

- Is there notice in the job announcement, bulletin, classified advertisement, internet site, etc. that you perform background checks?

**Reason:**

- Discourages applicants with something to hide and encourages applicants to be truthful.

**Procedures:**

- Is there a notice on the application form that a prospective candidate receives?
- Do applicants **sign a release** for a background check?

## 9. Does the Firm Use an Application Form? __

**Best Practice:**

- Utilize application forms, not resumes.

**Reasons:**

- Resumes are often not complete or clear.
- To applicant, a resume is a marketing tool.
- Applications ensure uniformity.
- Also, requires applicant to provide all necessary information, prevents employer having impermissible info, and gives places where applicants sign certain statements.
- If no application process, is there a supplemental form with necessary language?

## 10. Does the Application Form Have All Necessary Language? __

**Best Practice:**

- Specifically ask if person has been convicted or has pending charges.
- Use broadest legal language for both felonies and misdemeanors.
- Some limitation or controls on the use of misdemeanor records.

- Fraudulent statement or material omissions grounds to terminate the process, or employment, no matter when discovered.

## 11. If Using a Screening Service, are Procedures Being Used per FCRA? __

**Best Practice:**

- Make sure screening service is in compliance with FCRA.

**Procedures:**

- Obtain applicant's written release/disclosure on a stand-alone document.
- Pre-adverse action-copy of report and statement of rights so applicant can object if information inaccurate or incomplete.
- Second letter sent to applicant if decision is made final.
- Employer must also certify law will be followed, i.e. not discriminate, use for employment purposes only.
- If forms provided by screening firm, review for legal compliance.
- Be aware many states have their own rules on screening.

## 12. Reviewing Ten Potential Red Flags on Application __

**Procedures:**

- Review applications for—
    1. Does not sign application
    2. Does not sign release
    3. Leaves criminal questions blank – the honest criminal syndrome
    4. Applicant self-reports offense
    5. Fails to identify past employers
    6. Fails to identify past supervisors
    7. Fails to explain why left past jobs
    8. Excessive cross-outs and changes
    9. Unexplained employment gaps
    10. Explanations for employment gaps or leaving past jobs do not make sense

## 13. Does Firm Look for Employment Gaps? __

**Best Practice:**

- Critical to verify employment to determine where a person has been **even if you only get dates and job title**.

- Looking for unexplained gaps.

**Procedures:**

- Document that interviewer reviewed application for gaps and asked applicant.

- If can verify person gainfully employed last five-ten years, then less likely spent time in custody for serious offense.

## 14. Are Interviewers Trained in Legal Compliance? __

**Best Practice:**

- Train all interviewers to—

  o Question all applicants in a similar fashion

  o Not ask illegal questions, i.e., questions that are discriminatory or prohibited by law

  o Respond when an applicant volunteers impermissible information

  o Not to make statements to an applicant such as promises about the job

  o Not mark or make notes on resume

**Procedure:**

- Document the interviewer's training and audit results.

## 15. Five Critical Questions in a Structured Interview __

**Best Practice:**

- Since they have signed a consent and believe you are doing checks, powerful incentive to be truthful.

- "We do background checks on everyone we make an offer to. Do you have any concerns you would like to discuss?" (Good applicants will shrug this question off.)

- "We also check for criminal convictions for all finalists. Any concerns about that?" (Make sure question reflects what employer may legally ask in your state)

- "We contact all past employers. What will they say?"

- "Will past employer tell us…?" e.g., applicant was tardy, did not perform well, etc. (Questions must be on job-related issues only)

- Where gaps in the employment history are not explained, it is critical to ask, "Can you please tell us what you were doing during the periods between employments that you listed."

## 16. Does Firm Check References? __

**Best Practice:**

- Critical to verify employment to determine where a person has worked even if you only get dates and job title.

**Reasons:**

- Biggest mistake employer can make is *not* contact past employers— this is just as critical as criminal checks.
- Looking for unexplained gaps.
- To target locations to search for criminal records.
- If able to verify person gainfully employed last five-ten years, they are less likely to have spent time in custody for serious offense.
- Just attempting/documenting demonstrates due diligence.

**Case in Point:**

- See the case of the murderous carpet cleaner (page 15) or the case of the state sponsored computer school (page 116).

## 17. Does Firm Use Other Tools? __

**Best Practice:**

- Take these additional steps as necessary if related to job—
  - Criminal record checks
  - Civil records if relevant
  - Social Security trace
  - Education and past employment credentials
  - Credit report (if appropriate and if policies are in place to ensure that use of credit information is recent, relevant, and fair)
  - Driving record

## 18. If Outsourced to a Third-Party Firm, Can Employer Demonstrate Due Diligence? __

**Best Practice:**

- If background check failed due to screening firm, then employer may be liable if he or she failed to exercise due diligence in selection of firm.

**Factors:**

- Expertise/knowledge of the service provider

- Legal compliance — FCRA and state law compliance
- Personal service and consulting — providing professional consulting services
- Training/consulting services available
- References
- Pricing of secured internet order/reporting options.

## 19. Are the Mechanics of a Screening Program Documented? __

**Best Practice:**

- Document all procedures.
- Process to send requests to screening company, track progress, receive reports, maintain privacy, and restrict results to only authorized persons.
- Track the stages in the hiring process for screening
  (typically only the finalists are subject to screening).
- Degree of screening for each position
  (not every position needs to be screened at the same level).
- Uniform screening procedures – similarly situated applicants treated in the same non-discriminatory manner.
- Storage and retention of reports separately from personnel files.

## 20. Policies and Procedure for Use of Negative Information? __

**Best Practice:**

- Policies – are there written guidelines to follow?
- Documentation – are all procedures and decisions documented to file?
- Individualized review – flat policy can be discriminatory.
- Uniformity – are similarly situated applicants treated the same?
- Legal compliance – if third party utilized under the FCRA, have a procedure to ensure pre-adverse action and post-adverse letters?

## 21. Legal Use of Criminal Information __

**Best Practice:**

- Understand EEOC rules for use of criminal records based upon business necessity—
  - The nature and gravity of the offense
  - The amount of time that has passed since the conviction or completion of sentence
  - The nature of the job being held or sought
- Special rules considering arrests only.
- Did the applicant lie in the application?
- Criminal information was verified and information is current, belongs to applicant, employer has understanding of information, and there is no prohibition on the information's use.

## 22. Policy if Person with Negative Information Hired? __

**Best Practice:**

- Firm has examined the type of support, supervision, and structure needed to improve the chances of success within the organization.
- Firm has considered the nature of the job and the circumstances of the past offense to take appropriate measures to protect the firm, co-workers, and the public from harm.
- Firm has documented decision-making factors.

## 23. Procedures if Employment Before Background Check is Completed __

**Best Practice:**

- If employment begins before completion of a background check, is there a written statement that employment is conditioned upon receiving a report that is satisfactory to the employer?
- Does policy eliminate a possible debate over what is an acceptable background report?

**Issue:**

- May need to escort the person off premises if background check is negative.

## 24. Supervisor Policies Post-Hire __

**Best Practice:**

- Safe hiring also extends to retention, supervision, and promotion.

**Procedures:**

- Are supervisors periodically trained and educated regarding the employer's liability for negligent retention, supervision, or promotion?
- Are supervisors trained to recognize, report and deal appropriately with workplace misconduct?
- Are there procedures to investigate workplace misconduct?
- Is there a mechanism for workers or managers to report and record workplace misconduct?
- Is it part of written job descriptions for supervisors to record, report and address workplace misconduct and part of performance appraisal?

## 25. Are the Safe Hiring Policies, Practices and Procedures Reviewed and Updated Every Year? __

**Best Practice:**

- Audit and review a firm's entire Safe Hiring Program each year.

## Conclusion— How Do Your Practices Measure Up?

After taking the Safe Hiring Audit and assessing your practices, an employer should begin a program of improving those areas where there is potential litigation exposure. If there are areas where your firm needs improvement, utilize the resources in this book.

If your overall score was less than 3, you have quite a bit of work to do.

# Chapter 20

# Special Issues and Trends for Employers

## Employers Come in All Sizes

A 2001 study by the U.S. Census Bureau provides a breakdown of U.S. employers by number of employees. The study also shows the total number of persons employed by firms within a specific size range.[1]

| Size of Firm | Number of Firms | Employees |
|---|---|---|
| 1-4 employees | 2,697,839 | 5,630,017 |
| 5-9 employees | 1,019,105 | 6,698,077 |
| 10-19 employees | 616,064 | 8,274,541 |
| 20 to 99 employees | 518,258 | 20,370,447 |
| 100 to 499 employees | 85,304 | 16,410,367 |
| 500 to 999 employees | 8,572 | 5,906,266 |
| 1,000 to 1,499 employees | 2,854 | 3,474,455 |
| 1,500 to 2,499 employees | 2,307 | 4,419,771 |
| 2,500 to 4,999 employees | 1,706 | 5,904,452 |
| 5,000 to 9,999 employees | 871 | 6,064,760 |
| 10,000 employees or more | 936 | 29,715,945 |

The study underscores the importance of small businesses. The Office of Advocacy of the Small Business Administration (SBA) defines a small business for research purposes as an independent business having fewer than 500 employees.

---

[1] for more census data for small businesses, see www.census.gov/epcd/www/smallbus.html

According the SBA, small businesses—

- Employ nearly 50 million people
- Represent more than 99.7 percent of all employers
- Employ more than half of all private sector employees
- Pay 44.5 percent of total U.S. private payroll
- Generate 60 to 80 percent of net new jobs annually[2]

# Special Challenges Faced by Small Businesses

It is becoming a familiar story in the news — a small business owner hires a new employee, then the new hire is accused of a heinous crime. Only then does the employer realize the new employee had lied about their past; the employer had failed to perform a background check or check references!

Because small businesses operate with fewer employees, a single bad hire arguably has an even greater impact on small employers. Even though small businesses employ over 50% of all employees and the impact of a bad hire is significant, it is amazing that small businesses do not take meaningful precautions to know exactly whom they are hiring.

There are several reasons why small businesses may not perform background checks—

1. Safe hiring is focused on problem avoidance in the future. If a firm has not had a bad experience, then efforts at a Safe Hiring Program can seem like a waste of time and money. It is human nature to base future action on past experience; if a business has not had the issue arise, it's not a priority.

2. Some small firms have the ability to hire people that are known to the firm. Firms operating in a small community often hire individuals recommended by current employees. Hiring individuals who are known to the firm helps reduce the firm's risk of hiring a bad employee.

3. Some firms are so busy growing they simply do not take time to re-organize their processes as they expand. For a firm to initiate components of a Safe Hiring Program, someone in management must recognize that safe hiring is a core business practice and take the initiative to make it happen.

4. As firms get bigger, they hang onto methods that worked well when they were smaller. These methods often include "flying by the seat of the pants" hiring methods. As a firm matures, it should recognize that more methodical procedures are needed.

5. As a small business gets bigger, it will eventually hire a human resources professional to handle the many tasks necessary to hire and maintain a large workforce. The number of tasks placed on a new HR is immense, particularly if HR is a department of one. By the time a firm reaches fifty employees, an HR position probably is a necessity. Prior to that, someone who holds the position of "office manager" and/or "payroll" typically handles the HR functions.

[2] for more information, visit the SBA at www.sba.gov/advo/stats/sbfaq.pdf

# Why Safe Hiring is a Challenge for an HR Department of One

When a small business hires an HR professional, there are a myriad of tasks that the HR professional must address. Foremost concerns about background screening and safe hiring.

A. **Compliance.** A new HR practitioner must first ensure that a firm is in legal compliance with a number of federal and state regulations, including I-9 compliance, proper classification of employees into exempt or non-exempt status, leave of absences including maternity and family leaves, ADA, harassment and numerous other legal issues. Failure to address these issues leaves a firm with tremendous financial and legal exposure.

B. **Employee Manual.** Institute a handbook outlining formal practices and procedures.

C. **Employee Files.** A new HR practitioner must typically review existing employee files, assuming those exist. Every employee should have a file that includes at least an application form or resume, a W-2 form, performance reviews and basic employee data such as start date, salary, dates of promotions, and changes in status.

D. **Payroll.** An HR practitioner must review how payroll is performed and determine if the best procedure is to do it in-house or outsourced.

E. **Benefits.** Very complicated for an HR department of one! A new HR practitioner needs to review benefit concerns. Typical issues include selection of benefits to offer, cost control, selecting a benefits broker, reviewing enrollment periods, and dealing with employee complaints concerning benefits.

F. **New Client Orientation.** In a growing firm, an HR practitioner will also need to implement a new employee orientation, including explanations of company policies and benefits. The orientation should typically include a new hire checklist with various new hire forms such as I-9 compliance or tax forms.

G. **Compensation Review.** When a small firm hires an HR practitioner, the person must review the current compensation system. As a firm grows, a compensation strategy is necessary to make sure a firm is competitive and consistent.

H. **Job Descriptions.** Often a small business grows without ever having prepared job descriptions. Descriptions are vital in helping an employer hire employees with the right skill sets, to perform job performance appraisals, and to comply with the ADA by identifying essential job functions.

I. **Performance Appraisal System.** Most small businesses do not have a formalized performance appraisal system in place. Appraisals can be a critical factor to determine the proper compensation rate, to implement improvement plans for an employee, or to determine areas where additional training or supervision may be necessary to help an employee succeed.

J. **Information Mechanism for Employees.** Another important function of a new HR department is to institute a system for keeping employees informed of such things as changes in benefits, new laws, harassment training, even the company holiday schedule.

K. **Training.** A growing small business may not have sufficient training in place. This includes not only training specific for a job, but training for managers and workers in areas such as sexual harassment control.

L. **Recruiting and Hiring.** A new HR practitioner may be asked to help the "employer effort" to recruit, interview, hire, and train new employers.

M. **HR Software.** Another task often assigned to a new HR department is to consider automation procedures and software available to help the firm manage the employment aspects of a growing business.

For businesses with twenty employees or less, the challenges are even greater. Being a small business owner is one of the toughest jobs in America; not only does the owner of a small business have to make sure everything gets done, but the owner only gets paid after everyone else gets his or her money. The good news is that even a small employer can implement a Safe Hiring Program at very low cost. The AIR Process described earlier costs next to nothing. The one step that may cost the employer money is a criminal record search. An employer can either go the local courthouse or hire a screening firm that typically charges $20.00 or less to search per county.

A small business that hires negligently would be hard pressed to defend itself on the basis that it is too small to practice safe hiring. That defense has not proven successful. Although a small business may not be expected to perform at the same level as a Fortune 500 firm, the fact is that safe hiring can be performed at little or no cost. There is no reason why any small business has to hire blindly.

# Large Employer Issues

On the other side of the employment spectrum are large enterprises. While there is no generally accepted formula for what constitutes middle market and large or enterprise level employers, when an employer reaches a level of 1,000 employees, a whole new set of concerns and challenges develops.

Discussion of some special considerations that large employers face follows.

## 1. Large Employers Face Legal Complexities by Hiring in Multiple States

For large employers operating in a number of states, the first challenge is legal compliance. The complexity of compliance surfaces in two significant areas.

1. **Use of criminal records by employers.** Many states have their own rules concerning the use of criminal records; some of these rules are reviewed in Chapters 6 and 11. These restrictions are

typically set forth in a state's rules on discrimination in employment such as state fair employment guidelines. Some states have restrictions enacted by statutes. For example, in California it is a misdemeanor for an employer to—

> "...seek from any source whatsoever, or utilize, as a factor in determining any condition of employment including hiring, promotion, termination, or any apprenticeship training program or any other training program leading to employment, *any record of arrest or detention that did not result in conviction,* or any record regarding a referral to, and participation in, any pretrial or post trial diversion program." Cal. Labor Code § 432.7.

Individual state rules can affect any aspect of the hiring process including the language on applications, proper interview questions, and the ability of employers to obtain and use screening information on applicants. Operating in multiple states requires knowledge of the rules for each.

2. **State FCRA Laws.** As discussed in Chapter 6, there are a number of states with unique laws controlling background screening by third party professional background firms. An employer that intends to hire and screen in multiple state locations must be aware of the applicable laws. Also, employers must utilize the forms and procedures appropriate for each state. In California, using forms and procedures that work in the other 49 states could expose an employer to substantial damage awards in a civil lawsuit.[3]

3. **Understanding which state law to apply.** Operating in multiple states also creates complicated issues of which laws apply. Assume a firm incorporated in Delaware hires a Connecticut resident for a job in New York, and a screening firm in Atlanta improperly reports a criminal conviction when the applicant went to school in California, and the case was brought into federal court in New York alleging violations of a New York state law that protect employees. This is an actual case.[4]

## 2. Consistency Within the Organization; a Large Employer Issue

Another issue for large multi-state employers is consistency within the organization. Assume for example that an employer has a facility in Arizona that is performing in-depth background reports and utilizing the safe hiring techniques reviewed in previous chapters. Also assume the same firm has a facility in Ohio that is not doing nearly as much to ensure safe hiring. If a person is injured as a result of workplace violence in the less vigilant Ohio facility, then the injured party's attorney could use the practices and procedures at the more vigilant facility against the employer. The argument would be the employer knew how to hire safely but chose not to follow the higher standard in that particular facility. In other words, an employer may be held to the standard in the facility that exercises the greater degree of due diligence. As a result, management must be sensitive to the need to have a consistent company-wide policy when it comes to safe hiring and employment screening.

---

[3] California has set its own legal requirements; see the article in Appendix 5, Only In California

[4] The case was *Obabueki v. IBM and ChoicePoint,* 145 F. Supp. 2d 371 (S.D. N.Y. 2001). There were follow-up cases as well. A detailed discussion of the facts and legal issues involved are beyond the scope of this book. However, the general principles involved in considering which state's law to apply are summarized in Chapter 6 on the FCRA.

The same considerations come into play when utilizing negative information. If the Ohio facility hired an applicant with previous criminal records to be employed, then the Arizona facility could be accused of discrimination if a similarly situated person with a similar record is denied employment.

## 3. Automation, Integration with HR Information Systems and Applicant Tracking; a Large Employer Issue

Another consideration for large enterprise level firms is the automation and integration of the pre-employment process with their Human Resources Information Systems, or HRIS. Some firms will manage all of the human resources with some enterprise level application such as PeopleSoft, Oracle, or SAP. Other firms may coordinate background screening with an applicant tracking system, or ATS.

An ATS system is a database that is used to manage applicant information in a firm's hiring process. The software manages the receipt of resumes and applications (including online applications) as well as correspondence and contact between applicants and the firm. The software can track open positions, engage in some sort of matching process, and track the progress of each applicant. There are at least 100 providers of this service in a market that is estimated at somewhere between $250-500 million dollars, each ATS software provider touting any number of different bells and whistles. ATS software providers meet the needs of small, medium, large, and enterprise employers.

For large employers, one advantage of having a direct business-to-business (B2B) connection with a screening firm is the time saved by eliminating double data entry — since the applicant's name, Social Society Number, and data of birth are already in the employer's computer system, there is no need to visit the background screening firm's website to manually re-enter the same data. With a seamless B2B integration, employers can instantly send the required data electronically to the screening firm, and the data is automatically populated in the screening firm's HRIS or ATS system. The B2B seamless interface can also communicate the types of searches the employer is ordering. While the order is being processed, the employer can receive updates or status reports.

Although the technology involved in seamless B2B connections was complex and expensive at one time, the general rule that technology becomes less expensive and more readily available certainly applies to background screening processes for large firms. In a relatively short period of time, even a small regional background screening firm without an IT staff will be able to have the same ability to connect on a B2B basis with large employers. There is a danger for screening firms that adopted this technology years ago and at great expense — they are heavily invested in old technology and may be at a competitive disadvantage unless they adopt new approaches.

## 4. Large Employers and the Impact of HR-XML

The ability of background firms to develop software that will work with a number of HRIS and ATS systems has been furthered by the advent of the HR-XML Consortium. That industry group is developing a common communications framework for employers and suppliers of HR services. Here is an overall description of what they do[5]—

---

[5] see www.hr-xml.org/channels/about.cfm

- The HR-XML Consortium is an independent, non-profit organization dedicated to the development and promotion of a standard suite of XML specifications to enable e-business and the automation of human resources-related data exchanges.

- Human resources-related e-business — or any inter-company exchange of HR data — requires an agreement among participants about how the transaction or data exchange will be accomplished.

- The mission of the HR-XML Consortium is to spare employers and vendors the risk and expense of having to negotiate and agree upon data interchange mechanisms on an ad-hoc basis. By developing and publishing open data exchange standards based on Extensible Markup Language (XML), the Consortium provides the means for any company to transact with other companies without having to establish, engineer, and implement many separate interchange mechanisms.

In late 2003, the consortium released standards for pre-employment screening. Per their website—[6]

> **"Background Checking:** The Background Check schema supports background check requests to third-party suppliers of background checking services. The specification also supports the return of search results. A wide variety of screenings are supported, including searches of criminal records, education, employment, military service, professional licenses, professional sanctions, and credit."

The HR-XML schemas are not universally implemented. At this point they are only suggested standards yet to receive widespread adoption. However, the schema set the stage for a kind of universal translator between software systems used by employers to manage their human capital and the suppliers of various services.

Some applicant tracking systems have partnered with screening firms to provide a built-in connection between the ATS and a screening firm partner. The advantage is an employer can hit a button that says "Background Report," and the process commences automatically without going to a separate screen to enter the order or applicant data.

However, employers should be careful about selecting a background screening service merely because the firm happens to have bundled with an applicant tracking system. Background screening is a much more complicated service than applicant tracking due to the legal implications of each screening report. To select a background screening firm just because there is an applicant tracking system makes little sense. Both applicant tracking and background screening requires a separate competency. The selection of each service provider should be made based upon selection criteria unique to each service.

Some background screening firms have developed rudimentary online applicant tracking systems that seamlessly send data from the employer to the screening firm. These systems work well for small employers. However, if an employer wishes to have an ATS that is really designed to manage the recruitment and selection process, such add-ons are typically not very robust or useful. The best approach is to select the ATS that meets the criteria needed, and independently select a screening firm, then determine how the ATS and screening firm can communicate.

---

[6] see www.hr-xml.org/channels/projects_main.cfm

## 5. Managing Privacy and Reports Across Organizational Lines; a Large Employer Issue

Large employers have special privacy issues. With multiple facilities, each with multiple divisions and hiring managers, a large employer needs to be concerned about how privacy and confidentiality are maintained. Unless precautions are taken, reports may be viewed by co-workers, administrative staff or others who are not involved in the hiring process and do not have a need to review the reports. A screening report does not contain secret information, however, it does contain information confidential in nature that should not be made available to anyone who is not directly involved in the hiring decision. An argument can be made that even a hiring manager should not view a background screening report, but should only be advised by Security or Human Resources if there is a problem that needs to be addressed.

A solution would be a system whereby reports go only to one contact person in charge of reviewing the information. Also, the contact person should maintain the reports. If a firm utilizes an online system for reports, then only the contact person should have access to the online system. Most screening firms offer online systems where an employer can easily manage the process. There is typically a screen that indicates the status of all current reports and the degree of completion. An online system can also route reports to the right office.

Screening firms can set-up accounts that use parent-child relationships so that a supervisor can view all reports, but only the appropriate office or person can view the reports that pertain to them. That also allows a screening firm to set-up sub-accounts for an organization so that management reports and billing can be provided to the correct branch or office.

## 6. Training Hiring Managers Across the Organization; a large employer issue

Another issue in large organizations is training the various hiring managers to consistently follow the organization's safe hiring procedures. This is especially an issue for organizations that hire for a large number of branches, such as banks, hotels, or sales offices. Consistency and training are important for a number of reasons especially for documenting that a firm, in fact, follows safe hiring procedures, and also helps protect the firm against allegations of discrimination.

The best tool is the S.A.F.E. Program outlined in Chapter 4. Another critical tool helpful for large organizations is a Safe Hiring Checklist, which outlines the steps essential in a Safe Hiring Program. The hiring manager fills out the checklist as new hires are finalized. The checklist gives clear directions on what has to be done and enables an organization to audit, measure, and reward hiring managers for following the safe hiring procedures. A safe hiring checklist is found in Chapter 4.

## 7. Contracting for Safe Hiring Services Based Primarily on Price

There is an increasing trend among large firms to have purchasing or procurement departments involved in the selection of service providers, including background-screening services. In recent years, some organizations have even taken to awarding contracts based upon online auctions, where the finalists bid against each other in an effort to obtain the lowest possible price.

The difficulty for large employers with this approach is that purchasing a professional service on a purely price-driven model leaves the organizations vulnerable in the event the low cost provider fails to adequately perform. If a firm utilizes the auctions approach, then they need to recognize they are making a calculated risk-management decision that by spending the minimum now, they are doing enough. If the low cost provider fails to perform and the firm gets sued, then the employer would face a substantial challenge in attempting to prove they exercised due diligence.

The reason that an employer is vulnerable in a lawsuit is that selecting a provider purely on price hinges on the fact the biggest variable factor in screening is the cost of labor. The raw cost of data has a relatively narrow margin. If a screening firm is bidding low, the primary place to make up for the price reduction is the amount of staff time the screening firm devotes to the process, which in turn affects the level of service. A low-cost provider may also have to take "shortcuts" in obtaining or processing data. Shortcuts can include using untrained clerical workers to produce screening reports, or utilizing incomplete databases for criminal searches. Another example of a shortcut is when court researchers enter criminal information directly into the computer, so the employer sees data that has not been reviewed for accuracy, completeness, or legality by a screening professional. Another way large employers obtain cheap pricing is to utilize a service that offers screening services essentially as a "loss leader" in order to sell other HR products. Firms using auctions may also attract screening firms that are purely data houses willing to sell at or near cost to increase their volume, or willingly take a smaller profit per transaction as long as they can keep their costs down. Again, since the largest item of overhead is trained staff, a large employer who is driving down the price through an auction cannot count on having the level of professional service the task requires.

Firms using the auction method would probably not do so for other professional services such as finding a corporate attorney or an auditor. When using an auction for screening and safe hiring services, a large employer is essentially relegating safe hiring to a commodity product, ignoring the professional services aspect. One employer found out the hard way. In *Kay V. First Continental Trading, Inc.,* 976 F.Supp 772,774 (N.D. Ill 1997), a federal court ruled that an expert witness could give his opinion derived from his own experience, that a screening firm could not have effectively conducted a proper investigation for the low price that it charged the employer. The end result is that employers who focus solely on price may find themselves paying more later. As the saying goes, "You get what you pay for."

# Free Agent Nation and Corporate Me

The role of non-traditional workers was popularized during the internet bubble 1990-2002. One book popularized the notion of a "FreeAgent Nation" based upon the premise that a person is no longer defined by their job or job title. Instead, the new workers really work for themselves. They are their own corporation with their own brands. When they are on someone else's payroll, they are really "consultants" and every job should be an opportunity to increase their value.[7]

---

[7] see www.freeagentnation.com

# Special Issues With Hiring the Non-Traditional Workforce

According to a 1999 U.S. Department of Labor report[8]—

> "The age of 'just in time' production has given rise to 'just in time' workers—employees whom a business can hire on a moment's notice to fill a moment's need.

> Roughly one in ten workers fits into an *alternative arrangement*. Nearly four out of five employers use some form of non-traditional staffing arrangement.

> America's *alternative workers* number 13 million and they are a mixed group. The majority (8.5 million) are independent contractors. A growing number (1.3 million) are *agency temporary workers*."

Of course, not every independent contractor or non-traditional worker prefers that status. Even though a non-traditional job provides greater flexibility, at the same time it does not afford the same benefits or salary that a full time employee may typically enjoy.

The non-traditional workforce raises special considerations when it comes to safe hiring. Past employment history is harder to pin down when the applicant has had a number of positions.

When hiring a non-traditional worker, employers need to exercise the same safe hiring precautions they would for any other job applicant. If an employer decides to save costs by not attempting to verify every past work assignment in the past five to ten years, or search every past county in the past seven years for criminal records, then utilizing the AIR Process (as outlined in previous chapters) is even more important. In determining how much effort, money, and energy to put into background screening non-traditional workers, an employer should consider two factors—

1. **Use consistency.** The same level of screening used for similar positions should be used for a position that is to be filled by a non-traditional worker, or else the firm may be subject to allegations of disparate treatment of similarly situated people.

2. **The duty to hire with due diligence.** This basic rule still applies. An employer is negligent if they hire someone who the employer either knew or should have known, in the exercise of reasonable care, was dangerous or unfit or not qualified for the position.

# Special Problems With Large Hourly, Seasonal, Temporary Contract Workforces

Industries with large hourly, seasonal, or temporary contract workforces typically include hospitality and tourism, manufacturing, service, retail, food and restaurants, drug and groceries stores, call centers. Compounding their hiring problems are multiple locations and large turnovers.

---

[8] see www.dol.gov/asp/programs/history/herman/reports/futurework/report.htm

Unicru is an employment assistance firm that specializes in total workforce acquisitions solutions for specific industries, including industries with large hourly workforces. According to a 2002 special report by Unicru—

> "In the United States, over 90 million workers – more than 80 percent of the labor pool – are hourly or front-line employees. On an annual basis, large companies will hire far more hourly workers than salaried or professional staff.
>
> The mechanics of hiring from these two segments are vastly different. Hiring cycles for salaried personnel are longer than for hourly workers. The former tend to apply to positions and/or organizations in large numbers, while the latter tend to apply in much smaller numbers to locations within five miles of their homes. Psychologically, hourly workers feel much more pressure to find work quickly and tend to be on the market for only a few days, while a salaried candidate's shelf life is measured in months. A manager of salaried staff will typically interview only three candidates for a position and hire one person or less per year, but a location or store manager will hire more than 15 people per year, interviewing an average of five applicants per position. In the salaried workforce, turnover is less than 10 percent; it is 6 to 10 times that among hourly employees."[9]

The challenge is greater if the firm is engaged in providing services that have a greater degree of risk to third parties. For example, resorts hiring seasonally have greater exposure because of the fact children are present during their peak seasons. If temporary or seasonal employees are involved in higher risk activities in roles as lifeguards, ski instructors or other similar jobs, then the stakes are higher.

So, how do industries with significant turnover — or with large numbers of hourly, seasonal, temporary or contract workers — protect themselves in a cost-effective and efficient manner? Employers are under pressure to reduce the time and cost per hire by minimizing those costs and delays associated with pre-employment screening. A cost-effective solution is to devise a mechanism that incorporates the elements of the S.A.F.E. Hiring program outlined in Chapter 2 along with reasonable and appropriate background checks. One key element is to emphasize tools that discourage applicants with something to hide in the first place, then encourage early self-disclosure of negative information. The solution is to implement the AIR Process described in previous chapters in an assembly line fashion.

At a minimum, run a basic public records search. It is essential to run a Social Security trace, and at least a one county criminal record check. If any driving is involved, then a driving record should also be run. Of course, if it is a driving position regulated by the Department of Transportation, or for any other position that is regulated by federal or state rules, then all applicable laws must be followed.

---

[9] see www.unicru.com/literature/whitepapers/SalariedVsHourlyHiring.pdf. Unicru main website is www.unicru.com

# More About Hiring Juveniles

Hiring young workers or juveniles presents special problems. Juvenile records are typically not "public records" and criminal records are difficult to acquire unless the juvenile was tried as an adult. In addition, juvenile workers and young workers may not have a significant employment history. Employers, however, can require that they provide at least two letters of recommendation from non-family members or teachers who know them. This procedure helps eliminate those applicants without the initiative to obtain such letters, and helps an employer show *some* due diligence in hiring. Parental consent and state child labor laws are issues; if an employer is only obtaining public records, verifying past employment information or school attendance, parental consent is probably not required, in the absence of a specific state law. These procedures are not intrusive and there are FCRA protections. However, if parental consent is available, it does add extra protection.

Even though the cost of background checks can add up for large hiring programs, employers are still held to a standard of due diligence hiring for hourly, temporary, or seasonal employees. If sued, an employer might assert the defense that imposing the requirement of doing background checks was too costly of a burden to place on employers, but such a defense is not likely to succeed. Courts have taught employers that the cost of safe hiring is minor when compared to the possible harm not performing the check could cause. As explained in Chapter 2, the cost of litigation and attorney fees alone from one bad new-hire can negate the money saved on cutting corners.

**In conclusion— CEO's and CFO's that take the position that safe hiring and pre-employment screening are not important or too expensive need to carefully review the true economics of their firm and the risk factors involved from a single bad hire.**

# When Saving a Few Bucks is Just Not Worth What It Costs

A large employer may be tempted to save money by cutting corners on safe hiring. The theory is to "self insure," by taking a calculated risk that if something negative should happen, it is more cost-effective to pay out money later than to pay out upfront for screening.

An example of this corporate approach is the famous Ford Pinto case. The following excerpts are from an article from The Center for Auto Safety—

"In 1977, Mark Dowie of *Mother Jones Magazine*, using documents in the Center files, published an article reporting the dangers of the fuel tank design, and cited internal Ford Motor Company documents that proved that Ford knew of the weakness in the fuel tank before the vehicle was placed on the market but that a cost/benefit study was done which suggested that it would be 'cheaper' for Ford to pay liability for burn deaths and injuries rather than modify the fuel tank to prevent the fires in the first place. Dowie showed that Ford owned a patent on a better designed gas tank at that time, but that cost and styling considerations ruled out any changes in the gas tank design of the Pinto.

Closely following the publication of the *Mother Jones* article, a jury in Orange County, Calif., awarded Richard Grimshaw $125 million in punitive damages for injuries he sustained while a passenger in a 1971 Pinto which was struck by another car at an impact speed of 28MPH and burst into flames. Although the award was eventually reduced to $3.5 million by the trial judge, the jury's reason for the figure of $125 million was that Ford Motor Company had marketed the Pinto with full knowledge that injuries such as Grimshaw's were inevitable in the Pinto, therefore the punitive damages should be more than Ford had made in profit on the Pinto since its introduction, which was $124 million."[10]

Ford eventually recalled 1.5 million Ford Pintos and 30,000 Mercury Bobcats for fuel tank design defects, but not until Ford endured negative publicity and lawsuits. The lesson here is when it comes to fundamental questions of health and safety, the approach of saving money by hoping nothing goes wrong can work out very badly for employers and those at fault.

# Drawbacks to Using an Online Instant Database for Quick Hiring Decisions

Websites offering employers so called "instant searches" may include the following sample language—

"Human resource professionals can conduct extensive national pre-employment background checks in real time! Within seconds our system can reveal the following—

- Positively identify your candidate
- Validate their SSN's
- Secure all addresses the candidate used for the past 7-15 years
- Reveal their relatives and associates
- Determine if the applicant has been involved in litigation, bankruptcy, or has tax liens
- Confirm property ownership
- Verify the candidate's drivers license information (available in some states)
- Scan for any criminal records or sex offender listings."

Unfortunately, this type of instant search does provide as much coverage and protection as employers may believe, but exposes an employer to allegations for violation of federal and state laws.

---

[10] see this Ford story online at www.autosafety.org/article.php?scid=96&did=522

## Examples How Using These Databases Can Lead to Problems

The reason these internet searches do not provide a great deal of protection is these so-called "instant results" are essentially "data-dumps" based upon an automated search through billions of records. Criminal or sexual offender searches are subject to the database problems described in Chapter 12 — a database search is not necessarily complete, up-to-date, or accurate. For a number of reasons, an offender may not show up in a database, or a person may show up who is not an offender. This means an employer who relies upon search results for even an initial screening decision can face a difficult situation. They may eliminate someone who should not be eliminated, which may give rise to claims of discrimination, litigation, or an employer may give preliminary approval to someone who should not receive it. If the person is hired and causes harm, then that employer is a sitting duck in any resulting litigation since the use of these database searches by themselves are unlikely to demonstrate proper due diligence.

---

**Interesting Results from Two Studies—**

An April 11, 2004 article in the *Chicago Tribune* featured a story about a University of Maryland Associate Professor of Criminology who ran a test on an online database service. According to the article, Professor Bushway obtained the criminal records of 120 parolees in Virginia, and submitted these names to the popular online background check company. According to the article, sixty names came back showing no criminal record. Many other reports were so jumbled that the offenses were tough to pick out.[11]

The same article reported that the *Chicago Tribune* had conducted its own study. The Tribune selected an online data service and submitted the names and birthdates of 10 Illinois offenders whose sentences were in the media for crimes ranging from drunken driving and fraud to possession of child pornography. The online statewide search found no criminal records for any of the names, and flagged only one person as a sex offender, but provided little additional useful information.

---

Some information obtained from these internet databases can violate the Federal Fair Credit Reporting Act (FCRA) and state and federal discrimination laws. The use of conviction information found in a database is improper with compliance with FCRA section 613. Section 613 requires either the background service notify the applicant or take measures to visit the courthouse to ensure the report is accurate, up-to-date, and has proper identifiers.[12] Many of these internet services are only giving lip service to FCRA requirements, if mentioned at all.

On the other hand, employers need to be aware of all FCRA compliance issues if the internet site is in fact a Consumer Reporting Agency that genuinely, legally assembles and evaluates data. The employer must obtain consents, provide authorizations, and abide by the FCRA, but these instant internet sites

---

[11] see Chapter 12 for a more detailed explanation of why database searches can miss names
[12] see the detailed discussion in Chapter 6 on the FCRA

can lead an employer to believe that all they need is a credit card to obtain data. This can expose an employer to a serious threat of litigation.

Another factor employers must consider is compliance with federal and states discrimination laws. Some types of records sold by instant information vendors are not valid predictors of job performance. For example, a search that focuses on finding if someone had declared bankruptcy could violate a consumer's rights. Consideration of whether a person owns property is not likely to be a valid predictor of job performance, and can be discriminatory by creating a disparate impact on certain groups. Obtaining names and addresses of "relatives and associates" could be a violation of discrimination laws and an invasion of privacy.

In summary, employers need to be very careful about using online instant data brokers. Not only can there be issues with the accuracy, completeness, and applicability of the data, but there are also a number of FCRA, discrimination, and privacy considerations.

# Special Issues When Hiring in a Labor Shortage

Although the current economic environment has relatively high unemployment, experts tell us that the future will be very different. The news media reports that once the recession is over, the real story will be a **worker shortage**, especially for jobs requiring higher education. According to the Bureau of Labor Statistics, by 2010 there will be 10 million more jobs than people to fill them. Jobs requiring higher education or jobs that fall into the management/professional category are increasing significantly faster than the amount of available qualified workers to fill those positions.

When a shortage occurs, the pressure on employers and recruiters to fill positions is much greater. Delaying a new hire to wait for a background report could result in a good candidate being hired elsewhere.

However, when employers and recruiters become less selective and take a gamble, they tend to end up with new hires they may wish they could have avoided.

During a labor shortage an employer may wish to consider the following guidelines—

1. Resist the temptation to hire as fast as possible. Do not dispense with the fundamentals of a Safe Hiring Program. Shortcuts in hiring can come back to haunt the firm, the recruit, and the hiring manager in the future.

2. Understand that if a firm makes a bad hire, the "perceived need for speed" will likely not make much of an impact in front of a jury, if the employer is sued.

3. If time is of the essence, then make sure the no-cost suggestions made in this book about Applicant/Interview/Reference checking practices are followed. This helps to minimize problematic hires.

4. If the situation demands the applicant be hired without delay, then be certain to provide a written offer letter stating the new hire is conditional based upon receipt of a background report that is satisfactory to the employer.

# Special Issues With Safe Hiring and Job Boards

Although it is debated how many jobseekers actually find employment from online services, there is no question that large numbers of U.S. workers use the internet to look for job opportunities. Statistics suggest that fifty-two million Americans have looked online for information about jobs. Some services estimate there are as many as 10,000 job boards in the U.S. Although the "job board market" is dominated by large players — Monster, Careerbuilder, HotJobs — there are numerous job boards and career sites that focus on specific job niches or on geographic areas.

## Understanding the Job Board and Recruitment World

There are two useful websites that assemble, categorize, and analyze the various job boards, including recruiting and employment-related sites on the internet.

1.  Peter Weddles is a veteran of the online job world. He publishes guides to employment websites for recruiters and jobseekers. His recruiting guide has data on over 40,000 career-related sites. See www.weddles.com.

2.  Another service is offered by CareerXroads, publisher of a yearly book that reviews job and employment-related sites. See www.careerxroads.com.

The best cyberspace resource to follow major developments in the online employment scene is www.interbiznet.com. This site offers a daily newsletter for the recruiting industry, special employment reports, and a daily column by John Sumser, widely considered the leading source of analysis for the electronic recruiting industry.

## Verification of Resumes Found on Job Boards

One difficulty with the millions of resumes on job boards is verification. Resumes are not verified by a trusted third party. Although numerous job boards claim they "screen" candidates, the use of the word "screened" in the job board context is typically a process used to perform some sort of preliminary evaluation of candidate qualifications, at least on cyber-paper. The purpose is to eliminate unqualified candidates and guide employers to candidates more likely qualified. The catch is that job board screening tools are based on the premise that *what people say about themselves is true.*

If job boards independently verified facts on resumes, it would be immensely valuable. Employers could hire with a great deal more accuracy and confidence.

Consequently, the value of job boards is only as a tool for employers and jobseekers to find each other in the first place. Job boards, from the smallest local niche board to the biggest boards, are still essentially the electronic equivalent of a local supermarket bulletin board or the want ads in the newspaper. Using a job board does not relieve an employer of their safe hiring obligations — employers still have the same legal duty to exercise due diligence regardless of the source of the candidate.

> **Author Tip** ➡ On job boards, do not be confused by the use of the word "screened." Unless the employer knows for a fact the screening included safe hiring steps and verifiable background screening, the employer must take the same steps with job board candidates as they would with any other. Using proper safe hiring steps will also keep you in compliance with equal opportunity laws.

An excellent resource comes from The Privacy Rights Clearinghouse which published a special report by Pam Dixon, author and investigative researcher for the World Privacy Forum.

The report is titled *Fact Sheet 25: Privacy Tips for Online Job Seekers.*[13]

# A Job Board is Used to Commit Identity Theft

According to an article on MSNBC in November, 2002, job boards can be dangerous for the unwary. Here is the story—

"It was just the job lead Jim needed: a marketing manager position with Arthur Gallagher, a leading international insurance broker. Only days after Jim responded to the job posting on Monster.com, a human resources director sent along a promising email. 'We're interested in you,' the note said. 'The salary is negotiable, the clients big. In fact, the clients are so valuable and sensitive that you'll have to submit to a background check as part of the interview process.' Eager for work, Jim complied — and sent off just about every key to his digital identity, including his age, height, weight, Social Security Number, bank account numbers, even his mother's maiden name. It was all just an elaborate identity theft scam designed to prey on the most vulnerable potential victims — the increasing ranks of the unemployed."[14]

It was one big scam. The lesson here is for everyone to be careful about how you use your personal information on internet job boards, especially with your Social Security Number.

---

[13] *Fact Sheet 25: Privacy Tips for Online Job Seekers* is online at www.privacyrights.org/fs/FS25-JobSeekerPriv.htm

[14] see the online version of this MSNBC in November, 2002 story at http://msnbc.msn.com/id/3078533

# Special Issues With Safe Hiring and Recruiters

Recruiters are a source of applicants for employers. Recruiters are called upon to find highly qualified candidates appropriate for a particular job description. Employers use recruiters to economically and quickly find applicants interested in long-term job situations. Recruiters find applicants from a number of different venues, from job boards to cold calling to networking. Recruiters can be independent or work for a particular employer on an in-house basis.

The fees and reputations of independent recruiters and recruiting firms depend largely on the qualifications of the candidates they present. Although some recruiters may do some past employment checks themselves. The act of recruiters doing pre-employment screening before presenting candidates does not appear to be a wide spread practice. When balancing the relatively low cost of a screening report with the fees a recruiter can receive with the negative impact of just one bad candidate, it would seem to be an ideal due diligence service to have recruiters make a practice of screening all candidates.

Under the Fair Credit Reporting Act, there is no barrier to a recruiter obtaining a background report. A recruiter will need to follow the FCRA in terms of obtaining written authorization and providing the candidate with a disclosure of their rights. A screening firm can provide the necessary documents to the recruiter. There are two special considerations—

1. In the release form for a screening, the recruiter should add a provision indicating the candidate also releases the information to an employer who may wish to view the report. This allows the recruiter to share the background report with a potential employer.

2. There are restrictions in obtaining credit reports. The recruiter is not the end user of credit reports and the credit bureaus require the actual end-user be identified and to show a permissible purpose. However, there are no restrictions on other basic screening tools such as checking past employment or education or searching for criminal records.

In-house recruiters have different issues. Hiring managers will typically assign an in-house recruiter to fill a certain number of job positions. While Human Resources or security department dictates the safe hiring protocol for the employer — the background screening process that the firm may use — in-house recruiters typically are under pressure to complete the hiring quickly. As discussed in previous chapters, the process used for background screening usually takes up to three days. For large firms, even a one-day delay can have an impact since many employers have a preset new employee orientation schedule. If a new hire misses the start date, then the new hire may have to wait a week or more before the next new employee classes begin.

In-house recruiters can help speed up the process in several ways—

First, the recruiter must understand the process can be delayed if screening firms are sent incomplete information or forms that are not legible or completely filled out. Screening firms often face difficulty in deciphering an application in order to identify and locate past employers, but having a recruiter review and correct all candidate's applications before sending those applications to a screening firm will help eliminate delays. This is simply a good practice for any employer or recruiter.

Second, an in-house recruiter needs to communicate with hiring managers so there are not unrealistic expectations. A hiring manager may not understand, for example, that criminal records are searched at each relevant courthouse, or that delays can occur if there is a potential match that needs to be verified. Hiring managers must also be advised that employment and education verifications can be delayed for the all reasons discussed in Chapters 9 and 14. If there is a delay in receiving a completed screening report, the recruiter should examine the source of the delay.

Third, if a recruiter is working with a screening firm that has an online ordering system, the process is considerably faster, and with greater accuracy.

Finally, there are times when a recruiter may determine that even though the screening firm has not been successful in obtaining all of the information, enough data is available to make a hiring decision. Typically, delays happen when verifying previous employment, and past employment oldest in time is the most difficult to obtain, though the oldest employment may be the least relevant. If the applicant, for example, worked in a fast food restaurant six years ago after getting out of school, and the fast food place will not call back, then there may be no reason to delay the hiring decision if the screening firm has obtained the most recent and presumably more relevant job verifications.

# A New Emerging Tool— Use of Employment Kiosks

Another method for employers to find candidates is using job kiosks. Job kiosks are small, ATM type devices that jobseekers may use for applying online. Kiosks are usually controlled and operated by staffing firms or particular employers seeking employment applications.

---

**Results of Job Privacy Study**

The text below is taken from a 2003 Job Search Privacy Study conducted by Pam Dixon and published by the World Privacy Forum at www.worldprivacyforum.org.

Retailers, county and city workforce development centers, staffing firms, and other employers have deployed kiosks. Briefly, by way of example—

- Blockbuster deployed an estimated 4,000 employment kiosks in the year 2000.
- Albertson's deployed an estimated 2,300 kiosks across its retails stores in 2003.
- Sports Authority has deployed kiosks in its retail stores nationwide.
- Sears has employment kiosks in its retail stores.
- JobView has deployed at least 200 kiosks.
- Adecco has had at least 50 "jobshop" employment kiosks nationwide.
- Los Angeles County has deployed at least 13 job kiosks.
- The Dallas/Fort Worth area has 40 job kiosks deployed through the DFW employment centers.

---

An important issue in the process for applying for a job by kiosk or an online system is the applicant's consent for a background check. A kiosk will typically request private and sensitive data to process the request, which can include a Social Security Number and possibly date of birth. The use and storage of this information involves a myriad of compliance issues, mentioned throughout this book.

## Electronic Signatures and Applicant Consents

The Federal Trade Commission initially took the position that a mouse click was insufficient to meet the standards of the Fair Credit Reporting Act (FCRA) when written consent is required.[15]

FCRA Section 604(b)(2)(A)(ii) specifically requires that—

> "ii) the consumer has authorized in writing (which authorization may be made on the document referred to in clause (i)) the procurement of the report by that person."

Congress had carved out an electronic exception for the trucking industry, but this exception did not apply to other employers. See Section 604(b)(2)(B)(ii).

In October, 2000, the Electronic Signatures in Global and National Commence Act (ESIGN) was passed into law.[16] Section 101(a) of the act provides that—

> "(a) . . . Notwithstanding any statute, regulation, or other rule of law (other than this title and title II), with respect to any transaction in or affecting interstate or foreign commerce -(1) a signature, contract, or other record relating to such transaction may not be denied legal effect, validity, or enforceability solely because it is in electronic form."

The FTC revisited the issue of electronic authorization in the Zalenski letter issued May 24, 2001[17]. The FTC concluded that in view of the ESIGN Act, it was possible to use electronic signatures for authorization for a background check. The FTC indicated that whether or not the electronic signature is valid depends on the specific facts of each situation. Specifically—

- The electronic signature must clearly convey the consumer's instructions.
- The FTC stated that as specified by Section 101(e) of the ESIGN Act, that consumer's electronic authorization "must be in a form that can be retained and retrieved in perceivable form." In other words there must be a clear and reproducible record showing the electronic consent.

There are no approved or accepted standards on what type of procedure satisfies this requirement. In legal terms, the concept of authorization or consent means "an agreement to do something" or to "allow something to happen," and made with complete knowledge of all relevant facts such as the risks involved or any available alternatives.

At a minimum, any firm attempting to obtain electronic compliance online should go through a series of screens, each one giving the applicant the chance to continue or to exit.

---

[15] see the Landever letter, issued October 12, 1999, at www.ftc.gov/os/statutes/fcra/landever.htm

[16] see 15USC Sec. 7001 et. seq.

[17] view the 2001 Zalenski letter at www.ftc.gov/os/statutes/fcra/zalenski.htm

For each screen that conveys information, there should be an opportunity for an applicant to indicate by a mouse click if they "understand and agree" or "do not understand and agree." If they hit the "do not understand and agree," then they should be sent to a screen that makes it easy to obtain more information, either by providing phone numbers or a Frequently Asked Questions section, with the option to go back to the online screening process. In addition, it may be advisable to have the ability to go to an FAQ page from every screen.

In addition, the computer screens should clearly convey the following—

1. Clarify if using English or if other languages are available.

2. Statement that the employer will, consistent with the Americans with Disability Act and applicable state law, make reasonable accommodation for those applicants who are unable to complete the process using the kiosk or online system.

3. A clear explanation of exactly what the consumer is being asked to authorize, which includes an explanation of the background screening process and what information an applicant will need to provide.

4. A clear disclosure of the applicant's rights as set forth in the FCRA as well as any applicable state law.

5. A statement describing what security measures are in place, so a consumer can judge if risks are involved in sending confidential information electronically.

6. Additional websites and phone numbers a consumer can contact in order to obtain more information if necessary.

7. Indicate if a pre-employment background firm is being utilized. If so, a good practice would be to give the name, phone number, address, and website for that firm. It would also be advisable to explain to applicants that the screening firm makes no decisions on the application itself, and the screening firm should not be contacted for status or results of a hiring decision.

8. Clear instructions on how an applicant may withdraw consent in the future.

9. Information on how an applicant may receive a copy of the consent as well as a copy of the disclosure. It is in the best interest of the employer to devise a method to make that document instantly accessible. One technique is to allow an applicant to designate an email address to send a copy of the information to, including consent and disclosure of rights forms.

10. An option explaining how applicants can exercise any of their rights in person. A best practice would be to advise applicants they could receive copies of their rights, and apply or withdraw consent in person at a store or other physical location.

11. A screen that clearly indicates what the applicant is consenting to, with an option to opt out. It must be absolutely clear the consent or agree button authorizes the pre-employment screening. Every time there is an "agree" button, there should also be a "NO" button that takes the consumer to a screen explaining their rights.

12. An applicant should be clearly advised of his or her rights to obtain a free screening report. If the applicant is a resident of California, Oklahoma, or Minnesota, have a box to check for a free report.[18]

13. Indicate that when the applicant enters their Social Security Number, they consent to the background screening. It should be absolutely clear they have initiated the screening process, and once again, there should be an opt-out option.

Although not currently required by any law or statute, it may be a best practice to also have a procedure where an applicant can work around the online system and choose to provide the written consent and any data (such as their Social Security Number) by submitting a written form. This practice could help insulate a firm from allegations of any sort of discriminatory or unfair practices.

As a final protection, after the final "Yes" has been selected, there can be one last screening saying, "You have touched the I AGREE button. Is that what you intended?" with a YES or NO afterwards. Other practices can include a clear indication that if the applicant does not agree to any terms, the process will not be continued and they will not be considered for employment online.

If part of the screening process includes verification of past employment or education, there is still the issue of the need for a written authorization for occasions when a past employer or a school requires a written release. A screening firm may have to track down the applicant and ask for a written release, or provide the past employer or school with sufficient assurances that there was an electronic release.

Also, there is the issue of collecting a date of birth through the kiosk system; see Chapter 5, Complying with Discrimination and Privacy Laws.

# Candidates Presenting Their Own Verified Credentials

A new development is the concept of applicants proving their own credentials. A candidate self-credentialing website permits applicants to purchase a "verified" screening report.

One of the first websites to offer this service was MyJobHistory (see box below). Since the site was introduced, similar services have become available. Examples are HotJobs and Careerbuilder.com. The value of such a site is to help employers sort through a sea of resumes and focus on those candidates who are willing to have their qualifications scrutinized.

> **Author Tip** ➡ The FAQ section at www.myjobhistory.com gives an excellent overview of how these verified credentials services benefit both the applicant and the employer.[19]

---

[18] California and other states also have special disclosure rules that must be incorporated. See Chapter 5 for a discussion on the challenges of a fifty state complaint form.

[19] in the interest of full disclosure, the author of this book Les Rosen was the founder of MyJobHistory

Even if an employer hires an applicant that has a verification statement from such a website, an employer should still conduct whatever due diligence they normally perform — to take their normal steps to make sure a person is a good fit for the job and organization, including conducting a criminal record check.

Applicant-supplied criminal checks create a number of potential problems. First, the employer should decide where to conduct the search and how extensive it should be, not an applicant. An applicant with a criminal record may well decide to not request a criminal record check for that specific jurisdiction. Second, a criminal search is only good up until the day it is conducted. When an applicant supplies the criminal search, there is no way to know if the data is still current.

One website attempts to remedy that by only making the search available for ninety days. However, that still does not address the issue of applicants providing their own report, creating the potential for an applicant to hide his or her past. Another website provides a so-called "national database" search.[20] However, for the reasons reviewed in that chapter, such a search is only a secondary research tool and not a true criminal search.

There is one additional note of caution— an employer should not place a condition for employment upon the jobseeker to pay for such a report. Such a policy could be construed as discriminatory. In addition, charging an application fee may violate state law. For example, California Labor Code 450 can make it a criminal act to require an application fee.

# Looking Toward the Future— Background Screening and the Creation of a Human Capital Database

The ideal situation for an employer would be to have the ability to visit to a website, put in an applicant's name and Social Security Number, and instantly get a thumbs up or thumbs down — to hire or not to hire. Such a database does not exist and is not likely to for some time.

Conversely, from the point of view of a job applicant, life would be good if her or she could visit a website, input in their unique "profile," and instantly find the perfect job at the right location and salary.

In such a perfect world, where there was perfect information about job opportunities and applicants, employers and employees could find each other instantly. There would be a true labor market, where market forces would operate in such a way to instantly match the right person with right job at the right time, with a minimum of delay or transaction costs. There would essentially be a "just in time" system of employment.

Part of the reason there is not such a labor market in the United States is that markets operate on information. Part of what is lacking in the U.S. is a database of extensive pre-verified applicant information.

---

[20] plusses and minuses of national databases are described in detail in Chapter 12

Of course, background screening is only one part of such a database. Additional applicant information would be needed, including data as to "job fit." Verification of credentials and information about a criminal record would certainly be a major component of any such database.

The term used to describe this type of applicant data is a Human Capital Database. There are many definitions of "human capital." One definition is—

> *The set of skills which an employee acquires on the job, through training and experience, and which increase that employee's value in the marketplace.*

Additional definitions are provided by John Sumser at www.interbiznet.com/ern/archives/040601.html.

The future of safe hiring may well involve the creation of these large human capital databases, offering the ability to use the information intelligently and fairly. However, all sorts of issues arise from building a human capital database, including how to score, model, profile and predict without discriminating. Equally important is privacy and the ability of a consumer to fairly access, control and contest what is in the database. However, for the long run the future appears to be heading towards massive databases to facilitate employment.

## Useful Human Resource Sites for Employers

There are numerous Human Resources internet sites for employees. Websites listed below are extremely useful and will link to other websites.

**HR.com**— Aims to bring together experts and resources as a one-stop site for all Human Resources needs. www.HR.com

**SHRM**— The Society for Human Resource Management's home page. www.shrm.org/hrlinks

**Workforce Online Magazine**—HR Trends and Tools for Business Results. www.workforce.com

**HR Guide**— A selection of resources, separated into categories, including an HR guide to numerous websites as well as HR software, consultants, and resources. www.hr-guide.com

**The HR Screener**— A monthly publication with both online and print versions dedicated to pre-employment screening and safe hiring for HR Professionals. www.HRScreener.com

# Chapter 21

# International Background Checks

## Introduction

Increasingly, American firms find they need to conduct background screening on individuals who have spent time in other countries. U.S. government statistics show that 11.5 percent of the population consists of immigrants.[1] In 2000, there were approximately seven million unauthorized immigrants residing in the U.S.[2] There are also large numbers of workers from other countries here on temporary work visas. In addition, many U.S. citizens have spent time studying or working abroad.

What these figures tell employers is that only performing employment screening within the U.S. is probably not enough. With the mobility of workers across international borders, many employers find they need to obtain information from outside of the United States on such matters as criminal records, past employment, and educational accomplishments. These checks are generally described as "international background checks."

A need for an international background checks occurs in these situations—

- An applicant was born abroad and is either coming directly to the U.S. from another country or has not been in the U.S. long enough to rely solely upon checking American references and records;

- The applicant spent time in another country and the employer wants to obtain data for that time period;

International screening should not be confused with "global screening." International screening occurs when a U.S. firm hires someone in the U.S. for a U.S. based position, but part of the relevant work experience was outside of the U.S. In this situation, a U. S. based screening firm is typically utilized to make international inquiries. By comparison, when a U.S. employer opens an office or facility outside of the U.S. and wants to screen employees in that foreign county, this is known as "Global Screening." The U.S. employer may contact a screening firm with expertise in that particular country.

---

[1] See *Immigrants in the United States-2002, A Snapshot of America's Foreign Born Population*, by Center for Immigration Studies www.cis.org/articles/2002/back1302.pdf. In addition, the Citizenship and Immigration Services (USCIS) within the Department of Homeland Security (DHS) publishes numerous statistics on immigration related matters every year; see http://uscis.gov/graphics/shared/aboutus/statistics/index.htm

[2] estimates of the Unauthorized Immigrant Population Residing in the United States: 1990-2000; see http://uscis.gov/graphics/shared/aboutus/statistics/Ill_Report_1211.pdf

Because of the perceived difficulties in performing international employment screening, some employers have not attempted to verify international credentials. However, the mere fact that information may be more difficult or expensive to obtain from outside of the U.S. does not relieve an employer from the due diligence obligations associated with hiring. An employer cannot simply take a position that it is harder to exercise due diligence because the research is international.

Nor can an employer simply assume that the U.S. government has performed a background check if the worker was issued a visa. After the events of 9/11, the U.S. Government has increased checks on foreign visitors and workers by checking names against government "watch lists." However, these checks are primarily aimed at keeping terrorists and international fugitives from entering the U.S. These government checks are not necessarily aimed at lesser convictions that may be relevant to job performance, or verification of past employment or education credentials.

**Here is the bottom line.** If an employer hires someone without verifying their international background and the employer is sued for negligent hiring when it turns out that a due diligence check would have uncovered important facts, what is the defense? If a victim has been hurt or injured, then the employer's testimony will sound very hollow when they did nothing, believing it was too difficult or they did not know how.

Although international searches come with their own unique challenges and obstacles, employers have a number of options when it comes to exercising due diligence.

## The Extent of the Problem—

A global screening firm who performs international background screening for U.S. employers reports some interesting statistics. When verifying past employment around the globe, major discrepancies in employment information appeared 22% of the time. The overall discrepancy rate for education was 20%, consisting of a 16% rate of candidates claiming accomplishment they did not have and another 4% claiming degrees from fake schools or diploma mills. These figures include both U.S. citizens claiming international credentials as well as individuals from abroad. In every screening, candidates knew they were subject to screening and willingly signed consent forms. These statistics underscore the fact that by just accepting international credentials without questions, employers will have a 20-22% rate of potentially fraudulent credentials.

# Why Employers Cannot Assume the Government is Screening Workers from Abroad

There are essentially two legal ways for individuals to come to the U.S. to work or live — either apply for an immigrant visa or a non–immigrant visa. An example of a non-immigrant visa is an H1-B visa. This visa is issued for an initial three-year period to applicants with specialized professional skills to obtain permission to work in the U.S. In 2004, the U.S. authorized 65,000 H1-B visas. In previous years, the number was 195,000 per year. There are also F1 student visas.

According to government statistics, legal immigration in the U.S. was over a million people in 2002.[3] This figure does not count the individuals from abroad in the U.S. working on a temporary work visa.

Here is the crux of the matter for employers— employers cannot assume the U.S. government has performed a background check that relieves employers of their due diligence obligation to conduct their own screening. Government efforts are not foolproof. After the events of 9/11/2001, the U.S. Government has certainly increased checks on foreign visitors and workers, however, these checks are primarily aimed at keeping terrorists and international fugitives from entering the U.S. or deporting those non-citizens that commit crimes in the U.S. or overstay their visas. The efforts the government makes, although vital, do not substitute for what an employer needs to do. The government efforts are not aimed at lesser convictions that may be relevant to job performance, or verifications of credentials.

Part of the difficulty is this— when a person applies for either an immigration visa or a non-immigration visa, there are potential holes in the criminal background check process.

Criminal checks are done in different ways, depending on the type of visa. For a non-citizen applying for a visa in order to immigrate to the U.S. to live and to receive a "green card," there is a "police certificate" requirement. The applicant must obtain a police certificate from his or her home country's "appropriate police authorities." The applicant must include any prison records. That sounds good on paper; however, there are two points to consider.

The first problem is the time period for issuing police certificates may allow a person with a criminal record to evade detection. Under the State Department rules, the police certificate comes from a country, area, or locality where the alien has resided for six months. However, if a person has frequently moved around inside that country, criminal records can be missed, depending to how the records are kept. Recent offenses may not be reported. If a person has lived in other countries, then the relevant time period is one year, so records can be missed if the person was in the country for a short period of time or left after committing an offense. The consular officer — a State Department officer assigned to a local U.S. Consulate — may require a police certificate from additional jurisdictions regardless of length of residence in any country, if the officer has reason to believe a criminal record exists.[4]

---

[3] *2002 Yearbook of Immigration Statistics* by the U.S, Department of Homeland Security, Office of Immigration Statistics http://uscis.gov/graphics/shared/aboutus/statistics/Yearbook2002.pdf

[4] The definition is set forth in the Code of Federal Regulations (CFR), which is a codification of the general and permanent rules published in the Federal Register by the executive departments and agencies of the Federal Government. According to: 22 CFR 42.65: (c) Definitions. (1) Police certificate means a certification by the police or other appropriate authorities reporting information entered in their records relating to the alien. In the case of the country of an alien's nationality and the country of an alien's current residence (as of the time of visa application) the term "appropriate police authorities" means those of a country, area, or locality in which the alien has resided for at least six months. In the case of all other countries, areas, or localities, the term "appropriate police authorities" means the authorities of any country, area, or locality in which the alien has resided for at least one year. A consular officer may require a police certificate regardless of length of residence in any country if the officer has reason to believe that a police record exists in the country, area, or locality concerned. (2) Prison record means an official document containing a report of the applicant's record of confinement and conduct in a penal or correctional institution.

The second issue is that police certificates differ all over the world in terms of reliability, timelines, and completeness. Police certificates are still only as good as the efforts, resources, and abilities of the local law enforcement authorities in each country, so even when a police certificate is available, the completeness of the data can still be an open question.[5] In addition, a number of countries do not even have police certificates available, or police certificates are too difficult to obtain and not available as a practical matter.

The U.S. State Department recognizes this as an important issue. The State Department maintains the *Visa Reciprocity and County Document Finder*, an international listing by country of issues involved in obtaining necessary visa documents. For more, see http://travel.state.gov/visa/reciprocity/index.htm. Visa applicants can visit the website to find out how to obtain police certificates and court records from their own country.

The State Department recognizes the need to continuously update the availability of each country's criminal records information. *The State Department Foreign Affairs Manual and Handbook* is available online. According to the State Department rules—[6]

> "Consular officers should periodically discuss with the host government the availability and quality of police clearance information, as well as the procedures to be followed for visa applicants to obtain clearances both within and outside the country. Posts should provide information concerning the degree of automation and centralization of records, as well as any purge procedures followed by the host country. Posts should also determine how criminal records are indexed in their nation. The use of a unique national identification number as opposed to nonstandard spellings of names is also significant. Posts should provide background to the Department ((abbreviations omitted)) as well as draft language for inclusion in Appendix C ((the Visa Reciprocity and County Document Finder.)) Posts should coordinate with like-minded foreign embassies as appropriate."

A second type of visa application occurs when a person applies for a non-immigration visa. In other words, he or she is not applying to live permanently in the U.S. but to stay temporarily. An example is the H1-B visa. Another potential hole is that an applicant may come to the U.S. on student VISA and then change to an H1-B. In that case, it is not clear exactly what is being check and by whom.

In the situation of a non-immigrant visa, the applicant is asked about a criminal record on the non-immigrant visa form called a DS-156. Pursuant to 22 CFR 41.105(a) (4), a consular officer may request a police certificate if they have reason to believe a criminal record exists. Therefore, the police certificate is only required by the U.S. Consulate office on a per-case review. If an applicant coming to the U.S. decides to lie, and the U.S. Consulate does not have reason to challenge the lie, then a criminal record could exist and a person with a disqualifying criminal record could obtain a visa.

In addition, for some visas such as the H1-B, an applicant's past employment and education is a critical part of the visa process. However, given the fact that the Department of Homeland Security had a high ranking employee with worthless degrees from a diploma mill (see Chapter 14), this raises the question

---

[5] Chapter 12 discusses the drawbacks and deficiencies of criminal databases in the U.S, including the FBI national criminal database called the NCIC. Other countries have the same challenges when it comes to police databases.

[6] see http://foia.state.gov/masterdocs/09FAM/0942065PN.PDF

of how effective credentials verification can be when done for large numbers of applicants from all over the world. As discussed below, international degree fraud is an ongoing issue. Employers need to take steps to confirm past education and employment.

The essential lesson from this discussion is there are statistically a significant number of potential job applicants where the relevant background information will come from outside of the U.S. An employer cannot depend upon the visa process as protection. That means U.S. employers should consider what they can and should do internationally in the area of safe hiring and employment screening.

# Types of International Checks — Screening Versus Investigation

There are two types of international services an employer may utilize. The first type is an **international employment screening**. The second type is an **international investigation**.

For most employers, an international *employment screening* involves verifications of supplied information by an applicant who has given express written consent, as opposed to an active *investigation* to locate information. In other words, in a screening an employer will have already obtained from an applicant the names, addresses, and phone numbers of previous employers or schools. Also, the employer will have obtained a rough list of locations where an applicant has lived, worked, or studied, as it is important to know where to conduct criminal searches. If more information is needed such as the applicant's school identification number or some other data, then the applicant can be asked to supply the needed data. The employer does not need to hire an international investigator to locate that information. The applicant will help the employer obtain the information since the applicant has signed a consent form and wants to be hired.

Another way of distinguishing between an international screening and an international investigation is who conducts the check and where. An international investigation typically involves a trained and experienced investigator working in the country where the investigation is being conducted. When an employer utilizes a screening firm, there is not necessarily an agent on the ground in the country where the information is being obtained. The screening may be conducted by phone or email contact with courts, employers, and schools. The person available to assist in the foreign country may be a humble court runner as opposed to an experienced investigator.

Typically, an international investigation is considerably more expensive than a screening. Since international investigations may involve qualified personnel on the ground in the foreign country — doing in-person interviews or obtaining records — the cost can be thousands of dollars. If a business is filling a highly sensitive position or is conducting a due diligence investigation of a potential business partner, then the services of a qualified investigative firm may be needed. When the stakes are high, there is no substitute for having a trained investigator who knows the country, the language, the customs, and laws.

Screening, by comparison, is considerably less expensive. A typical international screening will consist of contacting the employers and schools supplied by the applicant, and conducting a criminal check to the extent possible in that country. A screening may also include, if available, a driving record and credit report. The overall cost, although greater than a typical U.S. screening, is less than an international investigation.

# The Special Challenges When Performing International Background Screenings

When performing international checks, there are a number of special challenges—

1.  **Each and every country is unique with differences in courts and legal systems.**

    Techniques and information that are taken for granted in the United States are oftentimes not available abroad. Outside the United States, there is often limited access to public records and the types of information needed for background screening. Each country has its own laws, customs, and procedures for background screenings, *and* its own legal codes, definition of crimes and court system. Keep this in mind when doing international court searches. International criminal checking requires an understanding of each country's court system, how criminal records are created and maintained, where searches should be conducted, the type of records available, and what the records mean. There are parts of the world where such records are not available without retaining local private investigators with their own resources.

2.  **Language barriers**

    In countries where English is not the primary language, expect communication barriers. Since past employment and education verifications are often done by verbal confirmation, language will likely be an issue in communication with foreign schools and employers. There can also be language issues in reviewing court documents. If a person not fluent in the language involved is conducting an interview, then services of a translator may be necessary.

    English is the second most used native language in the world, with over 400 million native speakers. English is the world's leading "second language." English is also generally considered to be the *lingua franca* — the language used for communication between people of different languages, but even among English speakers not everyone hears, speaks, and understands the same words. Technical words or matters of local knowledge can cause confusion. At times, Britons and Americans may not understand each other. In the U.S., regional dialects and pronunciations can have a person in New Hampshire trying to decipher what a person in Texas is saying.

3.  **Name variations**

    The issue of name variations when expressing foreign names in the English Alphabet is extremely complicated for two reasons. First, many cultures have naming conventions that are entirely different than the U.S. Some cultures may start the name with the family or clan name, where other cultures may utilize the mother's name as an integral part of the naming mechanism. Many cultures do not have the concept of a middle name.

    The second difficulty has to do with expressing a foreign name in an English format. For the languages that utilize the English alphabet, the expression of names is somewhat easier, names in

Italian, German, and Spanish — keeping in mind however that Spanish names can have cultural variations.

When it comes to expressing names that utilize a different alphabet, there is room for error and confusion. There is no easy way to translate Chinese, Korean, Arabic, or Japanese names into English.

The two techniques used to render names in foreign alphabets into English are transliteration and phonetic transcription.

**Transliteration** into English is based upon using a representation of the characters in the original language with English characters so that certain characters in one language always translate into English by use of agreed upon letters. It is analogous to using a codebook. Transliteration means mapping a name from one language into another. An example is Iraq, where the Q is pronounced as English CK.

**Phonetic transcription – or "transcribing"** – is based upon taking the sounds of a foreign name, and attempting to associate the same sounds to the sounds of the English alphabet.

With either method there can be any number of variations. For example, "Osama bin Laden" can be represented as both "Laden" with an "e" or "Ladan" with an "a." First name variations can be "Usama" or "Osama."

## 4. Time differences

Communicating with researchers, past employers, or schools around the world must take into consideration time differences. The added lag time can be very inconvenient; for employers attempting to conduct international past employment verification themselves, it is often necessary to have an employee wake up in the middle of the night to complete a call.

## 5. Means and cost of communications

Each country will have different means of communication. Although email would be preferable, not all countries have reliable email delivery. Communications can also be done by fax machine. Of course, an employer wants to be careful about simply picking up the phone and dialing international numbers. Without having an international calling card or an international phone plan, the employer may suddenly receive a very high bill.

## 6. Calendar

Keep in mind each country has its own holidays.

## 7. Locating phone numbers for employment and educational checks

To conduct an international verification efficiently, it is important to have the applicant provide as much information as possible. It is not practical for an American firm to attempt to call a foreign country to locate the past employer's phone number. When a better phone number is required, an international screening agency may need permission to contact an applicant directly to ask for better information.

# Manila Information, Please

One international firm reports having been asked to verify a high school degree in Manila in The Philippines. The school had a name similar to "Immaculate Heart" in its title. The exact school phone or address was not provided so the firm dutifully researched the high school and contacted it. The school indicated the person never attended much less graduated. The applicant insisted that she absolutely had graduated and supplied contact information and a copy of the diploma. Upon further investigation, the screening firm learned that there were numerous schools throughout Manila with similar names.

The lesson— screening internationally requires very precise information.

## 8. Fraud awareness

International screening carries an inherent risk of fraud. There is no guarantee that a past employer is a legitimate firm. In addition, just as the U.S. has a significant problem involving phony degree mills and fake degrees, there can be similar issues abroad. Although some steps can be taken to mitigate the possibility of fraud, firms that rely upon screening still face a risk. Engaging an investigator who is in the foreign country is likely to provide the best information, but the price is much higher. For firms seeking to make a critical hire, the additional cost may be worthwhile.

## 9. Equivalency evaluations

Another issue is an understanding of the quality of the candidate's school and the nature of his or her degree. For example, an applicant may have graduated from a foreign university, but is the required degree equivalent to a similar degree from a U.S. school?

## 10. Costs

International screenings are expensive when compared to screening in the United States. Since an employment screening normally consists of verifying supplied information, the costs can be kept more reasonable. However, even verifying supplied information can be expensive for the reasons indicated above. In some countries, a translation fee is involved.

In many countries, criminal searches must be conducted in each relevant location where a person has lived, worked, or studied. There are very few countries that have a true "national" or "official" criminal search. Searches are usually limited to felonies or serious matters.

Although the system for international criminal checks is not perfect, making the effort allows an employer to demonstrate due diligence. Checking records also discourages applicants with something to hide since all checks are conducted pursuant to a signed release under the Fair Credit Reporting Act.

## 11. Payments

If an employer utilizes the services of an investigator abroad, in many countries payment must be made in that country's currency. Some investigators require some or all of the fee be paid in advance. Employers who do their own background verifications and contract with an international investigator may find they need to have their bank do an international money transfer by wire (perhaps taking two weeks or more) or purchase a money order in the target country.

**12. Legal implications**

See the section below on key legal considerations involved.

# Performing International Criminal Checks

The problem of how to obtain international criminal records today is similar to the situation employers and screening professionals faced in the U.S. in the 1980's. When pre-employment screening emerged as a domestic industry, screening firms and private employers attempting to obtain criminal records had an uphill battle. Courts were not accustomed to the idea of employers and screening firms checking names in courthouses. Courts in more remote areas were a particular challenge, as screening firms and record retrievers devised various ways of checking courts, such as calling up court clerks on the phone, calling up local process servers or staffing agencies to go to the courthouse, or even calling up local newspapers and asking the reporter that handled the crime beat to stop at the courthouse. Of course, that has all changed today in the United States. Well-defined researcher networks are in place all over the U.S. that can literally cover any court within 24-48 hours. Researchers with wireless devices can return criminal results from select jurisdictions within hours. With computerization, many courts now provide in-person searchers with public access terminals.

There are firms currently involved in building resources around the world to locate criminal records. One pioneering firm, Straightline International at <u>www.search4crime.com</u>, offers a worldwide information database of court clerks and court access requirements.[7]

Overall, there are a number of critical issues when obtaining and using international records. One can imagine how these issues are magnified, given the potential number of countries where a search may occur and all of the different laws, languages, cultures, and access issues, each adding to the puzzle.

There are certain areas all employers should be knowledgeable about when it comes to international criminal records—

## Critical Issues With International Sources

Outside the United States there is less access to public records and the types of information needed for background screening. Each country has its own laws, customs, and procedures for background screenings. Records may be obtained from courts, police agencies or other government agencies depending upon the location involved, and not all courts are computerized.

In some countries there is confusion about the availability of searches and the legality of obtaining records. As a rule, employers should carefully analyze *any claim* that such-and-such country does not allow criminal background checks. *Nearly every country has multiple sources of criminal records* such

---

[7] Straightline founder and president Steven Brownstein built one of the first domestic criminal record retrieval networks in the U.S. and he is now doing the same on the international scale

as police authorities, government agencies, prosecution offices, and courts. There may be different levels of police akin to or different from the U.S. where local law, state, and federal enforcement officials abound. Some countries consider it illegal for the police to provide the criminal record information to a private firm, while the same documents may be available from the courts. Police records are typically broader and may include arrests for which there is no conviction; when the police are prohibited from providing such records, the courts are the next alternative.

Employers should distinguish when a complete prohibition on obtaining criminal records exists versus a lack of availability versus limitations in the manner and means of obtaining and utilizing criminal records. For example, read about EU Privacy Laws and the FCRA later in this chapter for the data privacy rules in effect for European Union members.

# The State Department List of Countries

As mentioned previously, a useful tool to determine what is legal and available in a country is the State Department website list called "Visa Reciprocity and County Document Finder."[8] The site advises immigrants and visitors coming to the U.S. on the availability of required visa documents. Although the information on the website is aimed at assisting individual visa applicants, it is useful for employers and screening firms to determine what information is available from what source. If an individual can obtain his or her own records, then presumably an employer or screening firm can use the same methods to obtain records from abroad, with consent. For each country listed, the website describes the availability of police certificates and court records.

## Scope of International Searches and Fees

Typically, searches for criminal records quote **per court** in a country and not for the entire country. Unless specifically noted, foreign searches are conducted in **each court** located where an applicant lived or worked. Very few countries have "national" criminal searches available to private employers. A criminal check may require multiple searches, for example, if an applicant merely indicated "London, England" a background firm may search the main criminal court in London. However, the main court covers very little of the actual jurisdiction of the London area and records can be missed.

Before ordering an international criminal record, an employer should carefully specify how many courts to search since the average price of an international criminal search will exceed $100 per court.

## Foreign Identifiers

In order to identify the person, an employer will need to supply the proper type of identification needed for each country. Identifiers can include—

---

[8] Visa Reciprocity and County Document Finder, see http://travel.state.gov/visa/reciprocity/index.htm

- Full name and date of birth

- A national ID number, if a country provides one

- Mother's maiden name

- Applicant's name in the primary language of that country. For example, use Chinese characters if doing a search in China

- Each state or city where a person has lived. Some countries only maintain criminal records by a single jurisdiction.

# American Rules May Apply Abroad

Employers obtaining criminal records from foreign countries need to be careful how it is done. The one thing that no American firm wants to do is pay money to a foreign official to obtain criminal records where the rules of the country do not permit such records to be released. Such actions could conceivably be prosecuted in the United States under the federal Foreign Corrupt Practices Act of 1977 (FCPA), 15 U.S.C. §§ 78dd-1, et seq.[9]

## Turnaround Time

The response time for a report can vary greatly depending upon the country. Responses can take, on the average, 48-98 hours. Courts in certain countries may take longer for the same reasons as in the U.S. — the court is located in a remote or less-populated region, usually.

## Translation of Court Documents

If there is a "hit," then the foreign criminal record must be translated into English. Remember, too, that British, Australian, and other nations with English as the primary language use different law terms that must be matched to the equivalent here to allow understanding of the facts of an offense.

## Level of Offenses

For most counties, the search is for felonies or major offenses. However, some courts do allow researchers to obtain records for misdemeanors or lesser offenses.

## Audit Trail and No Record Found

In the U.S., when court records are searched and there is no record found, there is typically no document provided by the court clerk. Court clerks do not normally confirm a lack of a finding. A "no record" is normally reported by the researcher, indicating they made the appropriate effort and there

---

[9] more information on Foreign Corrupt Practices Acts is available at www.usdoj.gov/criminal/fraud/fcpa/dojdocb.htm

were no results found. The same is true in doing court searches throughout most of the world. If the criminal record search is at a court and no record is found, there is not likely going to be a document or paper trail that says "No Record." To have a confirmation that there is, in fact, no record, an employer may need to have the applicant obtain a police certificate. That process can be subject to long delays.

# Countries Where Information Providers Indicate Criminal Records Are Available

Below is a list of countries where information providers indicate they can access criminal records.[10] Access to criminal records can range from having an agent in the country who works with the appropriate authorities, to remote contact through phone, fax, or mail. Keep in mind, because a firm is able to contact courts in a major city does not mean the entire country is readily available. Rural areas may not be.

Note: this list is subject to all of the inherent limitations on obtaining international criminal records. An employer should not assume that complete criminal records are available from all countries below merely because some data is available.

| | | | |
|---|---|---|---|
| Albania | Egypt | Liechtenstein | Sierra Leone |
| American Samoa | El Salvador | Lithuania | Singapore |
| Anguilla | England | Luxembourg | Slovakia |
| Antigua | Eritrea | Macedonia | Slovenia |
| Argentina | Estonia | Madagascar | Solomon Islands |
| Armenia | Ethiopia | Malawi | Somalia |
| Aruba | Fiji | Malaysia | South Africa |
| Australia | Finland | Maldives | Spain |
| Austria | France | Mariana Islands | Sri Lanka |
| Azerbaijan | French Guiana | Marshall Islands | St. Kitts & Nevis |
| Bahamas | French Polynesia | Martinique | St. Vincent & Grenadines |
| Bahrain | Gabon | Mauritania | Sudan |
| Bangladesh | Gambia | Mauritius | Swaziland |
| Barbados | Georgia | Mexico | Sweden |
| Barbuda | Germany | Micronesia | Switzerland |
| Belarus | Ghana | Moldova | Tajikistan |
| Belgium | Great Britain | Monaco | Taiwan |
| Belize | Greece | Mongolia | Tanzania |

---

[10] this county list is generated from lists found on screening firms advertisements

Benin
Bermuda
Bhutan
Bolivia
Botswana
Brazil
British Virgin Islands
Bulgaria
Burkina Faso
Burundi
Cambodia
Cameroon
Canada
Cayman Islands
Central African Republic
Chad
Chile
China; Shanghai & Beijing
Colombia
Cook Islands
Costa Rica
Croatia
Curacao
Cyprus
Czechoslovakia
Denmark
Djibouti
Dominica
Dominican Republic
East Timor
Ecuador

Greenland
Grenada
Guadaloupe
Guam
Guatemala
Guinea
Guinea Bissau
Guyana
Haiti
Honduras
Hong Kong
Hungary
Iceland
India
Indonesia
Ireland
Israel
Italy
Ivory Coast
Jamaica
Japan
Kazakhstan
Kenya
Korea
Kuwait
Kyrgyz Republic
Laos
Latvia
Lebanon
Lesotho
Liberia

Montserrat
Morocco
Mozambique
Myanmar
Namibia
Nepal
Netherlands
Netherlands Antilles
New Zealand
Nicaragua
Niger
Nigeria
Norway
Pakistan
Panama
Papua New Guinea
Paraguay
Peru
Philippines
Poland
Portugal
Puerto Rico
Qatar
Romania
Russia
Rwanda
Saint Lucia
Saudi Arabia
Scotland
Senegal
Seychelles

Thailand
Trinidad/Tobago
Tunisia
Turkey
Turkmenistan
Turks and Caicos Islands
Tuvalu
Uganda
Ukraine
United Arab Emirates
United Kingdom
Uruguay
Uzbekistan
Vanuatu
Venezuela
Vietnam
Virgin Islands
Yemen
Yugoslavia
Zaire
Zambia
Zimbabwe

# Verification of International Schools and Non-U.S. Employment

## Foreign Education Verifications

Verification of degree from abroad is an important, necessary tool for employers. The verification process has three parts—

1. Determine if applicant in fact attended the school claimed and received the degree claimed;
2. Determine if the school is accredited and authentic;
3. Determine the equivalency of a foreign degree in terms U.S. employers can understand.

### 1. Determine if the applicant in fact attended the school claimed and received the degree claimed

Did the applicant actually attend the listed school and receive the degree claimed? Verification can be done by an employer or by a screening firm. Internet resources offering lists of schools around the world are available. If the applicant presents a diploma or some other document, it should be sent to the issuing school for verification. (See www.ESRcheck.com/safehiringupdates.php for examples of fake international degrees.) Typically, schools can be contacted by phone or by email. Of course, challenges to overcome are language and time differences. Despite these handicaps, there is no question that the verification can certainly occur.

Before performing the verification it is helpful to obtain as much information as possible from an applicant. An employer needs to obtain the applicant's full name used while attending school, the exact spelling in the language utilized by the school, the dates the person attended the school, and any student ID number that was used. A copy of the degree or other documentation may be needed. It is helpful to obtain as much information as possible, such as school website and email.

### 2. Determine if the school is accredited and authentic

Is the school real? In other words, is the school an established and accredited institution? There is a significant problem with fake schools abroad. Employers in the United States have a difficult time detecting fraudulent degrees in America, let alone on an international scale. To resolve the authenticity issue, use the guidelines presented in Chapter 14.

There are numerous resources that can assist an employer. For example, the United States Network for Education Information is an interagency and public/private partnership, with a mission to provide official information assistance for anyone seeking information about U.S. education and for U.S. citizens seeking authoritative information about education in other countries. The network's website contains information on organizations worldwide who accredit schools; see www.ed.gov/about/offices/list/ous/international/usnei/edlite-index.html.

Another resource is the World Higher Education Database at www.unesco.org/iau/wadcd.html. This website is sponsored by the International Association of Universities, which is affiliated with the United Nations Educational, Scientific and Cultural Organization (UNESCO).[11] UNESCO has

---

[11] for more information about UNESCO, see www.unesco.org/iau/index.html

a database of schools but no contact information or details; see www.unesco.org/iau/world-universities/index.html.

# Fake Degrees and Credentials Flood the Market

An online story in the *Khaleej Times* in India on May 13, 2004, proclaimed "Fake India Degrees Flood Middle East Market."

> "India churns out brilliant graduates by the thousands every year. Unfortunately, it also churns out fake degrees by the thousands. Manufacturing fake certificates is a money-minting industry that has never stopped churning business for the people involved in it. The effect of such fakes is being felt globally."

Many agents also say it is quite difficult to spot a fake degree nowadays as it resembles an original one in every way — from the texture of the paper to the university stamp.

The story noted that not only are people claiming degrees they did not earn, but job applicants are also making up fake schools. As a result the process of obtaining actual verifications from schools can be time consuming and can cause harm to a real graduate who must take extra steps to prove his or her education credentials are genuine.

**3. Determine the equivalency of a foreign degree in terms U.S. employers can understand**

Understanding the equivalency of a foreign degree in terms U.S. employer can understand is not an easy task. However, there are several agencies offering services that provide an equivalency analysis. For example, for information about degrees issued by foreign medical schools, there is a well-established mechanism to make that determination — the **National Committee on Foreign Medical Education and Accreditation (NCFMEA)** was established under the Higher Education Amendments of 1992.[12]

## Tips on International Employment Verification

As outlined above, the challenges involved in international employment verification are similar to the challenges faced by employers in the United States, augmented by all the problems associated with working internationally. To obtain information, employers may need to schedule calls for the middle of the night, locate foreign phone numbers, and overcome language barriers.

There are two essential keys to successful international employment verifications—

1. **Obtain as much information as possible from the applicant.** Since locating past employers in a foreign county is difficult, the applicant must be asked to provide as much information as

---

[12] NCFMEA was established under the Higher Education Amendments of 1992 (Public Law 102-325). See www.ed.gov/admins/finaid/accred/ac creditation_pg21.html#NCFMEA

possible. Of course, there is always the possibility of a "set-up" or fake reference. Whenever possible, effort should be made to independently verify the existence and authenticity of past employers.

2. In order to obtain the best results, employment and **educational verifications should be conducted in the primary language of that country.** Even though there are international translation services, communicating with employers and schools in their native language improves the chances of completing a verification task.

3. If utilizing researchers or firms outside of the U.S. to obtain employment (or even education verification), be very careful about providing any personal and identifiable information (PII), such as date of birth, passport number or similar information. The best practice is to the extent possible to only utilize researchers outside of the U.S. to obtain contact information, but only provide PII directly to the employer or school.

There are other sources of international screening available to employers for applicants that have lived, worked, or studied abroad.

- International Wants and Warrants, and terrorist databases— See Chapter 22.
- Credit reports— Individual credit reports and bankruptcy reports available in some countries.
- Driving records— In some countries, an employer can obtain an applicant's driving record.
- Press search— A search of media and newspapers is available in some countries.

Another helpful resource is the book *Find It Online.*[13] Written by investigative reporter Alan Schlein, this excellent book profiles many useful international online resources.

# Additional International Due Diligence Steps

Other steps an employer can do when hiring a person who has spent time abroad—

1. Even though the person's time in the U.S. could be limited, do whatever background checking is possible based upon their time in the U.S. This effort demonstrates due diligence by documenting the fact an employer did what they *could do*.

2. Even if a person is relatively new to this country, ask for the names of personal references in the U.S. Be sure to document the relationship between the reference and the applicant. Although this is not a perfect solution, as in #1 above, an employer demonstrates due diligence by making and documenting an attempt to do a screening.

3. If hiring a number of applicants from abroad, then state in the release forms that you will also conduct background investigations in any countries where an applicant has lived in the past seven to ten years. This can at least have the effect of discouraging an applicant with something to hide. However, this should be worded carefully so that an employer does not imply that any hiring decisions are being made based upon country of origin or ethnicity.

---

[13] *Find It Online*, ©2004 Facts on Demand Press, BRB Publications, Tempe, AZ  www.brbpub.com

> **Author Tip** ➡ In order not to run afoul of EEOC rules, never refer to a screening in a foreign country as a search of "country of origin" or any other reference that implies that nationality or ethnicity is a consideration. "A search abroad" is simply a search in other countries where an applicant has live or worked.

# Legal Implications for Employers Doing International Background Checks

The legal implications of international background screening can be very complex and involve the intersection of U.S. domestic law and the operation of foreign law. Furthermore, international screening and the flow of information across borders is a relativity new and developing area of law. A discussion of some of the more significant considerations involved is in order.

There are three essential considerations. Employers must be aware of how the data is obtained, transmitted, and utilized.

## Obtaining Foreign Data

The essential rule for any employer in the U.S. is that information should be obtained in a manner consistent with the laws of the country where the data originated. If it is not legal in a particular country to obtain a criminal record from the police, then a U.S. employer should not do so either. A U.S. firm could be exposed to liability for obtaining foreign records that would be prohibited in the foreign country if the employer somehow obtained the records by illegal means in the applicant's home country. If a lawsuit arises, an applicant can claim an invasion of privacy or other violation of rights based upon the illegally obtained records. A complaint could be filed in the foreign country and the U.S. employer could face a lawsuit in the U.S. or the foreign country.

A key element in legally obtaining data is, of course, the applicant's written consent. In the context of pre-employment screening, the assumption is made that the applicant has not only consented, but wants to assist the employer in obtaining records in order to facilitate the employment decision.

## Transmitting Foreign Records

The concept of data transmittal has to do with data privacy protection rules in effect for many countries. That is discussed in more detail on the following pages. Data that may be obtained legally from a source may become improper to use if privacy rules are not followed.

## Utilization of Foreign Records

Utilization refers to rules that determine if and how a criminal record can be used in an employment decision. The first issue is whether the record was obtained legally. The next issue is whether an U.S. employer may legally consider information obtained from a foreign country for employment, especially in the context of criminal records.

**If the job and the applicant are both in a foreign country**, then it is likely the rule of the foreign country applies. As the old saying goes, "When in Rome, do as the Romans." In this situation the employer is best advised to consult legal counsel in the host country and follow the rules used in that country for any type of pre-employment screening.

**If the job and the applicant are in the U.S.,** then the best practice for the U.S. employer is to apply at the minimum the same rules they would to information obtained in the U.S. This means to follow the EEOC rules concerning the use of criminal data as outlined in Chapter 5. This also means a screening firm has the same obligations for accuracy and re-verification when it locates a criminal record in the U.S. For example, under FCRA section 607(b), there is an obligation to utilize reasonable procedures to assure maximum possible accuracy. If a record is found, then there is an obligation under FCRA section 613 to either utilize strict procedures to ensure the record is up-to-date or to give the applicant notice. Other specific adverse action notice procedures also apply.[14] However, when it comes to obtaining the data, employers should also take into account any privacy and data protection laws that exist in the country where the information is located, as discussed below.

**If the job is in the U.S. but the applicant is living abroad.** If there is a law in the foreign country that prohibits the use of criminal records in that country, but the job is to be performed in the U.S., then the employer needs to make a risk-management decision. The U.S. employer needs to exercise due diligence before bringing the worker to the U.S. Failure to exercise due diligence would leave the employer vulnerable in case the applicant committed some sort of harm, or if the employer had to defend their hiring practices in court. On the other hand, an employer does not want to be in the position of violating a foreign law. An employer may take the position that the use of the criminal record is regulated under U.S. law, since the employment is to be performed in the U.S. and that is where the employer stands the greatest chance of being sued. In addition, any criminal record obtained abroad is done so with express authorization of the applicant under the FCRA. Under general privacy principals, a valid consent goes a long way to protect an employer from a complaint that they violated an applicant's rights. In the interest of enforcing a consistent policy worldwide, an employer may also decide to operate under U.S. rules when considering how to utilize foreign criminal records on applicants who will be working in the U.S. However, this is still an emerging area of law.

# Privacy and Data Protection

Another consideration is the application of foreign privacy laws regarding the manner in which information is obtained, transmitted, and utilized. The central issues are data privacy and protection. A U.S. employer may legally obtain information from a foreign country and use the record in a legal manner, but still run afoul of privacy laws. Important privacy laws that concern U.S. employers are laws dealing with the European Union (EU). These rules went into effect in 1998. The European privacy rules impact the transmissions of "personally identifiable data" from offices in EU countries to businesses in the U.S. The European Commission maintains a website that lists all current members of the European Union, see http://europa.eu.int/abc/governments/index_en.htm.

---

[14] see Chapter 6 on the FCRA

Firms that acquire data on individuals from EU member countries without compliance with the EU rules can be in violation of EU law. This can have a serious impact on international firms or firms that do business in an EU country.

However, American firms that develop a privacy policy may enter what is called the "Safe Harbor" by certifying a privacy policy that includes adequate mechanisms to protect confidential personal data. The program is administered by the U.S. Department of Commerce.

In addition to the EU Privacy rules, other countries are in various stages of dealing with similar issues concerning personal and identifiable consumer information. Canada has privacy rules in effect, see below. A website called Privacy International outlines privacy rights and current status in countries around the world, see www.privacyinternational.org/index.shtml.

Countries that currently have either data privacy rules or are considering such rules include Argentina, Australia, Brazil, Bulgaria, Chile, Columbia, Finland, Iceland, Israel, Japan, Malaysia, Mexico, New Zealand, Paraguay, Russian Federation, Singapore, South Africa, South Korea, Taiwan, and Thailand.

# Introduction to The Safe Harbor[15]

According to the U.S. Department of Commerce— "The European Commission's Directive on Data Protection went into effect in October, 1998, and prohibits the transfer of personal data to non-European Union nations that do not meet the European 'adequacy standard' for privacy protection." While the United States and the European Union share the goal of enhancing privacy protection for their citizens, the United States takes a different approach to privacy from the approach of the European Union. The United States uses a sectoral approach that relies on a mix of legislation, regulation, and self-regulation. The European Union, however, relies on comprehensive legislation that requires creation of government data protection agencies, registration of databases with those agencies and, in some instances, prior approval before personal data processing may begin. Generally, the EU considers the U.S. as not having adequate privacy protections. As a result of these different privacy approaches, the Directive could have significantly hampered the ability of U.S. companies to engage in many trans-Atlantic transactions.

"In order to bridge these different privacy approaches and provide a streamlined means for U.S. organizations to comply with the Directive, the U.S. Department of Commerce, in consultation with the European Commission, developed a 'safe harbor' framework. The safe harbor — approved by the EU in July of 2000 — is an important way for U.S. companies to avoid experiencing interruptions in their business dealings with the EU or facing prosecution by European authorities under European privacy laws. Certifying to the safe harbor will assure that EU organizations know that your company provides 'adequate privacy protection,' as defined by the Directive."

---

[15] find the Department of Commerce Safe Harbor information online at www.export.gov/safeharbor/

A firm can become Safe Harbor certified by following the guidelines listed at the Department of Commerce website at www.export.gov/safeharbor/index.html. For compliance purposes, a background firm that obtains data from an EU country should be Safe Harbor certified. A listing of firms on the Safe Harbor list appears at http//web.ita.doc.gov/safeharbor/shlist.nsf/webPages/safe+harbor+list.

Under the category "Employment Services" three firms are listed that are primarily background screening firms at the time of the first printing of this book. They are—

1. Kroll Background America, Inc.  www.baionline.net

2. Verifications, Inc.  www.verificatinsinc.com

3. Employment Screening Resources  www.ESRcheck.com [16]

# European Union Privacy Laws and the FCRA

The text below shows how some of the main issues regarding the EU privacy laws compare to similar U.S. FCRA regulations.[17]

**Notice**— Individuals must have clear notice that personally identifiable information is being collected. This is not an issue for employment screening since the Fair Credit Reporting Act (FCRA) requires various notices and disclosures.

**Choice**— Individuals need the opportunity to exercise choice and to opt-out. Again, this is not an issue with employment screening per the FCRA since all screening is done with consent.

**Onward Transfer**— The EU laws deal with issues of how the data is protected when it is forwarded to other parties. In screening, the FCRA requires that an employer sign a certification concerning FCRA compliance. In addition, the individual's right to notice and choice are protected since the applicant is informed of the name of the employer seeking a consumer report and has the choice of signing or not signing consent.

**Access**— The EU privacy rules are concerned with an individual's ability to access his or her data. Under the FCRA, individuals have an extensive right to know what is being said about them, and to contest the contents of consumer reports.

**Security**— The EU rules also addresses the issue of security. Under the FCRA, there is an obligation to utilize data only for permissible purposes which means only those with a need to know may view and use data. U.S. screening firms are very pro-active in providing state-of-the-art security for employment screening data.

**Data Integrity**— The EU rules are concerned with the use of the data for the intended purpose. Under the FCRA, employment data can only be used for the permissible FCRA purpose it was collected.

---

[16] by way of disclosure, the author is the President of Employment Screening Resources
[17] see Chapter 6 for information regarding the FCRA

**Enforcement**— The EU rules address enforcement of privacy rules and individual recourse. In the U.S., employment screening under the FCRA is regulated by the Federal Trade Commission. In order to become safe harbor certified, a screening firm must also agree to an independent recourse mechanism. As example of such a mechanism is the service offered by the Council of Better Business Bureau's *BBB OnLine®* Privacy Program.[18]

These principles are outlined in more detail at www.export.gov/safeharbor/sh_workbook.html. For more information about international privacy, and best practice to protect confidential information, see www.ercheck.com/safehiringupdates.php.

# Canada's Strict Privacy Laws— PIPEDA

Effective January 1, 2004, a privacy law went into effect in Canada that has an impact on employment screening. The law is called the **Personal Information Protection and Electronics Document Act** or **PIPEDA.** PIPEDA privacy rules have a much broader application than just employment screening. For employment purposes, the law broadly applies to not only firms involved in a federal undertaking (such as governmental corporations or private firms involved in fields such as telecommunications, aeronautics, banks, communications, or transportation) but has been extended to nearly all employers unless their province already has such protections in place. Currently, British Colombia, Alberta and Quebec have laws substantially similar to the federal Canadian law.

Under PIPEDA, employers can still conduct pre-employment background screening, but only with some stringent privacy controls. PIPEDA identifies ten principals for privacy, which employers need to respect, including any modifications or clarifications of the Act itself.[19]

1. **Accountability**– employers are responsible for the personal information under their control, and must designate someone who is accountable for compliance with the Act.

2. **Identifying purposes**– employers must specify why they are collecting personal information from employees at or before the time it does so.

3. **Consent**– the employee's knowledge and consent is required for the collection, use, or disclosure of personal information.

4. **Limiting collection**– employers may only collect the personal information necessary for the purpose they have identified, and must collect it by fair and lawful means.

5. **Limiting use, disclosure, and retention**– unless they have the consent of the employee, or are legally required to do otherwise, employers may use or disclose personal information only for the purposes for which they collected it, and they may retain it only as long as necessary for those purposes.

6. **Accuracy**– the employees' personal information must be accurate, complete, and up-to-date.

7. **Safeguards**– all personal information must be protected by appropriate security safeguards.

---

[18] Council of Better Business Bureau's *BBB OnLine®* Privacy Program, see www.bbbonline.com

[19] these ten principles are set out in Schedule 1 of the Act

8. **Openness**– employers must make their personal information policies and practices known to their employees.

9. **Individual access**– employees must be able to access personal information about themselves, and be able to challenge the accuracy and completeness of it.[20]

10. **Challenging compliance**– employees must be able to present a challenge about the employer's compliance with the *Act* to the person that the employer has designated as accountable.

More information about the Privacy laws can be found at www.privcom.gc.ca/fs-fi/02_05_d_18_e.asp.

In many ways, the Canadian rules are similar to the FCRA. Both rules require notice, applicant consent, accuracy requirements, limitations on use of data, and the ability of consumers to know what is said about them and to contest it.

However, there are some important differences. First, under the Canadian rules, the obligation to utilize appropriate security safeguards is part of the law. In the U.S., electronic safeguards are critical but not necessarily mandated by statute. Under the Canadian law, a consumer has the right to request that data not be retained when no longer needed. Under the FCRA, the U.S. data is retained for six years. The Canadian rules require a posted privacy policy and the designation of an individual to be in charge of privacy matters. In the U.S. these are best practices but not mandates.

U.S. employers with offices or facilities in Canada need to review their compliance with the PIPEDA ACT for not only for employment screening purposes, but also for numerous other aspects of their businesses.

# Conclusion— International Background Checks

Although international screening can be challenging, it is not impossible. Given the statistics suggesting that 20-22% of applicants have substantial discrepancies in their education and employment credentials, employers can find themselves in hot water if they assume that international screening is too difficult or expensive and simply bypass the process.

Under the FCRA, both employers and screening firms still have certain obligations regarding international screening. If the task of international screening is outsourced to a screening firm, that firm has an FCRA obligation to take reasonable procedures to insure accuracy. If there is a negative public record, such as a criminal record "hit," then the firm must make certain the information is correct and up-to-date, and supplied in a way that does not violate any data or privacy protection rules.

---

[20] the *PIPEDA Act* permits some exceptions for individual access

# Chapter 22

# Terrorist Searches, Terrorist Databases, and The Patriot Act

## The Post 9/11 World and Terrorist Search Procedures for Employers

Prior to the events of September 11, 2001, the topic of how not to hire terrorists was not on the radar screen of most employers. Although most Americans would have acknowledged — if asked before 9/11 — that we live in a dangerous world, the danger had not significantly impacted American life to the extent it has after the attack on the United States.

Certainly employers with defense and other sensitive government contracts have long been involved in dealing with security clearance.[1] However, outside of security clearances, most employers were not focused on safe hiring from the point of view of keeping the U.S. safe from terrorists' harm. Employers in sensitive industries or sectors involved with the country's basic infrastructure have become concerned, post-9/11, with the potential risk that just one terrorist can have in their workplace. For example, a terrorist act could be aimed not only at airlines, but food and water supplies, transportation of hazardous materials, nuclear and other energy facilities, transportation, and a host of other vital industries.

As demonstrated by the events after 9/11, even small and medium employers that do not consider themselves involved in vulnerable sectors may need to be more alert in the future.

According to this 12/10/2003 article in the *Washington Times*—

> "U.S. authorities said sleeper cells also operate in at least 40 states from Florida and New York to California and Washington state – living low-profile lives, often in ethnic communities. The September, 2002 arrest of seven members of a terrorist cell in Lackawanna, N.Y., just south of Buffalo, was a first major clue to their existence.
>
> Between 2,000 and 5,000 terrorist operatives are said to be in the United States, many of whom are hiding in ethnic communities throughout the country, populated by millions of foreign immigrants, including illegal aliens for which the U.S. government cannot account."

---

[1] see Chapter 15 section on Security Clearances

It is difficult to verify these types of estimates. Even if the number was much smaller, it could still mean there is a high probability a terrorist with malicious designs toward the American way of life may well be applying to work at firms in the United States. A terrorist may apply for employment either with intent to do that firm harm in the future or to earn a livelihood while awaiting the orders to take some action against the U.S.

Part of the problem is identifying *who* is a terrorist. Terrorists applying for jobs with U.S. employers are going to take measures to hide their true intentions and possibly their true identity. There is not a single accepted definition of the term *"terrorist."* For purposes of American employers, the following definition from the Code of Federal Regulations is helpful. Terrorism is defined as—

> "...the unlawful use of force and violence against persons or property to intimidate or coerce a government, the civilian population, or any segment thereof, in furtherance of political or social objectives."[2]

The FBI further describes terrorism as either domestic or international, depending on the origin, base, and objectives of the terrorists. For example—

- Domestic terrorism is the unlawful use, or threatened use, of force or violence by a group or individual based and operating entirely within the United States or its territories without foreign direction committed against persons or property to intimidate or coerce a government, the civilian population, or any segment thereof, in furtherance of political or social objectives.

- International terrorism involves violent acts dangerous to human life that are a violation of the criminal laws of the United States or any state, or that would be a criminal violation if committed within the jurisdiction of the United States or any state. These acts appear to be intended to intimidate or coerce a civilian population, influence the policy of a government by intimidation or coercion, or affect the conduct of a government by assassination or kidnapping. International terrorist acts occur outside the United States or transcend national boundaries in terms of the means by which they are accomplished, the persons they appear intended to coerce or intimidate, or the locale in which the perpetrations operate or seek asylum.

Although employers currently tend to think of terrorists as being connected to events in the Middle East, the definition can be much broader. Another definition of terrorism from an online dictionary states—

> "...the systematic use of terror or unpredictable violence against governments, publics, or individuals to attain a political objective. Terrorism has been used by political organizations with both rightist and leftist objectives, by nationalistic and ethnic groups, by revolutionaries, and by the armies and secret police of governments themselves."

Identifying terrorists and keeping them out of the workspace is a significant task for employers. It would be made easier of course if employers could assume the efforts by the federal government to keep terrorists out of the U.S. in the first place were 100% effective. The U.S. government is taking a

---

[2] see 28 C.F.R. Section 0.85 which describes one of the functions of the FBI within the Department of Justice

number of measures to track terrorists in the U.S. and to prevent their entry in the first place. However, given the enormous numbers of people who are in the U.S. illegally, as well as the fact the U.S. has two very long borders — 4,121 miles with Canada and 1,940 miles with Mexico — employers cannot simply assume terrorists will not be in the U.S. applying for jobs. Even the new biometric databases being deployed at airports and seaports for foreign visitors, the US-VISIT program, and the planned database at airports called CAPPS 2 will likely have a margin of error due to the unruly nature of larger scale databases. See "The Bad News" section later in this chapter.

Employers, especially those in vulnerable and critical industries, have no real choice but to consider the importance of terrorism in their hiring program.

# The Patriot Act and Financial Institutions

In the aftermath of the events of 9/11, Congress passed the U.S. Patriot Act. Its official title is "Uniting and Strengthening America by Providing Appropriate Tools Required to Intercept and Obstruct Terrorism (USA PATRIOT ACT) Act of 2001."[3]

President George W. Bush signed the bill into law on October 26, 2001. The law gives sweeping new powers to both domestic law enforcement and international intelligence agencies. The complicated law is 342 pages long. For employers, it creates the need to deal with a wide range of issues such as access to business records by governmental agencies who have the power to request a judicial order to review records. The Act also provides procedures for the federal government to tap phones and internet use, and seize voicemail or emails, which raises additional workplace issues.

There are legal challenges to some aspects of the law. Although these laws are still subject to much debate over their effectiveness and their impact on civil liberties, there are valuable lessons for employers to be learned when it comes to hiring.

The Patriot Act also addresses the ease with which the September 11 terrorists were able to utilize holes in U.S. financial regulations to bring large sums of money into the U.S. to finance terrorists operations. According to reports following September 11, terrorists were able to transfer large sums to the U.S., including opening an account with a bank in Florida using false Social Security Numbers.

The use of documents such as foreign passports, visas, along with numerous variations of the spelling of last names can help terrorists slip through the cracks. Given the size and volume of financial transactions and records in the U.S., searching for suspicious transactions and looking for links and patterns is like looking for the proverbial needle in the haystack. The U.S. Internal Revenue Service (IRS) tracks suspicious transactions through forms that certain financial institutions must file, as well as cash transactions over $10,000, but the data must still be analyzed.[4] To help combat these problems, The Patriot Act in part creates a system whereby banks and financial institutions must now take much greater care *to know* their customers, and to report information to a central source.

Financial institutions are especially regulated under the Patriot Act with respect to controlling money laundering. The Act is aimed at controlling money that is used to finance terrorists' activities. Many

---

[3] see full text at www.epic.org/privacy/terrorism/hr3162.pdf

[4] of course, foreign terrorists are probably aware of this $10K ceiling

financial institutions have already been the subject of regulation when it comes to financial crimes. The Act increases these obligations. The Act also creates an obligation to report suspicious activities with the Federal Financial Crimes Enforcement Network (FinCEN).[5] The goal is to create a large database of information shared between the financial industry and law enforcement to help combat money laundering.

One of the most critical aspects of the Patriot Act is the definition of a financial institution, which has been considerably enlarged. The definition had included traditional institutions such as banks, mutual funds, credit card systems and SEC registered securities brokers. The Act also defines other institutions as *financial*, such as travel agencies, sellers of boats, planes, cars, precious metals, and even casinos.[6]

A key requirement of the Act dealing with fighting suspicious activity and money laundering is Section 326. This section centers on identifying customers and putting the obligation on financial institutions to match customer names against published lists of terrorists and terrorist organizations.[7] The Act essentially creates a form of "Know Your Client" obligations – or KYC obligations.

As broadly defined by the Patriot Act, when identifying clients, financial institutions must have the following—

- A program to verify the identity of customers.

- All new accounts need to be screened against a list maintained by the U.S. Treasury Office of Foreign Assets Control, commonly known as the **OFAC** list. Maintained by the U.S. Government, the OFAC is the primary list of known terrorists as well as others who engage in criminal activity such as drug trafficking or money laundering. OFAC is discussed throughout this chapter.

---

[5] see www.fincen.gov

[6] According to the Act, financial institutions include an insured bank; a commercial bank or a trust company; private bankers; an agency or branch of a foreign bank in the United States; any credit union; a thrift institution; a broker or dealer registered with the SEC under the Securities Exchange Act of 1934; a broker or dealer in securities or commodities (whether registered with the SEC or not); an investment banker or investment company; a currency exchange; an issuer, redeemer, or cashier of traveler's checks, checks, money orders, or similar instruments; an operator of a credit card system; an insurance company; a dealer in precious metals, stones, or jewels; a pawnbroker; a loan or finance company; a travel agency; a licensed sender of money or any other person who engages as a business in the transmission of funds, formally or informally; a telegraph company; a business engaged in vehicle sales, including automobile, airplane and boat sales; persons involved in real state closings and settlements; the United States Postal Service; an agency of the federal or any state or local government carrying out a duty or power of a business described in the definition of a "financial institution"; a state-licensed or Indian casino with annual gaming revenue of more than $1,000,000; and certain other businesses designated by Treasury (collectively "Financial Institutions"). See 31 USC 5312(a)(2)

[7] 7 Section 326 of the Act requires that: (l) IDENTIFICATION AND VERIFICATION OF ACCOUNTHOLDERS- (1) IN GENERAL- Subject to the requirements of this subsection, the Secretary of the Treasury shall prescribe regulations setting forth the minimum standards for financial institutions and their customers regarding the identity of the customer that shall apply in connection with the opening of an account at a financial institution. (2) MINIMUM REQUIREMENTS- The regulations shall, at a minimum, require financial institutions to implement, and customers (after being given adequate notice) to comply with, reasonable procedures for-- `(A) verifying the identity of any person seeking to open an account to the extent reasonable and practicable; `(B) maintaining records of the information used to verify a person's identity, including name, address, and other identifying information; and `(C) consulting lists of known or suspected terrorists or terrorist organizations provided to the financial institution by any government agency to determine whether a person seeking to open an account appears on any such list. Section(C) has been interpreted to refer to the list maintained by the U.S. Treasury Office of Foreign Assets Control (OFAC).

- Any document used to identify new accounts needs to be verified against a third party database, i.e. drivers license, Social Security card, etc.

The U.S. Treasury Department is in the process of issuing regulations for Sec. 326 compliance, and each industry needs to keep abreast of developments that affect them. Regardless of the specific rules for implementing section 326 for any industry, compliance will include an OFAC search.

Although the law does not mandate specific pre-employment screening or background checks for American workers, with the exceptions of those involved in transporting hazardous materials, the new law may well have a bearing upon employment practices, especially for those employers involved in the financial industry.

Prudent risk management would suggest that any firm the Patriot Act requires to exercise due diligence in identifying customers would also fall below a standard of care if they did not take the same precautions with their own employees. For example, financial institutions must perform due diligence on customers because of the harm customers can cause the U.S. if precautions are not taken. It is logical that financial institutions should know at least as much about their employees as they are required to know about their customers.

The current due diligence standard for financial institutions is that employees of financial institutions actually control the instrumentalities of commerce Congress has found to be vulnerable to abuse by terrorist, international drug dealers, and others who would harm the U.S. If the government is concerned that financial institution customers can adversely affect national security, then certainly the backgrounds of employees who run the institutions are just as critical.

To some extent, a criminal record check is already part of the hiring process for some financial institutions. For example, the Federal Deposits Insurance Corporation (FDIC) mandates insured banks may not hire, without the FDIC's consent, a person convicted of certain offenses involving dishonesty or breach of trust, money laundering, or drug trafficking.[8] Financial institutions covered by the Patriot Act without specific statutory duties to conduct criminal checks should also consider implementing a pre-employment screening program.

---

[8] see www.fdic.gov/regulations/laws/r ules/5000-1300.html

# Terrorist Searches and U.S. Vital Industries

A growing trend by the federal government is to protect America's vital interests and infrastructure by requiring background checks in sensitive industries.

## Food and Drug Administration Guidelines

In 2002 the U.S. Food and Drug Administration issued voluntary guidelines on workplace safety and security, urging virtually every business in the food industry – from "farmer to table" – to adopt more aggressive measures to protect the nation's food supply. The FDA's suggestions included asking employers to obtain and verify work references, addresses, and phone numbers, and to consider performing criminal background checks. In 2003, the FDA updated its guidance and suggested that various industries involved in the food chain should also follow the guidelines.

Although these guidelines are not mandatory, the FDA indicated the guidelines help minimize the possibility that items—

> "…under their control will be subject to tampering or other malicious, criminal, or terrorist actions. It does not create or confer any rights for or on any person and does not operate to bind FDA or the public."

FDA recommends that operators of food importing establishments consider—

> "…screening (pre-hiring, at hiring, post-hiring), examining the background of all staff (including seasonal, temporary, contract, and volunteer staff, whether hired directly or through a recruitment firm) as appropriate to their position, considering candidates' access to sensitive areas of the facility and the degree to which they will be supervised and other relevant factors."[9]

Further suggestions include obtaining and verifying work references, addresses, and phone numbers, having a criminal background check performed by local law enforcement or by a contract service provider, and participating in one of the pilot programs managed by the Immigration and Naturalization Service and the Social Security Administration.

These pilot programs provide electronic confirmation of employment eligibility for newly hired employees. For more information call the INS SAVE Program toll free at 1-888-464-4218, or fax a request for information to 202-514-9981, or write to: US/INS, SAVE Program, 425 I Street, NW, ULLICO-4th Floor, Washington, DC 20536.

The FDA recommended that screening procedures should be applied equally to all employees regardless of race, national origin, religion, and citizenship, or immigration status. For more information about these guidelines, See www.cfsan.fda.gov/~dms/secguid6.html.

The same guidelines issued to importers of food were also issued to operators of cosmetics establishments, including firms that process, store, repack, re-label, distribute, or transport cosmetics or cosmetics ingredients. See www.cfsan.fda.gov/~dms/secguid4.html.

---

[9] see Food Security Preventive Measures Guidance at www.cfsan.fda.gov/~dms/secguid7.html

# Purpose and Scope of FDA Laws to Thwart Terrorism

Below is a summary of materials found at www.cfsan.fda.gov/~dms/secguid5.html.

"This draft guidance is designed as an aid to operators of retail food stores and food service establishments (for example, bakeries, bars, bed-and-breakfast operations, cafeterias, camps, child and adult day care providers, church kitchens, commissaries, community fund raisers, convenience stores, fairs, food banks, grocery stores, interstate conveyances, meal services for home-bound persons, mobile food carts, restaurants, and vending machine operators). This is a very diverse set of establishments, which includes both very large and very small entities.

"This draft guidance identifies the kinds of preventive measures they may take to minimize the risk that food under their control will be subject to tampering or other malicious, criminal, or terrorist actions. Operators of retail food stores and food service establishments are encouraged to review their current procedures and controls in light of the potential for tampering or other malicious, criminal, or terrorist actions and make appropriate improvements.

"This draft guidance is designed to focus the operator's attention sequentially on each segment of the food delivery system that is within their control, to minimize the risk of tampering or other malicious, criminal, or terrorist action at each segment. To be successful, implementing enhanced preventive measures requires the commitment of management and staff. Accordingly, the FDA recommends that both management and staff participate in the development and review of such measures."

## Food Safety And Inspection Guidelines

The Food Safety and Inspection Service of the United States Department of Agriculture (USDA) has also issued safety and security guidelines The guidelines are the *FSIS Safety and Security Guidelines for the Transportation and Distribution of Meat, Poultry, and Egg Products*. According to the FSIS, "The second section of the guidelines deals specifically with security measures intended to prevent the same forms of contamination due to criminal or terrorist acts." Here is an example of one USDA guideline—

# USDA Asks to Screen & Educate Employees

Screen all potential employees, to the extent possible, by conducting background and criminal checks appropriate to their positions, and verifying references (including contract, temporary, custodial, seasonal, and security personnel). When this is not practical, such personnel should be under constant supervision and their access to sensitive areas of the facility restricted.[10]

---

[10] see www.fsis.usda.gov/oa/topics/transportguide.htm

## Bioterrorism and the Nation's Water Supply

Similar contamination concerns exist for the nation's water supply. On June 12, 2002, the President signed the Public Health Security and Bioterrorism Preparedness and Response Act of 2002 – The Bioterrorism Act. This act enhances federal and state efforts to prepare for and respond to the threat of bioterrorism and other public health emergencies. The act requires all community water systems serving a population greater than 3,300 to conduct a vulnerability assessment and provide a written copy of the assessment to the U.S. Environmental Protection Agency (EPA) administrator. One of the areas of inquiry under the act is the *security screening of employees or contractor support services.*[11]

These examples show federal agencies have put focus on background checks as weapons in the fight against terrorists. The list of affected industries likely to increase.

# Terrorist Databases— The Good and The Bad

## The Good News

For employers without access to non-public government terrorist data, the most frequently used tool is a list provided by the U.S. Treasury Office of Foreign Assets Control (OFAC). The OFAC publishes a list of individuals and companies owned or controlled by, or acting for or on behalf of, targeted countries. Also listed are individuals, groups, and entities such as terrorists and narcotics traffickers designated under programs that are not country-specific. Collectively, such individuals and companies are called Specially Designated Nationals or SDNs. Their assets are blocked and U.S. persons are generally prohibited from dealing with them. The OFAC list also has other designations, such as SDGT, standing for "Specially Designated Global Terrorist." There are approximately 3,000 names on the list.

According to the OFAC website at www.treas.gov/offices/eotffc/ofac/index.html—

> "U.S. persons are prohibited from engaging in any transactions with SDNs and must block any property in their possession or under their control in which an SDN has an interest. SDNs are designated primarily under the statutory authority of the Trading With the Enemy Act, the International Emergency Economic Powers Act, the Anti-Terrorism and Effective Death Penalty Act and the Foreign Narcotics Kingpin Designation Act."

There are public information provider firms who specialize in obtaining all the data that is publicly available from organizations that keep terrorist lists, and then assemble all the information into a proprietary database. These databases are useful search tools for employers since they contain the OFAC list and many of the public "most wanted lists" issued by various organizations and generally available on websites.

---

[11] see SEC. 1433. (42 USC 300i-2.) TERRORIST AND OTHER INTENTIONAL ACTS Section Services at www.fda.gov/oc/bioterrorism/PL107-188.html#title4

Below is a list of elements that could be found in a typical vendor's terrorist database—

- OFAC Specially Designated Nationals (SDN) & Blocked Persons
- OFAC Sanctioned Countries, including Major Cities & Ports
- Non-Cooperative Countries and Territories
- Department of State Trade Control (DTC) Debarred Parties
- U.S. Bureau of Industry & Security (formerly BXA)
- Unverified Entities List
- Denied Entities List
- Denied Persons List
- FBI Most Wanted Terrorists & Seeking Information
- FBI Top Ten Most Wanted
- INTERPOL Most Wanted List
- Bank of England Sanctions List
- OSFI - Canadian Sanctions List
- United Nations Consolidated Sanctions List
- Politically Exposed Persons List
- European Union Terrorism List
- World Bank Ineligible Firms

As a practical matter, an employer may want to consider at least searching the following databases, which are easily available either online or through information or software providers—

- OFAC List
- Denied Persons List— This is a list supplied by the United States Commerce Department and indicates individuals and entities restricted from exporting from the United States.[12]
- OSFI List— This is a list supplied by the Canadian Office of the Superintendent of Financial Institutions and contains names of individuals and organizations subject to the Regulations Establishing a List of Entities made under the Criminal Code or the United Nations Suppression of Terrorism regulations.[13]
- EU and UN Terrorist Lists— Lists supplied by the Bank of England,[14] the European Union, and the United Nations.

Interpol also publishes a web page to check international wants and warrants. See an example of a search for Bin Laden.[15] Note the name differentiation— "Usama" rather than "Osama."

---

[12] www.bax.doc.gov/dp/default.shtm

[13] www.osfi-bsif.gc.ca/eng/default.asp

[14] www.bankofengland.co.uk?Links/setframe.html – go to "QuickLinks" and click on "Financial Sanctions"

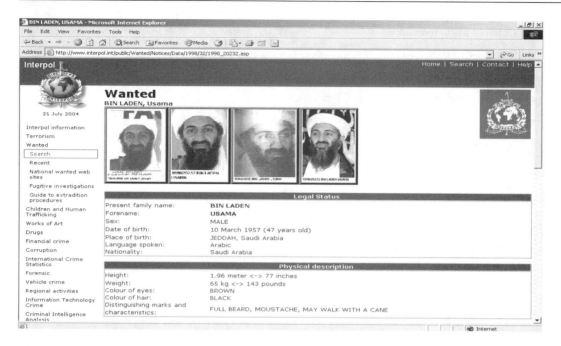

## The Not So Good News

It would be an easy procedure for businesses to avoid hiring or dealing with terrorists just by going online and looking up the OFAC list. Unfortunately, searching this list is easier said than done for the following reasons—

1. The online database is difficult for private employers to access efficiently. The OFAC data is maintained at www.treas.gov/offices/eotffc/ofac/index.html. Anyone can access it. However, as a practical matter, most private employers find the search difficult and time consuming. As alternatives, there are a number of private firms who provide Patriot Act compliance services that regularly assemble the OFAC data and make it available to employers and businesses through various web-based and computerized solutions.

2. The OFAC search, although valuable, does not include other "terrorist search" tools from other organizations and governments. For example, the Commerce Department maintains separate lists for the purposes of the programs it administers. Their Denied Persons List consists of individuals and companies that have been denied export and re-export privileges by the BIS. Their Entity List consists of foreign firms who pose an unacceptable risk of diverting U.S. exports and technology to alternate destinations for the development of weapons of mass destruction. Accordingly, U.S. exports to those entities may require a license. The two lists are maintained separately, because the BIS Entity List has a purpose different than the OFAC list. Some software firms that provide Patriot Act compliance services merge the two lists.

---

[15] www.interpol.int/Public/Wanted/Search/Form.asp

3. Positive identification can be difficult. The OFAC search provides as much data as possible, but it is not always sufficient. The names are often of Middle Eastern origin and the identifiers are not always sufficient to make a determination as to identity. Typically, international terrorists on the OFAC list do not have valid Social Security Numbers.

OFAC provides a Frequently Asked Questions webpage and outlines steps to take in the event of a possible match. The FAQ that follows tell financial institutions what to do if there is a "hit." The information is very useful for any employers as well.

---

# OFAC Frequently Asked Questions

If you are calling about an account—

1. Is the "hit" or "match" against OFAC's SDN list or targeted countries, or is it "hitting" for some other reason, i.e., "Control List" or "PEP," "CIA," "Non-Cooperative Countries and Territories," "Canadian Consolidated List (OSFI)," "World Bank Debarred Parties," or "government official of a designated country" ... *or* can you not tell what the "hit" is?

- If it is hitting against **OFAC's SDN list** or **targeted countries**, continue to #2 below.

- If it is hitting for some other reason, you should contact the "keeper" of whichever other list the match is hitting against. For questions about—

  - **The Denied Persons List and the Entities List**, please contact the Bureau of Industry and Security at the U.S. Department of Commerce at 202-482-4811.

  - **The FBI's Most Wanted List** or any other FBI-issued watch list, please contact the Federal Bureau of Investigation. (www.fbi.gov/contact/fo/fo.htm)

  - **The Debarred Parties List**, please contact the Office of Defense Trade Controls at the U.S. Department of State, 202-663-2700.

  - **The Bank Secrecy Act** and **the USA PATRIOT Act**, please contact the Financial Crimes Enforcement Network (FinCEN), 1-800-949-2732.

- *If you are unsure whom to contact*, then you should contact your interdict software provider which told you there was a "hit."

- *If you cannot tell what the "hit" is*, then you should contact your interdict software provider which told you there was a "hit."

2. Now that you have established that the hit is against OFAC's SDN list or targeted countries, you must evaluate the quality of the hit. Compare the name of your accountholder with the name on the SDN list. Is the name of your accountholder an individual while the name on the SDN list is a vessel, organization or company, or vice-versa?

- If yes, you do not have a valid match.

- If no, please continue to #3 below.

3. How much of the SDN's name is matching against the name of your account holder? Is just one of two or more names matching (i.e., just the last name)?

- If yes, then you do not have a valid match.

- If no, please continue to #4 below.

4. Compare the complete SDN entry with all the information you have on the matching name of your accountholder. An SDN entry often will have, for example, a full name, address, nationality, passport, tax ID or "cedula number," place of birth, date of birth, former names, and aliases. Are you missing a lot of this information for the name of your accountholder?

- If yes, then go back and get more information, then compare your complete information against the SDN entry.

- If no, then please continue to #5 below.

5. Are there a number of similarities or exact matches?

- If yes, then please call the hotline at 1-800-540-6322.

- If no, then you do not have a valid match.

6. If you have reason to know or believe that processing this transfer or operating this account would violate any of the Regulations, you must call the hotline and explain this knowledge or belief. [02-12-03]

Also see www.treas.gov/offices/eotffc/ofac/faq/index.html

## FCRA, EEOC, and Terrorist Searches

All employment screening is conducted under the federal Fair Credit Reporting Act (FCRA), which requires the use of reasonable procedures to assure maximum accuracy. A terrorist search may contain many common names and not provide the sufficient identifiers to determine if a match belongs to an applicant. As indicated in #5 above, OFAC also has a hotline to assist employers in the event of a possible match where there are insufficient identifiers on the search results.

In addition, employers need to be aware that a large number of names may be of Middle Eastern origin. Under the FCRA, a background screening may not be used in violation of any state or federal anti-discrimination laws. As a result, it is important that all efforts be made to determine if there is a positive match before taking any adverse action. This can prevent an employer from being the subject of a complaint for discrimination in hiring based upon national origin or ethnicity.

The EEOC issued a Press Release on this topic following the September 11, 2001 terrorist attacks—

# EEOC 9/14/2001 Press Release[16]

WASHINGTON - In the wake of this week's tragic events, Cari M. Dominguez, Chair of the U.S. Equal Employment Opportunity Commission (EEOC), called on all employers and employees across the country to promote tolerance and guard against unlawful workplace discrimination based on national origin or religion.

"We should not allow our anger at the terrorists responsible for this week's heinous attacks to be misdirected against innocent individuals because of their religion, ethnicity, or country of origin," Chair Dominguez said. "In the midst of this tragedy, employers should take time to be alert to instances of harassment or intimidation against Arab-American and Muslim employees. Preventing and prohibiting injustices against our fellow workers is one way to fight back, if only symbolically, against the evil forces that assaulted our workplaces Tuesday morning."

EEOC encourages all employers to do the following—

- Reiterate policies against harassment based on religion, ethnicity, and national origin;
- Communicate procedures for addressing workplace discrimination and harassment;
- Urge employees to report any such improper conduct; and
- Provide training and counseling, as appropriate.

Ms. Dominguez exhorted all individuals to heed the words of President Bush, who said yesterday: "We must be mindful that as we seek to win the war [against terrorism] we treat Arab-Americans and Muslims with the respect they deserve."

EEOC enforces Title VII of the Civil Rights Act of 1964, which prohibits discrimination in employment on the basis of race, color, religion, national origin, sex, and retaliation for filing a complaint. For example, Title VII precludes workplace bias based on the following—

- Religion, ethnicity, birthplace, culture, or linguistic characteristics;
- Marriage or association with persons of a national origin or religious group;
- Membership or association with specific ethnic or religious groups;
- Physical, linguistic or cultural traits closely associated with a national origin group, for example, discrimination because of a person's physical features or traditional Arab style of dress; and
- Perception or belief that a person is a member of a particular national origin group, based on the person's speech, mannerisms, or appearance.

---

[16] see online at www.eeoc.gov/press/9-14-01.html

"Our laws re-affirm our national values of tolerance and civilized conduct. At this time of trial, these values will strengthen us as a common people," Ms. Dominguez said. "The nation's workplaces are fortified by the enduring ability of Americans of diverse backgrounds, beliefs, and nationalities to work together harmoniously and productively."

## The Bad News

When private employers utilize publicly available lists for terrorist searches, there are four areas of "bad news."

1. As discussed in detail in Chapters 11 and 12, any criminal record database has inherent limitations. There are *issues as to timeliness, accuracy, and completeness.* Since the names on the lists are by necessity a judgment call, the list is certainly not complete or comprehensive. There is no way to know how long it takes for a name to be "approved" to be entered onto the list. In addition, the mechanics of a government agency making a decision that a person is a terrorist is not generally public information. Names can fall through the cracks.

2. Terrorists can *circumvent the databases.* If a person is a terrorist, then this person probably knows that he or she may be on a government watch list. A terrorist attempting to obtain employment at an American facility will have a fake name, driver's license, Social Security card, or other false identification. As a result, the bad news is that a determined terrorist may figure out a way around a terrorist database search.[17]

3. Employers need to understand that a terrorist database is subject to a high rate of *false positives and false negatives.* A false positive means someone is incorrectly identified as a terrorist or criminal. A false negative is where a person who should have been identified as a risk and stopped for further inquiry was not and was allowed through. This can happen for a number of reasons. Terrorist databases may have a number of name variations and spellings that can lead to names being mixed. Since many names on the terrorist lists are from other countries, there is the issue of translating the person's name into an English version. Terrorists may purposely alter spellings of their name. Since the terrorist may have false ID's or foreign IDS, the number that appears may not be a number consistent with numbering scheme of legitimate ID's — the terrorist's ID would be a false document. On the other end of the spectrum, it is entirely possible to have "computer twins," where two different people have the same names and the same birthday, which means at least one false positive.

4. A terrorist database search can potentially create a false sense of security if employers do not fully understand the *inherent limitations in a terrorist database.* As in a criminal database, just because a name is not in the database does not mean the applicant is not a threat. At the same time, just because a person's name is in a database does not mean it is *that* person. A database search is only one tool, and is most beneficial when used as part of a series of overlapping hiring tools.

---

[17] for a more detailed discussion on the problems associated with identity fraud, see Chapter 17

# Use All the Tools

As with all safe hiring techniques, no one tool is the complete answer. Besides using the terrorist databases and lists such as OFAC as a measure of safety against hiring terrorists, an employer should use the various employment screening procedures suggested in this book.

- A strong AIR (Application /Interview /Reference checking) Process.
- A seven-year criminal check for all jurisdictions where an applicant has lived, worked, or studied. Include both federal and state criminal convictions.
- A national criminal index search as described in Chapter 12.
- A Social Security trace (or an address information manager search) that utilizes a number of databases including credit bureaus' files for a list of all names and addresses associated with a particular Social Security Number. This is particularly important to guard against fake identification documents. It is also critical to review the times that addresses were reportedly used in conjunction with the SSN to look for unexplained gaps in a person's whereabouts.
- Verification of employment for the past 5-10 years.
- Verify education and any special credentials.
- A driver record search.
- Complete the I-9 process.

## The I-9 Process

If a person is made a conditional offer of employment, then it is also critical to make sure the I-9 process is completed. This process by which an employer verifies a person's eligibility to work in the U.S. is done pursuant to rules prepared by the Immigration and Naturalization Service. This also provides an employer a great deal of protection against someone who may be using a fake identity. As part of the I-9 process, the employer can also contact the Social Security Administration and verify the Social Security Number.[18]

---

[18] see Chapter 13 on how employers can contact the Social Security Administration after a conditional job offer has been made

# Past Employments Verification — The Key to Protecting Vital Industries from Terrorists

Of all the available tools an employer can use, verifying past employment is probably the most critical. As noted in Chapter 14 on References, this screening tool could have most likely raised a red flag had any of the 9/11 terrorists applied for employment in a critical industry.

In Chapter 17, we discussed the nature of identity. When it comes to knowing who a person really is and what history to attach to them, the least meaningful source of information is what the person says about himself. However, as you check public records, the reliability factor increases. Validations from past employment and education checks give us more confidence that a person is who he says he is — and has the history he claims.

The problems with spotting a potential terrorist, however, is as follows—

1. They are more likely than most to attempt to thwart safe hiring techniques by misrepresenting themselves and attempting to conceal their true identities and purpose.

2. They are more likely to be presenting false identification information and documents.

3. There is likely to be less info about the terrorist in the normal domestic database searches.

4. Terrorist databases can be circumvented.

The government has warned about "sleeper" terrorists, potential terrorists who have fit into American society and are waiting to be told to take some course of action. If a "sleeper" terrorist applies for a job not requiring a security clearance, then he or she may well be a perfectly honest applicant with nothing to indicate a secret mission. If the government with their resources cannot identify them, then employers are at a distinct disadvantage.

As a result, it is arguably more difficult for employers to prevent the hiring of terrorists than someone with an unsuitable criminal record or falsified credentials. Even though there are substantially less terrorists likely to apply to a vital infrastructure employer, the harm can be substantial.

The key is past employment calls. By calling to verify past jobs for the past 5-10 years, an employer verifies the applicant's general whereabouts and general accuracy of his or her job history.

> **Author Tip** ➡ Since information from applicants and databases may not be trusted sources, where can employers turn? The ultimate key to verification of identity and history stems from obtaining information from a "trusted source." For more information about the "trusted source rule" see page 265.

Where does the trusted source come in? A researcher doing a past employment check has the ability to access a directory assistance, a printed phonebook, or some other source of information that is generally considered reliable and would be extremely difficult to for an outsider to manipulate. By utilizing a telephone listing independently obtained and calling that past employer, it can be confirmed that the past employers exists and the phone number in fact belongs to a legitimate firm.

Although it may sound like a slender thread, the possibility of terrorists, such as the 9/11 hijackers, setting up a 5-10 year employment history just to weasel their way into a job in a sensitive industry is remote. It is not impossible, but it would require considerable effort.

To avoid such a possibility, employers in sensitive industries may consider the following certain steps. Once the information is obtained, the researcher should then review the confirmed information, matching it to data known about the applicant — developing a pattern for looking for consistencies or inconsistencies. The employer should develop a protocol to crosscheck applicants and other screening materials. For example—

- Does the job history match the address and the Social Security trace? The Social Security trace shows address and name associated with an applicant. If an applicant has a long job history, then the dates and locations should correspond to the information on the trace. The dates must be viewed as a whole to see if it is inherently consistent. In other words, the employer needs to see if the dots connect and all the information makes sense.

- A person claiming to have been self-employed for the past 5-10 years creates additional challenges, requiring verifications from a trusted sources in the information path. The recommended procedure is to contact customers of the applicant's businesses, and verifying the existence directly by phone. Even more important is to develop references. Call the references supplied by the applicant, and ask those supplied references if they know other clients of the self-employed applicant who can confirm if he was in business.

- With enough resources, know how, and planning, it is possible for a would-be terrorist to set-up an elaborate ruse. A person would need to start a company for the purpose of being in the phonebook, and then an accomplice posing as a legitimate reference would have to stand by to deliver a credible reference when the new prospective employer should happen to call. Of course, when calling past employers, a researcher needs to use common sense and be on the alert for conversations that do not sound businesslike and correct.

A suspected terrorist could set up an elaborate ruse to pass the reference check and this underscores the inherent difficulty faced by private employers. If the government, with all of its resources, did not detect the terrorist in the United States in the first place, then private employers are certainly at a disadvantage. However, employers can place as many barriers as possible in the way of potential terrorists in order to undermine their efforts, or to force would be terrorists to foul-up in their efforts to hide their identity or true purpose.

The bottom line— American employers must do what they are able to protect the United States.

**Chapter 23**

# Dealing With Fraud, Embezzlement and Integrity

## Screening for Honesty and Morality

Recently, corporate fraud and dishonesty have been major topics. The news media have focused on a variety of stories ranging from corporate fraud — Enron, MCI, and others — to the resume fibs of sports coaches. These stories all have one thing in common — applicants either lied to get their position or committed acts of dishonesty in the job, or employers were lax about hiring or exercising sound controls over unethical behavior.

How do firms hire honest employees? It would seem "Thou shall not steal" is not a hard thing to remember. A large part of the safe hiring process is to keep firms free of applicants and employees who are criminals, frauds, crooks, or who have a bent moral rudder.

Of course, honesty and morality are not easy traits to screen. There is no magic scanning machine that can read an applicant's soul or heart, or the synapses of the brain, declaring that an honest person is applying. Most often, in the hiring process, a firm is only able to look for manifestations of past or current dishonesty. These can include–

- Casting oneself in a false light by submitting an application that contains material lies or omissions. As noted in Chapter 1, it is estimated from various sources that up to one out of three applications and resumes contain material falsehoods or omissions, typically involving past education or employment.

- Lying in an interview, as discussed in Chapter 8.

- Having committed a criminal act which demonstrates dishonesty or a willingness to commit fraud or some other act of moral turpitude, or such an act that results in a civil lawsuit.

An additional complication is the very nature of honesty itself. For example, an applicant may be the type of person that tells a socially polite "little white lie," e.g. "that was delicious but I am full" when the meal did not taste very good. However, no one would suggest that this person is dishonest for purposes of employment.

The bigger issue is predicting future behavior. Honesty has multiple dimensions. One issue is what standards and moral values does a person have and to what level are they ingrained in a person? The past is often prologue. If a person had been honest in the past or is being honest now, then there is a very good chance he or she will be honest in the future. Will an employer be able to predict what guides a person's moral compass in the future under a variety of temptations? Some situations can be predicted since they are part of the job. For example, a bookkeeper will have access to assets and money. Can the new hire with no drug abuse history resist sampling the products at the pharmaceutical warehouse? Other situations cannot be predicted. In the future, a person may undergo sudden life changes or stress that may tempt dishonesty. Or, a supervisor may ask an employee to participate in a questionable act, such as document shredding — an act with an element of coercion or an implicit threat they would lose their job if they do not cooperate. Part of the complication is to discover ahead of time how a person may react when ordered to do something dishonest.

How does an employer know in advance if applicants will be influenced towards dishonesty if put into a situation where they feel an element of coercion if they do not go along, or are tempted by greed or succumb to life's pressures?[1]

Along with pre-employment screening of new hires, listed below are eight tools firms can use to help foster an environment that promotes and encourages future honesty.

1.  **Establish Clear Policies Regarding Conduct**

    According to the U. S. Declaration of Independence, "some truths are self-evident." That may be true but an employer should still have a clear written policy that theft, dishonesty, or unethical conduct will not be tolerated, no matter when discovered. Those negative behaviors are grounds for discipline, up to and including termination.

2.  **Have Adequate Controls and Auditing in Place**

    Having controls is useless if supervisors and management are asleep at the wheel, or the controls only exist on paper. As a general rule, an organization only accomplishes those things that are measured, audited, and rewarded. The same applies to controls in an organization to protect against dishonest or unethical behavior. If the job involves handling of cash or assets or reporting of financial activity *in any way*, then there are a number of controls that can be put into place. One of the main thrusts behind the Sarbanes-Oxley Act is an environment of control, discussed later in this chapter.

3.  **Immediate and Appropriate Response to Dishonest or Unethical Conduct**

    Employers need to make it clear that dishonest behavior is not tolerated, and will be the subject of swift and certain response by the employer.

4.  **Continuing Education on Success, Ethics, and Honesty**

    A continuing effort is critical to institutionalize honest and ethical dealing, and to remind all members of the team these concepts are essential to the firm's success and an individual's

---

[1] Peoples ability to resist life stress and act in an honest an ethical fashion may well depend upon their internal level of ethical development. However that is extremely difficult to test.

success. This can be accomplished through continuing education, staff meetings, videotapes, and other visible reminders of the firm's position.

5. **Atmosphere and Corporate Culture**

    The development of a corporate culture often starts at the top. If the leaders of an organization demonstrate honest and ethical dealings in both words and deed, then it should flow down throughout the entire organization.

6. **Anonymous Tip Hotline**

    The establishment of such a hotline is one of the provisions of the Sarbanes-Oxley Act. Experts agree that the ability of employees to give anonymous tips without fear of reprisals is a highly-effective, low-cost best practice.

7. **Ethics and Honesty Advisory Hotline**

    When a good employee is faced with a situation that falls into the category of dishonest or unethical conduct, the employee may simply have no one to talk to. Providing a safe haven for discussion — or where an employee can seek advice — is a best practice.

8. **Psychological Testing for Honesty and Ethics**

    The use of such tests is an attempt to predict who will act in an honest and ethical fashion in the future. These tests and their effectiveness are discussed later in this chapter.

The reasons that honesty and ethics are critical issues are demonstrated by the following facts and statistics drawn from various industry sources—

- Employee dishonesty alone causes 30% of all business failures.[2]

- Employee theft amounts to 4% of food sales at a cost in excess of $8.5 billion annually. 75% of inventory shortages are attributed to employee theft.[3]

- Employee theft costs between 1/2%-3% of a company's gross sales. Even if the figure was only 1%, it would still mean that employees steal over a billion dollars a week from employers.

According to a report issued by the highly regarded Association of Certified Fraud Examiners,[4] it is likely the loss toll is even higher. The report notes it is not possible to calculate the exact loss to the economy since not all fraud is detected or reported. According to the opinions of these highly-trained and experienced Certified Fraud Examiners, the loss to the U.S. economy from fraud can amount to as much as 6% of corporate revenue. This translates to an astounding 600 billion dollars.[5]

The above figures do not take into account *the fallout* from employee embezzlement, dishonesty, and fraud. The fallout can include destruction of a firm's reputation, the inability to stay in business, the damage to employee morale, and the time and energy taken from productive projects to deal with

---

[2] according to the U.S. Department of Commerce
[3] according to the National Restaurant Association
[4] in the Association of Certified Fraud Examiners *2002 Report to the Nation – Occupational Fraud and Abuse*
[5] see www.cfenet.com/publications/RttN.asp

dishonesty. For a small business, the personal loss experienced by the owners can be devastating, when a trusted employee is discovered to have been an embezzler or thief.

# How to Avoid Hiring an Embezzler

In terms of victims, embezzlement is an equal opportunity crime. It affects employers of all sizes as well as profit and non-profit firms.

At the root of embezzlement is a violation of trust. By definition, **embezzlement** is a crime where a person legally uses or possesses property belonging to the employer, then permanently converts this property to his or her personal use. Embezzlement differs from **theft**, where the culprit has no right to possession in the first place.

There are a number of ways an employee can steal or embezzle, from simply walking out with company equipment to more elaborate theft schemes such as siphoning off company resources.

Embezzlement is considered more serious and harder to detect. Embezzlement can range from simply stealing cash from the cash drawer to more elaborate schemes such as writing checks to oneself or to ghost employees, setting up and making payments to fake vendors, paying phony expense reimbursements, giving oneself a pay increase. Embezzlement typically occurs when there is a combination of motive, opportunity, and means. The opportunity and means portion is usually a result of a lack of proper internal controls. If an embezzler or thief has a co-conspirator, then the act becomes more difficult to guard against.

For purposes of safe hiring, the critical task is to look for a person who may have a motive for theft or a history of past financial misconduct.

## How to Spot an Embezzler

When embezzlement occurs, typically one or more of the following situations are true—

- The business did very little, if any, due diligence when hiring the embezzler. The firm did not determine if the applicant may be motivated to steal or had stolen in the past. Not following the rules of Safe Hiring, the employer made the decision based primarily upon the interview and subjective impression of the applicant. In a great number of embezzlement cases even the slightest due diligence could have revealed the danger signals. Often times, employers merely need to look deeper instead of handing over the keys to someone who had created a favorable impression during their hiring interview.

- The employer typically had very little, if any, internal controls in place. "Internal controls" typically refers to a system of cross checks so that no one person runs the company's finances. To accomplish an embezzlement, a criminal needs to control most if not all aspects of the firm's financial life, writing the checks, making deposits, reconciling bank statements, and/or opening mail. If any of these functions are interrupted by external controls or cross checks, then the ability of an embezzler to steal is diminished.

- Embezzlers often come disguised as the hard-working "perfect employee." They are perceived as hardworking and loyal. They never seem to take a vacation. They arrive first, leave last, and always volunteer to get the mail. Embezzlers put on their show for two reasons. First, since embezzlement is fundamentally a violation of an employer's trust, embezzlers need to earn that trust in order to have the opportunity to embezzle — employers are more likely to delegate responsibility and access to cash and assets to someone who is considered hardworking and loyal. Second, embezzlers need to control their environment as much as possible to accomplish their embezzlement and to hide their activities from others. Should an embezzler take a day off, then someone else could answer a call from an unpaid vendor, perhaps prompting the replacement to ask why bills are not being paid. Or, if the embezzler does not get to the mail first, incriminating letters cannot be intercepted. To keep the scheme going, an embezzler needs complete control.

There is no one profile of an embezzler. Embezzlers can be young or old, male or female, well-educated or high school dropouts. Disguised as perfect employees, embezzlers are very difficult to detect. However, there are some common traits—

- An embezzler is completely self-focused on ones own needs, wants, and desires. He or she is not overly concerned with betraying a trust or hurting co-workers — or the employer or the company.

- If they are prosecuted, embezzlers are more focused on their own pain caused by the prosecution and being put into an embarrassing position. There is often a mental disconnect between the fact that they violated trust and stole, and the position they find themselves in. "In denial" is the popular term.

- The embezzler almost immediately begins to blame the victim; their reasoning may be—

  o   I needed the money more than they did.

  o   I worked hard and they did not treat me right.

  o   I deserved the extra money.

  o   They made me take it — if they had treated me right it would not have happened.

- Embezzlers often do not want to give up even one cent of their ill-gotten gains. Even if it would keep them out of jail, embezzlers and white collar criminals are so focused on the money they will try to do anything to not have to pay it back.

- Many times the embezzled money is simply squandered. It is not uncommon for the stolen money to have already been wasted on clothes, travel, or general high living. Once the person is prosecuted or sued, little can be recovered for purposes of victim restitution.

There is always the possibility that the motivating event could be something totally out of the embezzler's control, such as the sudden illness of a family member requiring an expensive operation. However, this is unusual. More often, motivation for embezzlement is a need to have something the embezzler cannot otherwise afford. Quite often, the signs of this covetous attitude is spotted before the first time the person embezzles.

Also, the motivating factor can be an outgrowth of some personality trait of the embezzler, such as a drug habit or gambling habit. The problems caused by such habits may be discovered during a standard background check. A credit report may show a debt level incompatible with the salary for their position. Perhaps a past employment check reveals the applicant was habitually late to work, which can be associated with a problem employee profile.

As mentioned above, once an employer is a victim, there often is no ability to obtain restitution. An embezzler may have little left in the way of assets. Court proceedings often prove ineffective at returning property. It is not usual for an employer to attempt to resolve the matter by working out an agreement for restitution that calls for the employer not to contact the police. The result, of course, is that an embezzler is free to move on to yet another victim.

Of course, the best defense for an employer is to not hire the embezzler in the first place. To accomplish that, an employer needs to utilize all of the tools in their Safe Hiring Program. It is particularly important to contact past employers, to check for criminal cases, and to run a credit check.

# Corporate Fraud and Sarbanes-Oxley

When the Sarbanes-Oxley Act was signed into law on July 30, 2002, over 15,000 publicly held companies were given a new set of rules regarding corporate ethics. This far-reaching law radically changed the landscape of corporate governance, controls, audits and financial disclosures as follows—

- Chief executive officers and chief financial officers must personally attest to the accuracy of earnings reports and other financial statements.

- Curtailment of non-auditing consulting services must be provided by outside auditors.

- Whistle-blowers should receive protections.

- Criminal penalties are increased, including fines and jail terms for misdeeds by executives.

- Investment firms must take steps to improve the objectivity of reports performed by securities analysts.

- A Public Company Accounting Oversight Board was established to oversee the audits of companies that are subject to securities laws.

- The relationship between executives and directors to outside auditors was regulated.

Among the many critical provisions is Section 404[6] that requires public firms establish and maintain financial controls and processes. Public corporations are also required to conduct periodic evaluations of their current controls. Also under Section 404, merely having financial controls is inadequate — one

---

[6] SEC. 404. MANAGEMENT ASSESSMENT OF INTERNAL CONTROLS. (a) RULES REQUIRED.—The Commission shall prescribe rules requiring each annual report required by section 13(a) or 15(d) of the Securities Exchange Act of 1934 (15 U.S.C. 78m or 78o(d)) to contain an internal control report, which shall—(1) state the responsibility of management for establishing and maintaining an adequate internal control structure and procedures for financial reporting; and (2) contain an assessment, as of the end of the most recent fiscal year of the issuer, of the effectiveness of the internal control structure and procedures of the issuer for financial reporting. (b) INTERNAL CONTROL EVALUATION AND REPORTING.—With respect to the internal control assessment required by subsection (a), each registered public accounting firm that prepares or issues the audit report for the issuer shall attest to, and report on, the assessment made by the management of the issuer. An attestation made under this subsection shall be made in accordance with standards for attestation engagements issued or adopted by the Board. Any such attestation shall not be the subject of a separate engagement.

of the most important provisions of Section 404 is that external auditors must also attest to the effectiveness and adequacy of the controls in the annual report.

Under Sarbanes-Oxley, the Securities and Exchange Commission (SEC) issued rules on how Section 404 must be implemented. To ensure honesty and ethical dealings, public companies must have an ongoing effort aimed at instituting and documenting corporate controls.

There are a number of important tasks a public firm *must do* in order to be in compliance. Appearing on any list of 404 compliance tasks is the use of background checks. Experts agree that part of insuring that a firm engages in honest and ethical dealings is to hire honest and ethical people. Hence background screening has become a part of Sarbanes-Oxley compliance.

The need for background checks was confirmed with the November, 2003 publication of a white paper by PricewaterhouseCoopers titled *Key Elements of Antifraud Programs and Controls.*[7] The white paper outlines very specific steps a public firm should take in regard to creating the critical control environment as part of an overall framework of internal oversight roles for individuals with direct access to company assets or information systems. The white paper includes specific recommendations for background screening.

The emerging standards being compiled by the Open Standards and Ethics Group (OCEG) also supports employment background screening as a key business practice. OCEG was formed by a multi-industry, multi-disciplinary coalition that saw the need to integrate the principles of effective governance, compliance, risk management, and integrity into the practice of everyday business.[8]

The need for background checks as part of Section 404 requirements is not limited to new employees. According to an article in the *CareerJournal* "To meet new corporate governance requirements mandated by last year's Sarbanes-Oxley Act, legions of companies are also more rigorously investigating current employees via detailed background checks."[9] The Association of Certified Fraud Examiners (ACFE) also suggests steps for the prevention of corporate fraud and for compliance with Sarbanes-Oxley. According to an article by ACFE, part of a program of establishing a fraud detection process should include conducting background checks on all potential employees.[10]

# Psychological Testing for Honesty and Integrity

Another useful tool to find honest employees is psychological testing. An internet search will reveal a great many firms offering testing that not only measures attitude, skills, and compatibility for a job, but also purports to measure if a person can be reasonably anticipated to act in an honest and ethical fashion. Generally, an *honesty test* relies upon three different categories of questions. First, it looks for admissions by an applicant of prior acts of dishonesty. Second, it tests an applicant's attitudes toward

---

[7] *Key Elements of Antifraud Programs and Controls* published in conjunction with the Committee of Sponsoring Organizations of the Treadway Commission (COSO). That organization authored "Internal Control – Integrated Framework," widely accepted as a framework by which management and auditors evaluate **internal controls**; see www.pwcglobal.com/Extweb/NewCoAtWork.nsf/docid/D0D7F79003C6D64485256CF30074D66C/$file/PwC_Antifraud_Final.pdf

[8] see www.oceg.org

[9] www.careerjournal.com/recruiters/jungle/20030827-jungle.html *CareerJournal* published by the *Wall Street Journal*

[10] www.cfenet.com/media/releases/021203.asp

dishonest behavior. Third, it explores other personal characteristics of a person that may have a bearing on the potential for dishonest behavior. For example, some test vendors believe a person who feels alienated may be more likely to steal.

For Safe Hiring purposes, an honesty test is a written test designed to identify individuals applying for work who have a relatively high propensity to steal money or property on the job, or likely to engage in counter productive behavior. Chapter 8 describes "Integrity Interviews" where an applicant is asked point-blank questions about his or her past and habits. However, these interviews are conducted by professionally-trained interviewers and results are not scored or evaluated using psychological measurements, and not subject to the validity studies discussed below.

**Honesty tests** utilize two types of questions. **"Direct questions"** explore a person's own past dishonest acts. An example is "Describe what you have stolen in the past from an employer." Similar questions may explore an applicant's attitude toward theft or dishonesty such as "If you knew someone was stealing, would you report it to your supervisor?" or "Have you associated with employees who you knew stole from their employers?"

The second type is called **"indirect questions."** These indirect questions seek to discern attitudes or behavior that may have a bearing upon dishonesty. Sample questions include "Do you feel lonely even when with others?" or "How often do you make your bed?" or "Do you feel most people steal at least a few small things from their employer?"

Well-designed honesty tests have generally been shown to have a high degree of accuracy. In addition to using the tests as hiring tools, tests can help improve a firm's current culture when, for instance, tests are combined with leadership development training.

## Issues Surrounding Honesty Testing

Employers should be aware of certain issues associated with honesty tests.

1.  **Honesty is inherently a difficult character trait to nail down, since it can be situational**

    The basic premise behind a personality test is that it can help predict future behavior. The difficulty with predicting future honesty is that honesty may not be a permanent trait, but can be situational. It can be argued that everyone has told "little white lies." In some social situations, it would be considered rude not to lie when the truth would be unnecessary and hurtful. A dinner guest may say the soup is fine when in fact they dislike it. That does not mean this person would not be a good candidate for a job. On the other hand, if a person is dishonest about things that are more critical, this could have a bearing on how he or she will behave in the future. Factors that need to be considered when a lie is told are 1) the motive for the lie; 2) who is being lied to; 3) the methodology of the lie; 4) how effective the person is at lying; and perhaps the most critical, 5) the harm done to others by the consequences of telling the lie.

2.  **Too similar to a polygraph**

    Employers must be aware if their honesty testing comes too close to polygraph testing. Although legal in most states, most states do prohibit any test "similar to a polygraph," without defining what that means. Per the passage of the Employee Polygraph Protection Act of 1988, the use of polygraphs was barred for most employment-related situations. As a result, the number of firms offering some sort of honesty testing instrument has increased. An employer should consult legal counsel for the current law in the jurisdiction where the new hire will be employed.

### 3. Reliability

Reliability is simply a way of stating that if the test is repeated a short time later with the same group, the results would be consistent. In other words, a test is reliable if there is "consistency of measurement." If the same test on the same group produced widely different results, then the testing instrument would come under question.

### 4. Validity

A valid test is one which measures what it is truly stated. In the context of an employment test, validity means the test actually predicts who is going to be honest. However, if the test does not give job-related information, the test is not valid. The firm that prepares and sells the testing must convince the employer that their instrument is a valid predictor of future job honesty. The subject of demonstrating test validity is extremely complex and beyond the scope of this book, however, good advice to follow is that an employer should not use any test unless the developer is able to produce a substantial body of data as to the validity of the test.

### 5. EEOC considerations

Another critical consideration is whether the testing instrument is discriminatory and violates the rules of the Equal Employment Opportunities Commission. Even if the test is not discriminatory on its face, an employer needs to be aware that a test can have the effect of being discriminatory by the manner in which it is applied. Recall the discussion about the use of criminal records in Chapters 5 and 11 — The EEOC has ruled that the use of criminal records can have an adverse effect on certain protected groups. The short answer for employers is that firms selling the test instrument are responsible to provide the employer with documentation as to the Tile VII implications associated with the test.

### 6. Americans With Disabilities ACT (ADA)

A related issue is the Americans with Disabilities Act implications. A test for honesty will rarely contain a reference to a disability. However, the employer should require a vendor to document that vendor is not asking any questions that indirectly require an applicant to reveal or discuss a disability, or in some way discourage an applicant with a disability from applying.

### 7. Faking or distortion issues

A major issue with the validity of honesty tests is when applicants try to outsmart the test and give fake answers based upon what they believe the testmakers are looking for. Employers should review with testing vendors if psychologists have devised any methods that take such a distortion into account. Perhaps the test taker notices that, for every question, the best answer is always the third question.

8. **Administration of test**

Any employer using these tests will want its administration to be as quick and easy as possible. Even though there are pencil and paper tests, tests are also available over the internet and by phone. The costs for these tests are also very reasonable, as low as $10 or less per test for an off the shelf instrument. However, the development of a custom instrument is very expensive, such as those based upon modeling a firm's best current employee is very expensive.

9. **Security of results and privacy**

Of course, it is critical for an employer to ensure all results are confidential and that the privacy of an applicant is maintained. The vendor should demonstrate that their system is properly secured and all results are returned in a manner that protects privacy and confidentiality.

10. **Analysis and use of results**

Employers must be very careful using off-the-shelf instruments to make a hiring decision based upon a resulting numerical score. Psychological tests for honesty can be very complicated; a cookie cutter analysis can be deceptive. It is important to note certain cut-off points can be set while making sure not to hire any dishonest workers. For example, in order to make sure all of the potential "crooks" are eliminated, it is possible that some good candidates are eliminated along with the bad. The tests can also be prejudiced against an honest person. Perhaps one applicant may honestly admit he or she once took a pen home, but another applicant may consider that too trivial to report.

The lesson here is to very carefully review the instrument and the manner in which it is scored *before* using it to make any decision. Many experts suggest the results of an honesty test not be the sole deciding factor, but that they be just one of the factors. However, there are employers who have found these tests are highly accurate and do place a great deal of faith in them.

11. **Who is tested**

Another aspect of honesty testing is that they are typically used for hiring lower paid, hourly workers. Retail and manufacturing firms that hire unskilled or semi-skilled labor often use these tests; the tests are not typically used to the same degree for "white-collar" positions. However, given the emphasis on corporate honesty and ethics, a firm may want to consider using these tests for its salaried workers and professionals. The use of these tests serves to underscore the importance of honesty as well as possibly protect a firm from a bad hire in the executive offices.

12. **Possible negative consequences of honesty tests**

There are a number of negative consequences employers must consider and address before administering a testing program. These include—

   a. *False Sense of Security*— These tests could create a false sense of security among employers.

   b. *Hardship among Honest Workers*— If workers are denied employment based upon a test, there can be an inability to find a job. These tests can limit honest workers in an effort to find employment if they are unfairly tagged as not having passed a test.

   c.  *Invasion of Privacy*— Lawsuits have been filed based upon unfair or intrusive questions appearing on tests. An employer should review all questions carefully to ensure the tests do not offend applicants.

   d.  *The Employer-Employee Relationship*— It is important that applicants do not develop a negative first impression of a company due to a badly worded phrase, test item, or poor overall test. Typically, applicants receive indirect questions better than direct ones. Direct questions have been shown to offend a greater number of honest applicants. The goal of a test is to ultimately increase the odds of identifying those applicants that have more honest tendencies than others.

# Honestly! Do Honesty Tests *Really* Work?

## "Elevating Corporate Behavior One Test at a Time."

By John Schinnerer, PhD, President of InfiNet Assessment[11]

Honesty and integrity tests have been used ever since the polygraph, or lie detector, test was outlawed. The question that many people have is, "Do these tests really work?"

The short answer is "Yes, they do work." The proof that they work has been demonstrated by two concepts known as validity and reliability.

Validity is demonstrated when a test measures what it purports to measure, in this case – honesty and integrity. Most validity studies for honesty tests are done with two groups of people – an average group of people and a group of prison inmates. The idea being that prisoners have already demonstrated antisocial behaviors such as theft, assault, and deceit. The results from these two groups are then used to look at the items individually and collectively.

The major yardstick of honesty tests is predictive validity – a test's ability to predict who is more likely to have honest tendencies. The EEOC has set forth validity guidelines as to the usefulness of tests. These guidelines state that a validity of .21 to .35 is likely to be useful while anything above .35 is highly useful. On average, honesty tests have a validity of .41 (Ones, Chockalingan, & Schmidt, 1993) which has a great benefit to those looking to reduce shrinkage, theft of data, or other counterproductive behaviors.

The majority of these tests rely on very similar questions. These questions have been used over and over on different people (and occasionally the same person) over time. Certain questions

[11] contact email john@infinetassessment.com; website www.infinetassessment.com. Dr. John Schinnerer is President and Chief Strategist of Infinet Assessment, a psychological testing company founded in 1997. Dr. Schinnerer received his doctorate in educational psychology from U.C. Berkeley. His areas of expertise range from ethical and moral development to leadership development to psychometrics to the psychological constructs that influence job performance. He is a noted writer and speaker on topics such as the legal issues involved in pre-employment testing, optimizing brain functioning, leadership development, and creating an ethical workplace.

have been shown to repeatedly and consistently differentiate between individuals with antisocial tendencies and those who tend to obey the rules of society.

This brings us to the second concept, that of reliability. Reliability occurs when a test measures a concept, such as integrity, similarly in the same individual over time. A reliable integrity test should be able to consistently identify a felon as having more antisocial ideas today as well as one year from now.

Assuming we have a test that is reliable and valid, many people ask, "how do these questions work?" There are two main types of items in integrity and honesty tests – direct and indirect. Direct questions ask test-takers about their past behaviors in a direct manner. For example, "How many times in the past six months have you taken office supplies from your employer?" The answer choices for this question include "Zero", "Once or twice", "Three to five times", "Six to ten times", or "More than ten times."

Indirect items get at the same information in a more discrete manner. These items rely on a psychological concept known as projection. Projection is what humans do in an attempt to normalize their own behaviors. The assumption is that an individual will project his or her characteristic mode of responding into the question. These items are more or less disguised as to their true intent, thereby reducing the chances that the test-taker can deliberately create a desirable impression. An example of an indirect item is the following statement, "Borrowing office supplies from your employer is okay if you plan to replace them later." The test-taker is asked to what extent they agree with the statement above on a 1 to 5 scale. The greater the degree to which they agree with the statement, the more likely it is they are engaging in stealing or "borrowing" office items.

Another tool that test creators use is that of repetition. Most honesty tests will include similar items worded in different ways. Honesty is measured by the degree to which individuals remain consistent between these different items. This is one way to minimize our tendency to manage the impressions that other people have of us. To allow for this, most honesty tests are over 150 items in length to allow the test-taker adequate time and space to forget previous items measuring the same behavior (e.g., employee theft) that are worded differently.

While honesty tests have been shown to be valid, they are also situational. In other words, honesty is applied differently in different situations depending on the importance one places on the situation. Situations that are deemed important are more likely to be handled in an honest manner. For this and other reasons, honesty tests should never be used as the sole hiring criteria.

Honesty tests should be used as part of a battery of tests in an attempt to look at the entire applicant, not merely their honesty. Success on the job is comprised of much more than honesty. Success is usually a result of motivation, emotional intelligence, traditional intelligence, knowledge *and* honesty.[12]

---

[12] Ones, D., Chockalingan, V., & Schmidt, F. *"Comprehensive Meta-Analysis of Integrity Test Validities Findings and Implications for Personnel Selection and Theories of Job Performance"* from *Journal of Applied Psychology*. August 1993, 78, 4, 679-703.

# Chapter 24

# Workplace Violence

According to a Census of Fatal Occupational Injuries (CFOI) performed by the Bureau of Labor Statistics, 8,786 fatal work injuries occurred in the United States in 2001. 2,886 of these fatalities were attributed to the Sept 11th terror attacks. Of the remaining 5,900 deaths, 639 were homicides.

In other words, nearly 11% of on-the-job deaths were attributed to homicide, making it the third leading cause of workplace fatalities.[1]

The cost to America is staggering not only in personal terms, but in economic loss as well. In 1995, the Workplace Violence Research Institute[2] issued a report pegging the cost of work-related violence to the U.S. economy at $36 billion dollars. Since that figure is ten years old, the likelihood is that the current cost in today's dollars is even more significant.

Despite the shocking truth that over one-in-ten workplace deaths is the result of homicide, more appalling are the Occupational Safety and Health Administration (OSHA) statistics on workplace violence: two million American workers are the victims of workplace violence each year.

## Defining Workplace Violence

While the term is appropriate for a quick definition or diagnosis of a problem, "workplace violence" is a little nebulous. Many employers loosely define workplace violence as—

> *Assaults, other violent acts, or threats which occur in or are related to the workplace and entail a substantial risk of physical or emotional harm to individuals, or damage to company resources or capabilities.*

While this definition covers a fair degree of actions, a better interpretation should be used in order to create an effective, defensible policy. A better definition of workplace violence should account for the type of offense, circumstance — where and when an incident occurs, and whether it is considered to be "on-the-job" — and party or parties involved.

Workplace violence can take place anywhere employees are required to carry out a business-related function. The type of incident liable to occur varies by circumstance, but generally breaks down in the following manner—

---

[1] still the number one cause of deaths is vehicular or transportation-related fatalities

[2] Workplace Violence Research Institute www.workviolence.com

| Event or incident | Where it Occurs | Perpetrated by |
|---|---|---|
| Anger-related incidents<br>Arguments<br>Arson<br>Bullying/intimidation<br>Bringing a hand-gun on premises, and using it to intimidate, threaten or bully<br>Harassment<br>Murder<br>Physical assaults (biting, hitting, kicking, etc.)<br>Pranks<br>Property damage<br>Psychological trauma<br>Pushing<br>Rape<br>Robbery<br>Rumors<br>Sabotage<br>Suicide<br>Swearing<br>Theft<br>Vandalism<br>Verbal abuse<br>Written threats | At the traditional workplace (office, job site)<br><br>Off-site at a business-related function (conference, trade show, etc.)<br><br>At a social event related to work<br><br>In customer or client homes<br><br>Away from work but resulting from work (such as threats made by clients to employees at their residences) | An outsider with no legitimate relationship to the victim or workplace<br><br>A customer or someone who is a recipient of a service provided by the affected victim or workplace.<br><br>A current or former employee who has an employment-related relationship with the workplace victim.<br><br>Employee-related outsider who is a current/former spouse/lover, relative, acquaintance, etc. who has a dispute involving an employee of the workplace. Domestic violence can become workplace violence |

Obviously, there is a wide range in types of violence, and situations vary by circumstance. A case where a cashier is caught stealing from the register must be looked at differently than a case where an employee beats up a co-worker. Therefore, it becomes necessary to add a level of criteria to define the degree of severity of a behavior or action.

Most experts on the subject break down behaviors into three severity levels as follows—

**Level One**— Low-level acts or behaviors not severe enough to require disciplinary action, but which indicate that a problem may exist. This type of problem may not result in any significant damage to person or property, but acts as a warning sign that education or intervention may be necessary.

Level One behavior is most frequently seen in an employee's attitude. This type of behavior includes—

- **Argumentative or confrontational behavior**. Consistently moody, caustic, or mean behavior when dealing with co-workers or customers.

- **Uncooperative or arrogant behavior**. Consistent refusal to cooperate with co-workers or supervisors.

- **Inappropriate behavior**. Consistent use of profanity, spreading rumors, or comments of an off-color or sexual nature.

**Level Two**— Moderate-level actions that may merit . Level Two behavior indicates that a problem exists, and must be dealt with before it can escalate into more serious behavior. This includes—

- **Outbursts or "acting out."** Expressing a desire or intent to hurt others, slamming doors, punching walls, vandalism, verbal or written threats, etc.

- **Disobedience**. Open and intentional disregard of company policies and procedures.

- **Non-mutual displays of affection.** Persistent romantic overtures that are clearly one-sided and unwelcome, up to and including light sexual harassment.

- **Theft**

**Level Three**— Severe acts of violence against person or property, including—

- **Minor physical assault**. Hitting, fights, etc.

- **Major physical assault**. Murder, rape, etc.

- **Strong-arm or armed robbery**

- **Arson or major destruction of property**

A person acting inappropriately and violently may encounter a cycle of violence, where he or she goes though a progression. As the outbursts increase in intensity, the cycle can occur more quickly and the outbursts can become more pronounced. It is critical to deal with signs and symptoms of workplace violence as early as possible *before* it escalates into a heartbreaking statistic. See an excellent discussion on workplace violence expert W. Barry Nixon at the end of this chapter.

# Who Causes Workplace Violence?

Acts of workplace violence can come from two sources. First, the acts can be caused by external parties, such as robbery in the workplace by a stranger. In those circumstances, employers have certain duties to maintain a safe and secured workplace.

For purposes of this chapter, the concerns over workplace violence centers on workplace violence carried out by existing employees. Unfortunately, this leaves the employer largely liable for any problems that occur in the workplace under the Negligent Hiring Doctrine.

The Negligent Hiring Doctrine dictates that employers can be held liable for damages if they knowingly employ persons known to pose a potential threat to co-workers or the public. The Doctrine even goes so far as to state that if the employer *should have known* the employee was a threat, the employer is responsible.

That said, the question arises— how can an employer identify a potentially problematic employee?

Here is the problem. There is no magic formula that tells an employer in advance who will and will not be violent. Predicting future violence is a matter of considerable controversy.

However, experts have found some factors that are present in many cases of workplace violence. One important factor is a history of past violence.

For that reason, pre-employment background checks are widely regarded as an effective screening procedure because the process serves three major functions. First, screening job applicants can bring to light problems in a potential hire's past such as a history of violence, harassment, or extremely inappropriate behavior. Second, by making it standard policy to screen all job applicants on their way into the company, employers demonstrate due diligence, showing that all reasonable efforts have been made in determining whether or not the applicant poses a threat to the company or to the public. Third, pro-actively communicated background screening practices cause applicants to opt-out by discouraging prospective jobseekers with criminal or problematic backgrounds from applying. This idea is similar to the way 'We Test All Applicants for Drugs' has a chilling effect on drug users applying for positions.

As discussed in previous chapters, contacting past employers to ask about incidents of past violence may be difficult given the reluctance of many past employers to give any information beyond dates of employment and job title. That is why performing checks for past criminal acts is a critical step.

However, there is more to preventing workplace problems than screening at the door.

Factors in employees' lives change. A person who checked out in an initial screen may over time develop the traits or behaviors indicative of a potentially violent employee. It is up to the employer to maintain a constant eye on conditions and events in the workplace — to stay aware of employee attitudes and concerns in order to ensure the safety and security of everyone involved.

**Opportunity-motivated incidents** occur when an employee feels that he or she can get away with something. The motivation behind the action can vary from rationalization such as "I earned a little bonus, and besides, the boss won't miss $20 from the till" to desperation, "I'm way behind on my rent, and the landlord's going to evict me." With rationale like that, you have an employee who is willing to steal money, equipment, or goods from the employer. This type of action is seldom pre-meditated, occurring usually when the employee has unsupervised access to cash or materials.

**Stress-based incidents** are usually the result of frustration with work-related issues such as problems with management, co-workers, procedures, etc. These problems are often compounded by external stresses, including marital trouble, issues with sick or dependent family members, substance abuse problems.

Most employees who commit acts of stress-related workplace violence are not typically "bad employees." Violent employees can be dedicated, devoted individuals who take their jobs seriously. They can react violently to any perceived threat to work or employment. In a nutshell, their jobs are their life. Therefore, employment-related issues are elevated to "life and death" decisions. As a result, workplace violence often can be caused by the perpetrator's belief that some form of injustice has been inflicted and the violence is an attempt to regain a perceived loss of control or an attempt to get even for the perceived injustice or unfair treatment. If an employee defines their self worth by their job, then a perceived mistreatment by the employer can amount to their devaluation as human beings. The resulting stress that leads to violence can be driven by an intense need to defend themselves against what they perceive as such personal devaluation. Obviously, violence is not an acceptable response to stress, and employers must take appropriate measures to identify and protect against any employees who turn to violence.

A particularly sensitive area is termination. Losing a job can be a traumatic experience for anyone. For those people whose work is their life, termination can potentially set-off a lethal explosion of workplace violence even if the person being terminated had been warned and knew it was coming. As a result, every termination must be handled carefully, taking into account the potential for an outburst. Part of preventing workplace violence is a well thought out termination policy, which can be compiled with assistance from a labor attorney or a human resources consultant.

## What Work-Related Factors Increase the Risk of Violence?

The Canadian Centre for Occupational Health and Safety has assembled a list of examples of factors and situations that increase the potential for risk of workplace violence. The risk list is shown at www.ccohs.ca/oshanswers/psychosocial/violence.html and is also provided below.

### Situational Factors

- working with the public
- handling money, valuables or prescription drugs (e.g. cashiers, pharmacists)
- carrying out inspection or enforcement duties (e.g. government employees)
- providing service, care, advice or education (e.g. health care staff, teachers)
- working with unstable or volatile persons (e.g. social services, or criminal justice system employees)
- working in premises where alcohol is served (e.g. food and beverage staff)
- working alone, in small numbers (e.g. store clerks, real estate agents), or in isolated or low traffic areas (e.g. washrooms, storage areas, utility rooms)
- working in community-based settings (e.g. nurses, social workers and other home visitors)
- having a mobile workplace (e.g. taxicab)
- working during periods of intense organizational change (e.g. strikes, downsizing)

### Timing Factors

Risk of violence may be greater at certain times of the day, night, or year. For example—

- late hours of the night or early hours of the morning
- tax return season
- overdue utility bill cut-off dates

- Christmas
- paydays
- report cards or parent interviews
- performance appraisals

**Geographic Factors**

- near buildings or businesses that are at risk of violent crime (e.g. bars, banks)
- in areas isolated from other buildings or structures

# Preventing Workplace Violence

Unfortunately, there is no cure-all to eliminate the threat of violence. The unpredictable nature of human behavior makes it necessary for employers to keep a close watch on conditions and events in the workplace in order to ensure the safety and security of employees and customers.

This does not mean that employers are powerless to prevent workplace violence – far from it. The Safe Hiring Program (SHP) described in this book includes a range of tools, techniques, and services available to help employers mitigate the risk of hiring or retaining a potentially dangerous employee. The goal is to ensure that hiring managers company-wide follow procedures and pay attention to safe hiring.

Many employers consider background checks and reference checks to be the cornerstone of a Safe Hiring Program, effectively "weeding out" most potentially troublesome employees. By having a policy in place that lets job applicants know the information they provide to the company will be independently verified — and past employers will be contacted and criminal records checks may be conducted to search for any indication of violence in the past — the employer lets the applicant know that the company is serious about preventing problems in the workplace. Those applicants with a history of violent behavior may be considered ineligible for consideration based on past offenses or just simply dissuaded from applying in the first place.

Some employers go so far as to require that employees submit to a psychological profile to be considered eligible for hire. While this practice might indeed identify that an employee may have some obsessive tendencies or a propensity for violent or aggressive behavior, the number of faults with this type of screening immediately outweighs the benefits in all but the most extreme circumstances. For example, a negative hiring decision based on a psychological profile instead of an actual event or offense would be difficult to defend — the report may potentially identify the person as having a 'disability,' thus invoking ADA which explicitly prohibits not hiring someone unless there is a preponderance of current medical or other evidence indicating the person is a direct threat. In addition, the sheer cost of a psychological profile quickly puts the process beyond most employers' budgets. If psychological assessments are used, they should be only a part of all the factors considered among an array of selection processes determining a person's employability.

For the most part, the elements of a Safe Hiring Program are relatively basic, inexpensive, and easy-to-implement steps that, as a whole, can be instrumental in minimizing the potential for problems in the workplace. The typical elements of such a program include development of policies, procedures, and guidelines as well as employee training, policy implementation, and process evaluation.

One critical task is to have a clear workplace violence policy that everyone acknowledges and understands. In this way employees have a clear understanding the employer has a commitment to a safe workplace and enforces a policy that includes training for supervisors and consequences for failing to follow the policy.

An employer establishing a SHP should also assemble a team responsible and accountable for the process. The team should be comprised of employees and professionals from different functional areas to ensure all possible considerations are taken into account regarding the scope of establishing and implementing the program. The team will be responsible for administering the program, including the development and implementation of policy and practices, communicating the policies to all employees within the organization, and training employees in identifying and responding to problems. When or if a crisis occurs, they serve as the employer's response and intervention team.

**Team members** can include—

- Human Resources
- Security
- Attorney
- Psychologist or outside expert on violence

The team will need to address the following subjects—

## Policies, Procedure, and Guidelines

- Establish a detailed, precise definition of workplace violence, citing examples
- Clearly define the company's response to violence, both actual and threatened
- Identify and address all potential problem areas, including security elements currently missing and existing methods of dealing with incidents
- Assess which areas of security should be outsourced to a third-party vendor versus what can be done with the company's existing resources
- Have a termination policy, including policies on how a person is evaluated and terminated, and the physical termination process

## Implementation

- Make appropriate changes to the application/interview/hiring process — background or reference checks, requiring signed applications, etc.
- Communicate all necessary policy and procedural changes to all employees verbally, as a memo, and in the company manual

## Employee Training

- Train employees in recognizing and responding to situations
- Create an environment where employees are encouraged to report potential workplace violence issues, including a guarantee of confidentiality

- Train employees in prevention of possible volatile situations
- Provide an Employment Assistance Program (EAP) to encourage employees with personal problems to seek help
- For employees who are victims of violence or threats, EAP may assist in obtaining stay away orders from the court or police (such as in stalking or domestic violence cases).

### Evaluation

- Periodically audit all employees involved in the hiring process to ensure their adherence to the program.
- Evaluate elements involved in physical security, such as—
  o Making sure that public areas are set up to protect employees and to make them visible. This protects employees from external violence.
  o Consider physical barriers, controlling the number of entrances, controlling access, protective fencing, and adequate lighting and alarms.

### Crisis Response

- Prepare a crisis response plan, taking into account issues of physical security, premises evacuation. The crisis teams should include professionals to assess the stress, security expert to implement an immediate response, and HR and legal assistance to assess what action to take.

# Safe Workplace — Other Important Resources

This chapter was only a brief introduction to the issues involved. There are many excellent websites to assist employers in dealing with issues related to workplace violence. Resources listed below lead to voluminous research and materials on preventing workplace violence—

- www.osha-slc.gov/SLTC/workplaceviolence
  Workplace violence resources and sites from OSHA

- www.ccohs.ca/oshanswers/psychosocial/violence.html
  The Canadian Centre for Occupational Health and Safety

- www.workviolence.com
  Workplace Violence Research Institute

- www.opm.gov/workplace
  Dealing with Workplace Violence,
  A Guide for Agency Planners by the Federal Office of Personnel Management

- www.atapusa.org
  Association of Threat Assessment Professionals

- www.workplaceviolence911.com
  The National Institute for Prevention of Workplace Violence

- www.asisonline.org
  American Society for Industrial Security

# Intervening in Acts of Workplace Violence — the Supervisor's Role

By W. Barry Nixon

As Executive Director of the National Institute for Prevention of Workplace Violence, Inc.[3] and a recognized expert on workplace violence, we encourage preventative efforts and prepare clients to respond appropriately should an incident of violence occur. The adage "an ounce of prevention is worth a pound of cure" was never truer considering an average of 1,000 people annually have been killed on the job since 1990, up from an average of 750 in the 80's. Here is advice for supervisors faced with possible workplace violence situations—

Supervising people is a very challenging job particularly when potential violence enters the picture. The supervisor's job is to intervene when there are job performance and behavior problems. Knowing how to appropriately intervene in situations can make the difference in helping a troubled employee resolve an issue or 'fueling the fire' by mishandling the situation. Being able to resolve conflict situations amicably versus making an employee feel victimized or like he/she 'lost face' is a competence that is undervalued in most companies. Even more importantly, knowing how to de-escalate a hostile situation in today's turbulent workplace where workplace violence is prevalent could actually save your life.

Understanding the fundamental principles of positively engaging employees who are getting upset is an essential skill. First, it is important to understand the dynamics of how people react when they get angry so you know how to intervene.

In the "Normal" stage, a person may have anxiety, but their demeanor is calm and they are able to communicate. As the anxiety level increases, they may enter an "Escalation stage" that may be marked by defensiveness. The physical manifestation can be less rational communication and thought. A person can then enter the "Stress Release stage." During this stage their communication will be the least logical and rational as the stress levels are intensified and they are acting out. Eventually as the person loses steam, the person will enter a "recovery stage" where the tension is reduced.

The goal of intervening is to deal with the issue in the early stages to prevent it from escalating to a crisis level.

The technique we use to de-escalate an angry person is called the Stay Calm System .The system provides a mental roadmap and framework to follow when confronted with a potentially hostile

---

[3] The National Institute for Prevention of Workplace Violence, Inc., www.workplaceviolence911.com. A leader in occupational violence prevention, the Institute serves as a center for research, consulting, training, and communication. Their mission is to educate employers, unions and employees about the growing threat of violence in the workplace and how to effectively deal with it.

person. The three core skills incorporated in the system are active listening skills, asking open-ended questions and staying calm. It is also important to stay focused on what you can do to address the situation and not on what you can't do. By getting these necessary skills in advance you will be prepared and won't have to struggle with how to handle a situation.

Here is a summary of the Stay Calm System—

- Listen, listen and then listen some more
- Value and respect the angry person's view as being real for him/her
- Acknowledge their viewpoint
- Treat him/her in a respectful manner
- Don't let yourself get upset and emotional
- Manage your own behavior
- Avoid accusation and blame
- Be deliberate and conscious in your choice of words and phrases
- Don't take angry comments personally
- Get the person involved in a problem solving dialogue
- Allow the other person to "Save Face"
- Acknowledge the situation, admit mistakes, apologize, and take action

Supervisors need to know that one of the key ingredients in being able to resolve employee problems happens considerably before the situation ever becomes a problem. The development of a positive work environment and trusting relationships with employees are important ingredients that can help supervisors to be able to effectively dialogue with employees about problems. Once a problem arises, it is important that supervisors engage in an exchange of ideas with the employee where each person's view is valued and listened to. It helps to ask open-ended questions and to approach the situation with an open mind as opposed to preconceived notions and/or solutions. For example, say to the employee, "Over the last several months I have observed that your performance has slipped, is there something going on with you that we should talk about?" as opposed to "Your performance is at an unacceptable level and you had better get your act together." Just think about how you would react to these two different statements.

Learning to intervene before the situation escalates to the level of a major problem is also important. In the context of dealing with workplace violence, this means being aware of the 'early warning signs' — red flags that potential violence may be brewing. Many times supervisors prefer to avoid conflict and instead take the ostrich approach, hoping or perhaps praying the situation will go away. Behaviorists consistently report that failing to intervene in situations actually is a major contributor to the problem becoming more severe and may actually have the unintended consequence of putting you more in harms way. This is because these behavior patterns frequently are a cry for help. If the cry is unheard, the person in distress will find other, more aggressive means of calling attention to his or her problem. The key for the supervisor, therefore, is to take prompt action when they see the signs of a problem.

It is equally important to speak with an employee about a performance or conduct issue as close to the time of the incident as possible. If the employee's actions upset you, then your first goal should be to calm yourself down so that you are thinking effectively and non-emotionally. Never attempt to counsel an employee while you are angry. The result will likely worsen the situation.

During counseling, the employee should be treated with dignity and respect. This is especially true when dealing with an employee who may behave angrily or have violent tendencies. Your demeanor is important if you want the employee to understand your message and to follow through. It is best to put aside authority issues to make sure the employee knows you are in charge. Approach the dialogue in a manner that conveys your concern about the employee and your interest in helping. You should focus on assisting the employee and not on blaming or humiliating him or her. The quality of the counseling can make the difference between the employee seeking the help he or she needs or actually escalating the level of anger experienced by the employee.

An important point to understand is an effective counseling session is dependent on preparation. It is useful to have an agenda to guide you through all the points you need to discuss. Prepare for the session by outlining the factual issues you want to discuss. If you did not observe the occurrence personally, then you will first need to obtain information from others who were present and have the written details with you.

Your discussion should focus on *describing* rather than characterizing or judging behavior and conduct. Examples—

- *"You were speaking in a loud voice, and employees at the other end of the office heard you and came to see what was going on"* as opposed to *"you were screaming and out of control"*

- *"You threw the in-box so hard that it broke"* instead of *"you were a wild maniac on a rampage."*

It is important that you let the employee know you are aware that certain behaviors are being demonstrated, and that you need to find out why. By exploring the reason for the occurrence, you may be able to resolve the problem or determine what other actions need to be taken. Try to draw the employee out, and give him or her a full opportunity to express their concerns. It is very important for the troubled employee to feel they are being heard. You can reinforce that you have heard them out by repeating or summarizing the things the employee says. Also be sure to state that the behavior is not acceptable and must change. This does not have to be done in a threatening manner or tone, but more in a manner that is calm and firm.

If an employee demonstrates behaviors that may be indicative of potential violence tendencies, then you should refer him or her to the Employee Assistance Program (EAP.) Actively encouraging the employee to participate in counseling has better results than merely handing the employee a pamphlet. Here is an example of what a supervisor can say to influence the employee to seek counseling—

> "I can see you seem to be very angry, and this situation is bothering you. It troubles me also. I want to make sure you are going to be okay. I know your family wants you to be okay. I think it would be good for you to talk with someone about these problems. You know, someone who's not directly involved may be able to help you figure out what is going on. I have heard some good things about the Employee Assistance Program. Why don't we call them to make an appointment to see if they can help?"

In addition, supervisors should use the EAP as a key management tool. Many EAP contracts allow supervisors to contact the EAP and seek counsel on how to handle difficult employee situations. In essence, a supervisor can get personalized free coaching from behavioral experts in how to handle situations.

While the ultimate goal of counseling employees is to resolve problems and get an employee's performance or conduct in alignment with company standards, the stark reality is sometimes counseling will not succeed. When this happens you can be faced with terminating an employee. This is one of the most unpleasant and challenging situations a supervisor must face. Add to this the spectrum of the employee acting out in a violent manner makes it even more dreadful.

A key point to remember about a violent outbreak is that an individual's reaction to an event, whether real or perceived, is what is real in that person's mind. We also know that one of the top causes for a person to escalate to a violent reaction is the perception that the person has been 'wronged, disrespected, or treated unfairly.' Consequently, one of the basic actions that helps to prevent violent outbreaks during a termination is to make sure the entire process is a respectful one. We need to do this even when we feel the person being terminated does not deserve this treatment because, if we don't, our disrespectful treatment could be the stimulus for violence.

In developing a process that 'maintains the person's dignity,' think about it from the viewpoint of a person being terminated and how he or she will likely view each step of the your firm's process. Thinking about it this way will help you re-align the process from 'business as usual' to one that treats the terminated employee respectfully and allows them to depart with dignity. Blatant examples that violate this principle are: terminating someone in your office and then parading them through a crowded office for everyone to see; having him or her clean out their desk, then escorting them to the door; emailing the person their termination notice.

In the end, a supervisor plays a crucial role in assisting troubled employees to realign their performance to an acceptable level. It can unintentionally contribute to pushing an employee further towards the edge. Learning to treat employees in a respectful manner, maintaining their dignity and treating them in a fair manner is crucial to avoid escalating situations. Ironically, a supervisor can be their own best friend by handling these situations in a positive and pro-active manner which will help bring problematic situations to a winning solution for all involved.

# Chapter 25

# Drug Testing in the U.S.

Drug testing in the workplace is fast becoming a fact of life for many employers. Although the drug testing practice was initially adopted by the Fortune 500 companies, pre-employment drug testing is gaining increasing acceptance in all sizes of businesses looking to keep their workplaces safe and their costs down.

According to a study by the U.S. Department of Labor, drug use in the workplace costs an estimated $75 billion to $100 billion in lost time, absenteeism, accidents and on the job injuries, health care, and workers' compensation claims each year. Sixty-five percent of all accidents on the job are related to drugs or alcohol.

A 2002 survey of illicit drug use by the U.S. Substance Abuse and Mental Health Services Administration (SAMHSA) estimates that approximately 19.5 million Americans, or 8.3 percent of the population aged 12 or older, were considered to be *"current* illicit drug users" in 2002. By SAMHSA's definition, "current" drug use means use of an illicit drug during the month prior to the survey interview.

The National Institute on Drug Abuse reports that 77 percent of drug users are employed. By that math, there are over 15 million illicit drug users in the American workforce.

Almost all of the illicit drug users can be avoided as hires by establishing and enforcing a basic drug-testing program.

# The ABC's of Substance Abuse Testing

## Do I Need to Screen My Employees?

Although drug testing laws vary from state to state — in some cases, from county to county — only a handful of employers are required by law to screen their employees for illicit substances. The majority are in the transportation industry, and they tend to know who they are. For the remainder not bound by federal guidelines, the decision as to whether or not to screen employees is up to the discretion of the employer.

Many positions pose considerable risk to property, personnel, or the public. In these instances, drug or alcohol screening is often considered to be a necessary measure for preventing or mitigating potential mishaps.

## Mandatory Screening

Employers are legally required to screen employees for drugs and alcohol in certain cases, for example, truck drivers are regulated by the Department of Transportation (DOT) and must be tested if they drive a vehicle with a combination weight of over 26,002 pounds, or if the vehicle is designed to transport 16 or more passengers or hazardous materials. Testing requirements exist for workers in other regulated and safety sensitive industries such as aviation, rail, transit, maritime, and pipeline industries.

Another example centers on employers who operate under federal contracts and are subject to mandatory rules for a Drug Free Workplace. That applies to employers who do business with the federal government and have contracts in excess of a set minimum dollar amount.

## Recommended Screening

Employers not legally required to test for drugs or alcohol sometimes choose to require the procedure anyway. Many employers opt to screen employees in particularly safety-sensitive positions, such as any employee who—

- Works closely with children, the elderly, or the disabled
- Has extensive, unsupervised contact with the public
- Is required to operate a vehicle or heavy machinery
- Works in or has access to private residences and businesses
- Handles money or valuables
- Has access to weapons, drugs, or dangerous substances
- Works in a supervisory position

> **Author Tip** ➡ If an employer determines that a drug screening program is necessary, then screening should be implemented universally in order to avoid problems with discrimination.

## Pre-Employment and Post-Employment Drug Screens

Pre-employment drug screens are the most common *tests* used by employers. Courts have consistently upheld the legality of requiring a drug test as a condition of being considered for employment. Employers should consult their attorneys concerning any legal issues involved with drug testing. The federal Department of Labor provides a helpful guide to the laws of all fifty states, which is available online at http://said.dol.gov/StateLawList.asp.

Many employers utilize a single drug screen 'on the way in' to satisfy their requirement for demonstrating due diligence. For the most part, this is true. Screening a job applicant once prior to making a hiring decision does demonstrate that efforts have been made to prevent individuals with substance abuse problems from entering the workplace. However, maintaining a screening program that excludes existing employees from testing makes a potentially fatal presumption that employees' lives do not change past the moment of hire. Factors in any employee's life can change at a moment's notice and bad habits develop quickly. A drug test administered to a new hire on the way in is accurate only up to the moment that specimen was produced.

The decision to screen should be made considering all employees, not just candidates for the job.

## What About Consent?

Prior to the hire, express written consent should be obtained for a pre-employment drug test. When doing post-hire screening, the consent is often covered in the form of workplace rules and policies. Therefore, it is imperative that any firm intending to conduct post-accident testing or probable-cause testing have written polices and procedures in place before attempting to conduct post-hire drug tests.

An effective, comprehensive program covering post-hire testing should address such issues as—

- Communicating to the workforce about the need and advantages of a drug testing program – a safe workplace, lower health costs, improve productivity, etc.
- A well-written policy that has been reviewed by legal counsel
- Proof that all employees have received and are familiar with the policy
- Confidentiality of medical records
- The company's stance on workplace drug or alcohol use, i.e., Zero Tolerance
- The events or times at which testing takes place
- What constitutes a passed or failed drug test
- Having a policy on what to do in the event of a positive test, such as allowing the employee to explain or retest the sample
- Procedures involved if a person is suspected of violating the policy
- The consequences of a violation of the policy
- Options for treatment, counseling and rehabilitation and other employee assistance
- Supervisor training in drug testing procedures and policies
- Using medically approved tests and procedures
- Keeping all tests confidential and maintained separate from the personnel file
- Considering use of a Medical Review Officer (MRO) – mandatory for certain types of testing

Keep in mind that employers of certain size are subject to the rules and regulations of the Federal Americans with Disabilities Act (ADA) as well as similar state rules. Although the current use and abuse of drugs or alcohol is not considered to be a disability – and therefore not protected by the ADA – post-hire drug testing can be a very complicated legal area. Any employer looking to implement a post-hire screening program should first consult an attorney specializing in labor practices.

## Rules for Testing Other Than for Pre-employment?

The three major categories of testing other than pre-employment are *suspicion-less* testing, *post-accident* testing, and *reasonable suspicion* testing. Following are some points to consider.

| | |
|---|---|
| **Suspicion-less Testing** | • Applies to safety sensitive positions<br><br>• Normally government mandated, such as truck drivers, railroad workers, custom workers, security clearance, nuclear workers, jockeys, airline personnel, gas pipeline workers<br><br>• For example, Department of Transportation (DOT) has extensive rules and regulation including contacting past employers, random pools, special rules for testing, and the use of Medical Review Officers (MRO) |
| **Post-accident Testing** | • Announce the program in advance as part of company policy<br><br>• Offer counseling or treatment without fear of reprisal<br><br>• Will test safety sensitive positions<br><br>• Tested only after a serious accident<br><br>• Less intrusive testing possible, e.g. urine instead of blood test |
| **Reasonable Suspicion Testing** | • Employer may test if there is observable phenomena such as direct observation of drug use, or physical symptoms, pattern of abnormal conduct or erratic behavior, arrest for drug related offense, or information provided by credible sources<br><br>• Best practice is to have a drug policy in place and have supervisors formally trained to recognize signs of drug use<br><br>• On the issue of off-duty conduct justifying drug test—does it raise suspicion of on-duty impairment? |

# Not All Drug Tests Are Created Equal

For the most part, drug screens are separated into two categories— DOT (Dept. of Transportation) screens and Non-DOT screens (also called "forensic" or "non-regulated" screens). The two screens vary by criteria.

• In DOT screens, a limited panel of drugs can be tested for only in urine or breath testing with federally-mandated "cutoff levels" at specific times within the employee's time with the company.

- In non-DOT screens, employers are free to select the specimen to be tested — blood, breath, saliva, urine or hair — the panel of substances to be tested against, the cutoff level, and the times or circumstances at which the test may be taken.

DOT regulations require that employers test employees for a specific, limited panel of substances, under specific circumstances—

- Pre-employment
- Random selection
- Reasonable suspicion
- Post-accident
- Return-to-duty
- Follow-up

Typically a "5 panel" NIDA[1] test and DOT tests include—

- Marijuana (THC)
- Cocaine
- Phencyclidine (PCP)
- Opiates such as codeine and morphine, and
- Amphetamines, including methamphetamines

Nearly every testing facility and vendor in the testing industry refers to these five substances as their "basic 5-panel test." When facilities and vendors refer to "panels," they mean the number of substances for which they are screening, i.e. "5-panel" meaning a test for five substances, "10-panel" for ten substances.

Non-DOT drug tests do not satisfy DOT regulations, but the same laws governing privacy and disclosure still apply to these tests. Non-DOT tests can screen for more and different substances than DOT tests, including—

- Barbiturates
- Benzodiazepines
- Methadone
- Propoxyphene
- Methaqualone (Quaaludes)
- Hallucinogens (LSD, psilocybin)
- Designer drugs

---

[1] NIDA is the National Institute of Drug Abuse

## Drug Testing for Non-DOT Employers

While there are all varieties of illicit substances to be found in most major metropolitan areas — and just about anywhere else — most employers screen their applicants for the five most common "street drugs" using the "5 panel" screen. Some employers may replace the PCP screen with a screen for methamphetamines such as ecstasy.

Many additional tests are available on the market, including tests for prescription medications or "designer" drugs. A typical ten-panel screen may test for THC (Marijuana), Cocaine, PCP, Opiates, Methamphetamines (including Ecstasy), Methadone, Amphetamines, Barbiturates, Benzodiazepines, and Tricyclic Antidepressants (TCAs).

However, the standard five-panel screen serves its purpose – it weeds out those applicants found to have those substances in their systems, deters many more potentially problematic candidates from applying, and demonstrates due diligence in the event that an applicant with a substance-abuse problem slips through.

# How Does Drug Testing Work?

As drugs are processed by the user's system, they produce metabolites – substances produced as a byproduct of the user's body metabolizing or "digesting" the drug. While a drug will pass relatively quickly through the user's system, chemical traces of the metabolites produced by the person's body in processing the substance can remain afterwards for days or weeks. In general, drug tests do not screen for the drugs themselves, but instead test the user's system for the metabolites that were derived as a result of the drug passing through the user's system. In other words, drug tests don't test for drugs, instead for what the drugs leave behind.

When looking for evidence of illegal drug use, labs test bodily fluids (usually urine, but sometimes blood or saliva) or hair for traces of drugs or drug metabolites. Alcohol can be detected in blood, but is generally tested for in the breath.

## Drug Detection

Although each drug and each person is different, most drugs will stay in the system about two to four days. As mentioned above, chronic users of certain drugs such as marijuana or PCP may have results detected for up to fourteen days, and sometimes much longer.

The following chart illustrates the average detection window in which traces of drug use can be found in a user's system. While there is some "wiggle room" on either side of the specified time frames, this chart reflects the average retention periods of the average user.

| Drug | Detection Window |
|---|---|
| Marijuana | 3 – 15 days |
| Cocaine | 1 – 3 days |
| Opiates | 1 – 2 days |
| Methadone | 2 – 3 days |
| Phencyclidine | Up to 7 days |
| Amphetamines | 2 – 4 days |
| Barbiturates | Up to 14 days |
| Benzodiazepines | Up to 14 days |

Due to the limited detection windows of most drugs, one would think that the savvy drug user would seek to avoid detection by simply cleaning up for a few weeks prior to an anticipated test. Typically, this is not the case. Instead, a whole industry has surfaced purveying cheats, gimmicks, and products designed to help users defeat drug screening devices.

Laboratories and collection sites have countered this wave of anti-detection innovation with their own methods to determine whether or not the applicant has attempted to alter or replace the test specimen. The table below indicates the most common cheats and the most common countermeasures.

| Cheat | Countermeasure |
|---|---|
| System dilution (drinking excessive water, "flushing" the system) | Specific gravity tests measure the concentration of particles in urine. A significantly reduced result indicates tampering. |
| Specimen substitution (substituting clean urine from another individual or reconstituted "powdered" urine) | Measuring the specimen's temperature immediately can indicate whether or not the specimen was produced prior to or at the time of testing. |
| Prosthetic delivery devices | A firsthand witness is required to successfully prove that an individual used a prosthetic device to administer a false specimen. The usual giveaway is the "clunk" sound the device makes when it contacts the specimen cup. |
| Additives (doping the sample) | Doping the specimen to be tested only results in a polluted specimen, requiring a re-test. |
| Refuting results | An applicant refuting the results of a drug test is entitled to prove his or her innocence by having the specimen re-tested at the laboratory of choice. However, applicants typically are not allowed to retake a test since that simply gives time to clear out the system. |

## Cutoff Levels

The amount of a substance detected during the initial screen is important. The Mandatory Guidelines for Federal Workplace Drug Testing Programs published by SAMHSA (the Substance Abuse and Mental Health Services Administration) indicates a specific cutoff level for each drug. This is the set ratio of drug or drug metabolite to volume of liquid in the specimen that must be found in order for the specimen to legitimately qualify for positive detection. This applies to an initial screen and in a confirmatory screen. In urine analysis, cutoff levels are measured in nanograms per milliliter (ng/mL) – that is, Billionths of a gram of the substance per Thousandth of a liter of urine, more quantitatively translated into Millionths of a gram per liter — in any case, not very much is required for a positive result. Employers held to DOT regulations must follow the SAMHSA cutoff levels for the most commonly tested-for drugs, as follows—

**Initial Test Level (ng/mL)**

| | |
|---|---|
| Marijuana-metabolites... | 50 |
| Cocaine-metabolites... | 300 |
| Opiate-metabolites... | 300* |
| Phencyclidine... | 25 |
| Amphetamines... | 1,000 |

**Confirmatory Test Level (ng/mL)**

| | |
|---|---|
| Marijuana-metabolites... | 15 |
| Cocaine-metabolites... | 100 |

**Opiates**

| | |
|---|---|
| Codeine... | 2000 |
| Morphine... | 2000 |
| Heroin... | 10** |
| Phencyclidine.. | 25 |

**Amphetamines**

| | |
|---|---|
| Amphetamine... | 250 |
| Methamphetamine... | 250 |
| MDMA... | 250 |
| MDA... | 250 |
| MDEA... | 250 |

*25 ng/mL if immunoassay specific for free morphine

** the heroin metabolite is known as 6-acetylmorphine or 6-monoacetylmorphine. Because it rapidly metabolizes into morphine, it is rarely found during a screening.

In other words, if an initial urine screen shows marijuana metabolites in evidence in the amount of 26 nanograms per milliliter, and the cutoff level for marijuana metabolites is 50 ng/mL, the initial screen would come back negative for use of marijuana.

Basically, the more frequently a substance is used, the higher the volume will be seen in the specimen in ng/mL.

In order to suit the company's needs, "acceptable standards" may be established by any private employer. The Federal Workplace standards are not mandatory.

# When Results Are Positive

Labs have extensive procedures to reconfirm a positive test before reporting results to an employer. If a sample tests positive in the initial screening procedures, then the sample is subjected to testing by a **gas chromatography / mass spectrometry (GC/MS). This is considered the state-of-the-art science for the definitive testing of drugs.**

Most drug testing programs use the services of the MRO to review all test results. In the case of a positive result, the officer will normally contact the applicant to determine if there is a medical explanation. Some employers also review abnormal results. For example, a specimen that tests negative for drugs may show signs of having been tampered with. Specific gravity tests can be conducted to measure the concentration of particles in urine, which can indicate an applicant's attempt to mask drugs by drinking excessive fluids.

If the positive test is confirmed, then the job applicant can usually pay for a retesting of the sample at a laboratory of choice. In fact, labs retain all positive specimens they obtain for just that purpose. A re-test with a new sample may have been scheduled after the traces of the drug had been given adequate time to be flushed from the user's system. Certified laboratories will stand behind their results and make expert witnesses available.

# Pros and Cons of Testing Methods

The table below gives an excellent description of the pros and cons of the five most common test methods used by employers.

| Method | How it Works | Pros | Cons |
|---|---|---|---|
| Urine sample at third party collection site | Applicant is sent to third party collection sites. Is given a Chain of Custody (COC) or one is provided at site. Can use one of the national firms,[2] a regional firm, or a local drug-testing lab. The labs should be certified by the Substance Abuse and Mental Health Services Administration (SAMHSA) | There are over 20,000 third party collection sites. Test does not require the employer or HR to be involved in the physical collection procedures. Normally, negatives are returned in 24 hours. | Some employers feel it is unduly intrusive to have applicants provide a urine sample. Test window is only 2 to 4 days for some substances such as cocaine, opiates, and amphetamines. |
| On-site instant kits | The employer collects the urine sample at the job. Through some sort of manipulation, a 're-agent" is introduced into the sample, creating an instant result by some sort of color change. | Instant results. Relatively inexpensive. | If a positive, then the best practice is to send sample or applicant for a test where the results can be analyzed in a lab. Should not use a positive as an indication of drug use without further testing. Requires special care for the operator who handles body fluids. |
| Instant oral test | Relies upon a saliva test. Applicant places receptor in mouth under tongue (which is basically the size of a Q-tip). Operator then manipulates the device in order to place saliva onto a regent pad to view any color change. | Like the on-site instant kit, an instant oral kit is very accurate but less intrusive. | If a positive, then the best practice is to send sample or applicant for a test where results can be analyzed in a lab. Should not use a positive as an indication of drug use without further testing. Requires special care for the operator who handles body fluids. Of limited use past measurement. |

---

[2] national drug testing firms include Quest, Lab Corp, etc.

| Laboratory salvia test | Applicant handles entire procedure, from opening sealed applicator to sealing in a bag, to shipping to a lab. | No handling of body fluids by operators. Much less intrusive than a urine sample. Laboratory testing ensures accuracy. | Slow due to delay in mailing to lab. Not DOT approved as of 01/04. |
| --- | --- | --- | --- |
| Hair testing | Sample of hair is taken from crown of hair and mailed to laboratory. | Extremely accurate and not subject to contamination or efforts to mask the results. Goes back 90 days. | Some people find it an invasion of privacy to cut hair. Test needs sample from the crown of the head, about the size of pencil eraser. Mailing and testing takes longer than other tests and is more expensive. |

# Drug Testing Costs

Most small employers should expect to be able to get a standard, run-of-the-mill, 5-panel screen from a third-party vendor for somewhere in the $40.00 to $60.00 range or, for slightly more money, directly from the detection lab where third parties often receive volume discounts. The fee usually includes the handling and processing of the sample as well as monitoring chain-of-custody — tracking the specimen to ensure at no point is it possible for the specimen to be "switched" — and providing medical review services.

The availability of "home testing" kits — also called "quick and dirty" tests — from the internet is increasing. These products generally cost between $5.00 and $10.00 each, are usually sold by the box, and often allow the employer to "mix and match" the panel of substances for which the applicants will be tested.

These home testing kits, while a little cheaper, do have their drawbacks. First, they are non-DOT compliant, meaning the detection cutoff levels do not have to match those governed by the DOT. Second, the results cannot be confirmed. Positive results cannot be re-tested to confirm the presence of a substance, and negative results cannot be tested for tampering. The biggest drawback to these tests is the employer is required to manipulate the specimen, not to mention also witness the "donation" process in order to discourage cheating.

A final word of caution— all drug-testing results should be maintained on a confidential basis.

# Other Drug Testing Information Resources

This chapter was intended as a brief introduction to employment drug testing. A great deal more information is available from these government or non-profit websites.

- www.samhas.gov— Sponsored by the Substance Abuse and Mental Health Services Administration (SAMHSA), an agency of the U.S. Department of Health and Human Services
- www.nida.gov— Sponsored by the U.S. National Institute of Drug Abuse
- www.dot.gov— U.S. Department of Transportation site, covering tests mandated by that department, commonly referred to as DOT testing
- www.health.org— The national clearinghouse for drug and substance abuse information, sponsored by SAMHSA
- www.drugfreeamerica.org— Information concerning drug abuse and prevention
- www.drugfreeworkplace.org— Sponsored by the Institute for a Drug-Free Workplace
- http://said.dol.gov/StateLawList.asp— Summary of state laws, U.S. Department of Labor
- www.datia.org— Drug and Alcohol Testing Industry Association

# Chapter 26

# A Criminal Record Primer

## Crime and Punishment - The Abridged Version

The following is a brief introduction to the criminal justice system for employers, human resources professionals, and security professionals who utilize criminal records. The purpose is to assist a user in understanding a potential criminal record when making an employment decision. Keep in mind that, in addition to federal law, each state and U.S. territory has its own law. Consequently, our "Abridged Version" is intended as a general introduction to criminal law and procedures only, and users need to take additional steps to understand the appropriate rules and procedures in any relevant jurisdictions.

A crime is an act or omission that is prosecuted in a criminal court by a government prosecutor and can be punished by confinement, fine, restitution and/or a forfeiture of certain civil rights. Legislative bodies such as state legislature or the U.S. Congress decide what acts or omissions are against the law. Such prohibited criminal acts are published by a legislative body as part of a "code." For example, in California, criminal acts are published primarily in the California Penal Code. However, criminal acts can be defined in other codes as well — certain drug offenses are contained in the California Health and Safety Code. Federal crimes are defined in the United States Codes.

When a person is charged with a crime, the plaintiff is the prosecuting attorney who brings the criminal case in the name of The People or the government. In a civil case, a private party brings a tort action for monetary damages.

Here is an example— assume Jack D. Ripper assaults S. Victim with a knife in California. Jack is caught and arrested shortly afterward. If Jack is prosecuted for the crime in state court, the case is called, "The People of the State of California vs. Jack D. Ripper." If S. Victim sued Jack for damages in civil court, then that would be a TORT case. That case would be titled, "S. Victim vs. Jack D. Ripper."

A criminal case can be brought in either a federal court or a state court. When a criminal case is brought in a **state court**, a County Prosecutor initiates it. Every county has its own court. In some circumstances, a local law or ordinance may bring lesser charges by a city or municipal attorney. When charges are brought in **federal court**, a Federal Assistant U.S. Attorney (AUSA), who is part of the United States Justice Department, initiates it.

Some sort of **accusation** initiates a criminal charge. The accusation is typically brought by a prosecuting authority against the person arrested, either pursuant to an arrest warrant or a warrantless arrest by a law enforcement agent who had probable cause to believe a felony had been committed. In the case of a misdemeanor arrest, there is generally a requirement that it be committed in the presence of a law enforcement officer but there are certain exceptions.

Depending upon the jurisdiction, the accusation is commenced with some sort of **charging** document. The charging document may be known by such terms as a complaint, information, or indictment. For serious charges, called a felony, there is typically a "probable cause" determination before a trial in which there is a judicial determination that there is sufficient evidence for a trial to go forward. The standard of proof is just that it is more likely than not that a crime occurred and the defendant committed the crime. This is a much lower standard than proof beyond a reasonable doubt, which is needed in order to achieve a conviction. In some jurisdictions, the probable cause determination is accomplished by some sort of hearing before a magistrate or judge, sometimes referred to as a preliminary or probable cause hearing. In other jurisdictions, and typically in federal courts, there is a **grand jury indictment**.

State courts generally have three levels — the trial courts, an intermediate appellate court, and the highest appellate court. Furthermore, in many states, trial courts are further divided into a lower court[1] and felony trial courts.[2]

Federal courts also have three levels. The federal courts where trials are heard are called a **Federal District Court**. There are 94 Federal District Courts. Each state has at least one district court. Larger states will have up to four district courts. For example, New York state has four district courts– Eastern District, Northern District, Southern District, and Western District. Furthermore, district courts can have various divisions. The Southern District of New York for example has divisions in New York City[3] and White Plains.

The federal courts also have intermediate appellate courts called United States **Circuit Courts**. The U.S. Circuit courts are divided into thirteen circuits. For example, the Ninth Circuit hears appeals from the nine western-most states and two territories, Guam and the Marianas Is.

The highest court in the land is the United States **Supreme Court**, with nine members approved by Congress and headed by the Chief Justice of the United States.

# State Courts

If a person is **convicted** of a crime in STATE court, several things can happen—

1.  **Sentenced to State Prison.** A state prison is an institution that is administered by the state, as opposed to a local county jail. In other words, a state prison will accept a prisoner from any

---

[1] lower courts typically hear misdemeanor and preliminary criminal matters such as probable cause hearings

[2] note that certain states also have higher and lower civil courts, divided by a monetary limit.
Other states have unified the trial court system so there is no upper and lower trial court.

[3] New York City Federal District Court only covers Bronx and Manhattan boroughs. Other boroughs are under jurisdiction of the Eastern Division which includes Queens, Kings, Richmond boroughs and the 2 Long Island counties

county in the state. Sometimes the prison is referred to as the "Big House," such as San Quentin Prison in California, or Sing-Sing in New York. Depending upon your generation, think James Cagney in "White Heat," or Tim Robbins in "The Shankshaw Redemption."

2. **Sentenced to County Jail.** A county jail is run by the local sheriff and accepts prisoners from the local county. Every county, parish, or borough in the U.S. has a local jail.

3. **Fined.** A person convicted of a crime can have a fine imposed.

There are two other important terms to consider— **Probation** and **Parole**.

**Probation**— Probation means in exchange for not giving a defendant his or her full jail sentence, a judge has imposed terms and conditions of behavior on a convicted criminal defendant. Probation occurs on the county level at a state court. Assume for example a defendant is convicted of a drug crime that carries a potential sentence of one year in the county jail. Instead of sentencing the defendant to jail for the entire year, the judge can impose just 90 days, and hold the rest of the sentence in abeyance as long as the defendant obeys the terms of his or her probation.

Typical terms of probation may include—

- Violate no law or ordinance
- Participate in a drug rehabilitation program
- Pay a fine
- Pay restitution, if applicable
- Perform community service
- Submit to search and seizure upon request by a police officer without a warrant or probable cause
- Do not possess any item connected to the crime. For example, in a drug case a person will have a term and condition to not possess drugs or drug paraphernalia

If a defendant violates the probation by not adhering to the terms or conditions, then the defendant can be sentenced to jail for the remainder of the sentence. In other words, when a defendant is on probation, the unused jail time is like a reverse bank account being held in reserve — if he or she misbehaves, then the judge can impose more jail time.

**Parole**— When a person is sentenced to prison, he is placed on parole when released. That is an important difference when compared to probation. If a person violates his parole, then he can be sent back to state prison.

A parole officer is employed by the state, while the local county government employs a probation officer. As a practical matter, parole is out of the hands of the county judge or prosecutor and is instead handled by the state.

The actual sentence a defendant receives in state court depends upon a number of factors. There may be minimum or maximum penalties set forth by statute. For certain crimes, a defendant is not eligible for probation and MUST go to state prison. This can occur where the crime is serious such as certain sexual offenses or an offense using a weapon, or where by statute the person is classified as a repeat offender, such as a third strike in a three-strike case.

If a defendant is eligible for probation, a court will look a mitigating and aggravating factors of the crime and factors about the defendant to determine if probation is appropriate. If a person is sentenced to prison and a court has some sentencing discretion in terms of the length of sentence, the court again looks at mitigating and aggravating facts about the offender and the offense. A mitigating factor may be for example a lack of a record, the young age of a defendant, or the defendant's minor role in the offense. Example of aggravating factors are 1) the defendant has a history of committing offenses, 2) committed an offense while on panel or probation, 3) the offense was particularly violent.

# Federal Crimes and Federal Courts

Persons convicted in federal court and sentenced to prison fall under the authority of the Federal Bureau of Prisons (BOP). The BOP operates a federal prison system throughout the United States. Think of such institutions such as the old Alcatraz Federal Prison that housed such famous federal prisoners as the Birdman of Alcatraz and Al Capone, or the well-known Leavenworth Federal Penitentiary in Kansas, or "Club Fed," the popular name for the low security federal institutions where Watergate Conspiracy participants and white collar criminals like Martha Stewart have spent time.

Federal prisoners currently serve about 87% of their sentence. The remaining portion can be spent on parole, supervised by the U.S. Probation office. Federal defendants not sent to prison are supervised by the U.S. Probation office and subject to probation terms and conditions.

Similar to state systems, a federal defendant can also be sentenced to a federal version of probation. This may include "local time" on a supervised program under the direction of a federal probation officer.

The maximum and minimum sentences for federal crimes are set forth in the code section defining the crime. The factors that go into a sentence — and that serve to mitigate or aggravate a sentence — are found in the Federal Sentencing Guidelines.

# Crimes Are Classified Into Three Distinct Categories

1. A **Felony** is a serious offense that is punishable by a sentence to a state prison. Note the use of the word **punishable**, as opposed to actually **punished**. The distinction is important because a person can be convicted of a felony but may not go to prison. How does that work? Depending upon the state and the crime, there are certain felonies wherein a judge can give a defendant **felony probation**. This typically occurs with a relatively less-serious felony committed by a relatively less-serious offender. An example may be a first time felony drug offender convicted of a less-serious drug offense such as possession of a small amount of drugs for sale.

   If a defendant receives felony probation, the court can still sentence him to custody but in the local county jail. If the defendant violates his probation, the court then has the option of sending the defendant to state prison. That obviously creates a great deal of incentive for a felony defendant to not violate probation.

2. A **Misdemeanor** is a less serious offense that is only punishable by local jail time at the county level. Typically a misdemeanor may be punishable by up to one year in the county jail in the custody of the local county sheriff and a fine up to $1,000. A court can also impose terms and conditions of probation such as discussed above.

3. An **Infraction** is a public offense punishable only by a fine. This is typically a traffic violation such as an illegal left turn, speeding, or seat belt not fastened.

Actually there is a fourth category — Wobblers. The term designates an offense that can be either a misdemeanor or a felony offense, depending upon how the prosecuting attorney chooses to file the charges or how a judge views the offense or the offender. In California for example, a commercial burglary can be either a misdemeanor or a felony.

The table below indicates how state court offenses are carried out—

### State Court Offenses Table

|  | **Sentence** | **Supervisor** |
|---|---|---|
| **Felony** | State prison or local jail time or felony probation | If sentenced to prison – placed upon parole upon release from state prison and supervised by a parole officer. If given probation – supervised by local probation office. |
| **Misdemeanor** | Up to one year in a local county jail | If probation – supervised by local probation officer who works for the county where the sentence is imposed. |

# Criminal Sanctions

There are five general purposes for criminal sanctions.

1. **Punishment.** When a person violates the rules of society, imprisonment is used for pure punishment and revenge.

2. **Deterrence of others.** By punishing an offender, there is a possibility that others will be deterred from committing criminal offenses because they can see that such behavior results in certain punishment.

3. **Deterrence of the criminal in the future.** There is also an element of personal deterrence. If a person learns that criminal activity will result in punishment, then he or she may be less likely to commit a crime in the future.

4. **Rehabilitation.** Part of any sentencing scheme can be the goal of using punishment to effect rehabilitation. With the goal of dissuading future criminal conduct, the rehabilitation can be

either by means of personal deterrence as noted above, or use some program intended to actively assist an offender to resolve problems that create criminal behavior, such as a mandatory drug program or educational program.

5. **Protecting society.** Another use of punishment is to simply warehouse offenders so they cannot harm society.

# Other Important Criminal Record Terms

**Arrest vs. Conviction** — In discussing criminal records, it is also important to note the critical difference between an **arrest** and a **conviction**.

An **arrest** is an action by a police officer in taking a person into custody on suspicion of having committed a criminal violation. An arrest does not always result in a person being taken to jail. An arrest can also be a citation to appear in court.

A **conviction** occurs where there has been a factual adjudication of guilt. That can be done by a jury trial where 12 jurors[4] make a finding of guilt beyond a reasonable doubt. Or, a person can be found guilty by a judge in a court trial, where a judge makes the decision if the defendant waives the right to a jury trial. Guilt can also be judicially established where a defendant admits his or her guilt. This can occur when a defendant pleads *guilty* to the criminal charge. It can also occur if a defendant pleads *no contest*. In criminal courts, a no contest is the same as a guilty plea, but gives a defendant some protection in the event of a civil law suit.

**Delayed Adjudication/First Offender Programs** — Numerous states have case disposition rules that are somewhere between an arrest and a conviction. These can occur in a number of situations.

For example, some states have a disposition called a *Diversion Program*. This occurs where a first offender for a relatively less serious offense is literally "diverted" from the criminal justice system, and allowed to escape the criminal charge if he or she participates in and successfully completes certain court assigned tasks such as a counseling program or volunteer service. One of the most famous diversion case participants is O.J. Simpson. Prior to the death of his wife, Simpson was charged with domestic violence and allowed to participate in a domestic violence diversion program.

States also have diversion programs for such offenses as petty theft or drug use. If there is a violation of the terms of the program or a new arrest, then the court may terminate the diversion and re-instate charges, and the criminal case begins again.

A variation of the diversion program is a *delayed entry of judgment program*. In that program, the defendant actually enters a guilty plea to the offense. However, the court delays entry of the judgment in order to allow the defendant to participate in a prescribed program, which may include a course of counseling and volunteer work. Upon the successful completion of the court's requirements without having any additional violations, the criminal matter is dismissed. In some jurisdictions, there are special drug courts where defendants are given the opportunity to by-pass criminal drug charges if they participate in one or various programs.

---

[4] typically there are 12 jurors, but certain courts allow less

Many jurisdictions have first offender programs where a court will discharge the defendant and set aside the conviction upon completion of various conditions, as though the arrest and/or conviction had never occurred. The primary condition is often that the defendant must not get arrested again, or must stay away from a particular person. This is often used as a means of dealing with less serious misdemeanor offenses.

**Post-Offender Programs** — Many states also have various provisions to seal, expunge or somehow ease a criminal conviction *after* it occurs. Some states have procedures by which an offender can receive some sort of state pardon or a governor's pardon. There are procedures to have criminal records legally sealed, expunged, or judicially erased in some other fashion.

California has a provision called Penal Code section 1203.4, under which a misdemeanor offender who successfully completes probation can move to have his conviction set-aside and to be relieved of all penalties and dualities. Under California law, an employer may not consider the offense when making an employment decisions.

Under another California law, Labor Code Section 432.7, an employer has the following restrictions—

> *No employer, whether a public agency or private individual or corporation, shall ask an applicant for employment to disclose, through any written form or verbally, information concerning an arrest or detention that did not result in conviction, or information concerning a referral to, and participation in, any pretrial or post trial diversion program, nor shall any employer seek from any source whatsoever, or utilize, as a factor in determining any condition of employment including hiring, promotion, termination, or any apprenticeship training program or any other training program leading to employment, any record of arrest or detention that did not result in conviction, or any record regarding a referral to, and participation in, any pretrial or post trial program.*

Another type of program is called "deferred adjudication." Texas, for example, has a system whereby a person enters a guilty plea and a judge may defer the adjudication of guilt pending completion of a probation period. Upon completion of the deferred adjudication, the individual may request that the case be set aside. Tex. Code Crim. Proc. art. 42.12 provides further that the dismissal and discharge under this section may not be deemed a conviction for the purposes of disqualifications or disabilities imposed by law for conviction of an offense.

For additional state court procedures affecting the status of criminal convictions, see Chapter 11.

Keep in mind that usually these post-conviction processes do not result in a record being physically removed from the court's computer system. Once a unit of government creates a record, it is unlikely that anyone will physically destroy or delete it. It is unlikely that a clerk's office will have access to a "case delete" button, which means in most instances the record still exists. Even if a judge orders a record to be physically sealed, there is normally going to be some sort of record of the case somewhere in the public domain — the case number and the defendant's name will remain in some computerized index, which is available to a court researcher. In those instances the court record and the court public index will normally include documentation that there has been some sort of judicial or executive action to lessen the offense through some post-judgment procedure. If a screening firm comes across such a record, a competent screening firm should have a procedure in place to not report such a conviction. However, if an employer does his own search of the court records and comes across such a record, the employer is asked to wipe their own memory clean.

Another new wrinkle is Drug Courts. Drug courts use a post-conviction procedure where a court closely monitors and supervises a defendant with a personal drug abuse problem or who is accused of a drug-related crime. The court gives a defendant the opportunity to participate in a program and upon successful completion the defendant is relieved from criminal sanctions.

---

### Un-Ringing the Bell

In TV land, a lawyer makes an inflammatory statement in front of a jury, knowing it is inadmissible, prompting the other side to noisily object. The judge admonishes the jury to disregard the last comment. Of course, the jury heard it and the offending lawyer continues as though he scored some sort of victory. The TV viewer is wondering how a jury is supposed to un-remember something they just heard. Sometimes in court this is referred to as "un-ringing the bell." Once a bell has rung, it is hard to take it back. Another analogy is – how do you get a jury to not remember the word elephant after elephant is mentioned?

This happens much more on TV than in real life. In real life, judges take a dim view of lawyers who try to insert inadmissible evidence or arguments before a jury. In fact, judges have a great deal of latitude in making lawyers who do that sort of "unauthorized dramatics" regret having done so.

Employers can find themselves in a similar position. If they come across a record they cannot use or consider, how do they ignore it? If the record was located by in-house security or the HR Department, then the record should not be passed on to a hiring manager or a person with hiring authority. That of course assumes HR or internal security has received the proper training to recognize an impermissible record, and that there are policies and procedures in place.

---

## Conclusion— When Using Criminal Records

As the old saying goes, the devil is in the details. Although this chapter may assist employers in gaining an overall understanding of the criminal justice system, each and every case an employer encounters must be analyzed individually depending upon the state involved.

In order to analyze the meaning of a criminal record, an employer or background firm may also have to actually pull the case file to locate details. This is discussed in more detail in Chapter 12.

# Chapter 27

# Background on The Pre-Employment Screening Industry

Many employers outsource their pre-employment screening needs to professional service providers. In this chapter we will find out why, and what you should know if you do.[1]

The pre-employment screening industry has grown substantially in the past 25 years due to demand for service and advances in technology and widespread data availability, making large-scale screening possible. Although there is no exact count of the number of firms that provide employment-screening services, industry observers estimate that there are literally thousands of firms that are involved in some level of background screening. Firms range from large, publicly held companies to retired police officers and other one-person services. Using an internet search engine to look up the keyword "employment screening" or "background checks" will take an employer to literally thousands of web pages. Many firms are in adjacent industries such as security, human resources, drug or psychological testing, or payroll, and offer screening as a secondary service.

## A Multi-Billion Dollar Industry

The size of the employment screening industry has been estimated anywhere from two billion to five billion dollars.

The industry can be roughly broken down into four tiers—

**Tier One:** There are five tier one firms that can be distinguished in terms of revenues and assets. In alphabetical order, they are– Avert (part of ADP), ChoicePoint, First Advantage, Kroll, and United States Information Services. It is estimated that these top five firms each do nearly a billion dollars in sales of background screening services.[2] Tier one firms dominate in terms of technology, branding, breadth of services, resources, and the ability to provide large-scale, cost-effective solutions for large employers.

---

[1] for Frequently Asked Questions about working with a screening firm, see Chapter 28

[2] for analysis and data, see www.kpmgcorporatefinance.com/us/pdf/bkgd_screen.pdf

**Tier Two:** While substantial in size and revenue, tier twos are not as large as the tier one players. Tier two firms can roughly be placed in the 10 million to 50 million dollar sales range.[3] Tier two firms are characterized by large investments in technology and deep resources, and like the tier ones, tier twos have the ability to service large employers.

**Tier Three:** These are smaller firms with revenues roughly in the 1 million to 10 million dollar range. Typically, tier three firms have strong regional footprints as well as some national clients. Sometimes considered "boutique" firms, tier threes can compete in the screening marketplace by virtue of some niche service or a high level of customer service particularly within their geographical footprint. Many tier threes have begun offering technology solutions like their tier one and tier two competitors. A tier three's emphasis is less on being a low cost "data vendor" and more on customer service.

**Tier Four:** These are very small firms or sole practitioners that primarily serve a small local area. Tier four firms are typically private investigators, retired law enforcement, franchisees or agents of larger firms, or one and two person offices. Challenges for these firms include keeping up with advancing technology and staying on top of legal compliance issues.

# Industry Ratings

There has only been one published industry rating. The ratings are contained in a 467-page research report prepared by the Intellectual Capital Group, a division of HR.com. The report, titled *The 2002 Buyers' Guide to Drug Screening and Background Checking*.[4] was launched on November 19, 2002.

This report provides a comprehensive analysis of drug testing and background screening for Human Resources professionals, including a review and ratings of service providers. This was the first independent survey and rating of firms providing these services.[5]

The National Association of Professional Background Screeners (NAPBS), discussed later in this chapter, has plans to implement an accreditation system for screening firms. To earn an accreditation a screening firm would first be audited for compliance with various industry best practices.

---

[3] since tier two firms are primarily privately held, it is difficult to estimate revenue

[4] *The 2002 Buyers' Guide to Drug Screening and Background Checking* is available from www.HR.com. The in-depth industry report sold for $2,495.00.

[5] The report only rated firms that responded to requests for information. As an example, the report gave Employment Screening Resources (ESR) the highest rating - 19 out of a possible 20 - based upon an industry rating of service details and capabilities, facts about the company, and ESR's overall value proposition. By way of disclosure, the author of this book is the president of ESR.

# The Role of the Pre-Employment Screening Industry in the American Economy

Some courts and public officials have attempted, in recent years, to limit screening firm's access to public records in the mistaken belief that such restrictions protect privacy and serve the public good. Nothing could be less accurate.

Although screening firms are certainly private enterprise firms, the background screening industry operates under the strict guidelines of the federally-mandated Fair Credit Reporting Act (FCRA), which fully protects the rights of consumers and serves several critical national functions.

**The background screening industry—**

1.  helps employers comply with the legal hiring standards set by state and federal law.

2.  plays a critical part in helping public and private employers to comply with legal hiring standards in order to avoid legal exposure for negligent hiring

3.  makes a safer workplace for customers and employees, and helps employers avoid the nightmares associated with workplace violence, theft, hiring based upon fraudulent credentials, or hiring terrorists.

4.  plays a critical part in the homeland security effort by acting as a private sector version of law enforcement, but highly regulated by federal and state laws.

5.  improves both the profitability and productivity of American business by helping employers make better hiring decisions and lowering the high cost associated with employee turnover. This helps the U.S. economy.

These essential functions cannot be performed without reliable and timely access to criminal history information and public records. It is critical for employers, legislators, the courts, and public officials to understand that background screening is not in the same category as "data miners" and other entities who are "data profiteers." Screening firms provide a crucial public function in a highly-regulated environment where consumers have a full array of rights and remedies.

When providing background reports, screening firms do not work in an *inappropriate* manner to prevent employment for applicants with minor violations or misdemeanors unrelated to the work to be performed. As part of the hiring process, applicants have the opportunity up front to disclose minor violations and provide an explanation about such incidents.

The screening process ultimately works to *appropriately* prevent employment in those cases where 1) someone lies on an employment application or during the interview process, 2) the applicant or employee has criminal violations that may have serious consequences with respect to the integrity of job performance, or 3) does not have the claimed credentials needed for the position sought.

The Fair Credit Reporting Act (FCRA), which is the gold standard of privacy and consumer protection, controls the operations of background screening firms. Screening firms only obtain information on "consumers" who have given their full written authorization and have received an extensive written disclosure. Background reports are governed by detailed procedures designed to provide accuracy, transparency, and accountability.

Rules for the screening industry also include an extensive procedure to give consumers notice of any adverse information and recourse in the event a consumer considers any information contained in a consumer report to be inaccurate or incomplete. Consumers have a right to obtain reports and to have anything re-investigated that they disagree with. Furthermore, consumers are protected by the rules of the Equal Employment Opportunities Commission (EEOC) as well as numerous state laws.

Unreasonable restrictions on screening firms have only served to harm employers and taxpaying citizens seeking employment. When a public record-holder deletes dates of birth from files and the public index, they have inadvertently removed the primary identification – the date of birth – used by a screening firm to make a determination if a record belongs to a particular applicant. Although it is understandable that courts would desire to protect Social Security Numbers, masking a date of birth does not promote privacy or consumer protection, but only serves to delay employment decisions. This delay can ultimately hurt the very consumer who has signed a consent form and wants the potential employer to have the information. Other government restrictions and impediments that serve to hurt employers *and* job applicants are lengthy delays in providing access to public records and excessive court fees.

Conclusion— Employers depend upon pre-employment reports to make safe hiring decisions and to show due diligence to avoid litigation. Unreasonable restrictions to access public records (pursuant to the signed consent and authorization of an applicant) only work to the benefit of criminals, terrorists, and cheaters, and to the detriment of employers, employees, honest citizens, and taxpayers.

# How Pre-Employment Screening Companies Perform Their Tasks

Although there is no standard industry terminology, two separate terms can be used — PROFILE refers to all information about an applicant. The term ORDER means a particular search, such as a search in Santa Clara County, California, for a criminal record, or contacting the University of Kansas to verify a former student's past education. *One profile may contain a number of orders.*

When assembling and evaluating data on applicants, background firms fundamentally perform tasks in six areas—

## 1. Accept Requests from Employers

Usually, employers place their applicant background requests via fax or online. An employer placing requests online must certify to the background firm, pursuant to the FCRA, that the employer has and will retain the applicant's written authorization, and the applicant has been given an FCRA disclosure.[6] If the online request also includes an order for an employment or education verification, then written

---

[6] see Chapter 6 for full details about FCRA

consent form may still be necessary in order to allow the background firm to contact those schools or employers who require consent.

Background firms not using an online system to manage the workflow generally use a paper-based system where all work is monitored manually. A physical file is maintained for each applicant. The screening firm must wait to receive back information on each order and then enter the results into a written report to present to the employer. Each manual step adds time to the overall process and increases the possibility of clerical errors.

## 2. Engage in Various Workflows to Fulfill the Requests

Once a request for a screening is put into progress, each order must be routed to the proper source in order to obtain the information. For firms with a software system, the orders are normally routed automatically to the proper source. For background firms without a software system, some delays can occur.

The following is a brief description of some of the workflows involved—

### Criminal records from state courts

When a screening firm receives an order for a criminal search, the order is normally transmitted to the researcher who specializes in that specific court. Available to background firms is an entire industry — a virtual subculture — of court researchers covering every court in America, typically providing a turnaround time within 48 hours for record search requests. Some of the larger background firms have their own employee networks or hire court researchers to work for them. In most cases, court researchers work for multiple background firms. Again, employers may find that their report requests are subject to delay if they use screening firms that do not utilize web-enabling software.

Another important issue is determining who is in charge of reporting criminal hits to employers. Employers need to be certain that any criminal hit is reviewed by a knowledgeable member of the screening firm's staff. The complicated legal and factual determinations of what is and is not reportable should not be made by court researchers who are from all walks of life, including PIs, genealogists, and abstractors who have gone into the public record retrieval business. They are typically not lawyers, paralegals, or HR professionals. Their expertise is in looking for names and understanding court record indices. They are generally not experienced in the legal ramifications to the end users.

### Driving records, credit reports and Social Security trace reports

For the most part, background firms use online access to obtain these reports in a matter of moments, and can quickly pass results electronically to their clients by using a seamless business to business interface.

Although there are a few states where driving records cannot be obtained instantly, the majority of states do have instant access. Credit reports, if ordered online, offer immediate results. A Social Security trace can be immediate also, although it may entail additional time and workflow if an employer is using the trace to determine where to search for criminal records.

Some background screening firms offer enhanced software features that will automatically place orders for these specialty reports.

### Credentials verification – employment, education, and licenses

When an employer requests a credentials verification, the background firm must typically route the request to the specific company employee, department, or vendor handling these requests. Again, a firm with software systems is in a better position to track and manage the process. Firms without software systems must manually handle papers and files which can take longer.

## 3. Track the Status of All Orders and Manage Handling Delays

While the orders are being processed in various workflows, a screening firm must be able to track in real time the status of each order and keep the employer informed. Background firms with online systems give employers an advantage — the employer goes online to see the exact progress of each order and the likely time of completion. If there is a delay, then the employer is told exactly what is causing the delay.

It is important to understand that, for certain searches, there may be delays beyond the control of anyone. Hiring famous detective Sam Spade would not get results any sooner.

Sources of delays can be—

a.  Where courthouses require that the researcher give the county clerk a list of names to search and the county clerk in turn gives the researcher an estimated turnaround time. When there is a possible "hit," then the clerk needs to pull the file. No one has control over how long a court clerk takes to provide information. Court delays can be caused by the courthouse being closed for a holiday.

b.  The date of birth is required to obtain or verify some information has not been provided.

c.  On employment verifications, an employer may not return calls despite repeated attempts, or a past employer cannot be located, has no records, has moved or is no longer in business. After three attempts it is unlikely an employer will respond.

d.  On education verification, school record checks can be delayed where the school is closed or on break, or verification can only be done by mail, or advanced fee prepayment is required.

The critical part for employers is that they have real-time updates and status reports on any source of delays. They need to know the report is being worked on and when the information is expected back.

## 4. Assemble Orders into an Applicant Profile

From the screening firm's point of view, each aspect of the order must be monitored and usually completed within 72 hours. From the point of view of the employer, individual orders are not as relevant as obtaining the entire profile as soon as possible so a hiring decision can be made.

The profiling function requires a screening firm to re-assemble each order into a comprehensive report. Firms with more advanced software are able to assemble each of the components into a report automatically and quickly. If assembling reports becomes a manual process, then expect some lag time.

## 5. Provide the Profile Report to the Employer

How fast and how efficiently the employer receives the entire applicant profile is what separates the good screening companies from the not so good. Firms with sophisticated software programs that automatically send updates and final reports may provide a time advantage, but the real issue of concern to employers is— does the screening firm review what is being sent *or* does the screener's software merely sends raw data automatically to the employer? Firms that tend to be essentially data vendors simply dispense completed reports without review or "flag" potential areas of concern.

## 6. Handling Data "Exceptions"

The majority of consumer reports come back "clear." When there is a "hit," the employer may need assistance. A "hit" means the screening firm has located information potentially derogatory or adverse. This information may be derogatory on its face alone, such as a criminal record. There can be other instances when information only becomes derogatory when it is compared to other data. For example, if the screening firm reports the applicant was employed for a two-year period, that information alone is not derogatory. If the applicant falsely claims her or she was at the job for four years, then the report data could be adverse.

It is important for an employer to clearly understand how their screening firm operates. Some screening firms operate solely on the data vendor approach, giving employers whatever they find as a data pass, without regard to the limitations of federal or state laws, or without making any attempt at flagging potential discrepancies or providing any assistance regarding the use of the data. Other firms, though, follow a service model that has a policy of not providing employers with information they cannot legally possess.

Even though a screening firm cannot give legal advice, an employer may at least expect general industry guidance and some advice on the issues to consider. If the employer decides not to hire the applicant, then the employer may need assistance with the adverse action procedures; see Chapter 6 on adverse action procedures under the FCRA.

> **Author Tip** ➡ Chapter 10 contains more information on how to find and choose a screening firm. For Frequently Asked Questions about working with a screening firm, see Chapter 28. Appendix 3 has a form employers can use to request a bid for services from screening companies. The form is called an **RFP** – Request For Proposal.

# The Growth of the Industry— an Eyewitness Account

The pre-employment screening industry is relatively new. Industry consultant Bruce Berg[7] has been involved in the industry since 1990. The article below gives the history of the employment screening industry from his point of view.

## Background Checks— From an Afterthought to a Real Industry

By Bruce Berg

For twenty years as an executive for several Fortune 500 companies, I always would challenge my Human Resource Manager with the question "Isn't there some way we could have checked out this loser *before* we hired him!?" The response was always a blank stare. HR just had not been taught about background checks. Their job was to fill the position with the best candidate. The problem was they had to judge the candidate mostly on feelings because there was no easy way to verify that the candidate was, in fact, who they claimed to be.

In 1990, I was looking for a business opportunity and found a tiny company that was doing just this. They could check criminal, credit, address history, prior employment, education, workers' comp history, and professional licenses. For me this was a "Wow" — a company offering these "application verification" services actually existed! I though this would be a slam-dunk business success. What company wouldn't want this information? So I jumped into the screening industry.

What I very quickly learned was that while the security and loss prevention people understood the concept, it was an anathema to the HR side. Screening firms had to educate the profession as they improved their ability to provide relevant information. Industry software was developed that allowed customers to manage their search requests. All this time screening firms kept educating HR professionals through marketing, trade shows, and advertising in industry publications such as *HR Magazine, HR Executive Magazine,* and *Security Management Magazine.*

In 1995 the industry experienced heavy growth. What made it all happen? The increased demand for services came from a combination of things, including more and more negligent hiring lawsuits, big stories in the general press about people who were harmed by ex-cons who worked

---

[7] Berg Consulting, www.bergconsultinggroup.com

for companies that did not know the employee's past. Better and quicker access to county criminal data via the local court researcher networks was developed, violence and safety in the workplace became issues along with drug-free workplace programs, education sessions at SHRM and ASIS conferences — and more and more companies began offering these services. The "big boys" in the industry in the '80s and early '90s were doing background checks as a sideline. A number of small firms that jumped in and specialized in background checks helped to create an industry.

In 1997 the changes to the Federal Fair Credit Reporting Act defined us as Consumer Reporting Agencies and, while we were all at first uncomfortable operating under this law, once implemented, it really did tend to further legitimize the industry and create some much needed standards. It also brought a lot of national press to hiring issues and the need for pre-employment screening.

The screening industry grew dramatically between 1991 and 1998. Such fast growth attracted investor attention and the consolidation in the industry went into full swing. At the same time, because of the increased demand, more and more companies got into the business all serving to educate the end-user regarding the need and the value of screening. After 9/11, the words "background checks" were on everyone's lips. In 2002, at a pre-employment screeners conference, a grass roots call was made for a professional organization. As a result, the National Association of Professional Background Screeners was formed by some very dedicated members of the industry.

Now we are a full-fledged industry with estimated annual sales of $4-5 billion. There are about 1800 companies offering background checks to employers, from the smallest one person company through mid-sized and even very large-sized companies, some of them public firms. These companies have an established industry infrastructure with half a dozen suppliers of ready made software from which to choose. There are now several information wholesalers selling county criminal checks, prior employment verifications, education verifications, and even an instant, though limited, multi-state database of criminal convictions. The end user can order checks via the web, modem, fax, phone, or email. They can order a single search or submit the entire application to the background checking company, or simply send their candidates to the vendor for screening. The end user can receive back the results in various formats, including the actual details of the background check, a summary narrative, a "hire-no hire decision" or even a numeric score. Candidates can now pay to have his background pre-screened and certified via the web before even applying for a job.

Today the HR manager has a quick, easy, comprehensive outsourcing avenue to screen out the adverse employee. This is not just common practice; it has become a key tool in the pre-hire process — so key, in fact, that many HR departments have progressed to doing a preliminary screen on their applicants even before they invest their time in the interview process. Forewarned is forearmed.

# NAPBS— The Industry Trade Association

One of the most exciting developments in the pre-employment screening industry was the emergence of the first industry non-profit trade association in 2003. Called the National Association of Professional Background Screeners or NAPBS, the new association attracted nearly 300 of the nation's leading pre-employment screening companies. The association's website is found at www.NAPBS.com.

Per the website, the mission of NAPBS is—

> "The National Association of Professional Background Screeners (NAPBS) exists to promote ethical business practices, promote compliance with the Fair Credit Reporting Act and foster awareness of issues related to consumer protection and privacy rights within the background screening industry.

> The Association provides relevant programs and training aimed at empowering members to better serve clients and to maintain standards of excellence in the background screening industry.

> The Association is active in public affairs and provides a unified voice on behalf of members to local, state, and national lawmakers about issues impacting the background screening industry."

NAPBS began through the efforts of many people. Steve Brownstein, the editor of *The Background Investigator* (www.search4crime.com), a newspaper devoted to the screening industry, held the nation's first screening industry conference in Long Beach, CA in April, 2002. Brownstein encouraged the attendees to think in terms of a national association in order to promote and protect the screening industry. Sandra Burns agreed to head a committee to look into the possibility of forming an association. In November, 2002, Brownstein and *The Background Investigator* sponsored a large national conference in Tampa, Florida, attended by over 175 screening professionals. At this meeting there was widespread support for the formation of an association. Michael Sankey of BRB Publications joined Sandra Burns as a member of the interim board along with Bill Brudenell, Charlotte O'Neill, Jack Wallace, author Les Rosen, and Mike Cool. Les Rosen was designated chairperson of the steering committee that formed NAPBS. The interim board, along with other interested members of the screening industry, met in Arizona in January, 2003 and again in Washington D.C. in April, 2003. The interim Membership and Ethics committee met in Dallas, Texas in the Spring of 2003.

A membership drive was held in the last half of 2003, resulting in over 200 members. In order to provide seed money for the group, in early 2003 several screening firms stepped forward and generously donated the necessary funds to launch the association and to retain the services of a professional management firm.

NAPBS began its first full year of operations with an elected Board of Directors in 2004. There are now over 500 NAPBS members.

The first elected NAPBS Board of Directors is—

David Hein, **Co-chairman**

Les Rosen, **Co-chairman**

Jason B. Morris, **Co-chair elect**

Mary Poquette, **Co-chair elect**

Katherine Bryant, **Secretary**

Barry Nadell, **Co-treasurer**

Catherine Aldrich, **Co-treasurer**

Kevin G. Connell

Ann Lane

Larry Henry

Michael Sankey

A number of standing committees are also in operation—

Ethics/Accreditation

Finance

Membership

Provider Advisory

Best Practices and Compliance

Government Relations

Public Awareness and Communications

Resources Library

# First NAPBS Conference[8]

The first NAPBS conference was held in Scottsdale, Arizona in 2004. According to the NAPBS website at www.napbs.com—

Scottsdale, AZ, March 30, 2004— On March 29 and 30 more than 225 individuals representing over 175 companies converged on Scottsdale, AZ for the inaugural Annual Conference of the **National Association of Professional Background Screeners** (NAPBS).

**NAPBS** was formed to promote a greater awareness among employers nationwide of the growing importance of conducting background and reference checks. According to David Hein, NAPBS Board Co-chair, "It is estimated that fewer than 35% of employers are currently screening their applicants. Yet every day headlines across the country highlight the sometimes dire consequences that may result when prospective employees' backgrounds aren't thoroughly checked."

The Association's members are companies from across the country who provide *pre-employment/background screening, court records research, and tenant screening services.* Employers can be assured they are dealing with a screening firm that subscribes to the organization's goals and standards if the **NAPBS** logo appears in the screening firms collateral or on their website.

---

[8] author note– it is highly recommended that any employer who engages the services of a background screening firm ensure that the firm is a member of NAPBS. Although membership does not guarantee any a particular level of knowledge or service, it is valuable indicator that the firm has a commitment to the industry organization that is promoting professional standards and has promulgated a code of conduct.

Among its many missions, NAPBS will help *develop and coordinate training* and other relevant programs to enable its members to better serve their clients, to promote and maintain the highest standards of excellence and ethics in the background screening industry, to ensure compliance with the Fair Credit Reporting Act, and to foster awareness of issues related to consumer protection and privacy rights within the industry.

Joining the Association requires prospective members to abide by a Code of Ethics. Additionally, NAPBS is developing membership accreditation criteria to further insure member companies meet the high standards the Association has established.

For additional information concerning NAPBS, or for a list of Association members, call their offices at 1-888-686-2727.

The day-to-day activities of NAPBS are managed by an association management company which provides NAPBS with a professional staff dedicated to fulfilling the mission of the organization. NAPBS headquarters is located in Durham, NC.

NAPBS held its second industry conference in San Antonio, Texas in 2005, attended by over 300 members of the industry. Recent meetings include 2006 in Nashville, 2007 in Austin, and the 2008 meeting will be in New Orleans. Attendance now exceeds 500.

# Chapter 28

# FAQ's on Working With A Background Screening Company

This chapter outlines the mechanics of working with a background screening firm, legally known as a Consumer Reporting Agency, or "CRA."

## 1. How does an employer start the process?

Initially, an employer needs to sign a **Certification Form** with the CRA. This is required by the **Fair Credit Reporting Act (FCRA)**, and explained in detail in Chapter 6. **Certification** means the employer will utilize the information provided according to law. A typical certification form indicates 1) the employer understands the information can be used for employment purposes only, 2) that all information must remain confidential, 3) that information will not be used to discriminate unlawfully, and 4) the employer will follow the rules contained in the **FCRA** for the use of consumer reports.

Under the **FCRA**, a background firm is required to provide two documents to an employer. Document one is the "Notice to Users of Consumer Reports: Obligations of Users under the FCRA." The second document is, "A Summary of Your Rights under the Fair Credit Reporting Act," directed at job applicants. Both documents are available in Appendix 1.

One state, California, has additional special certification rules that must be followed. Those are contained in the California Investigative Consumers Reporting Agencies Act.[1] Any background firm or employer doing business in California, hiring in California, or using the consumer report in connection with a California resident or California employment location must be familiar with and *follow* the special California requirements.

## 2. What forms does an applicant sign or receive?

### A Disclosure Form

It is critical that employers utilize forms that are legally compliant under both federal law and state law. Although a CRA may provide an employer with forms, it is still the employer's responsibility to ensure the forms are legal in their state. A number of states have state-specific requirements. As of September

---

[1] the California Investigative Consumers Reporting Agencies Act - Civil Code section 1786 et. seq.

30, 1997, the **FCRA** says the **Disclosure form** is necessary for any background report whether or not it involves a credit report. Previously, release forms were contained in the back of employment applications. Congress was concerned that applicants were not made aware that a report might be prepared. As a result of the FCRA amendments effective in 1997, a separate stand-alone document is now required to perform backgrounds. The amended FCRA requires that an employer "make a clear and conspicuous written disclosure to the consumer before the report is obtained, in a document that consists solely of the disclosure, that a consumer report may be obtained." Under the FCRA, applicants do not necessarily sign the form, but that would be a best practice in order to show compliance.

## Release and Authorization Form

The **Release form** serves several purposes. First, it is the release of information so a CRA may obtain background information under the FCRA. Secondly, it is the place where the job applicant provides the necessary identifying information to the CRA to obtain public records. Third, this release may be needed when a former employer or school requests a release before information is given. Also, it can be used to reassure a job applicant that all of his rights are protected, and that screening is a sound business practice that is not to be taken personally. Whether or not it can be combined with the disclosure form depends upon how much information an employer wants to have in their release form. Too much information can violate the rule that the disclosure for cannot have excess verbiage that distracts from the plain meaning of the disclosure.[2]

The Release and Authorization typically does ask for the date of birth. The correct date of birth will be needed for positive identification.[3] If an employer does not want to have date of birth on the release form, then arrangements need to be made with a CRA to obtain it separately. The employer needs to be aware that without date of birth, there is likely to be delays.[4]

Any competent screening firm can provide all the necessary forms for pre-employment screening. If an employer's attorney or legal department already has forms, use those — assuming those forms fully comply with the requirements of the FCRA as well as applicable state rules. There is currently no nationally accepted set of forms for employment screening.[5]

There are some special issues involved with the forms— 1) the disclosures may not have excessive language that detracts from a clear understanding of the form; 2) whether a form may request that an applicant waive his rights to sue the employer or CRA. Per the FTC staff, an applicant *cannot* be required to waive his rights under the FCRA.[6] However a form may ask that an applicant waives his or her rights to the extent permitted by law. It is not clear that such waiver language however, gives a screening firm or the employer a great deal of protection against state torts such as defamation or

---

[2] see Chapter 6 for more details

[3] see Chapter 5 for a discussion of the "date of birth issue"

[4] see Chapter 6 on the FCRA for additional issues surrounding these forms
and the exception for "truck drivers" enacted by Congress in 1998

[5] One of the potential goals for the new National Association of Professional Background Screeners (NAPBS), the new screening association, is to formulate standards for forms utilized in employment screening. See Chapter 27 for more information about NAPBS.

[6] see staff letter to Richard Hauxwell, January 12, 1998 at www.ftc.gov/os/statutes/fcra/hauxwell.htm

invasion of privacy. Even if there is such a waiver, there is a problem of putting it on the disclosure form. For those reasons, some employers and CRA's will use two separate forms. First, the release form that contains the identifying information along with the waiver language, if utilized. Second, the disclosure form contains only the required language.

## Employer Order Form

If the employer is faxing an order to a CRA (instead of self-entry of the order into the CRA's internet system), then an **Employee Order form** is typically sent with each order. It tells the CRA what is being requested, who requested it and sending instructions. The CRA can customize the form for each employer so that paperwork is minimized. The customized form will reflect the type of screening program the employer requires and the employer's name, contact person, and contact information. To ensure accuracy and to avoid delays, the employer needs to confirm that the applicant's name, Social Security Number, driver's license number, and any other data needed to fulfill the order has been provided and is legible. Any information that is incorrect or not clear will cause a delay or result in inaccurate information returned. If a screening firm is given a name that is spelled wrong or a driver's license number or Social Security Number is not legible, say, a "3" looks like an "8," the result may be either bad data or data that is delayed. If the applicant has not given the names of past employers or provided the city and state, that can also cause a delay. The applicant's telephone number may be requested so the CRA may contact an applicant directly to clarify anything that is not clear on the form, however, having a screening firm contact the applicant is not always a good practice — an applicant may get concerned or confused, especially if the screening firm is calling to obtain the applicant's Social Security Number or other confidential data.

If an employer utilizes an online system to enter screening orders, the employer first needs to carefully review the application materials before placing the order online. For any material that is illegible or incomplete, the employer can contact the applicant to clarify. This not only saves time and avoids data errors, but also speeds up the screening process considerably since the screening begins as soon as the employer transmits the order electronically. If the order is faxed to the background firm, the order can be delayed pending the background firm entering the order into its computer system or by having to contact the employer to clear up any uncertainties.

## Applicant Resume and/or Application

When the CRA is asked to do an employment check or educational verification, it is a good practice to send the CRA both a copy of the full **application** and the consent even if the employer has entered the order online. This practice assists the screening firm when identifying past employers. Regardless if the employer uses a screening firm's online order entry system, many schools and past employers may require a **copy of a signed release** before providing information.

# 3. What language should be in the employer's employment application form?

In addition to the forms supplied by a **CRA**, an employer should also have two recommended sections in their own employment application forms. The language relates to criminal convictions, and truthfulness and honesty in the application process.[7] Many states have their own requirement and an employer should consult legal counsel on these.

# 4. When does the applicant sign the forms?

Typically, the actual screening begins after a company has decided that an applicant is a good prospect and wants to verify that their hiring assessment is correct. However, the forms can be signed ahead of time even if an applicant is not going to be submitted for screening.

Employers take two approaches. Many employers have all applicants sign the screening forms as part of the initial application process. There are several advantages. First, by having background forms in the standard application packet, it discourages applicants with something to hide. Secondly, applicants with a minor infraction in their past may still wish to apply and tend to self-disclose any negative information. That helps contribute to a very open interview. Third, employers find it much easier to administer the screening program if the candidate's necessary forms have already been signed.

The alternative approach is to have the finalist only sign the consent forms. Some firms wait until an offer has been made first. Firms use this approach if they feel a background screening may interfere with effective recruiting, although in this day and age, most job applicants understand that pre-employment screening is a standard business practice and is not a reflection upon them personally. This approach requires that HR, Security Department, or the hiring manager give the finalist the forms at a second interview. This can present administrative difficulties. Even if forms are not filled out as part of the initial application, it is suggested that applicants still be informed there will be a pre-employment background screening as a standard part of the hiring process.

# 5. During what step should applicants be screened and who should be screened – all applicants or just finalists?

Employers typically utilize pre-employment screening toward the end of the selection process — after the field has been narrowed down. Because of time and expenses involved, firms do not typically request screening on the entire applicant pool. Screening normally occurs after a company has decided that an applicant is a good prospect and wants to verify their hiring assessment is correct.

There are two directions that firms typically take. The more common approach is to have a CRA perform its screening function on a finalist or after a conditional job offer has been tendered. The

---

[7] see Chapter 7, Why Applications Are Vital for further discussion on applicant forms

purpose of pre-screening at that point is to demonstrate due diligence and to eliminate uncertainties about an applicant.

Alternatively, a firm will ask a CRA to screen the two or three finalists, then use the results in the selection process. The advantage is that a firm can make a selection with more facts. The disadvantages are— 1) multiple screens cost more; 2) adds two to four days to the selection process; and 3) there are possible FCRA and EEOC implications that can be triggered.[8] Essentially using pre-employment reports to choose among finalists can arguably impact EEOC considerations when EEOC-sensitive reports such as criminal history or credit reports are used.[9] An argument can be made that **the initial selection should be based upon the applicant's job qualifications and job fit only**; a pre-employment report is used only to eliminate an applicant with **a job-related criminal history, falsified credentials, or other negative history** that is uncovered.[10]

In addition, if any part of the selection process involves consideration of the pre-employment background report, then the "adverse action" rules apply. This means the applicant has the right to receive a copy of the report and the FCRA-compliant statement of his or her rights. Even if the information relied upon was not negative, the rejected applicant still has rights under the FCRA.

For these reasons, pre-employment screening reports are most often utilized at the very end of the selection procedure, after the company has selected a finalist.

# 6. Can an employer screen some finalists but not others?

Another important consideration in administering a screening program is that once a decision is made to screen for a particular opening, **all finalists** being considered for that opening should be screened. Selective screenings could raise an inference of discriminatory practice, particularly if the subject is a member of a legally protected group. Furthermore, all individuals who are screened should also be evaluated using the same criteria — for each position, the screening level must be the same for all candidates.

An employer may certainly have different screening requirements for different positions. A maintenance worker would not be screened at the same level as a bookkeeper. If there are different screening standards for different positions, an employer should be able to articulate a rational basis as to

---

[8] The FCRA implications are explained more fully in Chapter 6 and Appendix 1. Further EEOC considerations are detailed in Chapter 5 and EEOC statues appear in Appendix 2.

[9] see separate sections below for the EEOC considerations involved in criminal convictions and credit reports, and also EEOC in Chapter 5

[10] Under a new federal case form the Ninth Circuit, the timing of the background screening may also impact Americans with Disabilities Act (ADA). If a background report is necessary before a person becomes a finalist, then a firm may need to compete the background check before obtaining medical information or performing pre-employment physicals. The idea is that medical information should only be requested after there has been a real job offer, which means all relevant non-medical information has been evaluated. This enables an applicant to determine if there was a medical basis to a rejection, and to maintain medical privacy until later in the hiring process. See *Leonel v. American Airlines,* 400 F.3d 702 (9th Cir. 2005)

why some positions are screened differently than others. However, all maintenance workers should be screened the same way, and all bookkeepers screened the same way. In addition, not all positions in a firm must be screened. A firm can decide to stop pre-employment screening in the future. However, for any particular opening, all candidates must be treated the same.

# 7. What positions should be screened, and what information should be requested?

The level of pre-employment screening a firm should utilize is normally determined by the extent of the risk involved if a firm makes a bad hire. There are two primary reasons a company would perform pre-employment screening—

1. To exercise due diligence in the hiring process, primarily for the protection of co-workers, innocent third parties, and the public; and

2. To protect the company from the legal and financial harm stemming from a bad hire.

## Due Diligence

The law requires *an employer exercise reasonable care when selecting new employees*. Unless a firm is regulated by a state or federal law or by accepted industry standards, there is generally no single accepted industry standard as to what level of care is required in pre-employment screening. Whether a firm meets a standard of reasonableness would, under judgment, likely be determined based upon the totality of all the circumstances and the testimony of expert witnesses. However, given the relatively modest cost of pre-employment screening compared to the harm that can be caused by a bad hire, it is likely that a jury would hold an employer to a high standard. It would be difficult to defend a company against a charge of negligent hiring when the victim's attorney can argue that if the company had spent just another $20.00 on screening, some terrible crime would not have occurred, or a problem or loss could have been avoided.

## Protecting the Company

Any company needs to protect its own economic and legal interests, and companies with shareholders, in fact, have a duty to take reasonable steps to protect assets.

Employers should consider various levels of background screening that increase in depth as the risk for a bad hire also increases. Certainly an employer is not held to the standard of an FBI level check for each hire. However, given the relatively modest cost of screening compared to the protection afforded, a firm should probably error on the side of more screening than less.

Consider the following factors—

- Does the position have access to money or assets?
- Does the position carry significant authority, or fiduciary responsibility?
- Does the position have access to members of the public or co-workers so that any propensity to violence would cause harm?

- Does the position require the worker to go into someone's home?
- Does the person work with a vulnerable group such as children, the elderly, or people with disabilities?
- Would the position be difficult to replace in terms of recruitment, hiring and training?
- Would a falsification of skills, experience, or background put the firm at risk, or lower the firms productivity?
- Would a bad hire expose the firm to litigation or financial claims from the applicant, co-workers, customers, or the public?
- What degree of supervision is the worker under?
- Is the person full-time, part-time, seasonal, temporary, or a volunteer?

Using the above factors, an employer can create a risk matrix for each position. The employer needs to consider the risk inherent in the position and the amount of supervision the position needs.

The following are some suggested screening levels—

## Basic Screening

...for entry-level employees, retail, or manufacturing positions, or positions where the employer has internally checked references.

**Recommended search:** A full seven-year onsite criminal records check for felonies and misdemeanors, credit report or Social Security and identity check, and driver's license check. The number of counties searched depends upon the risk factors listed above. For maximum protection, an employer may consider doing ALL counties where a person has lived, worked, or studied.

## Standard Screening

...for more responsible positions and permanent hire.

**Recommended search:** The aforementioned Basic Screening *plus* verification of the last three employers and references,[11] and highest post high school education.

## Extended Screening

...for positions involving increased responsibility or supervision of others.

**Recommended search:** The Basic and Standard Screenings *plus* checking superior court civil cases for litigation matters that may be job related.

## The Integrity Check

...for any type of position involving significant responsibility, or access to cash or assets.

---

[11] that is, references if they are available

**Recommended search:** Includes everything previously mentioned *plus* TEN year searches 1) of federal court for criminal and civil cases, 2) of employment history, 3) to verify of all college degrees and professional licenses, and 4) for superior court civil lawsuits in the last two counties of residence.

For any position, the employer may wish to consider checking sexual offender databases if a worker will have access to children or vulnerable groups at risk. For positions involving access to money or assets, an employer may consider a credit report, subject to the limitations described in Chapter 13. In addition, an employer may consider a national "multi-jurisdictional database" as described in Chapter 12 as a "supplemental search." International searches may also be considered for applicants who have spent time outside of the U.S.

# 8. What about conditional hiring based upon receipt of the background report?

An employer can make an offer of employment or begin the employment relationship contingent upon the receipt of an acceptable background report. This may occur when an employer has a difficult position to fill and does not want to chance losing a good candidate.

It is recommended that the offer letter contain the following language—

> "This offer of employment is conditioned upon the employer's receipt of a pre-employment background screening investigation **that is acceptable to the employer at the employer's sole discretion."**

The suggested language specifies that the report must meet the employer's satisfaction so there can be no debate on what constitutes a satisfactory report.

# 9. How are forms and orders transmitted?

How an order makes it from the employer to the screening firm depends on the screening firm's methodology. If the screening firm has an internet system, then the employer has the ability to key in orders online. If the employer is connected in a seamless interface as described in Chapter 10, then the order's detail and data will automatically transmit without additional key-in. When paper documentation is a consideration, employers and screening companies may prefer the use of fax machines for order communications.

Even when electronic methods are used, there may still be occasion when a physical piece of paper must be handled. This occurs when a past employer, school, or DMV requires a written release form from the requestor. The screening company may need to contact the employer to obtain a physical copy of the release form.

# 10. How long does it take to get the report?

A CRA will normally return reports **within three full business days** after receiving the order. For reports involving credential checks on employment or education, extra time may be required — occasionally there is a delay in obtaining information in a situation where a CRA has no control. For example, it can take longer than three days if there is a potential name match in a criminal case and the court clerk must obtain records from storage. In addition, schools may be closed during Summer or holidays, or employers may not call back or may have merged, moved, or closed. If a form is unreadable, that can delay a report.[12]

# 11. How is the report sent back to the employer?

Screening firms using state-of-the-art web-based systems can make reports available to their clients in real time over the internet. Also, internet retrieval allows employers to have real-time access to the exact status of the report at anytime in order to monitor progress or answer questions from hiring managers. If a criminal search is delayed, an online system can advise the employer about the delay and the estimated time to obtain the information. Reports can also be faxed or emailed to the employer. A CRA will generally require the fax machine be private and secured. A faxed report should have a cover sheet to warn the unauthorized against seeing confidential information.

When a California, Oklahoma, or Minnesota applicant requests to receive a copy of his credit report, the CRA must provide a copy to the applicant at the same time the employer receives the report.

# 12. What should an employer do with the report when it comes back, and who sees the report?

Because the report contains sensitive and confidential information, all efforts must be made to keep the contents private and only available to decision-makers directly involved in the hiring process. The **Report** itself, along with the **Release and Authorization** forms signed by the applicant, should be maintained separately from the employee's personnel file. They should be kept in a relatively secured area, in the same fashion that medical files or sensitive employee matters are kept. These reports should definitely not be made available to supervisors or managers other than those in the hiring approval process. For example, during periodic *performance appraisals*, an employer would not want a supervisor to have access to a non-performance-related confidential background report.

For screening firms with advanced internet systems, there is in fact no need to physically download the report. It is available online.[13] However, an employer needs to be assured of internet security, and the employer needs to maintain a system of strong password protections. It is important that authorized users do not share passwords with those not authorized, nor reveal the password in any manner. Some screening firms require the user to change passwords every thirty days as a security measure.

---

[12] see Chapter 10 for a discussion on why some search results may be delayed

[13] the screening firm should be instructed to keep the report in case it may be needed later; see question #13

Typically, reports are returned to either Human Resources or Security Departments. Reports are reviewed for any negative information. If the report is clear, then the hiring manager is notified and the hiring proceeds. If there is a red flag or derogatory information, then the information itself is shared with the appropriate decision-makers. The physical report, however, normally stays with HR or Security. This protects against confidential information wrongfully being made known generally within the company.

## 13. What does a CRA do about information that an employer is not suppose to have?

Some CRA's carefully monitor their reports to ensure that no information is given to an employer that violates the various rules concerning limitations on what employers can and cannot use in making employment decisions. However, this is a tricky area. A CRA is not acting as an attorney and cannot make legal decisions. On the other hand, there are clear industry accepted practices about what an employer cannot have.

Some CRA's take the position they are primarily data conduits to the employer, and it is the employer's obligation to not utilize any information an employer should not have. An employer should carefully consider this issue in selecting a service provider.

## 14. How long should forms signed by applicants and applicant records be kept?

Record keeping requirements for employers can vary in accordance to the type of document in question. However, it is generally advisable for an employer to maintain all paperwork concerning the formation of the employment relationship for a period of at least three years from the termination of *any relationship*. That means if a person is hired, the report and all related screening documentation should be kept *during the entire employment relationship and for three years after it terminates*. If an applicant is screened and an employment relationship does not occur, then the reports and documents should be maintained for three years from the date of the report. The three-year period should cover any statute of limitations in the event of a claim or lawsuit.

However, as outlined in Chapter 6, a 2003 FCRA amendment changed the applicable statute of limitations for claims under the FCRA to up to five years. An employer and consumer reporting agency should maintain records concerning pre-employment screening by a CRA for at least six years following a screening, based upon the five-year statue, and an extra year to reflect the amount of time states generally allow to serve a lawsuit.

For employers that utilize the services of a CRA with an advanced internet system, that online system may be set up to archive the reports permanently.

There are two reasons why employer should also maintain the background screening authorization forms and disclosure forms as well as any other forms related to ordering a screening report for the same period of time. First, they may be needed to prove that the employer had consent for a screening report and a permissible purpose under the FCRA. Second, if a screening firm is audited by a data provider (such as a state motor vehicle department), the applicant's consent may be needed by both the background firm and the employer to demonstrate that the request for information was legal. Many background firms require in their contracts with employers that all such documents will be maintained by the employer and provided to the CRA if necessary for an audit. If there is an electronic signature, that data needs to be preserved as well.

## 15. What does an employer do if they decide not to hire an applicant?

If an employer decides to take any type of adverse action regarding an application for employment, based in any way upon information contained in a screening report, the provisions of the FCRA come into play. At that point, it is the employer's responsibility to first provide the applicant with a copy of the report and a statement of the consumer's rights. If the applicant does not contest the report and the decision stands, then the employer must send a second notice to the applicant under Section 615 of the FCRA notifying the applicant of a number of specific rights.[14]

An employer does NOT need to specify exactly why an applicant was rejected. The procedures set forth in the FCRA only require the applicant have an opportunity to review the background report prior to an adverse action being taken and be given a statement of his or her rights. If the decision is made final, the applicant then receives a letter indicating the action has been made final and was based in part upon the consumer report.

Some CRA's will provide all the necessary notices to the applicant. Under the rules of the FCRA, although it is the employer's responsibility to provide the pre-adverse and post-adverse action notices, that duty can be delegated to an agent such as a screening firm. If the applicant disagrees with any of the information contained in the report, then the applicant communicates directly to the CRA. **The CRA has a duty under the FCRA to re-investigate** within 30 days — up to 45 days under certain circumstances. The employer, however, has no obligation to keep the position open during the re-investigation period.

## 16. Is there the possibility of legal liability if an employer rejects an applicant as a result of a screening report?

When an employer follows the procedures in the FCRA, and also makes all hiring decisions utilizing legal and job related-reasons, the chances of a lawsuit from a rejected applicant is minimized. However, no employer can ever make itself immune from a lawsuit. Anyone with enough money to cover the court's filing fee can go to the court and file a lawsuit. The real issue is whether the benefits from a pre-employment screening program outweigh the risks.

---

[14] see Chapter 6 and Appendix 1 for FCRA details

Under the procedures in the FCRA, the chances of an applicant filing a lawsuit because of inaccurate or incomplete information have been minimized. If an employer intends to take adverse action based upon a background report, an applicant must first be provided with a copy of the report and a statement of his or her rights. Because of this procedure, an applicant will have the chance to correct anything in a report that is incorrect or inaccurate. If the information is inaccurate, the applicant will have the opportunity to object and to offer a correction. At that point, the employer can proceed with the hire. Under the previous system where applicants did not have to be told their reports contained negative or derogatory information, employers ran a greater risk of making hiring decisions based upon incorrect information.

The relatively small chance of a lawsuit from a rejected applicant must be weighed against the probability that, without pre-employment screening, a firm will almost certainly face workplace difficulties from a bad hire. Even one bad-hire can severely hurt a business. Given the national statistics that one-third of all applications contain material falsehoods, and approximately ten percent of job applicants have criminal records, the value of pre-employment screening has been proven. There are no court cases where an employer has successfully argued they did not exercise due diligence in their hiring because they were concerned about possible litigation from rejected applicants. Conversely, there are a large number of lawsuits stemming from lack of pre-employment screening.

## 17. How can a firm conduct pre-employment screening without interfering with recruitment or employee morale?

In performing pre-employment screening, it is important not to damage the bond of trust that a firm seeks to develop with their employees. Human Resources and Security departments are placed in a difficult position. On one hand, the company does not want to make bad hires. On the other hand, the company cannot afford to use a process that alienates its employees or interferes with recruiting. Furthermore, obnoxious background procedures will discourage good applicants. Some background investigators start with the proposition that all applicants are potential criminals until they prove otherwise — applicants may not want to work for a firm that treats them that way.

The solution is to make it clear to applicants that pre-employment screening is a sound business practice that not only benefits the company, but benefits all employees as well. No one wants to work with an unqualified person who obtained the job under false pretext or with a co-worker with a criminal record. Once an applicant understands the process is not a reflection on him or her, but is actually for their benefit as well, they will understand this is a good thing for a company to do.

A firm should make certain that applicants understand background screening benefits everyone. Furthermore, the applicant should be assured that all procedures used respect his or her rights to privacy, that all information is kept strictly confidential and is used only for employment purposes, and all legal rights are respected.

Furthermore, the scope of the investigation should be clearly job-related.

# Chapter 29

# For Job Applicants— Consumer Questions and Concerns

*Chapter 29 and Chapter 30*
*are written from the point of view of a Job Applicant.*

*Why is this information contained in a book written for employers?*

*First, job applicants often have questions about the procedures.*
*It is in the interest of employers that these questions be answered.*
*Second, while many applicants shrug off background checks as just another*
*part of the process, employers do not want to discourage otherwise good*
*applicants just because an applicant may be unaware of the details*
*of the procedures or their rights in the process.*

Employers are increasingly turning to background screenings of job applicants as a way of minimizing legal and financial exposure. Concerns about workplace violence, negligent-hiring lawsuits, wrongful termination and other problems are leading many employers to be more careful about who is hired in the first place.

Of course, a background screening is not a full-fledged FBI-type investigation. Screening companies are typically looking for red flags indicating potential problems or resumes that are not factual or omit important information.

In many cases, a background check is considered a prerequisite for eligibility in the application process. Many applicants understand, in this post-9/11 world, that background checking is a new fact of life.

## Applicants Have Protection

However, for some applicants, background screening can create an uneasy feeling of mistrust from the start — or "Big Brother is watching." This is exacerbated by the fact employers are not required by law to provide a great deal of hiring information to applicants. If an employer utilizes a third party service, the Fair Credit Reporting Act (FCRA) requires an employer to obtain the applicant's express written consent to perform a background or reference check, and the employer is also required to give certain legal disclosures.

However, unless the information is utilized to deny employment, very little additional information must be provided to the applicant. If the information is used in an adverse fashion, the applicant is entitled to a document called "A Summary of Your Rights," which focuses on what an applicant can do if he or she disagrees with the background report. A copy is in Appendix 1. If an employer does reference checks in-house — not using a screener of third parties — even less information must be given to an applicant, although the applicant's written consent is usually obtained.

The fact is, background screenings of job applicants benefit employers and employees alike, and with the recent changes in the FCRA, job applicants now have a greater legal protection.

For applicants, the advantages of working for a company that requires screening shows that efforts have been made to ensure co-workers have the qualifications and credentials they say they have. In addition, employers typically screen out those with criminal records, especially involving violence or dishonesty.

In order to minimize the risk of alienating prospective employees, employers may even consider making a policy to provide all applicants with detailed information about the background checking process and their rights. The following questions and answers cover most concerns an applicant might have regarding a pre-employment background check or drug screen — so they can understand the importance of this process and how their rights are protected.

# Applicants' Guide to Background Checks

### Why is a background check necessary?

A background check is more than keeping the employer out of trouble. Employers who screen their employees demonstrate their commitment to keeping employees safe on the job. In addition to the safety and well being of their employees, employers are being held responsible for the safety of their customers and anyone who may be affected or harmed by the actions or negligence of an on-duty employee.

It doesn't stop there. Employers can be held liable for damages if a court determines the employer *should* have known an employee posed a potential risk to person or property. Failing to make sure an employee is "safe" can land an employer in hot water as well as put innocent people at risk.

### Are background checks legal?

It is legal for an employer to perform a background check on an employee or job applicant. An employer has the right to select the most qualified applicant for a position, providing the employer is basing the decision on non-discriminatory factors that are valid predictors of job performance.

However, the employer must follow the guidelines set in the Federal Fair Credit Reporting Act (FCRA). Under the FCRA, when an employer uses a background screening company to prepare a report, several steps must occur—

- The employer must clearly disclose to the applicant that a report is being prepared. This disclosure must be a separate, stand-alone document and cannot be buried in the fine print of an application form.

- The employer must obtain the applicant's express written consent in order to obtain records such as criminal convictions or pending criminal cases, driving records, credit reports, past employment data, or educational credentials.

- An additional notice is required when a background firm checks references, such as asking previous employers about job performance.

- If an employer intends to deny employment based upon information in the report, the job applicant must receive a copy of the report and a notice of his or her legal rights.

- If the decision to deny employment is made final, an applicant is entitled to *some* additional information.

Employers are strictly bound by any state and local laws governing background checks. These laws vary from state to state and may place additional limits on the background checking process.

**Why do the same laws apply to credit reports and background checks?**

Even though the name of the Fair Credit Reporting Act uses the term "credit," this is actually misleading because the FCRA applies to much more than just credit applications. A credit report is just one type of consumer report governed by the FCRA. The FCRA defines a consumer report as any written, oral, or other communication of any information by a consumer reporting agency bearing on a consumer's "credit worthiness, credit standing, credit capacity, character, general reputation, personal characteristics, or mode of living which is used or expected to be used or collected in whole or in part" for various listed purposes, including credit, employment, or the underwriting of insurance.

Any employer or organization obtaining an applicant's driving records, employment records, or criminal records directly from a third party assembling this information into a consumer report is subject to the FCRA. A professional, third party background screening firm that gathers and assembles this information is called a Consumer Reporting Agency (CRA). Employers who fail to comply with the FCRA may be liable for damages or subject to other penalties.

**What information gets checked, and where does it come from?**

A background check is not a full-scale investigation into someone's private life. Instead, the process is used to confirm the information provided on an application, and that all relevant licenses, certifications, and degrees are in good standing. Previous employers and colleagues may also be contacted to confirm past employment and education. Employers and other references may be asked about job performance as well. A search may be conducted for criminal conviction records that may indicate that a person is unsuitable for a particular job. For example, if a person has a history of violent behavior, this tendency could possibly put employees, customers, or the business at risk. An applicant with a conviction for theft or fraud may not be suitable for a job that requires handling money or assets.

Some employers may attempt to collect this information themselves. Employers may contact past employers or schools. However, in order to access much of the information needed by employers, specialized search skills, knowledge, or resources are required. For that reason, many employers seek screening assistance from Consumer Reporting Agencies.

For the most part, background checks collect and verify information from state and federal agencies, credit bureaus, private institutions, and businesses. This information falls into two categories— public records checks and references/verifications.

### Public Records Checks

- Social Security Number (SSN) Trace is a check of names and addresses that are associated with a Social Security Number found in the databases maintained by the national credit bureaus. These checks may also include a check of other databases as well.

- Criminal records checks search for pending criminal cases or records of criminal convictions. Under federal law, the check for a conviction has no age limit, although some states do put a limit on how far back a screening firm may search. Criminal records are typically obtained from the relevant courthouse where the cases are held, and records must be manually retrieved by a researcher or clerk. Although there are some "canned" databases of criminal records available from vendors, records directly from the source are the most accurate and up-to-date.

- Driving records are typically accessed for up to three years of history and cover accident history and driver's license status. The driving records obtained for employment purposes come from the databases of individual states' Department of Motor Vehicles. Additionally, some trucking and transportation agencies will provide information about driver accidents.

- Workers' Compensation claims provide details about past injuries and Workers' Compensation claims filed by an individual. When an employee's claim goes through a state system or a Workers' Compensation Appeals Board (WCAB), the case becomes public record. An employer may only use this information for hiring purposes if an injury might interfere with one's ability to perform required duties.

- Credit reports retrieve a seven-year credit history, including high-low balances, trade lines, loans, mortgages, liens, bankruptcies, judgments, collections and summaries of the individual's payment patterns. Credit checks can reveal information such as fraudulent use of a Social Security Number, or general credit history, as well as provide current and previous addresses.

### References and Verifications

- Employment verifications confirm dates of employment, title, salary, and eligibility for rehire with each employer listed on the application. The information is verified with a supervisor or payroll/HR representative within the company.

- Education or degree verifications confirm dates of enrollment, programs of study, and degrees held. Generally, the information comes directly from the school attended or a licensed third-party records service, usually National Student Loan Clearinghouse. Some information, such as GED records, must be obtained from state agencies.

**What can my former employer say about me?**

Potential employers often contact an applicant's past employers for qualitative references. Contrary to popular misconception, employers are at liberty to provide information about a previous employee's performance and ability, provided the information is truthful, job-related, and accurate. However, in this litigious society, most employers have opted to implement a policy to only confirm dates of employment, job title, and in some cases, salary. Many employers are concerned that, if they give information beyond name, rank, and serial number, they could potentially be sued for defamation. Many large employers, in fact, have deposited past employment information on a telephone service, limiting new employers to hearing a computerized voice verifying just employment dates and job title.

# About Past Employer References...

The reluctance of employers to give information may actually work to the detriment of an applicant, making it more difficult to get a letter of recommendation. Applicants still have many avenues available to communicate about their past successes to new employers, even if past employers will not give a reference. The key is to plan ahead and to remember the importance of promoting your own career by obtaining the materials necessary to successfully market yourself—

- When leaving a job, clarify the past employer's policy on references and try to determine what will be said if a new employer calls.

- If the former employer has a "no comment policy," offer to sign a release of information.

- Before leaving a job, try to obtain personal letters of recommendation. Even if the firm does not give references, a supervisor or co-worker may be willing to write a favorable letter on the theory that it is a personal recommendation.

- Seek a letter of recommendation from someone no longer at the firm, who can verify your job performance.

- Keep copies of outstanding performance appraisals, or keep an example of your work to show at an interview, provided it was proper to retain it, i.e. not protected as a trade secret or by a non-disclosure agreement.

- Try to have references give specific examples. General statements like "great team player" are not nearly as strong as examples of behavior or performance in specific situations.

- Retain pay stubs and other documents as a means of verifying past employment. When firms merge, go out of business, or move, it can be difficult to confirm past employment.

If the previous employment involved a contract with an outside agency or was through an employee-leasing firm, then the actual workplace may not have records of you.

- It is also very important to accurately summarize the job duties and title for previous jobs on a resume. Although everyone wants a resume to shine, a resume that over-reaches can raise questions about your honesty.

In many states, employees have a right to review their own personnel files and make copies of documents they have signed. The personnel files of state or federal employees are protected under various state laws or the federal Privacy Act of 1974, and can only be disclosed under limited circumstances.

Most jobs involving the freight and transportation industries are regulated by the federal Department of Transportation. Employers are required to accurately respond to any inquiry from a prospective employer about whether an employee took a drug test, refused a drug test, or tested positive in a drug test while with the former or current employer.

### What if the information is wrong?

Despite the best efforts of record keepers and modern information storage systems, mistakes sometimes occur. However, applicants who genuinely are the victims of mistaken identity or bureaucratic errors are given the opportunity to know what is being said about them and to dispute errors or discrepancies that might otherwise unfairly deny them opportunity or eligibility for a position. Because of the rise of identity theft crimes, some applicants receive a very unpleasant surprise when a background check is conducted — they may discover that someone using their identity is the subject of a criminal record. If a person is arrested and uses your name, you becomes a double victim when a warrant for your arrest is issued after he fails to show up in court. Of course, since you – the applicant – was not the one arrested, you have no idea a warrant for your arrest is outstanding. There are even cases where the criminal stealing the identity pled guilty to a criminal charge using the stolen identity, creating a criminal conviction record for some unsuspecting ID theft victim. At that point, a job applicant must somehow correct the mess left by the identity thief.[1]

Under federal law, an employer intending to use information from the consumer report for an adverse action — such as denial of a job or promotion or terminating the employee — must take the steps outlined below.[2]

- **Before** the adverse action is taken, the employer must give the applicant a "pre-adverse action disclosure," including a copy of the report and an explanation of the applicant's rights under the FCRA.

- **After** the adverse action is taken, the individual must be given an "adverse action notice." This document must contain 1) the name, address, and phone number of the employment

---

[1] for more information on identity theft, see Chapter 17

[2] these steps are explained further in the Federal Trade Commission's website at
www.ftc.gov/bcp/conline/pubs/buspubs/credempl.htm

screening company, 2) a statement that the employer, not the background screening company, is responsible for making the adverse decision, and 3) a notice that the individual has the right to dispute the accuracy or completeness of any of the information in the report.

- A background checking company is required to remove or correct inaccurate or unverified information, usually within thirty days of notification.

**What can I do to prepare?**

Applicants who anticipate changing jobs in the near term can take several steps to ensure the information to be gathered is correct, and all precautions have been taken in the event contradictory information surfaces, or records cannot be located. The following tips are excerpted with permission from the Privacy Rights Clearinghouse, Fact Sheet 16, "Employment Background Checks: A Job Seeker's Guide,"[3]

# Tips from the Privacy Rights Clearinghouse

**Order a copy of your credit report.** If there is something you do not recognize or that you disagree with, dispute the information with the creditor and/or credit bureau before you have to explain it to the interviewer. Another individual's name may appear on your credit report. This happens when someone mistakenly writes down the wrong Social Security Number on a credit application causing that name to appear on your file, or you might be a victim of identity theft.[4]

**Check court records.** If you have an arrest record or have been involved in court cases, go to the county where this took place and inspect the files. Make sure the information is correct and up to date. Reporting agencies often report felony convictions when the consumer truly believes the crime was reduced to a misdemeanor, or that it was reported as a misdemeanor conviction when the consumer thought the charge was reduced to an infraction. Court records are not always updated correctly. For example, a signature that was needed to reduce the charges might not have been obtained or recorded by the court. Don't rely on what your attorney may have told you. If you think the conviction was expunged or dismissed, get a certified copy of your report from the court.

**Check DMV records.** Request a copy of your driving record from the Department of Motor Vehicles, especially if you are applying for a job that involves driving. Many employers ask on their application if you were ever convicted of a crime. Or they might word the question to ask whether you have ever been convicted of a felony or misdemeanor. Typically, the application says you do not have to divulge a case that was expunged or dismissed, or that was a minor

---

[3] Privacy Rights Clearinghouse, Fact Sheet 16, "Employment Background Checks: A Job Seeker's Guide," online at www.privacyrights.org/fs/fs16-bck.htm

[4] see PRC Fact Sheet 6 on your credit reporting rights, online at www.privacyrights.org/fs/fs6-crdt.htm, and Fact Sheet 17a on identity theft, online at www.privacyrights.org/fs/fs17a.htm

traffic violation. Don't be confused. A DUI (driving under the influence) or DWI (driving while intoxicated) conviction is *not* considered a minor traffic infraction. Applicants with a DUI or DWI who have not checked "yes" on a job application may be denied employment for falsifying the form – even when the incident occurred only once or happened many years before. The employer perceives this as dishonesty, even though the applicant might only have been confused by the question.

**Do your own background check.** If you want to see what an employer's background check might uncover, hire a company that specializes in such reports to conduct one for you. That way, you can discover if the databases of information vendors use contain erroneous or misleading information. Consult the Yellow Pages under "Investigators," of you may use one of the many online search services to find out what an employer would learn if conducting a background check online.

**Ask to see a copy of your personnel file from your old job.** Even if you no longer work there, state law might enable you to see your file. Under California law, you can access your file until at least a year from the last date of employment, and you are allowed to make copies of documents in your file that have your signature on them.[5] You may also want to ask if your former employer has a policy about the release of personnel records. Many companies limit the amount of information they disclose.

**Read the fine print carefully.** When you sign a job application, you will be asked to sign a consent form if a background check is conducted. Read this statement carefully and ask questions if the authorization statement is not clear. Unfortunately, jobseekers are in an awkward position, since refusing to authorize a background check may jeopardize the chances of getting the job. Notice of a background check has to be on a separate form. The only other information this form can include is your authorization and information that identifies you. Neither the notice of a background check nor any other form should ask questions on race, sex, full date of birth, or maiden name. Such questions violate the Federal Equal Employment Opportunity laws. You should *not* be asked to sign any document that waives your right to sue a screening company or the employer for violations of the law.

**Tell neighbors and work colleagues, past and present, that they might be asked to provide information about you.** This helps avoid suspicion and alerts you to possible problems. In addition, their prior knowledge gives them permission to disclose information to the investigator. Forewarning others will speed up the overall process and help you get the job faster.

---

[5] California Labor Code §432.

# Criminal Records and Getting Back Into The Workforce — Six Critical Steps For Ex-Offenders Trying to Get A Job

Employers have become increasingly concerned about knowing if an applicant has a criminal record. More and more employers are conducting pre-employment background checks for criminal records. Employers have been the subject of large jury verdicts for ***negligent hiring*** in cases where they hire a person with a criminal record who harms others, especially when the harm could have been avoided by a criminal record check. Employers have a legal duty to exercise ***due diligence*** in the hiring process, and that duty can be violated if an employer hires someone who they "either knew or should have known" in the exercise of reasonable care was dangerous or unfit for a job. The concern from the employer's point of view is that a person with a criminal past may have a propensity to re-offend in the future.

On the other hand, society also has a vested interest in helping people with a past criminal record obtain and maintain employment. It is difficult for an ex-offender to become a law abiding, taxpaying citizen without a job. Unless society wants to continue to spend its tax dollars on building more and more jails and prisons, ex-offenders need the opportunity to rejoin the workforce.

For an ex-offender, a job search can become a frustrating catch-22. Nearly every employment application will ask, in some fashion, if a person has a criminal record. If a person lies, then the person is always at risk of being terminated for lying upon such a criminal record being discovered. If a person is honest and admits the past misconduct, there is a risk of not getting the job.

Studies demonstrate what ex-offenders already know — it is significantly harder to get a job with a criminal record. According to a study conducted at Georgetown University in Washington,[6] only twenty percent of employers surveyed indicated a willingness to hire an ex-offender. Employers were most willing to hire ex-offenders for jobs that had little customer contact, such as in the construction or manufacturing industries.

The problem is getting worse. With the surging prison population, there are more than 600,000 people released from prison every year. Studies show that ex-offenders with jobs are less likely to re-offend. Society has a vested interest in keeping released prisoners from re-offending and going back into custody. Yet ex-offenders have the toughest time getting jobs, especially in a down economy.

There is no perfect answer. A person with a criminal record is going to face greater challenges in getting employment. However, **challenging** is not the same as **impossible**. The key is the right attitude and getting and keeping that first job, and, as time goes by, a person develops a successful job history that will outweigh past problems.

Described on the following pages are six approaches a person with a past criminal record can take to help obtain a job.

---

[6] quoted in *USA Today* 11/21/2003

## 1. Understand Your Rights

A person who has a criminal record and is looking for employment must understand his or her rights. There are instances where an applicant can legally and ethically answer NO to a question about a past offense. This may occur in some of the following situations—

- In many states, there is no obligation to report arrests not resulting in a conviction, or arrests with results not currently pending.

- There are limitations on reporting pre-trial adjudications where the conduct by statute is not considered a criminal offense. Some states have pre-trial diversion or delayed entry of judgment.

- There may be restrictions on the use of minor drug offense records. In California, for example, an employer may not ask about a minor marijuana offense for personal use older than two years.

- Some states have procedures to judicially "erase" a criminal offense. In another California example, if the matter is a misdemeanor and a person goes back to court and receives a certificate of rehabilitation under Penal Code 1203.4, the incident is not reportable.

Also, keep in mind most employment applications contain language stating the conviction of a crime will not automatically result in a denial of employment. Automatic disqualification could be a violation of state and federal discrimination laws. However, an employer may deny employment if the employer can establish a business-related reason for the refusal to hire.

## 2. See an Attorney

This is critical. Make sure you understand your rights. An attorney will help determine if you are eligible to get your conviction sealed, expunged, or legally minimized. An employer may not legally ask about or consider certain offenses. Each state has different rules on this, but all states have a mechanism for going back to court to try to seal or expunge certain offenses. Make sure you explore your options. The attorney who represented you or the local Public Defender or Probation Office should be able to assist.

## 3. Seek Professional Assistance

There are also organizations that assist past offenders. Some of these organizations have relationships with employers who are willing to give an ex-offender a chance. In addition, these organizations can help a person prepare a resume and practice interview techniques to deal honestly with the past offense. This helps a job applicant put his best foot forward by explaining why the applicant can perform the job and why the employer should hire him. Various re-entry or training programs will help ex-offenders develop new skills, or teach job search techniques.

## 4. Honesty is the Best Policy

When applying for a job, honestly is always the best policy. A criminal matter honestly explained during an interview may have much less negative impact than hiding it and having an employer discover it later. If an employer discovers an applicant is dishonest, the denial of a job could be based upon a lack of honesty, regardless of the nature of the criminal offense. However, a person who has made a mistake and is now motivated to do well at a job may be of great interest to some employers.

## 5. Rebuild Your Resume

The rebuilding of a resume is done one step at a time even if it involves taking a job that is not perfect. All employers know the best indicator of future job performance is past job performance. If a person with a criminal record can obtain whatever job he or she can, hold that job and do well, the next job becomes much easier to obtain. It is the building block approach — one block at a time.

It is critical to seek employment that can help rebuild your resume. You should first seek employment with people you know; they are more likely than a stranger to give you a chance. Ask everyone you know to recommend someone who might be willing to hire you. Yes, mention your conviction, but stress your professional strengths and how much "you have learned from your past."

You have to consider starting at the bottom. However, a few months of good work in an entry-level position can yield a good reference, which can start your career upward.

According to career coach Marty Nemko, an entry level-job can be a launch pad and a foot in the door. Do a great job, build up relationships with higher ups, express interest in moving up and before long, you many find yourself promoted.

> **Author Tip** ➡  Mr. Nemko also gives the following advice: "If you take an entry-level job in order to rebuild your resume, be sure it is one in which people with the power to promote you can observe the quality of your work. Avoid taking a job off-site or in a remote location. If you enjoy working for the organization, then ask questions, learn skills, and let them know you are interested in moving up."

There are certain industries that are in real need of workers. A fast food job, for example, may not be the job you want, but it is an example of a job that is widely available and allows a person to rebuild credentials and show what he or she can do.

Eventually, what a new employer sees is a person with great recommendations and an excellent job history. As the criminal conviction gets older, and the job history become stronger, a person who has made a mistake in the past will eventually find the criminal record is less of an issue.

It cannot be stressed enough — the best way to get a great job in the future is to get any job you can right now, and perform well.

# 6. Take the Long-Term View

This is the most difficult advice to follow. An ex-offender is anxious to get back into the workforce to start making a living. Ex-offenders may also be anxious to have their old life back, yet, the deck is stacked against a person with a criminal record. The jobs available may not be the ones you want. You may be qualified for something a great deal better. Doors may slam in your face. You may be subject to unfair assumptions. The frustration level could easily build with each disappointment encountered.

It comes down to this— ex-offenders need to take the long view and have the faith and patience that the criminal matter will eventually be put behind them. As frustrating as it is, the basic rule still applies — a person must rebuild a resume over time. As time goes by, the criminal offense becomes less of a factor in a person's life — but it is going to take time.

Even if it takes five years to rebuild your resume and get the job you want, five years will still go by. Five years later, what would you rather have — a new life with a good job or still living in frustration because you could not get what you wanted right away? Here are three case studies to consider—

> **Case Study One:** A schoolteacher was convicted of a misdemeanor offense that disqualified her from teaching. The person had dedicated her life to teaching, and suddenly it was no longer an option. She was very depressed and upset that she could no longer do what she loved and knew how to do so well. In order to qualify for a work-furlough program, she obtained a job with a friend in a retail store. It turned out she had a talent for the new job, and became very successful and happy with it and found a new and satisfying career.

> **Case Study Two:** A medical professional committed an offense that disqualified him from practicing his profession. He could not imagine not being employed in medicine. His career in medicine had been the most important aspect of his life and defined who he was. Over a long period of adjustment, he was very depressed and unhappy about how unfair it was he could not do what he did best. Out of necessity, he found a job in construction. It turned out he had a talent for this temporary job. He loved the hours and the freedom the job gave him. He also realized the pressures he had put himself under were the root cause of the criminal conduct. A few years later, when he would have been eligible to attempt to regain his license, he decided he enjoyed his new life and did not want to go back into medicine.

> **Case Study 3**: A young woman became involved in the wrong crowd at an early age. She was convicted of drug offenses and spent time in prison. In prison she obtained her GED. Upon release, she found a job in a fast food place. It was not the best job, but she worked hard and made herself the best worker there. She was always on time, cared about her job, respected her co-workers and supervisors, and she showed a real interest in succeeding. Since employers need that kind of worker, she was eventually promoted to the management trainee program. She then turned for assistance to a program that helped women get jobs, and was able to find a well-paying administrative job in a growing firm. It took time, but she did everything right.

These case studies have one critical element in common— the individuals could not have been more depressed and frustrated with their situations. By being patient, taking the long view, and believing things could improve, eventually their lives went in new and better directions.

# Chapter 30

# For Job Applicants –
# What To Do About Identity Theft

## The Extent of the Problem

In 2003, the Federal Trade Commission sponsored a study on the impact of identity theft in America. The results were astounding. According to the study, in 2002 there were nearly ten million Americans who were victims of some form of identity theft. The cost to American business was nearly fifty billion dollars. The loss to individuals was approximately five billion dollars.

There is also a large human toll as well, as victims try to dig out from underneath the economic damage. Repairing identity theft can take months of frustrating calls to police, merchants, financial institutions, and credit bureaus. According to the FTC study at www.ftc.gov/os/2003/09/synovatereport.pdf —

> "Victims of ID Theft also spend a considerable amount of their own time resolving the various problems that occurred because of the misuse of their personal information. On average, victims reported that they spent 30 hours resolving their problems. On average, victims of the "New Accounts and Other Frauds" form of ID Theft spent 60 hours resolving their problems. This suggests that Americans spent almost 300 million hours resolving problems related to ID Theft in the past year, with almost two-thirds of this time – 194 million hours – spent by victims of "New Accounts and Other Frauds" ID Theft."

For employers, the damage caused by identity theft has multiple dangers. A business loses productivity when one of it employees is sidetracked by serious personal financial worries. A business also faces liability if they are adjudged as the cause of the identify theft. Businesses have obligations not only to their customers but also their employees in terms of safeguarding the confidentiality of private information.

Most critically, the 2003 study found that early detection was the key. The economic losses were much smaller and the damage to individuals in both out-of-pocket costs and time spent resolving the problem were substantially smaller the sooner the victim discovered the theft.

## ID Theft – What is it?

Fundamentally, identity theft occurs when someone passes himself or herself off as someone else in order to gain a fraudulent advantage.

Identify theft typically occurs when the thief gains access to another person's personal information, such as Social Security Number, bank or credit card account numbers, then uses them to commit fraud or theft.

Here are three examples of identity theft—

1. The first is "**account takeover**." This occurs when a criminal literally takes over another person's existing accounts and makes purchases using a victim's credit cards.

2. The second type is what experts refer to as "**true name fraud**," or "**application fraud**." This involves a thief creating brand new accounts using someone else's personal information such as the Social Security Number. For example, a criminal may use the data to open a new American Express account.

3. A third type of identity theft is "**impersonation**," where an identity thief takes over another person's identity — by utilizing the victim's identification, the thief obtains documents to enable them to pass themselves off as the victim. If the ruse is successful, the ID thief has the ability to commit more sophisticated "application fraud," ranging from getting a job under the false name, to creating a whole life using someone else's identity. Another variation is "criminal identity theft" where a person who has stolen an identity is arrested and even convicted under the false identity. The victim of identity theft now has a criminal record in his or her name!

# How Identity Thieves Use the Information

The Federal Trade Commission publishes *ID Theft: When Bad Things Happen to Your Good Name* online at www.ftc.gov/bcp/conline/pubs/credit/idtheft.htm#intro.

On the following page is an excerpt from that document—

# How Identity Thieves Use Your Personal Information—

- They call your credit card issuer and, pretending to be you, ask to change the mailing address on your credit card account. The imposter then runs up charges on your account. Because your bills are being sent to the new address, it may take some time before you realize there is a problem.

- They open a new credit card account using your name, date of birth, and Social Security Number. When they use the credit card and don't pay the bills, the delinquent account is reported on your credit report.

- They establish telephone or wireless service in your name.

- They open a bank account in your name and write bad checks on that account.

- They file for bankruptcy under your name to avoid paying debts they've incurred under your name, or to avoid eviction.

- They counterfeit checks or debit cards and drain your bank account.

- They buy vehicles by taking out auto loans in your name.

- They give your name to the police during an arrest. If they are released from police custody, but do not show up for their court date, then an arrest warrant is issued in your name.

Criminal identity theft is especially worrisome. There have been numerous horror stories of innocent, law-abiding citizens arrested and tossed into jail for no apparent reason, only to find they have been the victims of identity theft. Someone who stole their identity committed some act resulting in a criminal charge or warrant, and gave the stolen name and information — your name, your information.

# How to Protect Yourself and What to Do If You Are A Victim

For a victim of identity theft, the immediate economic damages are generally limited. A victim may not be liable for any amount greater than the first $50.00, if that.

However, *the damage can go further*. Below is an excerpt of a special report by the Privacy Rights Clearinghouse[1]—

> "Even though victims are usually not saddled with paying their imposters' bills, they are often left with a bad credit report and must spend months and even years regaining their financial health. In the meantime, they have difficulty getting credit, obtaining loans, renting apartments, and even getting hired. Victims of identity theft find little help from the authorities as they attempt to untangle the web of deception that has allowed another person to impersonate them.

> Stealing wallets used to be the best way identity thieves obtained SSNs, driver's licenses, credit card numbers, and other pieces of identification. While still employed, identity thieves now use more sophisticated means—

> - "Dumpster diving" in trash bins for unshredded credit card and loan applications and documents containing SSNs.
>
> - Stealing mail from unlocked mailboxes to obtain newly issued credit cards, bank and credit card statements, pre-approved credit offers, investment reports, insurance statements, benefits documents, or tax information. Unfortunately, even locked mailboxes may not stop the most determined thief.
>
> - Accessing your credit report fraudulently, for example, by posing as an employer, loan officer, or landlord.
>
> - Obtaining names and SSNs from personnel or customer files in the workplace.
>
> - "Shoulder surfing" at ATM machines and phone booths in order to capture PIN numbers.
>
> - Finding identifying information on internet sources, via public records sites, and fee-based information broker sites.

The Privacy Rights Organization, along with many other private and governmental authorities, recommends numerous strategies individuals can take. A brief summary of their recommendations follows—

---

[1] for the full Privacy Rights Clearinghouse report, see www.privacyrights.org/identity.htm and go to *Fact Sheet No. 17*

## Check your own credit periodically

The best defense against suspected identify fraud is to obtain and review your credit report on a regular basis. The reports from all three bureaus should be reviewed. Consumers can contact all three bureaus and request reports. The contact numbers are listed at the end of this chapter.

There are also commercial services that offer a merged report with all three bureaus, as well as a commercial service that monitors a consumer's credit on an ongoing basis. The advantage is that a credit alert may warn someone who does not otherwise know he is the victim of identity theft, especially since many times a person does not discover the fraud until months after it has occurred. The downside is that a consumer has to pay to find information that should be readily available to them.

Fortunately, consumers now have more choice in the matter as a result of recent changes in the FCRA. Under recent 2003 amendments to the FCRA that took effect in 2004, the right to obtain a report has been broadened to allow a consumer to obtain a free report once a year. The procedures are explained on the Federal Trade Commission website at www.ftc.gov/bcp/conline/edcams/freereports/index.html

In addition, a consumer is entitled to a **free credit report** if he is a victim of identity theft, has been denied credit, receives welfare benefits, or is unemployed.

## Minimize access to personal data

Some ID theft prevention suggestions are—

- Do not carry excess identification that can be stolen, such as any document that contains your Social Security Number.
- Consider maintaining a low profile. This can be done by removing your name from marketing lists, getting on the "do not call" lists, and staying out of telephone books.
- Watch the mails. Do not have new checks mailed to your home, do not leave bills you are paying in a mailbox, don't let mail stack up if you are away from home.
- Guard your pin numbers and be careful about where you store passwords.
- Be extremely careful about your Social Security Number. It should be treated like a hundred dollar bill — not left around, given away, or shown unnecessarily.
- Carefully store any document with personal information. If something is being thrown away, make sure it is shredded. Dumpster divers can find a treasure trove of personal data in the trash, conveniently pre-printed on "free credit offers."

## Credit cards, credit reports, and financial papers

- Carry around just the minimum number of credit cards you need.
- Never give your Social Security Number or any credit card or any personal information to **anyone** unless you are confident that it is for a legitimate reason. If you would not give the person a $100 bill, then do not give out your Social Security Number. There are numerous stories of fake emails and even fake websites where consumers are defrauded into giving confidential information. A consumer may get an email claiming that his credit card for a trusted website has expired, or an email or phone call awarding a free trip in exchange for the

consumer providing his or her credit card or other personal information. A business that needs your Social Security Number will not be asking you for it again since you already given it to them.

- Never toss away credit card receipts that have credit card account information. Although the practice by credit card firms of putting account numbers on receipts is being phased out, consumers can never be too careful.

- Be aware of your right to place fraud alerts on your credit report.

- Carefully review your monthly financial records to make sure nothing unauthorized appears. Often, the first clue that you are the victim of identity fraud is when a bill shows up for something you never ordered, or unusual unexplained entries show up on your credit card statements or credit reports.

> **Author Tip** ➡ A substantial source of stolen personal data used for identity theft is information taken from businesses. Employers should help safeguard data concerning their employees and clients by adhering to responsible information handling practices, as discussed in Chapter 17.

## Hope to Repair the Damage

If a person is the victim of identity theft, then it can be a tremendous amount of work to unravel the damage. The topic of how to respond can be a book in itself; a number of websites give detailed advice on what to do. Some of these websites are listed as resources at the end of this chapter.

1. Report the theft to the three major credit bureaus immediately. Obtain a copy of your credit report and if necessary, place a fraud alert in your files.

2. Report the theft to the police immediately. Depending upon the state where a consumer lives, there may be helpful things the police can do. At a minimum, make a police report and get a copy of the report.

3. Review your credit report and credit card statements carefully for signs of fraudulent activity.

4. Get complete details on any fraudulent new account or any fraudulent use of an existing account.

5. Call your creditors or anyone where a fraudulent account has been opened, and tell them you are the victim of fraud. Most credit card issuers have a security department to help you. For more information on what to tell creditors, see the Federal Trade Commission's *When Bad Things Happen to Your Good Name*, available online at www.ftc.gov/bcp/conline/pubs/credit/idtheft.htm.

6. Fill out an identity theft affidavit. This may be needed by creditors who were also the victims of the identity thief. The form is available on the Federal Trade Commission website at www.ftc.gov/bcp/conline/pubs/credit/affidavit.pdf. The FTC is the federal agency leading the

fight on behalf of consumers against identity theft. You can also file a report concerning the identity theft with the FTC.

7. If an identification document is stolen, contact the issuing agency immediately. For example, if your driver's license is stolen or lost, go to your state Department of Motor Vehicles. If your mail is stolen, report it to the U.S. Postal Inspector office. If your passport is stolen, check with the State Department at the address at the end of this chapter.

8. If you are wrongly accused of a crime because a thief used your identity, check to see what program or procedures are available in your state to set the record straight. In California, for example, there is a special statewide repository where identity theft victims can register. You may need to contact your local police departments and courts to find out how to have any records corrected. Correcting the problem may involve having your fingerprints taken so that you can be eliminated as a suspect in a pending case.

9. If a bill collector contacts you, indicate you are a victim of identity theft and the debt is not yours. However, do not stop there. Write letters to bill collectors and creditors immediately — no later than 30 days — with all of the relevant information. Include as much documentation as possible in the letter, including your police report and identity theft affidavit. You have rights under federal law to stop a bill collector from bothering you.

# Helpful Resources in the War Against Identity Theft

## Credit Reporting Agencies

### Equifax
PO Box 105069, Atlanta, GA 30348.
Report fraud: Call 800-525-6285 and write to address above.
Order credit report: 800-685-1111
TDD: 800-255-0056
Website: www.equifax.com

### Experian (formerly TRW)
PO Box 9532 Allen, TX 75013
Report fraud: Call 888 EXPERIAN (888-397-3742) and write to address above.
Order credit report: 888 EXPERIAN
TDD: Use relay to fraud number above.
Website: www.experian.com

### TransUnion
PO Box 6790, Fullerton, CA 92834
Report fraud: 800-680-7289 and write to address above.

Order credit report: 800-888-4213
TDD: 877-553-7803
Email (fraud victims only): fvad@transunion.com
Website: www.transunion.com

# Additional ID Theft Related Agencies

### Federal Trade Commission Identity Theft Clearinghouse

Phone: (877) IDTHEFT (877-438-4338)

Website: www.consumer.gov/idtheft

FTC's free 34-page identity theft guide, *When Bad Things Happen to Your Good Name*, available by phone and online at www.ftc.gov/bcp/conline/pubs/credit/idtheft.htm

Learn about a free yearly credit report at www.ftc.gov/bcp/conline/edcams/freereports/index.html

### Identity Theft Resource Center

Phone: 858-693-7935

Website: www.idtheftcenter.org

### Privacy Rights Clearinghouse

Phone: 619-298-3396

Website: www.privacyrights.org

Test your identity theft risk factor online at www.privacyrights.org/itrc-quiz1.htm

### Compilation of Identity Theft Surveys

Website: www.privacyrights.org/ar/idtheftsurveys.htm

### U.S. Department of Justice

Website: www.usdoj.gov/criminal/fraud/idtheft.html

### FBI – Federal Bureau of Investigation

Website: http://norfolk.fbi.gov/1999/ident.htm

### Identity Theft Survival Kit

Phone: 800-725-0807

Website: www.identitytheft.org

### U.S. State Department, Passport Services

U.S. Dept. of State, Passport Services, Consular Lost/Stolen Passport Section, 1111 19th St., NW, Suite 500, Washington, DC 20036

# Section 5

# The Appendices

These Appendices consists of legal notices, forms, charts and other tools
to assist employers, applicants, and the pre-employment screening companies.

## Appendix 1   FCRA Summaries[1]

General Summary of Consumer Rights (Appendix F to Part 698)
Notice of Furnisher Responsibilities (Appendix G to Part 698)
Notice of User Responsibilities (Appendix H to Part 698)

## Appendix 2   Title VII EEOC Notices

Notice N-915.043 (July, 1989);     Notice N-915-061 (9/7/90);
Notice N-915 (7/29/87);     Notice N-915 (2/4/87)

## Appendix 3   Forms and Interview Questions

Telephone Interview Form;    Exit Interview Report;    Turnover Cost Calculator Form;
Employment Verification and Reference Worksheet;
Sample Request for Proposal (RFP) for Screening Services

## Appendix 4   Timelines and Tools

The Safe Hiring Timeline;    Description of Pre-Employment Screening Tools

## Appendix 5   Only in California

The Strange Saga of AB 655 - Critical New Rules Affecting Safe Hiring in California

---

[1] these documents may be viewed in the Federal Register at
http://a257.g.akamaitech.net/7/257/2422/06jun20041800/edocket.access.gpo.gov/2004/pdf/04-26240.pdf

# Appendix 1

# FCRA Summaries

## Appendix F to Part 698 - General Summary of Consumer Rights.

The prescribed form for this summary is a disclosure that it substantially similar to the Commission's model summary with all information clearly and prominently displayed. The list of federal regulators that is included in the Commission's prescribed summary may be provided separately so long as this is done in a clear and conspicuous way. A summary should accurately reflect changes to those items that may change over time (e.g., dollars amounts, or telephone numbers and addresses of federal agencies) to remain in compliance. Translation of this summary will be in compliance with the Commission's prescribed model, provided that the translation is accurate and that it is provided in a language used by the recipient consumer.

### A Summary of Your Rights Under the Fair Credit Reporting Act

Para informatcion en espanol, visite www.ftc.gov/credit o escribe a la FTC Consumer Response Center, Room 130-A 600 Pennsylvania Ave. N.W., Washington, DC 20580.

The federal Fair Credit Reporting Act (FCRA) promotes promote accuracy, fairness and privacy of information in the files of consumer reporting agencies There are many types of consumer reporting agencies, including credit bureaus and specialty agencies (such as agencies that sell information about check writing histories, medical records, and rental history records). Here is a summary of your major rights under the FCRA For more information, including information about additional rights, go to www.ftc.gov/credit or write to: Consumer Response Center, Room 130-A, Federal Trade Commission, 600 Pennsylvania Ave. N.W., Washington, DC 20580.

- **You must be told if information in your file has been used against you.** Anyone who uses a credit report or another type of consumer report to deny your application for credit, insurance, or employment – or to take another adverse action against you – must tell you, and must give you the name, address and phone number of the CRA that provided the information.

- **You have the right to know what is in your file.** You may request and obtain all the information about you in the files of a consumer reporting agency (your "file disclosure"). You will be required to provide proper identification, which may include your Social Security number. In many cases, the disclosure will be free. You are entitled to a free file disclosure if:

  o   a person has taken adverse action against you because of information in your credit report;

  o   you are a victim of identity theft and place a fraud alert in your file; your file contains inaccurate information as a result of fraud;

  o   you are on public assistance;

  o   you are unemployed but expect to apply for employment within 60 days.

- In addition, by September 2005 all consumers will be entitled to one free disclosure every 12 months upon request from each nationwide credit bureau and from nationwide specialty consumer reporting agencies. See www.ftc.gov/credit for additional information.

- **You have the right to ask for a credit score.** Credit scores are numerical summaries of your credit worthiness based on information from credit bureaus. You may request a credit score from consumer reporting agencies that create scores or distribute scores used in residential real property loans, but you will have to pay for it. In some mortgage transactions, you will receive credit score information for free from the mortgage lender.

- **You have the right to dispute incomplete or inaccurate information.** If you identify information in your file that is incomplete or inaccurate and report it to the consumer reporting agency, the agency must investigate unless your dispute is frivolous. See www.ftc.gov/credit for an explanation of dispute procedures.

- **Consumer reporting agencies must correct or delete inaccurate, incomplete, or unverifiable information.** Inaccurate, incomplete or unverifiable information must be removed or corrected, usually within 30 days. However, a consumer reporting agency may continue to report information it has verified as accurate.

- **Consumer reporting agencies may not report outdated negative information.** In most cases, a consumer reporting agency may not report negative information that is more than seven years old, or bankruptcies that are more than 10 years old.

- **Access to your file is limited.** A credit reporting agency may provide information about you only to people with a valid need -- usually to consider an application with a creditor, insurer, employer, landlord, or other business. The FCRA specifies those with a valid need for access.

- **You must give your consent for reports to be provided to employers.** A consumer reporting agency may not give out information about you to your employer, or a potential employer, without your written consent given to the employer. Written consent generally is not required in the trucking industry. For more, go to www.ftc.gov/credit.

- **You may limit "prescreened" offers of credit and insurance you get based on information in your credit report.** Unsolicited "prescreened" offers for credit and insurance must include a toll-free phone number you can call if you choose to remove your name and address from the lists these offers are based on. You may opt-out with the nationwide credit bureaus at 1-800-XXX-XXXX.

- **You may seek damages from violators.** If a consumer reporting agency, or, in some cases, a user of consumer reports or a furnisher of information to a consumer reporting agency violates the FCRA, you may be able to sue in state or federal court.

- **Identity Theft victims and active duty military personnel have additional right.** For more information, visit www.ftc.gov.credit.

State may enforce the FCRA, and many states have their own consumer reporting laws. In some cases, you may have more rights under state law. For more information, contact your state or local consumer protection agency or your state Attorney General. Federal enforcers are:

| TYPE OF BUSINESS: | CONTACT: |
|---|---|
| Consumer reporting agencies, creditors and others not listed below | **Federal Trade Commission: Consumer Response Center - FCRA**, Washington, DC 20580;  1-877-382-4357 |
| National banks, federal branches/agencies of foreign banks (word "National" or initials "N.A." appear in or after bank's name) | **Office of the Comptroller of the Currency** Compliance Management, Mail Stop 6-6, Washington, DC 20219;  1-800-613-6743 |
| Federal Reserve System member banks (except national banks and federal branches/agencies of foreign banks) | **Federal Reserve Board Division of Consumer & Community Affairs**, Washington, DC 205551 202-452-3693 |
| Savings associations and federally chartered savings banks (word "Federal" or initials "F.S.B." appear in the federal institution's name) | **Office of Thrift Supervision** Consumer Complaints, Washington, DC 20552;  800-842-6929 |
| Federal credit unions (words "Federal Credit Union" appear in institution's name) | **National Credit Union Administration** 1775 Duke St, Alexandria, VA 22314;  703-519-4600 |
| State-chartered banks that are not members of the Federal Reserve System | **Federal Deposit Insurance Corporation,** Consumer Response Center, 2345 Grand Ave, Suite 100, Kansas City, MO 64108-2638;  1-877-275-3342 |
| Air, surface, or rail common carriers regulated by former Civil Aeronautics Board of Interstate Commerce Commission | **Department of Transportation,** Office of Financial Management, Washington, DC 20590;  202-366-1306 |
| Activities subject to the Packers and Stockyards Act of 1921 | **Department of Agriculture,**  Office of Deputy Administrator - GIPSA, Washington, DC 20590;  202-720-7051 |

# Appendix G to Part 698 – Notice of Furnisher Responsibilities

The prescribed form for this disclosure is a separate document that is substantially similar to the Commission's model notice with all information clearly and prominently displayed. Consumer reporting agencies may limit the disclosure to only those items that they know are relevant to the furnisher that will receive notice.

All furnishers subject to the Federal Trade Commission's jurisdiction must comply with all applicable regulations, including regulation promulgated after this notice was prescribed in 2004. Information about applicable regulations currently in effect can be found at the Commission's website, www.ftc.gov/credit. Furnishers who are not subject to the Commission's jurisdiction should consult with their regulators to find any relevant regulations.

## Notices to Furnishers of Information: Obligations of Furnishers Under The FCRA

The federal Fair Credit Reporting Act (FCRA), 15 U.S.C. 1681-1681y, imposes responsibilities on all persons who furnish information to consumer reporting agencies (CRAs). These responsibilities are found in Section 623 of the FCRA, 15 U.S.C. 1681s-2. State law may impose additional requirements on furnishers. All furnishers of information to CRAs should become familiar with the law and may want to consult with their counsel to ensure that they are in compliance. The text of the FCRA is set forth in full at the website of the Federal Trade Commission (FTC): www.ftc.gov/credit.

Section 623 imposes the following duties upon furnishers:

**Accuracy Guidelines**

The banking and credit union regulators and the FTC will promulgate guidelines and regulations dealing with the accuracy of information provided to CRAs by furnishers. The regulations and guidelines issued by the FTC will be available at www.ftc.gov/credit when they are issued. Sections 623(e).

**General Prohibition on Reporting Inaccurate Information**

The FCRA prohibits information furnishers from providing information to a CRA that they know or have reasonable cause to believe is inaccurate. However, the furnisher is not subject to this general prohibition if it clearly and conspicuously specifies an address to which consumers may write to notify the furnisher that certain information is inaccurate. Sections 623(a)(1)(A) and (a)(1)(C).

**Duty to Correct and Update Information**

If at any time a person who regularly and in the ordinary course of business furnishes information to one or more CRAs determines that the information provided is not complete or accurate, the furnisher must promptly provide complete and accurate information to the CRA. In addition, the furnisher must notify all CRAs that received the information of any corrections, and must thereafter report only the complete and accurate information. Section 623(a)(2).

**Duties After Notice of Dispute from Consumer**

If a consumer notifies a furnisher, at an address specified by the furnisher for such notices, that specific information is inaccurate, and the information is, in fact, inaccurate, the furnisher must thereafter report the correct information to CRAs. *Section 623(a)(1)(B)*

If a consumer notifies a furnisher that the consumer disputes the completeness or accuracy of any information reported by the furnisher, the furnisher may not subsequently report that information to a CRA without providing notice of the dispute. *Section 623(a)(3)*

The federal banking and credit union regulators and the FTC will issue regulations that will identify when an information furnisher must investigate a dispute made directly to the furnisher by a consumer. Once these regulations are issued, furnishers must comply with them and complete and investigation within 30 days (or 45 days, if the consumer later provides relevant additional information) unless the disputer is frivolous or irrelevant or comes from a "credit repair organization." The FTC regulations will be available at www.ftc.gov/credit. Section 623(a)(8).

**Duties After Notice of Dispute from Consumer Reporting Agency**

If a CRA notifies a furnisher that a consumer disputes the completeness or accuracy of information provided by the furnisher, the furnisher has a duty to follow certain procedures. The furnisher must:

- Conduct an investigation and review all relevant information provided by the CRA, including information given to the CRA by the consumer. Sections 623(b)(1)(A) and (b)(1)(B).

- Report the results to the CRA that referred the dispute, and, if the investigation establishes that the information was, in fact, incomplete or inaccurate, report the results to all CRAs to which the furnisher provided the information that compile and maintain files on a nationwide basis. Sections 623(b)(1)(C) and (b)(1)(D).

- Complete the above steps within 30 days from the date the CRA receives the dispute (or 45 days, if the consumer later provides relevant additional information to the CRA). Section 623(b)(2).

- Promptly modify or delete the information, or block its reporting. Section 623(b)(1)(E).

### Duty to Report Voluntary Closing of Credit Accounts

If a consumer voluntarily closes a credit account, any person who regularly and in the ordinary course of business furnishes information to one or more CRAs must report this fact when it provides information to CRAs for the time period in which the account was closed. *Section 623(a)(4)*

### Duty to Report Dates of Delinquencies

If a furnisher reports information concerning a delinquent account placed for collection, charged to profit or loss, or subject to any similar action, the furnisher must, within 90 days after reporting the information, provide the CRA with the month and the year of the commencement of the delinquency that immediately preceded the action, so that the agency will know how long to keep the information in the consumer's file. *Section 623(a)(5)*

Any person, such as a debt collector, that has acquired or is responsible for collecting delinquent accounts and that reports information to CRAs may comply with the requirements of Section 623(a)(5) (until there is a consumer dispute) by reporting the same delinquency date previously reported by the creditor. If the creditor did not report this date, they may comply with the FCRA by establishing reasonable procedures to obtain and report delinquency dates, or, if a delinquency date cannot be reasonably obtained, by following reasonable procedures to ensure that the date reported precedes the date when the account was place for collection, charged to profit or loss, or subject to any similar action. Section 623(a)(5).

### Duty of Financial Institutions When Reporting Negative Information

Financial Institutions that furnish information to "nationwide" consumer reporting agencies, as defined in Section 603(p), must notify consumers in writing if they may furnish or have furnished negative information to a CRA. Section 623(a)(7). The Federal Reserve Board has prescribed model disclosures, 12 CFR Part 222, App. B.

### Duty When Furnishing Medical Information

A furnisher whose primary business is providing medical services, products, or devices (and such furnisher's agents or assignees) is a medical information furnisher for the purposes of the FCRA and must notify all CRAs to which it reports of this fact. Section 623(a)(9). This notice will enable CRAs to comply with their duties under Section 604(g) when reporting medical information.

### Duties When ID Theft Occurs

All furnishers must have in place reasonable procedures to respond to notifications from CRAs that information furnished is the result of identity theft, and to prevent refurnishing the information in the future. A furnisher may not furnish information that a consumer has identified as resulting from identity theft unless the furnisher subsequently knows or is informed by the consumer that the information is correct. Section 623(a)(6). If a furnisher learns that it has furnished inaccurate information due to identity theft, it must notify each consumer reporting agency of the correct information and must thereafter report only complete and accurate information. Section 623(a)(2). When any furnisher of information is notified pursuant to the procedures set forth in section 605B that a debt has resulted from identity theft, the furnisher may not sell, transfer, or place for collection the debt except in certain limited circumstances. Section 615(f).

**The FTC's website, www.ftc.gov/credit, has more information about the FCRA, including publications for business and the full text of the FCRA.**

# Appendix H to Part 698 - Notice of User Responsibilities.

The prescribed form for this disclosure is a separate document that is substantially similar to the Commission's notice with all information clearly and prominently displayed. Consumer reporting agencies may limit the disclosure to only those items that they know are relevant to the furnisher that will receive notice.

---

All users subject to the Federal Trade Commission's jurisdiction must comply with all applicable regulations, including regulations promulgated after this notice was prescribed in 2004. Information about applicable regulations currently in effect can be found at the Commission's website, www.ftc.gov/credit. Persons not subject to the Commission's jurisdiction should consult with their regulators to find any relevant regulations.

---

## Notice to Users of Consumer Reports: Obligations of Users Under the FCRA

The federal Fair Credit Reporting Act (FCRA), 15 U.S.C. 1681-1691y, requires that this notice be provided to inform users of consumer reports of their legal obligations. State law may impose additional requirements. The text of the FCRA is set forth in full at the Federal Trade Commission website at www.ftc.giv/credit. Other information about user duties is also available at the Commission's website. **Users must consult the relevant provisions of the FCRA for details about their obligations under the FCRA.**

This first section of this summary sets forth the responsibilities imposed by the FCRA on all users of consumer reports. The subsequent sections discuss the duties of users of reports that contain specific types of information, or that are used for certain purposes, and the legal consequences of violations. If you are a furnisher of information to a consumer reporting agency (CRA), you have additional obligations and will receive a separate notice from the CRA describing your duties as a furnisher.

## I. OBLIGATIONS OF ALL USERS OF CONSUMER REPORTS

### A. Users Must Have a Permissible Purpose

Congress has limited the use of consumer reports to protect consumers' privacy. All users must have a permissible purpose under the FCRA to obtain a consumer report. Section 604 of the FCRA contains a list of the permissible purposes under the law. These are:

- As ordered by a court or a federal grand jury subpoena. Section 604(a)(1).

- As instructed by the consumer in writing. Section 604(a)(2).

- For the extension of credit as a result of an application from a consumer, or the review or collection of a consumer's account. Section 604(a)(3)(A).

- For employment purposes, including hiring and promotion decisions, where the consumer has given written permission. Sections 604(a)(3)(B) and 604(b).

- For the underwriting of insurance as a result of an application from a consumer. Section 604(a)(3)(C).

- When there is a legitimate business need, in connection with a business transaction that is initiated by the consumer. Section 604(a)(3)(F)(i).

- To review a consumer's account to determine whether the consumer continues to meet the terms of the account. Section 604(a)(3)(F)(ii).

- To determine a consumer's eligibility for a license or other benefit granted by a governmental instrumentality required by law to consider an applicant's financial responsibility or status. Section 604(a)(3)(D).

- For use by a potential investor or servicer, or current insurer, in a valuation or assessment of the credit or prepayment risks associated with an existing credit obligation. Section 604(a)(3)(E).

- For use by state and local officials in connection with the determination of child support payments, or modifications and enforcement thereof. Sections 604(a)(4) and 604(a)(5).

In addition, creditors and insurers may obtain certain consumer report information for the purpose of making "prescreened" unsolicited offers of credit or insurance. Section 604(c). The particular obligations of users of "prescreened" information are described in Section VII below.

### B. Users Must Provide Certifications

Section 604(f) prohibits any person from obtaining a consumer report from a consumer reporting agency (CRA) unless the person has certified to the CRA the permissible purpose(s) for which the report is being obtained and certifies that the report will not be used for any other purpose.

### C. Users Must Notify Consumers When Adverse Actions Are Taken

The term "adverse action" is defined very broadly by Section 603 of the FCRA. "Adverse actions" include all business, credit, and employment actions affecting consumers that can be considered to have a negative impact as defined by Section 603(k) of the FCRA – such as denying or canceling credit or insurance, or denying employment or promotion. No adverse action occurs in a credit transaction where the creditor makes a counteroffer that is accepted by the consumer.

#### 1. Adverse Actions Based on Information Obtained From a CRA

If a user takes any type of adverse action as defined by the FCRA that is based at least in part on information contained in a consumer report, Section 615(a) requires the user to notify the consumer. The notification may be done in writing, orally, or by electronic means. It must include the following:

- The name, address, and telephone number of the CRA (including a toll-free telephone number, if it is a nationwide CRA) that provided the report.

- A statement that the CRA did not make the adverse decision and is not able to explain why the decision was made.

- A statement setting forth the consumer's right to obtain a free disclosure of the consumer's file from the CRA if the consumer requests the report within 60 days.

- A statement setting forth the consumer's right to dispute directly with the CRA the accuracy or completeness of any information provided by the CRA.

#### 2. Adverse Actions Based on Information Obtained From Third Parties Who Are Not Consumer Reporting Agencies

If a person denies (or increases the charge for) credit for personal, family, or household purposes based either wholly or partly upon information from a person other than a CRA, and the information is the type of consumer information covered by the FCRA, Section 615(b)(1) requires that the user clearly and accurately disclose to the consumer his or her right to be told the nature of the information that was relied upon if the consumer makes a written request within 60 days of notification. The user must provide the disclosure within a reasonable period of time following the consumer's written request.

### 3. Adverse Actions Based on Information Obtained From Affiliates

If a person takes an adverse action involving insurance, employment, or a credit transaction initiated by the consumer, based on information of the type covered by the FCRA, and this information was obtained from an entity affiliated with the user of the information by common ownership or control, Section 615(b)(2) requires the user to notify the consumer of the adverse action. The notice must inform the consumer that he or she may obtain a disclosure of the nature of the information relied upon by making a written request within 60 days of receiving the adverse action notice. If the consumer makes such a request, the user must disclose the nature of the information not later than 30 days after receiving the request. If consumer report information is shared among affiliates and then used for an adverse action, the user must make an adverse action disclosure as set forth in I.C.1 above.

### D. Users have Obligations When Fraud and Active Duty Military Alerts are in Files

When a consumer has placed a fraud alert, including one relating to identity theft, or an active duty military alert with a nationwide consumer reporting agency as defined in Section 603(p) and resellers, 605A(h) imposes limitation on users of reports obtained from the consumer reporting agency in certain circumstances, including the establishment of a new credit plan and the issuance of additional credit cards. For the initial fraud alerts and active duty alerts, the user must have reasonable policies and procedures in place to form a belief that the user knows the identity of the applicant or contact the consumer at a telephone number specified by the consumer; in the case of extended fraud alerts, the user must contact the consumer in accordance with the contact information provided in the consumer's alert.

### E. Users Have Obligations When Notified of an Address Discrepancy

Section 605(h) requires nationwide CRAs, as defined in Section 603(p), to notify users that request reports when the address for a consumer provided by the user in requesting the report is substantially different from the addresses in the consumer's file. When this occurs, users must comply with regulations specifying the procedures to be followed, which will be issued by the Federal Trade Commission and the banking and credit union regulators. The Federal Trade Commission's regulations will be available at www.ftc.gov/credit.

### F. Users Have Obligations When Disposing of Records

Section 628 requires that all users of consumer report information have in place procedures to properly dispose of records containing this information. The Federal Trade Commission, the Securities and Exchange Commission, and the banking and credit union regulators have issued regulations covering disposal. The Federal Trade Commission's regulations may be found at www.ftc.gov/credit.

## II. CREDITORS MUST MAKE ADDITIONAL DISCLOSURES

If a person uses a consumer report in connection with an application for, or a grant, extension, or provision of, credit to a consumer on material terms that are materially less favorable than the most favorable terms available to a substantial proportion of consumers from or through that person, based in whole or in part on a consumer report, the person must provide a risk-based pricing notice to the consumer in accordance with regulations to be jointly prescribed by the Federal Trade Commission and the Federal Reserve Board.

Section 609(g) requires a disclosure by all persons that make or arrange loans secured by residential real property (one to four units) and that use credit scores. These persons must provide credit scores and other information about credit scores to applicants, including the disclosure set forth in section 609(g)(1)(D)("Notice to the Home Loan Applicant").

## III. OBLIGATIONS OF USERS WHEN CONSUMER REPORTS ARE OBTAINED FOR EMPLOYMENT PURPOSES

### A. Employment Other Than in the Trucking Industry

If information from a CRA is used for employment purposes, the user has specific duties, which are set forth in FCRA Section 604(b). The user must:

- Make a clear and conspicuous written disclosure to the consumer before the report is obtained, in a document that consists solely of the disclosure, that a consumer report may be obtained.

- Obtain from the consumer prior written authorization. Authorization to access reports during the term of employment may be obtained at the time of employment.

- Certify to the CRA that the above steps have been followed, that the information being obtained will not be used in violation of any federal or state equal opportunity law or regulation, and that, if any adverse action is to be taken based on the consumer report, a copy of the report and a summary of the consumer's rights will be provided to the consumer.

- **Before** taking an adverse action, the user must provide a copy of the report to the consumer as well as the summary of the consumer's rights. (The user should receive this summary from the CRA.) A Section 615(a) adverse action notice should be sent after the adverse action is taken.

An adverse action notice also is required in employment situations if credit information (other than transactions and experience data) obtained from an affiliate is used to deny employment. Section 615(b)(2).

The procedures for investigative consumer reports and employee misconduct investigations are set forth below.

### B. Employment in the Trucking Industry

Special rules apply for truck drivers where the only interaction between the consumer and the potential employer is by mail, telephone, or computer. In this case, the consumer may provide consent orally or electronically, and an adverse action may be made orally, in writing, or electronically. The consumer may obtain a copy of any report relied upon by the trucking compnay by contacting the compnay.

## IV. OBLIGATIONS OF USERS OF INVESTIGATIVE CONSUMER REPORTS

Investigative consumer reports are a special type of consumer report in which information about a consumer's character, general reputation, personal characteristics, and mode of living is obtained through personal interviews by an entity or person that is a consumer reporting agency. Consumers who are the subjects of such reports are given special rights under the FCRA. If a user intends to obtain an investigative consumer report, Section 606 requires the following:

- The user must disclose to the consumer that an investigative consumer report may be obtained. This must be done in a written disclosure that is mailed, or otherwise delivered, to the consumer at some time before or not later than three days after the date on which the report was first requested. The disclosure must include a statement informing the consumer of his or her right to request additional disclosures of the nature and scope of the investigation as described below, and the summary of consumer rights required by Section 609 of the FCRA. (The summary of consumer rights will be provided by the CRA that conducts the investigation.)

- The user must certify to the CRA that the disclosures set forth above have been made and that the user will make the disclosure described below.

- Upon the written request of a consumer made within a reasonable period of time after the disclosures required above, the user must make a complete disclosure of the nature and scope of the investigation. This must be made in a written statement that is mailed, or otherwise delivered, to the consumer no later than five days after the date on which the request was received from the consumer or the report was first requested, whichever is later in time.

## V. SPECIAL PROCEDURES FOR EMPLOYEE INVESTIGATIONS

Section 603(x) provides special procedures for investigations of suspected misconduct by an employee or for compliance with Federal, state or local laws and regulations or the rules of a self-regulatory organization, and compliance with written policies of the employer. These investigations are not treated as consumer reports so long as the employer or its agent complies with the procedures set forth in Section 603(x), and a summary describing the nature and scope of the inquiry is made to the employee if an adverse action is taken based on the investigation.

## VI. OBLIGATIONS OF USERS OF MEDICAL INFORMATION

Section 604(g) limits the use of medical information obtained from consumer reporting agencies (other than payment information that appears in a coded form that does not identify the medical provider). If the report is to be used for an insurance transaction, the consumer must give consent to the user of the report or the information must be coded. If the report is to be used for employment purposes – or in connection with a credit transaction (except as provided in regulations issued by the banking and credit union regulators) – the consumer must provide specific written consent and the medical information must be relevant. Any user who receives medical information shall not disclose the information to any other person (except where necessary to carry out the purpose for which the information was disclosed, or as permitted by statute, regulation, or order.)

## VII. OBLIGATIONS OF USERS OF "PRESCREENED LISTS"

The FCRA permits creditors and insurers to obtain limited consumer report information for use in connection with unsolicited offers of credit or insurance under certain circumstances. Sections 603(l), 604(c), 604(e), and 615(d). This practice is known as "prescreening" and typically involves obtaining from a CRA a list of consumers who meet certain pre-established criteria. If any person intends to use prescreened lists, that person must (1) before the offer is made, establish the criteria that will be relied upon to make the offer and to grant credit or insurance, and (2) maintain such criteria on file for a three-year period beginning on the date on which the offer is made to each consumer. In addition, any user must provide with each written solicitation a clear and conspicuous statement that:

- Information contained in a consumer's CRA file was used in connection with the transaction.

- The consumer received the offer because he or she satisfied the criteria for credit worthiness or insurability used to screen for the offer.

- Credit or insurance may not be extended if, after the consumer responds, it is determined that the consumer does not meet the criteria used for screening or any applicable criteria bearing on credit worthiness or insurability, or the consumer does not furnish required collateral.

- The consumer may prohibit the use of information in his or her file in connection with future prescreened offers of credit or insurance by contacting the notification system established by the CRA that provided the report. The statement must include the address and the toll-free telephone number of the appropriate notification system.

In addition, once the Federal Trade Commission by rule has established the format, type size, and manner of the disclosure required by Section 615(d), users must be in compliance with the rule. The FTC's regulations will be at www.ftc.gov/credit.

## VIII. OBLIGATIONS OF RESELLERS

### A. Disclosure and Certification Requirements

Section 607(e) of the FCRA requires any person who obtains a consumer report for resale to take the following steps:

- Disclose the identity of the end-user to the source CRA.
- Identify to the source CRA each permissible purpose for which the report will be furnished to the end-user.
- Establish and follow reasonable procedures to ensure that reports are resold only for permissible purposes, including procedures to obtain:
  1. the identity of all end-users;
  2. certifications from all users of each purpose for which reports will be used; and
  3. certifications that reports will not be used for any purpose other than the purpose(s) specified to the reseller. Resellers must make reasonable efforts to verify this information before selling the report.

### B. Re-investigations by Resellers

Under Section 611(f), if a consumer disputes the accuracy or completeness of information in a report prepared by a reseller, the reseller must determine whether this is a result of an action or omission on its part and, if so, correct or delete the information. If not, the reseller must send the dispute to the source CRA for reinvestigation. When any CRA notifies the reseller of the results of an investigation, the reseller must immediately convey the information to the consumer.

### C. Fraud Alerts and Resellers

Section 605(f) requires resellers who receive fraud alerts or active duty alerts from another consumer reporting agency to include these in their reports.

## IX. LIABILITY FOR VIOLATIONS OF THE FCRA

Failure to comply with the FCRA can result in state government or federal government enforcement actions, as well as private lawsuits. Sections 616, 617, and 621. In addition, any person who knowingly and willfully obtains a consumer report under false pretenses may face criminal prosecution. Section 619.

---

**For More Information on the FCRA—**

The Federal Trade Commission website is filled with information, including Staff Opinion Letters, Educational Materials, and a complete copy of the Act. Visit www.ftc.gov/os/statutes/fcrajump.htm

# Appendix 2
# Title VII EEOC Notices

There are four important notices written by the Equal Employment Opportunities Commission (EEOC) that detail what an employer can and cannot do with criminal records.

- Notice N-915.043 (July, 1989)
- Notice N-915 (7/29/87)
- Notice N-915-061 (9/7/90)
- Notice N-915 (2/4/87)

For more information about the EEOC, visit their website at www.eeoc.gov

# Notice N-915.043 (July, 1989)

1. SUBJECT: Job advertising and Pre-Employment Inquiries Under the Age Discrimination In Employment Ace (ADEA).

2. PURPOSE: This policy guidance provides a discussion of job advertising and pre-employment inquiries under the ADEA. Additionally, certain defenses are discussed that may be proffered by respondents when impermissible practices appear to be involved.

3. EFFECTIVE DATE: Upon receipt.

4. EXPIRATION DATE: As an exception to EEOC Order 205.001, Appendix B, Attachment 4, § a(5), this Notice will remain in effect until rescinded or superseded.

5. ORIGINATOR: ADEA Division, Office of the Legal Counsel.

6. INSTRUCTIONS: File behind § 801 of Volume II of the Compliance Manual.

7. SUBJECT MATTER:

## I. JOB ADVERTISING

### A: GENERAL

The ADEA makes it unlawful, unless a specific exemption applies, for an employer to utilize job advertising that discriminates on account of age against persons 40 years of age or older. Specifically, sec. 4(e) of the ADEA provides as follows:

> It shall be unlawful for an employer, labor organization, or employment agency to print of publish, or cause to be printed or published, any notice or advertisement relating to employment by such an employer or membership in or any classification or referral for employment by such a labor organization, or relating to any classification or referral for employment by such an employment agency, indicating any preference, limitation, specification, or discrimination, based on age.   29 USC. § 623(e).

The commission interpretative regulation further develops the statutory language by providing the following guidance.

> When help wanted notices or advertisements contain terms and phrases such as "age 25 to 35," "young," "college student," "recent college graduate," "boy," "girl," or others of a similar

nature, such a term or phrase a violation of the Act, unless one of the exceptions applies. Such phrases as "40 to 50," "age over 65," "retired persons," or "supplement your pension" discriminate against others within the protected group and, therefore, are prohibited unless one of the exceptions applies. 29 C.F.R. S 1625.4(a).

Former Secretary of Labor, Willard Wirtz, in his 1965 report to Congress on age discrimination in employment was among the first to recognize a need to carefully assess employers' job advertisements, to assure that older workers are not arbitrarily discriminated against.

> The most obvious kind of discrimination in employment takes the form of employer policies of not haring people over a certain age, without consideration of a particular applicant's individual qualifications. These restrictive practices appear in announced employer policies (e.g., in help-wanted advertisements; or in job orders filed with employment agencies) or in dealing with applicants when they appear in the hiring office.1

Congress responded to this concern, in part, by enacting sec. 4(e). Covered entities are limited by sec. 4(e) of the ADEA with respect to the content of their job notices and advertisements. They must be careful to avoid not only explicit age based limitations, but also advertisements that implicitly deter older persons from applying. For example, a "job description can exert a subtle form of discrimination by setting qualifications of education that are completely appropriate for the young employee and completely irrelevant for someone with 30 years experience."[2]

Although the language of sec. 4(e) is relatively straightforward, and judicial and Commission interpretations have added insight as to its application, generally there remains the need for a careful, case-by-case assessment as to whether a particular job advertisement runs afoul of sec. 4(e). The analysis requires an examination not only of the language used in the advertisement but also the context in which it is used to determine whether persons in the protected age group would be discouraged from applying.

In Hodgson v. Approved Personnel Service Inc., 529 F.2d 760 (4th Cir. 1975), the court examined over fifty advertisements published by the defendant, an employment agency. The court held that some of the advertisements violated the ADEA while others did not. The defendant's advertisements used such words and phrases as: "recent college graduate." "those unable to continue in college," "1-2 years out of college," "excellent first job," "any recent degree," "recent high school grad," "young executive," recent technical school grad," "junior secretary," "junior accountant," "athletically inclined," "career girls," "young office group," and "all American type."

The court's analysis of each phrase involved close scrutiny of the advertisement in its entirety to determine whether sec. 4(e) had been violated. Specifically the court stated, "we are inclined to think that the discriminatory effect of an advertisement is determined no solely by "trigger words" but rather by its context."[3] In order to determine from its context whether the advertisement is in fact discriminatory, one must read the ad in its entirety, taking into consideration the results of the ad on the employer's hiring practices. The mere presence of "trigger words: does not constitute a violation of the ADEA.

---

[1] *The Older American Worker, Age Discrimination In Employment, Report of the Secretary of Labor to the Congress Under Section 715 of the Civil Rights Act of 1964*, 6 (1965)

[2] *Improving The Age Discrimination Law: A Working Paper, Senate Special Committee on Aging*, 93d Cong., 1st Sess. 6 (1973).

[3] *Hodgson v. Approved Personnel Serv.* At 765.

Those words and phrases found by the <u>Hodgson</u> court not to violate the ADEA are as follows: 1) "young executive seeks," refers to the age of the employer and does not state an age requirement for job applicants or suggest that older persons will not be considered; 2) "young office group," certainly carries an implication that an older person might not fit in but it tells the older applicant something he may want to know: that those already employed who will be his work associates are young; 3) "Athletically inclined" or "all American type," state qualifications relating to personal appearance and physical characteristics which can exist in persons at any age; 4) "junior," this adjective when applied to an employee's job description designates the scope of his duties and responsibilities. And does not carry connotations of youth prohibited by the Act; <u>Hodgson</u> at page 767 (Appendix). Of course, in a different context, the outcome with respect to any of the foregoing words and phrases might be different. As stated in the text, a case-by-case fact specific analysis is always required.

Read in context, "trigger words" may be innocent in some advertisements and clearly discriminatory in others. Hodgson at 765. The above concepts are demonstrated by the following examples.

EXAMPLE 1 = CP, a 65 year old, saw an ad in the newspaper for a cashier at a local supermarket ®. R's advertisement specified that "applicant must be young, energetic, and posses excellent customer relations skills. Applicants who are selected would be required to stand long periods of time and to lift 20-30 pounds." CP contacted the Commission to institute a charge against R, local supermarket. In this case the Commission would find a violation. By use of the word "young" the ad specifically indicates a preference, limitation, specification or discrimination based on age. Such an ad would almost certainly deter many qualified older persons from applying. Note that if the same ad appeared with only the word "young" deleted, it would probably be acceptable. Persona of all ages can be energetic and possess excellent customer relations skills. Further, the need to stand for long periods and to lift 20-30 pounds are not age related criteria and, in any event, appear to be legitimate requirements for the job in question.

EXAMPLE 2 – CP, a 57 year old graphic artist, claims that R, Advertising Firm, has discriminated against him based on age by publishing an advertisement which he feels clearly deters older persons from applying. R's ad stated, "Young-thinking, 'new wave' progressive advertising firm has openings for entry level position for graphic artist with no more than 3 years experience. We specialize in music videos and broadcast productions for a youthful audience. Our main focus is in the area of animation. Our clients include famous rock stars. If you have fresh, innovative ideas, and can relate to our audience, send your resume." While the ad does not contain explicit age limitations, read in its entirety, it does appear that persons in the protected age group would be discouraged from applying for the position. The employer contends that it does not discriminate against older persons and would hire a 75 year old applicant if he or she is qualified and willing to work for an entry level salary. However, on further investigation it was found that the employer has no employees over 30 years of age. It was also revealed that the firm recently turned down two fully qualified graphic artists X and Y, ages 47 and 67, who were willing to work at an entry level salary, though both possessed more that 3 years of experience. In this context the Commission would probably take the position that the ad is designed to deter older persons from applying. The Commission would seek to have R change the ad to read "young-thinking persons of any age with at least 3 years experience and willing to work at an entry level salary." The Commission would also attempt to contact X and Y to investigate the circumstances surrounding the denial of employment for the advertised position. The Commission has provided further specific guidance for investigating such incidents of "subtle" discriminatory advertising. See Volume I, Investigative Procedures Manual, § 8.6(b)(3)(i).

As indicated in sec. 1625.4(a), younger persons in the protected age group, for example, those individuals older than 40 but not old enough to retire, may be victimized by job advertising favoring older persons within the protected age group. The following example illustrates how this situation may occur.

> EXAMPLE 3 – CP, a 42 year old individual who is actively seeking part-time employment, contends that she was deterred from applying for a position because of the employer's ad. R, a local Laundromat, advertised in the newspaper as follows: "Opening for a person seeking to supplement pension. Part-time position available for Laundromat Attendant from 9:00 am – 2:00 PM, Monday-Thursday. Responsibilities include dispensing products sold on premises, maintaining washer, dryer, and vending machines. Retired persons preferred." This ad limits the applicant pool by indicating a preference based on age. Persons rarely receive pensions or attain retirement status before 55 and frequently not until age 65. Thus, the ad deters younger persons within the protected age group from applying. Therefore it is a violation of sec. 4(e) unless one of the exceptions to the Act applies.

Note, however, that the Commission would be unlikely to find a violation in situations where an age-neutral advertisement encourages individuals within the protected age group to actively seek the position(s) available.[4]

> EXEMPLE 4 – In response to a acute labor shortage that exists throughout the southeast region of the country, R, a large home improvement chain publishes the following advertisement:
>
> > WANTED; Individuals of all ages. Day and evening hours available. Full and part-time positions. All inquiries welcomed. Excellent secondary source of income for retirees.

While the ad mentions "retirees," the Commission would not find an illegal age-based discriminatory advertising practice in this instance. Individuals of all ages are welcomed for the employment opportunity. The reference to retirees in the ad does not, on its face, indicate a preference for this sub-grouping of the protected age group. Rather, it notifies them of an opportunity and invites them to participate. The language in this ad differs from the language used in Example 3 which suggests that only retired, pension eligible persons are considered for employment.

## B. EMPLOYMENT AGENCY ADVERTISEMENTS

Some courts have fashioned an exception to the general rules when the advertising in question is done by an employment agency and is intended to acquaint persons with the agency's services.[5] The Hodgson court held that when employment agencies use such phrases as "recent grad," or others of a similar nature to appeal acquaint such individuals with the agency's services, the ADEA is not violated. However, such an advertisement would seem to clearly indicate a preference, limitation, specifications, or discrimination based on age which is prohibited by the ADEA. The Commission, therefore, would not agree with the exception fashioned in the Hodgson decision. As a general enforcement principle, the Commission will closely scrutinize all ads that use words and phrases that would deter older persons from applying, including those used by employment agencies to inform the public of their services. An employment agency could as easily advertise generally for persons looking for employment by

---

[4] Section 2(b) of the ADEA states in pertinent part that "[I]t is therefore the purpose of this Act to promote employment of older persons based on their ability rather than age." See also EEOC Opinion Letter – 1, December 13, 1983 (ADEA rights of retirees).

[5] See Hodgson at 766

including in the advertisement language making it clear that both young and older applicants are wanted.[6]

In summary, a careful analysis of job advertising practices, whether by an employer or employment agency, is required in determining whether a violation of sec. 4(e) of the ADEA has occurred. If an ADEA charge/complaint raises the issue of an illegal age-based discriminatory advertising practice the following analytical scheme of investigation is suggested.

In some instances an advertisement may use a term or phrase which is listed in 29 C.F.R. § 1625.4(a). If an employer or employment agency resorts to the use of such terminology the advertising practice is per se illegal and a finding of a violation of sec. 4(e) of the ADEA is warranted, unless an exception (e.g., BFOQ) applies.

In many cases, however, the challenged advertisement will not contain direct age-based prohibited specifications or preferences and as such the legality of the advertising practice will depend upon the overall context, application and effect of discouraging individuals within the protected age group from applying or, in the alternative, generally limits, classifies or otherwise discriminates against an individual based on age. Specific attention in such instances should be given but not limited to charging party's/complainant's (1) explanation of why the ad served to discourage him or her from applying; (2) respondent's overall hiring practices, or; (3) a comparative analysis of respondent's applicant flow data with similar size employers using nondiscriminatory advertising practices. See generally Volume I, Investigative Procedures Manual, § 8.6(b)(3)(i)(ii).

## C. BONA FIDE OCCUPATIONAL QUALIFICAITON DEFENSE

Where an ad is per se discriminatory on the basis of age, a respondent may seek to invoke the :bona fide occupational qualification" defense, hereinafter referred to as "BFOQ," to justify the use of the ad.[7] If, because of the requirements of a job, an employer believes it must limit, specify, or discriminate based on age, an employer has the burden of proving that the position is a BFOQ.[8]

There are several elements which must be met in establishing a BFOQ defense. Whenever this defense is raised an employer must always show that the age limit is reasonably necessary to the essence of the business."[9] In proving that age must be used as a proxy for ability to perform the job, an employer must next show that either "all or substantially all individuals excluded from the job are in fact disqualified,"[10] or "some of the individuals so excluded possess a disqualifying trait that cannot be ascertained except by reference to age."[11]

Unless the employer can establish the existence of a BFOQ, the ad would have to be modified to eliminate any limitations based upon age.

---

[6] C. Edelman & I. Sigler, *Federal Age Discrimination in Employment Law, Slowing Down the Gold Watch*, 96 (1978). The Commission, for example, would encourage the use of such phrases as "state of the art knowledge" in lieu of "recent college graduate" or recommend to employment agencies the use of a specific disclaimer such as, "While we are skilled in assisting recent grads in finding positions, we encourage applicants of all ages and levels of experience – neither this agency nor any of our clients discriminate on the basis of an applicant's age."

[7] Section 4(f)(l) of the ADEA permits an employer "to take any action otherwise prohibited under subsection (a), (b), (c), or (e) of this section where age is a bona fide occupational qualification reasonably necessary to the normal operation of the particular business."

[8] 29 C.F.R.S 1625.6(b)

[9] 29 C.F.R. S 1625.6(b)(3)

[10] 29 C.F.R.S 1625.6(b)(2)

[11] 29 C.F.R. S 1625.6(b)(1)

EXAMPLE 5 – CP, a 43 year old fashion model, contends that she has been discriminated against based on age. R, a modeling agency, advertised in the newspaper as follows:" Experienced models between 20-30 for upcoming spring collection of 'junior sportswear.' Applicants must bring a portfolio and references to our New York Office. Only those persons in the specified age category need apply." CP auditioned and was rejected when the company found out her age. During the investigation, R raises the BFOQ defense and states that the "junior collection requires applicants who have a youthful appearance. R further alleges that traditionally the "junior" fashions are targeted to younger women, generally between 20-30. However, while CP is 43, she appears to be 23. In fact, R was in the process of completing the paperwork necessary to hire CP when its personnel manager noticed the date of birth on her driver's license. R is not able to prove that persons 40 or older have a disqualifying trait that cannot be ascertained except by reference to age. R has not established the existence of a BFOQ and its discriminatory ad must be changed. R has also violated the Act by its failure to hire CP on account of her age.

In sum, the employer has the burden of proving a bona fide occupational qualification. The Commission and the courts construe this defense very narrowly. If, however, the employer satisfies the requirements of the exemption, it can continue to express appropriate age limitations in its job ads.

## II. PRE-EMPLOYMENT INQUIRIES

Pursuant to sec. 4(a)(1) of the ADEA, 29 U. S. C. § 623(A)(1), "[I]t shall be unlawful for an employer to fail or refuse to hire or to discharge any individual or otherwise discriminate against any individual with respect to his compensation, terms, conditions, or privileges of employment, because of such individual's age." Although it is almost always unlawful to make employment decisions based on age, a pre-employment inquiry on the part of an employer for information such as "Date of Birth" or "State Age" on an application form is not, in itself, a violation of the ADEA.

However, because the request that an applicant state his age may tend to deter older applicants from applying, pre-employment inquires which request such information will be closely scrutinized by the Commission to assure that the request is for a permissible purpose and not for a purpose proscribed by the Act. There must be legitimate, non-discriminatory reasons for seeking the information and the information must not be used for an impermissible purpose.

The Commission has addressed the issue of pre-employment inquiries concerning age in two separate provisions. The first provision, 29 C.F.R. § 1625.4(b), Specifically addresses requests in help-wanted notices or advertisements for age or date of birth. The Commission's position in regard to help-wanted notices and advertisements is that although inquiries regarding age will be closely scrutinized, such inquiries are not per se violations of the Act.

The second provision, 29 C.F.R. § 1625.5, focuses on requests for age on employment application forms. The Commission regulation at 29 C.F.R. § 1625.5 provides in part:

A request on the art of an employer for information such as "Date of Birth" or "State Age" on an application form is not, in itself, a violation of the Act. But because the request that an applicant state his age may tend to deter older applicants or otherwise discriminate based on age, employment application forms which request such information will be closely scrutinized to assure that the request is for a permissible purpose and not for purposes proscribed by the Act. That the purpose is not one proscribed by the statute should be made known to the applicant. The term "employment applications" refers to all written inquiries about employment or application for employment or promotion including, but not limited to, resumes or other summaries of the applicant's background. It relates not only to written pre-employment inquiries, but to inquiries concerning terms, conditions, or privileges of employment as specified in section 4 of the Act.

The purpose of section 1625.5 is to insure that older applicants are judged on ability rather than age. To assure applicants in the protected age group that an inquiry as to age is for a permissible purpose, employers should include a reference on the application form stating that the employer does not discriminate on the basis of age. Another option would be to explain to each applicant the specific reason why the information concerning age is being requested. Most importantly, of course, employers must not use age related inquiries for an impermissible purpose.

EXAMPLE 6 – CP, a 55 year old radio announcer, sent a resume to R, WZAB, for the position of Program Director. WZAB's format is "hard rock." R responded by forwarding CP an employment application and scheduling an interview. The application requested CP to state his age, and also stated the statutory prohibition against age discrimination in employment. At the interview CP was introduced to the staff, all of whom appeared to be between the ages of 18 and 35. During the interview, CP discussed his past experience and talked at length about how the radio business had changed since he had begun his career. R asked CP if he would be opposed to having a younger supervisor and whether or not CP enjoyed working with younger people. Two days lager CP received a rejection letter from R. CP alleges that he was discriminated against based on age. It was later found that X, a 23 year old who was hired for the position of Program Director, did not submit an application and no inquiry was made as to her age. This evidence conflicted with R's statement that it was a standard practice to ascertain the age of all applicants. Despite the presence of the statutory prohibition against age discrimination on the application form, it would appear that in this particular instance, the inquiry about age was not applied uniformly and was used only to disqualify CP. Thus, even if an employer sets forth the statutory prohibition against age discrimination on the application form, when an age related inquiry is challenged, the employer must show that it has legitimate non-discriminatory reasons for seeking the information.

## III. CASE RESOLUTION

The Commission's position is that employment related inquiries requesting an applicant's age or date of birth will be closely scrutinized on a case-by-case basis to assure that they are for a lawful purpose.

Pre-employment inquiries as to age which are used for the purpose of disqualifying persons in the protected age group are prohibited. When the employer's inquiry does not serve any legitimate purpose, or the practice is not uniformly adhered to, it is quite likely that the information is being sought for purposes proscribed by the ADEA.[12]

[ Signed by Clarence Thomas on 07-02-89]

Date: _____     Signed:_____

Clarence Thomas

Chairman

---

[12]The ADEA principles and the BFOQ defense discussed in the text apply equally to Title VII. See, e.g., 29 C.F.R. S 1604.7. It should be noted, however, that the BFOQ defense under Title VII is limited to religion, sex, and national origin.

# Notice N-915-061 (9/7/90)

1. SUBJECT: Policy Guidance on the Consideration of Arrest Records in Employment Decisions under Title VII of the Civil Rights Act of 1964, as amended, 42 USC. § 2000e et seq. (1982).

2. PURPOSE: This policy guidance sets forth the Commission's procedure for determining whether arrest records may be considered in employment decisions.

3. EFFECTIVE DATE: September 7, 1990.

4. EXPIRATION DATE: As an exception to EEOC Order 205.001, Appendix B, Attachment 4, § a(5), this Notice will remain in effect until rescinded or superseded.

5. ORIGINATOR: Title VII/EPA Division, Office of the Legal Counsel.

6. INSTRUCTIONS: File behind the last Policy Guidance § 604 of Volume II of Compliance Manual.

7. SUBJECT MATTER:

## I. Introduction

The question addressed in this policy guidance is "to what extent may arrest records be used in making employment decisions?" The Commission concludes that since the use of arrest records as a absolute bar to employment has a disparate impact on some protected groups, such records alone cannot be used to routinely exclude persons from employment. However, conduct which indicates unsuitability for a particular position is a basis for exclusion. Where it appears that the applicant or employee engaged in the conduct for which he was arrested and that the conduct is job-related and relatively recent, exclusion is justified.

The analysis set forth in this policy guidance is related to two previously issued policy statements regarding the consideration of conviction records in employment decisions: "Policy Statement on the Issue of Conviction Records under Title VII of the Civil Rights Act of 1964, as amended 42 U.S.C. § 2000e et seq. (1982)" (hereinafter referred to as the February 4, 1987 Statement) and "Policy Statement on the use of statistics in charges involving the exclusion of individuals with conviction records from employment" (hereinafter referred to ad July 29, 1987 Statement). The February 4, 1987 Statement states that nationally, Blacks and Hispanics are convicted in numbers which are disproportionate to Whites and that barring people from employment based on their conviction records will therefore disproportionately exclude those groups.[1] Due to this adverse impact, an employer may not base an employment decision on the conviction record of an applicant or an employee absent business

---

[1] The July 29 Statement notes that despite national statistics showing adverse impact, an employer may refute this *prima facie* showing by presenting statistics which are specific to its region or applicant pool. If these statistics demonstrate that the policy has no adverse impact against a protected group, the plaintiff's *prima facie* case has been rebutted and the employer need not show any business necessity to justify the use of the policy. Statistics relating to arrests should be used in the same manner.

necessity.[2] Business necessity can be established where the employee or applicant is engaged in conduct which is particularly egregious or related to the position in question.

Conviction records constitute reliable evidence that a person engaged in the conduct alleged since the criminal justice system requires the highest degree of proof ("beyond a reasonable doubt") for a conviction. In contract, arrests alone are not reliable evidence that a person has actually committed a crime. Schware v. Board of Bar Examiners, 353 US 232, 241 (1957) ("[t]he mere fact that a [person] has been arrested has very little, if any, probative value in showing that he has engaged in misconduct.") Thus, the Commission concludes that to justify the use of arrest records, an additional inquiry must be made. Even where the conduct alleged in the arrest record is related to the job at issue, the employer must evaluate whether the arrest record reflects the applicant's conduct. It should, therefore, examine the surrounding circumstances, offer the applicant or employee an opportunity to explain, and, if he or she denies engaging in the conduct, make the follow-up inquiries necessary to evaluate his/her credibility. Since using arrests as a disqualifying criteria can only be justified where it appears that the applicant actually engaged in the conduct for which he/she was arrested and that conduct is job related, the Commission further concludes that an employer will seldom be able to justify making broad general inquiries about an employee's or applicant's arrests.

The following discussion is offered for guidance in determining the circumstances under which an employer can justify excluding an applicant or an employee on the basis of an arrest record.

## II. Discussion

### A. Adverse Impact of the Use of Arrest Records

The leading case involving an employer's use of arrest records is Gregory v. Litton Systems, 316 F. Supp. 401, 2 EPD ¶ 10,264 (C.D. Cal. 1970), modified on other grounds, 472 F.2d 631, 5 EPD ¶ 8089 (9th Cir. 1972). Litton held that nationally, Blacks are arrested more often than are Whites. Courts and the Commission have relied on the statistics presented in Litton to establish a prima facie case of discrimination against Blacks where arrest records are used in employment decisions.[3] There are, however, more recent statistics, published by the US Department of Justice, Federal Bureau of Investigation, which are consistent with the Litton finding.[4] It is desirable to use the most current

---

[2] The policy statements on convictions use the term "business necessity," as used by courts prior to the Supreme Court's decision in *Wards Cove Packing Co. v. Atonio*, 109 S. Ct. 2115 (1989). In *Atonio*, the Supreme Court adopted the term "business justification" in place of business necessity, but noted that "although we have phrased the query differently in different cases...the dispositive issue is whether a challenged practice serves, in a significant way, the legitimate employment goals of the employer, "citing, *inter alia, Griggs v. Duke Power Co.*, 401 US 424 (1971). 109 S. Ct. at 2125-2126.

[3] US v. City of Chicago, 385 F. Supp. 543, 556-557 (N.D. Ill. 1974), adopted by reference, 411 F. Supp. 218, aff'd in rel. part, 549 F.2d 415, 432 (7th Cir. 1977); City of Cairo v. Illinois Fair Employment Practice Commission, et al., 8 EPD ! 9682 (Ill. App. Ct. 1974); Commission Decision Nos. 78-03, 77-23, 76-138, 76-87, 76-39, 74-92, 74-90, 74-83, 74-02, CCH EEOC Decisions (1983) !! 6714, 6710, 6700, 6665, 630, 6424, 6423, 6414, 6386 and Commission Decisions Nos. 72-1460, 72-1005, 72-094 and 71-1950, CCH EEOC Decisions (1973) !! 6341, 6357 and 6274 respectively.

[4] The FBI's Uniform Crime Reporting Program reported that in 1987, 29.5% of all arrests were of Blacks. The US. Census reported that Blacks comprised 11.7% of the national population in 1980 and projected that the figure would reach 12.2% in 1987. Since the national percentage of arrest for Blacks is more that twice the percentage of their

available statistics. In addition, where local statistics are available, it may be helpful to use them, as the court did in Reynolds v. Sheet Metal Workers Local 102, 498 F. Supp. 952, 22 EPD ¶ 30,739 (D.C. 1980), aff'd., 702 F.2d 221, 25 EPD ¶ 31,706 (D.C. Cir. 1981). In Reynolds, the court found that the use of arrest records in employment decisions adversely affected Blacks since the 1978 Annual Report of the Metropolitan Police of Washington, D.C., stated that 85.5% of persons arrested in the District of Columbia were nonwhite while the nonwhite population constituted 72.4% of the total population. 498 F. Supp. At 960. The Commission has determined that Hispanics are also adversely affected by arrest record inquiries. Commission Decisions Nos. 77-23 and 76-03, CCH EEIC Decisions (1983) ¶¶ 6714 and 6598, respectively.[5] However, the courts have not yet addressed this issue[6] and the FBI's Uniform Crime Reporting Program does not provide information on the arrest records (see July 29, 1987 Statement), the employer may rebut by presenting statistics which are more current, accurate and/or specific to its region or applicant pool than are the statistics presented in the prima facie case.

## B. Business Justification

If adverse impact is established, the burden of producing evidence shifts to the employer to show a business justification for the challenged employment practice. Wards Cove Packing Co. v. Atonio, 109 S.Ct. 2115, 2126 (1989).[7] As with conviction records, arrest records may be considered in the employment decision as evidence of conduct which may render an applicant unsuitable for a particular position. However, in the case of arrests, not only must the employer consider the relationship of the charges to the position sought, but also the likelihood that the applicant actually committed the conduct alleged in the charges. Gregory v. Litton Systems, 316 F. Supp. 401; Carter v. Gallagher, 452 F.2d 315, 3 EPD ¶ 8335 (8th Cir. 1971), cert. Denied, 406 U.S. 950, 4 EPD ¶ 7818 (1972); Reynolds v. Sheet Metal Workers Local 102, 498 F. Supp. 952; Dozier v. Chupka, 395 F. Supp. 836 (D.C. Ohio 1975); US. V. City of Chicago, 411 F. Supp. 218 (N.D. Ill. 1974), aff'd. in rel. part, 549 F.2d 415 (7th Cir. 1977); City of Cairo v. Illinois Fair Employment Practice Commission et al., 8 EPD ¶ 9682 (Ill. App. Ct. 1974); Commission Decisions Mos. 78-03, 77-23, 76-138, 76-87, 76-54, 76-39, 76-17, 74-92, 74-83, 76-03, 74-90, 78093, 74025, CCH EEOC Decisions (1983) ¶¶ 6714, 6710, 6700, 6665, 6639, 630, 612, 6424, 6414, 6598, 6423, 6400 and Commission Decisions Nos. 72-0947, 72-1005, 72-1460, CCH EEOC Decisions (1973) ¶¶ 6357, 6350 and 6341, respectively.

---

representation in the population (whether considering the 1980 figures or the 1987 projections), the Litton presumption of adverse impact, at least nationally, is still valid.

[5] The statistics presented in Decision No. 77-23 pertain only to prison populations in the Southwestern United States. This data would, therefore, probably not constitute a prima facie case of discrimination for other regions of the country. In fact, there is no case law to indicate whether courts would accept this data as evidence of adverse impact for arrest records, even for cases arising in the Southwest, since all arrests do not result in incarceration. Decision No. 76-03 noted that Hispanics are arrested more frequently that are Whites, but no statistics were presented to support this statement.

[6] Cf. EEOC v. Carolina Freight Carriers, 723 F. Supp. 734, 751, 52 EPD ¶ 39, 538 (S.D. Fla. 1989) (EEOC failed to provide statistics for the relevant labor market to prove that trucking company's exclusion of drivers with, convictions for theft crimes had an adverse impact on Hispanics at a particular job site).

[7] Under Atonio, the burden of producing evidence shifts to the employer, but the burden of persuasion remains with the plaintiff at all stages of the Title VII case. 109 S.Ct. at 2116. Atonio thus modifies Griggs and its progeny.

## 1. A Business Justification Can Rarely Be Demonstrated for Blanket Exclusions on the Basis of Arrest Records

Since business justification rests on issues of job relatedness and credibility, a blanket exclusion of people with arrest records will almost never withstand scrutiny. Gregory v. Litton Systems, 316 F. Supp. 401. Litton held that employer's policy of refusing to hire anyone who had been arrested "on a number of occasions" violated Title VII because the policy disproportionately excluded Blacks from consideration and was not justified by business necessity. In Litton, an applicant for a position as a sheet metal worker was disqualified because of this arrest record. The court found no business necessity because the employer had failed to establish a business necessity for its discriminatory policy, it was enjoined from basing future hiring decisions on arrest records. Accord Carter v. Gallagher, 452 F.2d 315 (firefighter); Dozier v. Chupka, 395 F. Supp. 836 (firefighter); City of Cairo v Illinois Fair Employment Practice Commission, et al, 8 EPD ¶ 9682 (police officer).

The Commission has consistently invalidated employment policies which create a blanket exclusion of persons with arrest records. Commission Decision Nos. 78-03, 76-87, 76-39, 76-17, 76-03, 74-90, 74-25, 72-0947, 72-1005, CCH EEOC Decisions (1983) ¶¶ 6714 (laborer), 6665 (police officer), 6630 (cashier), 6612 (credit collector), 6598 (catalogue clerk), 6423 (uniformed guard commissioned by police department), 6400 (firefighter), 6357 (line worker) and 6350 (warehouse worker or driver). In several decisions, it appears that the arrest record inquiry was made on a standard company application which was used by the employer to fill various positions and there was no mention of any particular position sought. Commission Decision Nos. 76-138, 76-54, 74-82, 74-83, 74-02 and 72-1460, CCH EEOC Decisions (1983) ¶¶ 6700, 639, 6424, 6414, 6386 and 6341 and Commission Decision No. 71-1950, CCH EEOC Decisions (1973) ¶ 6274, respectively. An employer may not routinely exclude persons with arrest records based on the assumption that an arrest record will prevent an applicant from obtaining necessary credentials to perform a job without giving the applicant an opportunity to obtain those credentials. For example, in Decision 76-87, the Commission rejected an employer's assertion that employees' arrest records might hinder its ability to maintain fidelity (bond) insurance since it offered no proof to this effect.

Even where there is no direct evidence that an employer used an arrest record in an employment decision, a pre-employment inquiry regarding arrest records may violate Title VII. It is generally presumed that an employer only asks questions which he/she deems relevant to the employment decision. Gregory v. Litton Systems, 316 F. Supp. At 403-404. Noting that information which is obtained is likely to be used, the court in Litton enjoined the employer from making any pre-employment inquiries regarding arrests which did not result in convictions. Id.[8] But see EEOC f. Local 638, 532 F.2d 821 (2d Cir. 1976) (inquiry not invalidated where there was no evidence that union actually rejected applicants who had been arrested but not convicted); Jimerson v. Kisco, 404 F. Supp.

---

[8] Furthermore, potential applicants who have arrest records may be discouraged from applying for positions which require them to supply this information, thus creating a "chilling effect" on the Black applicant pool. Carter v. Gallagher, 452 F.2d at 330-331; Reynolds v. Sheet Metal Workers, Local 102, 498 F. Supp. At 964 n.12, 966 n.13, 967, 973; Commission Decision Nos. 76-138, 76-87, 76-17, 74-90, 74-25 and 74-02, CCH EEOC Decisions (1983) !! 6700, 6665, 612, 6423, 6400, 6386 and Commission Decision Nos. 74-1005 and 71-1950, CCH EEOC Decisions (1973) !! 6350 and 6274, respectively.

338 (E.D. Mo. 1975) (court upheld discharge for falsifying information regarding arrest record on a pre-employment application without considering the inquiry itself violated Title VII).[9] Numerous states have specifically prohibited or advised against pre-employment inquiries in their fair employment laws due to the possible misuse of this information.[10]

2. The Alleged Conduct Must Be Related to the Position Sought

As discussed above, an arrest record may be used as evidence of conduct upon which an employer makes an employment decision. An employer may deny employment opportunities to persons based on any prior conduct which indicates that they would be unfit for the position in question, whether that conduct is evidenced by an arrest, conviction or other information provided to the employer. It is the conduct, not he arrest or conviction per se, which the employer may consider in relation to the position sought. The considerations relevant to the determination of whether the alleged Conduct demonstrates unfitness for the particular job were set forth in Green v. Missouri Pacific Railroad Co., 549 F.2d 1158, 1160, 13 EPD ¶ 11, 579 (8th Cir. 1977) and reiterated in the February 4, 1987 Statement on Convictions, page 2:

- the nature and gravity of the offense or offenses;
- the time that has passed since the conviction[11] (or in this case, arrest) .; and
- the nature of the job held or sought.

See also Carter v. Maloney Trucking and Storage Inc., 631 F.2d 40, 43, 24 EPD ¶ 31,348 (5th Cir. 1980) (employer refused to rehire an ex-employee who had murdered a co-worker, not solely because of his conviction, but because he was a dangerous person and friends of the murdered man might try to retaliate against him while he was on the job); Osborne v. Cleland, 620 F.2d 195, 22 EPD on a charge of "sexual procurement" was unfit to be a nursing assistant in a psychiatric ward); Lane v. Inman, 509 F.2d 184 (5th Cir. 1975) (city ordinance which prohibited the issuance of taxicab driver permits to persons convicted of smuggling marijuana was "so obviously job related" that "it could not be held to be unlawful race discrimination," irrespective of any adverse impact); EEOC v. Carolina Freight, 723 F. Supp. 734, 52 EPD ¶ (S.D. Fla. 1989) (criminal history was related to position of truck driver who transported valuable property); McCray v. Alexander, 30 EPD ¶ 33,219 (D. Colo. 1982), aff'd 38 EPD ¶35,509 (10th Cir. 1985) (supervisory guard was discharged for killing a motorist, while off-duty, in a

---

[9] Note also that in Walls v. City of Petersburg, 895 F.2d 188, 52 EPD ! 39,602 (4th Cir. 1990), the court upheld an employer's policy of making an employment inquiry regarding the arrest records of employees' immediate family members. The court determined that under Atonio, the plaintiff was obligated to show not only that Blacks were more likely to have "negative" responses to this question, but also that the employer made adverse employment decisions based on such responses.

[10] New York, Hawaii, Oregon, Wisconsin, New Jersey, Ohio, Virginia, District of Columbia, California, Maryland, Minnesota, Utah, Washington, West Virginia, Arizona, Colorado, Idaho, Massachusetts, Michigan, Mississippi.

[11] But see EEOC v. Carolina Freight Carriers, 723 F. Supp. At 753 (court upheld trucking company's lifetime bar to employment of drivers who had been incarcerated for theft crimes since EEOC did not produce evidence that a 5-10 year bar would be an equally effective alternative). Note also that the court in Carolina Freight specifically rejected the Eighth Circuit's reasoning in Green, cautioning that Green could be construed too broadly. 723 F. Supp. At 752.

traffic dispute because employer concluded that, despite his acquittal, the conduct showed poor judgment on the use of deadly force).

Where the position sought is "security sensitive," particularly where it involves enforcing the law or preventing crime, courts tend to closely scrutinize evidence of prior criminal conduct of applicants. US. V. City of Chicago, 411 F. Supp. 217, 11 EPD ¶ 10,597 (N.D. Ill. 1976), aff'd in rel. part, 549 F.2d 415, 13 EPD ¶ 11,380 (7th Cir. 1977), on remand, 437 F. Supp. 256 (N.D. Ill. 1977) (applicants for the police department were disqualified for prior convictions for "serious" offenses); Richardson v. Hotel Corporation of America, 332 F. Supp. 519, 4 EPD ¶ 7666 (E.D. La. 1971), aff'd mem., 468 F.2d 951, 4 EPD ¶ 7666 (5th Cir. 1972) (bellman was discharged after his conviction for theft and receipt of stolen goods was discovered since bellmen had access to guests; rooms and was not subject to inspection when carrying packages); Haynie v. Chupka, 17 FEP Cases 267, 271 (S.D. Ohio 1976) (police department permissibly made inquires regarding arrest records and other evidence of prior criminal conduct).[12] (See Examples 3 and 4.)

Even where the employment at issue is not a law enforcement position or one which gives the employee easy access to the possessions of others, close scrutiny of an applicant's character and prior conduct is appropriate where an employer is responsible for the safety and/or well being of other persons. Osborne v. Cleland, 620 F.2d 195 (8th Cir. 1975) (psychiatric nursing assistant); Lane v. Inman, 509 F.2d 184 (taxi driver). In these instances, the facts would have to be examined closely in order to determine the probability that an applicant would pose a threat to the safety and well being of others. (See Examples 5 and 6).

3. Evaluating the Likelihood that the Applicant Engaged in the Conduct Alleged

The cases cited above illustrate the job-relatedness of certain conduct to specific positions. In cases alleging race discrimination based on the use of arrest records as opposed to convictions, courts have generally required not only job-relatedness, but also a showing that the alleged conduct was actually committed. In City of Cairo v. Illinois Fair Employment Practice Commission, et al., 8 EPD ¶ 9682, the court held that where applicants sought to become police officers, they could not be absolutely barred from appointment solely because they had been arrested, as distinguished from convicted. See also Commission Decision No. 76-87, CCH EEOC Decisions (1983) ¶ 6665 (potential police officer could not be rejected based on one arrest five years earlier for riding in a stolen car since there was no conviction and the applicant asserted that he did not know that the car was stolen). Similarly, in Decision No. 74083, CCH EEOC Decision (1983) ¶ 6424, the Commission found no business justification for an employer's unconditional termination of all employees with arrest records (all five employees terminated were Black), purportedly to cut down on thefts in the workplace. The employer could produce no evidence that the employee had been involved in any of the thefts or that persons who are arrested, but not convicted, are prone toward crime. Commission Decision No. 74-92, CCH EEOC Decisions (1983) ¶ 6424.

---

[12] See also *Quarrels v. Brown*, 48 EPD ! 38,641 (D.C. Mich. 1988) (recent conviction was related to position of corrections officer). Note however, that this action was brought under 42 USC. S 1983, rather than Title VII, and plaintiff alleged that he was discriminated against because he was an ex-offender, not because the policy adversely affected a protected group.

An arrest record does no more than raise a suspicion that an applicant may have engaged in a particular type of conduct.[13] Thus, the investigator must determine whether the applicant is likely to step because it requires the employer either to accept the employee's denial or to attempt to obtain additional information and evaluate his/her credibility. An employer need not conduct an informal "trial" or an extensive investigation to determine an applicant's or employee's guilt or innocence. However, the employer may not perfunctorily "allow the person an opportunity to explain" and ignore the explanation where the person's claims could easily be verified by a phone call, i.e., to a previous employer or a police department. The employer is required to allow the person a meaningful opportunity to explain the circumstances of the arrest(s) and to make a reasonable effort to determine whether the explanation is credible before eliminating him/her from employment opportunities.[14] (See Examples 1, 4, 5 and 6.)

III. Examples

The following examples are provided to illustrate the process by which arrest record charges should be evaluated.

Example 1: Wilma, a Black female, applies to Buss Inc. in Highway City for a position as a bus driver. In response to a pre-employment inquiry, Wilma states that she was arrested two years earlier for driving while intoxicated. Bus Inc. rejects Wilma, despite her acquittal after trial. But Inc. does not accept her denial of the conduct alleged and concludes that Wilma was acquitted only because the breatholizer test which was administered to her at the time of her arrest was not administered in accordance with proper police procedures and was therefore inadmissible at trial. Witnesses at Wilma's trial testified that after being stopped for reckless driving, Wilma staggered from the car and had alcohol on her breath. Wilma's rejection is justified because the conduct underlying the arrest, driving while intoxicated, is clearly related to the safe performance of the duties of a bus driver; it occurred fairly recently; and there was no indication of subsequent rehabilitation.

Contrast Example Number 1 with the facts below.

Example 2: Lola, a Black female, applies to Buss Inc. for a position as a bus driver. In response to an inquiry whether she had ever been arrested, Lola states that she was arrested five years earlier for fraud in unemployment benefits. Lola admits that she committed the crime alleged. She explains that she received unemployment benefits shortly after her husband died and her expenses increased. During this period, she worked part-time for minimum wage because her unemployment check amounted to slightly less than the monthly rent for her meager apartment. She did not report the income to the State Unemployment Board for fear that her payments would be reduced and that she would not be able to feed her three young children. After her arrest, she agreed to, and did, repay the state. Bus Inc. rejected Lola. Lola's rejection violated Title VII. The commission of fraud in the unemployment system does not constitute a business justification for the rejection of an applicant for the position of bus driver. The type of crime which Lola

---

[13] The employer's suspicion may be raised by an arrest record just as it would be negative comments about an applicant's conduct made by a previous employer or a personal reference.

[14] Although the number of arrests is not determinative (see *Litton*), it may be relevant in making a credibility determination.

committed is totally unrelated to her ability to safely, efficiently and/or courteously drive a bus. Furthermore, the arrest is not recent.

Example 3: Tom, a Black male, applies to Lodge City for a position as a police officer. The arrest rate for Blacks is substantially disproportionate to that of Whites in Lodge City. In response to an arrest record inquiry, Tom states that he was arrested three years earlier for burglary. Tom is interviewed and asked to explain the circumstances surrounding his arrest. Tom admits that although the burglary charge was dismissed for lack of sufficient evidence, he did commit the crime. He claims, however, that he is a changed man, having matured since then. Lodge City rejects Tom. Police officers are: 1) entrusted with protecting the public; 2) authorized to enter nearly and dwelling under the appropriate circumstances; and 3) often responsible for transporting valuables which are confiscated as evidence. The department is, therefore, justified in declining to take the chance that Tom has reformed. Even if the department is completely satisfied that Tom has reformed, it may reject him because his credibility as a witness in court could be severely damaged if he were asked about his own arrest and the surrounding circumstances while testifying against a person whom he has arrested. Since an essential element of police work is the ability to effect an arrest and to credibly testify against the defendant in court, the department would have two separate business justifications for rejecting Tom.

The above example is contracted with circumstances under which an arrest record would not constitute ground for rejection.

Example 4: John, a Black male, applies to Lodge City for the same position as does Tom. John was arrested three years earlier for burglary. The charges were dismissed. Lodge City eliminates John from consideration without further investigation and will not consider the surrounding circumstances of the arrest. If allowed to explain, John could establish that his arrest was a case of mistaken identity and that someone else, who superficially fit John's description, was convicted of the crime for which John was initially charged. Since the facts indicate that John did not commit the conduct alleged in the arrest record, Lodge City has not carried its burden of proving a business justification for John's rejection.

Example 5: David, a Black male, applies for a teaching position in West High School. In response to a pre-employment inquiry, David states that he was arrested two years earlier for statutory rape, having been accused of seducing a seventeen-year old student in his class when he taught at another high school The charges were dismissed. West High rejects David. David relies on Litton to establish a prima facie case of race discrimination, and West High is unable to rebut the case with more current, ac curate or specific statistics. David denies that there is any truth to the charge. West High decides to conduct a further investigation and learns that David was arrested after another teacher found him engaged in sexual activity with Ann, one of his students, in the school's locker room. This event occurred on Ann's eighteenth birthday, but in the confusion of the arrest, no one realized that Ann had just reached the age of majority. Ann's parents and other teachers believed that David had seduced Ann, who has a schoolgirl "crush" on him, prior to her eighteenth birthday. However, since Ann would not testify against David, the charges had been dismissed. West High may reject David. Irrespective of Ann's age, West High is justified in attempting to protect its students from teachers who may make sexual advances toward them. Although he might not have been guilty of statutory rape, his conduct was unbefitting a teacher.

The above example is contracted to the following circumstances.

Example 6: Paul, a Black male, applies for the same position as does David. Paul was arrested two years earlier for statutory rape, having been accused of seducing a seventeen year old student in his class at another high school. West High eliminates Paul from consideration without further investigation and refuses to consider the surrounding circumstances of the arrest. When filing his complaint, Paul states that when he taught at the other high school, he befriended a troubled student in his class, Alice, who was terrified of her disciplinarian parents. Paul insists that he never touched Alice in any improper manner and that on the day before his arrest, Alice confided in him that she had become pregnant by her seventeen-year old boyfriend, Peter, and was afraid to tell her parents for fear that her father would kill him. Paul states that the charges were dismissed because the district attorney did not believe Alice's statements. The district attorney and the principal of the high school, Ms. P., confirm Paul's assessment of Alice. Ms. P; states that Peter confided in her that he was the father of Alice's baby and that Alice had assured him that nothing sexual had ever happened between her and Paul. Ms. P. states that there were indications that Alice's father was abusive, that he had beaten her into giving him the name of someone to blame for the pregnancy and that Alice thought that Paul could handle her father better than could Peter. Since Paul denied committing the conduct alleged and his explanation was well supported by the district attorney and his former employer, West High has not demonstrated a business justification for rejecting Paul.

The examples discussed above demonstrate that whereas an employer may consider a conviction as conclusive evidence that a person has committed the crime alleged, arrests can only be considered as a means of "triggering" further inquiry into that person's character or prior conduct. After considering all of the circumstances, if the employer reasonably concludes that the applicant's or employee's conduct is evidence that he or she cannot be trusted to perform the duties of the position in question, the employer may reject or terminate that person.

9-7-90                                                          *Evan J Kemp, Jr.*

_____          Approved: _____

Date                                                          Evan J Kemp, Jr.

                                                              Chairman

# Notice N-915 (7/29/87)

1. SUBJECT: Policy statement on the use of statistics in charges involving the exclusion of individuals with conviction records from employment

2. PURPOSE: This policy statement sets forth the commission's view as to the appropriate statistics to be used in evaluating an employer's policy of refusing to hire individuals with conviction records.

3. EFFECTIVE DATE: July 29, 1987

4. EXPIRATION DATE: January 29, 1988

5. ORIGINATOR: title VII.EPA Division, Office of Legal Counsel.

6. INSTRUCTIONS: insert behind §S 604 of EEOC Compliance Manual, Volume II

7. SUBJECT MATTER:

INTRODUCTION

Green v. Missouri Pacific Railroad Company, 523 F.2d 1290, 10 EPD ¶ 10,314 (8th Cir. 1975), is the leading Title VII case on the issue of conviction records. In Green, the court held that the defendant's policy of refusing employment to any person convicted of a crime other than a minor traffic offense had an adverse impact on Black applicants and was not justified by business necessity. In a second appeal following remand, the court upheld the district court's injunctive order prohibiting the defendant from using an applicant's conviction record as an absolute bar to employment but allowing it to consider a prior criminal record as long as it constituted a business necessity. Green v. Missouri Pacific Railroad Company,549 F.2d 1158, 1160, 13 EPD ¶ 11,579 (8th Cir. 1977). See also Commission Decision No. 72-1497, CCH EEOC Decisions (1973) ¶ 6352, and Commission Decision Nos. 74-89, 78-10, 78-35, and 80-10, CCH EEOC Decisions (1983) ¶¶ 6418, 6715, 6720, and 6822, respectively.

It is the Commission's position that an employer's policy or practice of excluding individuals from employment on the basis of their conviction records has an adverse impact on Blacks [1] and Hispanics [2] in light of statistics showing that they are convicted at a rate disproportionately greater than their representation in the population. Policy Statement on the Issue of Conviction Records Under Title VII (February 4, 1987). However, when the employer can present more narrowly drawn statistics showing

Either that Blacks and Hispanics are not convicted at a disproportionately greater rate or that there is no adverse impact in its own hiring process resulting from the convictions policy, then a no cause determination would be appropriate.

---

[1] See, e.g., Commission Decision No. 72-1497, CCH EEOC Decisions (1973) ! 6352, and Commission Decision Nos. 74-89, 78-10, 78-35, and 80-10, CCH EEOC Decisions (1983) !! 6418, 6715, 6720, and 6822 respectively.

[2] See Commission Decision No. 78-03, CCH EEOC Decisions (1983) ¶ 6714.

1. Where the Employer's Policy is Not Crime-Specific

An employer's policy of excluding from employment all persons convicted of any crime is likely to create an adverse impact for Blacks and Hispanics based on national and regional conviction rate statistics. However, it is open to the respondent/employer to present more narrow local, regional, or applicant flow data, showing that the policy probably will not have an adverse impact on its applicant pool and/or in fact does not have an adverse impact on the pool. As the Supreme Court has stated,

> Although a statistical showing of disproportionate impact need not always be based on an analysis of the characteristics of actual applicants, Dothard v. Rawlinson, 433 U.S. 321, 330, evidence showing that the figures for the general population might not accurately reflect the pool of qualified job applicants undermines the significance of such figures. Teamsters v. United States, 431 U.S. 324, 340 n. 20.

New York City Transit Authority v. Beazer, 440 U.S. 568, 586 n. 29, 19 EPD ¶ 9027 at p. 6315 (1979). See also Costa v. Markey, 30 EPD ¶ 33,173 at p. 27,638 (1st Cir. 1982), vacated on other grounds, 706 F.2d 796, 32 EPD ¶ 32,622 (1st Cir.), cert. denied, 104 S. Ct. 547, 32 EPD ¶ 33,955 (1983).

If the employer provides applicant flow data, information should be sought to assure that the employer's applicant pool was not artificially limited by discouragement. For example, if many Blacks with conviction records did not apply for a particular job because they knew of the employer's policy and they therefore expected to be rejected, then applicant flow data would not be an accurate reflection of the conviction policy's actual effect. See Dothard v. Rowlinson, 433 US 321, 330 (1977). (Section 608, Recruitment, of Volume II of the Compliance Manual will provide a more detailed discussion of when and how to investigate for discouragement.

2. Where the Employer's Policy is Crime-Specific

In the past, when the Commission has evaluated an employer's "no convictions' policy dealing with a subcategory of crimes; e.g., theft, robbery, or drug-related crimes; the Commission has relied upon national or regional conviction statistics for crimes as a whole. See, e.g., Commission Decision No. 73-0257, CCH EEOC Decisions (1973) ! 6372, and Commission Decision Nos. 76-110 and 80-17, CCH EEOC Decisions (1983) !! 6676 and 6809, respectively. However, these statistics only show a probability of adverse impact for Blacks and Hispanics, while more narrow data may show no adverse impact.

If the employer can present more narrow regional or local data on conviction rates for all crimes showing that Blacks and Hispanics are not convicted at disproportionately higher rates, then a no cause determination would be proper. [3] Alternatively, the employer may present national, regional, or local data on conviction rates for the particular crime which is targeted in its crime-specific convictions policy. If such data shows no adverse impact, then a no cause determination would be appropriate. Finally, the employer can use applicant flow data to demonstrate that its conviction policy has not resulted in the exclusion from employment of a disproportionately high number of Blacks and Hispanics.

---

[3] However, if even more narrow statistics, such as regional or local crime-specific data, show adverse impact, then a cause finding would be appropriate absent a justifying business necessity.

# Notice N-915 (2/4/87)

1. <u>SUBJECT</u>: Policy Statement on the Issue of Conviction Records under Title VII of the Civil Rights Act of 1964, as amended, 42 U.S.C. § 2000e et <u>seq</u>. (1982).

2. <u>PURPOSE</u>: This policy statement sets forth the Commission's revised procedure for determining the existence of a business necessity justifying, for purposes of Title VII, the exclusion of an individual from employment on the basis of a conviction record.

3. <u>EFFECTIVE DATE</u>: February 27, 1987.

4. <u>EXPIRATION DATE</u>: September 15, 1987.

5. <u>ORIGINATOR</u>: Office of Legal Counsel.

6. <u>INSTRUCTIONS</u>: File behind page 604- 36 of EEOC Compliance Manual, Volume II, Section 604, Theories of Discrimination.

7. <u>SUBJECT MATTER</u>:

At the Commission meeting of November 26, 1985, the Commission approved a modification of its existing policy with respect to the manner in which a business necessity is established for denying an individual employment because of a conviction record. The modification, which is set forth below, does not alter the Commission's underlying position that an employer's policy or practice of excluding individuals from employment on the basis of their conviction records has an adverse impact on Blacks[1] and Hispanics[2] in light of statistics showing that they are convicted at a rate disproportionately greater than their representation in the population. Consequently, the Commission has held and continues to hold that such a policy or practice is unlawful under Title VII in the absence of a justifying business necessity.[3]

However, the Commission has revised the previous requirements for establishing business necessity[4] in the following manner. Where a charge involves an allegation that the Respondent employer[5] failed to

---

[1] See, e.g., Commission Decision No. 72-1497, CCH EEOC Decisions (1973) ¶ 6352, and Commission Decision Nos. 74-89, 78-10, 78-35, and 80-10, CCH EEOC Decisions (1983) ¶¶ 6418, 6715, 6720, and 6822, respectively.

[2] See Commission Decision No. 78-03, CCH EEOC Decisions (1983) ¶ 6714.

[3] See, e.g., Commission decisions cited *supra* notes 1-2.

[4] Prior to this modification, for an employer to establish a business necessity justifying excluding an individual from employment because of a conviction record, the evidence had to show that the offense for which the applicant or employee was convicted was job-related. If the offense was not job-related, a disqualification based on the conviction alone violated Title VII. However, even if the offense were determined to be job-related, the employer had to examine other relevant factors to determine whether the conviction affected the individual's ability to perform the job in a manner consistent with the safe and efficient operation of the employer's business. The factors identified by the Commission to be considered by an employer included:

1. The number of offenses and the circumstances of each offense for which the individual was convicted;
2. The length of time intervening between the conviction for the offense and the employment decision;
3. The individual's employment history; and
4. The individual's efforts at rehabilitation.

See, e.g., Commission Decision No. 78-35, CCH EEOC Decisions (1983) ! 6720. *continued next page*

hire or terminated the employment of the Charging Party as a result of a conviction policy or practice that has an adverse impact on the protected class to which the Charging Party belongs, The Respondent must show that it considered these three factors to determine whether its decision was justified by business necessity:

1.  The nature and gravity of the offense or offenses:

2.  The time that has passed since the conviction and/or completion of the sentence; and

3.  The nature of the job held or sought. [6]

This procedure condenses the Commission's previous standard for business necessity, substituting a one-step analysis for the prior two-step procedure and retaining some but not all of the factors previously considered. [7] The modification principally eliminates the need to consider an individual's employment history and efforts at rehabilitation. However, consideration is still given to the job-relatedness of a conviction, covered by the first and third factors, and to the time frame involved, covered by the second factor. Moreover, the first factor encompasses consideration of the circumstances of the offense(s) for which an individual was convicted as well as the number of offenses.

The Commission continues to hold that, where there is evidence of adverse impact, an absolute bar to employment based on the mere fact that an individual has a conviction record is unlawful under Title VII. 8 The Commission's position on this issue is supported by the weight of judicial authority [9]

---

Thus, under the previous procedure, business necessity was established by means of a two-step process: first, by showing that the conviction was job-related; then, by separately demonstrating that the conviction would affect the individual's ability to safety and efficiently perform the job upon consideration of the four factors enumerated above.

[5] Although the term "employer" is used herein, the Commission's position on this issue applies to all entities covered by Title VII. See e.g., Commission Decision No. 77-23, CCH EEOC Decisions (1983) ¶ 6710 (union's policy of denying membership to persons with conviction records unlawfully discriminated against Blacks).

[6] The Commission's revised business necessity analysis follows a decision by the United States Court of Appeals for the Eighth Circuit in the Green v. Missouri Pacific Railroad Company case. Green, 523 F.2d 1290, 10 EPD ¶ 10,314 (8th Cir. 1975), it the leading Title VII case on the issue of conviction records. In that case, the court held that the defendant's absolute policy of refusing employment to any person convicted of a crime other than a minor traffic offense had an adverse impact on Black applicants and was not justified by business necessity. On a second appeal in that case, following remand, the court upheld the district court's injunctive order prohibiting the defendant from using an applicant's conviction record as an absolute bar to employment but allowing it to consider a prior criminal record as a factor in making individual hiring decisions as long as the defendant took into account "the nature and gravity of the offense or offenses, the time that has passed since the conviction and/or completion of sentence, and the nature of the job for which the applicant has applied. Green v. Missouri Pacific Railroad Company, 549 F.2d 1158, 1160, 13 EPD ¶ 11,579 (8th Cir. 1977).

[7] See discussion supra note 4

[8] See, e.g., Commission Decision No. 78-35, CCH EEOC Decisions (1983) ¶ 6720

[9] See Green, 523 F.2d at 1298; Carter v. Gallagher, 452 F.2d 315, 3 EPD ¶ 8335 (8th Cir. 1971), cert. denied, 406 US 950, 4 EPD ¶ 7818 (1972) (brought under 42 U.S.C. §§ 1981 and 1983); and Richardson v. Hotel Corporation of America, 332 F. Supp. 519, 4 EPD ¶ 7666 (E.D. La. 1971), aff'd mem., 468 F. Supp. 951, 5 EPD ¶ 8101 (5th Cir. 1972). See also Hill v. United States Postal Service, 522 F. Supp. 1283 (S.D.N.Y. 1981); Craig v. Department of Health, Education, and Welfare, 508 F. Supp. 1055 (W.D. Mo. 1981); and Cross v. United States Postal Service, 483 F. Supp. 1050 (E.D. Mo. 1979), aff'd in relevant part, 639 F.2d 409, 25 EPD ¶ 31,594 (8th Cir. 1981).

It should be noted that the modified procedure does not affect charges alleging disparate treatment on a prohibited basis in an employer's use of a conviction record as a disqualification for employment. A charge brought under the disparate treatment theory of discrimination is one where, for example, an employer allegedly rejects Black applicants who have conviction records but does not reject similarly situated White applicants.

With respect to conviction charges that are affected by this modification—that is, those raising the issue of adverse impact—Commission decisions that apply the previous standard are no longer available as Commission decision precedent for establishing business necessity. To the extent that such prior decisions are inconsistent with the position set forth herein, they are expressly overruled.

Questions concerning the application of the Commission's revised business necessity standard to the facts of a particular charge should be directed to the Regional Attorney for the Commission office in which the charge was filed.


[Signed 2-4-87 by Clarence Thomas]

_____ Approved:_____

Date                                                   Clarence Thomas

                                                   Chairman

# Appendix 3

# Forms and Interview Questions

## Telephone Interview Form (page 1)

*For uniformity of treatment, all applicants should be asked the same questions, and the form filled out.*

**Applicant**:

**Date/Time called:**

**Caller:**

## Telephone Script—

Hello I am calling about a resume in sent us in response to our ad in the (*name of newspaper*) for (*job title*). Do you have a few minutes to talk on the phone?

1.  Can you tell me why you applied for this position and what interests you about it?

2.  May I ask you why you are looking for new employment?

3.  Can you describe your best five[1] skills?

4.  We are located in (*your town or city*) — is that convenient for you and can you get here? May I ask you what your salary history is in your current position?

---

[1] number of skills asked for can vary

**Phone Interview Form** (page 2)

5.   What hours are you available to work?

6.   May I ask you what your salary history is in your current position?

7.   If we would like to go into more detail and schedule an interview, what would be the best time and date for you?

*If the person sounds acceptable, schedule an interview for as soon as possible.*

*If the person does not appear to be a good fit, but further discussion with them may be an option, say—*

Thank you for your time. We need to review this information with the hiring manager, and if it looks like this is a match, we will call you back.

(*It is okay to give your phone number if the person requests it, but stress that* "we will call them.")

## Interview Rating and Impressions—

__ Excellent potential for position — *Interview is a priority*

__ Could be a good candidate — *Interview would be helpful*

__ *No further action necessary*

# Exit Interview Report

(page 1)

**EXIT INTERVIEW REPORT**

*ALL ANSWERS ARE HELD STRICTLY CONFIDENTIAL*

Employee's Name: _____  Employee #: _____

Department: _____  Position: _____

Dates of Employment:  From _____  To _____

Supervisor: _____

Reason for leaving Company: _____

Return of:

_____ keys              _____ company documents      _____ uniform

_____ I.D. card         _____ safety equipment        _____ tools

_____ credit card       _____ other company property  _____ company auto

Employee informed of restriction on:

_____ trade secrets            _____ employment with competitor (if applicable)

_____ patents                  _____ removing company documents

_____ other data               _____ other _____

Employee exit questions:

1.  Did management adequately recognize employee contributions? _____

_____

2.  Do you feel that you have had the support of management on the job? _____

_____

3.  Were you adequately trained for your job? _____

_____

4.  Did you find your work rewarding? _____

_____

**(Continued)**

**EXIT INTERVIEW REPORT**                                             **PAGE 2**

5.    Do you feel you were fairly treated by the company? _____
_____

6.    Were you paid an adequate salary for the work you did? _____
_____

7.    Were you content with your working conditions? _____
_____

8.    Do you feel your supervision was adequate? _____
_____

9.    Did you understand company policies and the reasons for them? _____
_____

10.   Have you observed incidences of theft of company property? _____
_____

11.   How can the company improve security? _____
_____

12.   How can the company improve working conditions? _____
_____

13.   What are the company's strengths? _____
_____

14.   What are the company's weaknesses? _____
_____

15.   Other comments: _____
_____
_____
_____

*USE ADDITIONAL SHEETS FOR FURTHER COMMENTS*

# Turnover Cost Calculator Form

(page 1)

| | |
|---|---|
| **Separation Costs—** | |
| Cost of time required to terminate the employee | $ |
| Cost of exit interviewer's time | $ |
| Employee's separation/severance pay | $ |
| Increase on unemployment taxes | $ |
| Termination-related administrative costs | $ |
| **Vacancy Costs—** | $ |
| Cost of overtime required of workers covering the vacancy | $ |
| Cost of any directly-hired temporary help in covering the vacancy | $ |
| Cost of any agency-based temporary help (agency costs and contracts) | $ |
| **Replacement Costs—** | |
| Pre-employment administrative expenses | $ |
| Cost of attracting applicants (recruitment advertising) | $ |
| Cost of entrance interviews | $ |
| Screening/testing (aptitude/skills test, drug screens, background/reference checks) | $ |
| Hiring-related travel expenses | $ |
| Moving or relocation expenses | $ |
| Post-employment medical exams | $ |
| Post-employment information gathering and dissemination costs (payroll, benefits, policies and procedures, time required to enter the individual into all relevant systems/programs, etc.) | $ |

**Turnover Cost Calculator Form** (page 2)

| | |
|---|---|
| **Training Costs—** | |
| Costs of informational literature (manual, employee handbook, brochures, policies) | $ |
| Formal training costs (classroom, instructor or specialty trainer) | $ |
| Informal training costs (supervisor, on-the-job training) | $ |
| Any overtime required by employee as s/he learns the job | $ |
| Additional overtime required of co-workers as new employee learns the job | $ |
| **Opportunity Costs—** | |
| Cost of difference in productivity between former employee and replacement | $ |
| Anticipated learning curve (time at which productivity returns to former standard) | $ |
| Cost of any customers or accounts lost in conjunction with loss of employee | $ |
| **Supervisory and Staff Costs—** | |
| Cost of first-line supervisors addressing turnover (problem solving, mentoring, troubleshooting) | $ |
| **Total Cost** → | $ |

# Employment Verification and Reference Worksheet

| | |
|---|---|
| Name Of Applicant | |
| Social Security Number | |
| Previous Employer Name | |
| City/State | |
| Phone Number | |
| Fax Number | |
| Contact Name | |
| Relationship To Candidate | |
| Title And Department | |

| | **Applicant Reported** | **Employer Reported** |
|---|---|---|
| Start Date | | |
| End Date | | |
| Starting Position | | |
| Ending Position | | |
| Ending Salary | | |
| Reason For Leaving | | |
| Eligible For Rehire? | | |

**Will Employer give reference? YES   NO**   If yes, see last page for reference information

## Call History

| Date | Time | Who Called | Results | Notes |
|---|---|---|---|---|
| | | | | |
| | | | | |
| | | | | |
| | | | | |
| | | | | |

1. Please record all efforts made to obtain a verification and reference for this applicant
2. Please note any changes in phone numbers or special instructions needed to obtain a reference on this applicant
3. If unsuccessful and no response to voicemail, contact the main number and send a fax to the employer. *Note time and date the fax request is sent.*

# EMPLOYMENT REFERENCE for: _____  page 2

*If reference is given by a source different than above, please note*

| | |
|---|---|
| Reference Name | |
| Phone Number | |
| Relationship To Candidate | |
| Title And Department | |
| Current Employer (If Different) | |

1. What were the applicant's job and the nature of his/her duties?

2. Is the applicant's resume description of their duties accurate and consistent?

3. Can you describe or give examples of the applicant's strengths?

4. What could the applicant do to improve his/her job performance?

5. How would you describe the quality of his/her work? Can you give examples?

6. Can you describe how he/she got along with others? ...teamwork, relationship to supervisors, etc.

7. Can you give examples of times when the applicant demonstrated leadership characteristics?

8. How would you describe the applicant's communication skills?
   (If the applicant was a supervisor, describe how he/she supervised others)

9.  How did the applicant show initiative or leadership on the job?

10. Were there any problems with attendance or punctuality?

11. Were there any work-related problems with this applicant?

12. On a scale of 1-10 (10 being the highest), overall, how would you rate the applicant's performance?

13. If you were responsible for the hiring process, would you consider him/her eligible for rehire?

14. Do you have any additional comments regarding this applicant?

## Additional Interview Questions to Ask a Past Employer

1.  In what areas did the applicant show need for improvement?

2.  How did the applicant get along with supervisors and managers?

3.  Did the applicant exhibit any tendency towards violence or inappropriate conduct/behavior that was workplace related? (this may include use of drugs, alcohol, or dishonesty)

4.  How did the candidate compare to the person now doing the job?

5.  Can you identify specific jobs this applicant would be better suited for?

6.  How did the candidate respond when confronted with an urgent assignment?

7.  Do you have any additional comments regarding this applicant?

8.  Why didn't you try to rehire or induce him/her to stay?

# Sample Request for Proposal (RFP) for Screening Services

Dear Service Provider,

You are invited to submit a proposal for providing our firm with pre-employment background screening services. Please submit all responses directly to the following address:

*{Place your contact person, company name, company address and telephone number here}*

Please note the following:

All proposals must be received by the followings date: _____

1.  All bids must be submitted in writing. Faxes are not accepted.
2.  Employer reserves the right to accept or reject any bid in its sole discretion and is not obligated to choose to lowest bid.
3.  Proposals must remain valid for a period of 180 days.
4.  Please direct all questions and comments to the person indicated above only.
    Communication with any other individual may be considered grounds for disqualification.
5.  The bid will be evaluated based upon the following criteria—
    - Price
    - Proven Ability to meet needs
    - Turnaround time commitment
    - Customer service
    - Supplier Personal
    - Understanding of legal requirements
    - Infrastructure, including the system for tracking and reporting
    - Ease of reading screening reports
    - Additional services provided
    - Quality and completeness of product provided
    - Knowledge of the process involved

**Sample Request for Proposal for Screening Services      (start of page 2)**

**I. Services offered**

1.  Indicate if you provide following services, describe them and your methodologies—
    a.  County felony and misdemeanor records
    b.  Credit reports
    c.  Social Security traces
    d.  Driving records
    e.  Federal Records
    f.  Employment verification
    g.  Education verification
    h.  Professional license
    i.  Sexual offender search
    j.  Terrorist databases

    k.   International criminal searches

    l.    International employment and education verification

    m.  Others

2.   Do you utilize the services of any subcontractors to fulfill criminal record searches, or any other search? If so, identify the methods used including quality control procedures.

3.   Do you use databases for any searches? If so, please describe:

    a)   The nature of the database

    b)   Any limitations on the usage of the database

    c)   Any legal compliance issues, such as FCRA Section 613

4.   Please describe any quality control procedures you follow to insure accuracy in your reporting of results.

5.   Does your firm have national capabilities? Describe.

6.   Does your firm have international capabilities? Describe.

7.   Describe your quality control procedures.

## II. Turnaround Time

1.   What is your turnaround time for each of the services above?

2.   Describe your methodology to ensure turnaround time of reports.

3.   Are you able to generate turnaround time reports for each order that is placed and for each search conducted?

4.   Do you notify employers if there is a delay and how long?

5.   Is there a performance guarantee?

## III. Reporting Format and Technology

1.   Describe the software or online system utilized by your firm.

2.   How does an employer send an order to your firm?

3.   How is an employer informed of results?

4.   How is an employer kept advised of status?

5.   What protection do you provide to keep customers limited to their candidate's data only?

6.   Please describe your ability to integrate with Applicant Tracking Systems or HR Information Systems.

7.   Please describe your ability to accept online candidate consents.

8.   Please provide a sample report.

## IV. Legal Compliance

1.   Describe your understanding of the laws that govern pre-employment screening and your methodology for compliance with those laws.

2.   How does your firm keep updated on applicable federal and state laws affecting employment screening?

3.   Do you maintain a guide to applicable laws in all 50 states?

4.   Describe what assistance you will give us, if any, in legal compliance.

5.   Describe how you keep your clients updated on important legal changes.

6.   If there is a criminal case found, who determines if it is reportable and describe the methodology used to determine whether it is reportable.

## V. Privacy and Security

1.   Does your firm have a Privacy and Data Security policy? If so, please provide.

2.   Describe your security and data protection practices, including any third party certifications.

3. Does your firm send PII outside of the United States for either for domestic or international screening? If so, please describe in detail.

4. How do you vet new clients to ensure your services are in compliance with the FCRA? Does your firm utilize any home based workers who have access to Personal and Identifiable Information (PII) about an applicant? If so, describe the process and describe how personal and identifiable applicant information is protected.

5. Does your firm utilize home operators to complete employment and education verifications? If so, describe the process and describe how personal and identifiable applicant information is protected.

## VI. Customer Service

1. Do you provide any customer training or continuing education? If so, please describe.

2. Do you provide an account executive that will handle our account?

3. Do you have an internal trouble ticket system? If so, describe how it works.

4. If there is not a trouble ticket system, describe your internal methodology to insure that customer service issues are addressed in a timely manner and that there is follow-through.

5. Describe your problem escalation procedures in the event of a service issue.

## VII. About Your Firm

1. Please describe the background and experience of your firm.

2. Please provide a short biography of the principals of your firm.

3. Do you require a contract?

4. Describe your account set-up procedures.

5. Are there set-up fees?

6. Can we set up a customized screening program?

7. How do you handle billing an employer with multiple locations, or different departments?

8. Do your have errors and omissions issuance? Describe.

9. Please list representative clients.

10. Please list three references. To the extent possible, choose references that have needs similar to our firm. Please provide full contact information.

11. Is your firm a member of the trade association for background firms (NAPBS)? If not a member, do you certify that you adopt and agree with their goals and standards?

12. Has your firm reviewed the proposed accreditation guidelines for NAPBS?

13. Is your firm in compliance with the proposed NAPBS Accreditation guidelines? If not, please indicate in detail where your firm is not in compliance, steps being taken to be in compliance or why such compliance should not be a factor in this RFP.

14. Describe how you train your employees.

15. Describe how you keep your employees updated on legal issues effecting screening.

## VIII. Pricing

1. Please provide pricing for each item listed above.

2. Do you have any package plans? Please describe.

3. Are there any other costs or expenses we should know about?

## IX. Other advantages

1. Are there any other advantages in selecting your firm to provide pre-employment background screening services?

2. There are many firms that provide this service. Why should we choose you?

# Appendix 4

# Timeline and Tables

## The Safe Hiring Timeline—

| Time | Event/Action | Notes |
|---|---|---|
| Pre-need stage (prior to vacancy or creation of new position) | Development of training policy and procedures. | Organizational assessments are made specifically targeting hiring policies and procedures that need to be in place before new hires are made.<br><br>Necessary managerial/HR/security training is outlined and begun.<br><br>Methods for auditing system progress and performance are reviewed/agreed upon. |
| Creation of New Position<br>or<br>Existing Position becomes open | Development of announcement of vacancy, employment classifieds, etc. | Method of job advertising is selected (print, electronic media, etc.[1])<br><br>Specific screening policy language is included in all announcements and classifieds ads mentioning employment. |
| Application stage | Applicants respond to job ad, begin to submit resumes/Curriculum Vitae (CV) to hiring firm. | Candidates should be asked to fill out and submit an application along with/instead of a resume or CV.<br><br>Application includes specific language discussing screening policies, also specific questions, releases, and standard statements. |

[1] Some job board software and application service provider solutions are available that allow some degree of assessment and/or skills testing to take place during the application process. These require that the specific needs – education, skills, etc. – be considered and addressed at the time the job advertisement is created.

| Time | Event/Action | Notes |
|---|---|---|
| Application Review stage | Sorting and weeding. Applicants are narrowed into candidates. | Hiring manager reviews all applications for red flags, including incomplete or ambiguous answers; reviews and considers applicants' reasons for leaving previous jobs. Hiring manager identifies suitable applicants, makes note of further required areas of questioning, and notifies candidates of their status. |
| Interview stage | More sorting and weeding. Candidates are selected conditional on passing a background check. | Interviewers ask candidates permissible questions designed to ensure honesty and integrity, making sure that all candidates are asked the same questions and treated equally. Candidates are again informed of company's screening policies. |
| Background Investigation stage | Candidate-provided statements and information are verified. Further information on the candidate's past is researched and collected. | References are checked, previous employers are contacted. Wages, credentials, degrees, licenses, etc. are verified. Court records are checked. Credit reports are requested. Workers' Comp claims are researched. All information is gathered in compliance with state/local laws and the FCRA. |
| Analysis of Information stage | Collected data is reviewed. | Information retrieved is reviewed and compared to candidate statements and claims. Discrepancies are identified. Negative information from a candidate's past is reviewed in the context of its impact on a candidate's ability to perform the required tasks or eligibility for employment. Ineligibility must be in compliance with EEOC, state and regional rules. |
| Post-hire stage | Policies and procedures are in place to maintain a safe workplace. | Screening is standard procedure for promotion, reassignment, and retention. Investigations are possible where necessary for claims of harassment, theft, violence, or other difficulties. |

# Description of Pre-Employment Screening Tools

| Type of Information | What It Will Tell | Reason You Need This Information | Limitations/Notes on Using This Information |
|---|---|---|---|
| Criminal Record Search (County Courts) | Felony and Misdemeanor convictions and pending cases, usually including date and nature of offense, sentencing date, disposition and current status. Generally goes back seven years. May also search federal court records.<br><br>It is critical to search both for felonies and misdemeanors in state court, since many serious job-related violations can be classified as misdemeanors. | Critical information to protect your business and employees. Protects employer from negligent hiring exposure and helps reduce threat of workplace violence, theft, disruption and other problems.<br><br>Failure to honestly disclose a prior criminal conviction can also be the basis not to hire.<br><br>For the maximum protection, all jurisdictions where an applicant has lived, worked or studied in the past seven years should be checked. | Some restrictions on having certain information (such as arrests not resulting in convictions), or certain minor offenses.[2] Employment cannot be automatically denied based upon a criminal record, but must show some sound business reason. Criminal records are not available by computer nationwide. Check public records at county courthouses[3] in locations where applicant resided or worked.. Be careful in using databases– if there is a "hit" then file must be reviewed for identifiers and details. |
| Driver's License Search | Driving history for three years.<br><br>Verification of driving privilege, and operator restrictions that might indicate the applicant's ability to perform job tasks. | Helps verify identity.<br><br>Gives insight on level of applicant's responsibility.<br><br>Determine if applicant keeps commitments to appear in court or pay fines, has a drug/alcohol problem, and current license status.<br><br>"Driving for work" is very broadly defined in most jurisdictions and is not limited to driving positions. | This information can be accessed by an outside agency on the employer's behalf. Background firms can also help interpret the DMV record. An alternative is having applicants go to the DMV to obtain their own records, which is not practical and is subject to fraud.<br><br>DMV may has a program for firms that would like record updates. |

---

[2] for instance, in New York state, misdemeanors cannot be considered — and all misdemeanors could not be found as there are over 1200 courts handling some sort of misdemeanor records in New York

[3] there can be delays when a court clerk pulls a file. Some courts charge a court search fee, copy fee, cert fee.

| Type of Information | What It Will Tell | Reason You Need This Information | Limitations/Notes on Using This Information |
|---|---|---|---|
| Social Security Number Trace/Check | Provides names and addresses associated with the applicant's Social Security Number and may indicate fraudulent use. Helps verify other applicant information. | Helps verify that applicants are who they say they are, critical to ensure employer not the victim of a fraudulent application by someone with something to hide. Can show where to search for criminal records. | Where employer does not have a sound business reason to obtain a business credit report, the Social Security trace gives information to help confirm identity and may uncover fraud. |
| Credit Report | Credit history and public records such as judgments, liens, and bankruptcies. May include previous employers, addresses, and other names used.[4] | Helps determine whether an employee is suitable for a position involving handling cash or the exercise of financial discretion. A possible way to gauge trustworthiness and reliability. | A credit report should only be requested when it is specifically relevant to a job function, and the employer has appropriate policies and procedures in place to ensure that the use of credit reports are relevant and fair. |
| Employment Verification | Basic verification includes dates of employment, job title, and reason for leaving. Some employers will verify salary. Usually obtained from HR, personnel, or payroll dept. Some employers provide reference information recorded on a 900 service. | This information confirms applicant's resume, and verifies their previous job history. Helps eliminate any *unexplained gaps* in employment, which ensures that appropriate jurisdictions have been checked for criminal records, reducing likelihood of incarceration for a serious offense. | Employers are often hesitant to give recommendations and may limit prior employment checks to release of basic information only. Limited results if— not allowed to contact current employer, employer will not return call, past employer is out of business or cannot be located, or if employee was working through an agency. |
| Employment Reference Check | This is a more in-depth reference check that seeks job duties, performance, salary history, strengths and weaknesses, eligibility for rehire, and other detailed information. | Allows an employer to have a realistic assessment of a candidate from former employers. It promotes a better "fit," confirms the hiring opinion, and protects the expensive hiring investment. | Although most employers would like references, few past employers give them due to concerns over legal liability. Always attempt to obtain verifications and references in order to demonstrate due diligence. |

---

[4] an employment credit report differs from commercial credit report-employment version.
The employment version does not have age, credit scoring, or account numbers of credit cards.

| Type of Information | What It Will Tell | Reason You Need This Information | Limitations/Notes on Using This Information |
|---|---|---|---|
| Personal Reference Check | Contact personal references to ascertain additional information about your applicant concerning fitness for the job in question. | Personal references can provide valuable information as to a person's character as it relates to the job opening. | Inquire about the applicant's relationship to the reference and how long they have known each other in order to judge the usefulness of the information provided. Contact "developed references" for a better picture of the applicant. |
| Education Verification | Will confirm degrees, diplomas or certificates, and dates attended. | Confirms that applicant has educational experience and professional ability to do the job. | Industry sources show that 30% of all job applicants falsify information about educational background. Expect to pay a fee for transcripts, but verifications generally free. Some schools require a verification fee, or only fax back documents to an 800 number. |
| Professional Licenses | The type of license, whether currently valid, dates issued, state licensing authority. | Confirms whether an applicant has the required credentials or licenses for the position. | There is a high rate of job applicants making up or falsifying licenses or credentials. |
| Civil Records (includes Litigation, Judgments, and Tax Liens) | Date of filing, case type, case number or file record, jurisdiction and, if available, identity of parties involved. | Discover whether your applicant has sued former employers or has been sued for reasons that are relevant to employment. | An employer should use this information where it is relevant to job performance. Have standard policies and procedures for civil records use. |
| Workers' Compensation Records | Information about Workers' Compensation claims and previous injuries. | This information allows the employer to conduct *post-job offer* reviews in compliance with strict standards of the Americans with Disabilities Act. | Federal and state laws regulate the use of these records. Have policies and procedures in place before requesting or utilizing Workers' Comp records. |

# Appendix 5

# Only in California…

## The Strange Saga of AB 655 — Critical New Rules Affecting Safe Hiring in California

The need to keep a close eye on what the legislatures in each of the fifty states are doing was never demonstrated as clearly than by the strange saga of changes in California law that occurred in 2002. California passed a bill known AB 655, which was a well-intended identity theft bill that went into effect largely unnoticed, and wreaked havoc on California employers because of its unintended consequences. Among other things, the law impacted reference checking and in-house investigation of applicants, and required employers to provide all background reports to applicants

In an effort to protect against identity theft, the bill amended the California Investigative Consumer Reporting Act (Civil Code Section 1786 et seq.), the law that governs pre-employment background screening in California. The legislature expressed concern that **identity theft** had become the fastest growing white-collar crime in America, and that providing pre-employment background reports to applicants would help people to protect themselves sooner.

Another factor behind AB 655 was the concern of privacy advocates that employers could conduct their own in-house background investigations without any regulation by the Federal Fair Credit Reporting Act (FCRA) or California state law. **Before AB 655, an employer had no obligation to inform an applicant that the employer found a criminal record if a background screening service was not used. This loophole has lead to documented cases of people being blacklisted because of incorrect records. AB 655 closed that loophole by requiring employers who do in-house investigations to provide certain notices to applicants.**

> Remember the story about Scott Lewis in Chapter 6? He was the unfortunate victim of an error in a vendor's database. Mr. Lewis could not get a job because prospective new employers would not let him respond to an adverse background check. The California legislation was, in part, spurred by the Scott Lewis story.

However, AB 655 placed an onerous burden on employers. Employers were placed under the obligation to provide *to all* applicants *any* information obtained about them as part of the hiring process, including past employment verifications and references that were obtained in-house. The law went beyond just providing criminal convictions or matters of public record. According to California Civil Code 1786.53, all information had to be provided at either the first meeting or interview between the employer and applicant or within seven days, whichever was sooner.

**This new burden created a nearly impossible task.** The physical process of hiring, especially for larger organizations with hiring managers and multiple locations, made it nearly impossible to comply. In addition, it added a new barrier to the already difficult task of obtaining employment references. It also made it more difficult for employers to conduct internal investigations of employees suspected of misconduct or wrongdoing.

**The law contained other requirements.** Any employer who obtained a background report had to provide a copy of the report to the applicant. Some law firms took the position that this task had to be performed by the employer, and could not be outsourced to a screening firm. AB 655 imposed additional requirements on disclosure forms to applicants, required employers to certify to background firms that they would comply with California law, and mandated a cover sheet on background reports. AB 655 also contained substantial damages that could be awarded to a consumer against an employer or background firm that failed to comply with the new rules.

After the author of the bill — Assemblyman Wright and his staff — was made aware of the unintended consequences of AB 655, they took up the task of gathering opinions from various parties, and crafting new legislation that addressed various concerns. They received input from employers, labor lawyers, HR and security professionals, staffing firms, background experts, and other groups that were affected. Assemblyman Wright and his staff then successfully shepherded the "clean-up" through the legislature. The author of this book worked with that office and assisted in drafting some sections of the clean-up bill and testified before a legislative committee.

Two clean-up bills AB 1068 and AB 2868 were passed unanimously by the California legislature and were signed by the Governor on September 28, 2002. The bills contained urgency clauses and they went into effect immediately.

Some of the more important changes in the legislation for employers and HR professionals are—

1.   **References**

The new law clarifies that under California Civil Code section 1786.53, **in-house references** obtained by an employer DO NOT have to be turned over to applicants. Under new AB 1068, an employer would have to turn over *any public records*, such as criminal convictions that it found on its own, but *not* reference checks.

2.   **Providing Reports to Applicants**

The law no longer requires employers to provide every background report to each applicant. Instead, each applicant will have the ability to check off a box on a disclosure sheet and have a background-screening firm send the report directly to the applicant. A similar rule already exists in California for credit reports. This is the same rule in effect currently in Oklahoma and Minnesota.

3.   **Special Cover Sheet**

The law revises the rules about a special cover sheet. The language was changed to say a screening firm is allowed to post the required notice on the first page of the report instead, in 12-point boldface type.

4.   **Employee Investigations**

There is also language in new section 1786.55 that clarifies that the new law is not intended to modify existing law concerning internal investigations of current employees suspected of misconduct or wrongdoing, or employer reference checking. However, the federal FCRA still applies to investigations by third parties.

5.   **Limitations on "do-it-yourself" investigations**

If an employer does their own investigation of an applicant or current employee without using the services of a background-screening provider and collects public records such as criminal records, there are new rules that are in effect. Any information must be turned over to the applicant/employee within seven days unless the employer suspects misconduct or wrongdoing in which case supplying the information may only be delayed. In addition, an employer who uses this procedure must provide a form to all applicants/employees with a checkbox that, if checked, permits a person to waive the right to receive the copy of any public record. If the investigation results in an adverse action, there are additional employer requirements as well. This procedure is only in effect if an employer does its own investigation.

6.   **Limitation on Criminal Record Searches**

The new law retains the seven year limitation on a background screening firm obtaining criminal records. However, the new law clarifies that there is an exception for employers that are required by a governmental agency to go back further when checking qualifications. This addresses a conflict between California law and situations where certain employers are required by other laws to go back further. Employers should also note there are many other California rules on background firm reporting and on employers utilizing criminal records.

7.   **Employer forms used for background screening**

Employers that utilize the services of a background screening firm should have received, shortly after AB 655 was effective, a revised certification form required of all California employers, as well as a revised Disclosure form that applicants must receive. There are very specific requirements for language that MUST be in the employer forms, particularly the applicant Disclosure form.

It is very important for employers and background screening firms to understand and follow the special California rules, since Civil Code Section 1786.50 provides that a background firm or employer who fails to comply with any requirement under this law can be liable for up to $10,000 or actual damages, whichever is greater, to each applicant who sues. If the violation is grossly negligent or willful, punitive damages are also allowed. There is also the possibility of class action lawsuits for failure to follow the California rules.

# Page Index

# Meet Author Lester S. Rosen...

**Lester S. Rosen** is an attorney at law and President of Employment Screening Resources, a national background screening company located in California, see www.ESRcheck.com. He is a consultant, writer and frequent presenter nationwide on pre-employment screening and safe hiring issues.

He is a former deputy District Attorney and defense attorney and has taught criminal law and procedure at the University of California Hastings College of the Law. His jury trials have included murder, death penalty, and federal cases. He graduated UCLA with Phi Beta Kappa honors and received a J.D. degree from the University of California at Davis, serving on the Law Review. He holds the highest attorney rating of A.V. in the national Martindale-Hubbell listing of U.S. Attorneys.

In 2002, he worked with the California legislature to amend AB 655, a law that adversely affected employers in the area of reference checks and hiring in California, and testified before the state legislature. He has qualified and testified in the California and Arkansas Superior Courts as an expert witness on issues surrounding safe hiring and due diligence. His speaking appearances have included numerous national and statewide conferences.

He is also featured as the narrator in a training video by Kantola Productions called "Safe Hiring: How You Can Avoid Bad Hires" which you can learn more about at www.esrcheck.com/safe_hiring_video.php

Mr. Rosen was the chairperson of the steering committee that founded the National Association of Professional Background Screeners (NAPBS), a professional trade organization for the screening industry with over 500 members. He was also elected to the first Board of Directors and served as the Co-chairman in 2004.

Mr. Rosen resides with his wife and daughter in Tiburon, California.

To contact Mr. Rosen for speaking or professional consultation for businesses, he may be reached at speaker@esrhire.com.